Welcome to
Georgia Social Studies!

Dear Georgia Student,

From the Civil War to Civil Rights, the history of the United States is an important story about people, places, and events. In this book, you'll read more about the actions of great leaders and the contributions of men and women, in the past and present.

As you study this year, you'll be achieving Georgia's standards. These learning goals will help you understand who has made a difference in your nation's history and why the events of the past are so important. The standards also help you develop geography, thinking, and personal finance skills.

The learning you accomplish this year in history, economics, citizenship, and geography will be yours for the rest of your life!

You are on your way!

Georgia's Social Studies Performance Standards are listed for you on the pages that follow. Your standards are covered in this special Georgia textbook.

Georgia's Social Studies Performance Standards Grade 5

United States History since 1860

In fifth grade, students continue their formal study of United States history. As with fourth grade the strands of history, geography, civics, and economics are fully integrated. Students study United States history beginning with the Civil War and continue to the present. The geography strand emphasizes the influence of geography on U. S. history. The civics strand emphasizes concepts and rights as outlined in amendments to the U. S. Constitution. The economics strand uses material from the historical strand to further understanding of economic concepts.

Historical Understandings

SS5H1 *The student will explain the causes, major events, and consequences of the Civil War.*

   a. Identify "Uncle Tom's Cabin," John Brown's raid on Harper's Ferry and explain how each of these events was related to the Civil War.

   b. Discuss how the issues of states' rights and slavery increased tensions between the North and South.

   c. Identify major battles and campaigns: Fort Sumter, Gettysburg, the Atlanta Campaign, Sherman's March to the Sea, Appomattox Court House.

   d. Describe the roles of Abraham Lincoln, Robert E. Lee, Ulysses S. Grant, Jefferson Davis, and Thomas "Stonewall" Jackson.

   e. Describe the effects of war on the North and South.

SS5H2 *The student will analyze the effects of Reconstruction on American life.*

   a. Describe the purpose of the 13th, 14th, and 15th Amendments.

   b. Explain the work of the Freedmen's Bureau.

   c. Explain how slavery was replaced by sharecropping and how African-Americans were prevented from exercising their newly won rights, to include Jim Crow laws and customs.

SS5H3 *The student will describe how life changed in America at the turn of the century.*

   a. Describe the role of the cattle trails in the late 19th century including the Black Cowboys of Texas, the Great Western Cattle Trail and the Chisholm Trail.

   b. Describe the impact on American life of the Wright brothers (flight), George Washington Carver (science), Alexander Graham Bell (communication), Thomas Edison (electricity).

    c. Explain how William McKinley and Theodore Roosevelt expanded America's role in the world including the Spanish-American War and the building of the Panama Canal.

    d. Describe the reasons people emigrated to the United States, from where the emigrated, and where they settled.

SS5H4   *The student will describe the U.S. involvement in World War I and post-World War I America.*

    a. Explain how German attacks on U.S. shipping during the war in Europe (1914-1917) ultimately led the U.S. to join the fight against Germany, including the sinking of the Lusitania and concerns over safety of U.S. ships.

    b. Describe the cultural developments and individual contributions in the 1920s of the Jazz Age (Louis Armstrong), the Harlem Renaissance (Langston Hughes), baseball (Babe Ruth), the automobile (Henry Ford), and the airplane (Charles Lindbergh).

SS5H5   *The student will explain how the Great Depression and New Deal affected the lives of millions of Americans.*

    a. Discuss the Stock Market Crash of 1929, Herbert Hoover, Franklin Roosevelt, the Dust Bowl, and soup kitchens.

    b. Analyze the main features of the New Deal including the significance of the Civilian Conservation Corps, Works Progress Administration, and the Tennessee Valley Authority.

    c. Discuss important cultural elements of the 1930's to include Duke Ellington, Margaret Mitchell, and Jesse Owens.

SS5H6   *The student will explain the reasons for America's involvement in World War II.*

    a. Describe Germany's aggression in Europe and Japanese aggression in Asia.

    b. Describe major events in the war in both Europe and the Pacific including Pearl Harbor, Iwo Jima, D-Day, VE and VJ Days, and the Holocaust.

    c. Discuss President Truman's decision to drop the atomic bomb on Hiroshima and Nagaskai.

    d. Identify Roosevelt, Stalin, Churchill, Hirohito, Truman, Mussolini, and Hitler.

    e. Describe the effects of rationing and the changing role of women and African Americans, including "Rosie the Riveter" and the Tuskegee Airmen.

    f. Explain the U.S. role in the formation of the United Nations.

SS5H7   *The student will discuss the origins and consequences of the Cold War.*

    a. Explain the origin and meaning of the term "Iron Curtain."

    b. Explain the how the United States sought to stop the spread of communism through the Berlin airlift, the Korean War, and the North Atlantic Treaty Organization.

    c. Identify Joseph McCarthy and Nikita Khrushchev.

SS5H8 *The student will describe the importance of key people, events, and developments between 1950-1975.*

    a. Discuss the importance of the Cuban Missile Crisis and the Vietnam War.

    b. Explain the key events and people of the Civil Rights movement including Brown v. Board of Education 1954, Montgomery Bus Boycott, the March on Washington, Civil Rights Act and Voting Rights Act, and civil rights activities of Thurgood Marshall, Rosa Parks, and Martin Luther King, Jr.

    c. Describe the impact on American society of the assassinations of President John F. Kennedy, Robert F. Kennedy, and Martin Luther King, Jr.

    d. Discuss the significance of the new technologies of television and space exploration.

SS5H9 *The student will trace important developments in America since 1975.*

    a. Describe U.S. involvement in world events including efforts to bring peace to the Middle East, the collapse of the Soviet Union, Persian Gulf War, and the War on Terrorism in response to September 11, 2001.

    b. Explain the impact the development of the personal computer and Internet has had on American life.

Geographic Understandings

SS5G1 *The student will locate important places in the United States.*

    a. Locate important physical features to include: the Grand Canyon, Salton Sea, Great Salt Lake, and the Mojave Desert,

    b. Locate important man-made places to include: the Chisholm Trail, Pittsburg, PA, Gettysburg, PA, Kitty Hawk, NC, Pearl Harbor, HI, Montgomery, AL.

SS5G2 *The student will explain the reasons for the spatial patterns of economic activities.*

    a. Identify and explain the factors influencing industrial location in the United States after the Civil War.

    b. Define, map, and explain the dispersion of the primary economic activities within the United States since the turn of the century.

    c. Map and explain how the dispersion of global economic activities contributed to the United States emerging from World War I as a world power.

Civic Understandings

SS5CG1 *The student will explain how a citizen's rights are protected under the U.S. Constitution.*

a. Explain the responsibilities of a citizen.

b. Explain the freedoms granted by the Bill of Rights.

c. Explain the concept of due process of law.

d. Describe how the Constitution protects a citizen's rights by due process.

SS5CG2 *The student will explain the process by which amendments to the U.S. Constitution are made.*

a. Explain the amendment process outlined in the Constitution.

b. Describe the purpose for the amendment process.

SS5CG3 *The student will explain how amendments to the U.S. Constitution have maintained a representative democracy.*

a. Explain the purpose of 12th and 17th amendments.

b. Explain how voting rights were protected by the 15th, 19th , 23rd, 24th , and 26th amendments.

SS5CG4 *The student will explain the meaning of and reason for the motto of the United States "e pluribus unum."*

Economic Understandings

SS5E1 *The student will use the basic economic concepts of trade, opportunity cost, specialization, voluntary exchange, productivity, and price incentives to illustrate historical events.*

a. Describe *opportunity costs* and their relationship to decision-making across time (such as decisions to remain unengaged at the beginning of World War II in Europe).

b. Explain how *price incentives* affect people's behavior and choices (such as monetary policy during the Great Depression).

c. Describe how *specialization* improves standards of living, (such as how development of specific economies in the north and south developed at the beginning of the 20th century).

d. Explain how *voluntary exchange* helps both buyers and sellers, (such as the G8 countries).

e. Describe how *trade* promotes economic activity (such as trade activities today under NAFTA).

f. Give examples of technological advancements and their impact on b̲ *productivity* during the development of the United States.

SS5E2 *The student will describe the functions of the three major institutions in the U.S. economy in each era of United States history.*

   a. Describe the *private business function* in producing goods and services.

   b. Describe the *bank function* in providing checking accounts, savings accounts, and loans.

   c. Describe the *government function* in taxation and providing certain goods and services.

SS5E3 *The student will describe how consumers and businesses interact in the United States economy across time.*

   a. Describe how *competition*, *markets*, and *prices* influence people's behavior.

   b. Describe how people earn *income* by selling their labor to businesses.

   c. Describe how *entrepreneurs* take risks to develop new goods and services to start a business.

SS5E4 *The student will identify the elements of a personal budget and explains why personal spending and saving decisions are important.*

HOUGHTON MIFFLIN

SOCIAL STUDIES

★ UNITED STATES HISTORY ★

CIVIL WAR TO TODAY

★ ★ ★ GEORGIA ★ ★ ★

★AUTHORS★

Senior Author
Dr. Herman J. Viola
Curator Emeritus
Smithsonian Institution

Dr. Cheryl Jennings
Project Director
Florida Institute of
    Education
University of North Florida

Dr. Sarah Witham
Bednarz
Associate Professor,
    Geography
Texas A&M University

Dr. Mark C. Schug
Professor and Director
Center for Economic
    Education
University of Wisconsin,
    Milwaukee

Dr. Carlos E. Cortés
Professor Emeritus, History
University of California,
Riverside

Dr. Charles S. White
Associate Professor,
School of Education
Boston University

Georgia Program Consultant
Glen Blankenship

Consulting Authors

Dr. Dolores Beltran
Assistant Professor
Curriculum Instruction
California State University, Los Angeles
(Support for English Language Learners)

Dr. MaryEllen Vogt
Co-Director
California State University Center for
the Advancement of Reading
(Reading in the Content Area)

HOUGHTON MIFFLIN
SOCIAL STUDIES

★ UNITED STATES HISTORY ★

CIVIL WAR TO TODAY

 HOUGHTON MIFFLIN BOSTON

GEORGIA

Consultants

Philip J. Deloria
Associate Professor
Department of History
   and Program in
   American Studies
University of Michigan

Lucien Ellington
UC Professor of Education
   and Asia Program
   Co-Director
University of Tennessee,
Chattanooga

Thelma Wills Foote
Associate Professor
University of California

Stephen J. Fugita
Distinguished Professor
Psychology and Ethnic
   Studies
Santa Clara University

Charles C. Haynes
Senior Scholar
First Amendment Center

Ted Hemmingway
Professor of History
The Florida Agricultural &
   Mechanical University

Douglas Monroy
Professor of History
The Colorado College

Lynette K. Oshima
Assistant Professor
Department of Language,
   Literacy and Sociocultural
   Studies and Social Studies
   Program Coordinator
University of New Mexico

Jeffrey Strickland
Assistant Professor, History
University of Texas Pan
   American

Clifford E. Trafzer
Professor of History and
   American Indian Studies
University of California

Teacher Reviewers

Skip Bayliss
Surfside Elementary
Satellite Beach, FL

Annette Bomba
Schenevus Central School
Schenevus, NY

Amy Clark
Gateway Elementary
Travelers Rest, SC

Melissa Cook
Machado Elementary
Lake Elsinore, CA

Kelli Dunn
Lindop School
Broadview, IL

Peggy Greene
Upson-Lee North
   Elementary
Thomaston, GA

Elyce Kaplan
Kumeyaay Elementary
San Diego, CA

Julia McNeal
Webster Elementary
Dayton, OH

Lesa Roberts
Hampton Cove Middle School
Huntsville, AL

Lynn Schew
Leila G. Davis Elementary
Clearwater, FL

Linda Whitford
Manning Oaks Elementary
Alpharetta, GA

Lisa Yingling
Round Hills Elementary
Williamsport, PA

Printed in the U.S.A.

ISBN-13: 978-0-618-49789-8
ISBN-10: 0-618-49789-7

3456789-KDL-13 12 11 10 09 08 07 06

Contents

Bringing the world to your classroom!

References

Citizenship Handbook R2

Resources R44

Extend Lessons

Connect the core lesson to an important concept and dig into it. Extend your social studies knowledge!

Readers' Theater

Geography

Economics

Citizenship

Technology

Biography

More biographies on Education Place—
www.eduplace.com/kids/hmss/

Primary Sources

More primary sources on Education Place—
www.eduplace.com/kids/hmss/

History

Skill Lessons

Take a step-by-step approach to learning and practicing key social studies skills.

North Pole
80°N
Arctic Circle
60°N
40°N
Tropic of Cancer
20°N
West — Equator — 0°East
Tropic of Capricorn
20°S
40°S
Antarctic Circle
60°S
80°S
South Pole

Visual Learning

Become skilled at reading visuals. Graphs, maps, and fine art help you put all the information together.

Diagrams and Infographics

Timelines

Interpreting Fine Art

About Your Textbook

① How It's Organized

Units The major sections of your book are units. Each starts with a big idea.

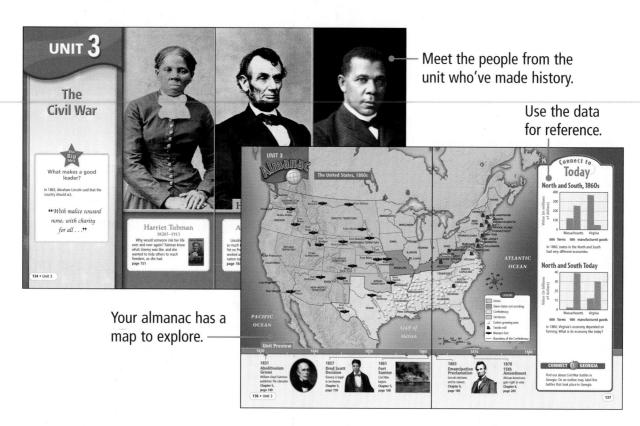

Meet the people from the unit who've made history.

Use the data for reference.

Your almanac has a map to explore.

Chapters Units are divided into chapters, and each opens with a vocabulary preview.

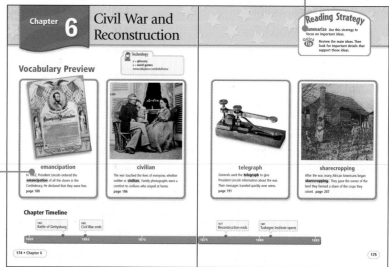

Get ready for reading.

Four important concepts get you started.

❷ Core and Extend

Lessons The lessons in your book have two parts: core and extend.

Core Lessons

Lessons bring the events of history to life and help you meet your state's standards.

Extend Lessons

Go deeper into an important topic.

Primary Sources

Core Lesson

Vocabulary strategies help with word meanings.

Before you read, use your prior knowledge.

Reading skills support your understanding of the text.

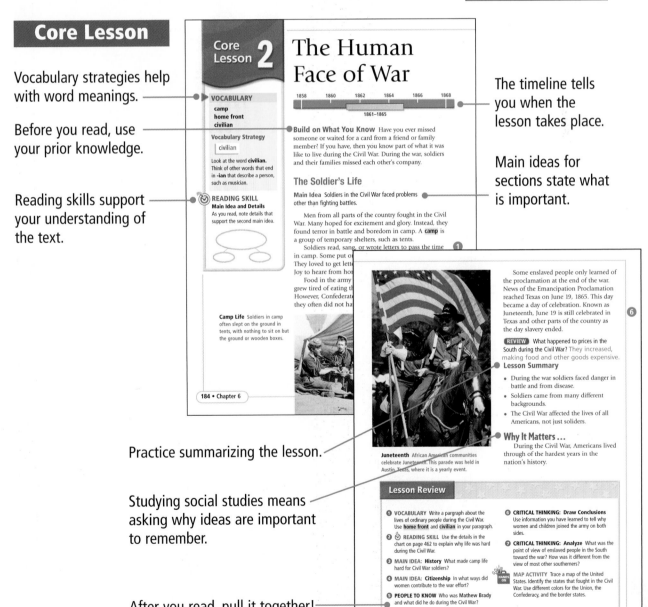

Core Lesson 2

The Human Face of War

| 1858 | 1860 | 1862 | 1864 | 1866 | 1868 |

1861–1865

VOCABULARY
camp
home front
civilian

Vocabulary Strategy

civilian

Look at the word **civilian.** Think of other words that end in **-ian** that describe a person, such as musician.

READING SKILL
Main Idea and Details
As you read, note details that support the second main idea.

Build on What You Know Have you ever missed someone or waited for a card from a friend or family member? If you have, then you know part of what it was like to live during the Civil War. During the war, soldiers and their families missed each other's company.

The Soldier's Life

Main Idea Soldiers in the Civil War faced problems other than fighting battles.

Men from all parts of the country fought in the Civil War. Many hoped for excitement and glory. Instead, they found terror in battle and boredom in camp. A **camp** is a group of temporary shelters, such as tents.

Soldiers read, sang, or wrote letters to pass the time in camp. Some put o[...]
They loved to get lette[...]
Joy to heare from hom[...]

Food in the army [...]
grew tired of eating t[...]
However, Confederat[...]
they often did not ha[...]

Camp Life Soldiers in camp often slept on the ground in tents, with nothing to sit on but the ground or wooden boxes.

184 • Chapter 6

The timeline tells you when the lesson takes place.

Main ideas for sections state what is important.

Some enslaved people only learned of the proclamation at the end of the war. News of the Emancipation Proclamation reached Texas on June 19, 1865. This day became a day of celebration. Known as Juneteenth, June 19 is still celebrated in Texas and other parts of the country as the day slavery ended.

REVIEW What happened to prices in the South during the Civil War? They increased, making food and other goods expensive.

Lesson Summary

• During the war soldiers faced danger in battle and from disease.
• Soldiers came from many different backgrounds.
• The Civil War affected the lives of all Americans, not just soliders.

Why It Matters ...

During the Civil War, Americans lived through of the hardest years in the nation's history.

Juneteenth African American communities celebrate Juneteenth. This parade was held in Austin, Texas, where it is a yearly event.

Lesson Review

❶ **VOCABULARY** Write a pargraph about the lives of ordinary people during the Civil War. Use **home front** and **civilian** in your paragraph.

❷ **READING SKILL** Use the details in the chart on page 462 to explain why life was hard during the Civil War.

❸ **MAIN IDEA: History** What made camp life hard for Civil War soldiers?

❹ **MAIN IDEA: Citizenship** In what ways did women contribute to the war effort?

❺ **PEOPLE TO KNOW** Who was Mathew Brady and what did he do during the Civil War?

❻ **CRITICAL THINKING: Draw Conclusions** Use information you have learned to tell why women and children joined the army on both sides.

❼ **CRITICAL THINKING: Analyze** What was the point of view of enslaved people in the South toward the war? How was it different from the view of most other southerners?

MAP ACTIVITY Trace a map of the United States. Identify the states that fought in the Civil War. Use different colors for the Union, the Confederacy, and the border states.

187

Practice summarizing the lesson.

Studying social studies means asking why ideas are important to remember.

After you read, pull it together!

Extend Lesson
Learn more about an important topic from each core lesson.

Dig in and extend your knowledge.

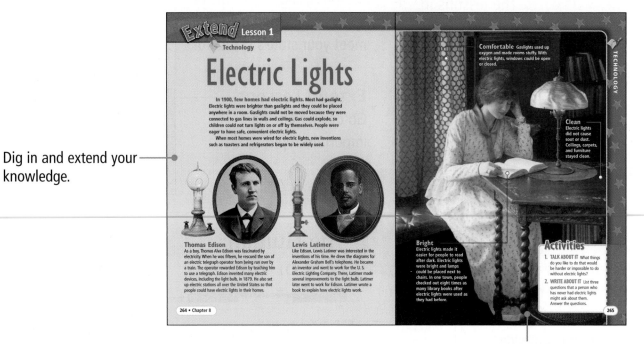

Look closely. Connect the past to the present.

Look for literature, readers' theater, geography, economics—and more.

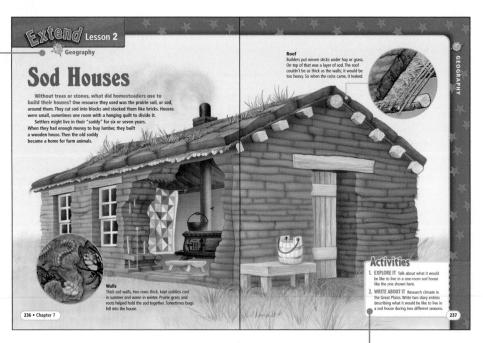

Write, talk, draw, and debate!

③ Skills

Skill Building Learn map, graph, and study skills, as well as citizenship skills for life.

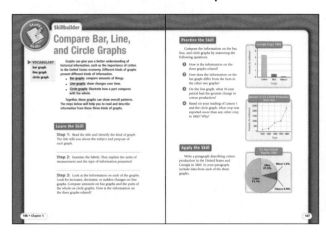

Each Skill lesson steps it out.

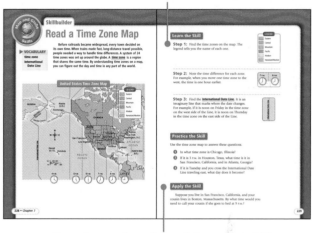

Practice and apply social studies skills.

④ References

Citizenship Handbook

The back of your book includes sections you'll refer to again and again.

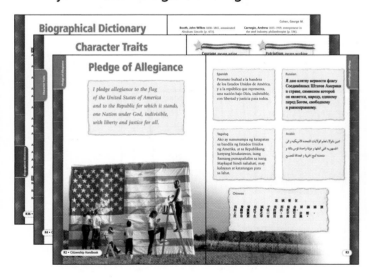

Resources

Look for atlas maps, a glossary of social studies terms, and an index.

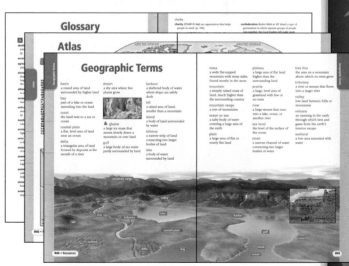

Reading Social Studies

Your book includes many features to help you be a successful reader. Here's what you will find:

VOCABULARY SUPPORT

Every chapter and lesson helps you with social studies terms. You'll build your vocabulary through strategies you're learning in language arts.

Preview
Get a jump start on four important words from the chapter.

Vocabulary Strategies
Focus on word roots, prefixes, suffixes, or compound words, for example.

Vocabulary Practice
Reuse words in the reviews, skills, and extends. Show that you know your vocabulary.

READING STRATEGIES

Look for the reading strategy and quick tip at the beginning of each chapter.

Predict and Infer
Before you read, think about what you'll learn.

Monitor and Clarify
Check your understanding. Could you explain what you just read to someone else?

Question
Stop and ask yourself a question. Did you understand what you read?

Summarize
After you read, think about the most important ideas of the lesson.

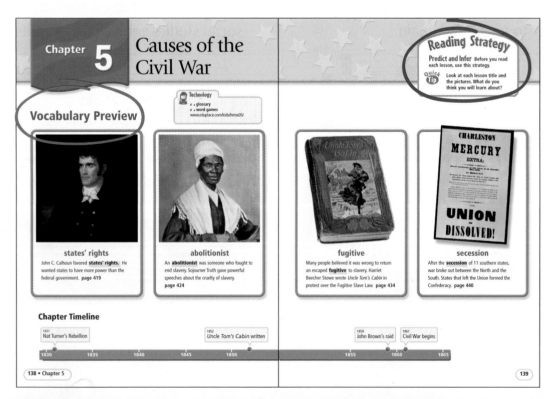

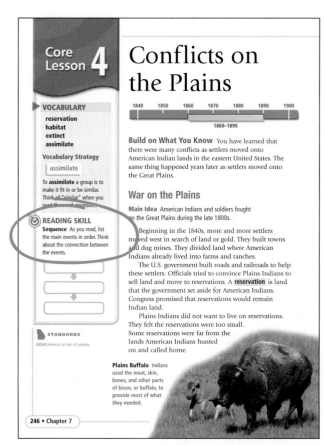

Core Lesson 4

Conflicts on the Plains

VOCABULARY

reservation
habitat
extinct
assimilate

Vocabulary Strategy

assimilate

To **assimilate** a group is to make it fit in or be similar. Think of "similar" when you read the word assimilate.

READING SKILL

Sequence As you read, list the main events in order. Think about the connection between the events.

STANDARDS

SSSH3 America at turn of century

1840 1850 1860 1870 1880 1890 1900

1860–1890

Build on What You Know You have learned that there were many conflicts as settlers moved onto American Indian lands in the eastern United States. The same thing happened years later as settlers moved onto the Great Plains.

War on the Plains

Main Idea American Indians and soldiers fought on the Great Plains during the late 1800s.

Beginning in the 1840s, more and more settlers moved west in search of land or gold. They built towns and dug mines. They divided land where American Indians already lived into farms and ranches.

The U.S. government built roads and railroads to help these settlers. Officials tried to convince Plains Indians to sell land and move to reservations. A **reservation** is land that the government set aside for American Indians. Congress promised that reservations would remain Indian land.

Plains Indians did not want to live on reservations. They felt the reservations were too small. Some reservations were far from the lands American Indians hunted on and called home.

Plains Buffalo Indians used the meat, skin, bones, and other parts of bison, or buffalo, to provide most of what they needed.

246 • Chapter 7

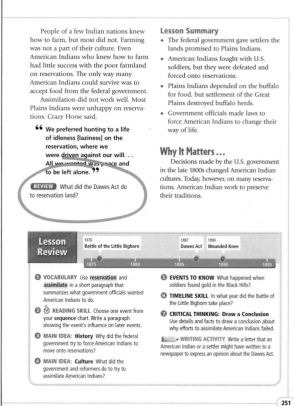

People of a few Indian nations knew how to farm, but most did not. Farming was not a part of their culture. Even American Indians who knew how to farm had little success with the poor farmland on reservations. The only way many American Indians could survive was to accept food from the federal government. Assimilation did not work well. Most Plains Indians were unhappy on reservations. Crazy Horse said,

> 66 We preferred hunting to a life of idleness [laziness] on the reservation, where we were driven against our will. . . All we wanted was peace and to be left alone. 99

REVIEW What did the Dawes Act do to reservation land?

Lesson Summary

- The federal government gave settlers the lands promised to Plains Indians.
- American Indians fought with U.S. soldiers, but they were defeated and forced onto reservations.
- Plains Indians depended on the buffalo for food, but settlement of the Great Plains destroyed buffalo herds.
- Government officials made laws to force American Indians to change their way of life.

Why It Matters . . .

Decisions made by the U.S. government in the late 1800s changed American Indian cultures. Today, however, on many reservations, American Indian work to preserve their traditions.

Lesson Review

1876 Battle of the Little Bighorn   1887 Dawes Act   1890 Wounded Knee

1875   1880   1885   1890   1895

1. **VOCABULARY** Use **reservation** and **assimilate** in a short paragraph that summarizes what government officials wanted American Indians to do.

2. **READING SKILL** Choose one event from your **sequence** chart. Write a paragraph showing the event's influence on later events.

3. **MAIN IDEA: History** Why did the federal government try to force American Indians to move onto reservations?

4. **MAIN IDEA: Culture** What did the government and reformers do to try to assimilate American Indians?

5. **EVENTS TO KNOW** What happened when soldiers found gold in the Black Hills?

6. **TIMELINE SKILL** In what year did the Battle of the Little Bighorn take place?

7. **CRITICAL THINKING: Draw a Conclusion** Use details and facts to draw a conclusion about why efforts to assimilate American Indians failed.

WRITING ACTIVITY Write a letter that an American Indian or a settler might have written to a newspaper to express an opinion about the Dawes Act.

251

READING SKILLS

As you read, organize the information. These reading skills will help you:

Sequence

Cause and Effect

Compare and Contrast

Problem and Solution

Draw Conclusions

Predict Outcomes

Categorize (or) Classify

Main Idea and Details

COMPREHENSION SUPPORT

Build on What You Know
Check your prior knowledge. You may already know a lot!

Review Questions
Connect with the text. Did you understand what you just read?

Summaries
Look for three ways to summarize–a list, an organizer, or a paragraph.

Social Studies:
Why It Matters

Learning social studies will help you know how to get along better in your everyday life, and it will give you confidence when you make important choices in your future.

WHEN I
- decide where to live
- travel
- look for places on a map—

I'll use the geography information I've learned in social studies.

WHEN I
- choose a job
- make a budget
- decide which product to buy—

I'll use economic information.

UNIT 1

Our Land and Early History

The Big Idea

Where would you like to explore?

"Gazing on such wonderful sights we did not know what to say."

A Spanish explorer, on arriving in the Aztec capital in 1519

Christopher Columbus
1451–1506

This explorer had a bold plan to sail west to Asia. Although he never reached his goal, his journeys to the Americas changed history for millions of people.
page 37

History Makers

Queen Isabella
1451–1504

Why did Queen Isabella take a chance on Columbus? She agreed to pay for his voyages because she thought they would bring power and wealth to Spain.

page 37

James Oglethorpe
1696–1785

This wealthy Englishman wanted to help people who owed money or were very poor. He started the colony of Georgia to give them a new beginning in North America.

page 54

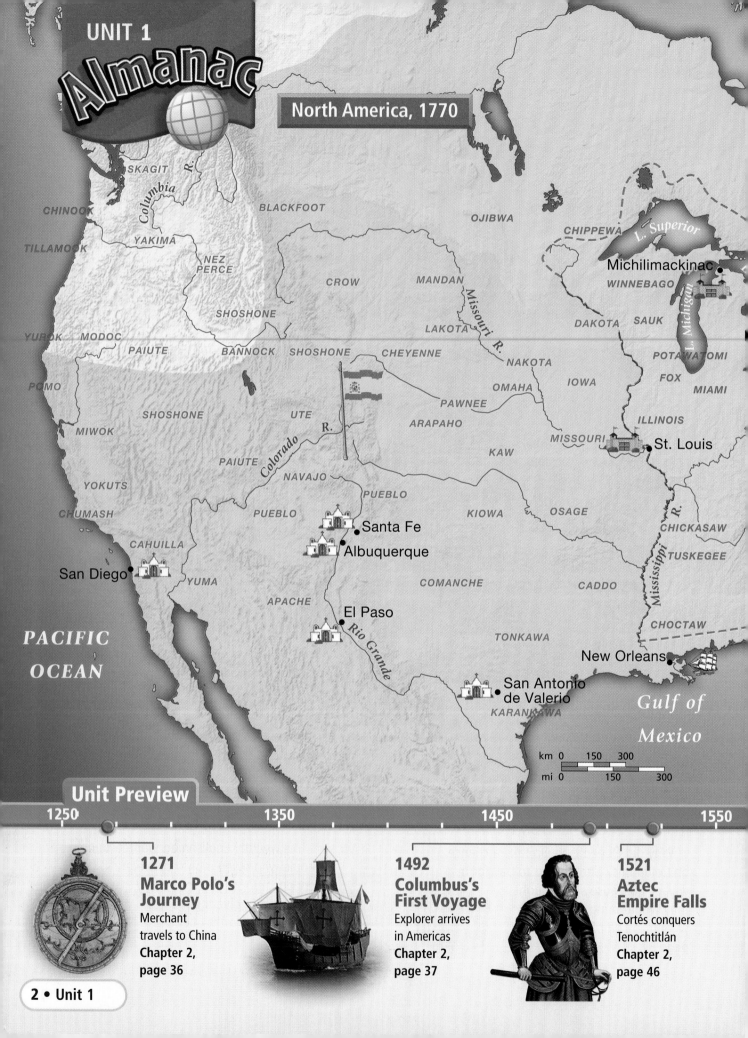

PACIFIC OCEAN

Gulf of Mexico

km 0   150   300
mi 0   150   300

Unit Preview

1250   1350   1450   1550

1271
Marco Polo's Journey
Merchant travels to China
Chapter 2, page 36

1492
Columbus's First Voyage
Explorer arrives in Americas
Chapter 2, page 37

1521
Aztec Empire Falls
Cortés conquers Tenochtitlán
Chapter 2, page 46

Quebec

Halifax

Montreal

ABENAKI

HURON

IROQUOIS NATIONS

L. Ontario

Niagara

L. Erie

Detroit

Boston

SUSQUEHANNOCK

New York

Philadelphia

DELAWARE

Ohio R.

POWHATAN

SHAWNEE

N
NW NE
W E
SW SE
S

CHEROKEE

TUSCARORA

ATLANTIC OCEAN

CATAWBA

Charleston

CREEK

YAMASEE

St. Augustine

TIMUCUA

CALUSA

LEGEND

The Thirteen Colonies

Other British territory

Spanish territory

Reserved for American Indians

Port

Mission

Trading post

HURON American Indians

1650   1750

1607 Jamestown Founded
First successful British colony in America
Chapter 2, page 50

1620 Mayflower Voyage
Pilgrims land at Plymouth
Chapter 2, page 51

Connect to Today

Exports to Britain in 1770s

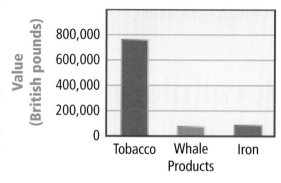

In the 1770s, the colonies' top exports were raw materials.

Exports to the World Today

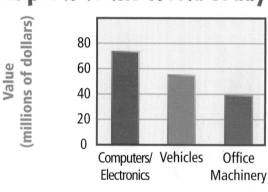

Today, the United States' top exports are manufactured products, such as computers.

Why do you think the kinds of exports have changed from the 1770s to today?

CONNECT to GEORGIA

Research an early European explorer who traveled throughout Georgia in the 1500s and 1600s. Create a journal describing the explorer's experiences.

3

Technology

e • **glossary**
e • **word games**
www.eduplace.com/kids/hmss05/

Vocabulary Preview

region

People think of canyons as a feature of the **region** called the West. Landforms are one feature that can define regions.

page 14

trade

Regions do not produce every item or food product that people want. **Trade** is the buying and selling of goods from other people or regions. **page 16**

Reading Strategy

Predict and Infer Use this strategy as you read the lessons in this chapter.

Quick Tip

Look at the pictures in a lesson to predict what it will be about.

ecosystem

Communities of plants, animals, soil, air, and water make up an **ecosystem.** These things all need one another to survive.

page 23

conservation

To protect the environment, people need to care for our natural resources. Practicing **conservation** benefits everyone.

page 23

The Land and Its Resources

VOCABULARY

resource
scarcity
opportunity cost
economic system

Vocabulary Strategy

scarcity

Scarcity comes from the word scarce, meaning "very little."

READING SKILL

Cause and Effect As you read, look for the causes and effects of scarcity.

CAUSE	EFFECT

Build on What You Know Where you live, can you ride a bike down a steep hill or along a smooth level road? Your answer depends on the landforms around you.

Geography of the United States

Main Idea The geography of the United States includes many kinds of landforms and major bodies of water.

The land and water of the United States make it different from any other place in the world. On either side of the country, long mountain ranges stretch from north to south. The Appalachian Mountains are in the east. They run from Maine to Alabama.

The mountains in the west include the Rocky Mountains and other ranges along the Pacific coast. Between the eastern and western mountains, wide plains stretch across the center of the country.

Rivers and lakes add to the variety of the country. The Mississippi River is the nation's longest river. Water flows into the Mississippi from other large rivers on the plains, including the Missouri, the Ohio, and the Tennessee rivers. The Great Lakes are on the northern side of the central plains. The Mississippi River system and the Great Lakes are important water routes in the middle of the nation.

Grand Canyon This landform is the biggest and deepest canyon in the United States.

STANDARDS

SS5G1a U.S. physical features
SS5E1a Opportunity cost
SS5E2a-c Private business, banks, government
SS5E3b Income

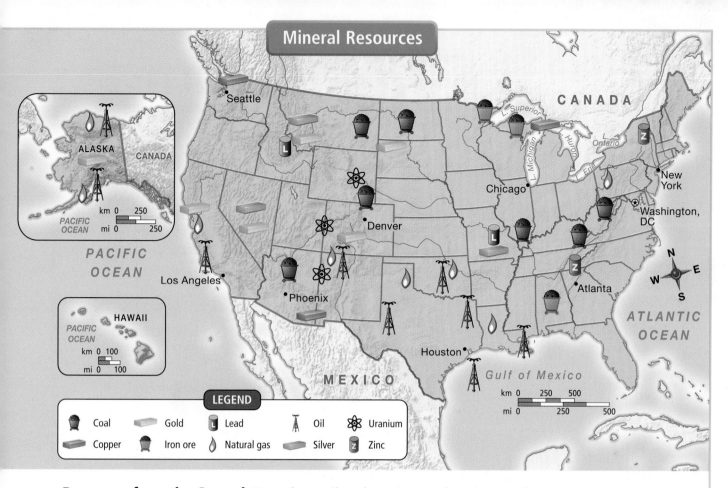

LEGEND

Coal	Gold	Lead	Oil	Uranium	
Copper	Iron ore	Natural gas	Silver	Zinc	

Resources from the Ground Natural gas, oil, and uranium are found across the United States and are used to produce energy. **SKILL** **Reading Maps** Which resources are found near Atlanta?

The Nation's Resources

Main Idea People use natural resources, capital resources, and human resources to produce goods and services.

Valuable resources are found all over the country — in the mountains, on the plains, and in the rivers and lakes. A **resource** is something people use to produce goods and services. Natural resources are one type of resource. A natural resource is a useful or necessary material found in nature, such as water or coal.

Some natural resources are renewable and some are nonrenewable. Renewable resources can be replaced. Fisheries are one example of a renewable resource.

A fishery is a place where many fish are caught. If people do not catch too many fish, new fish will be able to hatch and grow. The resource renews itself.

Nonrenewable resources cannot be replaced once they are used. For example, after oil is removed from the ground, no new oil will take its place.

Flow resources are another kind of natural resource. A flow resource can only be used where and when it is found. People can use wind power, for example, only while the wind is blowing. Wind, water, and sunlight are all flow resources that can be used to produce electricity.

REVIEW What is the difference between renewable and nonrenewable resources?

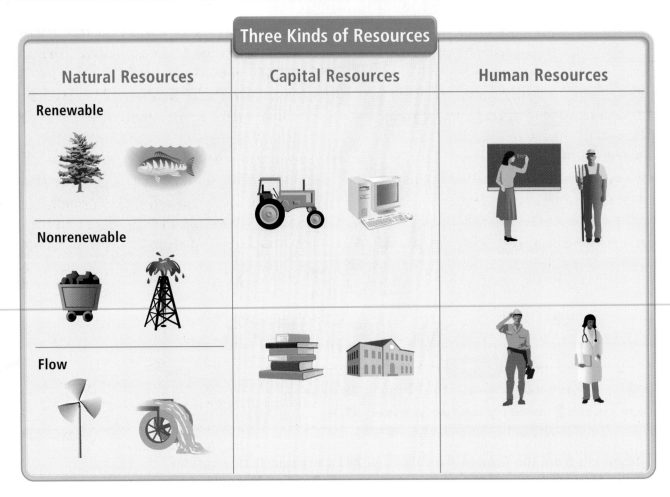

Three Kinds of Resources

Natural Resources	Capital Resources	Human Resources

Renewable

Nonrenewable

Flow

SKILL **Reading Charts** What are two more resources you could add to the categories of capital and human resources?

Capital and Human Resources

Producers use capital resources to make and sell goods and services. Capital resources are made by people and include tools, machines, and buildings. Some of the capital resources in your school are the computers, desks and books.

You are part of another type of resource: human resources. Human resources are people, along with the skills and knowledge they use in their work. Many people sell their labor, or work, to earn income. The teachers and principal are examples of human resources in your school.

Scarcity and Decision Making

Consumers are people who buy and use goods and services. Both consumers and producers face the problem of scarcity. **Scarcity** means not having enough resources to provide all the things people want.

Scarcity forces consumers to make choices. For example, you might want to buy a new book and a new T-shirt, but you don't have enough money for both. If you choose the book, you give up the opportunity to buy the T-shirt. The T-shirt is an opportunity cost. An **opportunity cost** is the thing you give up when you decide to do or have something else.

Economic Systems

Countries also face the problem of scarcity. No country has enough resources to make everything its people want. To solve this problem, each country has an economic system. An **economic system** is a set of rules that guides the use of resources and production of goods in a country.

Every country must answer certain economic questions:

- What goods will be produced and who decides what to produce?
- How will goods be produced?
- Who will receive or buy the goods?

In the economic system of the United States, it is the function of private business, not the government, to answer these questions. Private businesses produce most of the goods and services that people buy and use in the United States.

Other institutions also play important roles in the U.S. economic system. The functions of banks include providing accounts in which people and businesses can save their money. Banks also lend money to people and businesses. Government in the United States has many functions, but its main economic functions are to raise money through taxes and to use that money to provide certain goods and services.

REVIEW What is an economic system?

Lesson Summary

The United States has many types of landforms and natural resources. Resources are used to produce goods and services. Every society has an economic system that guides how people use resources and produce goods.

Why It Matters...

The resources of the United States, and the way they are used, affect people's lives every day.

Lesson Review

1 VOCABULARY Write a paragraph giving examples of the natural, capital, and human **resources** in your classroom.

2 READING SKILL What **effect** does scarcity have on the choices people make?

3 MAIN IDEA: Geography Give an example of a flow resource.

4 MAIN IDEA: Economics Why are capital resources important for producing goods and services? Give an example using details from the lesson.

5 CRITICAL THINKING: Decision Making Think about a recent decision you made, such as what to do after school. Write two sentences describing the opportunity cost of that decision.

 MAP ACTIVITY Use an atlas and an outline map of the United States to find and mark the location of the following places in the United States: Grand Canyon, Salton Sea, Great Salt Lake, Mojave Desert.

Making a Better Bike

It takes a big team to make a world-class bicycle. In fact, thousands of people have a role in making today's best bikes. Some mine the metal for the frame. Others collect the natural rubber used in the tires. Truckers move materials to factories, where workers shape and prepare the parts of the bike. Bankers, researchers, and even artists help make the bike a reality.

How do all these people come together to make the bike? In an economic system like ours, people's choices make it happen. Consumers look for the best bike they can afford. Bike manufacturers compete to sell consumers those bikes. To make the best bikes at the best prices, manufacturers search out materials, parts, and all the help they need. Choice by choice, decision by decision, the team comes together—and so does the bike.

Leather Seat
The seat of the bike is often made from leather. Racers need seats that provide comfort without adding too much weight.

Rubber Tires
The earliest bikes used wheels made of wood. Rubber tires filled with air were invented in 1888 and have been improved ever since. These tires grip the road and smooth the ride.

Early Bicycles
Called "high wheelers," these were hard to handle and much slower than today's racing bikes.

Aluminum
The frame of a modern bicycle is often made of aluminum or carbon fiber. Both materials are strong and much lighter than the metals used for earlier bike frames.

Activities

1. **THINK ABOUT IT** What is one thing you would like to improve in bicycles? Think of a way to make bikes stronger, faster, or less expensive.

2. **DEBATE IT** In a sport such as bicycle racing, better equipment gives some competitors an advantage. Debate whether rules should limit changes in equipment to keep the races fair.

Skillbuilder

Review Map Skills

Maps tell you many things about the world you live in. A **physical map** shows the location of physical features, such as landforms, bodies of water, or resources. A **political map** shows cities, states, and countries. A **historical map** shows information about places and events in the past. The map on this page is a physical map. Although different types of maps show different types of information, most maps share certain elements.

▶ **VOCABULARY**

historical map
physical map
political map

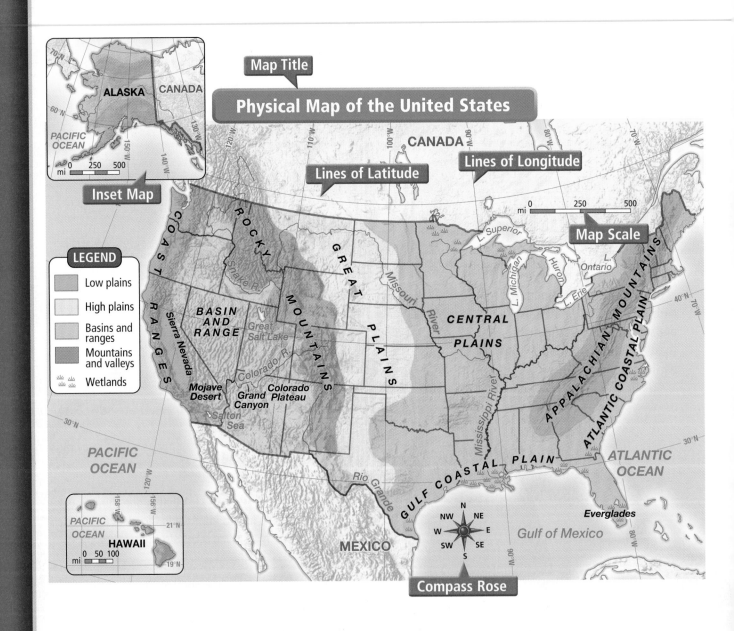

Map Title

Physical Map of the United States

Lines of Latitude

Lines of Longitude

Inset Map

Map Scale

ALASKA CANADA

PACIFIC OCEAN

mi 0 250 500

CANADA

LEGEND

Low plains
High plains
Basins and ranges
Mountains and valleys
Wetlands

COAST RANGES

ROCKY MOUNTAINS

GREAT PLAINS

L. Superior

L. Michigan

L. Huron

L. Ontario

L. Erie

APPALACHIAN MOUNTAINS

ATLANTIC COASTAL PLAIN

Snake R.

BASIN AND RANGE

Great Salt Lake

Sierra Nevada

Missouri River

CENTRAL PLAINS

Colorado R.

Mojave Desert

Grand Canyon

Colorado Plateau

Salton Sea

Mississippi River

PACIFIC OCEAN

Rio Grande

GULF COASTAL PLAIN

Everglades

ATLANTIC OCEAN

PACIFIC OCEAN

HAWAII

mi 0 50 100

MEXICO

Gulf of Mexico

Compass Rose

NW N NE
W E
SW S SE

Learn the Skill

Step 1: Read the map's title and labels to find the subject of the map. Look at the area shown on the map.

Step 2: Study the map legend. What symbols are used on the map?

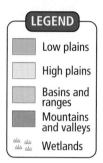

LEGEND

Low plains

High plains

Basins and ranges

Mountains and valleys

Wetlands

Step 3: Check cardinal and intermediate directions with the compass rose. Check distances with the map scale and a ruler.

Step 4: Note the lines of latitude and the lines of longitude. These lines form a grid to help you locate places on the map.

PACIFIC OCEAN

HAWAII

Practice the Skill

Use the map on page 12 to answer the following questions.

1 What type of landform covers the Hawaiian Islands?

2 In what direction would you travel to get from the Colorado Plateau to the Great Plains?

3 At approximately what latitude and longitude does the Mississippi River meet the Gulf of Mexico?

Apply the Skill

Make your own map of the neighborhood where you live. Include a title, a compass rose, and a legend. Use symbols to show places of interest, including the location of your home.

Regions of the United States

Build on What You Know Your school might have separate areas for a soccer field, a basketball court, and a playground. Each area is different from the others, but they are all part of the school. The United States can be divided into different areas, too.

VOCABULARY

region
specialization
trade
interdependent

Vocabulary Strategy

interdependent

Find the word **depend** in **interdependent**. People are interdependent when they depend on each other.

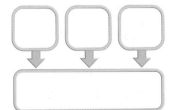 **READING SKILL**

Draw Conclusions As you read, note details that help you come to the conclusion that regions are interdependent.

What Is a Region?

Main Idea Geographers divide the United States into many types of regions.

Geographers study regions to learn more about the world around us. A **region** is an area that has one or more features in common. Those features make one region different from other regions. One way to divide the United States into regions is to group together states that are close to each other. The feature the states have in common is their location. The United States can be divided into four regions this way: Northeast, South, Midwest, and West.

Another way to look at the United States is to divide it into regions with similar landforms. The Rocky Mountain region stretches across several states and has thousands of steep mountains. Nearby, the Great Plains region is made up of flat or gently rolling land.

The Great Plains Much of the Great Plains is used to grow crops, such as wheat.

 **STANDARDS**

SS5E1c Specialization
SS5E1e Trade

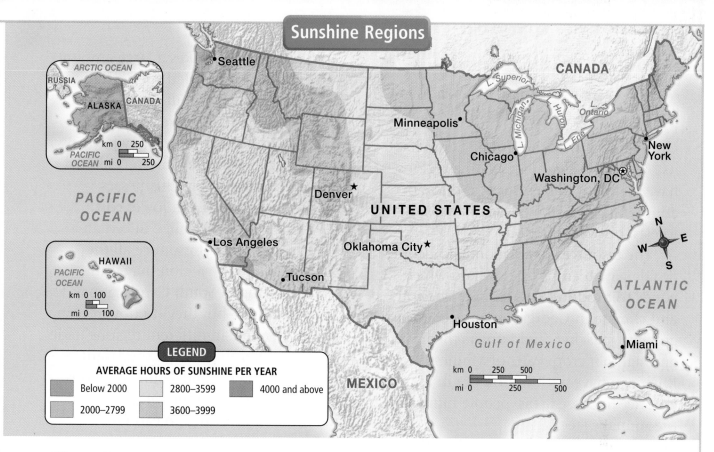

ARCTIC OCEAN
RUSSIA
ALASKA   CANADA
PACIFIC OCEAN
km 0   250
mi 0   250

Seattle

CANADA

L. Superior

Minneapolis

L. Michigan

L. Huron

L. Ontario

L. Erie

New York

Chicago

Washington, DC

Denver ★

UNITED STATES

PACIFIC OCEAN

Los Angeles

Oklahoma City ★

ATLANTIC OCEAN

Tucson

N
W   E
S

HAWAII
PACIFIC OCEAN
km 0   100
mi 0   100

Houston

Gulf of Mexico

Miami

LEGEND

AVERAGE HOURS OF SUNSHINE PER YEAR

Below 2000   2800–3599   4000 and above
2000–2799   3600–3999

MEXICO

km 0   250   500
mi 0   250   500

Climate Patterns Sunshine regions show which places have about the same amount of sunshine from year to year. **SKILL** **Reading Maps** Which city receives more sunshine, Houston or Los Angeles?

Other Kinds of Regions

The United States can be divided into climate regions, too. Regions in the Southwest receive much more sunshine than regions in the Northeast. The regions in the Southwest are usually warmer as well.

Regions can also be based on the goods people produce. The Corn Belt in the Midwest produces more corn than any other region in the country. At one time, the Cotton Belt in the South produced most of the cotton in the United States.

Regions can also be areas where most people speak the same language or share the same customs. All these ways of dividing the country into regions make it easier to compare places.

Regions and Change

Regions can change over time. For example, fruit orchards used to grow in a valley in northern California. In the 1970s, business owners started a few computer companies there. The companies were successful, and soon more were built nearby. Today the region is known for its many computer businesses and is called "Silicon Valley."

People's ideas of regions change over time, too. Americans used to call the Great Plains the "Great American Desert" because crops did not grow well there. When farmers learned new farming methods, the Great Plains blossomed with fields of crops. Now people call this region the "breadbasket" of the country.

REVIEW What are three kinds of regions in the United States?

15

Regions and the Economy

Main Idea Each region uses its resources to produce certain goods and services.

Each region of the United States has its own natural resources. Some regions have plenty of one resource and less of another. The Northwest region has large forests, but very little oil.

The resources in a region help people decide which crops to grow and which goods to produce. For example, the soil and climate in Georgia are perfect for growing peaches, and farmers there grow and sell that crop. Parts of Minnesota and Michigan have a lot of iron ore in the ground. In those areas, people mine iron ore to make steel.

When a region makes a large amount of one product it is called specialization. **Specialization** is the result of people making the goods they are best able to produce with the resources they have. By specializing, people become very skilled and work more quickly. Businesses produce more goods at a lower cost.

When regions specialize in certain products, they do not produce all the goods people in the region may want. Someone living in South Carolina may want pineapples, but they do not grow in that state. People in different regions trade with each other to get what they want. **Trade** is the buying and selling of goods. Trade increases the variety of goods that consumers in every region can buy.

Alabama Marble Alabama specializes in high-quality marble. People in the state mine it (below) and ship it all over the country. Alabama marble has been used in important buildings, such as the Lincoln Memorial (right).

Trade Routes The Mississippi River is an important trade route for shipping goods between regions.

Connected Regions

Today, people in different parts of the United States depend on trade with other regions for the goods and services they do not produce. All regions of the United States are interdependent. To be **interdependent** means to depend, or rely, on each other.

When someone in one region makes a decision about what to produce, people all over the country are affected by that decision. In recent years, fish farmers in the South have started raising more catfish. Goods such as catfish can be moved by truck, train, or airplane anywhere in the nation. Because of this, catfish are now available in supermarkets in cities all over the United States.

REVIEW In what way does trade affect what people can buy?

Lesson Summary

```
Regions share physical
or human features

Regions specialize          Regions trade
```

Why It Matters ...

Studying regions helps people see what places have in common and what makes them unique.

Lesson Review

1. **VOCABULARY** Write a paragraph about the way regions use their resources. Use **region, trade,** and **interdependent.**

2. **READING SKILL** Use your notes to explain how trade makes regions interdependent.

3. **MAIN IDEA: Geography** Why did people's ideas about the Great Plains change?

4. **MAIN IDEA: Economics** What effect does specialization have on workers' skills?

5. **CRITICAL THINKING: Analyze** Why does knowing about regions help people understand the United States better?

6. **CRITICAL THINKING: Synthesize** Why do interdependent regions need good transportation systems?

MAP ACTIVITY Use library resources to find out which climate regions your state is in. Create a map of your state that shows these regions.

EARTHQUAKE REGIONS

Thousands of earthquakes strike the United States each year. Most are so weak that people do not feel them. But the most powerful earthquakes can tear up streets and shake buildings apart.

Earthquakes occur where huge sections of the earth bump and scrape against each other deep underground. The region with the most earthquakes, and the strongest, is along the Pacific coast. In most years, California has more than 50 earthquakes strong enough to break windows and knock objects off shelves. In California, builders use special materials and designs to make structures that can withstand the state's frequent quakes.

Earthquake Facts

- Alaska and California are the states with the most earthquakes.

- Florida and North Dakota are the states with the fewest earthquakes.

- The biggest earthquake in the United States happened in Alaska in 1964.

- About 9,000 very small earthquakes occur around the world every day.

- Earthquakes are usually measured on a scale of 1 to 10 (the most powerful). This system is called the Richter (RIHK tur) scale.

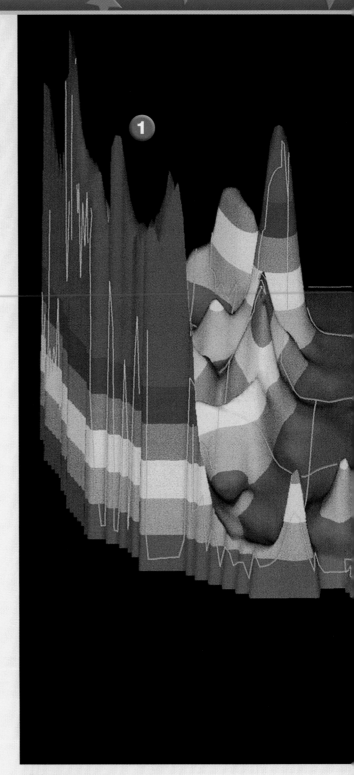

1 The Pacific Coast
Earthquakes are common along the Pacific coast. In the map above, the tall purple spikes show where earthquake activity is strongest.

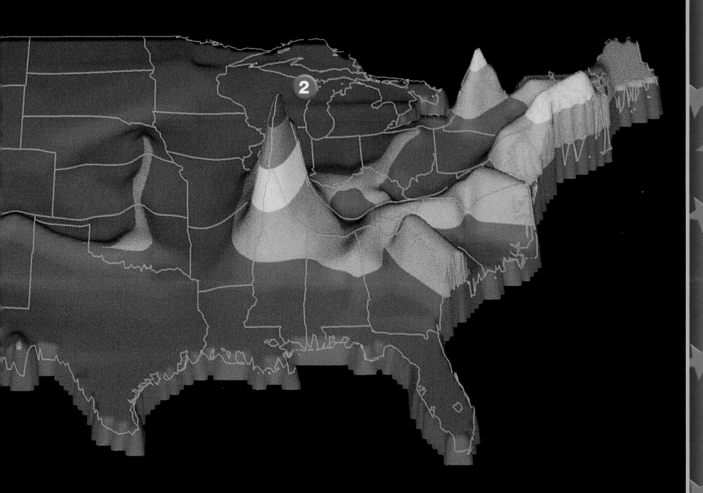

2 Missouri

One of the most powerful earthquakes in U.S. history struck near New Madrid, Missouri, in 1812. It rattled windows as far away as Washington, D.C. and made church bells ring in Richmond, Virginia.

Activities

1. **THINK ABOUT IT** Some regions of the United States have very few earthquakes. What five states would you choose to live in if you wanted to avoid earthquakes?

2. **CREATE IT** Find out what safety rules to follow in case of an earthquake. Create a poster that tells what to do.

People and the Environment

Build on What You Know Different parts of the United States have different resources. Maybe the area where you live has fresh water or good farmland. Resources in your region affect the people who live there and the kinds of work they do.

How Land Affects People

Main Idea The land and its resources affect where and how people live.

More than eight million people live in New York City. It is the largest city in the United States. Why is New York City so big? Geography is part of the reason. Like many large cities, New York has resources and a location that make people want to live there.

New York City is located on the Atlantic coast and has an excellent harbor. A harbor is a body of water where ships can load and unload goods. Shipping and trade gave the city its start and are part of its economy today. That economy provides jobs for millions of people.

Geography has affected the growth of other cities, too. San Francisco, California, grew partly because it has a harbor and because gold was discovered nearby. As thousands of miners moved to San Francisco, the number of stores, restaurants, and other businesses that served them increased. San Francisco's population grew as its economy grew.

New York City The largest city in the United States is a center of shipping, business, and entertainment.

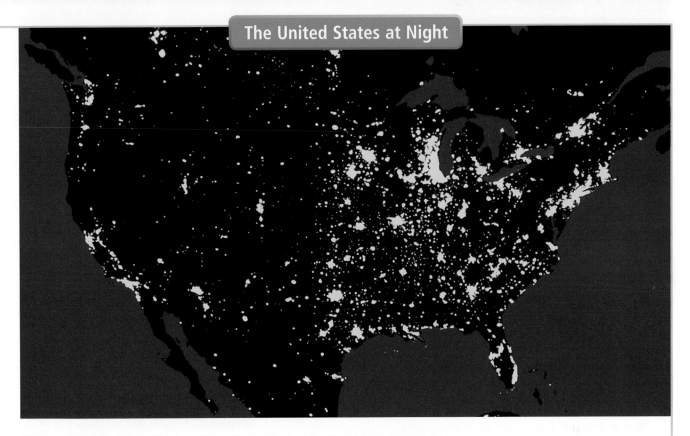

Where People Live This satellite photo shows the United States at night.

SKILL **Reading Maps** What do the light patterns tell you about where the most people live?

Geography and Choices

People settle in places where they are able to earn a living, but they also choose to settle in places they enjoy. Geography affects those choices, too. Many people live in Florida and Arizona because they like the environments there. The **environment** is the surroundings in which people, plants, and animals live. The environment in Florida and Arizona includes a warm, sunny climate.

Geography also affects the activities people do for fun. The mountain ranges in Vermont make downhill skiing a popular winter activity and hiking a popular summer activity in that state. People cannot ski on snow in Florida, but many people like to waterski on that state's lakes and rivers.

Changing the Environment

Main Idea Natural forces and human activities change the environment.

The environment is always changing. Natural forces such as earthquakes and volcanoes cause sudden changes. When volcanoes erupt, whole mountainsides can slide away and bury the land below.

Wind and rain change the land more slowly. The Appalachian Mountains, for example, were once much taller and steeper than they are today. Over time, wind and rain have worn away the soil and rock, leaving the mountains lower and more rounded.

REVIEW In what way did the geography of New York City help it grow?

Human Activities

People also change the land, usually to meet their needs. Their activities always affect the environment. When the United States government built the Interstate Highway System, for example, it made cross-country travel easier. However, the land for the highway could no longer be used for other purposes, such as farming.

People build dams to control the water level of rivers and create electricity. A dam can flood valuable land, though, including wetlands. A **wetland** is a moist area such as a swamp or marsh that provides a home for wildlife.

Strip mining for coal gives people a valuable source of energy. But strip mining can leave pollution in underground water. **Pollution** is anything that makes the water, air, or soil dirty and unhealthy. Pollution makes those resources less valuable and useful.

Clear-cutting forests is another example of people changing the environment. Clear-cutting means cutting down whole areas of forest at one time, to get wood at a low cost. After the trees are gone, rain can wash the soil away. To avoid this problem, logging companies plant trees to replace those they cut down.

Water Power Dams such as this one in the Tennessee River Valley produce energy. Other sources of energy are shown in the chart.

SKILL **Reading Graphs** Which energy source do people use more, water power or nuclear power?

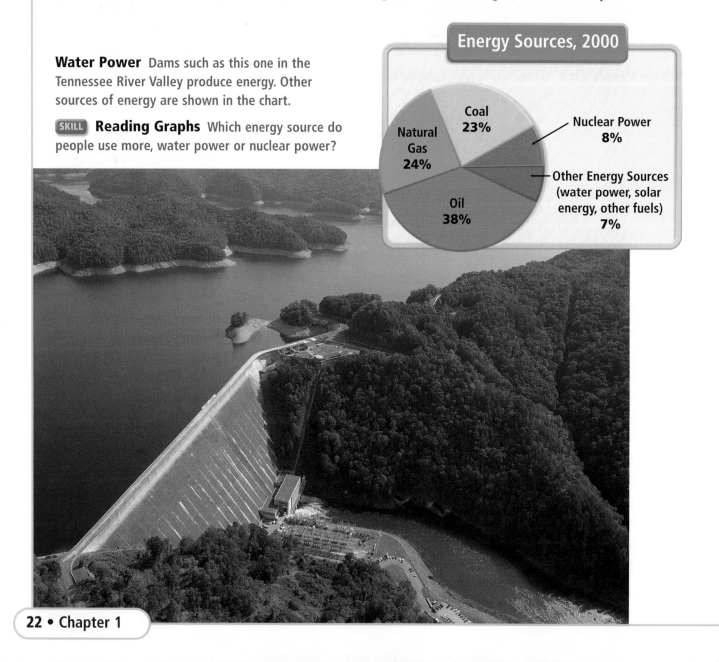

Energy Sources, 2000

- Coal 23%
- Nuclear Power 8%
- Other Energy Sources (water power, solar energy, other fuels) 7%
- Oil 38%
- Natural Gas 24%

The Environment and Conservation

The environment is made up of many ecosystems. An **ecosystem** is a community of plants and animals, along with nonliving things, such as soil, air, and water. Each part of an ecosystem affects the health of all the other parts. A lake is an ecosystem that has water, rocks, plants, fish, and birds. If the water in a lake becomes polluted, it can harm the plants and animals there.

Today people realize that the way they use natural resources affects the environment and its ecosystems. People will always need to use natural resources, but they also have to make sure there are enough resources for people to use in the future. One way to balance the needs of today with concern for the future is to practice conservation. **Conservation** is the protection and wise use of natural resources. The government supports conservation by passing laws to limit pollution.

Businesses can practice conservation by using containers that may be recycled, such as paper and cardboard. Everyone can practice conservation by not wasting water, gas, or electricity. In all these ways, people make choices that will preserve the environment for the future.

REVIEW In what way does conservation save resources?

Lesson Summary
- People change the environment to meet their needs.
- Building highways and digging mines are two of the many ways humans change their environment.
- Changing one part of an ecosystem affects other parts.

Why It Matters ...

People's lives are always connected to the land, and human activities can have lasting effects on the environment.

Lesson Review

❶ **VOCABULARY** Choose the correct word from the list below to complete each sentence.

   conservation   ecosystem   pollution

   _____ makes the river unhealthy for fish.

   When people turn off lights they are not using, they practice _____.

❷ **READING SKILL** How do wind and rain change the land?

❸ **MAIN IDEA: Geography** In what way does the environment influence people's activities?

❹ **MAIN IDEA: Geography** What are some ways people have changed the land?

❺ **CRITICAL THINKING: Compare and Contrast** How was the growth of San Francisco similar to the growth of New York City? How was it different?

❻ **CRITICAL THINKING: Draw Conclusions** Why is pollution harmful to an ecosystem?

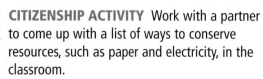

CITIZENSHIP ACTIVITY Work with a partner to come up with a list of ways to conserve resources, such as paper and electricity, in the classroom.

Okefenokee Ecosystem

The Okefenokee swamp is like a giant sponge. It lies on the border between Georgia and Florida, where it soaks up the area's frequent rain. The Okefenokee is full of plants and animals that have adapted to the wet location. Together they form an ecosystem. Every ecosystem has six basic parts. Look for them in this illustration.

Animals That Eat Other Animals
Alligators eat the turtles, birds, fish, and raccoons that live in the swamp. Alligators help keep animal populations in the ecosystem balanced.

Bacteria and Fungi
These tiny plants and animals are too small to see, but they have a big part in ecosystems. They break down dead plants and animals and enrich the soil.

Sun
Sunlight gives the energy that trees and other plants need to make food.

Trees and Plants
Cypress trees, longleaf pines, and plants such as cane grass give food and shelter for swamp animals.

Nonliving Things
All living things need nonliving things, such as soil, water, and air, to live.

Animals That Eat Plants
Deer, rabbits, turtles, and other plant-eating animals live around the swamp. They eat leaves, roots, and berries.

Activities

1. **TALK ABOUT IT** Choose an animal from the drawing and discuss how it fits into the ecosystem.

2. **WRITE ABOUT IT** All the parts of an ecosystem are connected. Write a prediction of what would happen if one part were taken away.

Visual Summary

1–4. ✏️ Write a description of each item named below.

🐟	**Renewable Resources**	
❓	**Economic Questions**	
South Carolina	**Regions**	
🌳	**Conservation**	

Facts and Main Ideas

✔️ **TEST PREP** Answer each question with information from the chapter.

5. **Geography** Why do people build communities in river valleys?

6. **Economics** Why does specialization cause regions to trade?

7. **Geography** Name two kinds of regions in the United States.

8. **Geography** What effect do wind and rain have on mountains over time?

9. **Citizenship** Why is it important for people to practice conservation?

10. **Government** How does the government help protect the environment?

Vocabulary

✔️ **TEST PREP** Choose the correct word to complete each sentence.

specialization, p. 16
trade, p. 16
interdependent, p. 17
environment, p. 21

11. The _____ in Florida includes a warm climate.

12. Regions that are _____ rely on each other.

13. Different regions _____ the goods they produce.

14. _____ is the production of goods based on what resources are available.

Apply Skills

✓ TEST PREP **Map Skill** Study the map of the Caribbean below. Then use your map skills to answer each question.

15. In what direction would you travel to get from Tampa Bay to the Yucatan Peninsula?

   A. northeast

   B. southwest

   C. northwest

   D. southeast

16. Which place is near 20°N 90°W?

   A. Tampa Bay

   B. St. Augustine

   C. Havana

   D. Campeche

Critical Thinking

✓ TEST PREP Write a short paragraph to answer each question.

17. **Cause and Effect** Name four effects human activity has on the environment.

18. **Draw Conclusions** A character in Willa Cather's novel *O Pioneers!* says, "We come and go, but the land is always here." Draw a conclusion about what this statement says about people and the land they live on.

Activities

 Connect to Georgia Research the physical regions of Georgia. Identify the regions on an outline map, using color and labels. Then describe each region.

 Writing Activity Human resources are important to every community. Write a description of the human resources at your school and the skills and knowledge that different people contribute to the school.

 Technology
Writing Process Tips
Get help with your description at
www.eduplace.com/kids/hmss/

Exploration and Settlement

Technology
e • **glossary**
e • **word games**
www.eduplace.com/kids/hmss05/

Vocabulary Preview

migration

Scientists believe that the first people to arrive in the Americas came from Asia. This early **migration** of people happened many thousands of years ago. **page 30**

navigation

In the 1400s, inventions in **navigation** allowed sailors to control the direction in which they traveled. Explorers traveled farther than before. **page 37**

Chapter Timeline

1535
New Spain founded

1607
Jamestown founded

1500   1550   1600

Reading Strategy

Summarize As you read, use the summarize strategy to focus on important ideas.

Review the main ideas to get started. Then look for important details that support them.

empire

The Aztecs ruled large areas of land and many people. Their **empire** included much of present-day Mexico.

page 44

self-government

Many settlers in the English colonies wanted to make laws for themselves. They believed that **self-government** was best for them.

page 55

1620
Plymouth founded

1664
English gain New York

1650

1700

First Americans

30,000 years ago   20,000   10,000   Today

27,000 years ago–500 years ago

VOCABULARY

migration
agriculture
culture

Vocabulary Strategy

culture

The oldest meaning of
culture is to take care of
something. In a **culture,**
people take care of their
traditions and pass them on.

READING SKILL
Compare and Contrast
Chart similarities between two
of the North American Indian
groups in this lesson.

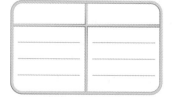

Build on What You Know Have you ever seen a
raccoon or a canoe? Do you know where Ohio and
Massachusetts are? These words and place names, like
many others, come from American Indian languages.
American Indians, also known as Native Americans,
were the first people in North America.

People Arrive in the Americas

Main Idea People first came to the Americas from Asia.

Thousands of years ago, the Earth was much colder
than it is today. Large amounts of water were frozen
in thick sheets of ice that covered almost half the world.

In some areas, the ocean floor was no longer covered
by water. At the Bering Strait, west of what is now Alaska,
the ocean floor turned into land covered by grasses. The
grassland formed a bridge between Asia and North
America. We call this land bridge Beringia.

Crossing into North America

Many scientists believe that the first people to come
to North America crossed this land bridge about 27,000
years ago. Other groups may have traveled in boats
across the sea. The people who crossed Beringia were
hunters following big animals. Scientists think they
traveled in groups from Asia over many thousands of
years. Movement like this, from one region to another, is
called **migration.** The migration over land to North
America ended about 10,000 years ago when the ice
began to melt and water covered Beringia.

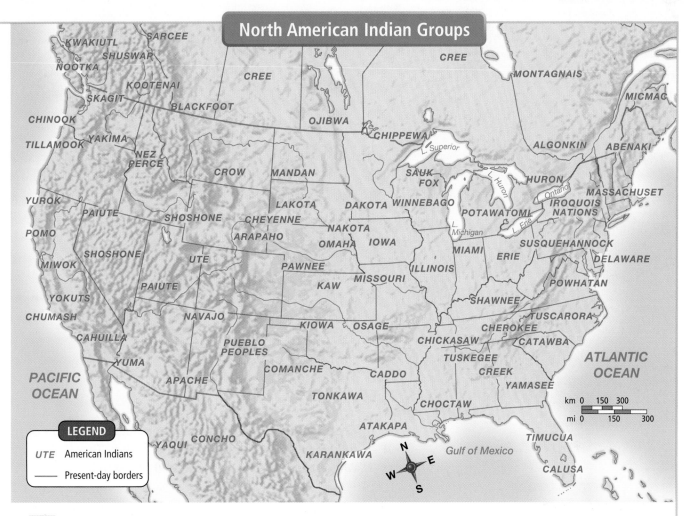

North American Indian Groups

KWAKIUTL
SARCEE
SHUSWAP
NOOTKA
KOOTENAI
SKAGIT
BLACKFOOT
CHINOOK
YAKIMA
TILLAMOOK
NEZ PERCE
CROW
MANDAN
YUROK
PAIUTE
SHOSHONE
CHEYENNE
LAKOTA
DAKOTA
POMO
NAKOTA
ARAPAHO
OMAHA
IOWA
SHOSHONE
MIWOK
UTE
PAWNEE
MISSOURI
PAIUTE
KAW
YOKUTS
CHUMASH
NAVAJO
KIOWA
OSAGE
CAHUILLA
PUEBLO PEOPLES
YUMA
APACHE
COMANCHE
CADDO
YAQUI
CONCHO
TONKAWA
KARANKAWA
ATAKAPA
CHOCTAW

CREE
CREE
MONTAGNAIS
MICMAC
OJIBWA
CHIPPEWA
L. Superior
ALGONKIN
ABENAKI
SAUK FOX
L. Huron
HURON
L. Ontario
MASSACHUSET
WINNEBAGO
DAKOTA
POTAWATOMI
IROQUOIS NATIONS
L. Michigan
L. Erie
MIAMI
ERIE
SUSQUEHANNOCK
ILLINOIS
DELAWARE
POWHATAN
SHAWNEE
TUSCARORA
CHEROKEE
CHICKASAW
CATAWBA
TUSKEGEE
CREEK
YAMASEE
TIMUCUA
CALUSA

PACIFIC OCEAN

ATLANTIC OCEAN

Gulf of Mexico

km 0 150 300
mi 0 150 300

LEGEND

UTE American Indians

— Present-day borders

SKILL **Reading Maps** Which American Indian group lived farthest south in what is now the United States?

Over time, American Indians migrated to all parts of the Americas. Around 9,000 years ago, people in present-day Mexico began to grow wild plants from seeds. This was the beginning of **agriculture,** or farming, in the Americas. As agriculture spread, some American Indian groups stopped moving around. They lived in one place all year round to care for the crops. Other groups continued to move, following the animals they hunted.

As they adapted to their environment, American Indian groups created their own cultures. A **culture** is the way of life that people create for themselves and pass on to their children.

North America in 1500

Main Idea Over time, American Indians developed many different ways of life.

The cultures of American Indians depended in part on the environment in which they lived. American Indian groups such as the Kiowa (KY uh wuh) traveled across the grasslands of the Western Great Plains. They hunted buffalo for food. Large herds of these woolly animals roamed the Plains.

Western Plains Indians depended on the buffalo for almost all of their needs. They ate buffalo meat and made shelter and clothing out of buffalo skin. They carved the bones into tools and weapons.

REVIEW What was Beringia?

Creek Village The Creek built their houses in groups of four. Families lived in each group of houses. They had a winter house, a summer house, and two storehouses.

The Southeast

In the Southeast, American Indians lived very differently. The mild weather and plentiful rainfall were good for farming. Southeast groups such as the Cherokee grew corn, beans, squash, tobacco, and other crops.

Southeast Indians usually lived in villages near their fields. Some groups surrounded their villages with walls made of logs for protection. A Cherokee village might have 50 homes, some buildings to store food, and a central open area for public events.

Unlike the Great Plains, the Southeast has mountains and valleys, rivers, swamps, and forests. American Indians hunted the many animals that lived in these environments, such as deer and bears. They also fished in the rivers and gathered wild plants for food.

The Northwest and Southwest

American Indian groups in other parts of North America also depended upon the environment for their survival. Along the Pacific Northwest coast, people lived near forests and along the sea. The region had many natural resources. For food, Northwest Indian groups such as the Chinook (shih NOOK) caught salmon, hunted deer and other animals, and gathered berries and plants. They built homes and canoes with wood from the forests.

In the Southwest, American Indian groups such as the Navajo (NAH vuh hoe) lived in a very dry climate with little rain and few trees. These groups learned how to farm by making the most of the scarce rainfall and water. They built homes with materials such as clay and stones, gathered from the surrounding land.

In all American Indian cultures, spiritual beliefs were very important. Plains Indians held ceremonies to show respect for the buffalo spirit and ask for a successful hunt. Southeast groups held the Green Corn Ceremony to give thanks for a good harvest. Indians of the Pacific Northwest honored the salmon in their spiritual practices. Southwest Indians held ceremonies to pray for rain and a good harvest. Though each group's beliefs were different, nature was important in the religious beliefs of all.

REVIEW How did the environment of the Southwest affect the lives of American Indians there?

Plains Indian Shield Warriors carried shields made from thick buffalo hide. These shields were strong enough to stop arrows.

Lesson Summary

Most scientists believe that people first came to the Americas when hunters crossed the Beringia land bridge to North America. These people migrated across the Americas and adapted to the many environments they found. The cultures of American Indian groups differed from region to region.

Why It Matters...

American Indians started the first civilization in the Americas. Their cultures are an important part of the history of the United States.

Lesson Review

① **VOCABULARY** Choose the correct word to complete the sentence.

       migration   culture   agriculture

People practiced _____ to grow plants for food.

② **READING SKILL Compare** and **contrast** the way Southwest and Northwest Indians got their food.

③ **MAIN IDEA: History** What effect did agriculture have on American Indian groups?

④ **MAIN IDEA: Culture** Why was the buffalo important to Western Plains Indians?

⑤ **PLACES TO REMEMBER** Where did people first start farming in the Americas?

⑥ **CRITICAL THINKING: Cause and Effect** Think about the climate and geography where you live. How might they have affected the lives of American Indian groups who lived there?

⑦ **CRITICAL THINKING: Infer** Why did the ceremonies of American Indian groups differ from region to region?

HANDS ON **RESEARCH ACTIVITY** Choose one American Indian group from the map on page 31 and find information about it. Make a fact sheet with drawings and captions about that group's culture.

AMERICAN INDIAN SHELTERS

In a harsh climate, good shelter can mean survival. American Indians across the continent faced severe weather at times. Blizzards swept the Plains, hurricanes and rainstorms pounded the coasts, and long winters froze the Northeast.

In every region, American Indians built shelters for protection and comfort. Using local resources, they created homes that suited their needs and their environment.

Pacific Northwest

Type of Shelter
Large house

Materials Used
Boards cut from cedar trees

Unique Features
Totem poles were placed at entrances or used to support a roof. House heated by central open fireplaces.

Southwest

Type of Shelter
Pueblo

Materials Used
Stone and adobe bricks

Unique Features
Ladders connected several stories. Rooms heated by coal fires instead of wood.

Western Great Plains

Type of Shelter
Teepee

Materials Used
Buffalo skins and wooden poles

Unique Features
Easy to pack up and move. Flaps on teepee acted as vents to let out smoke or let in fresh air.

Northeastern Woodlands

Type of Shelter
Longhouse

Materials Used
Bark and wooden poles

Unique Features
Long enough to hold several families and keep several fires going.

Southeastern Woodlands

Type of Shelter
Roundhouse

Materials Used
Wooden poles covered with clay and bark

Unique Features
Used for dances and ceremonies. Sometimes used as shelter for the elderly.

Activities

1. **TALK ABOUT IT** In what ways were the shelters of American Indian groups the same? How were they different?

2. **RESEARCH IT** Research information about the shelters of a group of American Indians from the region where you live. Write and illustrate a one-page report.

Europeans in America

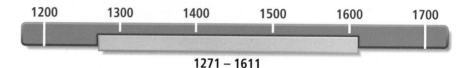

1200   1300   1400   1500   1600   1700

1271 – 1611

Build on What You Know Have you ever read a book that made you want to visit a new place? Around the year 1300, some Europeans read a book by Marco Polo that sparked their interest in a distant land.

The Age of Exploration

Main Idea European explorers began to travel great distances in search of trade routes to Asia.

Marco Polo was an Italian merchant. A **merchant** buys and sells goods to earn money. In 1271, he began a journey from Italy across Europe and Asia to China to trade goods. When he returned, he wrote a book describing the wonders he saw while traveling. This book increased Europeans' interest in Asia.

Over the next 100 years, other European merchants set up trade routes to Asia. They bought goods such as silk and spices from traders in Asian cities. The merchants sold these goods at higher prices in Europe. They earned large profits from this trade. A **profit** is the money left over after expenses have been paid. European rulers tried to find faster and safer trade routes to Asia to increase their nations' wealth and power.

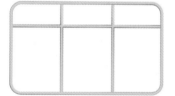

Astrolabe
Sailors used astrolabes to find their way on ocean voyages.

Portugal Leads the Way

European merchants knew that traveling by sea was faster than traveling by land. **Prince Henry** of Portugal believed that sailors could find a new route to Asia by sailing south around the tip of Africa and then northeast to India. To help meet this goal, he started a school for navigation. Navigation is the science of planning and guiding the route of a ship at sea.

Sailors at this school developed new, faster ships called caravels to send on expeditions. An expedition is a journey with an important goal. With improvements in navigation and shipbuilding, expeditions became safer as well as faster.

In 1498, Portuguese explorer **Vasco da Gama** became the first European to sail around Africa to Asia. His ships landed on the coast of India. This new sea route helped Portugal become rich from its trade with Asia.

Columbus's Ships These ships were made for the 500th anniversary of Columbus's voyage to the Americas. They are copies of the *Niña*, *Pinta*, and *Santa Maria*.

Arriving in the Americas

Main Idea Christopher Columbus and other explorers searched for trade routes to Asia.

An Italian sailor named **Christopher Columbus** thought there might be a way to reach Asia by sailing west across the Atlantic Ocean. At that time, Europeans did not know that North and South America existed.

In the late 1400s, Spain's rulers **Queen Isabella** and **King Ferdinand** were looking for ways to expand Spain's power. They also wanted to spread Christianity to other parts of the world. Queen Isabella agreed to pay Columbus to lead an expedition west over the Atlantic. Columbus sailed from Spain in 1492 with three ships.

Two months later, the ships arrived at an island that Columbus named San Salvador. This island is in the Caribbean Sea between North and South America. Columbus wrongly believed he had reached the Indies, a group of islands off the Asian coast. He called the people he met there Indians.

REVIEW Why did European rulers want to find safer and faster trade routes to Asia?

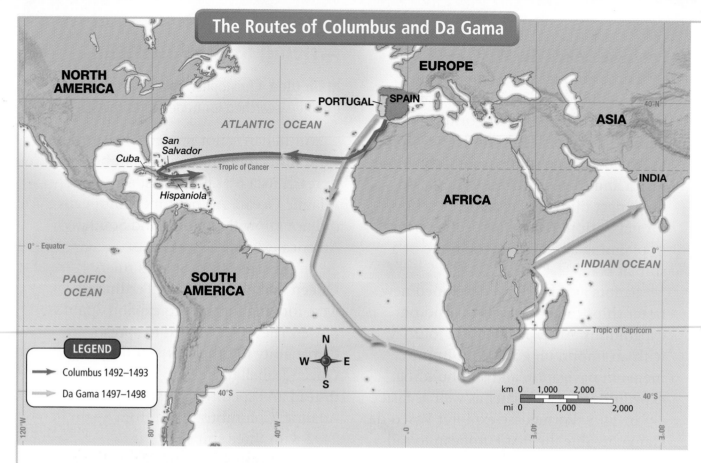

The Routes of Columbus and Da Gama

LEGEND
→ Columbus 1492–1493
→ Da Gama 1497–1498

Routes of Exploration Columbus and da Gama both looked for new trade routes to Asia. **SKILL** **Reading Maps** Use cardinal and intermediate directions to describe da Gama's route to India.

More Voyages to the Americas

Columbus sailed back to Spain, but he returned three times to the Americas. He claimed all the lands he explored for Spain. In time, other Spanish explorers and settlers sailed to the Americas. Each journey increased Spain's power there.

England, Portugal, and France also joined the search for a western trade route to Asia. England hired a sea captain named **John Cabot** to lead an expedition. In 1497, he landed in Newfoundland on the coast of present-day Canada. He claimed this land for England.

Portugal hired **Pedro Álvares Cabral** to find a new route to India. On his expedition he found a land that was unknown to Europe—present-day Brazil. Cabral claimed this land for Portugal.

About forty years later, French explorer **Jacques Cartier** (kahr TYAY) explored part of the St. Lawrence River. He claimed the surrounding land for France. That land is now part of Canada.

English explorer **Henry Hudson** was hired by the Dutch and then by the English to find a water route across North America to Asia. Between 1609 and 1611, he explored a wide river in present-day New York and a large bay in northern Canada. Both were later named after him.

The Columbian Exchange

Once Europeans reached America's shores, both Europe and the Americas were changed forever. Europeans found crops they had never seen before, such as corn, potatoes, tomatoes, and beans. They took these plants back to Europe.

Europeans brought new plants and animals to the Americas. These included wheat, sugar, horses, cattle, and pigs. This movement of goods between the Western Hemisphere and the Eastern Hemisphere is named after Columbus. It is called the **Columbian Exchange.**

Europeans also brought much suffering to American Indians. They carried diseases that were new to the Americas, such as smallpox and measles. Over time, European diseases would kill millions of American Indians.

The Columbian Exchange, however, made life better for American Indians in some ways. Plains Indians began using horses to hunt and travel. Many European plants and animals provided Indians with new sources of food and clothing.

REVIEW What new crops did Europeans find in the Americas?

Lesson Summary

> Marco Polo's book led to European interest in Asian trade.

> In search of a new route to Asia, Christopher Columbus sailed to the Americas.

> French, Portuguese, and English explorers came to the Americas after Columbus.

> The Columbian Exchange carried plants, animals, and diseases between the Western and Eastern Hemispheres.

Why It Matters ...

When Europeans came to the Americas, they had contact with American Indians for the first time. This contact changed life in both places forever.

Lesson Review

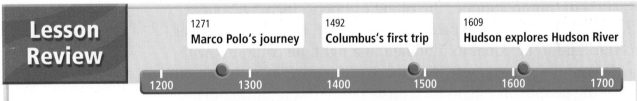

1271
Marco Polo's journey

1492
Columbus's first trip

1609
Hudson explores Hudson River

| 1200 | 1300 | 1400 | 1500 | 1600 | 1700 |

① **VOCABULARY** Why is **navigation** important to an **expedition?** Write a brief explanation using both words.

② 🕑 **READING SKILL** Review the **categories** you used for your chart. Write a paragraph about one of the explorers in this lesson, using information you have gathered.

③ **MAIN IDEA: History** In what ways did Prince Henry help European exploration?

④ **MAIN IDEA: Economics** What was the Columbian Exchange?

⑤ **TIMELINE SKILL** How many years after Marco Polo's journey did Columbus sail to the Americas?

⑥ **CRITICAL THINKING: Infer** European explorers found continents they had never known before. Why do you think they began claiming land there for their countries?

HANDS ON

GRAPH ACTIVITY Using the map of European explorers' travel routes in the lesson, estimate the distance each traveled. Create a bar graph to show your results.

Juan Ponce de León

by Jean Fritz

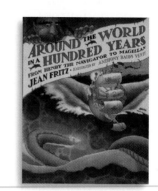

After Columbus reached the islands of the West Indies, explorers of the early 1500s were curious about the land that lay to the north. Juan Ponce de León was a Spanish explorer living on the island of Hispaniola (now Haiti and the Dominican Republic). Stories he heard about that land sparked his imagination.

Juan Ponce de León had been living in Hispaniola since arriving with Columbus in 1493, and he was interested in that land. And not only the land. Somewhere on that land there was supposed to be a magic fountain that made old people young and kept young people young if they drank from it. People said it might be on an island called Bimini. Or on another nearby island.

But before Ponce de León could look for the fountain, the king of Spain sent him to conquer the island of Puerto Rico. Of course his famous red-coated dog, Bercerillo, went with him. Not only was Bercerillo said to be equal to fifty men in a fight, he could tell with a single sniff if a stranger was friendly or unfriendly. As it turned out, most of the people on Puerto Rico (also Tainos) were unfriendly, but Ponce de León himself was not friendly either. In any case, he conquered the Tainos and for three years ruled the island. Still, off in the distance he kept hearing that gush of water, that splash of promise—the sound of old age washing away.

On March 3, 1513, with the permission of the king, Ponce de León set out at last to follow his dream. And none too soon. He was thirty-nine years old now, not really old but not really young either. With three ships he sailed north, picking his way among the islands scattered like grazing sheep across the sea.

On April 3, after just a month at sea, he dropped anchor and went ashore on what seemed to be a large island. A beautiful island so ablaze with wildflowers and blossoming trees, it appeared to be the very home of springtime. The air smelled sweet. And young. Just the kind of place a person might expect to find a magic fountain. Ponce de León planted a cross and claimed the land for Spain. Because it was Easter season (Pascua florida, or "flowering Easter"), he called it La Florida. But there was no sign of gushing water.

Down the coast he sailed, stopping at every village to ask about a fountain. Not only did the people not know about any fountain, they didn't like Spaniards bursting in on them. They didn't want Spaniards even to come near. Actually, Ponce de León need not even have asked. If there had been a magic fountain nearby, there would not have been old people in the village. And there were. Still, he kept asking. Only once did his hopes rise. Stopping at a tiny island known now as Key Biscayne, he came upon a clear, bubbling spring. It was not a fountain but it was so crystal-like, so dancing with sunlight, it looked as if it might have been a fountain once. Eagerly, Ponce de León and his men leaned down and scooped up handfuls of water. They slurped it down. Then they stood, looking at each other, waiting for something to happen. Nothing did.

On they sailed. Around the southern tip of Florida. Up the west side. Before going back to Puerto Rico, Ponce de León sent one of his ships to search for the island of Bimini while he went south and west. Still hoping. When he came to land, he mistook it for Cuba or an island off Cuba. Just in case, he named it Bimini, but when he and his men left, they were all just as old as when they had come. As it happened, this land was the Yucatan peninsula, and without knowing it, Ponce de León was the first European to step on what would later be called Mexico.

Back in Puerto Rico, Ponce de León kept thinking about Florida. Not about the Fountain of Youth. As the years went by, he gave up on that. Perhaps people teased him about his early dreams. That fountain, they would have said, was just a story. Too strange to be true. But what was too strange? Was it any stranger than a new world suddenly popping out of the Ocean Sea?

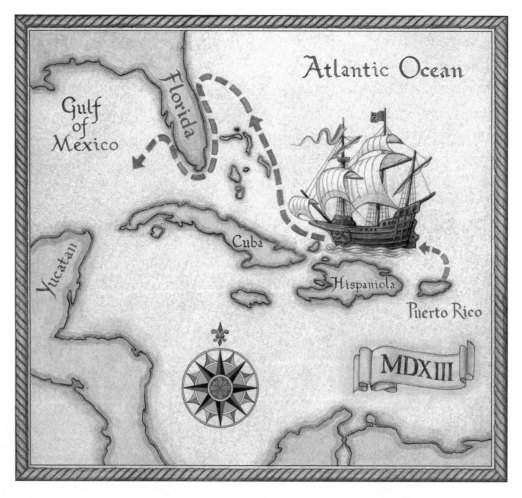

The map shows Ponce de León's route in 1513. Where did his journey start?

By the time Ponce de León was forty-seven years old, he had resigned himself to the idea of old age, but he did want to spend his last years in Florida. After all, he'd found the place, claimed it, and now he wanted to plant a colony on it. He also wanted to find out if Florida was an island or not. On February 21, 1521, he set out with two hundred men, fifty horses, cattle, sheep, and swine and landed on the beautiful shell-strewn beach that we now call Sanibel Island. But the native people of Florida were no happier to see Spaniards now than they had ever been. Hardly had the colonists started to put up their houses before angry natives descended upon them, bows drawn, arrows flying. One of the arrows buried itself deep in Ponce de León's flesh. It was a serious wound that not only wouldn't heal but became dangerously infected. The colonists decided that Florida was not for them. So they boarded their ships and sailed to the nearest settlement in Cuba. Ponce de León's wound never did heal and he died in Cuba, still not sure if Florida was an island or not.

Alonso Alvarez de Pineda was the one who settled the island question. He was one of many explorers looking for a strait that would lead quickly to China. There must be such a strait, explorers figured—some way through this inconvenient mass of land that was keeping them from where they wanted to go. On his search Pineda mapped the shore of the Gulf of Mexico and encountered a mighty river which would later be called the Mississippi. Pineda came upon no strait, but he did determine that Florida was part of the mainland.

Activities

1. **MAP IT** The map on page 42 shows only part of Ponce de León's route. Trace the map and draw a route that shows the other places where he went.

2. **WRITE ABOUT IT** What were Ponce de León's strengths and weaknesses as a leader? Write two paragraphs that answer this question. Include specific examples.

New Settlements

| 1500 | 1550 | 1600 | 1650 | 1700 | 1750 | 1800 |

1519 – 1664

VOCABULARY

empire
colony
convert
mission

Vocabulary Strategy

mission

The word **mission** has more than one meaning. In this lesson, it means a religious community.

READING SKILL

Predict Outcomes Note what you think will happen as a result of the European explorations.

PREDICTION:

OUTCOME:

Build on What You Know Have you ever competed against others for something you really wanted? During the 1500s and 1600s, European countries competed with each other to gain land in North America.

New Spain

Main Idea After the Spanish conquered the Aztec Empire in present-day Mexico, they started the colony of New Spain.

In the early 1500s, the Aztecs ruled an empire that covered much of present-day Mexico. An **empire** is a group of nations or territories ruled by a single government or leader. The Aztecs built their empire by conquering nearby Indian nations. Many Aztec people lived in the capital city of Tenochtitlán (teh nawch tee TLAHN).

The Aztecs and Cortés

In 1519, the powerful Aztecs faced a new challenge. **Hernán Cortés** (kohr TEHS), a Spanish explorer, landed on the east coast of Mexico. Cortés and his 600 soldiers planned to conquer the region, claim land for Spain, and take gold back to his home country.

The Aztec ruler **Moctezuma** (mock teh zoo mah) welcomed Cortés at first. The Spanish explorer's greed for gold soon angered Moctezuma. The Aztecs attacked the Spanish and drove them from Tenochtitlán.

Moctezuma He was the last leader of the Aztecs, ruling from 1502 to 1520.

Defeat of the Aztecs

Cortés returned with an army that included thousands of men from nearby Indian nations. The Spanish also had horses, guns, and steel armor, and the Aztecs did not. With the Aztecs weakened by smallpox, a European disease, Cortés was able to defeat them in 1521.

Cortés took gold and other Aztec treasures back to Spain. His expedition encouraged more Spanish to come to the Americas. In 1535, the king of Spain made Mexico a colony called New Spain. A **colony** is a territory that is ruled by a distant country.

In 1540, **Francisco Vásquez de Coronado** (kor oh NAH doh) led an expedition north of Mexico in search of gold. Coronado did not find gold, but he claimed large areas of what is now the southwestern United States for Spain. **Hernando de Soto**'s exploration in present-day Florida led to Spanish claims there as well.

Life in New Spain

New Spain attracted thousands of Spanish settlers. The Spanish government gave land to the first settlers. The government also allowed colonists to force Indians to work for them without pay. Indians worked under harsh conditions on Spanish farms and in Spanish mines.

Priests followed the explorers into the Southwest. They believed they could improve the lives of American Indians by converting them from their religions to Roman Catholicism. To **convert** means to convince someone to change his or her religion or beliefs. In order to do this, the priests built missions throughout New Spain. A **mission** was a religious community where priests taught Christianity. Through these missions, the Spanish tried to change the American Indians' religions. They also tried to change their culture, language, and farming methods.

REVIEW Why was Cortés able to defeat the Aztecs?

Spanish Mission Church buildings were at the center of missions.

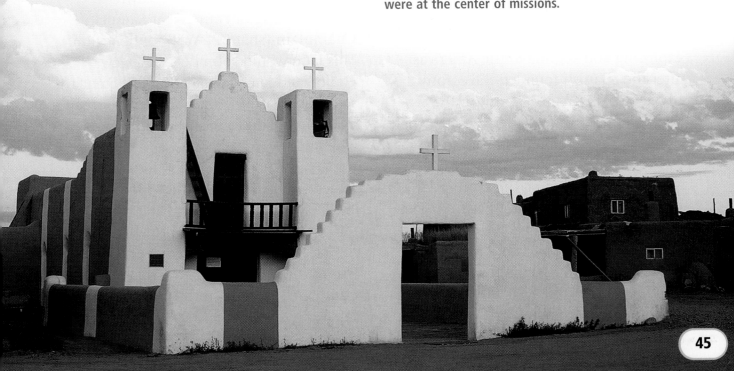

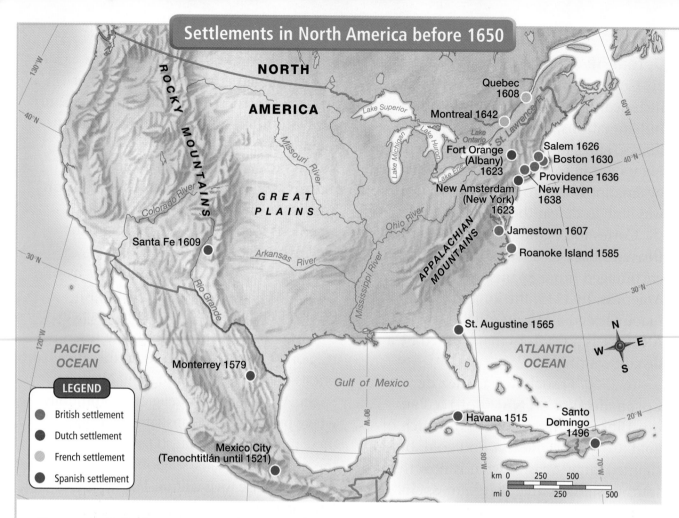

NORTH

AMERICA

Quebec
1608

Montreal 1642

ROCKY MOUNTAINS

Lake Superior

Lake Michigan

Lake Huron

Lake Ontario

Lake Erie

St. Lawrence R.

Missouri River

GREAT
PLAINS

Colorado River

Ohio River

APPALACHIAN MOUNTAINS

Fort Orange
(Albany)
1623

Salem 1626
Boston 1630

Providence 1636
New Haven
1638

New Amsterdam
(New York)
1623

Jamestown 1607

Roanoke Island 1585

Santa Fe 1609

Arkansas River

Mississippi River

Rio Grande

St. Augustine 1565

PACIFIC
OCEAN

ATLANTIC
OCEAN

N
W E
S

Monterrey 1579

Gulf of Mexico

LEGEND

● British settlement

● Dutch settlement

● French settlement

● Spanish settlement

Havana 1515

Santo
Domingo
1496

Mexico City
(Tenochtitlán until 1521)

km 0   250   500

mi 0   250   500

European Colonies Four European countries claimed different parts of
North America. **SKILL** **Reading Maps** Which country settled farthest south?

Challenges to New Spain

Main Idea European countries explored and
claimed land in North America.

Other European countries began
exploring and settling in the Americas
after the Spanish founded the colony
of New Spain. France, Portugal, the
Netherlands, and England wanted a share
of the riches that had made Spain the
most powerful country in the world.

When settlers from these other
nations arrived, a new age began in the
Americas. Spain now had to compete
with other Europeans for land and
wealth. New languages, religions, and
customs were brought to North America.

New France

About 75 years after **Jacques Cartier**
claimed land around the St. Lawrence
River, the king of France sent **Samuel de
Champlain** (sham PLAYN) to the region.
This land would soon be called New
France, and later Canada. But few French
settlers had arrived since Cartier's journey,
and Champlain found no major towns
when he arrived.

Champlain started a fur-trading
settlement on the St. Lawrence River in
1608. He called it Quebec. Later, it became
the capital of the colony of New France.

Far fewer colonists came to New
France than to New Spain. Those who
came often worked in the fur trade or
made a living fishing.

The French traded with the Huron and other American Indians living near the Great Lakes. Many French traders learned American Indian languages and customs.

Over the next 100 years, French traders and explorers traveled across large parts of North America. They claimed much of it for France, including the Mississippi River and the surrounding lands.

New Netherland

After Henry Hudson's explorations, the Dutch claimed all the land along the Hudson River. They called it New Netherland. Dutch colonists were mostly farmers and fur traders. Many settlers lived in New Amsterdam, which was the largest city in the colony.

Dutch control of New Netherland lasted only 42 years. In 1664, English ships sailed into the harbor at New Amsterdam to attack the colony.

The Dutch colony of New Netherland became an English colony. The English renamed New Amsterdam and called it New York.

REVIEW What country did New France become?

Lesson Summary

- After Cortés's defeat of the Aztecs, Spain created the colony of New Spain.
- The Spanish forced many American Indians to work for them. They also built missions to teach Christianity to American Indians.
- The French and Dutch started colonies in North America. The settlers there fished, traded for furs, and farmed.

Why It Matters ...

The creation of colonies brought European languages and cultures to the Americas.

Lesson Review

| 1521 Cortés defeats Aztecs | 1608 Champlain founds Quebec | 1664 English control New York |

1500   1600   1700

❶ **VOCABULARY** Describe New Spain in a short paragraph, using the words **colony** and **mission.**

❷ 🕐 **READING SKILL** Review your chart. Did your **predictions** agree with the actual outcomes of the explorations?

❸ **MAIN IDEA: History** Why did so many settlers come to New Spain?

❹ **MAIN IDEA: Geography** Why did other European nations start colonies in North America after Spain?

❺ **PEOPLE TO KNOW** Who was **Hernán Cortés** and what was the result of his voyage?

❻ **TIMELINE SKILL** How many years passed between Cortés's defeat of the Aztecs and the founding of Quebec?

❼ **CRITICAL THINKING: Cause and Effect** What effect did the Spanish have on the lives of Indians in New Spain?

HANDS ON

CHART ACTIVITY Make a chart comparing the Spanish, French, and Dutch colonies in the Americas. Include information on when and where these colonies were settled. Add details and illustrations of the kinds of work people did.

EUROPEAN EXPLORERS

Three explorers each had different goals. Hernán Cortés of Spain, Samuel de Champlain of France, and Henry Hudson of England all claimed lands in North America for their countries. One wanted gold, one wanted to trade, and one searched for a shortcut to China.

Hernán Cortés * 1485–1547

In his shining armor, Hernán Cortés may have looked like a god to the Aztec people. Cortés was eager to find gold, which he had heard about from Christopher Columbus. After conquering the Aztec empire in 1521, Cortés became governor of Mexico. Later, he led an expedition to Central America. When he returned to Mexico from a trip to Spain, he found other officials had taken over some of his power. Cortés continued to explore Mexico, searching for gold.

Samuel de Champlain ✳ 1567–1635

Should France create a colony on the St. Lawrence River? Samuel de Champlain thought so. He knew the St. Lawrence region was rich in beaver and bear pelts. In 1603, Champlain looked for good sites for a French colony. Champlain built a successful fur trade with the help of the Algonquian and Huron Indians. He became the leader of the colony of New France. Throughout his travels, Champlain kept a detailed journal. Today, his journal shows what life was like four hundred years ago.

Henry Hudson ✳ 1575?–1611

Henry Hudson was a determined man. Again and again he tried to find a water route from England to China. On his first two trips he sailed near Greenland, but his passage was blocked by ice. In 1609, a third voyage brought him to the Atlantic coast of North America, where he entered New York Bay. He sailed up the Hudson River, now named after him. The river narrowed and Hudson's hopes died again. On a fourth expedition, he explored a part of the Atlantic Ocean now called Hudson Bay. Although Henry Hudson never found the sea passage that he was looking for, he sailed farther north than any other explorer.

Activities

1. **THINK ABOUT IT** Which explorer was most successful at achieving his goal and why? Why do you think the others were less successful?

2. **CONNECT IT** Choose a voyage taken by one of these explorers. List the challenges of that trip and how long it would have taken. Then list the challenges and length of the same trip taken today.

 Technology Visit Education Place for more biographies of people in this unit. www.eduplace.com/kids/hmss05/

English Colonies

1500   1550   1600   1650   1700   1750   1800

1607 – 1732

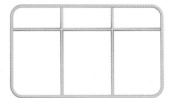
Build on What You Know Have you ever grown a plant from a seed? If so, you probably found that the soil and climate had to be just right for the plant to grow. When English colonists moved to North America, they had to learn which crops grew best in their new lands.

The First English Settlements

Main Idea The first successful English settlements in North America were in Virginia and Massachusetts.

When English settlers came to North America in the late 1500s and early 1600s, they hoped to find gold, silver, and other riches. These first settlers did not find riches, but they did claim land for England on the east coast of what is now the United States.

Jamestown and Plymouth

The first successful English colony in North America was Jamestown, in present-day Virginia. Jamestown was founded in 1607 by a group of English men and boys who came to look for gold.

Most of the Jamestown settlers did not know how to farm, and many colonists soon died from disease or lack of food.

John Smith He was the leader of the settlement at Jamestown. He helped the colony survive its difficult early years.

Plimoth Plantation At Plimoth Plantation (as it was originally spelled), actors show the way early settlers lived. **SKILL** **Reading Visuals** What activities are the settlers doing?

A Jamestown settler named **John Rolfe** began to grow tobacco in 1612. The crop grew well in Virginia's hot, humid climate. Before long, Jamestown merchants were selling thousands of pounds of tobacco to England. Tobacco became Jamestown's first cash crop. A **cash crop** is a crop that is grown and sold to earn income. The sale of tobacco gave the colony enough money to buy much-needed food and supplies from England.

In 1620, another group of English settlers sailed to North America on a ship called the *Mayflower*. These settlers became known as the Pilgrims. Their group was part of the Puritan movement in England. The Puritans were people who wanted to change and purify the Church of England.

The Church of England was the only legal church in England at that time. The Pilgrims decided to leave England to form a settlement where they could live and worship freely. They founded the colony of Plymouth, in present-day Massachusetts.

During the first winter in Plymouth, nearly half of the Pilgrims died from lack of food. The following spring, the Pilgrims met an American Indian named **Squanto** (SKWAHN toh). Squanto taught the colonists how to raise crops such as maize (corn), pumpkins, and beans. He also guided them in hunting and fishing. Squanto's lessons helped the Pilgrims survive.

REVIEW What cash crop helped Jamestown settlers create a lasting settlement?

Three Regions

Main Idea Colonists built settlements and adapted to the different climates and resources in their regions.

During the 1600s, many more English settlers moved to North America. They started new colonies in the three regions of New England, the Middle Colonies, and the Southern Colonies.

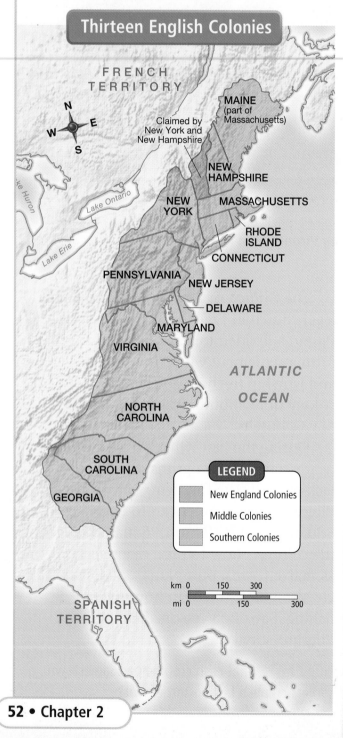

Thirteen English Colonies

FRENCH TERRITORY

MAINE (part of Massachusetts)

Claimed by New York and New Hampshire

NEW HAMPSHIRE

NEW YORK

MASSACHUSETTS

RHODE ISLAND

CONNECTICUT

PENNSYLVANIA

NEW JERSEY

DELAWARE

MARYLAND

VIRGINIA

ATLANTIC OCEAN

NORTH CAROLINA

SOUTH CAROLINA

GEORGIA

Lake Huron

Lake Ontario

Lake Erie

SPANISH TERRITORY

LEGEND
New England Colonies
Middle Colonies
Southern Colonies

km 0   150   300
mi 0   150   300

New England

After the Pilgrims founded Plymouth, other groups of Puritans came to the region. They also disagreed with the Church of England and hoped to start a community based on their religious beliefs. These Puritans settled north of Plymouth. The Puritan settlement was known as the Massachusetts Bay Colony and included the town of Boston.

In the Massachusetts Bay Colony, religion shaped the government. Only church members could vote or serve in town government. Many towns made laws that controlled the way people worshiped. Some colonists did not like these laws and were forced to leave the colony.

Roger Williams was a Puritan minister who wanted more religious freedom in the Massachusetts Bay Colony. Puritan leaders forced him out of the colony because of his beliefs. In 1636, Williams started a new colony that became known as Rhode Island.

Along the Coast England's thirteen colonies stretched along the Atlantic coast. People in cities such as Philadelphia (below) used rivers to ship goods to the coast.

The Massachusetts Bay Colony and other nearby colonies grew quickly. The area became known as New England. Most New England colonists were farmers. Farming was difficult in New England, because the area had rocky soil, long cold winters, and a short summer for growing crops. Farm families usually grew only enough food to feed themselves.

New England colonists found other ways to earn a living. Some caught fish or hunted whales in the nearby Atlantic Ocean. Others used lumber from the region's forests to build ships. New England became a center for fishing, whaling, shipbuilding, and trading.

Middle Colonies

After the English took control of New York, their settlements spread through the area south and west of New England. They divided the land into several colonies. The region became known as the Middle Colonies.

Proprietors owned these Middle Colonies. A **proprietor** was a person who owned and controlled all the land of a colony. In Pennsylvania, **William Penn** was the proprietor. Penn was a member of a religious group called the Society of Friends, or Quakers. Quakers practiced religious tolerance. To practice **tolerance** is to respect beliefs that are different from your own.

Quakers believed that all Christians should be free to worship in their own ways. Some Quakers in England were put in jail or killed because they did not share the beliefs of the Church of England. Penn wanted Pennsylvania to be a place of religious tolerance for all Christians.

As in New England, most people in the Middle Colonies were farmers. The Middle Colonies, however, had better soil and a warmer climate than New England. Farmers there could grow enough crops to feed their families and still have plenty to sell.

REVIEW What did New England colonists do to earn a living?

The Plantation This painting of a Southern plantation shows the main house at the top of the hill where the owners lived. Ships brought goods to the plantation and carried cash crops and other products away.

Southern Colonies

While colonies were being founded in New England and the Middle Colonies, Virginia continued to grow. Several other colonies were founded near Virginia on the rich lands of the South.

In 1632, Cecilius Calvert, who was also known as **Lord Baltimore**, founded Maryland. He wanted to establish a colony where Catholics could worship freely. Like Quakers, Catholics in England were punished for their religious beliefs.

In 1663, **King Charles II** of England decided to start a new colony south of Virginia. He hoped the new colony would increase England's power in the area. This colony was later split into North Carolina and South Carolina.

James Oglethorpe founded the colony of Georgia in 1732. Oglethorpe wanted Georgia to be a place where poor English people could start new lives.

The warm, damp climate of the Southern Colonies made the region perfect for growing tobacco and rice. Indigo, a plant used to make a blue dye for cloth, also grew well in the South. These crops were grown in large amounts on plantations. A **plantation** is a big farm on which crops are raised by workers who live there.

Many workers did the hard labor that kept a plantation running. Plantation owners often used enslaved Africans for this work. Although enslaved Africans lived in all the English colonies, most were in the Southern Colonies.

The South was known for its large plantations, but small farms were much more common. Most southern colonists lived on family farms with few slaves or none at all.

The Beginnings of Democracy

Main Idea Many of the colonies had some form of democratic government.

Settlers throughout the English colonies believed in self-government. **Self-government** happens when a group of people make laws for themselves.

In 1619, Virginia colonists formed the House of Burgesses (BUR jihs iz). The House of Burgesses was the first representative government in the English colonies. In a representative government, voters elect people to run the government.

In Massachusetts, Pilgrims signed the Mayflower Compact in 1620. This agreement set up a government for the colony of Plymouth. The Mayflower Compact was the first written plan for self-government in North America.

Even in colonies owned by proprietors, voters usually had a voice in the government. Proprietors chose governors, but voters elected people to help make laws.

The representative governments in the colonies were not fair to everyone. Only men who owned property could vote. Even so, colonists had more control over their governments than most people in Europe.

REVIEW What was the Mayflower Compact?

Lesson Summary

English colonists in North America lived in three regions: New England, the Middle Colonies, and the Southern Colonies. Each region had its own climate, resources, and way of life. Many colonists had some form of self-government.

Why It Matters ...

Self-government in the English colonies led to democratic government in the United States.

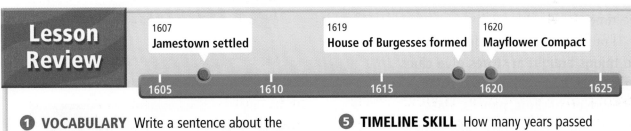

Lesson Review

| 1607 Jamestown settled | 1619 House of Burgesses formed | 1620 Mayflower Compact |

1605   1610   1615   1620   1625

❶ **VOCABULARY** Write a sentence about the Southern Colonies using the words **cash crop** and **plantation.**

❷ **READING SKILL** Using information from your chart, write a paragraph that contrasts the three colonial regions.

❸ **MAIN IDEA: Geography** Which region was better for farming, New England or the Middle Colonies? Why?

❹ **MAIN IDEA: Economics** What were the most important cash crops in the South?

❺ **TIMELINE SKILL** How many years passed between the founding of Jamestown and the signing of the Mayflower Compact?

❻ **CRITICAL THINKING: Decision Making** What were the short-term effects of the Pilgrims' decision to settle in America? What were the long-term effects?

HANDS ON

MAP ACTIVITY A number of state and city names in the United States came from the names of their founders. Look at a map or book and make a list of state or city names and the people after whom these places were named.

SLAVERY'S PAST

How did enslaved people live day by day? Narratives and clues dug up from historical sites are helping to answer this question.

In the 1700s, most slaves worked in the rice fields of South Carolina and the tobacco plantations of Virginia and Maryland. Researchers digging near Williamsburg, the colonial capital of Virginia, have found important information about the food that enslaved people ate, items they owned, and how they may have used the little free time they had.

Thousands of handmade objects and things bought in stores give clues to the past. Personal items such as hand-woven baskets, pencils, slates, and reading glasses show how people tried hard to keep part of their lives free from the burden of slavery.

Slave Quarters These cabins near Williamsburg, Virginia, have been restored to the way they looked in the 1700s.

Reading History's Clues

Dr. Theresa Singleton is a professor of archaeology at Syracuse University. She has a special interest in the lives of slaves. "To me," Singleton says, "the most important discoveries have been usable objects made from broken and discarded materials, such as fish-hooks from nails." Such findings prove that the people were not just victims, Singleton explains:

66 *They were thinkers and doers who improved their situations as best they could despite the odds against them.* 99

— Dr. Theresa Singleton

① **Inside the Cabins**
Fireplaces were made of clay and wood. As many as nine adults may have slept in one cabin on mattresses filled with corn husks.

② **Possessions**
Furniture was simple: barrels, old tables, and chairs. This pewter plate may have been purchased through extra labor.

Activities

1. **TALK ABOUT IT** What questions would you like to ask Dr. Singleton about her discoveries?

2. **WRITE ABOUT IT** Why is it difficult for historians to find information about the daily lives of enslaved people? Write a one-page paper that answers this question.

Skillbuilder

Make a Timeline

A **timeline** shows events in the order in which they happened. Placing important dates on a timeline can help you to organize and understand what you read.

▶ **VOCABULARY**

timeline

Learn the Skill

Step 1: Look back at the lesson you just read. Make a list of four important events from the lesson. Put the events in order, listing the earliest event first.

1607	Jamestown founded
1619	House of Burgesses formed
1620	Pilgrims arrive in Plymouth
1636	Rhode Island founded

Step 2: Timelines are divided into sections that show equal periods of time. Draw a horizontal line and divide it into equal sections. Label the end of each section with a month or a year.

1600   1610   1620   1630   1640

Step 3: Place each event on the timeline on the date it occurred. When an event occurred between two dates marked on the timeline, estimate where to place it.

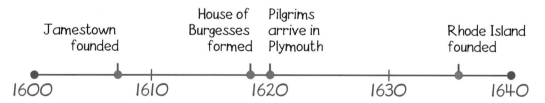

Jamestown founded   House of Burgesses formed   Pilgrims arrive in Plymouth   Rhode Island founded

1600   1610   1620   1630   1640

Practice the Skill

Read the following paragraph about the Pilgrims and answer the questions. Then make a timeline of the events. The dates on your timeline should start with the month and year of the first event and end with the month and year of the last event.

About 100 Pilgrims set sail across the Atlantic Ocean on the Mayflower in September 1620. In November of that year, the Pilgrims landed on the coast of Massachusetts and created their own plan for government called the Mayflower Compact. The next month, they settled in Plymouth, Massachusetts. The Pilgrims had a hard time in the new colony. Then, in March 1621, the Pilgrims met Squanto, a member of the Wampanoag nation. He helped the settlers plant crops and showed them where to hunt and fish.

1 In the paragraph, how many events have dates given?

2 Should you divide your timeline into days, months, or years?

3 Which event came first? Which event came last?

Apply the Skill

Reread Chapter 2, Lesson 3, "New Settlements," on pages 44–47. List four events in the lesson. Then create a timeline that includes those events.

Visual Summary

1.–3. Write a description of each journey named below.

Journeys

Columbus's First Voyage	Hudson's Search for Asia	The Mayflower
_____	_____	_____
_____	_____	_____
_____	_____	_____

Facts and Main Ideas

TEST PREP Answer each question with information from the chapter.

4. **Geography** Why did American Indians in the Northwest and Southwest build their homes with different materials?

5. **History** Name one advantage that helped Hernán Cortés defeat the Aztecs.

6. **Economics** What made Jamestown the first successful English colony?

7. **Citizenship** What were two ways in which English colonists practiced self-government?

8. **Government** In what way did religion shape the government in Massachusetts Bay Colony?

Vocabulary

TEST PREP Choose the correct word from the list below to complete each sentence.

profit, p. 36
colony, p. 45
tolerance, p. 53

9. After Cortés defeated the Aztecs, the Spanish started a _____ named New Spain.

10. The Quakers practiced religious _____ by respecting different beliefs.

11. If a company earns a _____, it means that there is money left over after all expenses have been paid.

1535 New Spain founded	1607 Jamestown founded	1620 Plymouth founded	1664 English gain New York

1500   1550   1600   1650   1700

Apply Skills

✓ **TEST PREP** **Chart and Graph Skill**
Read the passage below. Then use what you have learned about timelines to answer each question.

> In 1271, Marco Polo traveled by land to China. Then in 1492, Columbus tried to reach Asia by sailing west across Atlantic Ocean. Five years after Columbus, John Cabot tried to find a western route to Asia. In 1609, Henry Hudson also searched for a water route around North America to Asia.

12. If you were making a timeline of the events in the paragraph above, how many years would it have to cover?

   A. 17

   B. 23

   C. 147

   D. 338

13. On your timeline, which event would be to the right of John Cabot's voyage?

   A. Vasco de Gama finds a route to Asia.

   B. Henry Hudson searches for a route to Asia.

   C. Marco Polo travels to Asia.

   D. Christopher Columbus searches for a route to Asia.

Critical Thinking

✓ **TEST PREP** Write a short paragraph to answer each question.

14. **Compare and Contrast** In 1500, how was American Indian life on the Western Great Plains different from life in the Southeast?

15. **Fact and Opinion** What changes did the Columbian Exchange bring to European and American Indian cultures? State your opinion about these changes.

Timeline

Use the Chapter Summary Timeline above to answer the question.

16. Which settlements were founded in the 1600s?

Activities

 Connect to Georgia Find out how early colonists in Georgia earned their living. List and describe different jobs that men, women, and children did.

 Writing Activity Write a persuasive essay that an early settler in North America might have used to convince friends in Europe to join him or her.

 Technology
Writing Process Tips
Get help with your essay at
www.eduplace.com/kids/hmss/

Review and Test Prep

Vocabulary and Main Ideas

✓ **TEST PREP** Write a sentence to answer each question.

1. In what way does **scarcity** affect people's choices?

2. Why are different **regions** of the United States **interdependent?**

3. How does **pollution** affect an **ecosystem?**

4. In what ways was the buffalo important to the **culture** of Plains Indians?

5. Why did Spain's rulers support Christopher Columbus's **expedition** to the Americas?

6. Why did Catholic priests build **missions** throughout New Spain?

Critical Thinking

✓ **TEST PREP** Write a short paragraph to answer each question.

7. **Cause and Effect** What effect did new navigation tools in Europe have on the people of the Americas?

8. **Infer** Why do you think self-government was important to English colonists? Explain your point of view.

Apply Skills

✓ **TEST PREP** **Chart and Graph Skill** Read the paragraph below. Use what you know about making a timeline to answer each question.

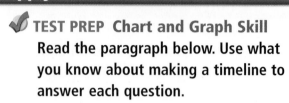

In 1619, Virginia colonists formed the house of Burgesses. The Pilgrims in Massachusetts signed the Mayflower compact in 1620. In 1621, the Pilgrims met Squanto, who taught them how to plant crops.

9. If you were making a timeline for this paragraph, what period of time would each section of the timeline show?

    A. 1 year
    B. 2 years
    C. 3 years
    D. 10 years

10. Which event would you place farthest left on the timeline?

    A. Mayflower Compact signed
    B. Pilgrims meet Squanto
    C. House of Burgesses formed
    D. Pilgrims plant crops

Connect to Georgia

Unit Activity

Create a Journal

- Research a European explorer who traveled through Georgia in the 1500s and 1600s.

- Create a journal describing where the explorer went, what he saw, and American Indians living in Georgia where he traveled.

- Use facts and details in your descriptions. Draw a map of the explorer's route.

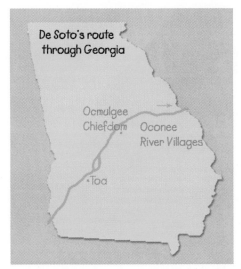

De Soto's route through Georgia

Ocmulgee Chiefdom

Oconee River Villages

Toa

Personal Finance

In this unit, you read that scarcity means not having enough of some resources. Because people have scarce resources, they have to make economic choices. (p. 9)

Write a paragraph about a time that you had either a scarcity of time or a scarcity of money and had to make a choice about how to use that resource. How did you make your choice? Share your paragraph with a partner. Discuss what might have happened you if had made a different choice.

CURRENT EVENTS
WEEKLY (WR) READER

Connect to Today

Create a bulletin board showing American Indians in your state.

- Find information about American Indians who have lived or live in your state.

- Write a brief description of each group, including where they lived in the past or live now.

- Place a map of your state on the bulletin board. Then put the descriptions of each group around the map.

Technology

Weekly Reader online offers social studies articles. Go to:
www.eduplace.com/kids/hmss/

Read About It

Look for these Social Studies Independent Books in your classroom.

Pocahontas
by Carl W

On Board the
Santa Maria
by Becky Cheston

Wind and Water
Two Great Powers
by Susan Ring

UNIT 2

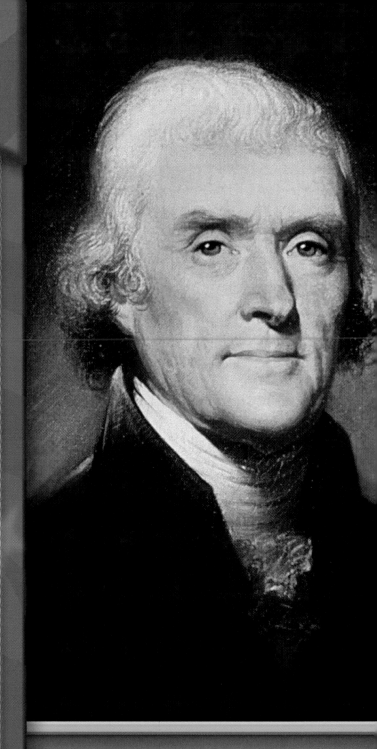

The New Nation

The Big Idea

How did the United States become independent?

"These United Colonies are, and of Right ought to be Free and Independent States."

The Declaration of Independence, 1776

Thomas Jefferson
1743–1826

Thomas Jefferson wrote words that are known all around the world—the Declaration of Independence. While President, he doubled the size of the United States.
page 73

History Makers

Abigail Adams
1744–1818

While her husband planned the new nation, Adams wrote to him about liberty. "Remember the Ladies," she urged. She also said that people who owned slaves could not value liberty. **page 77**

James Madison
1751–1836

Madison gathered books and read all he could about different forms of government. At the Constitutional Convention, he used this knowledge to propose a new government for the nation. **page 86**

OREGON TERRITORY–1846
Ceded (given up) by Great Britain

Portland

Columbia R.

RED RIVER CESSION–1818
Treaty of 1818
with Great Britain

L. Superior

L. Michigan

Milwaukee

Chicago

Indianapolis

Missouri R.

**LOUISIANA
PURCHASE–1803**
Bought from France

Salt
Lake
City

San Francisco

Colorado R.

St. Louis

Kansas City

MEXICAN CESSION–1848
Treaty of Guadalupe Hildago

Nashville

Memphis

Mississippi R.

TEXAS ANNEXATION–1845

GADSDEN PURCHASE–1853
Bought from Mexico

Rio Grande

Mobile

PACIFIC

OCEAN

San Antonio

**WEST FLORIDA
ANNEXATION–
1810, 1813**

Gulf of Mexico

Unit Preview

1770 — 1790 — 1810

**1776
Liberty
Declared**

Declaration of
Independence
**Chapter 3,
page 73**

**1788
Constitution
Ratified**

U.S. system of
government is
established
**Chapter 3,
page 89**

**1803
Louisiana
Purchase**

Jefferson purchases
territory from France
**Chapter 4,
page 108**

Map Labels

WEBSTER ASHBURTON TREATY–1842
Border adjustment with Great Britain

Portland
Boston
Buffalo
Detroit
L. Huron
L. Ontario
L. Erie
Cleveland
Philadelphia
Pittsburgh
New York
Baltimore
Washington, D.C.
Ohio R.

UNITED STATES–1783
Lexington
Louisville
Norfolk

Wilmington

Atlanta
Charleston
Savannah

ATLANTIC OCEAN

Jacksonville
EAST FLORIDA –1819
ceded (given up) by Spain

N NE E SE S SW W NW

km 0 150 300
mi 0 150 300

LEGEND
• Major city, 1850

Timeline

1830

1850

1838 Trail of Tears
Cherokee forced to leave their homes
Chapter 4, page 111

1849 Gold Rush
Forty-niners rush to California
Chapter 4, page 124

Connect to Today

House of Representatives, 1800–1850

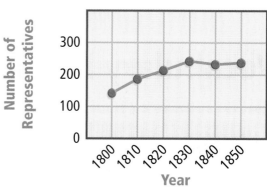

Number of Representatives
300
200
100
0

1800 1810 1820 1830 1840 1850
Year

Between 1800 and 1850, the number of members of the House of Representatives increased as the U.S. population increased.

House of Representatives Today

Since 1910, the number of members of the House has remained at 435, while the U.S. population has greatly increased.

CONNECT to GEORGIA

Learn about Georgia's delegates to the Constitutional Convention. Write a report summarizing the contributions of two of the delegates.

Chapter 3

Creating a New Nation

Vocabulary Preview

revolution

A **revolution** is a complete change of government. In the American Revolution, the colonies overthrew their British rulers and created a new government. **page 72**

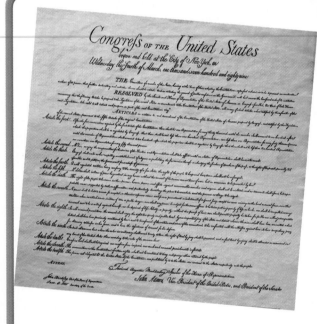

rights

Every person has **rights.** The laws of the United States recognize and protect these freedoms.
page 73

Chapter Timeline

1765	1773	1776
Stamp Act	Boston Tea Party	Declaration of Independence

1765   1770   1775

Reading Strategy

Monitor and Clarify Use this strategy to check your understanding.

Quick Tip Stop and ask yourself if what you are reading makes sense. Reread, if you need to.

treaty

In 1783, the United States and Britain signed a **treaty** saying that the United States was independent of Britain. This document was called the Treaty of Paris. **page 79**

compromise

People make a **compromise** to reach an agreement. Each side gives up something to settle their differences.
page 87

1783
Treaty of Paris signed

1787
Constitution signed

1780   1785   1790

Moving Toward Independence

VOCABULARY

tax
revolution
congress
independence
rights

Vocabulary Strategy

| rights |

The word **rights** means freedoms that a government should protect. Colonists felt that it was correct, or "right," to have rights.

READING SKILL

Cause and Effect As you read, list causes of the American Revolution.

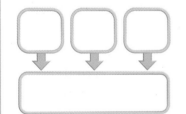

Build on What You Know You know that the older you get, the more you want to decide things for yourself. In the 1770s, the American colonies had been ruled by Britain for nearly 150 years. Colonists were ready to make their own decisions.

Conflicts Begin

Main Idea Colonists protested when Britain tried to force them to help pay for the French and Indian War.

In the 1750s, Britain and France both wanted to control the Ohio River Valley. In 1754, their conflict turned into a war called the French and Indian War. Most Indian nations fought on the French side against the British and American colonists.

After almost ten years of fighting, Britain won the war. Now Britain controlled most of the land east of the Mississippi River, but the war had cost Britain a lot of money. Parliament, which made the laws in Britain, wanted American colonists to help pay those costs.

Parliament passed laws to make colonists pay a tax. A **tax** is money citizens pay to their government for services. In 1765, Parliament passed the Stamp Act. This tax made colonists buy a stamp for everything they bought that was printed on paper.

The Stamp Act This act, or law, made colonists pay to have stamps like these put on printed items such as newspapers.

STANDARDS

SS4H4 Review Causes of Revolution

The Boston Tea Party To protest the Tea Act, Boston colonists dressed as Mohawk Indians and dumped thousands of pounds of tea overboard.

Protesting Taxes

Many colonists objected to the Stamp Act. They were used to running their own governments. They did not want Parliament to tax them because they could not elect representatives to speak for them in Parliament. Across the colonies people cried,

> **❝ No taxation without representation! ❞**

Groups of colonists called the Sons of Liberty organized protests throughout the colonies. A protest is a public show of dissatisfaction. The Sons of Liberty and other groups attacked tax collectors and broke into their houses.

Colonists also boycotted, or refused to buy, British goods such as cloth. Groups of women called the Daughters of Liberty wove their own cloth instead of buying it from Britain.

British businesses lost money because of these boycotts. Parliament canceled the Stamp Act but taxed other goods instead. Again, colonists protested. These taxes were removed, too.

When Parliament passed a tax called the Tea Act, protesters climbed aboard ships and dumped British tea into Boston Harbor. After this event, now called the Boston Tea Party, British leaders sent soldiers to Boston.

To punish Boston, Parliament passed laws that took power away from colonial governments in Boston and Massachusetts. Colonists called these laws the Intolerable Acts. Something that is intolerable cannot be accepted.

REVIEW Why did the colonists protest the taxes that Britain made them pay?

Breaking Away from Britain

Main Idea Conflicts with Britain grew and colonists declared independence.

Colonists became more united against Britain when they learned how Parliament had punished Boston. Many felt that it was time for a revolution. A **revolution** is an overthrow, or a forced change, of a government.

In September 1774, representatives from all the colonies except Georgia met in Philadelphia. This meeting is called the First Continental Congress. A **congress** is an official gathering of people to make decisions.

The congress sent a letter to Britain to protest the taxes and the Intolerable Acts. It also stopped trade between the colonies and Britain. Throughout the colonies, people prepared for war by gathering weapons and training to fight.

The Revolutionary War Begins

In April 1775, British troops marched from Boston to Lexington and Concord to look for weapons. **Paul Revere** and several others rode through the night to warn colonial fighters, called Minutemen, that British soldiers were coming.

Minutemen gathered in Lexington. When the British soldiers arrived at dawn, shots were fired and fighting began. The British troops marched on to Concord where more fighting took place. The Minutemen drove the British back to Boston and kept shooting at them as they marched. Minutemen from all over New England gathered near Boston after they heard about these battles.

In June 1775, Minutemen and British soldiers fought again at the Battle of Bunker Hill. The British won, but nearly half of their soldiers were killed or wounded. Colonists started to believe that they could beat the well-trained British.

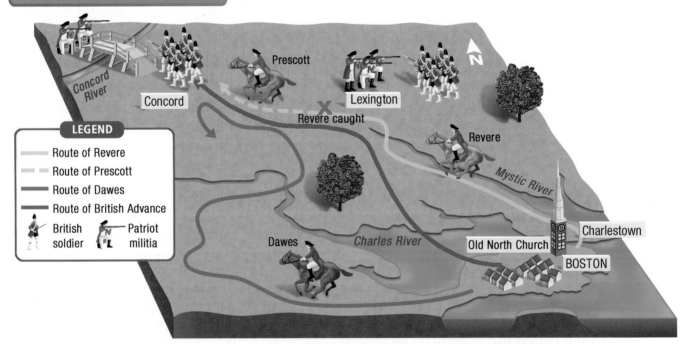

Lexington and Concord

LEGEND
— Route of Revere
- - Route of Prescott
— Route of Dawes
— Route of British Advance
British soldier   Patriot militia

Lexington and Concord Paul Revere, Samuel Prescott, and William Dawes warned Minutemen that the British troops were coming. **SKILL** **Reading Maps** What river did Paul Revere ride along on his way to Lexington?

The Declaration of Independence

In April of 1776, the colonies sent representatives to the Second Continental Congress. This congress chose **Thomas Jefferson** to write an official statement called the Declaration of Independence. **Independence** is freedom from being ruled by someone else.

In this declaration, Jefferson wrote that all people have rights to "life, liberty, and the pursuit of happiness." **Rights** are freedoms protected by law. If a government does not protect those rights, Jefferson wrote, people have the right to start a new government.

The Declaration of Independence said that the colonies were starting a new country because Britain had not protected colonists' rights.

Liberty Bell This national symbol rang out on July 8, 1776 when the Declaration of Independence was read aloud.

The Declaration of Independence was approved on July 4, 1776. The Fourth of July is celebrated today as the birthday of the United States. The Declaration still promises equal rights to all U.S. citizens.

REVIEW Why did the colonists declare independence?

Lesson Summary

> Britain made colonists pay taxes to help with the costs of the French and Indian War.

> Colonists protested the taxes.

> Minutemen and British soldiers fought near Boston in 1775.

> Thomas Jefferson wrote the Declaration of Independence in 1776.

Why It Matters...

Conflicts with Great Britain led to the birth of the United States.

Lesson Review

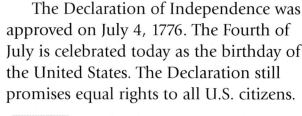

1773
Boston Tea Party

1776
Declaration of Independence

| 1773 | 1774 | 1775 | 1776 | 1777 |

1. **VOCABULARY** Write a paragraph about the American colonies using two of the words below.

   tax independence rights

2. **READING SKILL** For each **cause** you listed, name an **effect** it had on the colonies.

3. **MAIN IDEA: Economics** Why did Parliament want the colonists to pay taxes?

4. **MAIN IDEA: History** Why did the American colonies declare independence from Britain?

5. **TIMELINE** Which event on the timeline happened in 1776?

6. **CRITICAL THINKING: Infer** Colonists lost the Battle of Bunker Hill, but they considered it a success. Explain why.

WRITING ACTIVITY Write a journal entry that a person at the Boston Tea Party might have written describing the event. Do research to find details and facts you can use in your entry.

Thomas Jefferson

1743–1826

Thomas Jefferson is deep in thought. He must find the right words. Congress has chosen Jefferson to tell the king why the American colonies no longer belong to Britain. These are dangerous words, and they could cost Jefferson his life. Yet he loves his country and is writing the words that will create a new nation.

He dips his quill pen into the inkwell and rewrites a sentence in his draft. At this amazing moment in his life, he applies to his writing what he has learned and what he cares so much about.

All his life, Jefferson wanted to know the why and how of everything. He played the violin, studied the stars, invented things, and designed buildings.

He had read about government, history, and science as a young man. In his draft of the Declaration, he used ideas he had learned. The result was one of the most important documents in history.

Major Achievements

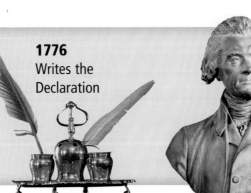

1768
Designs Monticello, a U.S. landmark

1776
Writes the Declaration

1801
Elected U.S. President

A Declaration by the Representatives of the UNITED STATES OF AMERICA, in General Congress assembled.

When in the course of human events it becomes necessary for one people to dissolve the political bands which have connected them with another, and to assume among the powers of the earth the separate and equal station to which the laws of nature & of nature's god entitle them, a decent respect to the opinions of mankind requires that they should declare the causes which impel them to the separation.

We hold these truths to be self-evident, that all men are created equal & independent, that from that equal creation they derive rights inherent & inalienable, among which are the preservation of life, & liberty, & the pursuit of happiness; that to secure these ends, governments are instituted among men, deriving their just powers from the consent of the governed.

Look Closely

In his draft, Jefferson put brackets around words he was not sure of.

We hold these truths to be self-evident; **created equal** that **they are endowed** rights; that **inherent & inalienable, among** **life, liberty, & the pursuit of happiness; that to**

Portable Desk

Jefferson wrote his draft on a portable desk, which he designed himself.

Activities

1. **TALK ABOUT IT** How might Jefferson's patriotism have helped him write an important document like the Declaration of Independence?

2. **WRITE ABOUT IT** What happens on June 28, 1776, when delegates in Congress hear the Declaration draft for the first time? Write a one-page story in the present tense.

 Technology Visit Education Place at www.eduplace.com/kids/hmss05/ for more biographies of people in this unit.

1803
Doubles size of United States with the Louisiana Purchase

LOUISIANA PURCHASE

1804
Sends Lewis and Clark to explore the West

The War for Independence

1770   1775   1780   1785   1790

1776–1783

Build on What You Know Have you ever had to make a difficult choice? After the colonies declared independence in 1776, ordinary people had to decide whether to support Britain or the Americans. Some took no side at all.

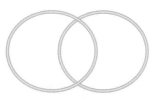
Patriots and Loyalists

Main Idea Americans had different views about independence.

In 1776, the American colonies were at war against Britain. Colonists disagreed about which side to support. About half were Patriots. **Patriots** wanted independence from Britain. A smaller group called **Loyalists** believed Britain should rule the colonies. Many people were neutral. To be **neutral** means not to take sides.

Nearly 5,000 free and enslaved African Americans joined the American army, called the Continental Army. Many enslaved African Americans were Loyalists, however, because the British promised them freedom.

Most American Indian nations were neutral. Many who did fight chose the British side. They believed the British would make settlers stop taking Indian land. American Indians trusted the British because the British had tried to stop colonists from moving west.

Joseph Brant He was a Mohawk leader who urged his people to side with the British.

 STANDARDS

SS4H4 Review Events of Revolution

Phillis Wheatley This poet was among the women who supported the Patriots by writing poems, letters, and plays.

Many women were Patriots. Some cooked and carried water for the army. Some even fought or served as spies. Women also ran family farms and businesses during the war. **Abigail Adams,** wife of future President **John Adams,** managed their farm while he was at the Second Continental Congress.

The Continental Army

The British army was one of the strongest in the world. The Continental Army was smaller than the British army. The colonies had little money for soldiers or equipment. British soldiers had better training and weapons.

The Continental Army did have some strengths, however. Its commander was General **George Washington,** a strong, respected leader. Many soldiers in the Continental Army knew the land. British soldiers were far from home and were unfamiliar with the land. Many Patriots fought hard because they believed in their cause. For many in the British army, fighting was just a job.

Fighting the War

Main Idea Americans won their independence after a long and difficult war.

In the spring of 1776, the Continental Army drove the British out of Boston. After that success, however, things went badly for the colonists. The British defeated Washington's army in a series of battles near New York City. The Americans had to retreat, or move back, all the way to Pennsylvania.

After these losses, Washington was desperate for a victory. On December 26, 1776, Washington and his soldiers crossed the icy Delaware River. They surprised and defeated British soldiers camped at Trenton, New Jersey. That victory lifted the spirits of Washington's army and the nation.

REVIEW Why did some people living in the colonies support the British?

Surprise Attack Washington caught British forces off guard by crossing the frozen Delaware River.

Victory at Yorktown General Washington accepts the British surrender at Yorktown, Virginia. American soldiers were overjoyed by this victory.

Help from Europe

Americans won another important victory near Saratoga, New York, in June of 1777. This victory helped to convince France that the United States could win the war. The French decided to send money, soldiers, and a navy.

People from other countries came on their own to fight for the American side, too. A French soldier, the **Marquis de Lafayette** (mahr KEE duh laf ee ET), wanted to help the American struggle for freedom. He led Americans in many battles. A German officer named **Baron von Steuben** (SHTOY ben) trained American soldiers to fight better.

Marquis de Lafayette

Winning the War

By 1779, neither side was winning the war. The British invaded the South. They hoped the many Loyalists there would help them. By 1780, they controlled Georgia and South Carolina. Led by General **Charles Cornwallis** (Korn WAHL iss), they won more battles.

Just when it seemed Americans might lose the war, southern Patriots began using new ways of fighting. **Francis Marion** was a commander called the Swamp Fox because he was so good at sneaking up, attacking the enemy, and then escaping through swamps.

Nathanael Greene, commander of the Continental Army in the South, also frustrated the British. He made Cornwallis's forces chase his army until British soldiers were worn out and had used up all their supplies. In the spring of 1781, Cornwallis moved his troops to Virginia.

Led by **George Rogers Clark,** the Americans also won victories in present-day Indiana and Illinois. In 1779, the Patriots were helped when the Spanish General **Bernardo de Gálvez** captured British forts near the Gulf of Mexico.

In late 1781, Washington's army surrounded General Cornwallis's troops, who were camped at Yorktown, Virginia. The French navy blocked the harbor so the British could not retreat. Cornwallis was trapped. After a week of fighting he surrendered. The Americans had defeated Cornwallis's entire army and won the last major battle of the war.

Bernardo de Gálvez

In 1783, the United States and Britain signed the Treaty of Paris, ending the war. A **treaty** is an agreement between countries. The treaty stated that the United States now stretched north to British Canada, west to the Mississippi River, and south to Spanish Florida. Americans had won their independence.

REVIEW What led to Cornwallis's defeat?

Lesson Summary

Colonists were divided into Patriots and Loyalists. After its victory at Saratoga, the Continental Army received valuable help from France. By 1779, most fighting had shifted to the South. Americans won the war after the Battle of Yorktown. In 1783, the Treaty of Paris ended the war.

Why It Matters …

The United States became a new, independent country when it won the Revolutionary War.

Lesson Review

1777 Battle of Saratoga	1781 Battle of Yorktown	1783 Treaty of Paris

1776 1778 1780 1782 1784

❶ **VOCABULARY** Write two sentences about the American Revolution. Use either **Patriot** or **Loyalist** in each one.

❷ 🖐 **READING SKILL** List two advantages the British army had over the Continental Army.

❸ **MAIN IDEA: History** Why did many enslaved African Americans support the British in the war?

❹ **MAIN IDEA: Geography** How did **Francis Marion** use the land to help him beat the British in the South?

❺ **EVENTS TO KNOW:** Why was the victory at Yorktown so important?

❻ **TIMELINE SKILL** Which event happened first, the Battle of Yorktown or the Treaty of Paris?

❼ **CRITICAL THINKING: Cause and Effect** What effect did the Battle of Saratoga have on the war? Why was this important?

HANDS ON **RESEARCH** Research a person from this lesson and create a fact file about him or her. Draw a picture of the person to illustrate the fact file.

Winning the War

Could the United States have lost the Revolutionary War? Colonial soldiers did not have enough food, warm clothing, or equipment. They were usually outnumbered and they lost many battles.

Several events changed the course of the war. At these turning points, colonial troops gained the strength and support they needed to win the war.

Four Turning Points

1 SARATOGA
September–October 1777

British General John Burgoyne lost two battles at Saratoga because it took so long for his troops to travel through the forests. American soldiers had time to gather until they outnumbered and defeated the British. Benjamin Franklin used this victory to convince the French to help the colonists win the war.

2 VALLEY FORGE
December 1777–June 1778

Washington's army spent the winter at Valley Forge, where many soldiers died from the cold and from lack of food. Yet that winter was a turning point because German officer Baron von Steuben taught the soldiers how to fight.

3 GUILFORD COURT HOUSE
March 1781

The British won the battle at Guilford Court House, but they did not stay to defend the land they had won. British troops left for Yorktown, Virginia. Colonial soldiers led by Nathanael Greene then recaptured most of the South.

4 YORKTOWN
September–October 1781

By 1781, General Washington needed an important victory. His soldiers were discouraged and lacked supplies. Washington decided to attack Cornwallis at Yorktown because the French could help him. After ten days, the British surrendered. Yorktown was the last major battle of the war.

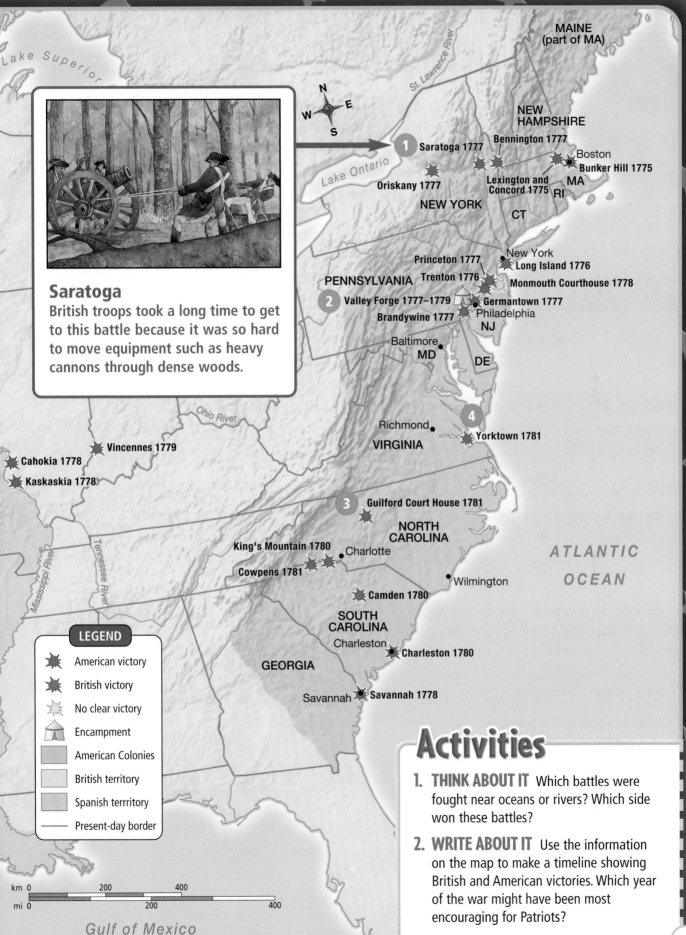

MAINE
(part of MA)

St. Lawrence River

Lake Superior

N
W E
S

Lake Ontario

NEW
HAMPSHIRE

1 Saratoga 1777

Bennington 1777

Boston
Bunker Hill 1775

Oriskany 1777

Lexington and
Concord 1775

MA
RI

NEW YORK

CT

Princeton 1777

New York
Long Island 1776

Trenton 1776

Monmouth Courthouse 1778

PENNSYLVANIA

2 Valley Forge 1777–1779

Germantown 1777

Brandywine 1777

Philadelphia

NJ

Baltimore

MD

DE

Ohio River

Richmond

4

VIRGINIA

Yorktown 1781

Vincennes 1779

Cahokia 1778

Kaskaskia 1778

3 Guilford Court House 1781

NORTH
CAROLINA

King's Mountain 1780

Charlotte

Cowpens 1781

Wilmington

ATLANTIC
OCEAN

Camden 1780

SOUTH
CAROLINA

Charleston

Charleston 1780

GEORGIA

Savannah

Savannah 1778

Mississippi River

Tennessee River

Saratoga

British troops took a long time to get to this battle because it was so hard to move equipment such as heavy cannons through dense woods.

LEGEND

* American victory
* British victory
* No clear victory
* Encampment
* American Colonies
* British territory
* Spanish terrritory
* — Present-day border

km 0   200   400
mi 0   200   400

Gulf of Mexico

Activities

1. **THINK ABOUT IT** Which battles were fought near oceans or rivers? Which side won these battles?

2. **WRITE ABOUT IT** Use the information on the map to make a timeline showing British and American victories. Which year of the war might have been most encouraging for Patriots?

Citizenship Skills

Skillbuilder

Make a Decision

► **VOCABULARY**
consequence

Colonists had to think about many things before deciding to support the American Revolution. Their decisions had consequences for themselves and for others. A consequence is a result of a decision or an action. It can be positive or negative. The steps below will help you understand one way to make decisions.

Learn the Skill

Step 1: Describe or summarize the decision to be made.

Step 2: Gather information. What do you need to know to make the decision? You may need to do research or talk with other people.

Step 3: Think of the options that you have.

Step 4: Consider the positive or negative consequences of each option.

Step 5: Choose an option. Which one has the most positive consequences and fewest negative consequences?

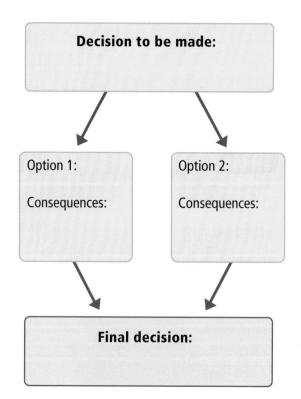

Decision to be made:

Option 1:

Consequences:

Option 2:

Consequences:

Final decision:

Practice the Skill

Think about the choices people had when deciding to support the American Revolution. Consider each person described below. Decide whether each one should become a Patriot, become a Loyalist, or remain neutral. Use a chart like the one on page 82 as you think about the positive or negative consequences of each person's options.

1 Tea merchant who is losing business because of the Tea Act

2 Tax collector who is protected by British soldiers

3 Farmer who recently came to the colonies from Germany

Apply the Skill

Choose a current issue that people must make a decision about. You might choose a topic about the environment, an upcoming election, or some other important issue. Fill out a chart like the one on page 82. Then write a paragraph explaining what you think the right decision is, and why.

Learn About the Candidates for Mayor

Creating the Constitution

1770   1775   1780   1785   1790   1795   1800

1781–1789

Build on What You Know Have you ever made something that didn't turn out as you had hoped? You may have learned from your mistakes and then created something even better. When the United States chose its first plan for government, it, too, had to try again.

Articles of Confederation

Main Idea The Articles of Confederation created a weak national government.

After the American states declared independence, they needed a government for their new nation. The first plan for a national government was called the Articles of Confederation. A **confederation** is a group of nations or states that joins together. Americans did not want a national government that was as powerful as the British system they were fighting. The Articles made Congress the national government but gave more power to the states than to the national government. The plan was approved in 1781.

State Money Under the Articles of Confederation, each state had its own money.

The Articles gave Congress very few powers. It could declare war and make peace treaties and agreements with other nations. It could print and borrow money. Congress could not have an army, however, and it could not make laws about trade. It had no way to make people obey its laws and it had no power to raise money through taxes.

The states did not work well together under the Articles of Confederation. Each state had one vote in Congress, and nine votes were needed to pass a law. All 13 states had to agree on any major changes to the Articles. The states rarely agreed on anything. States argued about land, taxes, and trade. Partly because of these disagreements, the nation's economy suffered. An economy is a nation's system for buying, selling, and making things.

Shays's Rebellion

While members of Congress argued, people grew frustrated. They owed money to the merchants who sold them supplies. Those who could not pay these taxes or debts risked going to jail. Banks or the state government could take their farms.

In August of 1786, a Massachusetts farmer named **Daniel Shays** led protests to stop the state government from taking farms. After several months, about 1,100 farmers tried to capture weapons belonging to the U.S. government. Congress had no army to stop what became known as Shays's Rebellion. The Massachusetts militia, or state volunteer fighters, ended the rebellion in January 1787.

REVIEW What problems did the Articles of Confederation cause?

Shays's Rebellion Daniel Shays and other farmers protest at a courthouse.

SKILL Reading Graphs About how many more people were taken to court for debt in Worcester County between 1784 and 1786 than between 1770 and 1772?

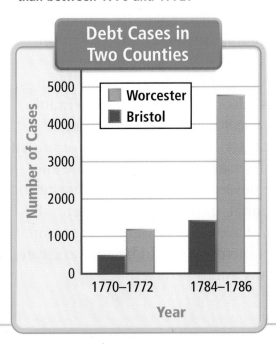

Debt Cases in Two Counties

Birth of the Constitution An exhibit at the National Constitution Center in Philadelphia shows models of delegates debating at the Constitutional Convention.
1 Roger Sherman 2 James Madison 3 George Washington

The Constitution

Main Idea Delegates to the Constitutional Convention created a new plan of government called the Constitution of the United States.

Shays's Rebellion showed that the national government was too weak to keep order. **George Washington** worried about his country's future. He wrote,

> 66 Wisdom, and good examples are necessary at this time to rescue the political machine from the impending [gathering] storm. 99

In February 1787, Congress asked the states to send delegates to a convention, or meeting, in Philadelphia to fix the Articles of Confederation. A **delegate** is someone who speaks and acts for others.

In May of 1787, 55 delegates from 11 of the 13 states arrived in Philadelphia. They included **Benjamin Franklin, Alexander Hamilton,** and George Washington, who led the convention.

Delegates to this Constitutional Convention decided to do more than change the Articles of Confederation. **James Madison**, a delegate from Virginia, had a plan for a whole new government.

Madison's plan, called the Virginia Plan, was for a federal system. In a **federal** system, the national government and the state governments divide and share power. The Virginia Plan proposed a national, or federal, government, that would have more power than the state governments. It would be able to create an army and raise taxes.

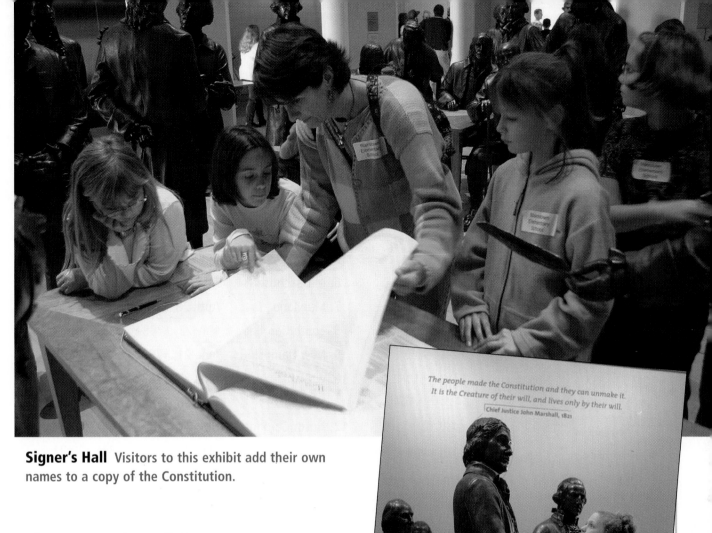

Signer's Hall Visitors to this exhibit add their own names to a copy of the Constitution.

> The people made the Constitution and they can unmake it. It is the Creature of their will, and lives only by their will.
> Chief Justice John Marshall, 1821

Three Branches of Government

The Virginia Plan divided the national government into three parts, or branches. The legislative branch, Congress, would make national laws. The executive branch, headed by the President, would make sure laws were obeyed. The judicial branch, the courts, would decide the meaning of laws and settle legal arguments. So that no one branch could become too powerful, each branch had ways to limit the power of the others.

The delegates accepted most of the Virginia Plan. But delegates from small states worried that their states would have less power because larger states would have more votes in Congress. This plan based the number of representatives a state sent to Congress on the state's population.

Delegates from smaller states proposed the New Jersey Plan, which called for each state to send the same number of representatives to Congress. Under this plan, states would have the same number of votes in Congress.

The delegates argued bitterly about representation. **Roger Sherman** of Connecticut offered a compromise. In a **compromise,** both sides give up something to settle a disagreement.

REVIEW What three branches of the national government did the Virginia Plan create?

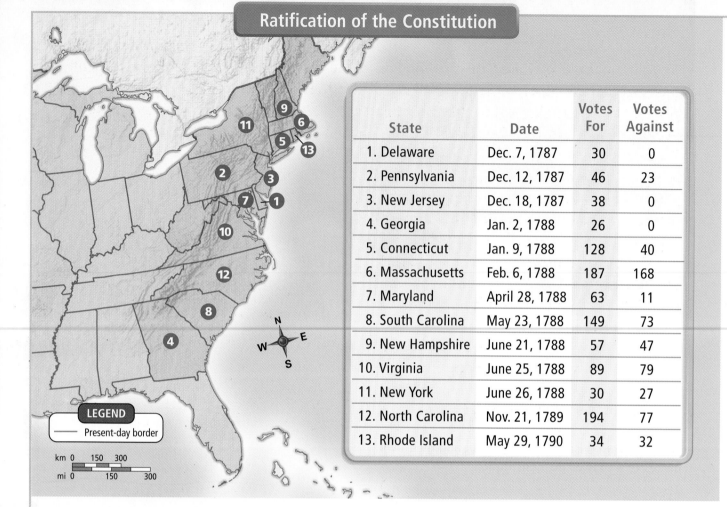

Ratification of the Constitution

State	Date	Votes For	Votes Against
1. Delaware	Dec. 7, 1787	30	0
2. Pennsylvania	Dec. 12, 1787	46	23
3. New Jersey	Dec. 18, 1787	38	0
4. Georgia	Jan. 2, 1788	26	0
5. Connecticut	Jan. 9, 1788	128	40
6. Massachusetts	Feb. 6, 1788	187	168
7. Maryland	April 28, 1788	63	11
8. South Carolina	May 23, 1788	149	73
9. New Hampshire	June 21, 1788	57	47
10. Virginia	June 25, 1788	89	79
11. New York	June 26, 1788	30	27
12. North Carolina	Nov. 21, 1789	194	77
13. Rhode Island	May 29, 1790	34	32

LEGEND

——— Present-day border

km 0   150   300

mi 0   150   300

Ratification States are numbered in the order in which they ratified the Constitution. **SKILL** **Reading Charts** Which state had twice as many votes for ratification as it had against ratification?

The Compromises

Sherman suggested dividing Congress into two parts, or houses. In one house, states with larger populations would have more representatives. In the other house, each state would have the same number of representatives. The delegates agreed to this plan, called the Great Compromise.

Delegates also argued about counting enslaved people as part of the population. Southern states wanted to count them to get more representatives in Congress. Northern states opposed this plan. The delegates compromised, agreeing that three-fifths of each state's enslaved people would count for representation.

Delegates also argued about ending slavery. Southern states wanted the slave trade, or the buying and selling of slaves, to continue. Northern states did not. Delegates compromised by agreeing that the slave trade could continue until 1808.

After four months of debate, the delegates finally agreed on their new plan for government. They signed the Constitution on September 17, 1787. It could not go into effect, though, until at least nine states approved it.

States held their own conventions to vote on the new plan. Throughout the 13 states, people debated whether to accept the Constitution.

Changing the Constitution

Some people said the Constitution gave the national government too much power. They worried it could threaten the freedoms they had won from the British. Those who supported the Constitution promised to add a Bill of Rights to protect people's freedoms. The Bill of Rights is the first ten amendments to the Constitution. An amendment is a change.

The Constitution describes the process of adding amendments. Amendments are usually proposed by two-thirds of the House of Representatives and the Senate. Three-fourths of the states must **ratify,** or officially accept, an amendment. Only then is it part of the Constitution.

The purpose of the amendment process was to make sure that most people approve of any changes to the Constitution. Because changes need the support of Congress and three-fourths of the states, small groups of people cannot pass amendments.

In June 1788, the Constitution became the country's new system of government. In the end, a Bill of Rights was added and all 13 states ratified it. No system like it had ever been tried before, but the Constitution succeeded. It has become a model for countries around the world.

REVIEW What compromises did delegates make?

Lesson Summary

- The first government of the United States was too weak to be effective.
- The Constitution created a federal system in which the national and state governments divide and share power.
- All 13 states approved the Constitution and a Bill of Rights was added.

Why It Matters ...

The Constitutional Convention created the government that the United States still has today.

Lesson Review

1781 — Articles of Confederation
1787 — Constitution signed
1788 — Ninth state ratifies

1780   1782   1784   1786   1788   1790

1. **VOCABULARY** Write a short summary of the lesson using **compromise** and **ratify.**

2. **READING SKILL** Which **problem** do you think was the most difficult for delegates to **solve**? Why?

3. **MAIN IDEA: History** How did Shays's Rebellion lead to a Constitutional Convention?

4. **MAIN IDEA: Government** What were the main points of the Virginia Plan?

5. **PEOPLE TO KNOW** What did **James Madison** contribute to the Constitutional Convention?

6. **TIMELINE** How many years after the adoption of the Articles of Confederation was the Constitution ratified?

7. **CRITICAL THINKING: Decision Making** For a small state like New Jersey, what were the costs and benefits of the decision to accept the Great Compromise?

WRITING ACTIVITY Write an editorial that someone might have written for or against ratification.

First in Peace

by John Rosenburg

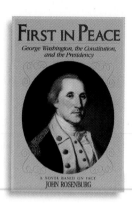

In 1789, George Washington was sworn in as the first American president in Federal Hall in New York City. This description of Washington's inauguration is based on what really happened.

New York awakened to the boom! boom! of cannon fire that cool and cloudy morning of April 30, 1789. Thirteen evenly spaced shots in all made a fitting salute to what would be an auspicious day in American history. By nine o'clock, when church bells rang throughout the city to summon people to prayer, the skies had cleared, and bright sunshine warmed the air.

In his quarters on Cherry Street, Washington prepared himself for the big day, all the while regretting that Martha had decided to stay home with her grandchildren.

He dressed in a plain, brown broadcloth suit that had been made in Hartford, Connecticut, and purchased for him by Henry Knox. And with the metal buttons, which bore the likeness of an eagle with its wings spread, proclaiming "liberty," the suit clearly said "Made in America."

Washington also wore white silk stockings and black shoes adorned with well-polished silver buckles. To complete this simple costume, he fastened a dress sword in a steel scabbard to his waist.

During the short trip, Washington rode alone in a sumptuous carriage pulled by four handsome horses in gleaming harness.

Well aware of what was taking place, hundreds of New Yorkers clogged the narrow streets, forcing the procession to move slowly and carefully.

The two houses of Congress were waiting for Washington in the Senate chamber, a handsome, newly decorated room that measured forty feet by thirty feet and featured a ceiling painted with the sun and stars.

A portrait of George Washington ▶ **at Yorktown**

As Washington walked from a door at the back of the room toward a platform and three chairs at the front, he found the Senators on his right and the members of the House on his left. All were standing and applauding politely.

Following directions given earlier, Washington sat in the center chair. Now, Congress, with much scuffling and scraping of feet, became seated.

After a long moment of silence, John Adams rose and said solemnly, "Sir, the Senate and the House of Representatives are ready to attend you to take the oath required by the Constitution. It will be administered by the Chancellor of the State of New York."

Washington stood, gave a short bow to Adams and said simply, "I am ready to proceed."

Washington took the oath of office on a portico of Federal Hall that overlooked Wall Street and Broad Street. It was a covered balcony of some 480 square feet with three doors at the rear, a window at either end, and an iron railing across the open side.

When Washington stepped through the center door to the railing, a roar went up from the hundreds of upturned faces in the streets below and from the rooftops and windows facing Federal Hall.

Touched, he put his right hand on his heart and bowed repeatedly to right and left. This simple gesture, intended only to acknowledge his welcome, intensified the acclaim.

Finally, Washington pulled back and sat in an armchair as members of Congress crowded onto the portico, and the Chancellor of New York, Robert R. Livingston, prepared to administer the oath.

When all seemed ready, Washington rose and moved close to the balcony, his right side to the street. Livingston, who had been a member of Congress when Washington was appointed commander in chief in 1776, faced him a few feet away, his left side to the street.

Between them, facing the street, stood Samuel Otis, secretary of the Senate. Otis held a small red cushion in his hands. Atop the cushion rested a large leather Bible.

When Otis lifted the Bible, Washington immediately placed his right hand on it, palm down. At that moment, it was so quiet that Washington, Otis, and Livingston could have been alone.

"Do you solemnly swear," asked Livingston, breaking the silence, "that you will faithfully execute the office of President of the United States and will, to the best of your ability, preserve, protect, and defend the Constitution of the United States?"

**George Washington taking
the oath of office**

In a low voice tinged with emotion, Washington responded:

"I solemnly swear that I will faithfully execute the office of the President of the United States and will, to the best of my ability, preserve, protect, and defend the Constitution of the United States."

Then he added, "So help me God." At the last word, he quickly bent forward and kissed the Bible.

"It is done!" cried Livingston, his hands pumping skyward.

The crowds outside Federal Hall applauded and cheered wildly as a cacophony of cannon shots, horns, and whistles erupted in the harbor. Suddenly, however, a hush fell over those in the immediate area of the Hall. A fluttering object sliding slowly but smoothly upward above the building's cupola drew every eye. It was the American flag.

Activities

1. **TALK ABOUT IT** Look closely at the painting on page 91. What details show that the painter thought Washington was a great man?

2. **REPORT IT** Write a newspaper article that might have appeared in a New York newspaper on April 31, 1789, reporting on Washington's inauguration.

Visual Summary

1–4. Write a description of each item below.

French and Indian War, 1755

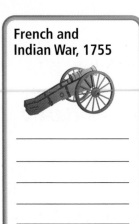

_____
_____
_____
_____
_____

Patriots

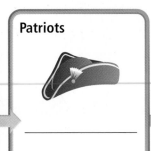

_____
_____
_____
_____
_____

Loyalists

_____
_____
_____
_____
_____

Shays's Rebellion, 1786

_____
_____
_____
_____
_____

Facts and Main Ideas

TEST PREP Answer each question with information from the chapter.

5. **Citizenship** Name two ways that the Sons of Liberty and the Daughters of Liberty protested British taxes.

6. **History** What happened at the First Continental Congress?

7. **History** What strengths did the Continental Army have that the British army did not?

8. **Geography** Where was the last major battle of the American Revolution fought?

9. **Government** Why did delegates at the Constitutional Convention want to change the Articles of Confederation?

Vocabulary

TEST PREP Choose the correct word to complete each sentence.

tax, p. 70
rights, p. 73
treaty, p. 79
federal, p. 86

10. The Virginia Plan called for a _____ system of government.

11. The Declaration of Independence states that all people have _____, including "life, liberty, and the pursuit of happiness."

12. The Revolution ended with a _____ signed by the United States and Britain.

13. The Stamp Act placed a _____ on anything that was printed on paper.

1765	1773	1776	1783
Stamp Act	**Boston Tea Party**	**Declaration of Independence**	**Treaty of Paris**

1765   1770   1775   1780   1785

Apply Skills

✔ TEST PREP **Citizenship Skill** Use the information below and what you have learned about making decisions to answer each question.

> A delegate to the Constitutional Convention needs to make a decision about the plan of government. He agrees with James Madison's plan for a federal system of government. However, he still needs to decide which plan to support: the Virginia Plan, the New Jersey Plan, or the Great Compromise.

14. What would be the best first step for the delegate to take?

   A. Ask others which plan they support.

   B. Flip a coin to make a decision.

   C. Wait to see if someone else makes the decision.

   D. Gather as much information as possible about each plan.

15. Which of the following is the best reason for choosing one particular plan?

   A. The plan leads to the most positive consequences.

   B. The plan leads to the most negative consequences.

   C. Friends are voting for the plan.

   D. The plan is the easiest to understand.

Critical Thinking

✔ TEST PREP Write a short paragraph to answer each question.

16. **Cause and Effect** Why did British taxes cause American colonists to protest?

17. **Compare and Contrast** Explain the difference between the Federalists and the Antifederalists.

Timeline

Use the Chapter Summary Timeline above to answer the question.

18. Which came first, the Stamp Act or the Treaty of Paris?

Activities

 Connect to Georgia Research Revolutionary War battles that took place in Georgia. Use an outline map of your state to label where the battles occurred. Include an important fact about each battle.

 Writing Activity Find out more about one of the key figures in the Revolution, such as George Washington or Francis Marion. Then write a one-page research report about the person.

 Technology
Writing Process Tips
Get help with your report at
www.eduplace.com/kids/hmss/

Principles of DEMOCRACY

★ ★ ★

All nations have governments. A government is a group of people who make and enforce the laws of a political region, such as a country. Just as your school has rules, the nation has laws to govern its citizens.

Life in the United States would be difficult without government. The government sets up ways to choose leaders and makes laws to protect people at home and in the community. Governments run public schools and libraries and print stamps and money. When governments work well, they protect freedom and keep order.

Democratic Government

Governments take many forms. The United States is a democracy. A democracy is a government in which people govern themselves. In a democracy, citizens have the power to make political decisions.

The United States has a form of democracy called representative democracy. That means citizens elect representatives who speak or act for them in making laws.

Majority and Minority

In the United States, the majority of voters usually decides who will win an election. Majority means more than half. Many important decisions are made by majority rule. For example, the majority of lawmakers in Congress must agree on a law before it is passed.

Even though most decisions are made by majority rule, the rights of the minority are protected. Minority means fewer than half. The majority cannot take away the rights of small groups of people to express unpopular views or take part in the government. This limit on majority rule is sometimes called minority rights.

The Rule of Law

The Constitution is the plan for the United States government. It is also the supreme, or highest, law of the United States. Everyone, including the President, must obey the country's laws. This is known as the rule of law. The rule of law is a system in which laws are made by elected representatives, not one or two individuals. The rule of law promises justice to all. In other words, it promises that laws will protect everyone equally.

We the People

Two Hundred Years Thousands of balloons were released to celebrate the 200th anniversary of the U.S. Constitution in 1987.

REVIEW What does the rule of law promise to everyone?

Structure of the GOVERNMENT

★ ★ ★

The federal government is our national government. The Constitution created a federal government with three branches. These branches, or parts, are the legislative, executive, and judicial branches.

The three branches of government work together, but each branch has its own powers. A system of checks and balances prevents any one branch from having too much power. In this system, each branch limits the power of the other two branches.

For example, the President can veto, or reject, laws passed by Congress. Congress can refuse to approve treaties made by the President. The courts of the judicial branch can rule that laws made by Congress or actions taken by the President are unconstitutional.

All three branches are supposed to work toward the common good of the country's citizens. The common good means what is best for the whole country, not just for a few individuals.

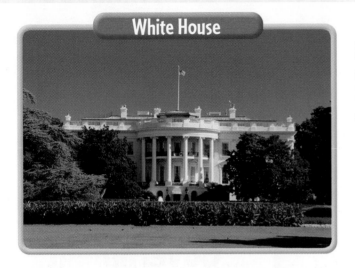
White House

Executive Branch The head of the executive branch is the President. The Vice President and the heads of government departments give advice to the President.

★ proposes, approves, and enforces laws made by Congress

★ makes treaties with other countries

★ leads the military

Capitol

Legislative Branch The legislative branch is called Congress. Congress has two parts: the Senate and the House of Representatives.

★ makes laws

★ raises money by collecting taxes or borrowing money

★ approves the printing of money

★ can declare war

Supreme Court

Judicial Branch The Supreme Court and other courts make up the judicial branch. One Chief Justice and eight Associate Justices serve on the Supreme Court.

★ decides whether laws follow the guidelines of the Constitution

★ decides what laws mean

★ decides whether laws have been followed

REVIEW Why is it important that a balance of power exist among the three branches of government?

Levels *of* GOVERNMENT

★ ★ ★

The federal government is not the only government in the United States. Every state has a government, which is led by a governor. Some decisions are made by the federal government, while others are made by a state government.

Each state is broken into smaller units that have local governments. These units may include counties (parts of states made up of several towns), townships (small parts of counties), cities, and school districts. Local governments take many forms. Some are headed by a mayor. Others are run by a city manager or by a group of people such as a town council.

Federal, state, and local governments have their own powers, but they also share some powers. For example, both the federal and state governments collect taxes, set up courts, and make and enforce laws.

Federal Government

★

Main Powers

★ prints money

★ declares war

★ runs the postal system

★ makes treaties with other countries

★ collects income taxes

State Government

⭐

Main Powers

★ issues licenses, such as marriage licenses and driver's licenses

★ runs elections

★ sets up local governments

★ collects income and sales taxes

Local Government

⭐

Main Powers

★ provides police and fire protection

★ runs public schools and public libraries (with help from the state)

★ provides public transportation, such as buses and subways

★ collects sales and property taxes

REVIEW Which level of government has the power to run elections?

The Bill of Rights

★ ★ ★

The first 10 amendments to the Constitution are called the Bill of Rights. An amendment is an official change or addition to a law. The Bill of Rights is like a promise to the people of the United States. It lists many of the individual rights the U.S. government promises to protect. This chart explains each amendment.

The First Amendment says we have the right to speak our minds.

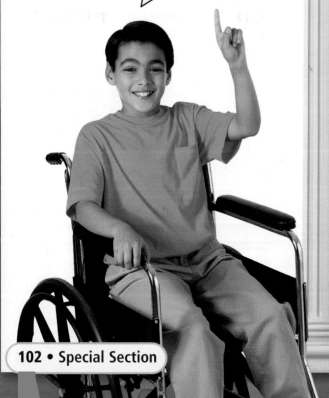

1 First Amendment The government cannot support any religion above another. It may not prevent people from practicing whichever religion they wish. People have the right to say and write their opinions, and the press has the right to publish them. People can also meet together and ask the government to make changes.

2 Second Amendment Because people may have to fight to protect their country, they may own weapons.

3 Third Amendment People do not have to allow soldiers to live in their homes.

4 Fourth Amendment The police cannot search people or their homes without a good reason.

5 Fifth Amendment People accused of a crime have the right to a fair trial. They cannot be tried more than once for the same crime. Accused people do not have to speak against themselves at a trial.

⑥ **Sixth Amendment** People accused of a crime have the right to a speedy, public trial by a jury. A jury is a group of people who hear evidence and make a decision. Accused people also have the right to a lawyer, to be told what crime they are accused of, and to question witnesses.

⑦ **Seventh Amendment** People who have a disagreement about something worth more than $20 have the right to a trial by a jury.

⑧ **Eighth Amendment** In most cases, accused people can remain out of jail until their trial if they pay bail. Bail is a sum of money they will lose if they don't appear for their trial. Courts cannot demand bail that is too high or punish people in cruel ways.

⑨ **Ninth Amendment** People have other rights besides those stated in the Constitution.

⑩ **Tenth Amendment** Any powers the Constitution does not give to the federal government belong to the states or the people.

REVIEW List three rights that are protected by the Bill of Rights.

Review

★ ★ ★

Complete two of the following activities.

Art Activity Work with a group to create a poster titled, *What Democracy Means to Me.* Cut out pictures from newspapers and magazines that illustrate some part of government or something government does.

Writing Activity Choose one of the branches of government and write a short report about it. Give an example of how the branch provides for the common good of the American people.

Research Activity A state capital is a city in which a state's government is located. Make a list of every state's capital. Write a fact card for one capital on your list, including its population and the year it was founded.

Writing Activity Find out who your leaders are at each level of government. Write the names of the President and your senators, representatives, and local leaders. Write to a local leader. Ask questions about that person's job.

Speaking Activity The Bill of Rights still matters today. Prepare an oral report on one of the amendments, explaining how it has affected a current event.

A Growing Nation

Technology

e • **glossary**
e • **word games**
www.eduplace.com/kids/hmss05/

Vocabulary Preview

suffrage

When territories became new states, all white men in those states were allowed to vote. Even those who did not own land were given **suffrage.** page 110

productivity

With the use of machines, goods could be produced more quickly. Factories increased the **productivity** of the United States.
page 115

Chapter Timeline

1803
Louisiana Purchase

1812
War of 1812 begins

| 1800 | 1810 | 1820 |

Reading Strategy

Question As you read, ask yourself questions to check your understanding.

Quick Tip Write down a question you have and answer it when you finish reading.

republic

After winning its independence, Texas was a **republic.** Citizens elected leaders to represent them in the government. **page 122**

forty-niner

Most of those who were part of the California Gold Rush arrived in 1849. They were known as **forty-niners.** page 125

1825
Erie Canal built

1833
National Road completed

1838
Trail of Tears

1830

1840

The Country Grows

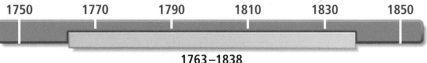

Build on What You Know Today you can travel across a mountain range by plane in less than an hour. In the late 1700s and early 1800s, travel was not so easy. It took weeks for people to make that same trip.

Pioneers Cross the Appalachians

Main Idea Pioneers settled land west of the Appalachian Mountains in the late 1700s.

The first colonists who came to the British colonies from Europe settled between the Atlantic Ocean and the Appalachian Mountains. This 2,000-mile-long mountain range was difficult to cross. In addition, a British law called the Proclamation of 1763 made it illegal for colonists to settle on American Indian lands west of the mountains. But this did not stop people from trying to go there. As more of the East filled in with farms and towns, settlers found new ways to cross the Appalachians.

VOCABULARY

pioneer
frontier
interpreter
doctrine
suffrage

Vocabulary Strategy

inter**preter**

The prefix **inter-** means between or among. An interpreter goes between people who don't speak the same language to explain what they are saying to each other.

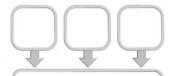 **READING SKILL**

Cause and Effect As you read, list reasons that tell why the United States grew during the late 1700s and early 1800s.

THE NATION GROWS

 STANDARDS

SS4H6 Review Westward expansion
SS5CG3a 12th Amendment

The Cumberland Gap This opening, or gap, in the rugged Appalachian Mountains made it easier for colonists to move into the Ohio River Valley.

The Cumberland Gap

Daniel Boone was a hunter and pioneer who was curious about the land west of the Appalachians. A **pioneer** is one of the first of a certain group to enter or settle a region. In 1769, Boone and five other hunters followed an American Indian trail through a narrow opening, or gap, in the mountains. This opening, called the Cumberland Gap, led from Virginia to thickly forested land in present-day Kentucky. In 1775, Boone helped build a road called the Wilderness Road through the Cumberland Gap.

Thousands of people crossed the Appalachians on the Wilderness Road. Pioneers traveled by wagon and on foot. The Wilderness Road was just a rocky dirt path barely wide enough for a wagon to pass. The road was so bumpy that wagons often broke apart.

Once across the mountains, settlers journeyed farther west on rivers. Most traveled on the Ohio River. Flatboats carried families, their animals, and their belongings down the river. A flatboat was a large, rectangular boat partly covered by a roof.

The people who built new settlements in the fertile Ohio River Valley thought of the land farther west as a frontier. A **frontier** is the edge of a country or a settled area. But the land beyond the frontier was not empty. It was already settled by American Indians. The Shawnee, Choctaw, Cherokee, and other people lived between the Appalachians and the Mississippi River. They didn't want settlers moving onto their lands. On the frontier, American Indians and settlers fought over land, but they also borrowed ideas and customs from one another.

REVIEW Why was the Cumberland Gap so important to settlers wanting to cross the Appalachians?

Daniel Boone Settlers saw Boone as a hero. Below, Boone leads his team of explorers through the Cumberland Gap.

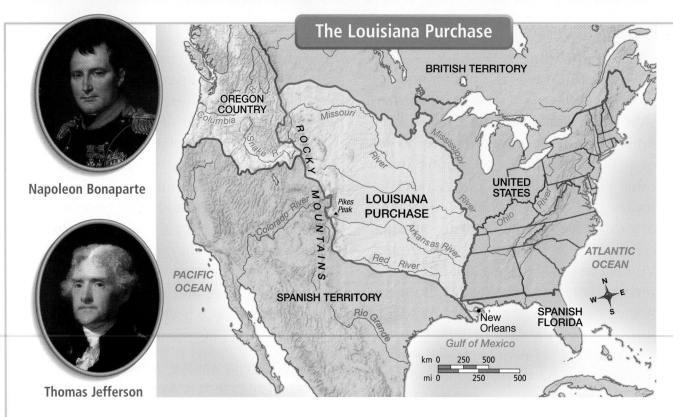

Napoleon Bonaparte

Thomas Jefferson

BRITISH TERRITORY

OREGON COUNTRY

Columbia R.

Missouri River

ROCKY MOUNTAINS

Snake R.

Pikes Peak

LOUISIANA PURCHASE

UNITED STATES

Mississippi River

Ohio River

Colorado River

Arkansas River

Red River

PACIFIC OCEAN

ATLANTIC OCEAN

SPANISH TERRITORY

Rio Grande

New Orleans

SPANISH FLORIDA

Gulf of Mexico

km 0   250   500
mi 0   250   500

Louisiana Purchase Napoleon Bonaparte of France sold Louisiana to the United States for $15,000,000. President Thomas Jefferson bought this land to increase the size the United States.

Thomas Jefferson

Main Idea President Jefferson added territory to the United States and sent explorers there.

Thomas Jefferson ran for President in 1800. At that time, a group of people called electors chose the President. Each elector cast two votes. The person with the most votes became President. The person with the second most votes became Vice President. In 1800, though, **Aaron Burr**, another Republican, received the same number of votes as Jefferson. The two men were tied. The House of Representatives had to choose the President. They chose Jefferson.

To avoid any more ties between two people from the same party, the nation ratified the 12th Amendment in 1804. It said that electors would vote for the President and Vice President separately.

The Louisiana Purchase

When **Thomas Jefferson** became President, the French claimed a large area of land west of the Mississippi River. They called this land Louisiana. France also controlled the port of New Orleans.

Jefferson asked the French government to let American ships use New Orleans. To his surprise, the French offered to sell all of Louisiana to the United States.

The President quickly accepted the offer. The Louisiana Purchase of 1803 doubled the size of the country.

President Jefferson sent a group of soldiers led by **Meriwether Lewis** and **William Clark** to explore the land the United States had bought. He asked them to look for a water route to the Pacific Ocean. He also told them to gather information about the geography, plants, animals, climate, and peoples of the West.

Corps of Discovery Lewis and Clark (above) lead the way through the cold Bitterroot Mountains. The United States Mint honored the 200th anniversary of the Lewis and Clark expedition with a new nickel (right).

The Lewis and Clark Expedition

In May of 1804, Lewis and Clark set out from St. Louis, Missouri. Their group was called the Corps (kor) of Discovery. A corps is a team of people working together. A Shoshone (shoh SHOH nee) woman named **Sacagawea** (sah KAH guh WEE uh) later joined the team and became an interpreter. An **interpreter** explains what is said in one language to people who speak a different language.

The Corps traveled up the Missouri River, over the Rocky Mountains, and down the Columbia River to the Pacific Ocean. The explorers returned to St. Louis in September 1806. American Indians along the way suggested travel routes and traded for supplies and horses.

Lewis and Clark described the people, wildlife, and the land in their journals. They had learned that there was no water route across the country to the Pacific Ocean. They had shown, however, that it was possible to cross over the Rocky Mountains. The Corps had also made contact with western Indians. These discoveries created interest in the West and would help future pioneers and traders for years to come.

REVIEW What did Lewis and Clark learn about the West?

War of 1812

Main Idea As the United States grew, so did conflicts with Britain and American Indians.

People from the United States continued to move west. Fighting increased between settlers and American Indians trying to protect their land. Some people believed that British colonists in Canada were giving weapons to American Indians.

At this time, France and Britain were at war. The United States was neutral, but the British navy seized American ships to stop them from trading with France. The British captured American sailors and forced them to join the British navy. Forcing sailors to serve in the British navy was called impressment.

The United States declared war against Britain in 1812. The two countries fought along the Canadian border and in cities on the east coast.

Late in the war, British soldiers attacked Washington, D.C. They burned the White House and the Capitol.

By 1814, neither country was winning, so both sides agreed to end the war. Although neither side won any land, Americans were proud that their country had not lost to powerful Britain.

The War of 1812 gave the leaders of the United States confidence. In 1823, President **James Monroe** issued a warning called the Monroe Doctrine. A **doctrine** is an official statement or position. Monroe warned European nations not to start new colonies in the Americas. This warning showed that the United States saw itself as a major power.

After the War of 1812, many new states were added to the United States. All adult white men in these new states were given suffrage. **Suffrage** is the right to vote. For the first time, men who did not own land could legally vote.

War of 1812 In this painting, an American ship captures a British ship in one of the many sea battles of the War of 1812.

President Andrew Jackson

These new voters helped elect President **Andrew Jackson** in 1828. Jackson grew up on the frontier. He was seen as a hero of the War of 1812 and was admired by many as a tough fighter.

Jackson wanted more settlers to own frontier land. To get the land, he signed the Indian Removal Act in 1830. This law ordered people of Indian nations east of the Mississippi River to move west to present-day Oklahoma. The U.S. Army forced thousands of American Indians to leave their homes.

People of the Cherokee nation argued that the Indian Removal Act was illegal. Chief **John Ross** took this case to the Supreme Court. The Court agreed that it was against the law to force the Cherokee to move, but President Jackson ignored the ruling. In 1838, the U.S. Army forced the Cherokee to make the nearly 1,000-mile trip west.

Thousands of Cherokee died from the terrible conditions along the way. This heartbreaking journey became known as the Trail of Tears.

REVIEW What was the result of the War of 1812?

Lesson Summary

In the late 1700s, pioneers traveled on the Wilderness Road to cross the Appalachians. President Jefferson arranged to buy the Louisiana Territory in 1803, and the next year, Lewis and Clark set off to explore the West. The United States and Britain fought each other in the War of 1812, but neither side won or lost any land. President Jackson forced American Indians east of the Mississippi to move west in 1830.

Why It Matters ...

In the early 1800s, the United States grew larger and more powerful. Conflicts with American Indians over land, however, would continue throughout the 1800s.

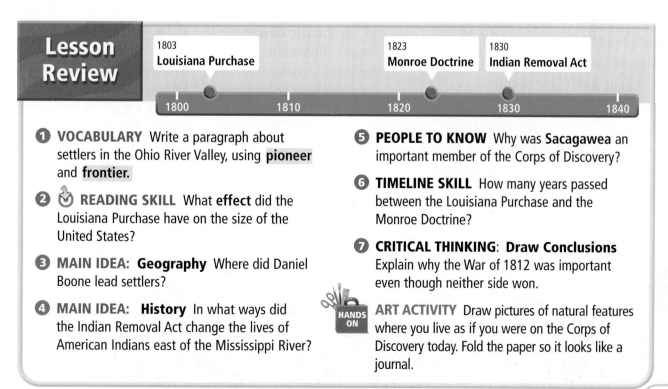

Lesson Review

Timeline:
- 1803 **Louisiana Purchase**
- 1823 **Monroe Doctrine**
- 1830 **Indian Removal Act**

1800 — 1810 — 1820 — 1830 — 1840

1 VOCABULARY Write a paragraph about settlers in the Ohio River Valley, using **pioneer** and **frontier.**

2 READING SKILL What **effect** did the Louisiana Purchase have on the size of the United States?

3 MAIN IDEA: **Geography** Where did Daniel Boone lead settlers?

4 MAIN IDEA: **History** In what ways did the Indian Removal Act change the lives of American Indians east of the Mississippi River?

5 PEOPLE TO KNOW Why was **Sacagawea** an important member of the Corps of Discovery?

6 TIMELINE SKILL How many years passed between the Louisiana Purchase and the Monroe Doctrine?

7 CRITICAL THINKING: **Draw Conclusions** Explain why the War of 1812 was important even though neither side won.

HANDS ON ART ACTIVITY Draw pictures of natural features where you live as if you were on the Corps of Discovery today. Fold the paper so it looks like a journal.

Journey of Discovery

OREGON COUNTRY

PACIFIC OCEAN

Fort Clatsop **4**

Columbia River

Canoe Camp

Great Falls

Clearwater River

3

Camp Fortunate

Shoshone villages

Snake River

They had paddled unmapped rivers and scrambled over mountain passes for more than a year. Finally, the explorers in the Corps of Discovery caught sight of the Pacific Ocean. President Jefferson had asked Lewis and Clark to find a route across the continent to the Pacific. Along the way, they filled their journals with drawings of plants and animals. They described the time that Lewis's dog, Seaman, scared away an attacking bear and the time that Sacagawea saved precious tools and papers from the waters of the Missouri after a boat tipped over.

Lewis and Clark covered thousands of miles. How did the Corps of Discovery travel over this rugged land? Look at the map to find out. Their journey begins on the right side of the map.

4 **Pacific Ocean, 1805-1806**

The Corps traveled down the Columbia River and reached the Pacific Ocean in early November 1805. They spent a rainy winter there. In his journal, Clark described his joy at seeing the "immense ocean."

3 **Bitterroot Range, 1805**

At Camp Fortunate, Sacagawea helped Lewis and Clark trade for horses with the Shoshone. The explorers needed these horses to cross the steep Bitterroot Range of the Rocky Mountains.

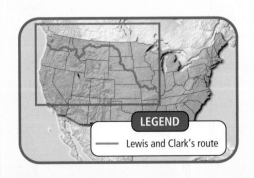

LEGEND

—— Lewis and Clark's route

LEGEND

- Travel by boats
- Travel by horses
- Travel by walking
- American Indian settlement

- Louisiana Purchase
- Oregon Country
- Spanish territory

Missouri River

Yellowstone River

2 Fort Mandan

Hidatsa and Mandan villages

ROCKY MOUNTAINS

LOUISIANA PURCHASE

G R E A T   P L A I N S

Platte River

Missouri River

Mississippi River

START HERE

Camp Dubois
St. Louis

1

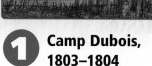

2 Fort Mandan,
1804–1805

After traveling more than a thousand miles, the explorers spent a cold winter at Fort Mandan on the Great Plains.

1 Camp Dubois,
1803–1804

In May, the Corps of Discovery journeyed up the Missouri River from the point where it joins the Mississippi. The travelers had to paddle or pole their boats to keep moving upriver against the strong current.

Activities

1. **EXPLORE IT** Find the Missouri and Columbia rivers. Follow the route on the map. What places or events made the trip difficult? Why?

2. **WRITE ABOUT IT** Choose one of the photographs. Write a journal entry to describe it. Think about the things the Corps of Discovery needed to do to get past this landmark. List the steps.

The Industrial Revolution

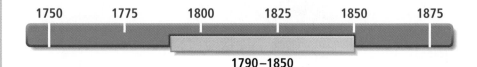

1750   1775   1800   1825   1850   1875

1790–1850

Build on What You Know Most of the things you use are made by machines. People first used machines to make cloth and tools in the late 1700s.

VOCABULARY

textile
entrepreneur
interchangeable parts
mass production
productivity

Vocabulary Strategy

inter**change**able

The word **interchangeable** includes the word **change.** When an interchangeable part breaks, it's easy to change it with a new one.

READING SKILL

Categorize List inventions of the Industrial Revolution in two categories on a chart.

FACTORIES	TRANSPORTATION

The Industrial Revolution Begins

Main Idea New inventions and ways of working changed how goods were made.

In the early 1700s, people made cloth, tools, and furniture by hand in homes or small shops. That changed in the late 1700s as people began to use machines to produce more goods. Also, new forms of transportation moved people and goods faster than ever before. These changes in manufacturing and transportation are known as the Industrial Revolution.

Some of the first machines of that time spun cotton into yarn. Machines could spin cotton much faster than people could do it by hand. In 1790, a British mechanic named **Samuel Slater** opened the first cotton-spinning textile mill, or factory, in the United States. **Textile** means cloth or fabric.

In 1813, an entrepreneur (AWN trah PAH noor) named **Francis Cabot Lowell** built a mill near Boston. An **entrepreneur** takes risks to start new businesses. Lowell's mill had both cotton-spinning machines and power looms that wove yarn into cloth. It was the first mill in the world to turn raw cotton into finished cloth. Entrepreneurs opened more textile factories, and New England became the center of a growing textile industry.

STANDARDS

SS5E1f Productivity
SS5E3c Entrepreneurs take risks

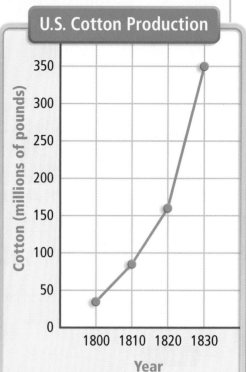

Textiles Some mills could produce 30 miles of cloth a day. After cloth was woven, designs were printed on it.

SKILL **Reading Graphs** In which decade did the largest jump in cotton production occur?

Eli Whitney

New mills turned cotton into yarn very quickly, but getting cotton ready for these mills took a lot of work. The seeds in the cotton had to be removed before the cotton could be spun into yarn.

In 1793, **Eli Whitney** invented a cotton engine, or gin, that used wire teeth to remove seeds. The gin could do work in minutes that once took a full day.

The United States hired Whitney to make 10,000 guns for the army. At that time, guns were made one at a time by hand. To make the guns quickly and cheaply, Whitney used interchangeable parts. **Interchangeable parts** are parts made by a machine to be exactly the same so that any of them can fit into another product with the same design.

Whitney used mass production to make the guns. Mass is another word for many. **Mass production** means making many products at once. Instead of making a complete gun, each worker added a certain part to many guns. These parts were always the same. Fitting the same parts over and over was faster than making a single gun from start to finish.

Workers using new machines, interchangeable parts, and mass production produced goods more quickly. The productivity of the whole country increased. **Productivity** is the amount of goods produced in a certain amount of time by a person, machine, or group.

REVIEW Why was Whitney able to manufacture guns quickly and cheaply?

115

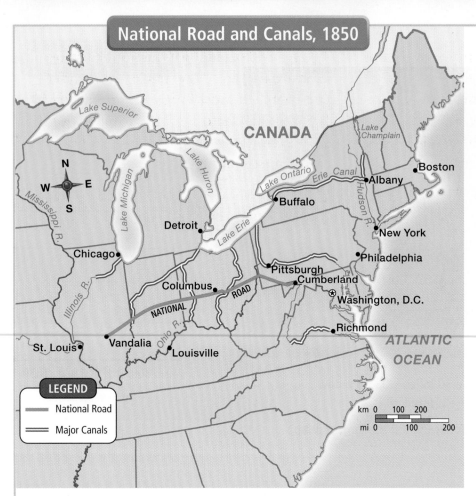

National Road and Canals, 1850

LEGEND
— National Road
═ Major Canals

Better Travel Routes
New roads and canals improved travel. By 1840, more than 3,000 miles of canals crossed the eastern United States.

SKILL **Reading Maps** Which land and water routes could a farmer in Vandalia, Illinois, take to move goods to New York City?

Changes in Transportation

Main Idea Roads, canals, and railroads improved travel in the 1800s.

Travel was slow and expensive in the early 1800s. Most roads were narrow dirt paths. Snow and rain made roads icy and muddy. Because travel over these roads was difficult, it took a long time and cost a lot of money for farmers to move their goods to cities to be sold.

In 1815, the United States began building a road to connect Ohio with the East. The first section of the road followed an American Indian trail. By 1833, this road, the National Road, went from Maryland to Ohio and was paved with stone. It became the most heavily traveled road in the country. People built towns and businesses all along the National Road.

Steam Power

In the 1700s and early 1800s, shipping goods by water was easier than using roads. But travel by water was slow, too. Boats could move only by wind or water currents. Then, in 1807, **Robert Fulton** invented the steamboat, which could travel against currents. Steam power gave boats more speed. Within a few years, steamboats became common on rivers.

Canals made water travel possible to more cities and towns. Canals are waterways built to link rivers to other bodies of water. The Erie Canal was finished in 1825. It connected the Hudson River to Lake Erie. This canal allowed farmers and manufacturers near the Great Lakes to move their goods directly to New York City's ocean port by water.

Travel over land also improved. Trains pulled by steam locomotives were fast. They could run in snow and ice, and travel up and down hills easily. A trip from New York City to Albany, New York, took only 10 hours by railroad instead of 32 hours by steamboat.

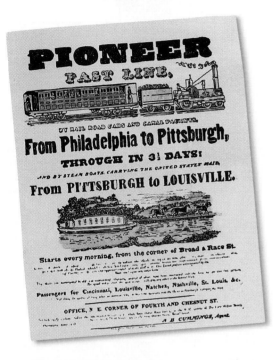

Full Steam Ahead! This poster (above) advertised a speedy ride to Kentucky.

By 1850, the nation had 9,000 miles of railroad track. New tracks were added every day. As more cities were connected by railroads, factories and farmers could ship their goods to almost any city or town in the country.

REVIEW Why were steam locomotives better than other forms of transportation?

Lesson Summary

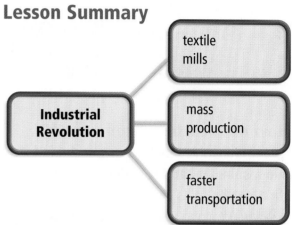

Industrial Revolution
- textile mills
- mass production
- faster transportation

Why It Matters ...

New machines and ways of working that were invented during the Industrial Revolution affect the way products are made today.

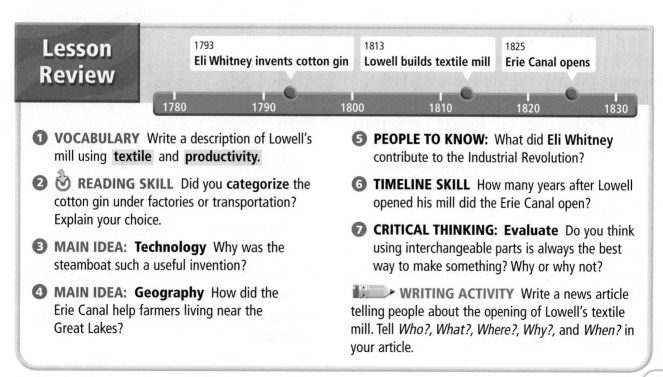

Lesson Review

1793	1813	1825
Eli Whitney invents cotton gin	Lowell builds textile mill	Erie Canal opens

1780　1790　1800　1810　1820　1830

1 VOCABULARY Write a description of Lowell's mill using **textile** and **productivity.**

2 READING SKILL Did you **categorize** the cotton gin under factories or transportation? Explain your choice.

3 MAIN IDEA: Technology Why was the steamboat such a useful invention?

4 MAIN IDEA: Geography How did the Erie Canal help farmers living near the Great Lakes?

5 PEOPLE TO KNOW: What did **Eli Whitney** contribute to the Industrial Revolution?

6 TIMELINE SKILL How many years after Lowell opened his mill did the Erie Canal open?

7 CRITICAL THINKING: Evaluate Do you think using interchangeable parts is always the best way to make something? Why or why not?

WRITING ACTIVITY Write a news article telling people about the opening of Lowell's textile mill. Tell *Who?*, *What?*, *Where?*, *Why?*, and *When?* in your article.

Inside a Cotton Mill

How does cotton become cloth?
The process involves many steps, including cleaning, spinning, and weaving the cotton. The first cotton mills only spun cotton into yarn. Weavers wove yarn into cloth in homes or small shops. When Francis Cabot Lowell put power looms in his Massachusetts textile factory, he made it possible to do all of the steps of making cloth in one building.

The cloth-making process began on the bottom floor of the mill. After the raw cotton was cleaned, cotton fibers were carded, or combed into loose ropes. These ropes were spun into thread on the second floor of the mill. Next, the thread was prepared for weaving. This process, called warping, took place on the third floor. Finally, the thread was woven into finished cloth. Each of these steps required a different machine.

The mill's machines used water power. Lowell's company built canals along the Merrimack River. The canals carried rushing water to the mills where it turned waterwheels. The waterwheels were attached to belts that powered the machines in the factory.

Bales of Cotton
Workers rip open huge bales of cotton weighing about 500 pounds. The raw cotton is run through machines that clean and sort the cotton fibers.

Spinning

Loose strings of cotton are spun into yarn or thread. The thread is wound onto wooden sticks called bobbins.

Weaving

Looms turn yarn into cloth by weaving thousands of threads under and over each other.

Activities

1. **TALK ABOUT IT** Look at the pictures of workers and machines. Which step do you think took the most time? Why?

2. **DESCRIBE IT** Look at the picture and read the captions. Write the steps for making cloth in a numbered list. Use your list to write a paragraph describing how cloth is made.

Skillbuilder

Draw Conclusions

▶ **VOCABULARY**

conclusion

Writers don't always make connections among the different pieces of information they present. To make these connections, you may need to draw conclusions. A **conclusion** is a judgment or decision based on facts and ideas. To draw a conclusion, use your own experience to decide how facts are connected.

Learn the Skill

Step 1: Study the facts and ideas that the author presents.

Step 2: Look for connections among the facts.

Step 3: Draw a conclusion. Your conclusion should state your observation or opinion about the facts and ideas.

Practice the Skill

Read the following paragraphs about two major changes in transportation in the 1800s. Then answer the questions.

It took almost 8 years and about $7 million to build the Erie Canal. Because of the canal, the cost of shipping products across New York dropped from $100 to $5 a ton. The trip between Albany and Buffalo took only 5 days, instead of 20 days by wagon. The cost of building the canal was repaid in just two years.

Steamboats allowed people to move upstream as well as downstream without the help of poles, sails, or ropes. They carried farm products to the cities. Steamboats also carried manufactured goods to small towns in the country. People who traveled on steamboats admired their speed but often found them noisy and crowded.

1 What can you conclude about the effects of the Erie Canal?

2 What would you conclude about the invention of the steamboat? Would you say it was a good or bad way to travel?

3 What details support your conclusion about steamboats?

Apply the Skill

In a paragraph, explain your conclusions about transportation in the 1800s. Support your conclusions with information from each paragraph above.

Moving West

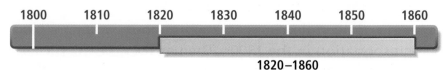

1800   1810   1820   1830   1840   1850   1860

1820–1860

VOCABULARY

republic
annexation
forty-niner
boomtown

Vocabulary Strategy

forty-niner

Many people went to California in 1849. They were called **forty-niners.**

READING SKILL

Sequence Note the order of important events in this lesson.

1	
2	
3	
4	

STANDARDS

SS4H6 Review Westward expansion

Build on What You Know You have learned that colonists fought for independence from Britain during the Revolutionary War. When Texas was part of Mexico, Texans also fought for independence.

Texas and the Mexican War

Main Idea After Texas became a state, the United States gained more western land from Mexico.

In the 1820s, settlers from the United States began to move to Texas. Texas was then a part of Mexico. By 1830, more Americans than Mexicans lived in Texas. Mexico passed laws to stop Americans from settling there, but Americans continued to come.

Americans in Texas sometimes disagreed with the Mexican government and disobeyed Mexican laws. They wanted to make their own laws. In March of 1836, Texans declared independence from Mexico to form a new government. Mexico sent soldiers to stop them.

Mexican Texans, known as Tejanos (teh HAHN ohs), fought alongside American Texans during the Texas War for Independence. After about six months of fighting, **Antonio López de Santa Anna**, the ruler of Mexico, was captured. He agreed to give Texas its independence.

From 1836 to 1845, Texas was an independent republic, no longer part of Mexico. A **republic** is a government in which the citizens elect leaders to represent them.

Lone Star Flag This is the earliest flag for the independent Republic of Texas.

Texans elected **Sam Houston** as their president. In 1836, they voted to join the United States. Congress approved the annexation of Texas in 1845. **Annexation** means the addition of an area to a country.

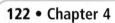

The Mexican War

After Texas was annexed, Mexico and the United States disagreed on the boundary between Texas and Mexico. President **James Polk** sent troops to the Rio Grande (REE oh GRAHN deh), the river that he believed should be the border. U.S. leaders hoped a war against Mexico would give the United States a chance to gain land in the present-day southwestern United States. The United States declared war on Mexico on May 13, 1846.

The fighting lasted about 15 months. Battles were fought in Texas and Mexico, including the present-day states of California and New Mexico. The United States won the war when its army captured Mexico's capital, Mexico City.

In 1848, the two nations signed a peace treaty. Mexico agreed to make the Rio Grande the border between Mexico and Texas. The United States paid Mexico $15 million for a vast area of land called the Mexican Cession. All Mexicans living in the Cession could become citizens of the United States.

Moving West

Main Idea Pioneers traveled west for land and for gold.

While some Americans settled in Texas, others went across the continent to find new places to live. Those pioneers followed trails that led to the Oregon Territory, California, and other areas of the West.

Explorers and missionaries were among the first to reach the Oregon Territory. **John Frémont** explored a route to Oregon in 1842. His reports created interest in the Northwest region. Missionaries traveled west to teach American Indians about Christianity. Their descriptions of a rich and beautiful land made farmers want to move there.

REVIEW What were the results of the United States' victory in the Mexican War?

The Alamo In 1836, Texans fought the Battle of the Alamo in San Antonio. Texans lost, but their courage inspired the battle cry, "Remember the Alamo!"

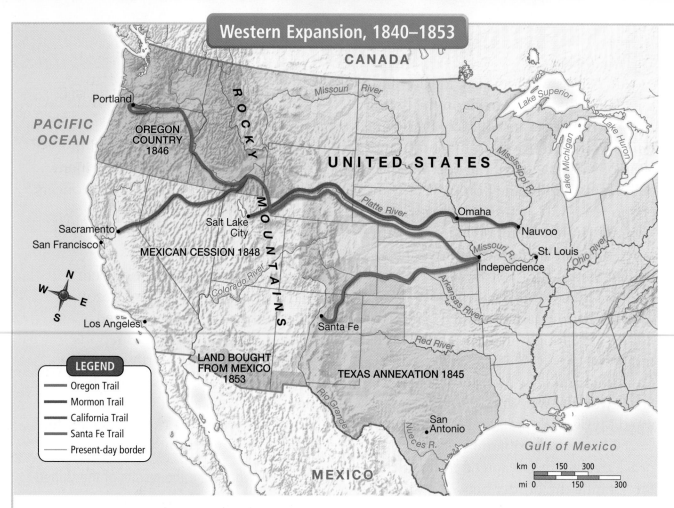

Western Expansion, 1840–1853

CANADA

Missouri River

PACIFIC OCEAN

Portland

OREGON COUNTRY 1846

R O C K Y

UNITED STATES

Lake Superior

Lake Michigan

Lake Huron

Platte River

Omaha

Sacramento

Salt Lake City

M O U N T A I N S

Nauvoo

San Francisco

MEXICAN CESSION 1848

Missouri R.

St. Louis

Independence

Ohio River

Colorado River

N
W   E
S

Los Angeles

LAND BOUGHT FROM MEXICO 1853

Santa Fe

Arkansas River

Red River

TEXAS ANNEXATION 1845

Rio Grande

Nueces R.

San Antonio

Gulf of Mexico

LEGEND
— Oregon Trail
— Mormon Trail
— California Trail
— Santa Fe Trail
— Present-day border

MEXICO

km 0   150   300
mi 0   150   300

Overland Trails Many trails led settlers west. After the Mexican Cession, the United States stretched from the Atlantic to the Pacific Ocean.

SKILL **Reading Maps** Which trail led to Portland?

In 1843, the first large group of about 1,000 settlers headed west along the Oregon Trail. Most were families who were looking for good, inexpensive farmland. Several trails led west, but the Oregon Trail was used the most.

Pioneers traveled in lines of covered wagons called wagon trains. Wagons were pulled by oxen. Settlers traveled in these groups for safety.

Settlers faced injuries, diseases, bad weather, and lack of food and water on the long journey. River crossings could also be dangerous for wagon trains. Despite such hardships, thousands of pioneers settled in the West and began new lives.

California Gold Rush

On January 24, 1848, a worker found gold in the American River in California. News of the discovery spread quickly. By 1849, thousands were hurrying to California. This rush of excited gold seekers was called the California Gold Rush. One miner wrote,

66 A frenzy seized my soul...
piles of gold rose up before
me at every step... I had a very
violent attack of the gold fever! 99

During the gold rush, more than 250,000 people poured into California. They came from the United States, Mexico, China, South America, and Europe.

The miners were called forty-niners because most of them came in 1849. A **forty-niner** is someone who took part in the California Gold Rush. Miners built boomtowns near the mines. A **boomtown** is a town that grows very quickly. People who wanted to sell goods and services to the miners also flocked to boomtowns.

Panning for Gold Miners used special pans to collect sand from rivers. They then drained the water and sand hoping to find a shiny nugget of gold.

The California Gold Rush lasted about five years. When it ended, many miners returned home with no gold, but thousands stayed in California. By 1850, California had enough people to become a state. The United States now stretched all the way across the continent.

REVIEW What kind of people went to boomtowns?

Lesson Summary

- After gaining independence from Mexico, Texas was annexed by the United States.
- The United States won the Mexican War and gained a large area of land.
- Pioneers made long trips on overland trails to settle the West.
- The California Gold Rush brought so many people to California that it became a state in 1850.

Why It Matters...

The United States expanded to the Pacific coast after the Mexican War.

Lesson Review

1836	1846	1850
Texas gains independence	Mexican War begins	California becomes a state

1820　　　　　1830　　　　　1840　　　　　1850　　　　　1860

1 **VOCABULARY** Is the United States a **republic?** Give a reason for your answer.

2 **READING SKILL** Write a short paragraph summarizing the **sequence** of events in this lesson.

3 **MAIN IDEA: History** What made so many people want to move to the West?

4 **MAIN IDEA: Geography** What effect did the Mexican Cession have on the United States?

5 **EVENTS TO KNOW** In what ways did the Gold Rush lead to the growth of California?

6 **TIMELINE SKILL** Which event occurred first, the Mexican War or Texan independence?

7 **CRITICAL THINKING: Decision Making** What were costs and benefits of deciding to go to California to search for gold in 1849?

HANDS ON

RESEARCH ACTIVITY In a small group, look up cities and geographic features with Spanish names in the states of the Mexican Cession. Choose one place and find out what its name means and other facts about it. Then make a fact card about the place you chose.

Wagon Train

What was it like to travel by wagon train? In the 1840s, settlers began traveling overland to California and Oregon. The journey took many months. The travelers, like these families bound for California, had to work as a team to overcome problems.

Characters

Narrator

Henry Dalton: Illinois farmer

Cecelia Dalton: Illinois doctor

Jane Dalton: 16-year-old daughter of Henry and Cecelia

Sarah Dalton: 12-year-old sister of Jane and Daniel

Daniel Dalton: 10-year-old brother of Jane and Sarah

Anna Getz: Illinois farmer, Cecelia Dalton's sister

Will Getz: Illinois farmer, Anna Getz's husband

Jesse Getz: Will Getz's cousin

Narrator: It is a brutally hot day in August, 1851. The settlers have halted at the bank of the Humboldt River in Nevada. They must cross the river to continue west to California.

Henry Dalton: Looks like we've got trouble.

Cecilia Dalton: What's wrong, Henry?

Henry: Look at those rocks. The river is full of them. How are we supposed to get the wagons past those?

Will Getz: The wheels and axles will be splinters by the time we get to the other side.

Jane Dalton: What if one of the oxen slips? We can't lose an ox. We still have to get across the desert and over the mountains.

Sarah Dalton: Can't we cross the river somewhere else?

Jesse Getz: This is the shallowest part, Sarah. We talked it over with the scout. It's too deep to cross anywhere else.

Anna Getz: Well, let's get some food ready while we figure this out. Jesse, why don't you and Jane put up some canvas between our wagons for shade?

Cecilia: Sarah and Daniel, bring us some water, please.

Daniel Dalton: Can I go for a swim first? I've been walking behind the wagon all day. Sarah and I have been helping the Weber family, and I'm all dusted out.

Cecelia: I'm not sure the river's safe, Dan. Why don't you take the bucket and cool yourself off?

Sarah Dalton

Jane Dalton

127

Narrator: A short time later, Sarah comes running, gasping for breath.

Sarah: Mama! Hannah's brother got stung by something.

Cecelia: Oh, dear! No time to waste. Jane, hand me that big green bottle and a roll of bandages. The rest of you, do what Anna tells you till I get back.

Narrator: Cecelia Dalton hurries away and the families finish preparing the noon meal. Over their food, they discuss the river crossing.

Anna: So, what have you decided about the wagons?

Will: Old Captain Coombs says we'll carry them across the river.

Jane: You'll do what?

Daniel: Can I help, Pa?

Henry: You can help unload the wagon, son. After we've lightened the load, we'll walk each wagon into the river, grab hold of it, and lift it across. Then we'll guide the oxen.

Henry
Dalton

Cecelia
Dalton

nna
Getz

Anna: We'll need to make sure there's plenty of tar on the wagon boards. We don't want any leaks. Jane, Sarah—you can help me with the tar bucket, too.

Narrator: The families empty the wagons and a dozen people carry each wagon around the rocks until the whole train is safely across. It takes all day. The oxen make it across without injury. The next morning, the Daltons wait for the signal for the wagon train to move on.

Daniel: Come on, let's go! I want to get to California before the gold is all gone!

Jesse: Be patient, cousin. Gold might not be so easy to find. But you can always come to work for me. I hear California is a farmer's paradise.

Will: Almost as good as Illinois.

Sarah: Mama, may I walk with the Webers and Hannah? Oh—John's doing fine now, isn't he?

Cecelia: Yes, he'll be all right. Be back by noon.

Anna: I wish we could have waited here one more day, Cecelia. How about you, Jane?

Jane: I agree, but Captain Coombs says we have to get over the Sierra Nevadas before the first snow, or we'll all be in danger.

Henry: There's the signal! Everybody ready? Let's move out!

Will Getz

Activities

1. **TALK ABOUT IT** What character traits did pioneers need to make the journey west?

2. **ACT IT OUT** Create a short additional scene about the wagon train. Show what happens when the Daltons and Getzes cross the desert or the mountains, or use your own ideas.

Visual Summary

1.–3.  Write a description of each item named below.

Transportation

Wilderness Road

_____
_____
_____

Erie Canal

_____
_____
_____

Oregon Trail

_____
_____
_____

Facts and Main Ideas

✓ **TEST PREP** Answer each question with information from the chapter.

4. **Geography** How did the Cumberland Gap help western settlement?

5. **Government** What was the Indian Removal Act, and why did President Jackson sign it?

6. **Economics** What was the advantage of making goods with interchangeable parts?

7. **History** What caused the Mexican War in 1846?

8. **History** Why did many people move to California in 1849?

Vocabulary

✓ **TEST PREP** Choose the correct word from the list below to complete each sentence.

doctrine, p. 110
entrepreneur, p. 114
republic, p. 122

9. From 1836 to 1845, Texas was an independent _____.

10. Francis Cabot Lowell was an _____ who built a mill near Boston.

11. The Monroe _____ warned European nations not to start new colonies in the Americas.

CHAPTER SUMMARY TIMELINE

1803 Louisiana Purchase	1812 War of 1812 begins	1825 Erie Canal built	1833 National Road completed	1838 Trail of Tears

1800   1810   1820   1830   1840

Apply Skills

✅ **TEST PREP** **Reading and Thinking Skill** Read the passage below. Then use what you know about drawing conclusions to answer each question.

> The Gold Rush began in 1848. By 1852, California's population was twenty times larger than it had been in 1848. Boomtowns sprang up overnight and grew into cities. Some people found gold, but many others discovered that they could make money by selling supplies to the miners. The Gold Rush ended after five years, but many people stayed in California.

12. Which of the following statements is a conclusion you could draw from this paragraph?

   A. The Gold Rush had little effect on California.

   B. The Gold Rush had a big effect on California.

   C. The Gold Rush made everyone rich.

   D. It took a long time to settle California after the Gold Rush.

13. Explain which details in the paragraph helped you to draw your conclusion.

Critical Thinking

✅ **TEST PREP** Write a short paragraph to answer each question.

14. **Fact and Opinion** A newspaper criticized the Louisiana Purchase, saying "we are to give money of which we have too little, for land of which we already have too much." Do you think the Purchase was a good idea at the time?

15. **Summarize** For what reasons did settlers go west during the mid-1800s?

Timeline

Use the Chapter Summary Timeline above to answer the question.

16. Which was completed first, the Erie Canal or the National Road?

Activities

 Connect to Georgia Research why Georgians began moving to new parts of the state during the early 1800s. Write a letter describing the experiences of a pioneer who moved to a new part of Georgia.

 Writing Activity Learn more about the Trail of Tears. Write a paragraph for a research report about the event.

 Technology **Writing Process Tip** Get help with your report at www.eduplace.com/kids/hmss/

Vocabulary and Main Ideas

 TEST PREP Write a sentence to answer each question.

1. Why did many people in the colonies want **independence** from Britain?

2. What was the **Treaty** of Paris?

3. What powers do national and state governments share in a **federal** system?

4. Why might a **pioneer** have wanted to cross the Appalachian Mountains in the late 1700s?

5. What did Francis Cabot Lowell do to help New England become a center of the **textile** industry?

6. Why did someone who moved to California during the Gold Rush become known as a **forty-niner?**

Critical Thinking

TEST PREP Write a short paragraph to answer each question.

7. **Cause and Effect** What effect did interchangeable parts have on the production of goods?

8. **Analyze** Why do you think the Constitution, which was written in 1787, has lasted so many years? What makes it a good plan for government? Use details from the unit to support your answer.

Apply Skills

TEST PREP **Reading and Thinking Skill** Read the paragraph below. Then use what you know about drawing conclusions to answer each question.

When Lewis and Clark started their journey across the country in 1804, they were joined by more than 30 people. Most of them were soldiers. The group had many different skills. Some hunted, while others served as interpreters. Together, they formed the Corps of Discovery and succeeded in traveling across the country.

9. Which conclusion could you draw from this paragraph?

   A. The members of the Corps of Discovery helped the Lewis and Clark expedition succeed.

   B. The Corps of Discovery did not work well together and fought often.

   C. Many of the members of the Corps of Discovery were unskilled and lazy.

   D. Lewis and Clark could have completed their journey alone.

10. What details in the paragraph helped you to draw your conclusion?

Connect to Georgia

Unit Activity

Write a Report

- Research Georgia's delegates to the Constitutional Convention.

- Choose two of the delegates and write a report summarizing their contributions.

- Discuss issues that were important to each of the Georgia delegates.

Personal Finance

In this unit, you read that taxes are money that people pay to the government for services. (p. 70) You also read that different levels of government provide different services. (p. 100)

How do you think the government's decisions about what services to provide are similar to individuals' decisions about how to spend their money? In what ways do you think government spending and savings decisions are different from individuals' decisions?

Create a Venn Diagram to compare and contrast government finance decisions with personal finance decisions.

CURRENT EVENTS
WEEKLY (WR) READER

Connect to Today

Write a speech about a symbol of freedom.

- Find information about places or monuments in the United States.

- Choose a place or a monument that you think symbolizes freedom.

- Write a speech explaining what the place or monument means to you.

- Share your speech with the class.

Technology

Weekly Reader online offers social studies articles. Go to: **www.eduplace.com/kids/hmss/**

Read About It

Look for these Social Studies Independent Books in your classroom.

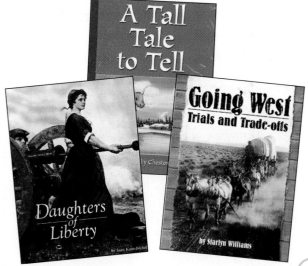

UNIT 3

The Civil War

The Big Idea

What makes a good leader?

In 1865, Abraham Lincoln said that the country should act,

"With malice toward none, with charity for all . . ."

Harriet Tubman
1820?–1913

Why would someone risk her life over and over again? Tubman knew what slavery was like, and she wanted to help others to reach freedom, as she had.
page 151

History Makers

Abraham Lincoln
1809–1865

Lincoln's election angered southern states so much that they broke away from the Union. Yet no President had ever worked as hard to keep the nation together.
page 164

Booker T. Washington
1856–1915

This teacher helped former slaves gain new skills. At his Tuskegee Institute in Alabama, students of all ages learned to make and grow the things they needed.
page 208

Almanac

The United States, 1860s

Seattle

WASHINGTON TERRITORY

Portland

Columbia R.

Fort Benton

Fort Union

L. Superior

MICHIGAN

Fort Walla Walla

Snake R.

DAKOTA TERRITORY

MINNESOTA

L. Michigan

OREGON

Fort Boise

WISCONSIN

Fort Hall

Fort Pierre

Missouri R.

Fort Bridger

Fort Randall

IOWA

Chicago

Fort Laramie

NEBRASKA TERRITORY

INDIANA

Platte R.

ILLINOIS

NEVADA TERRITORY

Fort Kearny

San Francisco

UTAH TERRITORY

Colorado R.

COLORADO TERRITORY

Fort Riley

St. Louis

CALIFORNIA

KANSAS

Fort Leavenworth

MISSOURI

Bent's New Fort

Arkansas R.

Los Angeles

Fort Defiance

Santa Fe

Fort Union

INDIAN TERRITORY

Fort Smith

ARKANSAS

San Diego

Fort Yuma

NEW MEXICO TERRITORY

MISSISSIPPI

Pecos R.

Fort Belknap

LOUISIANA

Fort Davis

TEXAS

Brazos R.

PACIFIC OCEAN

Rio Grande

New Orleans

Gulf of Mexico

Unit Preview

| 1830 | | 1840 | | 1850 | | 1860 |

1831
Abolitionism Grows
William Lloyd Garrison publishes *The Liberator*
Chapter 5, page 149

1857
Dred Scott Decision
Slavery is legal in territories
Chapter 5, page 158

1861
Fort Sumter
Civil War begins
Chapter 5, page 168

The Map

MAINE

VERMONT

NEW HAMPSHIRE

Boston
MASSACHUSETTS

NEW YORK

RHODE ISLAND

CONNECTICUT

New York

PENNSYLVANIA

NEW JERSEY
Philadelphia

Baltimore

DELAWARE

OHIO

Washington, D.C. MARYLAND

Cincinnati

WEST VIRGINIA

Louisville

VIRGINIA

KENTUCKY

TENNESSEE

NORTH CAROLINA

SOUTH CAROLINA

GEORGIA

ALABAMA

FLORIDA

L. Huron

L. Ontario

L. Erie

ATLANTIC OCEAN

N NE NW E W SE SW S

LEGEND
- Union
- Slave states not seceding
- Confederacy
- Territories
- Cotton growing area
- Textile mill
- Western fort
- Boundary of the Confederacy

km 0 150 300
mi 0 150 300

Timeline

1870   1880

1863
Emancipation Proclamation
Lincoln declares end to slavery
Chapter 6, page 180

1870
15th Amendment
African Americans gain right to vote
Chapter 6, page 200

Connect to Today

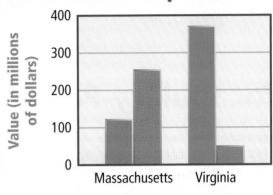

North and South, 1860s

Value (in millions of dollars)

400
300
200
100
0

Massachusetts   Virginia

■ farms   ■ manufactured goods

In 1860, states in the North and South had very different economies.

North and South Today

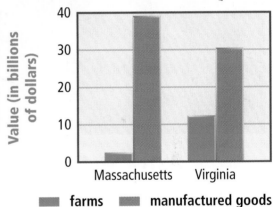

Value (in billions of dollars)

40
30
20
10
0

Massachusetts   Virginia

■ farms   ■ manufactured goods

In 1860, Virginia's economy depended on farming. What is its economy like today?

CONNECT to GEORGIA

Find out about Civil War battles in Georgia. On an outline map, label five battles that took place in Georgia.

Chapter 5

Causes of the Civil War

Technology
e • glossary
e • word games
www.eduplace.com/kids/hmss/

Vocabulary Preview

states' rights

John C. Calhoun favored **states' rights.** He wanted states to have more power than the federal government. **page 143**

abolitionist

An **abolitionist** was someone who fought to end slavery. Sojourner Truth gave powerful speeches about the cruelty of slavery. **page 148**

Chapter Timeline

1831
Nat Turner's Rebellion

1852
Uncle Tom's Cabin written

1830   1835   1840   1845   1850

Reading Strategy

Predict and Infer Before you read each lesson, use this strategy.

Quick Tip Look at each lesson title and the pictures. What do you think you will learn about?

fugitive

Many people believed it was wrong to return an escaped **fugitive** to slavery. Harriet Beecher Stowe wrote *Uncle Tom's Cabin* in protest over the Fugitive Slave Law. **page 158**

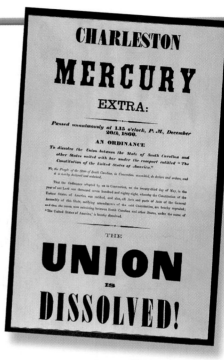

secession

After the **secession** of 11 southern states, war broke out between the North and the South. States that left the Union formed the Confederacy. **page 164**

1859
John Brown's raid

1861
Civil War begins

1855   1860   1865

Worlds Apart

| 1760 | 1780 | 1800 | 1820 | 1840 | 1860 | 1880 |

1793–1860

VOCABULARY

tariff
states' rights
sectionalism

Vocabulary Strategy

sectionalism

Find the word **section** in **sectionalism**. Sectionalism is loyalty to one section, or part, of a country.

READING SKILL
Compare and Contrast
What differences were there between the North and South in the early 1800s? Write them down as you read.

NORTH	SOUTH

Build on What You Know When people have very different ideas from one another, it can seem as if they live in separate worlds. In the early 1800s, the South and the North were worlds apart from each other in many ways.

Slavery in the United States

Main Idea Slavery grew in the South after the invention of the cotton gin.

Slavery had a long history in the United States. The thirteen colonies had all allowed slavery, though slaves were less common in the North than in the South. After the War for Independence, several northern states passed laws to abolish, or end, slavery. Southern states chose not to.

At the Constitutional Convention, some delegates tried to stop slavery in all states. As one delegate said, slavery did not fit with "the principles of the Revolution."

The Growth of Slavery

George Mason, a slaveowner from Virginia, called slavery a "national sin." Delegates at the Continental Congress could not agree to end slavery. Many hoped that it would soon die out. However, changes in southern farming caused slavery to grow in coming years.

After the invention of the cotton gin in 1793, southern farmers wanted more enslaved people to work in their cotton fields. The cotton gin made cotton much easier to produce. At the same time, the value of cotton was rising. New textile mills in Britain and New England needed more cotton, and the South could grow it.

Cotton became the South's most important crop. By 1840, the South was growing most of the world's cotton. Plantation owners used their profits to buy more land and more slaves. Slavery grew rapidly. In 1790, there were about 700,000 enslaved people in the South. By 1860, there were nearly four million.

Resistance to Slavery

Sometimes enslaved people fought against slaveowners. In Virginia in 1831, an enslaved African American named **Nat Turner** led a rebellion against slave owners. He and his followers killed 59 people before being stopped by the local militia. After Nat Turner's Rebellion, southern states passed laws to control both enslaved and free blacks. For example, black ministers were no longer allowed to preach without a white person present. By the 1850s, slaves and free blacks had fewer rights than ever.

Slavery became a source of deep conflict between the North and South. Many southerners argued that slavery was too important to their economy to give up. Some people in the North argued that slavery kept the country's economy from growing faster. They also believed that slavery was unfair and wrong.

REVIEW What led to the growth of slavery in the early 1800s?

Cotton Plantations

1. Enslaved people worked in the fields, picking cotton.

2. Cotton was packed into bales before being shipped.

3. Many plantations were near the Mississippi River, where steamboats carried the cotton south to New Orleans.

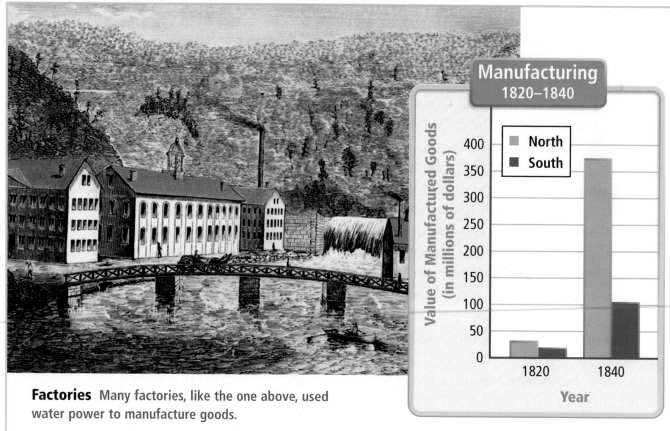

Manufacturing
1820–1840

Value of Manufactured Goods (in millions of dollars)

North
South

Year

Factories Many factories, like the one above, used water power to manufacture goods.

SKILL **Reading Graphs** What was the value of goods made in the North in 1840?

North and South

Main Idea The many differences between the North and South divided the two regions.

The North and the South had different economies. The South's economy was agricultural, or mostly based on farming. Some southerners worked on large cotton plantations. Many more had small farms and grew food crops such as corn, or raised cattle and pigs. These farmers usually had only a few enslaved people or none at all.

Northern states had many farmers as well, but the economy of the North was changing. Cities in the North were growing quickly and factories were being built throughout the region. In factories, people made textiles, shoes, tools, and other goods. By 1860, fewer than half of people in the North were farmers.

The Tariff

The different economies in the North and South led to disagreements between the regions about tariffs. A **tariff** is a tax on imported goods.

Between 1816 and 1832, Congress passed high tariffs on goods made outside the country. British textiles, for example, became very expensive. The only cloth most people could afford came from the mills of New England.

Congress used tariffs to help American manufacturing. Tariffs were good for northern industry, but they did not help the South, where there was less industry. Southerners, like all consumers, had to pay higher prices for manufactured goods they wanted, such as steel and cloth. When prices of these goods went up, southerners blamed it on tariffs and the North.

States' Rights

One southerner who argued against tariffs was **John C. Calhoun** of South Carolina. Calhoun was Vice President in 1828. He believed the Constitution did not allow the federal government to create tariffs. He argued for states' rights. **States' rights** is the idea that states, not the federal government, should make the final decisions about matters that affect them. Calhoun believed that states had the right to veto tariffs. States' rights became a popular idea in the South.

John C. Calhoun
He became a U.S. senator after serving as Vice President. Calhoun argued for slavery and states' rights.

Disagreements over slavery, tariffs, and other economic issues increased sectionalism in the North and South. Loyalty to one part of the country is called **sectionalism.** As conflicts grew, it seemed that many people cared more about their own section of the country than for the country as a whole.

REVIEW Why did southerners dislike tariffs?

Lesson Summary

> Slavery grew with the demand for cotton.

> Tariffs helped the growing number of northern factories.

> The North and South argued over slavery, tariffs, and states' rights.

Why It Matters ...

The North and South were headed toward war. It began with arguments about slavery and the power of the national and state governments.

Lesson Review

1793
Cotton gin invented

1831
Nat Turner's Rebellion

1790 — 1800 — 1810 — 1820 — 1830 — 1840

❶ **VOCABULARY** Show that you understand the meaning of **sectionalism** and **states' rights** by using these words in a paragraph about disagreements between the North and South.

❷ **READING SKILL** What were the views on slavery in the South and North? Use your notes to **compare** and **contrast.**

❸ **MAIN IDEA: Economics** Why did cotton become the South's most important crop?

❹ **MAIN IDEA: Economics** What did tariffs do to help northern industries?

❺ **TIMELINE SKILL:** When was Nat Turner's Rebellion?

❻ **CRITICAL THINKING: Infer** Tell what you think might have happened if the cotton gin had not been invented.

WRITING ACTIVITY Write one or two math questions based on the graph on page 418. Trade questions with a partner and try to answer your partner's questions.

King Cotton

In the 1840s and 1850s, cotton was called "king." It was the most valuable crop raised in the South and an important part of the North's growing industrial economy. In some years, more than two million bales of cotton were harvested. Bales weighed about 500 pounds. All that cotton was turned into shirts, pants, jackets, and other useful products.

Each step of the process of turning cotton into clothing was done separately by workers who did only that step. This specialization made each part of the process faster. As the cotton industry became more productive, people could buy more and more cotton goods.

1 **Working in the Fields** Cotton grows in the South's fertile soil and mild climate. It is often grown on large plantations and picked by enslaved workers.

3 **Unloading at the Docks** Bales of cotton arrive in northern ports such as Boston. The North has most of the nation's mills, including some of the biggest in the world.

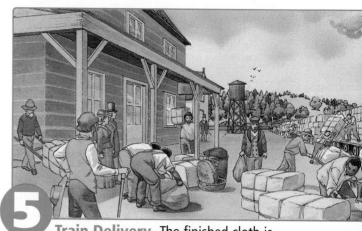

5 **Train Delivery** The finished cloth is loaded onto trains and shipped to buyers throughout the United States and other countries.

2 **Shipping North** Bundled into bales, the cotton is sent by wagon and steamboat to port cities such as New Orleans and Charleston. Then it is loaded onto ships and sent to the North and to other countries.

4 **Weaving the Thread** The cotton arrives at the mills. There, it is spun into thread and woven into cloth by women and girls working at huge spinning and weaving machines.

Cotton boll

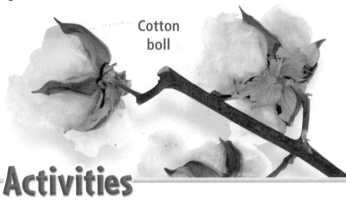

Activities

1. **DISCUSS IT** Use the pictures to compare all of the different places cotton traveled, from when it was picked to the finished cloth.

2. **REPORT IT** Where does cotton come from today? Using library resources, research cotton and write a summary of what you find out.

Graph and Chart Skills

Skillbuilder

Compare Bar, Line, and Circle Graphs

▶ **VOCABULARY**

VOCABULARY
bar graph
line graph
circle graph

Graphs can give you a better understanding of historical information, such as the importance of cotton to the United States economy. Different kinds of graphs present different kinds of information.

- **Bar graphs** compare amounts of things.
- **Line graphs** show changes over time.
- **Circle graphs** illustrate how a part compares with the whole.

Together, these graphs can show overall patterns. The steps below will help you to read and describe information from these three kinds of graphs.

Learn the Skill

Step 1: Read the title and identify the kind of graph. The title tells you about the subject and purpose of each graph.

Step 2: Examine the labels. They explain the units of measurement and the type of information presented.

Step 3: Look at the information on each of the graphs. Look for increases, decreases, or sudden changes on line graphs. Compare amounts on bar graphs and the parts of the whole on circle graphs. How is the information on the three graphs related?

Practice the Skill

Compare the information on the bar, line, and circle graphs by answering the following questions.

1. How is the information on the three graphs related?

2. How does the information on the bar graph differ from the facts in the other two graphs?

3. On the line graph, what 10-year period had the greatest change in cotton production?

4. Based on your reading of Lesson 1 and the circle graph, what crop was exported more than any other crop in 1860? Why?

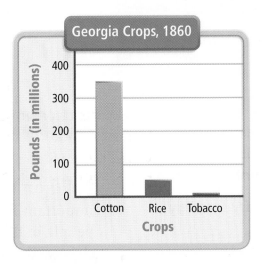

Georgia Crops, 1860

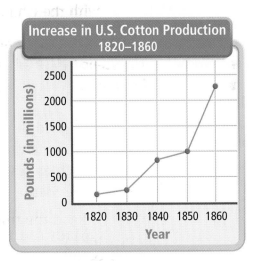

Increase in U.S. Cotton Production 1820–1860

Apply the Skill

Write a paragraph describing cotton production in the United States and Georgia in 1860. In your paragraph, include data from each of the three graphs.

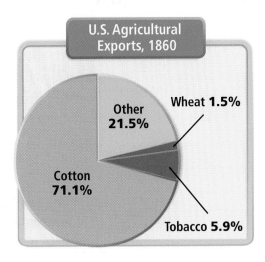

U.S. Agricultural Exports, 1860

Other 21.5%
Wheat 1.5%
Cotton 71.1%
Tobacco 5.9%

The Struggle for Freedom

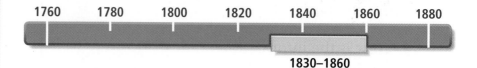

| 1760 | 1780 | 1800 | 1820 | 1840 | 1860 | 1880 |

1830–1860

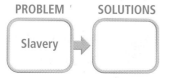
Build on What You Know Think about how important freedom is to you. In the early 1800s, not all people in the United States were free. Many lived in slavery. They struggled to win freedom, with help from the antislavery movement.

The Antislavery Movement

Main Idea Groups against slavery formed in the mid-1800s.

People could not agree about the issue of slavery. Some felt that slavery was needed to grow cash crops such as cotton and tobacco. As cotton farming spread in the South, they wanted slavery to spread as well.

Other people felt it was wrong to enslave people. Many of them became abolitionists. An **abolitionist** is someone who joined the movement to abolish, or end, slavery. Most abolitionists felt that slavery went against the ideas of Christianity.

Abolitionists included people in the North and South, whites and free blacks, men and women. They wrote pamphlets and traveled across the country, speaking against slavery. The abolitionist movement grew quickly in the 1830s and 1840s.

Slavery Some enslaved people had to wear tags that told where they lived and what they did.

SKILL Primary Sources What city is stamped on this tag?

William Lloyd Garrison
"I will not retreat a single inch —
AND I WILL BE HEARD," Garrison
wrote in *The Liberator*.

Frederick Douglass
After escaping to the North,
Douglass raised enough
money to buy his freedom.

Sojourner Truth
When she preached against
slavery, she attracted
large crowds.

Leading Abolitionists

In 1831, **William Lloyd Garrison** began printing an antislavery newspaper called *The Liberator*. In it, he demanded that all enslaved people be freed.

Frederick Douglass was a well-known black abolitionist. Douglass had escaped from slavery. He was a writer and often spoke to white audiences about slavery. He told one audience,

66 **I can tell you what I have seen with my own eyes, felt on my own person, and know to have occurred in my own neighborhood.** 99

Sojourner Truth, another important abolitionist, had also been born into slavery. Truth spoke in favor of abolition and women's rights.

Sarah Grimké (GRIM kee) and **Angelina Grimké** of South Carolina saw the cruelty of slavery from another point of view. They were daughters of a slave-owner. As adults, the sisters moved north and spoke out against slavery.

Free Blacks

By 1860, about 500,000 free blacks lived in the United States. About half lived in the North, half in the South.

Free blacks in the South often faced discrimination. **Discrimination** is the unfair treatment of particular groups. State laws limited the rights of free blacks. For example, they could not travel without permission or meet in groups without a white person present.

African Americans in the North also faced discrimination. However, they could travel freely, organize groups, and publish newspapers. These rights made it possible for free blacks in the North to work openly against slavery. Free black leaders joined whites in creating the American Anti-Slavery Society in 1833. This group called for the immediate end of slavery. Many free blacks gave money to the group. *The Liberator* also received most of its money from free blacks.

REVIEW What did free blacks in the North do to convince people that slavery was wrong?

The Underground Railroad

Main Idea The Underground Railroad helped people escape from slavery.

Some abolitionists worked in secret to help slaves escape to freedom. They set up a system known as the Underground Railroad. The **Underground Railroad** was a series of escape routes and hiding places to bring slaves out of the South.

Runaways, the people who fled slavery, could head for the North and Canada, or go south to Florida, Mexico, or the Caribbean.

Runaways often walked at night. Sometimes they hid in carts driven by members of the Underground Railroad. Escaping took great courage. Runaways who were caught would be punished and returned to slavery.

Escape to Freedom The Underground Railroad was not really underground, and not really a railroad. It was the routes that led slaves to freedom.

Underground Railroad

LEGEND
→ Routes of escape
Slave states in 1860
Free states in 1860

Harriet Tubman This photograph shows Harriet Tubman (left) with a group of enslaved people she helped to escape.

Stations and Conductors

Free blacks gave most of the money and did most of the work to support the Underground Railroad. Members of the Railroad gave food, clothing, and medical aid to runaways. They hid them until it was safe to move on. Hiding places were known as stations. "Conductors" guided runaways on to the next station.

The most famous conductor was **Harriet Tubman**, who escaped from slavery in Maryland. She then returned 19 times to lead others to freedom. Each time, she risked being caught and enslaved again. Tubman helped about 300 people escape to the North. She became a symbol of the abolitionist movement.

REVIEW What was the purpose of the Underground Railroad?

Lesson Summary

Abolitionists worked to end slavery. Free blacks and women played important roles in the abolitionist movement. Many people worked against slavery by helping enslaved people escape to freedom on the Underground Railroad.

Why It Matters ...

As abolitionists struggled to free enslaved people, they convinced others that slavery was wrong.

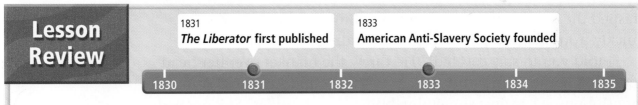

Lesson Review

1831
The Liberator first published

1833
American Anti-Slavery Society founded

1830   1831   1832   1833   1834   1835

❶ **VOCABULARY** Use the words below to write a short paragraph about the fight against slavery.

abolitionist   Underground Railroad

❷ **READING SKILL** What was one **solution** used to fight slavery?

❸ **MAIN IDEA: History** In what ways were Frederick Douglass and Sojourner Truth alike?

❹ **MAIN IDEA: Geography** Where did the Underground Railroad take runaways?

❺ **PEOPLE TO KNOW** Who was **Sojourner Truth**, and what did she do to fight slavery?

❻ **TIMELINE SKILL:** How long after *The Liberator* was the American Anti-Slavery Society founded?

❼ **CRITICAL THINKING: Decision Making** What were the possible consequences for Harriet Tubman when she helped slaves escape along the Underground Railroad? Why do you think people like her made the decision to help runaways?

RESEARCH ACTIVITY Research an abolitionist you read about in the lesson. Look for characteristics such as courage or persistence. Write a short report about his or her life.

Stealing Freedom

by Elisa Carbone

This story is based on the life of a real person, Ann Weems, an enslaved servant who lived in the Maryland home of Charles Price in the 1850s. Ann, age thirteen, hopes to be freed. A lawyer, Jacob Bigelow, promised to help her escape on the Underground Railroad. But tonight a man whom Ann saw at the county fair has kidnapped her from the Prices and bundled her into the back of a carriage. She has been riding in the carriage a long time. Where is he taking her?

⁕

The horse stopped. In an instant, Ann threw off the blanket and grasped the handle of the carriage door. But the man leaped so quickly from his seat, he was already standing over her.

"I told you to stay covered!" He threw the blanket over her head and lifted her in it, his arms tight as a vise around her chest. Ann's mouth bumped against something bony—his shoulder? She opened her mouth wide and, blanket and all, bit him as hard as she could.

The man yelped and dropped her. She landed on her rump and struggled to get untangled from the blanket. He grabbed her again and, this time with no blanket to cushion him, she bit down on his arm.

A door opened and a slice of yellow light brightened the dark street.

"Help!" Ann cried.

But the blanket came down over her head again.

"Are you mad?" It was another man's hushed voice. "The constable patrols this street every hour all night!"

"The wench bit me!"

Ann found herself being held tightly by two pairs of strong hands.

"Just get her inside."

She heard a door shut and as it did, her heart sank. She was trapped.

"You've scared her half to death, is what you've done."

"I got her here, ain't I?" came the voice of her captor.

The blanket was lifted off her head. A hand grasped hers and helped her to her feet. She blinked, uncomprehending. She was standing in the foyer of a narrow row house. One candle flickered on a table nearby. In the dancing light she saw the stubbly face of the tobacco-chewing man from the fair. He was calmly picking his teeth. When she turned to see the other man who'd helped him drag her inside, she let out a yelp and stepped back, her hands covering her mouth. It was Jacob Bigelow.

"Welcome to my home," said Mr. Bigelow.

Ann took in a sharp breath. "You're . . . I mean . . ." She pointed to the other man. "He's . . ."

Mr. Bigelow smoothed the sweaty hair away from her forehead. "There will be time for explanation," he said. "Are you in one piece?"

She nodded.

Mr. Bigelow handed the man a fat wad of paper money. "You got her here safely. Now be off before the constable comes by to find out why there's a brawl going on in my foyer at three A.M."

The man tipped his hat to Ann and slipped out the door.

"I apologize for his conduct," said Mr. Bigelow, "but often it's only the roughest sort who are willing to do such risky work. And I'm sure you understand why we had to do it this way."

Ann screwed up her face. "I don't think I understand anything," she said, bewildered.

Mr. Bigelow helped her to a chair in the parlor, carrying the candle with them. She sat stiff and uncomfortably. It was the first time she'd ever sat in a parlor.

"We had to steal you from your master this way," he said.

Ann felt a quiver go from her throat to her belly as it dawned on her what had actually happened this night.

"You see—" Mr. Bigelow adjusted his spectacles. "If you'd known that you were escaping, you would not have played the part so convincingly. But as it was, if you'd been taken up by the sheriff, what would you have told him?"

"That I'd been kidnapped!"

"Exactly," said Mr. Bigelow. "And you would have been returned to your master without harm or suspicion."

Ann's eyes widened as the plan began to make sense.

"And if anyone has seen you, the rumor mill will serve us well. You were not seen running away. You were being carried away against your will."

Ann rubbed the bump on her head—what a small price to pay for a clean escape! "Thank you," she said. She held her hands together toward him in a gesture like prayer. "Thank you so much."

Mr. Bigelow pressed his fingertips together. "Ah, yes," he said. "A lawyer by day, a lawless kidnapper by night. It's a wonder I get any sleep at all."

There was the sound of footsteps in the street. They stopped briefly outside the door, then moved on.

"That's Sergeant Orme on his parol," Mr. Bigelow said quietly. "I'd better show you to the guest quarters now."

He led Ann into the hallway and, with one wiry eyebrow raised, pointed to the ceiling. "There you are," he said. "The most comfortable lodging in town for kidnapping victims."

The candlelight flickered and Ann squinted at the place where he'd pointed. All she could see was wide ceiling boards that fit tightly together. Was he playing a joke on her?

Mr. Bigelow hummed as he opened a nearby closet and pulled out a ladder.

Then he climbed up and pushed carefully on the ceiling. Ann's mouth dropped open as a piece of the ceiling lifted up and he slid it aside.

"Up you go," he said, stepping down off the ladder. He gave her the candle.

Ann climbed up until her head entered a stuffy, attic-like room. She lifted the candle and saw a pitcher of water, a dish of corn bread, a straw mat and quilt, and a chamber pot over in the corner. She looked down at Mr. Bigelow. "No one will know I'm here!" she exclaimed.

"My thoughts exactly," he replied.

Ann scrambled up, then lay on her stomach to peer down before closing up the opening. "May I know his name?" she asked. "The man who brought me here?" He had given her several hours of terror and a rather large bump on her head, but he had, in fact, been her savior. She wanted to remember him.

Mr. Bigelow rested one foot on the bottom rung of the ladder. "The Powder Boy," he answered. "He takes both gunpowder and fugitives on his sailing vessel. Of course, that's not his real name, but that is how he's known on the road—and since you are now a passenger on the road, that is how you should know him."

The Powder Boy. She would never forget. She looked quizzically at Mr. Bigelow. "The road?" she asked, shaking her head slightly.

"The Underground Railroad. You have just begun to ride it, my dear. I am one of the conductors, and this is your first stop. It runs all the way to Canada."

Canada. She felt the quiver run through her again. She could not turn back now. And Canada was so far away.

They said good night, and Ann slid the ceiling boards back into place. They fit perfectly. The hiding place must have been built, she thought, like a hidden closet behind one of the upstairs bedrooms.

When she blew out the candle the room went quite dark. Her stomach had been through too much this night for her to eat the corn bread, but she drank thirstily from the pitcher. The air was hot and close. Sweat dripped down her neck as she lay on the mat. Her heart pounded in her ears with a new rhythm—one she'd never heard before. It said, "I'm free, I'm free, I'm free . . . ."

Activities

1. **TALK ABOUT IT** Why was Ann kidnapped? What do you think of Joseph Bigelow's plan?

2. **MAP IT** Where will Ann go next? Plan a route that Ann might follow from Baltimore, Maryland to Canada. Show the route on a map. Mark places on the map where she might stop along the Underground Railroad.

Compromise and Conflict

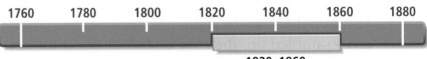

1760	1780	1800	1820	1840	1860	1880

1820–1860

VOCABULARY

slave state
free state
Union
popular sovereignty
fugitive

Vocabulary Strategy

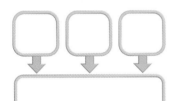

fugitive

Fugitive and refuge come from a word meaning to flee. A fugitive flees to find refuge, or safety.

READING SKILL

Cause and Effect Note the causes that made the conflict over slavery grow worse.

Build on What You Know To solve a disagreement, you give a little to get something back. That is a compromise. During the 1800s, Congress made several compromises over slavery to keep the country together.

Would Slavery Spread?

Main Idea Congress had to decide whether to allow slavery in new territories and states.

The United States grew in the 1800s. The Louisiana Purchase and the Mexican War had opened new lands to settlers. Congress set up governments for these lands, and some of the regions became territories. When a territory's population was large enough, it could become a state.

Congress had to decide whether to allow slavery in each territory. Territories that allowed slavery became slave states. A **slave state** permitted slavery. Territories where slavery was illegal became free states. A **free state** did not permit slavery. For a time, Congress tried to keep an equal number of free and slave states.

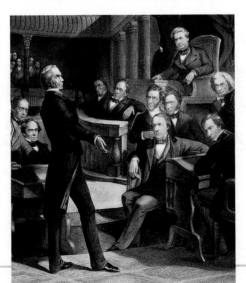

Henry Clay Known as the Great Compromiser, Kentucky senator Henry Clay tried to keep arguments over slavery from dividing the nation.

Compromises in Congress

Through the first half of the 1800s, Congress argued over which territories would have slavery. Northerners wanted free states to have a majority of representatives in Congress, so they could pass laws against slavery. Southerners wanted more slave states.

Missouri wanted to join the Union as a slave state. The **Union** is another name for the United States. To satisfy both sides, Congress created the Missouri Compromise in 1820. It accepted Missouri as a slave state and Maine as a free state. Congress then created an invisible line across the rest of the territories. Only territories south of that line would allow slavery.

Congress continued to debate the spread of slavery into new territories. In the Compromise of 1850, Congress allowed settlers in some territories to make the decision for themselves. The right of people to make political decisions for themselves is called **popular sovereignty.**

In 1854, Congress passed the Kansas-Nebraska Act. This law gave popular sovereignty to the Kansas and Nebraska territories. Abolitionists opposed the act because it allowed slavery north of the line created in the Missouri Compromise. Settlers supporting and opposing slavery rushed into Kansas. Both sides wanted to win the vote on whether to allow slavery. Soon the two sides fought for control of the territory. In 1861, Kansas joined the Union as a free state.

REVIEW What compromises did Congress make as the nation grew?

Growth and Compromise Compromises in Congress affected where slavery was allowed.

SKILL **Reading Maps** Which state joined the Union as a free state in 1850?

MISSOURI COMPROMISE, 1820

MAINE

UNORGANIZED TERRITORY

MISSOURI

LEGEND

Free state or territory

Slave state or territory

Decision on slavery left to territory

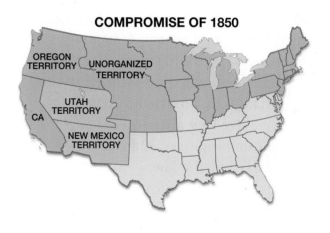

COMPROMISE OF 1850

OREGON TERRITORY

UNORGANIZED TERRITORY

UTAH TERRITORY

CA

NEW MEXICO TERRITORY

KANSAS-NEBRASKA ACT, 1854

NEBRASKA TERRITORY

UTAH TERRITORY

KANSAS TERRITORY

NEW MEXICO TERRITORY

Harriet Beecher Stowe
Her book, *Uncle Tom's Cabin*, described the suffering of slaves. Many people in the North began to feel new sympathy for enslaved people after reading the book.

The Growing Crisis

Main Idea Events in the 1850s made the split between the North and South worse.

As part of the Compromise of 1850, Congress passed the Fugitive Slave Law, which upset northerners. A **fugitive** is a person who is running away. The law said that slaves who had escaped to the North had to be returned to slavery. The Fugitive Slave Law also ordered citizens to help catch fugitives. Many northerners refused to obey the law.

Harriet Beecher Stowe, a writer from New England, was against the Fugitive Slave Law. She decided to write a story describing the cruelty of slavery. Her book, *Uncle Tom's Cabin*, sold 300,000 copies in one year. Stowe pointed out in the book that slavery was not just the South's problem. It was the nation's problem. *Uncle Tom's Cabin* convinced many northerners that slavery was wrong. Some southerners insisted that Stowe's picture of slavery was false. The arguments over the book pushed the North and South further apart.

Dred Scott

A legal case about slavery came to the Supreme Court in 1857. **Dred Scott,** an enslaved man from Missouri, asked the court for his freedom. Scott argued that he should be free because he had once lived in Illinois, a free state, and Wisconsin, a free territory. The Supreme Court disagreed. It said that enslaved people were property, and that living in a free state did not make them citizens. The Supreme Court also said that the government could not keep slavery out of any territory, because that would prevent slaveowners from moving their property to new territories.

The Dred Scott decision was a victory for slaveowners. It meant that slavery had to be legal in all territories, even if most settlers did not want it. Abolitionists feared that slavery would spread over the whole country.

Dred Scott

Attack at Harpers Ferry

John Brown's Raid

An abolitionist named **John Brown** decided to fight slavery on his own. In 1859, he tried to start a rebellion against slavery by attacking a U.S. Army post at Harpers Ferry, Virginia. Soldiers quickly surrounded his group and captured Brown. The government accused Brown of treason. At his trial, he insisted that he had done "no wrong but right." Brown was found guilty and hanged. Many northerners saw Brown as a hero. Southerners saw him as a violent man out to destroy their way of life.

By 1860, the North and South were deeply divided. As antislavery feeling grew stronger in the North, some southerners argued that they should leave the Union to protect their way of life.

REVIEW Why did John Brown attack Harpers Ferry?

Lesson Summary

> Americans disagreed about whether slavery should be allowed to spread.

> Congress tried to settle the slavery issue with a series of compromises.

> The Fugitive Slave Law and John Brown's raid drove the North and South further apart.

Why It Matters ...

Over time, it became much harder for Americans to compromise over slavery. This conflict started to split the nation.

Lesson Review

Timeline:
- 1852 *Uncle Tom's Cabin* written
- 1857 Dred Scott decision
- 1859 John Brown's raid

(1852 — 1854 — 1856 — 1858 — 1860)

1. **VOCABULARY** Write a short paragraph, using the words **free state**, **slave state**, and **fugitive** to describe the United States in the 1850s.

2. **READING SKILL** What **effect** did the Kansas-Nebraska Act of 1854 have on the conflict over slavery?

3. **MAIN IDEA: Government** Why did the Fugitive Slave Law upset some people in the North?

4. **MAIN IDEA: Government** What did the Dred Scott decision say?

5. **TIMELINE SKILL** What important event took place in 1859?

6. **PEOPLE TO KNOW** What effect did **Harriet Beecher Stowe's** book have on the debate over slavery?

7. **CRITICAL THINKING: Infer** Why did the compromises made in Congress fail to end the conflict over slavery?

WRITING ACTIVITY John Brown's raid on Harpers Ferry was an important event in the debate over slavery. Write a news report telling people what happened and why it happened.

A Troubling Law

Was the Fugitive Slave Law a bad law? The setting is dusk in a northern town in 1850. Citizens have gathered to decide how to respond to the new  Slave Law, meant to help slave owners. Should people in free states follow it or resist it?

Characters

Annabella Smith: teacher

Charlotte Pressman: elderly writer

Patrick James: stable owner

John Chase: storekeeper

Mary Chase: storekeeper

Edward Lester: law student

James Eglin: printer

Catherine Giles: baker

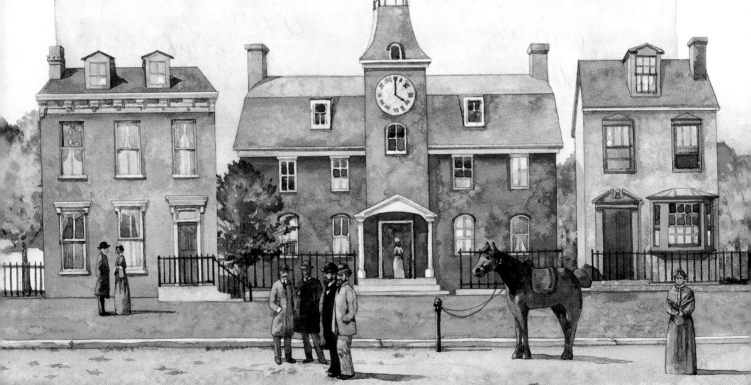

Annabella Smith: I have bad news. Robert Simms has been arrested — taken from his house last night!

John Chase: What happened? What was his offense?

Charlotte Pressman: I'm sure he did nothing wrong. We all know Robert. He has lived in this town for five years since he came here from Virginia.

Patrick James: It's that new slave law! He will be dragged back to slavery unless we do something.

Edward Lester: It is a very troubling law. It strikes a blow to the heart of our efforts to free people.

John Chase: That's easy for you to say, Edward. Mary and I are storekeepers, and radical talk about abolition isn't good for business.

Patrick James: But Simms worked in our town, John, and he is a human being.

Mary Chase: I used to say that slavery was a southern evil, no concern of mine. I live in a free state. But this new law…

Catherine Giles: This law is a danger to all of us. I am a free woman, born of free parents. But because I am black, I could be kidnapped and sold into slavery, and there would be no help for me.

James Eglin: It's true! I ran away from slavery. I earn an honest living as a printer. Now the law says my old master can come after me, and you have to help him.

Annabella
Smith

Charlotte
Pressman

Annabella Smith: Help him?

James Eglin: And if my old master catches me, I don't get a trial. I can't speak in my own defense. Just his word alone can send me back in chains.

Edward Lester: Did you know that the judge who hears the case is paid $5 when he frees a fugitive and $10 when he sends him back to slavery?

Annabella Smith: We must disobey this law. We must help Mr. Simms.

John Chase: I hear the punishment for helping a fugitive is a $1,000 fine or six months in jail.

James Eglin: That's nothing compared to a person's freedom.

John Chase: A thousand dollars is still a lot of money. If I spent six months in jail, my business would collapse.

Patrick James: I am willing to risk it.

Edward Lester

Mary Chase

ABOLITION
Meeting Tonight
ewbury Hall
:00 p.m

LAW

Charlotte Pressman: The question is, what can we do? It's too late to hide him. He has already been caught.

Patrick James: Then we must rescue him by force. Don't look so shocked! It has already happened in Boston. A group broke into the courthouse and rescued a fugitive.

John Chase

James Eglin: It wouldn't be easy. My uncle says a slaveowner and his hunters tried to capture some fugitives in Pennsylvania. People were badly wounded. A man died.

Annabella Smith: This could be dangerous.

Catherine Giles: It could lead to terrible violence.

Edward Lester: Then we will set out to rescue Mr. Simms without violence. We will gather a group large enough to overpower the guards and try to persuade them to let Robert go. We will carry no firearms.

James Eglin: I will do it.

Patrick James: You know I will.

Mary Chase: So will I.

John Chase: What if you get hurt? What if you are thrown in jail? I just don't know what to do.

Mary Chase: This is a free state, John. We cannot let the slaveholders take away our freedom.

Charlotte Pressman: I will defy this law, no matter what may come of it!

Activities

1. **THINK ABOUT IT** In what ways do you think the townspeople showed **courage**?

2. **WRITE ABOUT IT** Write a letter to the editor of a newspaper in 1850 telling your beliefs about the Fugitive Slave Law.

Civil War Begins

1840　1845　1850　1855　1860　1865　1870

1854–1861

VOCABULARY

secession
Confederacy
civil war

Vocabulary Strategy

Confederacy

A confederation is a group that unites for a purpose. The **Confederacy** was a confederation formed by 11 southern states.

 READING SKILL

Sequence As you read, note in order the events that began the Civil War.

Build on What You Know You know that strong beliefs can make a difference in people's lives. President Abraham Lincoln strongly believed that the Union should not be allowed to split apart. When southern states tried to leave the Union, Lincoln went to war to stop them.

Abraham Lincoln

Main Idea Many people joined a new political party that opposed the spread of slavery.

By 1860, the conflict over slavery was becoming worse. **John Brown's** raid on Harpers Ferry in 1859 had worried people in the South. They thought abolitionists wanted to start a slave rebellion. Some southerners believed secession was the only way to protect their states' rights and continue as a slave-owning region. When part of a country leaves or breaks off from the rest it is called **secession.**

Northerners were upset as well. Many disliked the Kansas-Nebraska Act and the **Dred Scott** decision. They feared that slavery would spread across the country. Some formed a new political party, the Republican Party. Republicans wanted to keep slavery out of the territories. **Abraham Lincoln** was a famous Republican. In these difficult years, he became one of the most important leaders the United States has ever had.

Abraham Lincoln He earned a reputation for hard work and honesty.

 STANDARDS

SS5H1c Fort Sumter
SS5H1d Lincoln, Davis

Log cabin This is a copy of the cabin where Lincoln was born. As a boy, he studied math, grammar, spelling, and history. A page of his math homework is on the right.

Lincoln's Early Years

Abraham Lincoln was born in a small cabin in Kentucky, a slave state. His father was a farmer there. The family later moved to Indiana and then to Illinois, both free states. As a boy, Lincoln worked hard on his father's farm. He did not have much time to go to school. He loved reading, though, and read all the books he could.

Lincoln did not want to be a farmer. He studied law and became a lawyer. Lincoln also wanted to be a member of the Illinois legislature. He first won an election at age 25 and served four terms. Each term was for two years.

Later, Lincoln served one term as a representative in the United States Congress. He argued against allowing slavery to expand into new territories. After his time in Congress, Lincoln returned to his job as a lawyer.

REVIEW Why did some southerners want their states to leave the Union?

Lincoln's Campaigns

Main Idea Abraham Lincoln opposed slavery when he ran for the Senate and for President.

After Congress passed the Kansas-Nebraska Act, Lincoln decided to run for office again. In 1858, he ran for the Senate in Illinois as a Republican against **Stephen Douglas.** The two men held seven debates. In the debates, they argued about slavery.

Lincoln saw slavery as a "moral, social, and political evil." He argued that the United States could not go on forever divided by slavery. He said,

> **66** A house divided against itself cannot stand. I believe this government cannot endure [last] permanently half slave and half free. . . . It will become all one thing, or all the other. **99**

Douglas wanted popular sovereignty in the territories. He did not believe slavery was wrong and thought it should be legal if people wanted it. Douglas also thought the country could remain split over slavery. He asked, "Why can it not exist divided into free and slave states?"

Lincoln hated slavery, but he did not think that the national government had the power to end slavery in slave states. The Constitution did not mention slavery. He said, "I have no purpose . . . to interfere with the institution of slavery in the states where it exists. I believe I have no lawful right to do so."

Although Lincoln did not argue for abolition, he wanted to keep slavery from spreading into the territories. Like many Republicans, Lincoln believed that slavery would end on its own if it were not allowed to spread across the country.

A Divided Nation

Lincoln lost the election to Douglas, but the debates made Lincoln famous. Reporters printed what the two men said. Across the country, people read Lincoln's words. Many northerners agreed with his views on slavery. In the South, people saw him as an enemy.

In 1860, the country held an election for President. The Democratic Party was split and could not agree on only one candidate. Northern Democrats chose Stephen Douglas. Southern Democrats chose **John Breckinridge** of Kentucky. Breckinridge owned slaves. He wanted slavery allowed in all the territories.

The Republican Party chose Abraham Lincoln as its candidate. Lincoln was the only candidate against slavery. He had support in the North, but very little in the South. In 10 southern states, voters were not given Lincoln's name as a choice.

Lincoln won the election, but the result showed how divided Americans were. He did not win in a single southern state. To southerners, Lincoln's election was a disaster. One southern newspaper called it "the greatest evil that has ever befallen [happened to] this country."

Many southerners felt that the federal government had become too powerful. When the government passed tariffs or tried to limit slavery, southerners argued that their states' rights were under attack. With Lincoln as President, they feared that the government would grow stronger and that Lincoln would try to end slavery. They believed that secession was the only way to protect their rights.

REVIEW Why did southerners see Lincoln as an enemy?

Lincoln–Douglas Debates

THE CAMPAIGN IN ILLINOIS.
THE LAST JOINT DEBATE.
DOUGLAS AND LINCOLN AT ALTON.
5,000 TO 10,000 PERSONS PRESENT!

The seven debates made history, attracting large crowds each time. The newspaper headline tells of their last one, which was on October 15, 1858. After two months of traveling around the state of Illinois and debating, Lincoln spoke these famous lines...

"Has anything ever threatened the existence of this Union save and except this very institution of slavery?... That is the real issue."

Antislavery Medals, 1860s

Union and Confederacy

PACIFIC OCEAN

WASHINGTON TERRITORY

OREGON

NEVADA TERR.

UTAH TERRITORY

COLORADO TERRITORY

NEW MEXICO TERRITORY

CALIFORNIA

MEXICO

DAKOTA TERRITORY

NEBRASKA TERRITORY

KANSAS

INDIAN TERRITORY

TEXAS

MINNESOTA

WISCONSIN

IOWA

MICHIGAN

ILLINOIS

MISSOURI

AR

LA

MS

AL

GA

IN

OHIO

KENTUCKY

TENNESSEE

CANADA

ME

VT

NH

NEW YORK

MA

RI

PA

CT

NJ

MD

DE

WV

VIRGINIA

NORTH CAROLINA

SOUTH CAROLINA

FLORIDA

ATLANTIC OCEAN

Gulf of Mexico

LEGEND
- Union free states
- Union slave states
- Confederate slave states
- Territories
- Boundary of the Confederacy

km 0 150 300
mi 0 150 300

Secession Eleven slave states decided to secede from the Union. Five slave states chose to stay in the Union. **SKILL** **Reading Maps** How many states were part of the Union?

Secession Begins

Main Idea Eleven southern states left the Union and formed their own government.

South Carolina withdrew from the Union first. People there voted to leave the Union on December 20, 1860. Mississippi, Florida, Alabama, Georgia, Louisiana, and Texas soon did the same.

On February 4, 1861, delegates from the seven states met in Montgomery, Alabama. They voted to form their own confederation. In this confederation, the states would have more power than the central government. These states called themselves the Confederate States of America, or the **Confederacy.** The delegates elected **Jefferson Davis** as President.

Attack on Fort Sumter

President Lincoln was determined to find a way to hold the country together. "We are not enemies, but friends," he said. "We must not be enemies."

It was too late. In Charleston, South Carolina, the state militia had surrounded Fort Sumter, a federal fort with United States soldiers inside. The Confederate government wanted control of the fort, but Lincoln refused to surrender it. Instead, he sent a ship with supplies to the fort.

Jefferson Davis After serving as an officer in the Mexican War, he became a senator from Mississippi and argued for states' rights.

Lincoln wanted to show that he would not give in to the Confederacy. However, he also did not want to start a war. He hoped that the southern states would return to the Union peacefully.

Confederate leaders saw the refusal to surrender Fort Sumter as an act of war. They ordered cannons to fire on the fort. The first shot was fired on April 12, 1861.

The cannons fired on Fort Sumter for 34 hours. At last, the soldiers in the fort had to surrender. The attack on Fort Sumter marked the beginning of the Civil War. A **civil war** is a war between two groups or regions within a nation.

Fort Sumter

President Lincoln called for 75,000 soldiers to fight the rebellion. Some states refused to send men to help Lincoln. Arkansas, North Carolina, Tennessee, and Virginia joined the Confederacy instead. Citizens in the North and the South prepared to fight.

REVIEW What event began the Civil War?

Lesson Summary

- Americans who opposed slavery formed the Republican Party.
- Abraham Lincoln became famous for his speeches against slavery.
- After Lincoln's election, southern states began to leave the Union.

Why It Matters...

For the first time in United States history, states tried to leave the Union. This began a terrible war.

Lesson Review

1860 **Lincoln elected**

1861 **Fort Sumter attacked**

| 1858 | 1859 | 1860 | 1861 | 1862 |

❶ **VOCABULARY** Use **secession** and **civil war** in a paragraph describing the election of 1860.

❷ **READING SKILL** Use your **sequence** chart to tell what happened after the election of 1860.

❸ **MAIN IDEA: Citizenship** What were Lincoln's reasons for wanting to keep slavery out of the territories?

❹ **MAIN IDEA: History** Why were southerners upset about Lincoln's election?

❺ **TIMELINE SKILL** In what year did the Confederates attack Fort Sumter?

❻ **PEOPLE TO KNOW** Who was **Jefferson Davis**? What was his role in the Confederacy?

❼ **CRITICAL THINKING: Infer** Why do you think Virginia, North Carolina, Arkansas, and Tennessee waited before joining the Confederacy?

HANDS ON **SPEAKING ACTIVITY** Lincoln and Douglas helped make debating an important part of American politics. With a partner, prepare a short debate on a topic in the news today.

Blue and Gray

"I fear our happy days are gone," wrote Sarah Rousseau Espey of Alabama in her diary in March, 1861. The threat of war was tearing the United States apart. States, towns, and even families were divided over which side to support. Only a few people guessed how terrible the war would be.

Americans in the North and South wrote many letters and diary entries expressing their feelings about the causes of the war and what had to be done. Many of these letters have been saved. Today, we can read the words and think about how the writers felt.

Confederate Soldier
After South Carolina and six other southern states seceded, Americans wondered whether war was coming. One young Virginian wrote home to his mother in February 1861:

" I believe we will have war with the North in less than sixty days... I am a man who knows my rights... One of those rights is secession... But like that gallant Henry [Patrick Henry] who rose in rebellion against the mightiest empire on earth my words are 'give me liberty or give me death.' "

—John H. Cochran

Gray
Confederate soldiers often wore uniforms that were gray, or a shade of brown called butternut.

Union Soldier Once the Confederacy fired on Fort Sumter, people all across the North prepared for war. A young man on his way to join the Union army wrote to the people of his home town in Middle Spring, Pennsylvania:

" I think it is my duty as well as those of my neighbors to go and join with those that have gone before; and help to fight the battles of our country… And every young single man that is healthy and will not go when his country needs him is either a coward or a rebel and I don't care which. No good country loving Patriot will stay at home when he hears of his country's flag being trampled in the dust by the Southern confederacy. "

—George Traxler

Blue

At the beginning of the war Union soldiers wore many different uniforms, but soon they all wore blue.

Activities

1. **TALK ABOUT IT** How are the Union and Confederate uniforms the same? How are they different? Why are the differences important?

2. **WRITE ABOUT IT** Write a personal narrative from the point of view of one of the letter writers. Describe his feelings about going to war. Include setting, events, and other people.

 Technology Learn about other primary sources for this unit at Education Place. www.eduplace.com/kids/hmss05/

Visual Summary

1–3. ✏️➤ Write a description of each event named below.

Conflicts before the Civil War

Nat Turner's Rebellion	
Attack on Harpers Ferry	
Attack on Fort Sumter	

Facts and Main Ideas

✔️ **TEST PREP** Answer each question with information from the chapter.

4. **Economics** What happened to slavery as states grew more cotton?

5. **History** What effect did Nat Turner's rebellion have on southerners and their opinion of freedom for African Americans?

6. **Geography** What were the results of the Kansas-Nebraska Act?

7. **History** How did the Underground Railroad help people escape slavery?

8. **Government** Why were many southerners unhappy when Abraham Lincoln was elected President?

Vocabulary

✔️ **TEST PREP** Choose the correct word from the list below to complete each sentence.

tariff, p. 142
popular sovereignty, p. 157
fugitive, p. 158

9. In some territories, settlers had _____ and decided for themselves whether to allow slavery.

10. When Congress passed a _____, people had to pay higher prices for imported goods.

11. An escaped slave was called a _____.

1831
Nat Turner's rebellion

1852
Uncle Tom's Cabin written

1859
John Brown's raid

1861
Civil War begins

1830 1835 1840 1845 1850 1855 1860 1865

Apply Skills

✔ TEST PREP **Chart and Graph Skill**

Use the graphs about African American population before the Civil War to answer each question.

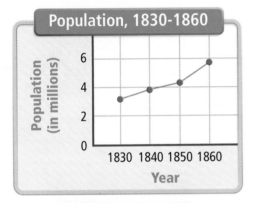

Population, 1830–1860

Population (in millions)

6
4
2
0

1830 1840 1850 1860
Year

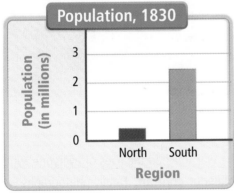

Population, 1830

Population (in millions)

3
2
1
0

North   South
Region

12. Which statement is most accurate?

   A. The number of African Americans in the North grew quickly.

   B. The number of African Americans in the North and South was equal in 1830.

   C. The number of African Americans decreased over time.

   D. The number of African Americans in the South was greater than in the North.

13. What do the two graphs have in common?

Critical Thinking

✔ TEST PREP Write a short paragraph to answer each question.

14. Cause and Effect What were the causes of sectionalism in the United States?

15. Compare and Contrast In what way was Abraham Lincoln's view of slavery different from that of Stephen Douglas?

Timeline

Use the Chapter Summary Timeline above to answer the question.

16. Which events took place during the 1850s?

Activities

Connect to Georgia Research cotton in Georgia during the 1800s. Write a paragraph describing the importance of cotton in the conflict between the North and the South.

Writing Activity Write a dialogue for a story in which a member of the Underground Railroad asks friends to help rescue enslaved people. Have the characters discuss the dangers and importance of the work.

Technology
Writing Process Tips
Get help with your story at
www.eduplace.com/kids/hmss/

Chapter 6

Civil War and Reconstruction

Technology

e • **glossary**
e • **word games**
www.eduplace.com/kids/hmss/

Vocabulary Preview

emancipation

In 1862, President Lincoln ordered the **emancipation** of all the slaves in the Confederacy. He declared that they were free.
page 180

civilian

The war touched the lives of everyone, whether soldier or **civilian.** Family photographs were a comfort to civilians who stayed at home.
page 186

Chapter Timeline

1863
Battle of Gettysburg

1865
Civil War ends

1860   1865   1870

Reading Strategy

Summarize Use this strategy to focus on important ideas.

Quick Tip Review the main ideas. Then look for important details that support those ideas.

telegraph

Generals used the **telegraph** to give President Lincoln information about the war. Their messages traveled quickly over wires. **page 191**

sharecropping

After the war, many African Americans began **sharecropping.** They gave the owner of the land they farmed a share of the crops they raised. **page 207**

1877
Reconstruction ends

1881
Tuskegee Institute opens

1875   1880   1885

A Nation at War

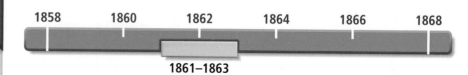

| 1858 | 1860 | 1862 | 1864 | 1866 | 1868 |

1861–1863

VOCABULARY

border states
casualties
draft
emancipation

Vocabulary Strategy

draft

Draft is a homograph, a word with more than one meaning. In this lesson, it means a system for bringing people into the military.

READING SKILL

Classify List the advantages and disadvantages that the North and the South had at the start of the war.

NORTH	SOUTH

STANDARDS

SS5H1c Major battles
SS5H1d Lincoln, Lee, Grant, Jackson
SS5G1b Locate Gettysburg, PA

Build on What You Know Have you ever started a task that was harder than it seemed at first? At the start of the Civil War, both sides thought they could win quickly. Soon, they knew that winning would be far from easy.

North Against South

Main Idea The Union and Confederacy had different strengths.

When the Civil War began, 11 southern states seceded and formed the Confederacy. Four other slave states, Missouri, Kentucky, Maryland, and Delaware, stayed in the Union. Slave states that stayed in the Union were known as **border states.**

The North had many advantages in the war. About 22 million people lived in the North. The South only had around nine million people, and about one-third of them were enslaved and could not become soldiers. The North had more factories for making weapons and supplies. It also had more railroad lines than the South. Soldiers and supplies could move quickly by railroad.

The Confederate states had some advantages, too. Most of the fighting took place in the South, and Confederate soldiers were defending land they knew. The South also had excellent military leaders, such as General **Robert E. Lee.**

General Lee He was a skilled and respected Confederate general who had fought in the Mexican War.

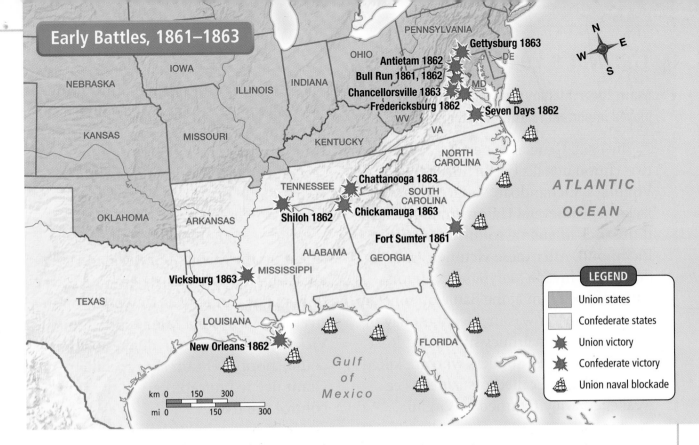

Early Battles, 1861–1863

Gettysburg 1863
Antietam 1862
Bull Run 1861, 1862
Chancellorsville 1863
Fredericksburg 1862
Seven Days 1862
Chattanooga 1863
Shiloh 1862
Chickamauga 1863
Fort Sumter 1861
Vicksburg 1863
New Orleans 1862

PENNSYLVANIA
OHIO
DE
MD
WV
VA
NORTH CAROLINA
SOUTH CAROLINA
TENNESSEE
ALABAMA
GEORGIA
MISSISSIPPI
LOUISIANA
TEXAS
OKLAHOMA
ARKANSAS
KANSAS
MISSOURI
KENTUCKY
NEBRASKA
IOWA
ILLINOIS
INDIANA

ATLANTIC OCEAN

Gulf of Mexico

FLORIDA

LEGEND
Union states
Confederate states
Union victory
Confederate victory
Union naval blockade

km 0   150   300
mi 0   150   300

Early Battles The Union plan to block Confederate ports and attack by land was called the Anaconda Plan, after a snake that squeezes its prey.

SKILL **Reading Maps** In which state were most of the Confederate victories?

Plans for War

Union leaders created a strategy, or plan, to defeat the South. The navy would block southern seaports so that the Confederacy could not trade with other countries. The navy would also take control of the Mississippi River. Then the Union army would attack in the East and West at the same time.

The South's strategy was to fight off northern attacks until the Confederacy could survive as a separate nation. Southerners knew that many people in the North were already against the war. If the Union lost too many battles, northerners might give up. Southerners also hoped for help from Britain and France because those countries needed southern cotton.

The War in the East

At the start of the war, both sides expected a quick, easy victory. Thousands of men from the North and South joined the Union and Confederate armies.

In July 1861, a Union army marched south from Washington. Its goal was to capture the Confederate capital of Richmond, Virginia. On July 21, the two armies fought at a stream called Bull Run, near the town of Manassas. At this battle, called the First Battle of Bull Run, General Thomas Jonathan Jackson led Confederate troops from the top of a hill. An onlooker said he looked "like a stone wall." He became known as Stonewall Jackson. Although the Confederate army won this battle, it was worse than expected. People realized the war would not end soon.

REVIEW What was the Confederacy's plan for winning the war?

The War's Leaders

Main Idea Military and political leaders played important roles during the war.

In 1862, General Robert E. Lee defeated two Union attacks on Richmond. In Virginia's Shenandoah Valley, Stonewall Jackson beat several Union armies. He kept thousands of enemy soldiers away from Richmond. After these victories, Lee decided to invade Maryland. A Union army stopped him at the Battle of Antietam (an TEE tam). It was the deadliest day of the war. The two armies suffered at least 23,000 casualties. Soldiers who are killed or wounded are called **casualties.** Lee's weakened army returned to Virginia.

The War in the West

In the West, the Union army and navy had more success. General **Ulysses S. Grant** led a Union army south from Illinois into Tennessee. He captured several Confederate forts along the way. In the Battle of Shiloh, he defeated a large Confederate army.

At the same time, the Union navy sailed up the Mississippi River and attacked New Orleans. By early 1863, the only major Confederate town left on the river was Vicksburg, Mississippi. From Vicksburg's cliffs, Confederate soldiers could shoot at Union ships on the river. Grant needed to capture Vicksburg to control the river.

Battle of Antietam Look at the map and the description on the next page to learn more about this fierce battle.

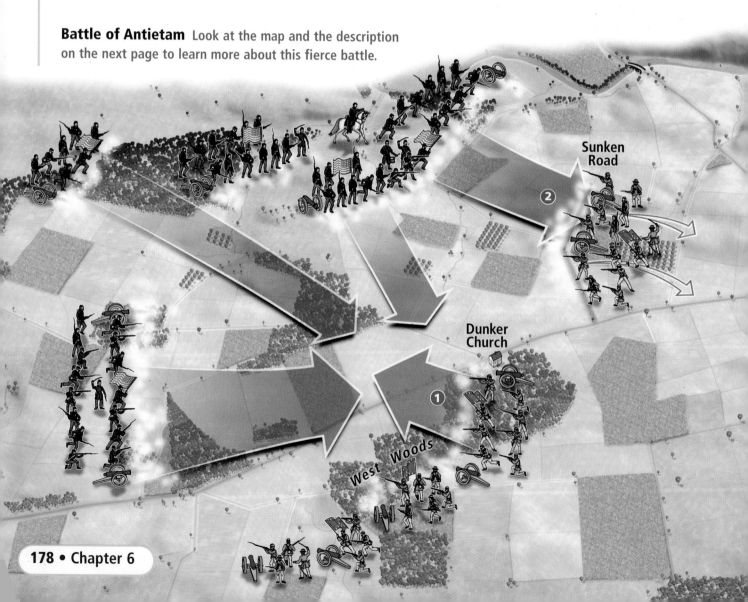

Sunken Road

Dunker Church

West Woods

The Governments Respond

Jefferson Davis, the president of the Confederacy, faced many problems. The Union blockade closed most Confederate ports. The South had trouble getting enough food, weapons, or money to fight. Not enough people wanted to join the army. To find more soldiers, Davis had to start a draft. During a **draft,** a government selects people to serve in the military. The Confederate states often ignored Jefferson Davis's orders.

President **Abraham Lincoln** also faced challenges. As the number of casualties rose, he had to work hard to win support for the war.

Like the Confederacy, the Union had to start a draft. Rich people could pay to get out of the draft. This upset people who could not afford the money and those who were against the war. In New York City, people opposed to the draft started a riot that lasted for days. A riot is a violent protest. The government had to send in thousands of soldiers to stop the riots.

REVIEW Why did people in the North oppose the draft?

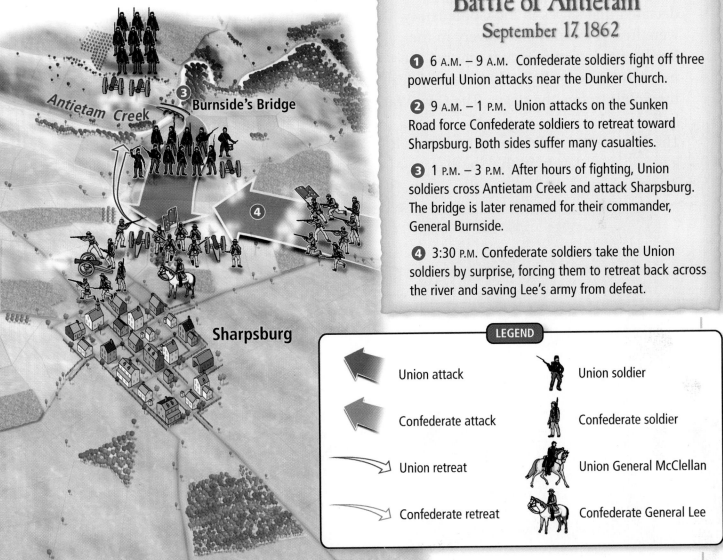

Antietam Creek

Burnside's Bridge

Sharpsburg

Battle of Antietam
September 17, 1862

1 6 A.M. – 9 A.M. Confederate soldiers fight off three powerful Union attacks near the Dunker Church.

2 9 A.M. – 1 P.M. Union attacks on the Sunken Road force Confederate soldiers to retreat toward Sharpsburg. Both sides suffer many casualties.

3 1 P.M. – 3 P.M. After hours of fighting, Union soldiers cross Antietam Creek and attack Sharpsburg. The bridge is later renamed for their commander, General Burnside.

4 3:30 P.M. Confederate soldiers take the Union soldiers by surprise, forcing them to retreat back across the river and saving Lee's army from defeat.

LEGEND

Union attack

Confederate attack

Union retreat

Confederate retreat

Union soldier

Confederate soldier

Union General McClellan

Confederate General Lee

Turning Points

Main Idea Events in 1863 helped the Union become stronger in the Civil War.

At the start of the war, President Lincoln's only goal was to keep the Union together. He did not plan to free enslaved people. By 1862, however, he changed his mind. Many people in the North wanted him to end slavery, and freeing enslaved people could weaken the Confederacy. He also hoped that freed slaves would work to help the Union.

Lincoln put the Emancipation Proclamation into effect on January 1, 1863. **Emancipation** is the freeing of enslaved people. This proclamation declared that slaves in the Confederacy were free. It did not end slavery in the border states. Confederates ignored the new law. The North would have to defeat the South to free the slaves. The Civil War had started as a war to save the Union. The Emancipation Proclamation made it a war to end slavery in the South.

Vicksburg and Gettysburg

In 1863, the Union won two important battles. In the West, General Grant's army surrounded Vicksburg and fired cannons into the town for six weeks. On July 4, Vicksburg surrendered. The Union now controlled the Mississippi River. This cut off Texas and Arkansas from the rest of the South.

The Union also won a major battle in the East. After stopping two more attacks on Richmond, General Lee decided to invade the Union again. He marched north into Pennsylvania. The Union army met Lee's soldiers on July 1, near the town of Gettysburg.

For two days the armies battled back and forth. On the third day, Lee ordered a final attack. Nearly 14,000 Confederate soldiers charged across open fields towards the Union army.

The Union soldiers were ready. They stopped the attack with rifle and cannon fire. The heavy fire killed or wounded about half of the Confederate soldiers. Lee's weakened army had to retreat.

July 1863 was the turning point of the war. The Union victories at Vicksburg and Gettysburg gave the Union a better chance of winning.

Emancipation Proclamation
President Lincoln decided to issue the proclamation to free the slaves. This is a copy that was made so that people could put it up in their homes and schools.

Later that year, President Lincoln gave a short speech at Gettysburg, known as the Gettysburg Address. He declared that the Union was fighting to make sure that American democracy would survive. The speech is famous as a powerful statement about the purpose of the Civil War.

REVIEW Why was the victory at Vicksburg important to the Union?

Lesson Summary

At first, the Confederacy won most battles in the East, while the Union won battles in the West. However, victories at Vicksburg and Gettysburg gave the Union the advantage in the war.

Why It Matters...

With the Emancipation Proclamation, the Civil War became a fight to end slavery in the Confederate States.

Gettysburg This painting shows the Confederate attack on the third day of the battle. The attack is known as Pickett's Charge, after one of the generals who led it.

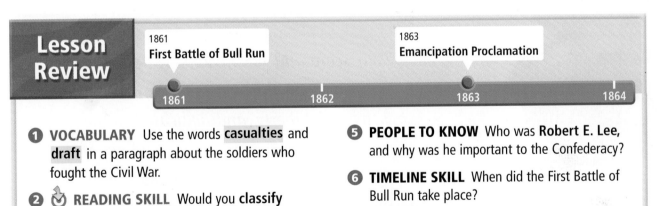

Lesson Review

1861
First Battle of Bull Run

1863
Emancipation Proclamation

1861   1862   1863   1864

① **VOCABULARY** Use the words **casualties** and **draft** in a paragraph about the soldiers who fought the Civil War.

② **READING SKILL** Would you **classify** having control of Vicksburg as an advantage or disadvantage for the Union? Why?

③ **MAIN IDEA: History** What was the Union strategy in the Civil War?

④ **MAIN IDEA: Government** Why did both the Union and the Confederacy need to use the draft?

⑤ **PEOPLE TO KNOW** Who was **Robert E. Lee,** and why was he important to the Confederacy?

⑥ **TIMELINE SKILL** When did the First Battle of Bull Run take place?

⑦ **CRITICAL THINKING: Infer** Why do you think having a larger population was an advantage for the Union?

WRITING ACTIVITY News of the Civil War was very important to Americans. Prepare a news report about an event from the Civil War from the Union or Confederate point of view.

Primary Source

The GETTYSBURG ADDRESS

The speech President Lincoln gave on that November day in 1863 was short. It took him barely two minutes to read it. The speech that came before his had lasted for two hours. But Americans still remember the Gettysburg Address more than 140 years later.

Lincoln gave the address just four months after the Battle of Gettysburg. In a ceremony honoring the Union soldiers who had died in the battle, Lincoln spoke about the meaning of the war and its terrible cost. His words captured the feelings of Americans as they struggled to meet a serious danger to their country.

① *Four score and seven years ago our fathers brought forth on this continent, a new nation, conceived in Liberty, and dedicated to the proposition that all men are created equal.*

② *Now we are engaged in a great civil war, testing whether that nation, or any nation so conceived and so dedicated, can long endure.*

③ *We are met on a great battle-field of that war. We have come to dedicate a portion of that field, as a final resting place for those who here gave their lives that that nation might live. It is altogether fitting and proper that we should do this.*

④ But, in a larger sense, we can not dedicate—we can not consecrate—we can not hallow—this ground. The brave men, living and dead, who struggled here, have consecrated it, far above our poor power to add or detract. The world will little note, nor long remember what we say here, but it can never forget what they did here. It is for us the living, rather, to be dedicated here to the unfinished work which they who fought here have thus far so nobly advanced. It

⑤ is rather for us to be here dedicated to the great task remaining before us—that from these honored dead we take increased devotion to that cause for which they gave the last full measure of devotion—that we here highly resolve that these dead shall not have died in vain—that this nation, under God, shall have a new birth of freedom—and that government of the people, by the people, for the people, shall not perish from the earth.

① Eighty-seven years ago, our nation was founded on the ideals of freedom and equality.

② Now we are fighting a war to see if our nation and our ideals can survive.

③ We are here to honor soldiers who died fighting in this war.

④ The best way we can honor them is to stay dedicated to our ideals.

⑤ We promise to uphold freedom so that our democracy will survive.

Activities

1. TALK ABOUT IT What do you think Lincoln meant by "unfinished work"?

2. WRITE ABOUT IT Explain why you think Lincoln's speech is famous today. Choose two of his ideas and write a one-page paper about why they are still important.

 Technology Learn about other primary sources for this unit at Education Place. www.eduplace.com/kids/hmss05/

The Human Face of War

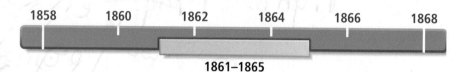

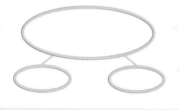
Build on What You Know Have you ever missed someone or waited for a card from a friend or family member? If you have, then you know part of what it was like to live during the Civil War. During the war, soldiers and their families missed each other's company.

The Soldier's Life

Main Idea Soldiers in the Civil War faced problems other than fighting battles.

Men from all parts of the country fought in the Civil War. Many hoped for excitement and glory. Instead, they found terror in battle and boredom in camp. A **camp** is a group of temporary shelters, such as tents.

Soldiers read, sang, or wrote letters to pass the time in camp. Some put on shows or printed newspapers. They loved to get letters. "It made the boys shout with Joy to heare from home once more," wrote one soldier.

Food in the army was usually poor. Union soldiers grew tired of eating the same food almost every day. However, Confederate soldiers suffered more because they often did not have enough to eat.

Camp Life Soldiers in camp often slept on the ground in tents, with nothing to sit on but the ground or wooden boxes.

New Soldiers African American soldiers fought for the Union in many battles. Several won the Congressional Medal of Honor, shown at right, for their courage.

Who Were the Soldiers?

Civil War soldiers came from many different backgrounds. At first, almost all were white and born in the United States. As the war went on, the Union allowed African Americans to join the army. About 180,000 African Americans served in the Union army. They fought in many battles, including Vicksburg.

Immigrants also joined the Union army. They included people from Germany, Ireland, and Italy. American Indians fought on both sides.

Thousands of boys went into battle even though they were too young. Some served as drummers who sent signals to soldiers in battle. Hundreds of women on both sides disguised themselves as men and joined the army. Women also worked as spies for one side or the other.

Casualties of War

The Civil War was the deadliest war in American history. Rifles could shoot farther and more accurately than ever before. Casualties were much higher than people had expected. However, battle was not the only danger of war. Disease killed twice as many soldiers as the fighting did.

Women helped care for the sick and wounded. More than 3,000 northern women served as nurses. One was **Clara Barton,** who later founded the American Red Cross. Southern women also cared for wounded soldiers in hospitals and in their homes.

The Civil War affected the lives of most Americans. Soldiers had to face the dangers of battle and disease, as well as the boredom of camp life. Thousands of families lost loved ones.

REVIEW What did women on both sides of the war do to help their side?

On the Home Front

Main Idea The Civil War was difficult for people at home, especially in the South.

Many soldiers left families behind when they went to war. Those families were part of the home front. When a country is at war, the **home front** is all the people who are not in the military. Soldiers and their families did not want to be separated. "My Dear Dear Father," wrote the daughter of one officer, "I do miss you so much. . . ." With men gone, women took on new tasks. They ran farms and businesses. Thousands of women sewed uniforms, knitted socks, made bandages, and raised money for their armies.

Most of the battles in the Civil War took place in the South. Few people in the North could see the war happening. The new technology of photography let civilians see what the war looked like. A **civilian** is a person who is not in the military. **Mathew Brady** took pictures of soldiers, camp life, and battlefields. He showed his photographs in the North. Civilians there saw that war was much worse than they had realized.

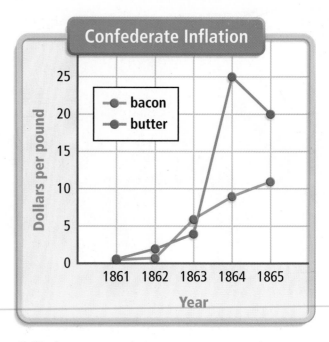

Inflation Food and other necessary goods became too expensive for many southerners to afford. **SKILL** **Reading Graphs** How expensive was butter in 1864?

The Southern Home Front

Life on the home front was especially hard in the South. Their farms became battlefields. Their cities, homes, and barns were destroyed.

In the South, soldiers and civilians often did not have enough to eat. Inflation, or a rise in prices, made food very expensive. The money printed by the Confederate government became almost worthless. A barrel of flour that cost $6 in 1861 might cost $1,000 in 1865. In Richmond and other towns, hungry women attacked shops in search of food.

Enslaved people in the South suffered as well, but most still welcomed the war. The Emancipation Proclamation in 1863 gave them the hope of freedom.

Money Each Confederate state printed its own money. Because of inflation, most of the bills became almost worthless.

Juneteenth African American communities celebrate Juneteenth. This parade was held in Austin, Texas, where it is a yearly event.

Some enslaved people only learned of the proclamation at the end of the war. News of the Emancipation Proclamation reached Texas on June 19, 1865. This day became a day of celebration. Known as Juneteenth, June 19 is still celebrated in Texas and other parts of the country as the day slavery ended.

REVIEW What happened to prices in the South during the Civil War?

Lesson Summary

- During the war soldiers faced danger in battle and from disease.
- Soldiers came from many different backgrounds.
- The Civil War affected the lives of all Americans, not just soliders.

Why It Matters ...

During the Civil War, Americans lived through some of the hardest years in the nation's history.

Lesson Review

1. **VOCABULARY** Write a pargraph about the lives of ordinary people during the Civil War. Use **home front** and **civilian** in your paragraph.

2. **READING SKILL** Use the details in the graph on page 186 to explain why life was hard during the Civil War.

3. **MAIN IDEA: History** What made camp life hard for Civil War soldiers?

4. **MAIN IDEA: Citizenship** In what ways did women contribute to the war effort?

5. **PEOPLE TO KNOW** Who was **Mathew Brady** and what did he do during the Civil War?

6. **CRITICAL THINKING: Draw Conclusions** Use information you have learned to tell why women and children joined the army on both sides.

7. **CRITICAL THINKING: Analyze** What was the point of view of enslaved people in the South toward the war? How was it different from the view of most other southerners?

MAP ACTIVITY Trace a map of the United States. Identify the states that fought in the Civil War. Use different colors for the Union, the Confederacy, and the border states.

Courageous Women

Many women are remembered today for their role in the Civil War. Few women fought, but many on both sides did take part in the war. Some braved serious dangers to nurse wounded soldiers on the battlefields. Others took risks by acting as spies. For many, especially in the South, simply living through the war took courage.

CLARA BARTON
1821–1912

When Clara Barton volunteered as a Union army nurse, she saw that hospitals had no medicines or bandages. She wrote letters to newspapers asking people to make donations. When she arrived at battlefields with loads of supplies, she sometimes risked her life. But the troops cheered. "I went in while the battle raged," she once recalled. After the war, in 1881, she was asked to start the American Red Cross, an organization that still helps people in times of war and peace.

ELIZABETH VAN LEW
1818 – 1890

Even before the Civil War began, Elizabeth Van Lew opposed slavery. She lived in Virginia, a southern state, and she convinced her mother to free the family's slaves. During the war, Van Lew became a spy for the Union army. She got important information from Confederate sources. She asked her servants to carry her secret coded messages in hollow eggshells or in the soles of their shoes. In 1865, when Union troops arrived in Richmond, Van Lew flew the Union flag for all to see.

MARY CHESNUT
1823 – 1886

Mary Chesnut kept a diary during the Civil War. She was a wealthy South Carolinian whose husband was a Confederate general. In her diary, she described the collapse of the Confederate government. She recorded the thoughts and fears of people involved in the war, including her own true beliefs—she was against slavery. Her writing is valued today as a full portrait of the Confederacy, and a rich source of information for historians.

Activities

1. **TALK ABOUT IT** Discuss how each of these women showed **courage** during the Civil War.

2. **DEBATE IT** Do you think it was harder or easier for women to take part in the war than for men? Debate your opinion. Support your opinion with facts.

Technology Visit Education Place for more biographies of people in this unit. www.eduplace.com/kids/hmss/

The War Ends

1858　　1860　　1862　　1864　　1866　　1868

1864–1865

telegraph
total war
desert

Vocabulary Strategy

telegraph

The prefix **tele-** in the word **telegraph** means "far away." A telegraph sends messages to distant places.

READING SKILL
Predict Outcomes

As you read, make a prediction about how the Civil War will finally end.

PREDICTION

OUTCOME

STANDARDS

SS5H1c Atlanta, Sherman's March, Appomattox

Build on What You Know To finish a job, you need to have enough supplies. In the Civil War, the Union had more soldiers, weapons, and food than the Confederacy. These supplies helped the Union win the war.

Union Victories

Main Idea The Union tried to force the South to surrender by destroying southerners' resources.

By the end of 1863, the Union had won several important battles in the Civil War. Victories at Vicksburg and Gettysburg gave northerners hope of winning the war. But the Confederate armies were still fighting hard. To end the war, the North had to destroy the South's ability to fight.

President Lincoln needed a tough army general to defeat the South. He chose **Ulysses S. Grant.** Grant proved in the West that he could fight hard. Lincoln made him the commander of all Union armies.

Grant planned to lead an army into Virginia to defeat General **Robert E. Lee's** army and capture Richmond. Grant also ordered General **William Tecumseh Sherman** to lead the Union army in Tennessee. Sherman planned to attack Atlanta, Georgia, a major Confederate city.

General Grant Little known before the war, he became famous for his determination to win.

Later Battles, 1864–1865

PENNSYLVANIA
MARYLAND DELAWARE
ILLINOIS INDIANA OHIO WEST
VIRGINIA
Ohio River
KENTUCKY
VIRGINIA
Wilderness 1864
Spotsylvania 1864
Cold Harbor 1864
Appomattox Court House 1865
Petersburg 1864–1865
NORTH
CAROLINA
ATLANTIC
OCEAN
TENNESSEE
Nashville 1864
Franklin 1864
Chattanooga
SOUTH
CAROLINA
Columbia
Atlanta
Charleston
Atlanta 1864
ALABAMA GEORGIA
Savannah
MISSISSIPPI
Mobile Bay 1864
New Orleans
FLORIDA
Gulf of Mexico
Mississippi River

N
W E
S

LEGEND
Union states
Confederate states
Union victory
Confederate victory
No clear victory
Sherman's route

km 0 150 300
mi 0 150 300

Later Battles This map shows the major battles from the last two years of the Civil War. During their march through Georgia, Union soldiers wrecked railroads (above) by bending the rails.

The Atlanta Campaign

Sherman began his attack on Atlanta in May 1864. The city was a center for southern supplies, factories, and railroads. Experienced Union soldiers marched into Georgia. The Confederates fought back all summer. They used the mountains and rivers of northern Georgia as defenses. However, Sherman's larger army finally captured Atlanta in September. Sherman sent a message to President Lincoln by telegraph. A **telegraph** is a machine that sends electric signals over wires. Sherman's message said "Atlanta is ours, and fairly won."

Lincoln welcomed this news. He was running for reelection in 1864 and worried about losing. He needed victories like Atlanta to gain voters' support.

Sherman's March to the Sea

From Atlanta, Sherman's soldiers marched to Savannah. This march became known as the March to the Sea. Along the way, they destroyed anything southerners needed for the war. They stole food, killed animals, and wrecked railroad tracks and factories. Sherman used total war to make southerners so tired of fighting that they would give up. **Total war** is the strategy of destroying an enemy's resources.

After reaching Savannah, Sherman's army turned north, once again ruining everything in its path. One woman described how the soldiers "roamed about setting fire to every house . . ."

REVIEW Why did Sherman decide to use total war against the South?

191

Grant and Lee

Main Idea Grant's attacks in Virginia wore down Lee's army and forced it to surrender.

While Sherman marched into Georgia in 1864, Grant led a huge army toward Richmond, Virginia. He was opposed by Robert E. Lee's army. Lee was a brilliant general who had defeated larger armies. Grant's strength was his determination. He kept attacking, even after a defeat.

Lee used all of his skill to fight off Grant's army. The Union suffered terrible losses, but Grant kept attacking. His attacks wore down the Confederate army in a series of battles. Lee was forced farther and farther south.

In June 1864, the two armies faced each other near Richmond. They stayed there for almost a year. Neither side could defeat the other. However, the Union army was growing stronger.

Lee's Surrender

The Union's resources helped Grant. He received a steady supply of food and equipment. The North sent thousands more soldiers to join his army. President Lincoln said, "We have more men now than we had when the war began."

At the same time, Lee's army was struggling. The Confederate government had no more soldiers or supplies to send Lee. Confederate soldiers went hungry, and some began to desert. To **desert** means to leave the army without permission.

By early April 1865, Lee's army was too weak to defend Richmond any longer. Lee retreated. The Union army captured Richmond and chased Lee's army west. Finally, near a town called Appomattox Court House, Lee made a hard decision. His starving army was nearly surrounded. He had to surrender. He said,

❝ There is nothing left for me to do but go and see General Grant... ❞

Surrender Lee surrendered to Grant on April 9, 1865 at Appomattox Court House. "We are all Americans," one of Grant's officers told Lee afterwards.

Lee's Chair

On April 9, 1865, Grant and Lee met in a home in the village of Appomattox Court House. Grant said that Lee's soldiers could go home. Lee agreed to surrender. Grant then sent 25,000 meals to the hungry Confederate soldiers.

Grant told his soldiers not to celebrate. "The war is over," he said. "The rebels are our countrymen again." A few days later, Lee's soldiers marched past the Union army to surrender. As they passed, the Union soldiers saluted their old enemies.

News of Lee's surrender spread quickly. In Washington, people celebrated in the streets. Confederate soldiers in North Carolina surrendered to Sherman. Fighting continued in a few places, but by late June all was quiet. The war was over at last.

REVIEW Why did Lee have to surrender?

Lesson Summary

> General Sherman used total war to destroy the South's ability to fight.

> General Lee's army could not get enough food or equipment.

> Lee had to surrender to General Grant.

Why It Matters...

The victory of the Union made certain that the United States would remain one nation.

Lesson Review

1864 **Grant invades Virginia**

1865 **Lee surrenders**

1864 — 1865 — 1866

1 **VOCABULARY** Choose the correct word to complete each sentence.

total war   telegraph   desert

Sherman used the _____ to communicate with President Lincoln. Lee's army shrank as his soldiers began to _____.

2 **READING SKILL** Check your **prediction**. Compare it to the description in the lesson of how the war ends.

3 **MAIN IDEA: History** What was Sherman's plan for making the South surrender?

4 **MAIN IDEA: Economics** In what way did lack of resources affect the Confederate army?

5 **PEOPLE TO KNOW** Who was **Ulysses S. Grant**, and why was he important during the Civil War?

6 **TIMELINE SKILL** In what year did Grant invade Virginia?

7 **CRITICAL THINKING: Decision Making** What were the effects of Sherman's decision to march from Atlanta to Savannah?

HANDS ON

MATH ACTIVITY At Appomattox Court House, the Union army had about 103,000 soldiers and the Confederate army had about 28,000 soldiers. How many more soldiers did the Union have? Draw a bar graph to compare the size of the two armies.

A Global View, 1865

During the 1860s, the Civil War changed life for most Americans. At the same time, changes were taking place elsewhere. Powerful nations in Europe tried to conquer land in other continents. Some countries grew more wealthy. People in other countries rebelled against their leaders and governments.

New technology made travel and communication easier, so trade among continents grew. Goods and ideas spread more quickly than ever before. Look on the map to see what was happening around the world.

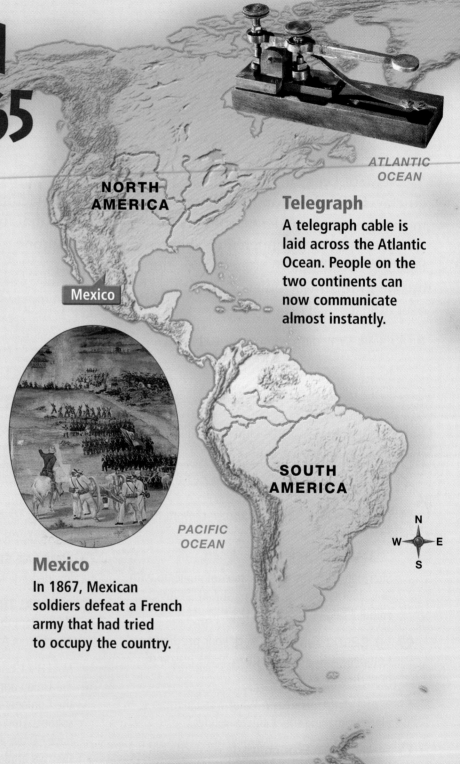

NORTH AMERICA

Mexico

ATLANTIC OCEAN

Telegraph

A telegraph cable is laid across the Atlantic Ocean. People on the two continents can now communicate almost instantly.

SOUTH AMERICA

PACIFIC OCEAN

Mexico

In 1867, Mexican soldiers defeat a French army that had tried to occupy the country.

Italy

Italy, which had been made up of many small states, is united for the first time in almost 1,500 years.

EUROPE

Italy

Egypt

AFRICA

India

The British government takes over large parts of India. India is ruled by Britain until 1947.

ASIA

India

PACIFIC OCEAN

Egypt

The Suez Canal opens in 1869. Ships traveling between Europe and Asia no longer have to sail all the way around Africa.

INDIAN OCEAN

Australia

The discovery of gold in Australia brings thousands of new settlers to the colonies there.

AUSTRALIA

ANTARCTICA

Activities

1. **TALK ABOUT IT** How do you think the Suez Canal or a telegraph across the Atlantic Ocean changed people's lives?

2. **CREATE IT** Find out the different ways people could travel and communicate in 1865. Make a poster comparing travel and communication in 1865 and today.

Reconstruction

1860   1865   1870   1875   1880

1865–1877

VOCABULARY

Reconstruction
assassination
Freedmen's Bureau
impeach

Vocabulary Strategy

Reconstruction

Find the word **construct** in **Reconstruction.** When you reconstruct something, you construct, or build, it again.

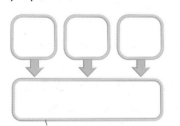

READING SKILL
Draw Conclusions
Use facts and details to come to a conclusion about how Reconstruction affected people's lives.

Build on What You Know Have you ever had a moment when you knew that your life has changed forever? That is a turning point. The Civil War was a turning point for the United States. After the war, the nation would never be the same again.

Plans for Reconstruction

Main Idea President Lincoln and Congress disagreed about how to rebuild the South.

As the Civil War ended, Americans faced a challenge. The nation had nearly split apart. During Reconstruction, the country had to be reunited. The period when the South rejoined the Union is called **Reconstruction.**

Americans could not agree on how to bring the South back into the Union. Some wanted to use Reconstruction to punish the South. Others wanted to make it easy for southern states to rejoin. **President Lincoln** did not want to punish the South. He said,

66 **With malice [meanness] toward none, with charity for all . . . let us strive on [try] to finish the work we are in, to bind up the nation's wounds . . .** 99

President Lincoln Saving the Union was Lincoln's greatest concern. He wanted to reunite the nation quickly.

STANDARDS

SS5H1e Effects of war
SS5H2a 13th, 14th, 15th Amendments
SS5H2b Freedmen's Bureau
SS5CG1c-d Due process
SS5CG3b 15th Amendment

War Department, Washington, April 20, 1865,

$100,000 REWARD!

THE MURDERER

Of our late beloved President, Abraham Lincoln,

IS STILL AT LARGE.

$50,000 REWARD

Will be paid by this Department for his apprehension, in addition to any reward offered by Municipal Authorities or State Executives.

$25,000 REWARD

Will be paid for the apprehension of JOHN H. SURRATT, one of Booth's Accomplices.

$25,000 REWARD

Will be paid for the apprehension of David C. Harold, another of Booth's accomplices.

EDWIN M. STANTON, Secretary of War.

Funeral Train
Large crowds gathered for parades honoring President Lincoln after his death.

Lincoln's Death

Lincoln planned to let the defeated states set up new state governments and rejoin the Union quickly. Many people disagreed with Lincoln, especially Radical Republicans. These representatives and senators wanted to change the South.

Lincoln and Congress did not have a chance to reach an agreement. On the evening of April 14, 1865, Lincoln went to a play in Washington. **John Wilkes Booth,** an actor who had supported the Confederacy, shot the President. Abraham Lincoln died the next day.

Lincoln's assassination shocked the nation. **Assassination** is the murder of an important leader. Lincoln had become a hero to many people. His death filled them with sadness. They would miss his leadership during the difficult years of Reconstruction.

Effects of the War

The Civil War had caused suffering across the nation. Hundreds of thousands of people on both sides had died. It also changed both regions, though the changes were very different.

The war was a disaster for the South. Its farms, cities, and factories were ruined. People had to rebuild their homes and businesses. The war brought freedom to enslaved people, but most had no homes or jobs. Southerners needed to find new ways to make their economy work.

The North grew stronger as a result of the war. There had been little fighting there to damage cities or farms. Northern industries and railroads grew quickly during and after the war.

REVIEW What was Lincoln's plan for Reconstruction?

Reconstruction

Main Idea Congress took control of Reconstruction from President Andrew Johnson.

After Lincoln's death, Vice President **Andrew Johnson** of Tennessee became President. Johnson put Lincoln's plan for Reconstruction into action in 1865. The southern states quickly set up new state governments. The federal government forced them to abolish slavery in their state constitutions. At the same time, though, most southern states passed harsh laws called Black Codes. The Black Codes limited the rights of former slaves to travel, vote, and work in certain jobs.

Radical Republicans in Congress were unhappy about the Black Codes. President Johnson upset them more by allowing southern states to elect former Confederate leaders to Congress.

Congress fought back. Members voted not to let the new southern representatives join Congress. They passed a law to protect the rights of freedmen, who were the people freed from slavery. Congress also created the Freedmen's Bureau. The **Freedmen's Bureau** provided food, clothing, medical care, and legal advice to poor blacks and whites. It set up hospitals and schools and found jobs for many.

Reconstruction The mural below shows several scenes from Reconstruction: ❶ Students attend a new school opened by the Freedmen's Bureau. ❷ Radical Republicans impeach President Johnson. ❸ African Americans vote for the first time. ❹ African Americans serve in Congress.

Congress Takes Control

In 1867, Congress began its own Reconstruction plan. It put the South under military rule. Soldiers from the national army marched into the region. When they arrived, they forced southern states to obey Congress. The states had to allow all men, including blacks, to vote.

After taking over Reconstruction, Congress tried to remove President Johnson. In 1868, the House of Representatives voted to impeach Johnson. To **impeach** means to charge a government official with a crime. They accused him of breaking one of their new laws. Congress almost forced Johnson out of office, but they did not succeed, and he finished his presidency.

Carpetbaggers and Scalawags

Some southerners supported the Republicans during Reconstruction. Those southerners were very unpopular in the South. Southerners who helped the government during Reconstruction were known as scalawags. Scalawag was a slang word for an old worthless horse.

Many northerners traveled south during Reconstruction. Some wanted to help rebuild the South, but others just wanted to make money. These people were known as carpetbaggers, because they often carried suitcases made of carpet material. Southerners disliked carpetbaggers and did not want them there.

REVIEW Why were soldiers sent to the South?

The Constitution Changes

Main Idea Congress changed the Constitution to protect the rights of African Americans and to guarantee all citizens due process of law.

During Reconstruction, Congress created three new amendments to the Constitution. The new amendments gave the national government more power over the states. They also protected the rights of African Americans.

The first of the new amendments, the Thirteenth Amendment, ended slavery throughout the United States. In 1865, the states ratified the amendment, which means they approved it.

Black Codes still limited the rights of African Americans. To protect those rights, Congress passed the Fourteenth Amendment, which gave citizenship to African Americans. It said a citizen's life, liberty, or property cannot be taken away without a fair trial. This is called "due process of law." It also said all citizens must be treated equally under the law.

Almost every southern state refused to ratify the Fourteenth Amendment. They did not want the national government to interfere with their state laws. Congress declared that southern states had to ratify the Fourteenth Amendment to rejoin the Union. The states then agreed to the demands of Congress.

In 1870, Congress passed the Fifteenth Amendment, guaranteeing African American men the right to vote. The Fifteenth Amendment had an effect right away. African Americans began taking part in government. Religious leaders, former soldiers, and others ran for office. Some became leaders in community and state government.

Many African Americans served in state legislatures. They worked to create the first public schools for whites and blacks in the South. Sixteen African Americans joined the United States Congress. **Blanche K. Bruce** and **Hiram Revels** of Mississippi became two of the first black senators.

Three New Amendments

Thirteenth Amendment

The Thirteenth Amendment declared that slavery would not be allowed to exist in the United States. It ended the long argument in the United States over whether slavery should be legal.

Fourteenth Amendment

The Fourteenth Amendment declared that the states could not limit the rights of citizens. States could not take away life, liberty, or property without due process of the law, or deny equal protection of the law.

Fifteenth Amendment

The Fifteenth Amendment gave all men the right to vote, no matter what their skin color was or if they had been enslaved. Women were still not allowed to vote until 1920.

The Struggle for Rights Continues

The amendments passed during Reconstruction helped all Americans. They protected people's rights and made laws fairer. For example, the Fourteenth Amendment requires both the federal and the state governments to treat all citizens equally and fairly.

The amendments, however, did not solve all of the nation's problems. Some people, both in the North and in the South, did not want African Americans to vote or to have equal rights.

Hiram Revels
He served in the Mississippi state senate, and later became the first African American elected to the U.S. Senate.

Sometimes laws protecting rights were ignored. The struggle for equality would continue for African Americans.

REVIEW Why did Congress pass the Fourteenth Amendment?

Lesson Summary

- Congress and President Lincoln had different plans for Reconstruction.
- President Lincoln was assassinated just after the war ended.
- Congress took control of Reconstruction from President Johnson.
- Three important amendments were ratified during Reconstruction.

Why It Matters...

During Reconstruction, the nation's laws became fairer, with new constitutional protection for citizens' rights and freedoms.

Lesson Review

1865 Lincoln assassinated	1868 Congress impeaches Johnson	1870 15th Amendment

1865 — 1867 — 1869 — 1871

1 **VOCABULARY** Write a paragraph about the actions of the United States government after the Civil War, using the words **Reconstruction, Freedmen's Bureau,** and **impeach.**

2 **READING SKILL** Review your **conclusion.** What effect do you think Reconstruction had on the lives of freedmen?

3 **MAIN IDEA: Government** Why did Congress fight against President Johnson?

4 **MAIN IDEA: Citizenship** What right did the Fifteenth Amendment protect for African American men?

5 **PEOPLE TO KNOW** Why was **Andrew Johnson** important after Lincoln's death?

6 **TIMELINE SKILL** What did Congress do in 1868?

7 **CRITICAL THINKING: Compare and Contrast** How were the effects of the war different for the North and the South?

HANDS ON

RESEARCH ACTIVITY The Fourteenth Amendment guarantees due process of law and equal protection under the law. Use library or Internet resources to find out more about this amendment and create a mural explaining it.

The South After the War

After the Civil War, the economy of the United States grew faster than ever before. The South, however, did not see as much growth as other regions. Manufacturing in the South grew more slowly than in the rest of the country. Southern farmers struggled to produce as much as they had before the war.

The economy of the South suffered for many reasons. The region lost two-thirds of its wealth. Many young men who would have been farmers or workers lost their lives in the war. The war ruined homes, farms, machinery, factories, and railroads.

People in the South worked hard to rebuild their homes, cities, and factories. Cities such as Atlanta, Richmond, and Charleston became centers of trade and industry again.

Charleston (above) was left in ruins by the end of the Civil War. However, people rebuilt quickly. By 1893, Charleston (below) had grown into a large and busy city.

In 1870, the value of a southern farm was only one-third of what it had been before the war.

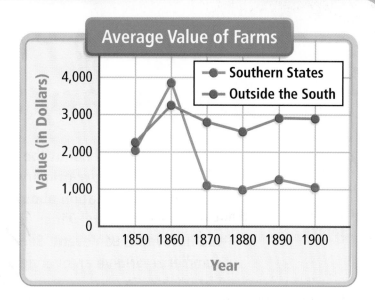

Average Value of Farms

Southern States
Outside the South

Value (in Dollars)

4,000
3,000
2,000
1,000
0

1850 1860 1870 1880 1890 1900

Year

The economy of the South improved after the war. However, the value of goods made in the South remained lower than in the rest of the country.

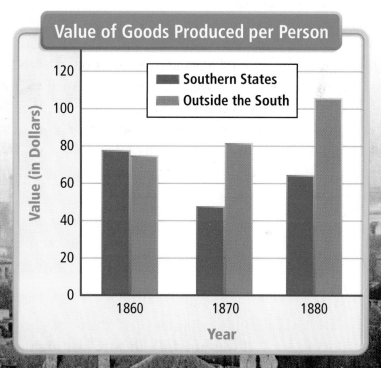

Value of Goods Produced per Person

Southern States
Outside the South

Value (in Dollars)

120
100
80
60
40
20
0

1860 1870 1880

Year

Activities

1. **THINK ABOUT IT** Why do you think so much property was destroyed in the South, but not in the North?

2. **MAKE YOUR OWN** Look at the line graph of farm values. Make a bar graph showing farm values.

Skillbuilder

Compare Primary and Secondary Sources

▶ **VOCABULARY**

primary source

secondary source

People learned about the death of President Lincoln from two types of sources: primary and secondary. A primary source is firsthand information about an event, a place, or a time period. A secondary source is information from someone who did not witness an event. Secondary sources sometimes summarize or give an overview of what happened.

The New York Herald

J. Wilkes Booth, the Actor, the Alleged Assassin of the President

War Department – Washington, April 15, 1865 – 1:30 a.m. – Major General Dix, New York:

This evening, at about 9:30 p.m., at Ford's Theatre [Washington, D.C.], the President, while sitting in his private box with Mrs. Lincoln,... was shot by an assassin, who suddenly entered the box and approached behind the President.

The assassin then leaped upon the stage, brandishing [waving] a large dagger or knife, and made his escape in the rear of the theatre.

...I was at Ford's theatre last night, seated in the left hand side nearly opposite the President's box. About half past ten I heard a shot. I thought it was in the play. A man appeared in front of the President's box and got upon the stage swinging himself down partly by the curtains and partly jumping. I noticed he had a large dagger in his left hand I think. He appeared to stagger but recovered himself. He held the dagger up just as he got upon the stage and said in a tragical tone very clearly...sic semper tyrannis [thus always to tyrants].

- Will T. Kent, testimony given to Supreme Court on April 15, 1865

Learn the Skill

Step 1: Read the sources. Look for clue words such as *I* and *my*, which are sometimes used in primary sources.

Step 2: Identify the information as a primary or secondary source. Ask yourself, Who wrote the information? Was the writer at the event?

Step 3: Make a list of the similarities and differences in the sources. Does the primary source give a different account of the event than the secondary source? What information did you learn from each source?

Practice the Skill

Read the two accounts of President Lincoln's assassination on page 480. Then answer these questions.

1. Is the news article a primary or a secondary source? How do you know?

2. Is Will T. Kent's account a primary or a secondary source? How do you know?

3. What facts do the two accounts share?

4. What differences do you see between sources?

Apply the Skill

Find an example of a primary source in a book, newspaper, or magazine article. Then find an article that is an example of a secondary source. In a paragraph, explain how you identified each one.

The Challenge of Freedom

1860	1865	1870	1875	1880	1885	1890

1865–1881

VOCABULARY

sharecropping
Jim Crow
segregation

Vocabulary Strategy

sharecropping

In **sharecropping,** a farmer only gets to keep a part, or **share,** of a crop and gives the rest to the landowner.

READING SKILL

Problem and Solution
Take notes to identify the problems facing African Americans after the Civil War and their solutions.

PROBLEMS	SOLUTIONS

Build on What You Know You know how important freedom is to people in the United States. Millions of African Americans were free after the Civil War. Freedom brought new opportunities, but also new challenges.

Freedom and Hardship

Main Idea Freed African Americans looked for ways to make a living after the end of slavery.

❝ **No more iron chain for me, no more, no more!** ❞

African Americans sang with joy to celebrate their new freedom. Reconstruction was a time of hope for them. Slavery had ended at last. They had the chance to make new lives for themselves.

Freedom was exciting, but it was not easy. Newly freed African Americans had to struggle to make a living. They also had to prepare for their new roles as full citizens. They worked to educate themselves and took part in politics. However, times were hard in the South and some people did not want African Americans to be truly free.

Sharecropping This photograph shows sharecroppers at work in the fields they rent from a landowner.

STANDARDS

SS5H2c Sharecropping, Jim Crow laws
SS5H3b Impact of Carver

The Rise of Sharecropping

Reconstruction ended the plantation system in the South, leaving many people there very poor. Freed people wanted to farm for themselves. However, few had enough money to buy land.

Landowners set up a system called sharecropping that let poor whites and former slaves become farmers. In **sharecropping,** poor farmers used a landowner's fields. In return, the farmer gave the landowner a share of the crop. Landowners often loaned sharecroppers tools and seeds as well.

Sharecropping gave African Americans some independence. It also kept poor farmers in debt. After selling their crops, many sharecroppers did not have enough money to pay the landowners what they owed. They had to keep borrowing and could not get out of debt. Sharecropping made it hard for poor farmers to save money and provide a good life for their families.

Responses to Reconstruction

Reconstruction angered some people in the South. They opposed the new laws that protected African Americans' rights. They also disliked having federal soldiers in the South to enforce the laws.

Some people wanted to stop African Americans from taking part in government. They formed secret organizations, such as the Ku Klux Klan. The Ku Klux Klan threatened, beat, and even killed African Americans to keep them from voting. The Ku Klux Klan also attacked people who helped African Americans. In 1871, African Americans in Kentucky asked Congress for protection. They described the Klan's "riding nightly over the country . . . robbing, whipping . . . and killing our people."

REVIEW Why did many freed African Americans become sharecroppers?

Debts Landowners often charged high prices. This chart shows how much a sharecropper might owe after a year of hard work.

SKILL **Reading Charts** How much more did this farmer need to earn to make a profit?

Sharecropper's Account for the Year 1870

Money Borrowed		Money Earned		Debt
Food	-$83.25	Cotton	+$90.45	
Clothing	-$64.75			
Farm Supplies	-$75.08			
Medicine	-$2.17			
TOTAL:	-$225.25		+$90.45	-$134.80

The End of Reconstruction

Main Idea African Americans worked and studied to overcome new laws that limited their rights.

People grew disappointed with Reconstruction over time. They did not feel that it had successfully reunited the nation. In 1877, the new President, **Rutherford B. Hayes**, ended Reconstruction and ordered government soldiers to leave the South. Without protection, many African Americans were unable to vote and they lost their political power.

Southern states began passing Jim Crow laws. **Jim Crow** was a nickname for laws that kept African Americans separate from other Americans. These laws made segregation legal. **Segregation** is the forced separation of the races. Jim Crow laws segregated schools, hospitals, and even cemeteries. States usually spent less money on schools and hospitals for African Americans.

New Schools

African Americans did not want to let Jim Crow laws ruin their hopes for the future. Many believed that education would give them a chance for a better life. Eager students filled the new schools and colleges for African Americans that opened in the South. Churches in the North sent money and teachers to support these new schools. African American churches in the South also took a leading role. These churches became important centers in African American communities.

In 1881, a former slave named **Booker T. Washington** opened the Tuskegee Institute in Alabama. All of Tuskegee's students and teachers were African Americans. Washington believed that African Americans would receive equal treatment in time if they were educated and learned useful skills. Students at the Tuskegee Institute studied writing, math, and science. They also learned trades such as printing, carpentry, and farming.

Tuskegee Schools such as the Tuskegee Institute (right) gave African Americans the education they had not received under slavery. Booker T. Washington, (below) was the president of Tuskegee.

The most famous teacher at Tuskegee was **George Washington Carver**. Carver studied how to improve the lives of poor southern farmers. He taught them to grow crops such as peanuts, pecans, and sweet potatoes instead of cotton.

Carver invented over 300 products made from peanuts. His inventions included peanut butter, peanut cheese, and peanut milk. Carver's discoveries helped farmers across the South.

REVIEW What was the purpose of the Tuskegee Institute?

Lesson Summary
- Many freed African Americans became sharecroppers.
- The Ku Klux Klan used violence to stop African Americans from voting.
- Reconstruction ended when government soldiers left the South in 1877.
- After Reconstruction, Jim Crow laws required segregation in many public places in the South.

Why It Matters ...

After Reconstruction, African Americans had to continue their struggle for freedom. They were no longer enslaved, but many became sharecroppers. For decades, Jim Crow laws prevented African Americans from exercising their rights.

George Washington Carver
He worked at the Tuskegee Institute for more than 40 years. He invented new products that could be made from common crops.

Lesson Review

1877 **Reconstruction ends**

1881 **Tuskegee Institute opens**

1877 — 1878 — 1879 — 1880 — 1881 — 1882

1. **VOCABULARY** Write a paragraph that describes life in the South after the Civil War, using **sharecropping** and **segregation.**

2. **READING SKILL** In what ways did sharecropping **solve** a **problem** for poor farmers? What new problem did it create?

3. **MAIN IDEA: Economics** Why was it difficult for many southerners to earn a living as farmers after the Civil War?

4. **MAIN IDEA: Government** What were Jim Crow laws?

5. **PEOPLE TO KNOW** Who was **Booker T. Washington,** and what did he do to improve African American education?

6. **TIMELINE SKILL** When did Reconstruction end?

7. **CRITICAL THINKING: Compare and Contrast** In what ways was sharecropping different from slavery? In what ways was it similar?

RESEARCH ACTIVITY Use library resources to learn more about George Washington Carver. Then make a web of some of his inventions. Include pictures of the ones we still use.

African American Education

The Freedmen's Bureau closed, but African Americans kept their schools open. After the Civil War, the Freedmen's Bureau gave money to set up schools and colleges for African Americans in the South. The head of the bureau said that they helped start 4,239 schools. More than 240,000 students attended these schools.

When the Freedmen's Bureau closed in 1872, African Americans raised money to keep their schools open. Their efforts increased the number of African American colleges to 34 by the year 1900. Many of these schools are still open today.

A Freedmen's Bureau School

Tuskegee One of the most famous Freedmen's Bureau schools was the Tuskegee Institute, shown above. It specialized in practical education. Students learned skills such as shoemaking, carpentry, and cabinetmaking.

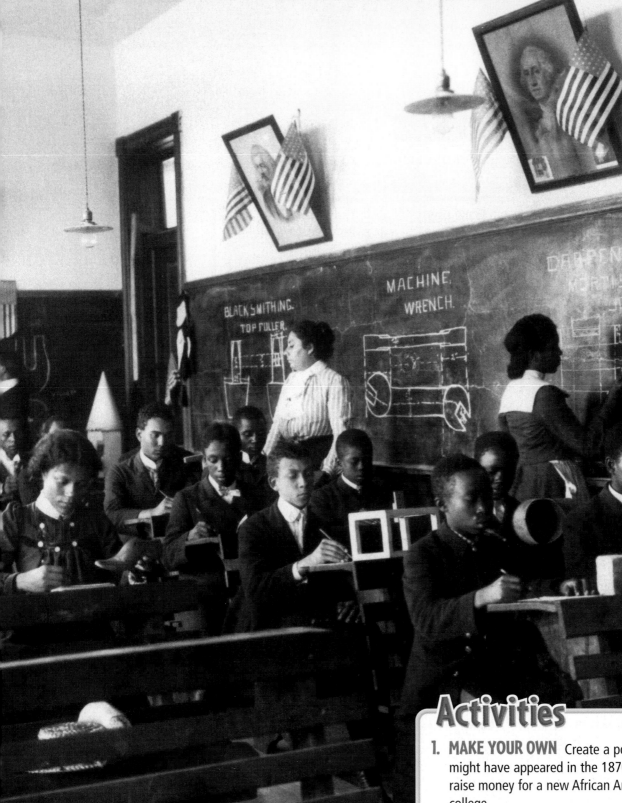

The Institute Grows
The Institute started in a small building with 30 students. By 1915, it had 100 buildings and 1500 students.

Activities

1. **MAKE YOUR OWN** Create a poster that might have appeared in the 1870s to raise money for a new African American college.

2. **WRITE ABOUT IT** What courses do you think would have been important for elementary school students to learn in the 1870s? Write a brief description of a typical school day.

Visual Summary

1–4.  Write a description of each item named below.

Emancipation Proclamation, 1863

_____
_____
_____
_____
_____

Jim Crow Laws

_____
_____
_____
_____
_____

Three New Amendments

_____
_____
_____
_____
_____

Tuskegee Institute

_____
_____
_____
_____
_____

Facts and Main Ideas

✔ **TEST PREP** Answer each question with information from the chapter.

5. **Citizenship** What were the effects of the Civil War on civilians in the South?

6. **Geography** Why did the Union army want to control the Mississippi River?

7. **History** Why did General Robert E. Lee decide to surrender?

8. **Economics** What were some advantages and disadvantages of sharecropping?

9. **Government** Why did Congress create the Freedmen's Bureau?

Vocabulary

✔ **TEST PREP** Choose the correct word to complete each sentence.

draft, p. 179
home front, p. 186
total war, p. 191
segregation, p. 208

10. People who are not in the military when a country is at war are part of the _____.

11. After the Civil War, some states passed laws making _____ legal.

12. Sherman used the strategy of destroying an enemy's resources known as _____.

13. Jefferson Davis started a _____ to get enough soldiers for his army.

CHAPTER SUMMARY TIMELINE

1863
Battle of Gettysburg

1865
Civil War ends

1877
Reconstruction ends

1881
Tuskegee Institute opens

1860   1865   1870   1875   1880   1885

Apply Skills

✔️ **TEST PREP** **Study Skill** Read the quotes about the final charge at Gettysburg to answer the question.

> We saw the enemy with colors [flags] flying…until this moment I had not gazed upon so grand a sight as was presented by that beautiful mass of grey.
>
> — Thomas Galwey, Union soldier

> About 13,000 troops advanced across an open field and up Cemetery Ridge in what has become known as "Pickett's Charge."…Only a few of the Southern troops reached the top of the ridge.
>
> — from the *World Book* encyclopedia article for the Battle of Gettysburg

14. What does the first source tell you that the second source does not?
    A. who led the charge
    B. when the charge took place
    C. how many soldiers were in the battle
    D. how the charge looked to the soldiers

15. How do you know that the *World Book* article is a secondary source?

Critical Thinking

✔️ **TEST PREP** Write a short paragraph to answer each question.

16. **Analyze** In what ways was life during the war harder in the South than it was in the North?

17. **Categorize** What two categories could you use to group the following?

    Abraham Lincoln, Robert E. Lee, Jefferson Davis, Ulysses S. Grant, William T. Sherman

Timeline

Use the Chapter Summary Timeline above to answer the question.

18. Did the Civil War end before or after the end of Reconstruction?

Activities

 Connect to Georgia Research the lives of former enslaved people in Georgia after the Civil War. Summarize ways their lives changed and ways their lives stayed the same.

 Writing Activity Write a short story about the first day for students at a Freedmen's School in the South. Include details about what life was like after the Civil War.

 Technology
Writing Process Tips
Get help with your story at
www.eduplace.com/kids/hmss/

213

Review and Test Prep

Vocabulary and Main Ideas

✓ **TEST PREP** Write a sentence to answer each question.

1. What issues increased **sectionalism** in the United States during the early 1800s?

2. Why was **popular sovereignty** an important issue as the United States grew?

3. Why did some people in the South argue for **secession**?

4. What did the **Emancipation Proclamation** say?

5. What did General Sherman's army do when it used **total war** against the South?

6. How did **segregation** and **Jim Crow** laws affect life for African Americans?

Critical Thinking

✓ **TEST PREP** Write a short paragraph to answer each question.

7. **Contrast** In what ways was life in the South after the Civil War different from life before the Civil War?

8. **Synthesize** Explain how the Thirteenth, Fourteenth, and Fifteenth Amendments changed the U.S. Constitution. Use details from the unit to support your answer.

Apply Skills

✓ **TEST PREP** **Study Skill** Use the two sources about John Brown's raid on Harpers Ferry below to answer each question.

...before me stood four men, three armed with Sharpe's rifles. ...I was then told that I was a prisoner.
— Colonel Washington, Harpers Ferry, 1859

The next appearance... was at the house of the Colonel Lewis Washington, a large farmer and slave-owner. ...A party [group] rousing Colonel Washington, told him he was their prisoner...
— R.M. DeWitt, New York, 1859

9. What piece of information tells you that Colonel Washington's account is a primary source?

   A. the description of the type of rifles

   B. the words "I was"

   C. the description of the number of men

   D. the date it was written

10. What does the secondary source tell you that the primary source does not?

    A. what time the event occurred

    B. where the event took place

    C. who Colonel Washington was

    D. why Colonel Washington was taken prisoner

Unit Activity

 GEORGIA

Make a Civil War Battle Map

- Research Civil War battles that took place in Georgia.

- Choose four battles.

- On an outline map of Georgia, label where and when the battles took place and include an important fact for each one.

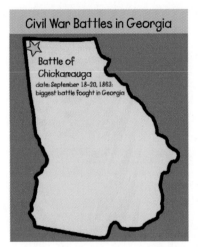

Civil War Battles in Georgia

Battle of Chickamauga
date: September 18–20, 1863;
biggest battle fought in Georgia

Personal Finance

In this unit, you read that tariffs are taxes that make imported goods more expensive. (p. 142)

When choosing between two items that are very similar, but one costs more, which item would most people choose? Would there ever be a reason why someone might choose the one that costs more? Explain.

For one week, record purchases made by you or family members. What is the cost of each item? What is the amount of tax? Review the list and explain what you observe about which items are taxed and by how much.

CURRENT EVENTS
WEEKLY (WR) READER
Connect to Today

Create a poster about the leaders of different countries today.

- Find information about the leader of another country.

- Write a short biography of this leader. Draw or find a picture of him or her.

- Display your poster in your classroom.

Technology

Weekly Reader online offers social studies articles. Go to: **www.eduplace.com/kids/hmss/**

Read About It

Look for these Social Studies Independent Books in your classroom.

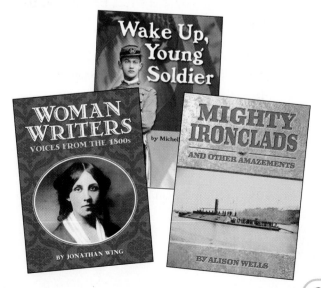

UNIT 4

Transforming the Nation

The Big Idea

How can people change the world they live in?

"If there is no struggle, there is no progress."

Frederick Douglass, 1857

Chief Joseph
1840?–1904

How far did this man walk in search of freedom? Chief Joseph led the Nez Pere a journey of more than 1,200 miles to escape being forced onto a reservation.

page 248

History Makers

Jane Addams
1860–1935

As a young women, Jane Addams wanted to change the lives of immigrants. She founded Hull House, a settlement house in Chicago that provided services to people in need.
page 275

W.E.B. Du Bois
1868–1963

This man led the fight for equal rights for African Americans. Almost 100 years ago, he started an organization that is still working for people's rights today.
page 281

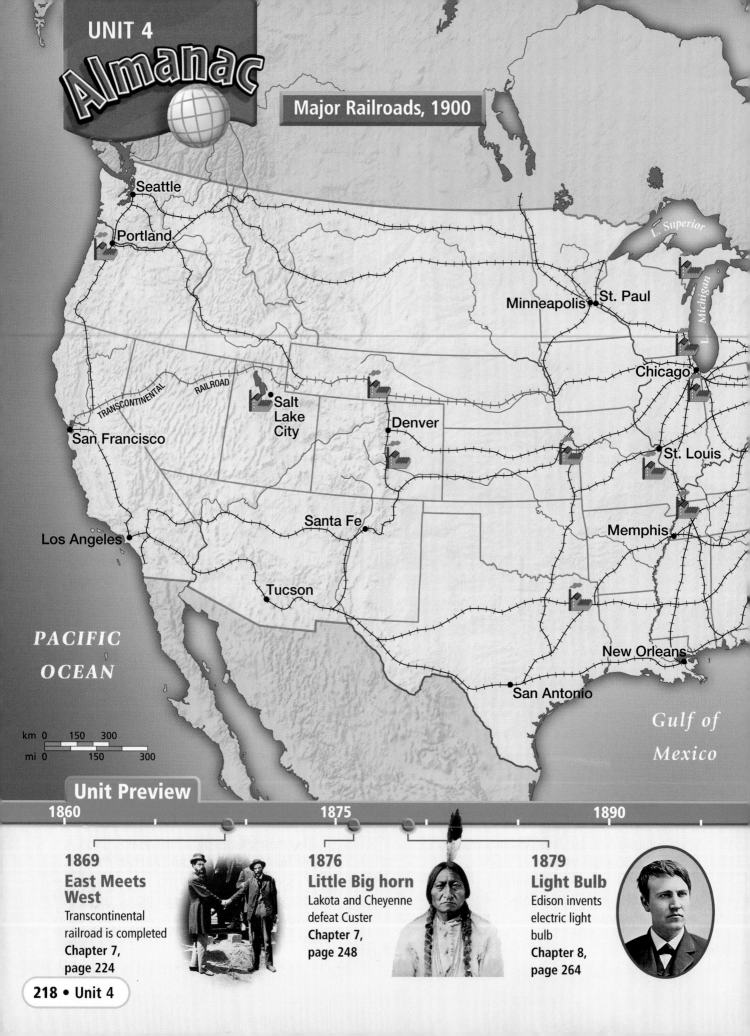

Major Railroads, 1900

Seattle

Portland

Minneapolis St. Paul

L. Superior

L. Michigan

Chicago

Salt Lake City

Denver

St. Louis

San Francisco

Santa Fe

Memphis

Los Angeles

Tucson

New Orleans

PACIFIC OCEAN

San Antonio

Gulf of Mexico

TRANSCONTINENTAL   RAILROAD

km 0   150   300
mi 0   150   300

Unit Preview

1860   1875   1890

1869
East Meets West
Transcontinental railroad is completed
Chapter 7, page 224

1876
Little Big horn
Lakota and Cheyenne defeat Custer
Chapter 7, page 248

1879
Light Bulb
Edison invents electric light bulb
Chapter 8, page 264

Map labels:
L. Huron
L. Ontario
L. Erie
Detroit
Cleveland
Buffalo
Pittsburgh
Cincinnati
Baltimore
Philadelphia
New York
Boston
Atlanta
Savannah

ATLANTIC OCEAN

Compass rose: N, NE, E, SE, S, SW, W, NW

LEGEND
┼┼┼ Major Railroad
┼┼┼ Transcontinental Railroad, completed 1869
🏭 Iron or steel mill

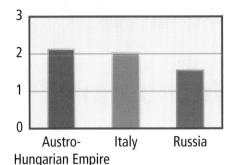

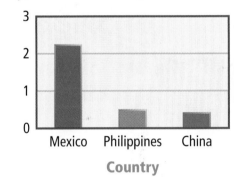

Connect to Today

Immigration, Early 1900s

Immigrants (in millions)

3
2
1
0

Austro-Hungarian Empire | Italy | Russia

Country

In the early 1900s, most immigrants came from eastern and southern Europe.

Immigration Today

Immigrants (in millions)

3
2
1
0

Mexico | Philippines | China

Country

Today, most immigrants come from Latin America and Asia.

Which bar graph shows more immigrants coming to the United States?

CONNECT to GEORGIA

Research important events that happened in Georgia from 1870 to 1920. Create a timeline showing five of these events.

Timeline: 1905 ———— 1920

1909 NAACP Founded
African Americans struggle for equality
Chapter 8, page 280

1920 19th Amendment
Women gain the right to vote
Chapter 8, page 280

Vocabulary Preview

Technology
e • **glossary**
e • **word games**
www.eduplace.com/kids/hmss/

transcontinental

In 1869, the first **transcontinental** railroad was completed. People could travel and send goods across the continent.
page 224

homestead

Settlers paid a small amount of money for a home and land on the Great Plains. After five years, they became the owners of their **homestead.** **page 231**

Chapter Timeline

| 1862 Homestead Act | 1869 Transcontinental Railroad | 1876 Battle of the Little Bighorn |

1860   1865   1870   1875

Reading Strategy

Monitor and Clarify Check your understanding with this strategy.

quick Tip Stop and check that you understand what you are reading. Reread, if you need to.

railhead

Ranchers brought the cattle they wanted to sell to towns called **railheads.** These towns were located at the beginning or end of railroad tracks. **page 239**

habitat

Buffalo once lived on the Great Plains in large numbers. The grasslands of the plains were their **habitat.**
page 249

1887
Dawes Act

1880   1885   1890

Linking East and West

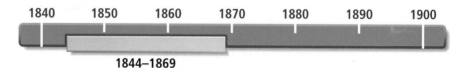

| 1840 | 1850 | 1860 | 1870 | 1880 | 1890 | 1900 |

1844–1869

VOCABULARY

transcontinental
prejudice

Vocabulary Strategy

| trans | continental |

The prefix **trans-** comes from a word that means across. A **transcontinental** railroad goes across a continent.

READING SKILL

Predict Outcome Think about who will use the transcontinental railroad when it is finished. Write your predictions and look for the outcome.

> PREDICTION

> OUTCOME

Build on What You Know Have you ever had to wait for news from friends or family? In the early 1800s, people often waited weeks to receive messages from far away.

The Telegraph Helps Communication

Main Idea The telegraph made it much faster to send messages over long distances.

In the early 1800s, letters and news traveled by horse, stagecoach, or steamboat. It could take days or weeks to send a message from one city to another. Newspaper stories might be weeks old by the time they were printed.

In 1844, **Samuel Morse** amazed people by sending a message from Washington, D.C., to Baltimore, Maryland, in seconds. Morse used a telegraph to send his message. A telegraph is a machine that sends electric signals over wire telegraph lines. Morse invented a code of dots and dashes to send such messages.

Samuel Morse Morse is shown here holding an early version of his telegraph. The chart shows Morse Code, which uses electric signals to stand for letters of the alphabet.

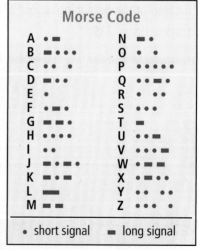

Morse Code			
A	• ▬	N	▬ •
B	▬ • • •	O	• • •
C	• • ▬ •	P	• • • • •
D	▬ • •	Q	• • ▬ •
E	•	R	• • •
F	• ▬ •	S	• • •
G	▬ ▬ •	T	▬
H	• • • •	U	• • ▬
I	• •	V	• • • ▬
J	• ▬ ▬ ▬	W	• ▬ ▬
K	▬ • ▬	X	• ▬ • •
L	▬ • • •	Y	• • • •
M	▬ ▬	Z	• • • •

• short signal   ▬ long signal

At that time, the telegraph was the quickest way to send a message over long distances. Many companies built telegraph lines throughout the country. By October 1861, over 20,000 miles of telegraph wires carried messages from the East Coast to the West Coast.

Few inventions had changed people's lives as greatly as the telegraph. People could tell each other about important events soon after they took place.

Reporters used the telegraph to send stories to their newspapers. Other people used it to send messages to family and friends. Bankers used it to get business information. During the Civil War, generals sent battle plans by telegraph.

A Transcontinental Railroad

Main Idea Transcontinental railroads made traveling and shipping easier and faster.

Remember that many pioneers were heading west by the 1840s. Some were searching for gold. Others were looking for new places to settle. To get to the West, many people sailed around South America. Others traveled as far as they could on railroads and then continued overland in wagons pulled by horses, mules, or oxen. When people go overland they travel on land. Either way, the trip was slow, unsafe, and expensive.

REVIEW How did people travel west in the 1840s?

Transcontinental Railroad This railroad linked California to places east of the Mississippi River.

SKILL **Reading Charts** About how many weeks longer did it take to travel from coast to coast by ship than by the first transcontinental railroad?

Transcontinental Travel, 1869

Method of Travel	Travel Time
Ship	Six months
Railroad and wagon	Five months
Transcontinental railroad	Eight days

Major U.S. Railroads, 1869

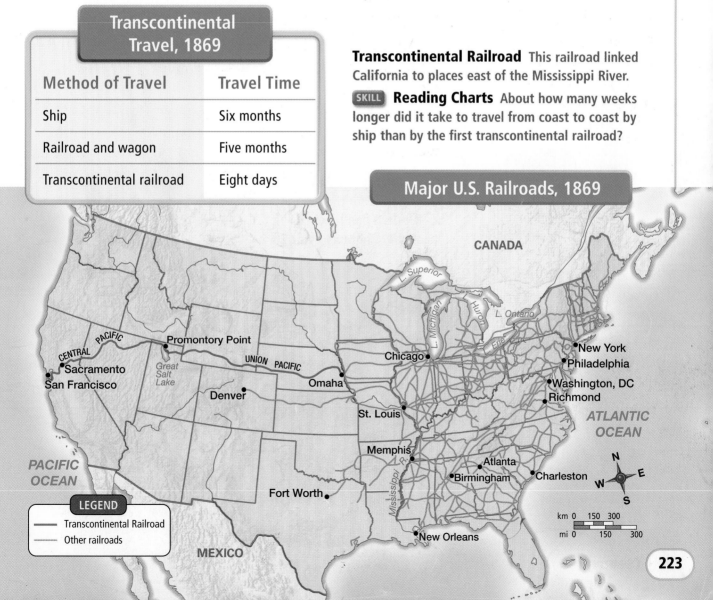

LEGEND
— Transcontinental Railroad
— Other railroads

km 0 150 300
mi 0 150 300

Two Railroad Companies

A group of entrepreneurs in California planned to earn money by building a transcontinental railroad. A **transcontinental** railroad is a railroad that crosses a continent. This railroad would make travel easier from California to the East. The group asked Congress to help by giving them money and land.

In 1862, Congress passed the Pacific Railway Act. This law said the government could loan money to the Union Pacific and the Central Pacific railroad companies. Congress told the Union Pacific to build a railroad from east to west, starting in Nebraska. The Central Pacific was to build a railroad from west to east, starting in California. Rails built by the two companies would meet to create a transcontinental railroad.

After the Civil War, the Union Pacific hired thousands of former soldiers and freed African Americans. Irish immigrants also moved west to work on the railroad.

The Central Pacific hired many Chinese workers. Thousands of Chinese had come to California to search for gold. The Chinese faced prejudice from other railroad workers. **Prejudice** is an unfair, negative opinion that can lead to unjust treatment. The Chinese were paid less than other workers. Sometimes they were given dangerous jobs such as using explosives to blast away rock.

On May 10, 1869, both tracks were joined at Promontory Point, Utah. Railroad officials tapped spikes of gold and silver into the last piece of track. Then two railroad locomotives, one traveling west, the other traveling east, slowly moved forward until they met.

Completing the Railroad
Locomotives for the Central Pacific (left) and Union Pacific meet at Promontory Point, Utah.

The Effects of the Railroads

Telegraph wires instantly carried the exciting news from Promontory Point throughout the United States. People around the country held parades and gave speeches to celebrate. The 1,800-mile transcontinental railroad was finally finished.

This railroad was the first of several transcontinental railroads that would be built in the United States. These railroads made it easier to move people and goods across the country.

Transcontinental railroads helped settlers in the West earn money by shipping their goods to markets. Trains carried cattle and wheat and other western crops to eastern cities. Western farmers and ranchers could sell their products for more money in the East, where there were more people and fewer farms.

In the East, businesses and factories used the railroads to ship clothing, tools, and other goods to western towns and mining camps.

REVIEW What kinds of goods were shipped on transcontinental railroads?

Lesson Summary

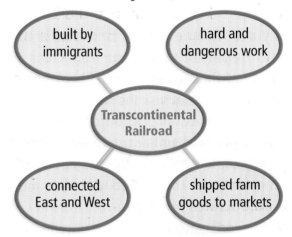

Why It Matters…

Improvements in communication and transportation helped unite the country and made the economy of the West grow.

Lesson Review

1844 Morse sends telegraph message

1862 Pacific Railway Act

May 10, 1869 Transcontinental Railroad

1840 — 1850 — 1860 — 1870 — 1880

❶ **VOCABULARY** Use the words **prejudice** and **transcontinental** in a paragraph about Chinese railroad workers.

❷ **READING SKILL** Review the predictions you made. Who used the new railroad?

❸ **MAIN IDEA: Technology** List three ways people used the telegraph in the 1800s.

❹ **MAIN IDEA: Economics** In what ways did the transcontinental railroad make it easier for settlers in the West to earn money?

❺ **PLACES TO KNOW** Where did the Central Pacific and Union Pacific meet to finish the first transcontinental railroad?

❻ **TIMELINE SKILL** How many years after Congress passed the Pacific Railway Act was the first transcontinental railroad finished?

❼ **CRITICAL THINKING: Decision Making** What were some short-term effects of the decision to build the transcontinental railroad? What were some long-term effects?

HANDS ON

MATH ACTIVITY If two people left the East on June 1, 1869, one traveling by ship and the other by transcontinental railroad, when would each arrive in California? Use the chart on page 499 to find the answer. Ask a partner two more math questions using information from this chart.

Railroad Workers

Why did people travel thousands of miles from their homelands? Some came from China, crossing the Pacific in the hope of finding gold to send back home. Others came from Ireland, driven across the Atlantic by famine.

Once they arrived, they faced prejudice and discrimination. Discrimination means unfair treatment. For these immigrants it meant they could not live in the neighborhoods where others lived. It meant they could not buy land, or mine gold, or work in certain jobs. Men from China and Ireland did hard and dangerous work, such as building the railroads that would someday link every corner of the United States.

As Irish workers built the Union Pacific Railroad, they sang this song. "Tay" means tea, and the U.P. railway is the Union Pacific.

Drill, my heroes, drill
Drill all day, no sugar in your tay
Workin' on the U.P. railway.

Transcontinental
railroad workers

By 1867, 90 percent of the workers on the Central Pacific Railroad were Chinese immigrants. The company paid thousands of Chinese workers much less than they paid other workers. When the Chinese refused to work unless they were treated fairly, the company cut off food to their camp. After the railroads were built, many Chinese worked in factories in San Francisco. They still faced unfair treatment.

Activities

1. **TALK ABOUT IT** What planning might it take to build the track shown in this picture?

2. **CHART IT** Find out what kinds of work Chinese immigrants did after the railroads were built. Show your findings on a chart.

227

Skillbuilder

Read a Time Zone Map

▶ **VOCABULARY**

time zone
International
Date Line

Before railroads became widespread, every town decided on its own time. When trains made fast, long-distance travel possible, people needed a way to handle time differences. A system of 24 time zones was set up around the globe. A **time zone** is a region that shares the same time. By understanding time zones on a map, you can figure out the day and time in any part of the world.

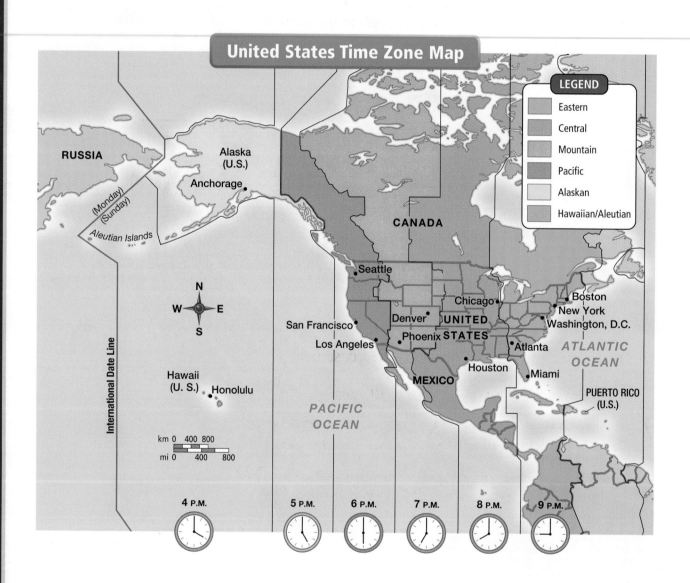

United States Time Zone Map

LEGEND
- Eastern
- Central
- Mountain
- Pacific
- Alaskan
- Hawaiian/Aleutian

Learn the Skill

Step 1: Find the time zones on the map. The legend tells you the name of each one.

LEGEND

☐ Eastern
☐ Central
☐ Mountain
☐ Pacific
☐ Alaskan
☐ Hawaiian/Aleutian

Step 2: Note the time difference for each zone. For example, when you move one time zone to the west, the time is one hour earlier.

7 P.M.   8 P.M.

Step 3: Find the **International Date Line.** It is an imaginary line that marks where the date changes. For example, if it is noon on Friday in the time zone on the west side of the Line, it is noon on Thursday in the time zone on the east side of the Line.

International Date Line

Practice the Skill

Use the time zone map to answer these questions.

1. In what time zone is Chicago, Illinois?

2. If it is 3 P.M. in Houston, Texas, what time is it in San Francisco, California, and in Atlanta, Georgia?

3. If it is Tuesday and you cross the International Date Line traveling east, what day does it become?

Apply the Skill

Suppose you live in San Francisco, California, and your cousin lives in Boston, Massachusetts. By what time would you need to call your cousin if she goes to bed at 9 P.M.?

Life on the Great Plains

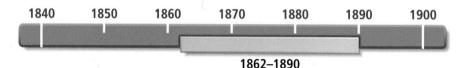

1840   1850   1860   1870   1880   1890   1900

1862–1890

Build on What You Know Have you ever seen people rush to buy something because the price has been lowered? During the late 1800s, settlers rushed to the Great Plains because land was inexpensive.

Settling the Great Plains

Main Idea During the late 1800s, large numbers of settlers moved onto the Great Plains and started farming.

The Great Plains are in the middle of the United States. They stretch from Texas to Canada and from east of the Rocky Mountains to the Mississippi River. This vast area is mostly flat and covered by grasses. It has few trees and gets less than 20 inches a year of rain. At first, most settlers moving west passed through the Great Plains without stopping. They thought the dry land would be bad for farming and that they would have trouble building homes or fences because wood was hard to find.

Land for Sale This railroad company pamphlet was used to sell millions of acres of land.

SKILL **Primary Source**
Read the advertisement. Where is the land located?

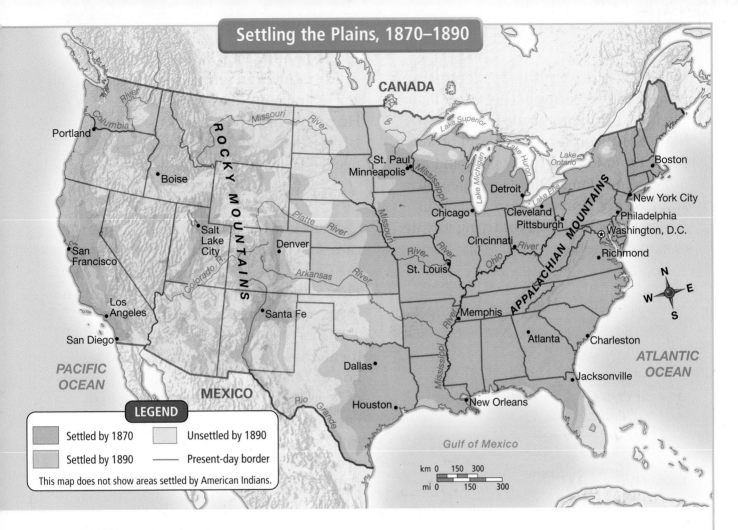

Settling the Plains, 1870–1890

CANADA

Portland

Columbia River

Boise

R O C K Y   M O U N T A I N S

Missouri River

St. Paul
Minneapolis

Mississippi

Lake Superior

Detroit

Chicago

Lake Michigan

Lake Huron

Lake Erie

Cleveland
Pittsburgh

Lake Ontario

APPALACHIAN MOUNTAINS

Boston

New York City

Philadelphia

Washington, D.C.

Salt Lake City

Denver

Platte River

Cincinnati

Ohio River

Richmond

San Francisco

Colorado R.

Arkansas River

St. Louis

Los Angeles

Santa Fe

Memphis

Atlanta

Charleston

San Diego

Dallas

Mississippi River

PACIFIC OCEAN

MEXICO

Rio Grande

Houston

New Orleans

Jacksonville

ATLANTIC OCEAN

Gulf of Mexico

N W E S

LEGEND

Settled by 1870

Unsettled by 1890

Settled by 1890

Present-day border

This map does not show areas settled by American Indians.

km 0 150 300
mi 0 150 300

Moving West Large areas of the United States were still unsettled after 1870. **SKILL** **Reading Maps** By what year was most of the land east of the Mississippi river settled?

The Homestead Act

In 1862, Congress passed a law called the Homestead Act. A **homestead** is a settler's home and land. The Homestead Act offered 160 acres of land to adults who were U.S. citizens or wanted to become citizens. To claim land, settlers had to pay a small amount of money and farm the land for five years. After that, it was theirs.

The Homestead Act is an example of a price incentive. When prices affect the decisions people make, they are called incentives. By offering land at a low price, Congress encouraged more people to settle the Great Plains.

Many settlers came from the eastern United States where good farmland was expensive. Homesteaders also came from Europe, where most farms were much smaller than farms on the Great Plains.

European settlers came to the Great Plains from Germany, Sweden, Norway, Denmark, and the Netherlands. For a time, some parts of the Great Plains had more European-born people than people born in the United States. Between 1860 and 1890, the population of Nebraska alone had increased by over a million.

REVIEW Why did settlers from Europe and the East move to the Great Plains?

231

The Exodusters

African Americans in the South also wanted to start farms on the Great Plains. After Reconstruction ended in the 1870s, life was difficult for African Americans in the South. Most were very poor and did not own any land. They faced prejudice and violence. Some African Americans were attacked or killed for trying to vote or start businesses.

Benjamin "Pap" Singleton was an African American who visited Kansas in 1873. Singleton liked Kansas very much. He printed advertisements for Kansas land. He said that African Americans needed to leave the South because

66 starvation is staring us in the face. 99

Tens of thousands of African Americans moved to Kansas and other parts of the Great Plains between 1877 and 1879. They started towns where they made their own laws and felt safe from injustice.

These African American settlers called themselves **Exodusters,** after *Exodus*, a book of the Bible. *Exodus* tells the story of how the people of ancient Israel left Egypt to escape slavery. Many African Americans felt that they were like the people of Israel. They, too, were trying to find a place to be free.

New Settlers The Speese family was among the thousands of Exodusters who settled on the Great Plains. This photo was taken in Nebraska in 1888.

Settlers Face Hardships

Main Idea Settlers had to learn new ways of farming on the Great Plains.

Settlers had different reasons for moving to the Great Plains, but once there, they all shared the same hardships. The area's harsh climate made life difficult.

Winters were long and bitterly cold. Temperatures could sink as low as 40 degrees below zero. Blizzards of snow and wind could last for days. Spring often brought violent thunderstorms, heavy rains, floods, tornados, and hailstones as big as baseballs.

Summers were hot and dry and droughts were common. A **drought** is a long period with little or no rain. This extreme dry weather could destroy crops for many years in a row because plants did not get the water they needed.

During dry weather, farmers had to watch out for prairie fires. Flames from campfires or lightning strikes could quickly spread across miles of prairie grasslands. Settlers even had to worry about grasshoppers. Millions of the insects appeared on the Great Plains in the 1870s. They ate crops, clothing, and even the wood handles of farm tools.

Some homesteaders thought that life on the Great Plains was too difficult and moved away. One Kansas settler said that he did not want to stay in a land

❝ **where it rains grasshoppers, fire, and destruction.** ❞

Other settlers stayed and adapted to the Great Plains. They found ways to adjust to the environment.

REVIEW Why was life on the Great Plains so difficult?

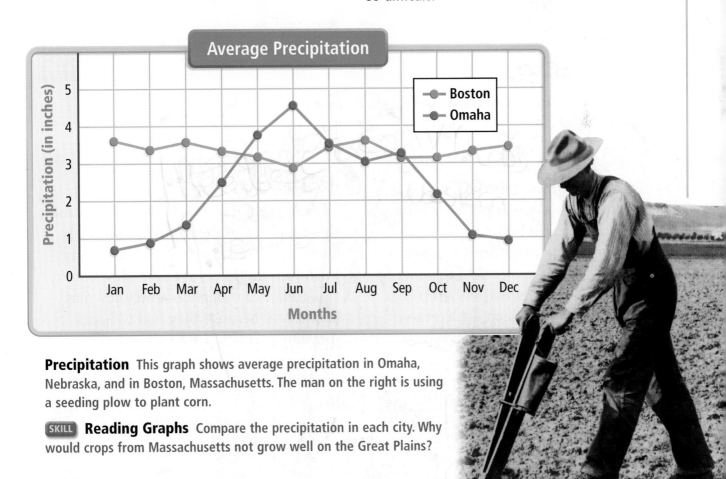

Precipitation This graph shows average precipitation in Omaha, Nebraska, and in Boston, Massachusetts. The man on the right is using a seeding plow to plant corn.

SKILL **Reading Graphs** Compare the precipitation in each city. Why would crops from Massachusetts not grow well on the Great Plains?

Homesteaders Settlers used natural resources and new machines to adapt to the Great Plains.

Settlers Adapt to the Great Plains

The first problem settlers faced was how to build a house. Wood was very scarce on the Great Plains, so most settlers made their first homes out of sod. Sod is grass-covered dirt held together by a thick mass of roots. Settlers cut pieces of sod from the prairie and used them like bricks. Sod kept the settlers' homes cool in summer and warm in winter. Unfortunately, sod also leaked during rainstorms. Sometimes snakes and other small animals dug through the sod walls.

Sod was much harder to plow than the soil of the eastern United States or Europe. Farmers had to slice through the thick sod before they could plant seeds. They used iron or steel plows to slowly push into the ground. Some plows broke. Great Plains farmers became known as **sodbusters** because they had to break through so much thick soil.

Life in a sod house could get lonely. If a sodbuster family needed help from a neighbor, or just wanted some company, they might have to travel for miles.

Growing Crops

Another challenge sodbusters faced was finding crops that would grow in such a dry climate. The wheat that grew in the eastern United States grew poorly on the Great Plains. Farmers tried seeds brought to the United States by European settlers. These seeds came from the dry grasslands of Eastern Europe. The wheat grown with these seeds was even better than wheat grown in the East.

Because there was little rainfall, farmers carried water from streams or springs. Settlers who lived far from streams dug deep wells and pumped water by hand. Both ways of getting water were difficult and took a lot of time. Settlers who could afford windmills attached them to the pumps in their wells. Wind power operated the water pumps and made getting water easier.

Farmers could not hire extra workers because few people lived on the Great Plains. Nearly all the early settlers were part of homesteading families.

New and improved farming machines replaced extra workers. Machines such as plows, planters, reapers, and threshers made it faster and easier to grow crops.

In 1840, it took 35 hours of work to produce an acre of wheat. In 1880, after better farm machines had been invented, producing an acre of wheat took only 20 hours. These machines made farmers more productive. They could farm more land and grow more wheat.

REVIEW How did settlers adapt to the lack of extra workers on the Great Plains?

Lesson Summary

Large numbers of farmers settled the Great Plains in the late 1800s. Most came from Europe and the eastern and southern United States. The climate of the Great Plains was harsh, but many settlers adapted.

Why It Matters ...

Farmers turned the Great Plains into vast fields of wheat.

Lesson Review

1 **VOCABULARY** Write a paragraph about the Great Plains using **homestead, drought,** and **sodbuster.**

2 **READING SKILL** How did settlers solve the **problem** of getting water for their crops? Describe their **solutions.**

3 **MAIN IDEA: Geography** Describe the climate of the Great Plains.

4 **MAIN IDEA: History** In what ways did settlers adapt to the Great Plains?

5 **PEOPLE TO KNOW** Who were the **Exodusters,** and why did they move to Kansas?

6 **CRITICAL THINKING: Draw Conclusions** Do you think Congress wanted people to settle on the Great Plains? Why or why not?

7 **CRITICAL THINKING: Generalize** Settlers had to adapt to life on the Great Plains. Why is learning to adapt to new and difficult situations an important skill?

WRITING ACTIVITY Many settlers on the Great Plains wrote to relatives in other parts of the United States and Europe. Write a description that a settler might have sent to a relative about life on the Great Plains.

Sod Houses

Without trees or stones, what did homesteaders use to build their houses? One resource they used was the prairie soil, or sod, around them. They cut sod into blocks and stacked them like bricks. Houses were small, sometimes one room with a hanging quilt to divide it.

Settlers might live in their "soddy" for six or seven years. When they had enough money to buy lumber, they built a wooden house. Then the old soddy became a home for farm animals.

Walls
Thick sod walls, two rows thick, kept soddies cool in summer and warm in winter. Prairie grass and roots helped hold the sod together. Sometimes bugs fell into the house.

Roof

Builders put woven sticks under hay or grass. On top of that was a layer of sod. The roof couldn't be as thick as the walls; it would be too heavy. So when the rains came, it leaked.

Activities

1. **EXPLORE IT** Talk about what it would be like to live in a one-room sod house like the one shown here.

2. **WRITE ABOUT IT** Research climate in the Great Plains. Write two diary entries describing what it would be like to live in a sod house during two different seasons.

237

Cattle Ranchers

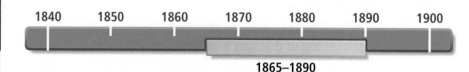

1840   1850   1860   1870   1880   1890   1900

1865–1890

VOCABULARY

demand
supply
railhead
barbed wire

Vocabulary Strategy

barbed wire

A **barb** is a sharp point.
Barbed wire is wire with
sharp points attached to it.

READING SKILL

Cause and Effect Note the
reasons why cattle drives
began and ended.

CAUSE	EFFECT

Build on What You Know You may have seen exciting
movies or paintings about cowhands. A cowhand's work,
however, was mostly hard, dirty, and boring.

Texas Cattle

Main Idea In the 1800s, ranchers in Texas raised and sold
longhorn cattle.

In the 1860s, millions of wild longhorn cattle lived
on the Texas plains. Longhorns were tough, strong
animals that were first brought to North America by
Spanish settlers. The cattle could live far from water and
shelter, eating nothing but grass.

Remember that Texas had been part of Mexico, which
was once ruled by Spain. After Texas became part of the
United States in 1845, Mexicans in Texas became U.S.
citizens. Many Mexican Americans faced prejudice from
other Americans. Some had their lands taken away. But
vaqueros (vah KEH rohs), or Mexican cowhands, were
respected for their skill at herding cattle. Vaqueros taught
their methods of herding on horseback to other
cowhands and ranchers in the Southwest.

Vaqueros at Work This painting
shows vaqueros leading a herd of
cattle. These cowhands often took
care of thousands of cattle.

STANDARDS

SS5H3a Role of cattle trails
SS5G1b Locate Chisholm Trail
SS5E3a Markets, prices influence behavior

Demand and Supply The point on this graph where the demand and supply lines meet shows where the amount of cattle that sellers are willing to supply equals the amount that buyers demand. This point is what the price would be.

SKILL **Reading Graphs**
What would be the price of cattle if the supply were at 30,000?

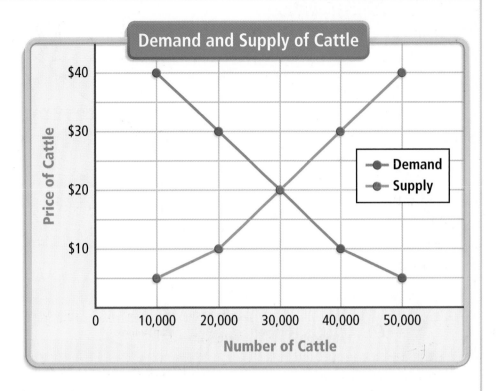

Demand and Supply of Cattle

Price of Cattle / *Number of Cattle*

— Demand
— Supply

Demand and Supply for Cattle

Texas had many cattle, but it was not a good cattle market. A market is a situation in which people buy and sell goods. In a market, producers find buyers for their goods, and consumers find goods to buy.

In Texas, cattle sold for only about $4 each. In the eastern and northern United States, people wanted cattle products such as beef and leather. In those regions, cattle sold for about $40 each.

The price of cattle was partly set by demand and supply. **Demand** is the amount of something that people want to buy at certain prices. When the price of something is low, people usually buy more of it. **Supply** is the amount of something that people want to sell at certain prices. When the price of something is high, people want to produce and sell more of it.

The Cattle Drives

Main Idea Cowhands led cattle to railroads, where the cattle were shipped to eastern and northern cities.

Demand and supply affected the price of cattle. Texas ranchers wanted to sell their cattle where they could get the highest prices. They shipped their cattle to eastern and northern cities. To get to these cities, the cattle first had to be led to railheads. A **railhead** is a town where railroad tracks begin or end. At the railheads, cattle were loaded onto trains.

Railheads were often hundreds of miles away from the cattle ranches. Beginning in the 1860s, cowhands led cattle to the railheads. These cattle drives took weeks or months to complete. Cattle drives followed trails where water and grass were available.

REVIEW Why did Texas cattle ranchers want to sell their animals in the East and North?

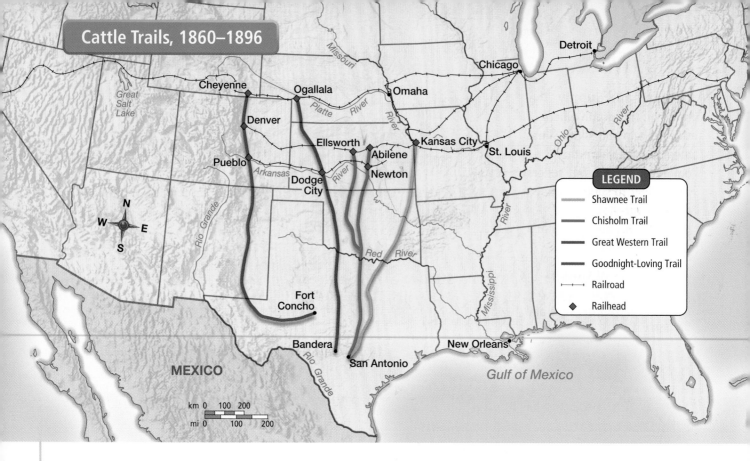

Cattle Trails, 1860–1896

LEGEND
- Shawnee Trail
- Chisholm Trail
- Great Western Trail
- Goodnight-Loving Trail
- Railroad
- Railhead

Cattle Trails Five major cattle trails led from Texas to Great Plains railheads.
SKILL **Reading Maps** Which major rivers did the cattle trails cross?

Life on the Drives

Life on the cattle drives was hard. The work was sometimes dangerous, often boring, and always dirty. A dozen cowhands had to care for about 3,000 longhorns. Cowhands spent 10 to 14 hours a day on horseback. They rode slowly next to the herd to keep the cattle together. Usually nothing much happened. When cattle were startled by lightning or sudden noises, however, they might stampede, or run away. A cattle stampede was dangerous. Riders had to race after the cattle to round them up again. Lost cattle meant lost money.

Nat Love This cowhand wrote a book about his adventures on the trail.

Many cowhands were African Americans or Mexicans. Nat Love, an African American, wrote about a stampede at night. He asked readers to imagine

❝ chasing an immense [big] herd of maddened [upset] cattle which we could hear but could not see . . . It was the worst night's ride I ever experienced. ❞

Cowhands slept on the ground, wrapped in blankets. At night, they took turns guarding the herd from animals and thieves. By the end of a cattle drive, the cowhands were exhausted. They were happy to reach the railheads where their journey ended.

The End of the Drives

The cattle drives lasted for only about 20 years, from the late 1860s to the late 1880s. They ended for several reasons.

The first reason was the invention of barbed wire. **Barbed wire** is twisted wire with a sharp barb, or point, every few inches. Barbed wire fences, put up by new settlers, blocked the cattle trails that crossed the Great Plains.

The next reason was the growth of railroads. After railroads were built in Texas in the 1870s, ranchers used nearby railheads to ship cattle to eastern cities. They no longer had to drive their cattle hundreds of miles to reach a railhead.

Another reason was that by the mid-1880s, too many cattle grazed on crowded ranges. There was not enough grass to feed all the cattle. Sheepranchers also wanted this scarce land for their flocks.

Finally, during the terrible winter of 1886–1887, freezing cold temperatures killed thousands of cattle. Cattle were still very important in Texas, but by the 1890s, the days of the long cattle drives were over.

REVIEW What led to the end of the big cattle drives?

Lesson Summary

- Cattle ranchers sent their herds on long cattle drives to railheads so that the cattle could be shipped to the East and North.
- The price of cattle was affected by demand and supply.
- By the 1890s, big cattle drives had mostly ended.

Why It Matters...

Cattle drives lasted for only about 20 years, a short time in U.S. history. Yet people still think of cattle drives when they think of the West.

Lesson Review

1 VOCABULARY Choose the correct word to complete each sentence.

  demand   supply

The price of milk was so low that the _____ fell.
The _____ for cheap land was high.

2 READING SKILL What effect did railroads have on the beginning and ending of cattle drives?

3 MAIN IDEA: Geography Why did the cattle business develop in Texas?

4 MAIN IDEA: Economics Use demand and supply to explain why Texas ranchers sent their longhorns on cattle drives.

5 CRITICAL THINKING: Summarize What was the life of a cowhand like?

6 CRITICAL THINKING: Infer When the supply of a product is large, people often have to sell it for a low price. What would probably happen to that product's price if the supply decreased?

HANDS ON

MUSIC ACTIVITY Cowhands sang songs about life on the cattle drives. Using library resources, find a cowhand song. Act out the song and describe what it is about.

IN THE DAYS OF THE
VAQUEROS
by Russell Freedman

Mexican vaqueros are known as the first cowhands of America. They rode across the open range looking for stray cattle. Their work was often hard. Sometimes they went without food, and they often slept on the ground. The vaqueros developed a style of dress that fit their rugged way of life.

In the early days, the vaquero wore any clothes he happened to own, but as the years passed, he developed a distinct and practical way of dressing. While his clothing varied from one region to the next, according to the terrain he rode, and changed appearance over the years, it always singled him out as a working cowhand.

To shield his head and eyes from the Mexican sun, he wore a sombrero, from the word *sombrear,* "to shade"—a wide-brimmed hat made of straw, leather, or felt. Held in place with a *barbiquejo,* a chin strap, it often was decorated with a colorful band. A sombrero might have a low flat crown with a straight stiff brim, or a tall crown, several inches high, with a soft floppy brim. Whatever its shape, it was always impressively large, with a brim wide enough to shade the wearer's face.

Because of its practicality, the big wide-brimmed hat became a familiar cowboy trademark.

Under his sombrero, the vaquero wore a kerchief tied over his head. His hair was parted in the middle and brushed back into a long braid that might hang down his back, or be folded up and tucked under his hat.

A vaquero usually carried a brightly colored sarape, or poncho, which was thrown over his shoulder like a shawl or carried on the back of his saddle. A sarape offered protection when it rained and warmth when it was cold. It served as a bed at night when the vaquero slept under the stars. Waved wildly in the air, it was used to haze cattle during roundups and stampedes.

When the gold rush ended, cattle raising in California began a slow decline as ranches gradually gave way to farms. But on the sparsely settled Texas prairie, cattle were multiplying faster than anyone could count. These animals had descended from herds left behind by missionaries who had gone back to Spain, and from herds abandoned by Mexican ranch owners who had fled across the Rio Grande when Texas broke away from Mexico, leaving both their cattle and their vaqueros behind.

Texas cattle were not at all like the tame and docile animals that Anglo settlers in Texas were accustomed to raising back East. These cattle were as wild as buffalo and antelope, and now millions of them were wandering around loose. They clustered together in bunches, hiding in thickets by day and running by night. They could go days without water. Their sense of smell was keener than a deer's. And they had long, sharp, dangerous horns.

If a man tried to approach on foot, a bull would paw the earth, toss his head in anger, lower his horns, and charge. The animals could be approached only on horseback. And even then, bulls often tried to attack both man and horse.

American settlers considered the wild cattle they found in Texas fair game, free for the taking. Yet they had little idea how to manage large numbers of fierce, far-ranging longhorns. Most of the early Texas settlers were farmers who raised a few cattle on the side. They had never practiced large-scale ranching, as the Spaniards and Mexicans had on their ranchos and haciendas.

A Mexican vaquero, photographed around 1900 in Berino, New Mexico

Handling wild cattle on the open range was new to the Americans but old to the Mexican vaqueros. And so the Americans turned to the vaqueros for help. "They are universally acknowledged to be the best hands that can be [found] for the management of cattle, horses, and other livestock," a Texas settler reported.

Mexican vaqueros still living in Texas began to capture mustangs for the newcomers and round up wild steers. As the Americans watched the vaqueros work, they too became skilled at taming mustangs and roping steers. In this way, the North American cowboy learned his trade from the Mexican vaquero.

Activities

1. **TALK ABOUT IT** Look closely at the painting on page 243. What skills does the vaquero need to catch the horse? What tools does he need?

2. **PRESENT IT** Prepare an oral report or multimedia presentation on the vaqueros. Include what the settlers learned from them.

Conflicts on the Plains

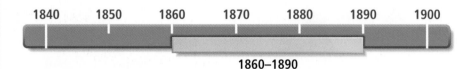

1840   1850   1860   1870   1880   1890   1900

1860–1890

VOCABULARY

reservation
habitat
extinct
assimilate

Vocabulary Strategy

assimilate

To **assimilate** a group is to make it fit in or be similar. Think of "similar" when you read the word assimilate.

READING SKILL

Sequence As you read, list the main events in order. Think about the connection between the events.

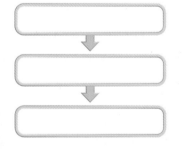

STANDARDS

SS5H3 America at turn of century

Build on What You Know You have learned that there were many conflicts as settlers moved onto American Indian lands in the eastern United States. The same thing happened years later as settlers moved onto the Great Plains.

War on the Plains

Main Idea American Indians and soldiers fought on the Great Plains during the late 1800s.

Beginning in the 1840s, more and more settlers moved west in search of land or gold. They built towns and dug mines. They divided land where American Indians already lived into farms and ranches.

The U.S. government built roads and railroads to help these settlers. Officials tried to convince Plains Indians to sell land and move to reservations. A **reservation** is land that the government set aside for American Indians. Congress promised that reservations would remain Indian land.

Plains Indians did not want to live on reservations. They felt the reservations were too small. Some reservations were far from the lands American Indians hunted on and called home.

Plains Buffalo Indians used the meat, skin, bones, and other parts of bison, or buffalo, to provide most of what they needed.

Sand Creek This painting shows the Colorado militia attacking a Cheyenne village near Sand Creek. **SKILL** **Reading Visuals** What details does the artist show about this battle?

Government officials hoped that Plains Indians would move to reservations and become farmers. People of Indian nations such as the Lakota and Arapaho did not want to farm. They were nomads, which means they moved from place to place to find food and water. They rode horses over miles of open prairie to hunt bison. Bison, also known as buffalo, provided Plains Indians with most of what they needed, such as food and clothing. Without large areas of land, Plains Indians would not be able to find the resources they needed to live.

Plains Indians fought soldiers who tried to force them onto reservations. Sometimes they attacked settlers and miners to make them leave Indian territory. Most of this fighting on the Great Plains happened in the 1860s and 1870s.

Sand Creek

In 1864, volunteer fighters of the Colorado militia attacked a Cheyenne village near Sand Creek, Colorado. The Cheyenne were asleep when the attack began. **Chief Black Kettle** raised a white flag and an American flag to surrender. The soldiers ignored him and killed almost half of the men, women, and children in the village.

After the Sand Creek Massacre, many Plains Indians thought that peace with the U.S. government was impossible.

Fighting among Indians, soldiers, and settlers increased after Sand Creek. By the 1870s, however, most Indian nations had been forced onto reservations. Only a few nations, including the Lakota and the Cheyenne, were still fighting for their land and traditions.

REVIEW Why did Plains Indians need large areas of land?

Battle of the Little Bighorn

The Black Hills of South Dakota and Wyoming are sacred, or holy, to the Lakota. In the early 1870s, a lieutenant colonel named **George Custer** led soldiers to the Black Hills and found gold. Thousands of Lakota and Cheyenne gathered to protect the Black Hills.

In June 1876, Custer and his soldiers tried to force the Lakota and Cheyenne onto a reservation. The soldiers attacked them at their village on the Little Bighorn River in Montana. Led by **Crazy Horse, Gall,** and **Sitting Bull,** the Lakota and Cheyenne won what became known as the Battle of the Little Bighorn. All of the U.S. soldiers were killed.

Little Bighorn was one example of how American Indians fought efforts to move them to reservations. The Nez Perce of Oregon resisted being moved to Idaho.

Chief Joseph was among those who tried to lead the Nez Perce to Canada. The Nez Perce fought several battles with the soldiers before they surrendered, 30 miles from the Canadian border in 1877.

Within a few years, almost all Plains Indian nations were on reservations.

Wounded Knee

In the late 1880s, Plains Indians hoped for some way to improve their lives. Many of them began to follow a religion called the Ghost Dance. This religion taught that the buffalo would return and dead Indians would come back to life. As more and more Plains Indians turned to the Ghost Dance, government officials worried that the Ghost Dancers would start another war.

Chief Joseph (right) Government soldiers chased Chief Joseph and the Nez Perce for 1600 miles, through Idaho, Wyoming, and Montana. The photograph below shows a Plains Indian village in the late 1800s.

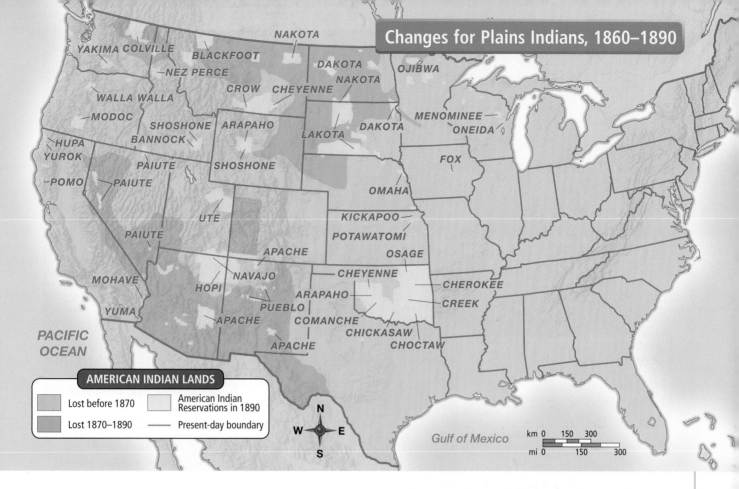

AMERICAN INDIAN LANDS

Lost before 1870

American Indian Reservations in 1890

Lost 1870–1890

Present-day boundary

PACIFIC OCEAN

Gulf of Mexico

km 0   150   300
mi 0   150   300

N W E S

Indian Lands By 1870, American Indians had already lost most of their lands to the U.S. government. **SKILL** **Reading Maps** What color is used on this map to show reservation lands in 1890?

When Sitting Bull became a Ghost Dancer, government officials sent police to arrest him. During the struggle, Sitting Bull was killed.

Sitting Bull's death frightened the Ghost Dancers. They were afraid that they would be killed as well. Led by **Chief Big Foot,** many Ghost Dancers went to hide in the Badlands of South Dakota.

U.S. soldiers captured Big Foot and his followers near Wounded Knee Creek. On the morning of December 29, 1890, the soldiers tried to take the Indians' guns. In the fighting that followed, the soldiers killed women and children, as well as men. This event became known as the Massacre at Wounded Knee.

Destruction of the Buffalo

Reservations changed Indian life. So did the destruction of the buffalo. At one time, millions of buffalo lived on the Great Plains. As more people crossed the Great Plains, wagon trails and railroad tracks cut across buffalo habitat. A **habitat** is the area where an animal or plant normally lives or grows.

The settlers killed buffalo for meat. Their cattle carried diseases that were deadly to the buffalo. Hunters shot buffalo for sport or for the skins, which were made into coats or leather products.

As more and more settlers moved onto the Great Plains, buffalo herds kept shrinking. Soon the buffalo were nearly extinct. When a certain type of plant or animal becomes **extinct** it no longer exists. By 1889, only about 1,000 buffalo were left.

REVIEW Why did the buffalo herds shrink?

Indian Schools The children above were students at an Indian school in Pennsylvania around 1900.

Before and After At Indian schools, students had to cut their hair and could not wear their traditional clothing. These photos show the same three Navajo children before and after they entered an Indian school.

Government Policy

Main Idea Government officials tried to force American Indians to change their way of life.

Even though Plains Indians were on reservations, government officials were afraid of more fighting. They hoped Indians would be less likely to fight if they gave up their old ways. Reformers and lawmakers tried to make American Indians assimilate into American life. **Assimilate** means changing a group's culture and traditions so that it blends with a larger group.

One way the government tried to force American Indians to change was to make religious practices such as the Ghost Dance illegal. Another way was to send children to schools where they were not allowed to speak American Indian languages or wear traditional clothing.

In 1887, Congress passed the Dawes Act to make American Indians become farmers. This law took reservation land away from Indian nations and split it into smaller pieces. Some of this land was given to individual American Indians to farm. The rest was sold to settlers.

People of a few Indian nations knew how to farm, but most did not. Farming was not a part of their culture. Even American Indians who knew how to farm had little success with the poor farmland on reservations. The only way many American Indians could survive was to accept food from the federal government.

Assimilation did not work well. Most Plains Indians were unhappy on reservations. Crazy Horse said,

> 66 **We preferred hunting to a life of idleness [laziness] on the reservation, where we were driven against our will. . . . . All we wanted was peace and to be left alone.** 99

REVIEW What did the Dawes Act do to reservation land?

Lesson Summary

- The federal government gave settlers the lands promised to Plains Indians.

- American Indians fought with U.S. soldiers, but they were defeated and forced onto reservations.

- Plains Indians depended on the buffalo for food, but settlement of the Great Plains destroyed buffalo herds.

- Government officials made laws to force American Indians to change their way of life.

Why It Matters ...

Decisions made by the U.S. government in the late 1800s changed American Indian cultures. Today, however, on many reservations, American Indians work to preserve their traditions.

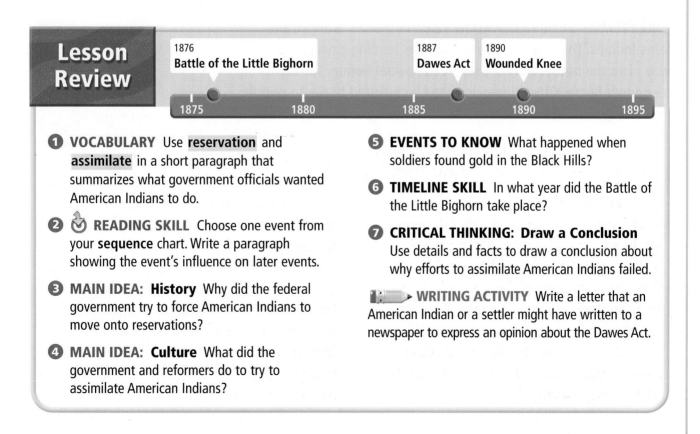

Lesson Review

1876 **Battle of the Little Bighorn**
1887 **Dawes Act**
1890 **Wounded Knee**

1875   1880   1885   1890   1895

❶ **VOCABULARY** Use **reservation** and **assimilate** in a short paragraph that summarizes what government officials wanted American Indians to do.

❷ **READING SKILL** Choose one event from your **sequence** chart. Write a paragraph showing the event's influence on later events.

❸ **MAIN IDEA: History** Why did the federal government try to force American Indians to move onto reservations?

❹ **MAIN IDEA: Culture** What did the government and reformers do to try to assimilate American Indians?

❺ **EVENTS TO KNOW** What happened when soldiers found gold in the Black Hills?

❻ **TIMELINE SKILL** In what year did the Battle of the Little Bighorn take place?

❼ **CRITICAL THINKING: Draw a Conclusion** Use details and facts to draw a conclusion about why efforts to assimilate American Indians failed.

➤ **WRITING ACTIVITY** Write a letter that an American Indian or a settler might have written to a newspaper to express an opinion about the Dawes Act.

Battle of the Little Bighorn

How do we know what happened at the Battle of the Little Bighorn in 1876? Lakota, Cheyenne, and Arapaho Indians who survived the battle told stories about it. These stories were later recorded by historians. Some survivors drew pictures to tell about the battle.

Red Horse, a Lakota who was at the Little Bighorn, drew what he saw. He used colored pencils and ink to create a series of 41 pictures on large sheets of paper. These drawings are an important primary source.

Red Horse's pictures show how valuable horses were to the Plains Indians. This drawing shows warriors leading cavalry horses away after the battle. Warriors received special honors for capturing an enemy's horse. Often a warrior gave a captured horse to people in his village.

Crazy Horse
1840?–1877

Crazy Horse was a Lakota leader who refused to accept life on a reservation. Crazy Horse led a charge against Custer during the Battle of the Little Bighorn.

Sitting Bull
1831?–1890

After Little Bighorn, Sitting Bull led his followers to Canada. He returned to the United States, where he was forced to live on a reservation, but he kept working for justice for the Lakota.

George Armstrong Custer
1839–1876

Custer fought in the Civil War. He began fighting American Indians in 1867. He had such confidence in his abilities as an Indian fighter that he thought he would win at the Little Bighorn.

Activities

1. **THINK ABOUT IT** What can you find out about the Lakota by looking at the drawing on this page?

2. **WRITE ABOUT IT** List three ways that this picture shows that horses were important to the Lakota.

 **Technology** Visit Education Place for more primary sources. www.eduplace.com/kids/hmss05

Visual Summary

1–4. Write a description of the four items in the web below.

Homesteaders

Railroads

Changes in the
Great Plains

Reservations

Cattle drives

Facts and Main Ideas

TEST PREP Answer each question with information from the chapter.

5. **Technology** Why was the invention of the telegraph important to the United States?

6. **Economics** What were two effects of the transcontinental railroad on the United States?

7. **History** Why did Exodusters move to the Great Plains?

8. **History** What brought about the end of the cattle drives?

Vocabulary

TEST PREP Choose the correct word to complete each sentence.

prejudice, p. 226
drought, p. 233
demand, p. 239

9. Some railroad workers who felt _____ toward Chinese workers treated them unfairly.

10. Ranchers wanted to sell their cattle where the _____ and price for beef were high.

11. The hot and dry weather on the Plains often created a _____.

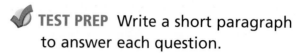

1862
Homestead Act

1876
Battle of the Little Bighorn

1887
Dawes Act

1860 · 1865 · 1870 · 1875 · 1880 · 1885 · 1890

Apply Skills

🗹 **TEST PREP** **Map Skill** Use the time zone map below to answer each question.

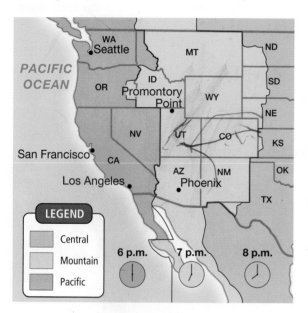

WA
Seattle

MT

ND

PACIFIC OCEAN

OR

ID
Promontory Point

SD

WY

NE

NV

UT

CO

KS

San Francisco

CA

AZ

NM
Phoenix

OK

Los Angeles

TX

LEGEND
- Central
- Mountain
- Pacific

6 p.m.   7 p.m.   8 p.m.

12. If the Central Pacific Railroad workers started working at 8 A.M. in Nevada, what time was it in California?

   A. 7 A.M.

   B. 10 A.M.

   C. 8 A.M.

   D. 9 A.M.

13. If golden spikes were tapped into the track at Promontory Point, Utah, around 11:45 A.M., what time was it in Seattle, Washington?

   A. around 12:45 P.M.

   B. around 5:45 P.M.

   C. around 8:45 A.M.

   D. around 10:45 A.M.

Critical Thinking

🗹 **TEST PREP** Write a short paragraph to answer each question.

14. **Decision Making** What would be the costs and benefits of a European immigrant's decision to settle on the Great Plains?

15. **Draw Conclusions** Which event in this chapter do you think caused the biggest changes on the Great Plains? Explain your conclusions.

Timeline

Use the Chapter Summary Timeline above to answer the question.

16. How many years after the Homestead Act was the Dawes Act passed?

Activities

 Connect to Georgia The transcontinental railroad changed the nation. Research and write a report about how railroads changed Atlanta after the Civil War.

 Writing Activity Think of two questions about the sodbusters that you would like answered. Write two paragraphs of a research report answering the questions.

 Technology
Writing Process Tips
Get help with your research report at **www.eduplace.com/kids/hmss/**

Technology

e • **glossary**
e • **word games**
www.eduplace.com/kids/hmss/

Vocabulary Preview

labor union

Workers formed the first **labor union** to demand change from big companies. Union members acted as a group to get more pay and better working conditions. **page 262**

tenement

Immigrants came to the United States with little money for food and rent. Most lived in crowded and unsafe buildings called **tenements.** page 268

Chapter Timeline

1869
Knights of Labor Union

1882
Chinese Exclusion Act

| 1860 | 1870 | 1880 | 1890 |

Reading Strategy

Summarize Use this strategy to focus on important information.

Quick Tip Take notes as you read. Then highlight the most important information.

rapid transit

Electricity made it possible for people to travel quickly on streetcars and subways. These **rapid transit** systems were built in many large cities. **page 274**

progressive

Jane Addams was a **progressive.** She started a community center that helped people in Chicago improve their lives.
page 278

1909
NAACP founded

1920
Nineteenth Amendment

1900   1910   1920

The Rise of Big Business

VOCABULARY

corporation
competition
monopoly
labor union
strike

Vocabulary Strategy

| labor union |

Union and unite are related words. A **labor union** brings together, or unites, workers.

READING SKILL

Classify Make a column for each main idea. Classify information and list inventions in the correct column.

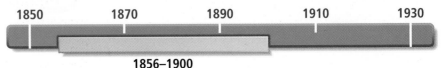

| 1850 | 1870 | 1890 | 1910 | 1930 |

1856–1900

Build on What You Know You probably enjoy talking to your friends and relatives on the phone. In the late 1800s, the telephone was a brand-new invention. Few Americans had one.

A Time of Invention

Main Idea Inventions of the late 1800s changed people's lives.

The last half of the 1800s was full of wonderful inventions. These inventions allowed people to do things that had been impossible before, such as recording sound. New machines saved time and money and improved life for many people.

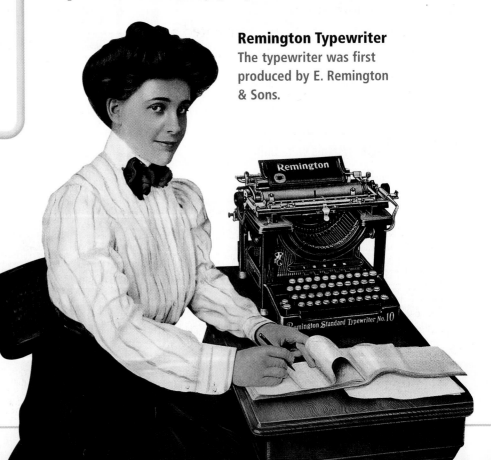

Remington Typewriter
The typewriter was first produced by E. Remington & Sons.

 STANDARDS

SS5H3b Impact of Bell, Edison
SS5E1f Productivity
SS5E2a Private business function
SS5E3a Competition
SS5E3c Entrepreneurs

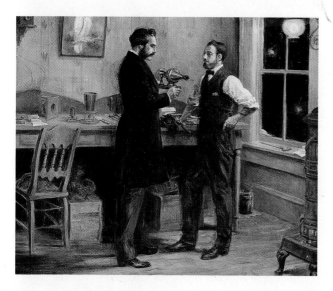

Alexander Graham Bell In his laboratory in Boston, Bell (left) works on his new invention, the telephone. His assistant is Thomas Watson.

Inventions for Home and Work

In 1872, **Elijah McCoy** invented an oil cup. The oil cup kept trains and other machines running longer by dripping oil over moving parts.

In 1874, E. Remington & Sons became the first company to make and sell type-writers. Office workers saved time by typing letters and reports.

In 1867, **Margaret Knight** invented a machine that made paper bags with a flat bottom, so they could hold more. Her paper-bag-making machine is still in use.

Granville Woods Woods improved the telephone, telegraph, and transportation systems. His inventions made streetcars like the one below faster and safer.

Alexander Graham Bell invented the telephone in 1876. Workers in large buildings used the telephone to talk to people on other floors. People at home used telephones to talk to friends and relatives hundreds of miles away.

Thomas Edison created over 1,000 inventions. In 1877, he invented the phonograph, or record player. For the first time, sounds such as music and speech could be recorded and played back.

Edison developed the electric light bulb in 1879. Before electric lighting, people used gaslights. These lights were smoky and could start fires. Electric lights were cleaner and safer than gas lamps. They kept city streets bright and allowed factories and shops to stay open after dark.

These inventions increased productivity in businesses. Some inventions kept machines running longer, or made it possible for workers to do more work. More goods could be produced. During the last half of the 1800s, new inventions allowed businesses to change and grow.

REVIEW In what ways did inventions of the late 1800s save time?

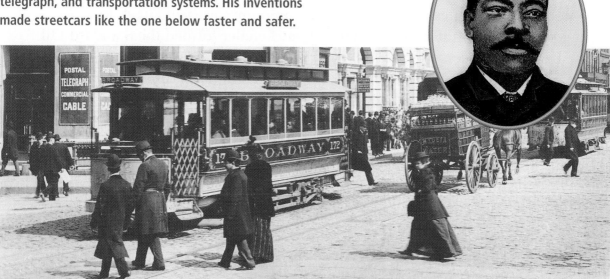

Steel Mills Andrew Carnegie (left) was an entrepreneur, a person who takes risks to start a business. He owned many steel mills. The painting above shows workers inside a steel mill.

Big Business

Main Idea Businesses in the late 1800s produced more goods, hired more people, and earned more money than before.

In 1856, British scientist **Henry Bessemer** invented a process to make steel. The Bessemer process made steel much less expensive to produce.

Andrew Carnegie was one of the first people in the United States to use the Bessemer process. He built a factory that used the Bessemer process to make steel rails for railroads. Steel rails lasted much longer than the iron rails that other American factories sold. Railroad companies bought Carnegie's steel rails, and his business grew. To help his steel company succeed, Carnegie bought fuel companies, railroads, and ships.

Because he owned these companies, he could get fuel for his factories and shipping for his goods at a lower price. By 1900, Carnegie's steel company produced about one quarter of all the steel made in the United States.

Corporations

Andrew Carnegie's steel company was big, but **John D. Rockefeller's** oil company was even larger. In 1870, Rockefeller formed the Standard Oil Company, which made products such as fuel and lamp oil. Standard Oil was a corporation. A **corporation** is a business in which many people own shares, or parts, of the business. Corporations pay part of their profits to their share owners. A profit is the money earned by a business after all the costs of machinery, workers, and raw materials are paid.

Companies Grow Larger

Corporations such as Standard Oil grew and became more common in the late 1800s. A corporation could raise money by selling lots of shares to many people. Business owners wanted to raise money to build factories and buy expensive machines. A small business could not afford the factories or machines needed to produce many products.

Another way Standard Oil grew was by buying other oil companies. It soon controlled 90 percent of the oil sold in the United States. One reason Rockefeller bought these companies was to reduce competition. **Competition** occurs when more than one business tries to sell the same goods or service.

When there is competition, a company has to keep prices low and quality high to get customers to buy its goods. When there is little competition, consumers have fewer choices about where to get the goods and services they want. A company with few competitors may raise prices or provide poor service.

Rockefeller bought so many oil companies that Standard Oil almost became a monopoly. A **monopoly** is a company that has no competition. Entrepreneurs such as Carnegie and Rockefeller earned large profits for their companies. They were accused, however, of using business practices that hurt consumers and smaller businesses.

Both Carnegie and Rockefeller became philanthropists. A philanthropist is a person who gives money to projects that help other people. Carnegie and Rockefeller believed wealthy people should use some of their money for good causes. Carnegie paid for libraries in nearly 3,000 towns. He gave away about $350 million. Rockefeller donated over $500 million to schools, colleges, churches, and hospitals.

REVIEW What is a monopoly?

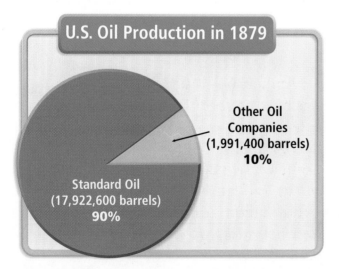

U.S. Oil Production in 1879

Other Oil Companies (1,991,400 barrels) **10%**

Standard Oil (17,922,600 barrels) **90%**

Oil Production In 1879, Standard Oil controlled most of the oil production in the United States. Rockefeller (right) became one of the richest people in the United States as a result.

Workers' Lives Change

Main Idea Workers united to improve working conditions.

In the late 1800s, businesses used mechanization to speed up the process of producing goods. Mechanization is the use of machines to do work. Machine-made goods could be sold at lower prices than handmade goods.

Consumers bought large quantities of these inexpensive machine-made products. Businesses made more goods and hired more workers to run the machines. Factories and businesses grew bigger. Some had thousands of workers.

Workers in factories did the same thing for ten or twelve hours a day, six days a week. Few factories had safe working conditions and many workers were injured or killed in accidents.

The Labor Movement

Factory workers were poorly paid. Many families struggled to pay for a place to live and food to eat. Children as young as 10 to 15 years old worked because their families needed the money they earned.

Anyone who complained about poor pay or bad working conditions could be fired. Workers formed labor unions so they could act as a group and have more power. A **labor union** is an organization of workers that tries to improve pay and working conditions for its members.

The Knights of Labor was the first large labor union. It was formed in 1869. Its goals were safer working conditions and an eight-hour workday. The Knights of Labor also wanted to stop businesses from hiring children. The labor union used strikes to try to force business owners to make changes. During a **strike,** workers refuse to work.

Striking Workers Labor unions included workers from different countries. The striking workers in this photo hold signs written in several languages.

SKILL **Reading Visuals**
Read the English signs in the photo. What do the workers want?

Some workers thought the Knights of Labor was not doing enough. In 1886, these workers formed the American Federation of Labor (AFL). They elected **Samuel Gompers** as the AFL's president. The AFL was a large group of trade unions. A trade union is an organization of workers who do the same type of job, such as plumbing, or are in the same industry, such as steelworking. Trade unions in the AFL wanted better wages, safer conditions in the workplace, and shorter workdays.

Samuel Gompers
An immigrant from England, Gompers believed that workers needed to act together to improve their working conditions.

The first labor unions did not have much success. Strikes failed when businesses fired the strikers. People were hurt or killed in fights between police or soldiers and striking workers. Powerful monopolies often blocked progress for workers. Labor unions, however, continued to bring workers together.

REVIEW Why did workers form labor unions?

Lesson Summary

- In the late 1800s, many inventions changed people's lives.
- Businesses became larger and earned bigger profits.
- Workers formed labor unions to improve poor working conditions.

Why It Matters ...

Inventions allowed people to save time and made life easier. Changes in business created more profits and led to the first labor unions.

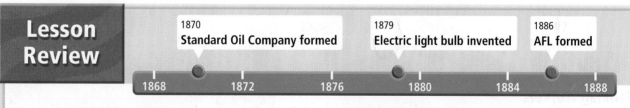

Lesson Review

Timeline:
1870 Standard Oil Company formed
1879 Electric light bulb invented
1886 AFL formed
1868 — 1872 — 1876 — 1880 — 1884 — 1888

1 **VOCABULARY** Which of the following does not describe Standard Oil?
corporation   monopoly   labor union

2 **READING SKILL** Use the information you **classified** under the column of inventions to write a summary paragraph about changes in the late 1800s.

3 **MAIN IDEA: Technology** Why was the electric light bulb such an important invention?

4 **MAIN IDEA: Economics** What did John D. Rockefeller do to make his oil company grow?

5 **PEOPLE TO KNOW** Who was **Samuel Gompers**?

6 **TIMELINE SKILL** How long before the AFL began was the Standard Oil Company formed?

7 **CRITICAL THINKING: Infer** Why do you think that most business owners did not like labor unions?

HANDS ON **ART ACTIVITY** Make a Then and Now poster. Use images from library resources to show an invention from the late 1800s and what it looks like today.

Electric Lights

In 1900, few homes had electric lights. Most had gaslight. Electric lights were brighter than gaslights and they could be placed anywhere in a room. Gaslights could not be moved because they were connected to gas lines in walls and ceilings. Gas could explode, so children could not turn lights on or off by themselves. People were eager to have safe, convenient electric lights.

When most homes were wired for electric lights, new inventions such as toasters and refrigerators began to be widely used.

Thomas Edison

As a boy, Thomas Alva Edison was fascinated by electricity. When he was fifteen, he rescued the son of an electric telegraph operator from being run over by a train. The operator rewarded Edison by teaching him to use a telegraph. Edison invented many electric devices, including the light bulb, in 1879. He also set up electric stations all over the United States so that people could have electric lights in their homes.

Lewis Latimer

Like Edison, Lewis Latimer was interested in the inventions of his time. He drew the diagrams for Alexander Graham Bell's telephone. He became an inventor and went to work for the U. S. Electric Lighting Company. There, Latimer made several improvements to the light bulb. Latimer later went to work for Edison. Latimer wrote a book to explain how electric lights work.

Comfortable Gaslights used up oxygen and made rooms stuffy. With electric lights, windows could be open or closed.

Clean
Electric lights did not cause soot or dust. Ceilings, carpets, and furniture stayed clean.

Bright
Electric lights made it easier for people to read after dark. Electric lights were bright and lamps could be placed next to chairs. In one town, people checked out eight times as many library books after electric lights were used as they had before.

Activities

1. **TALK ABOUT IT** What things do you like to do that would be harder or impossible to do without electric lights?

2. **WRITE ABOUT IT** List three questions that a person who has never had electric lights might ask about them. Answer the questions.

Immigrants in America

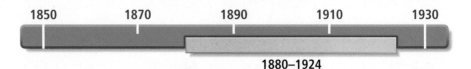

| 1850 | 1870 | 1890 | 1910 | 1930 |

1880–1924

Build on What You Know Do you know anyone who has moved to your neighborhood from another place? Many people moved to the United States about 100 years ago.

Arriving in America

Main Idea Millions of immigrants moved to the United States in the late 1800s and early 1900s.

About 25 million immigrants moved to the United States in the years between 1880 and 1924. Most immigrants before 1880 came from Ireland, Germany, England, Sweden, Denmark, and other countries of northern or western Europe. The newer immigrants, however, were usually from southern or eastern Europe. They came from Italy, Russia, Hungary, Greece, and Poland. Some also came from Mexico.

Immigrants were looking for work. Growing businesses like those of **Andrew Carnegie** and **John D. Rockefeller** offered plenty of jobs. Some immigrants also came to escape war or persecution. **Persecution** is unfair treatment or punishment. For example, many Jews in eastern Europe were hurt or killed because of their religion. Jewish people hoped to escape persecution by moving to the United States.

Most immigrants found greater political freedom in America as well. A man from Slovenia expressed immigrants' feelings when he said,

> 66 **In America everything was possible.** 99

VOCABULARY

persecution
ethnic group
tenement

Vocabulary Strategy

ethnic group

Ethnic comes from a word that means people. An **ethnic group** is a group of people who share the same language or culture.

 READING SKILL

Draw Conclusions List facts and details you can use to draw a conclusion about why immigrants came to the United States.

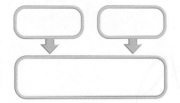

Immigration Stations

Once immigrants arrived in the United States, they went through immigration stations, such as Ellis Island in New York Harbor. Government workers at the stations asked newcomers about where they planned to live and work. Doctors examined the immigrants to be sure they didn't have diseases that could spread to others. Almost all European immigrants who came to the United States were allowed to enter.

Coming to America Immigrants fill a ship crossing the Atlantic Ocean. These children (right) are coming to the United States from Italy.

Asians moved to the United States to find jobs, too. Large numbers of Chinese immigrants first arrived on the West Coast in the 1850s. They also had to go through immigration stations, such as Angel Island in San Francisco Bay. They faced more prejudice than European immigrants. Asian immigrants on Angel Island had to stay for weeks, months, or even years before being allowed to enter the United States. About 25 percent were forced to return to their home countries.

REVIEW In what ways were Asian immigrants treated differently than immigrants from Europe?

Living in a New Country

Main Idea Many immigrants moved to large cities and worked in factories.

After entering the United States, most immigrants settled near family or friends. Immigrant communities in big cities grew quickly. In some cities whole neighborhoods were made up of a single ethnic group. An **ethnic group** is a group of people who share a culture or language. In ethnic neighborhoods, immigrants spoke their native languages, practiced their religions, and kept their country's customs.

Immigrants' lives were not easy. Some worked in dangerous steel mills. Others had jobs in noisy and dirty factories where they sewed clothing or made thread. Nearly all worked long hours for low pay, making so little money they could barely buy food for themselves or their families.

Many newcomers lived in tenements. A **tenement** is a poorly built apartment building. Tenements were crowded and unsafe. They often had no windows or running water. Several families might live in one small apartment.

Hard Times for Immigrants

As neighborhoods changed, immigrants faced prejudice from people who were frightened by unfamiliar languages and customs. Employers liked to hire immigrants because they worked hard for little pay. For the same reason, some people worried about losing their jobs to immigrants and wanted immigration stopped.

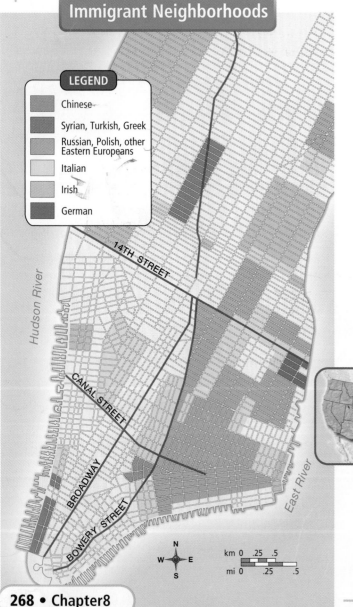

Immigrant Neighborhoods

LEGEND
- Chinese
- Syrian, Turkish, Greek
- Russian, Polish, other Eastern Europeans
- Italian
- Irish
- German

Hudson River
14TH STREET
CANAL STREET
BROADWAY
BOWERY STREET
East River

Anna Rosenberg Born in Hungary, Rosenberg was the first female Assistant Secretary of Defense for the United States.

New York City This map shows ethnic neighborhoods in New York City in 1920.

SKILL **Reading Maps** Which ethnic groups lived along Bowery Street?

Laws Against Immigration

In 1882, Congress limited immigration by passing the Chinese Exclusion Act. This law excluded, or kept out, almost all new Chinese immigrants. Later laws limited the number of people from other countries. In 1921 and 1924, Congress passed laws that greatly lowered the number of Europeans allowed into the United States. These same laws also kept out most people from Asia.

Laws made it hard for immigrants to enter the United States, and they faced prejudice when they arrived. Immigrants overcame these hardships and helped the United States become one of the richest and fastest-growing countries in the world. They constructed thousands of miles of railroad tracks, dug deep coal mines, and worked in factories.

REVIEW What did immigrants do to help the United States grow?

Lesson Summary

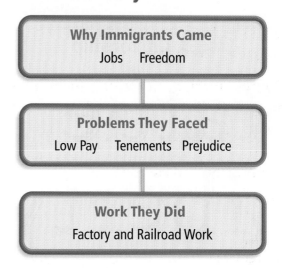

Why Immigrants Came
Jobs   Freedom

Problems They Faced
Low Pay   Tenements   Prejudice

Work They Did
Factory and Railroad Work

Why It Matters ...

The United States today includes the great-grandchildren of immigrants who came in search of freedom and better lives in the 1800s and early 1900s.

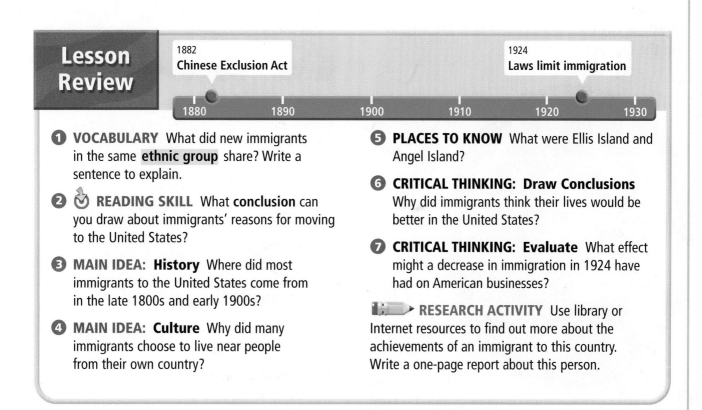

Lesson Review

1882
Chinese Exclusion Act

1924
Laws limit immigration

1880   1890   1900   1910   1920   1930

❶ **VOCABULARY** What did new immigrants in the same **ethnic group** share? Write a sentence to explain.

❷ **READING SKILL** What **conclusion** can you draw about immigrants' reasons for moving to the United States?

❸ **MAIN IDEA: History** Where did most immigrants to the United States come from in the late 1800s and early 1900s?

❹ **MAIN IDEA: Culture** Why did many immigrants choose to live near people from their own country?

❺ **PLACES TO KNOW** What were Ellis Island and Angel Island?

❻ **CRITICAL THINKING: Draw Conclusions** Why did immigrants think their lives would be better in the United States?

❼ **CRITICAL THINKING: Evaluate** What effect might a decrease in immigration in 1924 have had on American businesses?

RESEARCH ACTIVITY Use library or Internet resources to find out more about the achievements of an immigrant to this country. Write a one-page report about this person.

Statue of Liberty

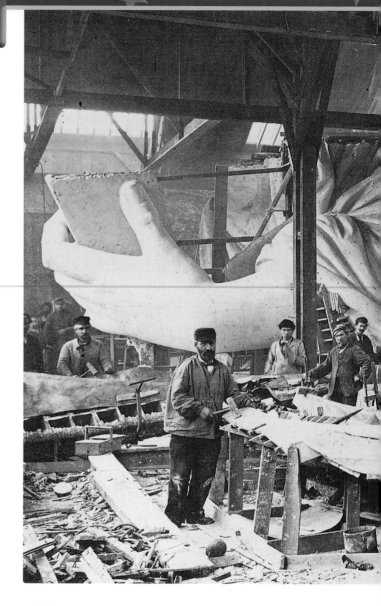

French sculptor Frédéric Auguste Bartholdi loved America. He wanted to build an enormous statue as a symbol of the long friendship between France and the United States.

Bartholdi called the 225-ton statue "Liberty Enlightening the World," but today it is known as the Statue of Liberty. It stands in New York harbor. It is a symbol of friendship between nations, of hope for immigrants, and of freedom for all Americans.

Poet Emma Lazarus was invited to write a poem about the statue. Her words are engraved on the statue's base.

> " *Give me your tired, your poor,*
> *Your huddled masses yearning to breathe free,*
> *The wretched refuse of your teeming shore.*
> *Send these, the homeless, tempest-tost to me.*
> *I lift my lamp beside the golden door!* "
>
> —*Emma Lazarus*

Torch

The right arm and torch were completed first. By 1949, the torch's lamps beamed 13,000 watts of light. The torch is a symbol of freedom.

Crown

The seven spikes on the crown stand for the seven seas and seven continents.

Tablet

The tablet in Liberty's left hand is engraved with July 4, 1776, in Roman numerals.

JULY
IV
MDCCLXXVI

Making the Statue of Liberty

Bartholdi and his assistants started by making clay models of the statue. They created models that were larger and larger until they made a model that was as big as the final statue—151 feet high.

Activities

1. **THINK ABOUT IT** Why do people visit the Statue of Liberty today?

2. **DESIGN YOUR OWN** Draw your idea for a monument about citizenship. What words of inspiration would be on the monument? What parts of the monument would be symbols? Use captions to explain the symbols.

Growing Cities

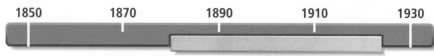

1850   1870   1890   1910   1930
1880–1924

VOCABULARY

stockyard
skyscraper
rapid transit
slum
settlement house

Vocabulary Strategy

stockyard

Stockyard is a compound word. **Stock,** or farm animals used for food, are kept in a **stockyard.**

READING SKILL

Cause and Effect As you read, take notes to show the effects that new technology had on cities.

STEEL	ELECTRICITY

STANDARDS

SS5H3d Where emigrants settled
SS5G1b Locate Pittsburgh, PA
SS5G2a Factors influencing industrial location
SS5E1c Specialization in North and South

Build on What You Know When you think about cities, do you think about millions of people and very tall buildings? In the late 1800s, millions of people moved to cities and built the first tall buildings.

Moving to Cities

Main Idea Cities in the United States grew quickly in the late 1800s and early 1900s.

Most of the millions of immigrants who came to the United States between 1880 and 1910 lived and worked in cities. Many people who lived on farms or in small towns also moved to urban areas during this time. There were not many jobs for them in the rural United States. Fewer farm workers were needed after new machines increased productivity on farms.

Urban Growth By 1920, over 50 million people lived in cities.

SKILL **Reading Graphs** What percentage of people in the United States lived in cities in 1920?

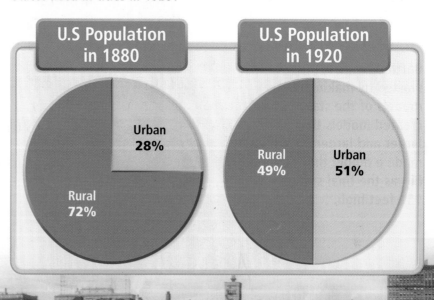

U.S Population in 1880

Urban 28%

Rural 72%

U.S Population in 1920

Rural 49%

Urban 51%

LEGEND

+++ Railroad	Logs		Corn
= Canal			
— Shipping	Hogs		Cattle

km 0   100   200
mi 0   100   200

Chicago's Resources This map shows natural resources and transportation routes in 1900.

Good Locations

Industry grew quickly after the Civil War. People built factories all across the country. Many were in cities that were near natural resources or transportation routes. Although the South's economy remained highly dependent on agriculture, cities in both the North and the South specialized in making goods using the resources in their area. Better transportation made this specialization possible. Railroads and canals made it easy to ship raw materials and finished goods into and out of cities.

Chicago, 1913

Chicago Booms

Chicago grew quickly because of its location near transportation routes, natural resources, and Lake Michigan. Factories in Chicago cut logs into lumber. Mills turned wheat and corn into food. Stockyards held thousands of animals. A **stockyard** is a fenced area where large numbers of animals, such as pigs and cattle, are kept until they are used as food or moved to another place. Many people moved to Chicago to find jobs.

REVIEW What factors helped Chicago grow?

Changes in Cities

Main Idea Technology allowed cities to grow, but crowding caused problems.

The first skyscraper in the United States was built in Chicago in 1885. A **skyscraper** is a very tall building. Skyscrapers with strong steel frames towered over city streets in the late 1800s and early 1900s.

The growth of the steel industry made skyscrapers possible. Structures with steel frames could be taller than buildings with heavy iron or brick frames. In 1883, a magazine writer called skyscrapers

> **tower-like structures that have sprung up as if by magic.**

Electricity also changed cities. Inventors **Thomas Edison** and **Nikola Tesla** thought of new ways to make electricity and send it through wires.

Inventions that used electricity could now be found everywhere in big cities. Electric elevators carried people quickly from floor to floor in skyscrapers. Electric lights lit theater stages and electric signs attracted shoppers. Electricity powered rapid transit vehicles, such as streetcars and subways. **Rapid transit** is a system of trains used to move people around cities. Rapid transit moved large numbers of people faster than ever before. Growing cities were exciting places.

Growing cities had problems, too. As cities got busier, they grew noisier and more crowded. Those who could not find good housing lived in slums. A **slum** is a poor, crowded part of a city. Buildings in slums were built quickly and cheaply. Slum buildings, also called tenements, were not safe. They could catch fire easily, and many had no fire escapes.

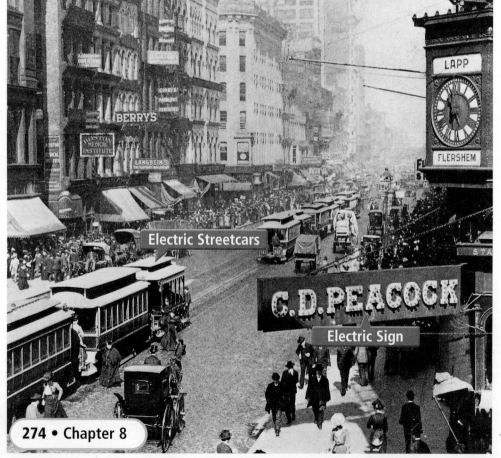

Electric Streetcars

G.D. PEACOCK

Electric Sign

Electricity By the early 1900s, city streets were full of signs and streetcars powered by electricity. Nikola Tesla (above), an immigrant from Croatia, found ways to send electricity through wires.

Helping Each Other

City people, especially immigrants, helped each other find jobs and places to live. Reformers helped as well.

Jane Addams and **Ellen Gates Starr** were reformers who opened Hull House in Chicago in 1889. Hull House was one of the first settlement houses in the United States. A **settlement house** is a community center for people in cities.

Jane Addams Reformers such as Addams helped immigrants.

People came to Hull House to learn English, get medical care, or find jobs. Hull House had clubs for girls and boys. Working mothers left babies in the Hull House nursery. Reformers in other cities liked the work Hull House did and they started settlement houses themselves.

REVIEW What kinds of help did immigrants find in settlement houses?

Lesson Summary

- In the late 1800s and early 1900s, immigrants and people from rural areas moved to cities.

- Technology changed urban life.

- Settlement houses helped people in cities solve their problems.

Why It Matters . . .

During the late 1800s and early 1900s, skyscrapers and electricity made cities start to look more like they do today.

Lesson Review

1885	1889	1910
First skyscraper built	Hull House opened	Almost half of U.S. population is urban

1880　1885　1890　1895　1900　1905　1910　1915

1. **VOCABULARY** Write a description of cities in the late 1800s and early 1900s, using **skyscraper, slum,** and **rapid transit.**

2. **READING SKILL** What was the **effect** of electricity on rapid transit?

3. **MAIN IDEA: Geography** Why did Chicago grow quickly in the late 1800s and early 1900s?

4. **MAIN IDEA: History** What problems did people face in growing cities?

5. **PEOPLE TO KNOW** What did **Thomas Edison** and **Nikola Tesla** do to change cities?

6. **TIMELINE SKILL** How many years after the first skyscraper was built were nearly half of all Americans living in cities?

7. **CRITICAL THINKING Decision Making** For a farmer in the late 1800s, what were some of the consequences of the decision to move from the farm to the city?

WRITING ACTIVITY Write a newspaper editorial from 1889 about the work of Hull House for the citizens of Chicago.

STEEL CITY

Pittsburgh was just the right place to produce steel. It had two major rivers. It had natural resources nearby, such as coal. Steel was in demand in the late 1800s and early 1900s. The nation needed steel for railroads, bridges, skyscrapers, and factories. Pittsburgh soon got the nickname "Steel City."

Iron ore and a mineral called lime were the ingredients used to make steel. Tons of coal were burned to melt the ore, and the smoke blackened the skies of Pittsburgh as the city grew. Rivers and railroads carried raw materials into the city and carried finished steel out of it.

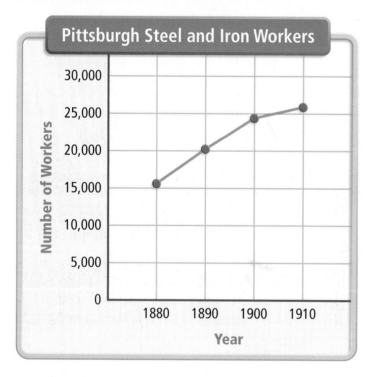

The number of Pittsburgh steel and iron workers increased by how many between 1880 and 1910?

The Carnegie Steel Company owned these Pittsburgh factories, shown in the early 1900s.

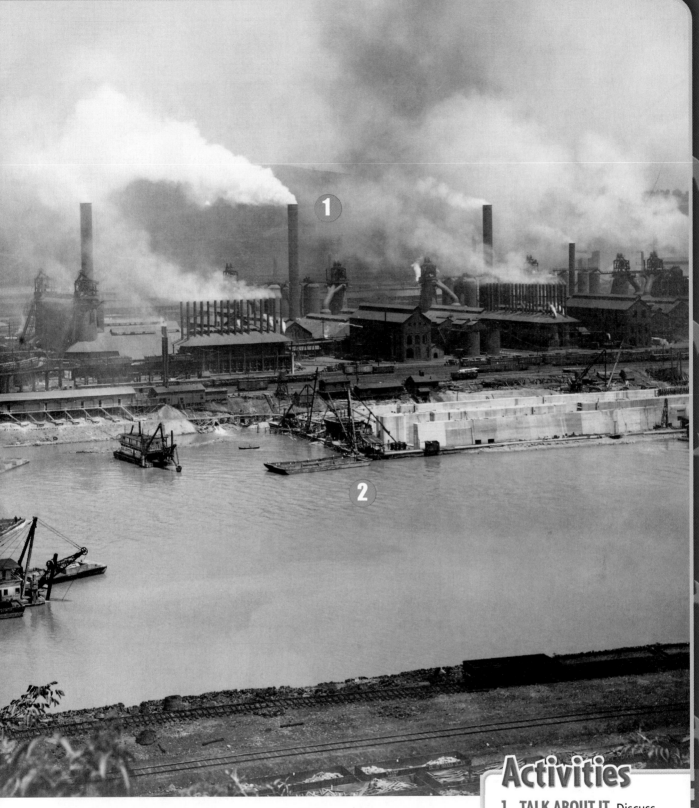

1. **Smokestacks**
Smoke from burning coal blows into the sky. Rain carries some of this pollution back into the river.

2. **River** Boats take coal up the Monongahela River, pictured above. The city's other major river is the Allegheny.

Activities

1. **TALK ABOUT IT** Discuss how you think the making of steel changed Pittsburgh.

2. **WRITE ABOUT IT** Write a paragraph describing the scene in the picture.

277

Time of Reform

1850   1870   1890   1910   1930

1900–1920

Build on What You Know You have probably tried to fix something that wasn't working well. In the early 1900s, people called progressives wanted to fix what they thought was wrong with the country.

The Progressives

Main Idea Progressives tried to improve life in the United States.

As cities and businesses grew, more adults and children went to work in factories. Jobs in factories were not always safe. People could slip on dirty floors or get hurt while working with unsafe machines.

Factories dumped dirt and poisons into city water. Smokestacks blew soot and smoke into city air. People who lived near factories got sick from drinking dirty water and breathing dirty air.

Progressives wanted to make cities and factories cleaner and safer. **Progressives** were reformers. They did not always agree with one another, but most thought governments should make laws to protect workers, consumers, and citizens' rights.

VOCABULARY

progressives
muckraker

Vocabulary Strategy

progress**ives**

Find the word **progress** in progressives. **Progressives** wanted progress, or improvement in society.

READING SKILL
Problem and Solution
Chart the problems that reformers tried to solve. Then look for the solutions they offered.

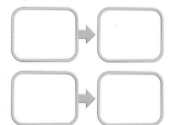

Working Children
Some children worked long hours in factories. This girl is making stockings.

 STANDARDS

SS5H3 America at turn of century
SS5CG3a 17th Amendment

Making Changes

Progressives wrote about workers who were hurt in accidents. They took pictures of children working in unsafe places. They convinced state lawmakers to protect workers and keep children from working.

Progressives who wrote about the need for change were called muckrakers. Muck is something dirty or unpleasant. A **muckraker** is someone who "rakes up," or points out, unpleasant truths.

In 1906, a muckraker named **Upton Sinclair** published his book, *The Jungle.* This fictional description was based on Sinclair's observations of unsafe and dirty conditions in meatpacking plants. It told about the use of chemicals to cover the taste of rotten meat. Sinclair wrote,

66 **There was never the least attention paid to what was cut up for sausage . . . rats, bread, and meat would go into the hoppers [containers] together.** 99

Government Reforms

President **Theodore Roosevelt** worked with Congress to pass two laws in 1906 to make food safer. The Pure Food and Drug Act and the Meat Inspection Act stated that medicine and foods had to be made without harmful chemicals. The factories where they were made had to be clean.

Roosevelt also wanted to preserve wilderness areas. He was influenced by **John Muir,** a conservationist who believed that natural areas were precious resources. Muir took President Roosevelt to visit present-day Yosemite (yoh SEHM ih tee) National Park in California in 1903. After seeing Yosemite, Roosevelt set aside millions of acres for national parks and wilderness areas.

REVIEW What did the Pure Food and Drug Act and the Meat Inspection Act do to make food safer?

Constitutional Amendments

Progressives' Goal	Result	What It Did
Make people who earned more money pay more of the cost of government	16th Amendment	Allowed Congress to pass an income tax
Allow voters to choose their lawmakers	17th Amendment	Allowed citizens to elect senators
Reduce violence and crime they thought was caused by drinking alcohol	18th Amendment	Made it against the law to make or sell alcoholic beverages
Allow women to vote	19th Amendment	Recognized the right of women aged 21 or older to vote

Progressive Amendments Between 1913 and 1920, the time known as the Progressive Era, Congress passed several amendments to the Constitution.

SKILL **Reading Charts** What did the 19th Amendment do?

Working for Equal Rights

Main Idea In the early 1900s, women and African Americans worked to gain equal rights.

New laws helped workers and made food safer. Yet women and African Americans could not vote in many states. They also faced discrimination in getting jobs and education. For example, most colleges and universities did not take women or African American men as students.

Voting Rights for Women

Women first called for the right to vote before the Civil War. They wanted Congress to amend the Constitution to recognize this right. In 1878, Congress voted against such an amendment. Leaders of the women's suffrage movement, however, did not give up. Women such as **Carrie Chapman Catt** gave speeches and wrote letters to lawmakers. Thousands of women marched in protest in New York, Chicago, and Washington, D.C.

For decades, women fought for suffrage. They won the right to vote in a few states, but they could not vote in national elections. Finally, Congress passed the Nineteenth Amendment, which guaranteed women the right to vote. In 1920, three-quarters of the states approved the amendment and it became law.

Women's Suffrage On a crowded street in 1916, women march for the right to vote. Women worked hard to win the support of President Wilson for their cause.

Struggle for Racial Equality

In the early 1900s, African Americans, Mexican Americans, American Indians, and Asian Americans faced prejudice when they applied for jobs or tried to rent or buy homes. Some states had laws that kept people in these groups from voting, or forced their children to go to separate schools. Many organizations fought against unfair laws and prejudice.

The National Association for the Advancement of Colored People (NAACP) was founded in 1909 to work for equality for African Americans. Advancement means improvement. "Colored People" was a term used at the time for African Americans.

One of the NAACP's leaders was **W.E.B. Du Bois.** Du Bois was an African American writer and professor. His writings on African American life helped persuade many Americans that change was needed. **Booker T. Washington** was another African American leader. He started a school to educate and give job training to southern African Americans.

Around 1910, a growing number of African Americans left the south for jobs in northern cities. In the early 1920s, the Ku Klux Klan, the group that attacked African Americans, grew larger.

The Klan's increasing violence made life even more difficult for southern African Americans. Between 1910 and 1930, about 1.5 million African Americans left the rural South. Most went North to work in large factories and businesses. This movement of people became known as the Great Migration.

REVIEW What is the NAACP and what is its purpose?

Lesson Summary

During the early 1900s, progressives wanted laws to protect workers, consumers, and citizens' rights. Laws were passed to make food safer and conserve land. Women won the right to vote. Many organizations, including the NAACP, fought prejudice and injustice.

Why It Matters...

The laws that progressives worked for made life in the United States safer and more just.

W.E.B. Du Bois
He worked for equal rights for African Americans.

Lesson Review

Timeline:
1906 — Pure Food and Drug Act
1909 — NAACP founded
1905 | 1906 | 1907 | 1908 | 1909 | 1910

❶ **VOCABULARY** Write a paragraph about the Pure Food and Drug Act and the Meat Inspection Act, using **progressives** and **muckraker.**

❷ **READING SKILL** What was the **solution** to the **problem** of women not being allowed to vote?

❸ **MAIN IDEA: History** Name three things progressives tried to change in the early 1900s.

❹ **MAIN IDEA: Citizenship** What did Booker T. Washington do for African Americans in the South?

❺ **PEOPLE TO KNOW** What did **Theodore Roosevelt** do to support conservation?

❻ **TIMELINE SKILL** When was the NAACP started?

❼ **CRITICAL THINKING: Synthesize** Why were progressives important to millions of people in the United States?

HANDS ON **ART ACTIVITY** Create a poster that a person in the early 1900s might have made about voting rights for women.

The Great Migration

Why did millions of African Americans leave their homes in the South? The answer is jobs and opportunities. Jobs in steel mills and railroad yards and in the automobile, meatpacking, and food processing plants of the North and Midwest paid much better than jobs open to African Americans in the South.

Although African Americans faced prejudice in the North, they had new opportunities, too. Adults could vote. Children could go to public schools.

Ready to Leave
The Great Migration occurred in several waves from the 1910s through the 1950s. This family is moving north in 1940.

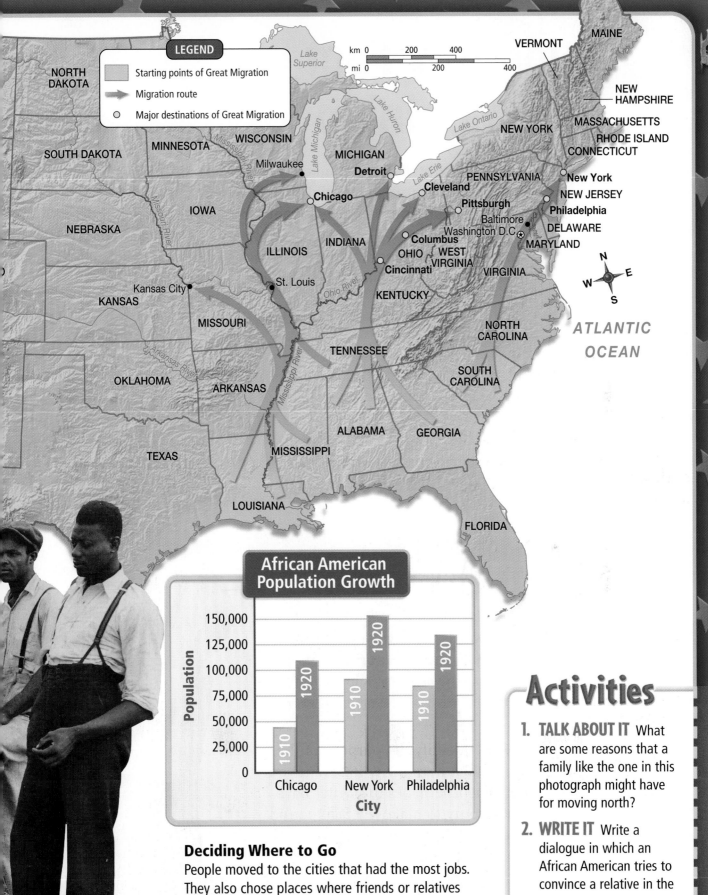

LEGEND

Starting points of Great Migration

Migration route

○ Major destinations of Great Migration

African American Population Growth

Population

	1910	1920
Chicago	~45,000	~110,000
New York	~90,000	~155,000
Philadelphia	~85,000	~135,000

City

Deciding Where to Go
People moved to the cities that had the most jobs. They also chose places where friends or relatives were already living.

Activities

1. **TALK ABOUT IT** What are some reasons that a family like the one in this photograph might have for moving north?

2. **WRITE IT** Write a dialogue in which an African American tries to convince a relative in the South to move North.

Skillbuilder

Identify Fact and Opinion

▶ **VOCABULARY**

fact

opinion

When you study social studies, it helps to be able to identify the difference between fact and opinion. A **fact** is a piece of information that can be proved. Proof can come from sources such as observation, books, or artifacts. Facts answer questions such as *Who, What, When,* and *Where.* An **opinion** is a personal belief. It expresses someone's thoughts or feelings and cannot be proved.

Learn the Skill

Step 1: Read the piece of writing. Look for specific names, events, dates, and numbers. These often signal facts.

Step 2: Look for theories, feelings, and thoughts. These are opinions. Sometimes opinions contain phrases such as *I believe* or *I think.* Other opinion words are *might, could, should,* and *probably.* The words *best, worst, greatest,* or *extremely* also signal opinions.

Step 3: Identify the purpose of the writing. What does the writer want you to do or believe? Does the writer have a reason to try to make the facts sound different from what they really are?

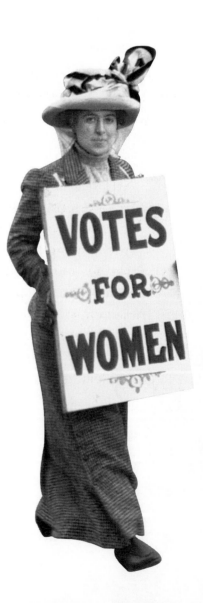

Practice the Skill

Read the following statements. Then identify each one as a fact or an opinion. Explain how you made your decision.

1 It seems to me that the Pure Food and Drug Act was terrible for the business of meat factories.

2 Creating and protecting national parks is the best thing a President can do for the country.

3 When the NAACP was created, its members worked to educate people about the unfair treatment of African Americans. They made speeches, started a newspaper, and handed out flyers.

Apply the Skill

Read the following paragraph about women's suffrage and the Nineteenth Amendment. Identify the facts and opinions. Then explain your choices. What did the writer want you to believe?

Women had been calling for suffrage since the Seneca Falls Convention in 1848. It was surprising that by the end of World War I, women still were not allowed to vote. During the war, thousands of women filled the jobs of men who had gone off to fight. They worked in airplane factories, drove trucks, and operated elevators. These women put an end to the silly argument that women should stay in the home and let men do the voting. In 1920, the Nineteenth Amendment was passed, guaranteeing women the right to vote.

Visual Summary

1.–4. Write a description of how each person below improved others' lives.

Samuel Gompers

TRADE **AFL** UNION

Jane Addams

The Reformers

Booker T. Washington

Carrie Chapman Catt

VOTES FOR WOMEN

Facts and Main Ideas

✓ **TEST PREP** Answer each question with information from the chapter.

5. **Economics** What did John D. Rockefeller do to make Standard Oil grow?

6. **Citizenship** Why did immigrants settle in ethnic neighborhoods?

7. **Geography** Why did the location of Chicago cause it to grow quickly?

8. **History** What new kinds of technology helped cities grow?

9. **Government** What did women do to gain support for the Nineteenth Amendment?

Vocabulary

✓ **TEST PREP** Choose the correct word from the list below to complete each sentence.

corporation, p. 260
persecution, p. 266
rapid transit, p. 274
progressives, p. 278

10. Some immigrants came to the United States to escape _____.

11. People own shares, or parts, of a _____.

12. Reformers like Upton Sinclair were _____ who wanted to improve society.

13. Streetcars and subways are part of a _____ system.

CHAPTER SUMMARY TIMELINE

| 1869 | 1882 | | 1909 | 1920 |
| Knights of Labor Union | Chinese Exclusion Act | | NAACP founded | Nineteenth Amendment |

1860   1870   1880   1890   1900   1910   1920

Apply Skills

✓ **TEST PREP** **Reading and Thinking Skill** Read the paragraph below from *The Bitter Cry of the Children* by John Spargo. Then use what you have learned about fact and opinion to answer each question.

> I shall never forget my first visit to a glass factory….The boys employed, [were] about forty in number, at least ten of whom were less than twelve years of age….The hours of labor for the "night shift" were from 5:30 P.M. to 3:30 A.M….The work of these…boys was by far the hardest of all.

14. Which of the following is an opinion?

   A. About 40 boys were employed.

   B. Ten boys were less than twelve years old.

   C. Boys worked from 5:30 P.M. to 3:30 A.M.

   D. The work of these boys was by far the hardest of all.

15. Which of the following best summarizes what Spargo wants you to believe about child labor?

   A. Children worked hard jobs for long hours.

   B. Child labor laws protected children.

   C. Visitors did not see the worst sights.

   D. Children only worked at night.

Critical Thinking

✓ **TEST PREP** Write a short paragraph to answer each question.

16. **Cause and Effect** Why did labor unions organize strikes?

17. **Infer** What changes did the Great Migration bring to the lives of African Americans?

Timeline

Use the Chapter Summary Timeline above to answer the question.

18. What events took place in the 1800s?

Activities

 Connect to Georgia Progressives tried to improve life in the United States. Research and write a short biography of a Georgian who fought for change.

 Writing Activity Learn more about one of the inventions of the late 1800s, such as the oil cup, typewriter, or telephone. Write a description of the invention, explaining its effect on life in the United States.

 Technology
Writing Process Tips
Get help with your description at
www.eduplace.com/kids/hmss/

Vocabulary and Main Ideas

 TEST PREP Write a sentence to answer each question.

1. What effect did **transcontinental railroads** have on life in the United States?

2. What did the U.S. government do to make American Indians **assimilate?**

3. In what way does **competition** help to keep prices low?

4. Why did workers believe that **labor unions** were important?

5. Why did new immigrants to the United States often live with members of **ethnic groups?**

6. Who was Upton Sinclair and why was he called a **muckraker?**

Critical Thinking

TEST PREP Write a short paragraph to answer each question.

7. **Evaluate** Do you think immigrants' lives were better or worse after they arrived in the United States? Why or why not?

8. **Cause and Effect** How was the growth of cities a cause of the Progressive movement?

Apply Skills

TEST PREP Reading and Thinking Skill
Use what you have learned about fact and opinion to answer each question.

Settlers on the Great Plains faced many hardships. Winter temperatures could sink to 40° below zero. No one should have to live with that kind of freezing weather. Summers were hot and dry. Millions of grasshoppers ate the crops. The settlers probably wanted to live someplace else. But they had no right to complain, because land was so inexpensive.

9. Which statement is a fact?

   A. Settlers had no right to complain.

   B. Winter temperatures could sink to 40° below zero.

   C. Summers were pleasantly cool.

   D. No one should have to live with that kind of freezing weather.

10. Which statement is an opinion?

   A. Millions of grasshoppers ate the crops.

   B. Settlers on the Plains faced many hardships.

   C. The settlers probably wanted to live someplace else.

   D. Summers were hot and dry.

Connect to Georgia

Unit Activity

Create a Timeline

- Research Georgia events during the years 1870–1920.

- Choose five events that affected the lives of Georgians.

- Make a timeline. Include the date and an important fact for each event.

Personal Finance

In this unit, you read that competition in business means that more than one person or group tries to sell the same good or service. (p. 261)

Suppose you wanted to earn money by walking dogs in your neighborhood. How would you make decisions about what to charge people?

What might happen if someone else offered to walk the same dogs for less money than you charged? How would this competition affect decisions you might make?

CURRENT EVENTS
WEEKLY (WR) READER

Connect to Today

Create a bulletin board that connects an important event from this unit to events going on today.

- Choose an event or topic from the unit, such as new inventions, and write a description of it. Then find information about a similar topic.

- Write a paragraph or draw a picture showing the connections between the events.

- Display your paragraphs and illustrations on a bulletin board.

 Technology
Weekly Reader online offers social studies articles. Go to: **www.eduplace.com/kids/hmss/**

Read About It

Look for these Social Studies Independent Books in your classroom.

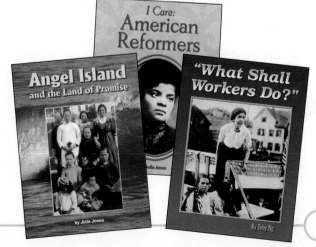

I Care: **American Reformers**

Angel Island and the Land of Promise
by Julia Jones

"What Shall Workers Do?"
By Toby Ng

289

UNIT 5

The Early Twentieth Century

The Big Idea

How do different people show their courage?

"The only thing we have to fear is fear itself."

President Franklin D. Roosevelt,
First Inaugural Address, 1933

Queen Liliuokalani
1838–1917

This queen fought to hold onto power in Hawaii. She lost her throne when Hawaii became part of the United States, but she did all she could to preserve Hawaiian traditions.
page 297

History Makers

The Wright Brothers
Wilbur, 1867–1912
Orville, 1871–1948

Two brothers made their dream of flight come true. After years of persistence and determination, they built and flew the first practical airplane.
page 332

Franklin D. Roosevelt
1882–1945

After millions of people lost their jobs during the Great Depression, Roosevelt offered Americans a "New Deal." His programs helped the nation survive this hard time.
page 345

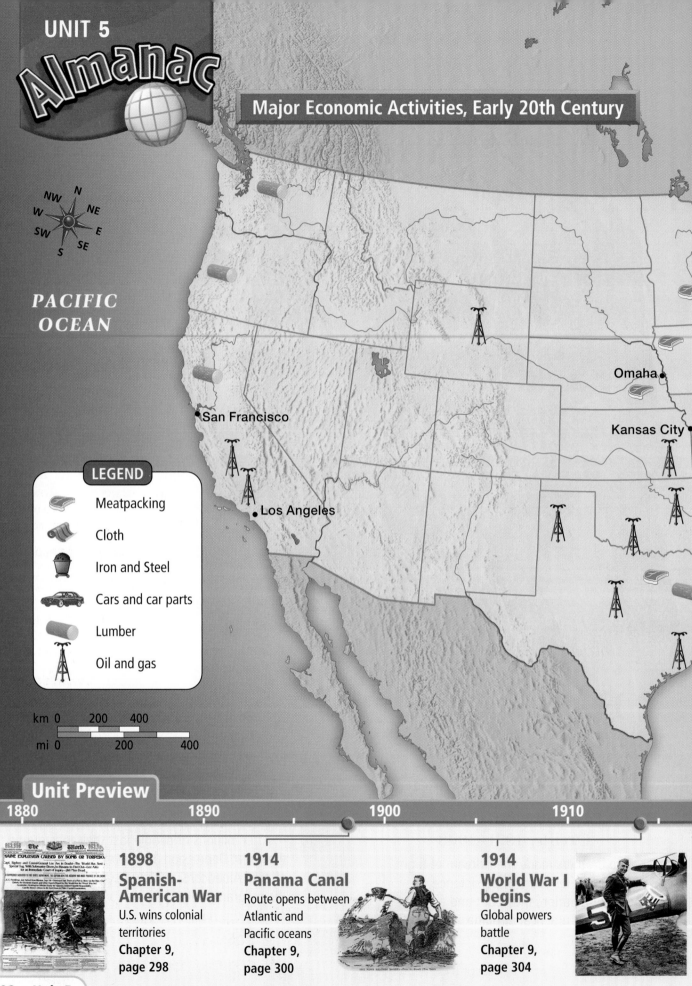

Major Economic Activities, Early 20th Century

N
NW   NE
W   E
SW   SE
S

PACIFIC
OCEAN

LEGEND

- Meatpacking
- Cloth
- Iron and Steel
- Cars and car parts
- Lumber
- Oil and gas

Omaha

San Francisco

Kansas City

Los Angeles

km 0   200   400
mi 0   200   400

Unit Preview

1880   1890   1900   1910

1898
Spanish-American War
U.S. wins colonial territories
Chapter 9, page 298

1914
Panama Canal
Route opens between Atlantic and Pacific oceans
Chapter 9, page 300

1914
World War I begins
Global powers battle
Chapter 9, page 304

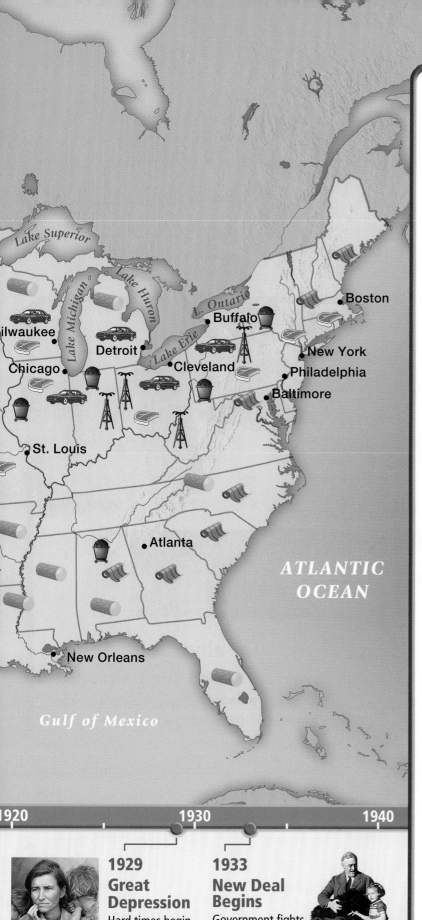

Boston
Buffalo
Detroit
Cleveland
New York
Philadelphia
Baltimore
Chicago
Milwaukee
St. Louis
Atlanta
New Orleans

Lake Superior
Lake Michigan
Lake Huron
Lake Erie
L. Ontario

ATLANTIC OCEAN

Gulf of Mexico

Connect to Today

Employment by Industry
1929

Government
Agriculture
Transportation and Utilities
Mining and Construction
Services
Manufacturing
Wholesale and Retail Trade

Employment by Industry
2003

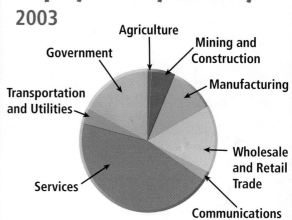

Agriculture
Government
Mining and Construction
Transportation and Utilities
Manufacturing
Services
Wholesale and Retail Trade
Communications

Economic activity in the United States has changed over time. What changes do the map and circle graphs show?

CONNECT to GEORGIA

Current events on the web!

Research how the New Deal helped Georgians through the Great Depression. Organize your findings in a multimedia presentation.

1920   1930   1940

1929
Great Depression
Hard times begin
Chapter 10, page 337

1933
New Deal Begins
Government fights unemployment
Chapter 10, page 345

Chapter 9

A New Role for America

Technology

e • **glossary**
e • **word games**
www.eduplace.com/kids/hmss05/

Vocabulary Preview

imperialism

In this cartoon, European leaders show **imperialism.** They are dividing the world into colonies as though they were slicing a cake. **page 298**

alliance

In the early 1900s, Britain, France, and Russia formed an **alliance.** They agreed to defend one another if attacked. **page 304**

Chapter Timeline

1898
Spanish-American War

1901
Theodore Roosevelt elected

1895 — 1900 — 1905

Reading Strategy

Question Ask yourself questions as you read this chapter.

Quick Tip Ask yourself whether you understand what you have just read.

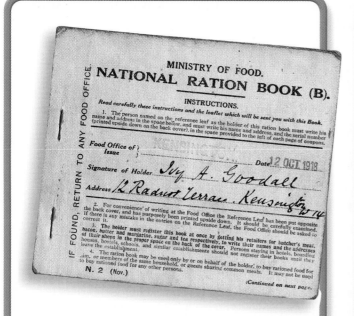

rations

During World War I, each person was allowed their **rations,** a measured amount of foods and supplies. Fewer goods for civilians meant more for soldiers. **page 313**

armistice

When World War I ended, people celebrated the **armistice** with parades. People were glad that the war was over. **page 314**

1914
World War I begins

1919
Treaty of Versailles

1910   1915   1920

New Territories

1860   1870   1880   1890   1900   1910   1920

1867–1914

READING SKILL
Compare and Contrast
Note the way each new territory was added to the United States.

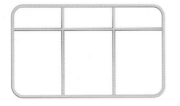

STANDARDS

SS5H3c America's role in the world

Build on What You Know Have you noticed that some people with a special talent or strength like to show others what they can do? At the end of the 1800s, the United States wanted to show the world it was a powerful country. Some Americans thought that adding new lands was a way to do that.

The Nation Expands

Main Idea The United States added Alaska and Hawaii to the country.

For much of the 1800s, the United States gained territory in western North America. During those years, settlers from the East moved to the new lands of the West. They began to mix with the American Indians, Mexicans, and others who already lived there. By the late 1800s, the country could no longer expand west. Some people believed the United States had reached the "end of the frontier." In the late 1800s and early 1900s, however, the nation found new ways to continue to gain land.

Alaska The vast region of Alaska is twice the size of Texas. It includes glaciers, volcanoes, grassland, and rain forest.

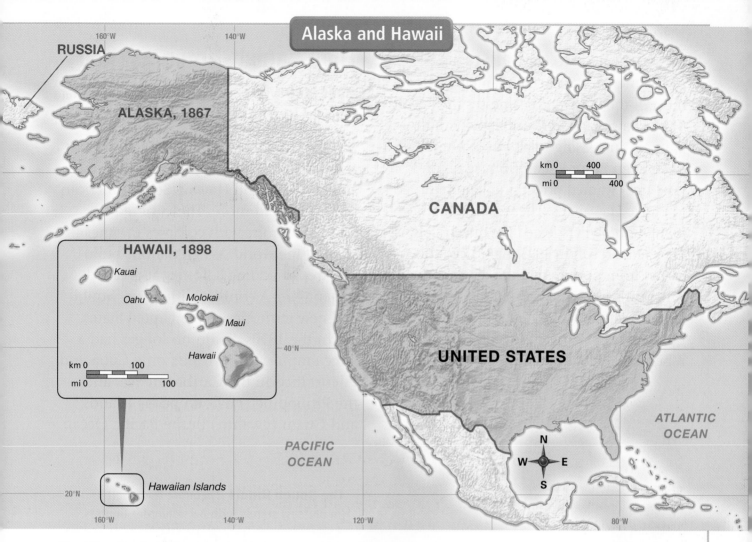

RUSSIA

ALASKA, 1867

CANADA

km 0   400
mi 0   400

HAWAII, 1898

Kauai

Oahu   Molokai

Maui

Hawaii

km 0   100
mi 0   100

40°N

UNITED STATES

PACIFIC
OCEAN

ATLANTIC
OCEAN

N
W   E
S

20°N   Hawaiian Islands

160°W   140°W   120°W   80°W

New Territories The United States bought Alaska in 1867. Hawaii joined the nation in 1898. **SKILL** **Reading Maps** What countries are close to Alaska?

Alaska and Hawaii

In 1867, Russia offered to sell its colony of Alaska to the United States. The Secretary of State, **William Seward**, convinced Congress to buy Alaska.

Most Americans believed that buying Alaska was not a good idea. They called Alaska "Seward's Folly."

Then, in 1896, miners found gold in the region. Thousands of people went to the region hoping to get rich. Very few discovered gold. What people did discover was that Alaska's fish, forests, and minerals turned out to be worth much more than its gold. In 1912, Alaska became a United States territory. In 1959, Alaska became the 49th state.

Hawaii is a group of islands in the Pacific Ocean several thousand miles west of California. The first people to settle there came from Asia, probably more than 1,500 years ago. The first Americans to come to Hawaii were mostly traders and missionaries who arrived in the late 1700s. Afterwards, Americans began setting up sugar and pineapple plantations there.

REVIEW How did Alaska become a U. S. territory?

Queen Liliuokalani
She became the queen of Hawaii in 1891.

Hawaii Joins the United States

By the late 1800s, the planters owned most of the land and businesses in Hawaii. Many Hawaiians were unhappy with the planters' increasing wealth and power.

Queen Liliuokalani (luh lee uh oh kuh LAH nee) wanted power and land returned to native Hawaiians. The wealthy American plantation owners feared the queen's plans. They led a revolt in 1893 that forced the queen from power. After the revolt ended, Americans in Hawaii asked to join the United States. In 1898, Hawaii became a U.S. territory. In 1959, it became the 50th state.

The Spanish-American War

Main Idea Victory in the Spanish-American War made the United States a world power.

The United States showed the world it was becoming more powerful when it added Alaska and Hawaii. Some American leaders wanted more. They wanted to build an empire with colonies in other parts of the world. When nations build empires by adding colonies, it is called **imperialism**. A conflict with Spain would add new territories to the United States.

In the 1890s, Spain no longer had a large empire. It controlled only Cuba and Puerto Rico in the Caribbean Sea, and the Philippine (FIHL uh peen) Islands and Guam (gwahm) in the Pacific Ocean.

The Rough Riders Theodore Roosevelt (in glasses) stands with his volunteer fighters.

CUBA

In 1895, the people of Cuba revolted against Spain. American newspapers wrote about Spain's cruel treatment of Cubans during the revolt. The news stories were shocking, but not always true. News reporting of this kind became known as yellow journalism. **Yellow journalism** is a kind of writing that exaggerates news to shock and attract readers.

In February 1898, the U.S. Navy ship *Maine* exploded in Havana harbor, Cuba. No one knew how the explosion happened, but American newspapers blamed Spain. President McKinley soon asked Congress to declare war on Spain.

The fighting began in the Philippine Islands. The U.S. Navy sank most of Spain's fleet in the Battle of Manila Bay. Then, the war shifted to Cuba.

Roosevelt and the Rough Riders

Theodore Roosevelt, the Assistant Secretary of the United States Navy, strongly supported American imperialism. He wanted to help fight the war against Spain. He quit his job and formed a volunteer fighting group known as the Rough Riders. They went to Cuba to fight. There, they were joined by a group of African American soldiers known as the Buffalo Soldiers. Together, they won a famous battle called the Battle of San Juan Hill.

Spain surrendered in August 1898. In the peace agreement, Spain gave Puerto Rico, the Philippines, and Guam to the United States. Cuba became independent.

REVIEW What was the effect of the explosion of the *Maine?*

Manila Bay The Battle of Manila Bay lasted just a few hours. When it was over, Spain's fleet was in ruins.

PHILIPPINES

Building the Panama Canal

Main Idea The United States built the Panama Canal to open a route between the Atlantic and Pacific oceans.

After the Spanish-American War, Theodore Roosevelt returned to the United States. He became President in 1901 and served until 1909. President Roosevelt believed that the United States should build a canal linking the Atlantic and Pacific oceans. The canal would save ships the long, expensive trip around the southern tip of South America when traveling from the east coast of the United States to the west coast.

The best place for a canal was at the narrowest point in Central America, which is the Isthmus (IS muhs) of Panama. An **isthmus** is a narrow strip that links two larger pieces of land. It has water on both sides.

Panama was a part of the South American country of Colombia. Roosevelt tried to buy land for the canal from Colombia. The Colombian government would not sell the land. Roosevelt tried another plan. He helped the people of Panama win their independence from Colombia. The new leaders of Panama agreed to let the United States build the Panama Canal.

Political Cartoon The title of this cartoon is "The News Reaches Bogotá." Bogotá is the capital of Colombia. **SKILL** **Primary Sources** Look at the details of the cartoon, such as the size of President Roosevelt and what he is doing. What is the artist saying?

Panama Canal
Ships in the canal sail through narrow passages that connect wider natural lakes.

Building the canal was difficult, dangerous, and expensive. It took about 10 years to complete. In August 1914, the Panama Canal finally opened. For ships that used the canal, the trip from coast to coast took only weeks instead of months.

REVIEW Why did the United States build the Panama Canal?

Lesson Summary

Alaska and Hawaii became part of the United States in the late 1800s. Victory in the Spanish-American War gave the United States the territories of Guam, Puerto Rico, and the Philippines. President Roosevelt built the Panama Canal to shorten the trip from coast to coast.

Why It Matters...

By the early 1900s, the United States had become an international power.

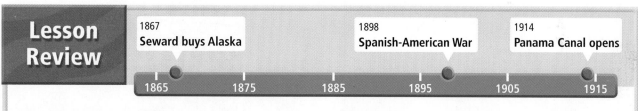

Lesson Review

1867 Seward buys Alaska	1898 Spanish-American War	1914 Panama Canal opens

1865   1875   1885   1895   1905   1915

① **VOCABULARY** Write a paragraph about how **imperialism** and **yellow journalism** led to the Spanish-American War.

② **READING SKILL** What was the difference between the ways Alaska and Puerto Rico became territories of the United States?

③ **MAIN IDEA: Geography** In which two Spanish colonies did the major battles of the Spanish-American War take place?

④ **MAIN IDEA: Economics** Why did the United States want to make the ocean trip from coast to coast shorter?

⑤ **PEOPLE TO KNOW** Who was **Theodore Roosevelt,** and what did he do during the Spanish-American War?

⑥ **TIMELINE SKILL** Which event took place in the 1900s?

⑦ **CRITICAL THINKING: Analyze** Why did adding Alaska and Hawaii increase the wealth of the United States?

HANDS ON

MATH ACTIVITY Find out how long it takes to travel from New York to San Francisco by ship. Compare the time it takes with and without using the Panama Canal. Calculate the difference and put your data in a chart.

PANAMA CANAL

The Panama Canal changed the geography of an entire region. How? The builders of the Panama Canal faced an almost impossible job on the isthmus of Panama. They had to dig and blast through 50 miles of jungle, swamp, and mountains to build a canal that would connect the Atlantic and Pacific Oceans. When the canal opened in 1914, it was said to be one of the greatest engineering achievements in history.

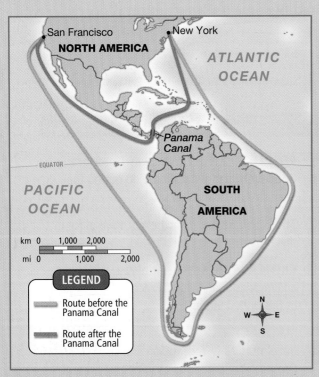

The Panama Canal turned a 13,000-mile trip into a trip of fewer than 5,200 miles.

Machinery
Enormous steam shovels were used to dig the canal. Billions of tons of rock and earth were hauled away in 4,000 wagons pulled by 160 steam locomotives.

Workers
More than 45,000 people worked for ten years on the canal. The use of dynamite and heavy machinery made the work dangerous.

Health and Climate

Workers lived in buildings like these. They slept with fine nets around their beds to protect them from mosquitoes. Thousands of workers died from the jungle heat, accidents, and disease during the building of the canal.

Trade

In 1914, the new 51-mile-long channel sped up the flow of people and goods. Today, hundreds of ships pass through the canal daily, carrying goods from all over the world.

Activities

1. **EXPLORE IT** Put yourself in this picture. Talk about what it would be like to be working on the canal.

2. **CHART IT** Use a world map to estimate distances between four countries for ships using the Panama Canal. Then estimate distances between the same countries for ships not using the canal. Show the differences on a chart.

World War I

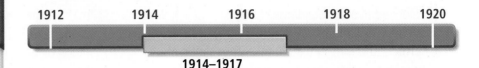

1912   1914   1916   1918   1920

1914–1917

VOCABULARY

nationalism
militarism
alliance
trench warfare

Vocabulary Strategy

| alliance

A synonym for the word
alliance is "partnership."
When people make alliances,
they become partners.

READING SKILL

Sequence List the events
that led to the start of World
War I. Put them in the order in
which they happened.

1	
2	
3	
4	

Build on What You Know When your friend has a
problem, you probably try to help solve it. In the same
way, the nations of Europe tried to help their friends
during World War I.

Causes of the War

Main Idea Struggles for power among European empires
caused a world war.

In the early 1900s, nationalism was leading European
countries toward war. **Nationalism** is the belief that your
country deserves more success than others.

Nationalism in Europe made countries such as
Germany, Russia, and France compete for land and power.
Several European nations followed a policy of imperialism,
starting colonies in other parts of the world.

To protect their empires, the nations of Europe
strengthened their armies and navies. Militarism became
popular with Europeans. **Militarism** is the building of a
strong military to frighten or defeat other countries.

The War Begins

As countries in Europe built up their armies, they also
made alliances with one another. An **alliance** is an
agreement nations make to support and defend each
other. The two most important alliances were the Allied
Powers, or Allies, and the Central Powers.

In 1914, Austria-Hungary, one of the Central Powers,
declared war on Serbia. Serbia had an alliance with
Russia, so Russia fought on Serbia's side. Then Germany,
also a Central Power, invaded Belgium and France.
France was allied with Russia. World War I, or the Great
War, had begun.

The Battlefield

Many people were eager for war. Because of the strong nationalism in Europe, thousands of young men signed up to serve in the military. They did not know how terrible the fighting would be or how long it would last.

Soldiers on both sides fought from long, narrow ditches called trenches. The fighting was called **trench warfare** because soldiers crouched down in the trenches for protection and fired their weapons from there. Sometimes they tried to capture the enemy by crossing the land between trenches.

Millions of soldiers were killed in these battles. The fighting lasted for four years. By the end of the war, Europe was covered with thousands of miles of trenches.

In most earlier wars, soldiers fought on battlefields but didn't live on them. With trench warfare, soldiers lived in the trenches day and night. The mud, cold weather, and rats made life hard. One soldier voiced the feelings of millions:

66 It was no place for a human being to be. . . 99

REVIEW Why did so many countries join the war?

Europe in 1914 This map shows the alliances of the European countries. **SKILL** **Reading Maps** Which countries were Central Powers?

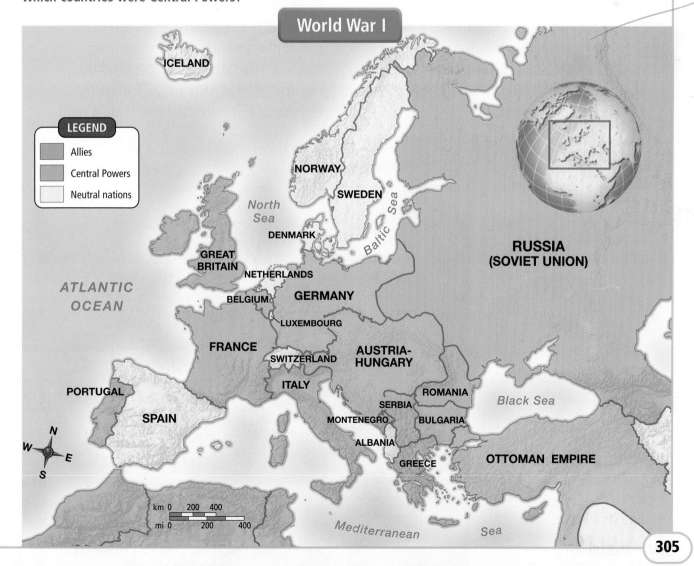

World War I

LEGEND
- Allies
- Central Powers
- Neutral nations

ICELAND

NORWAY

SWEDEN

North Sea

Baltic Sea

DENMARK

GREAT BRITAIN

NETHERLANDS

BELGIUM

GERMANY

LUXEMBOURG

ATLANTIC OCEAN

FRANCE

SWITZERLAND

ITALY

AUSTRIA-HUNGARY

RUSSIA (SOVIET UNION)

Black Sea

ROMANIA

SERBIA

MONTENEGRO

BULGARIA

ALBANIA

PORTUGAL

SPAIN

GREECE

OTTOMAN EMPIRE

N W E S

km 0   200   400
mi 0   200   400

Mediterranean Sea

America Enters the War

Main Idea The United States entered World War I in 1917 on the side of the Allies.

When World War I started in 1914, most Americans wanted to stay out of it. President **Woodrow Wilson** said,

66 The United States must be neutral… in thought as well as action. **99**

During the first year of the war, German submarines sank British ships carrying trade goods. Then, in 1915, a German submarine sank the *Lusitania*. The *Lusitania* was a British passenger ship with many Americans on board. People were shocked and angry.

After the sinking of the *Lusitania*, Germany agreed not to attack any more passenger ships. In 1917, however, Germany broke this promise and began attacking U.S. ships. Soon afterwards, in April 1917, the United States declared war on the Central Powers.

The first American troops landed in France in June. "Lafayette, we are here," said an American military officer in Paris. These now-famous words reminded people of the help France gave to the United States during the Revolutionary War.

New Weapons

The Allies and the Central Powers fought with new weapons in World War I. Soldiers used machine guns that could shoot hundreds of bullets per minute. They threw small bombs called hand grenades and fired cannon shells miles through the air.

Other technologies changed the fighting, too. Submarines sank ships in the Atlantic Ocean. The British invented the tank to attack across the land between trenches. Both sides used poison gas to harm and kill one another. Later in the war, airplanes were used to drop bombs. World War I was the most destructive war in history at that time.

A Soldier's Life These American soldiers had to eat their meals in the trenches. Below is the food kit that a World War I soldier used.

Eddie Rickenbacker Civilians admired fighter pilots because of their skill and daring.

Heroes of the War

The war produced many military heroes. An American pilot named **Eddie Rickenbacker** was a hero in the United States. A German pilot named **Manfred Von Richthofen** (RIKHT hoh fehn) was also famous. He flew a bright-red airplane and was called The Red Baron.

Many heroes of the war were never famous. Thousands of American soldiers fought bravely. Doctors and nurses worked hard to save soldiers' lives. As the fighting continued, ordinary people helped the millions of European civilians who needed food and shelter.

REVIEW What caused the United States to enter the war?

Lesson Summary

- European countries competed with one another to gain land and power.
- Alliances forced many countries to take part in the war.
- The two main alliances were the Allies and the Central Powers.
- The United States entered the war on the side of the Allies in 1917.

Why It Matters...

At the time, World War I was the largest and most destructive war that had ever been fought. The war directly affected millions of soldiers and civilians.

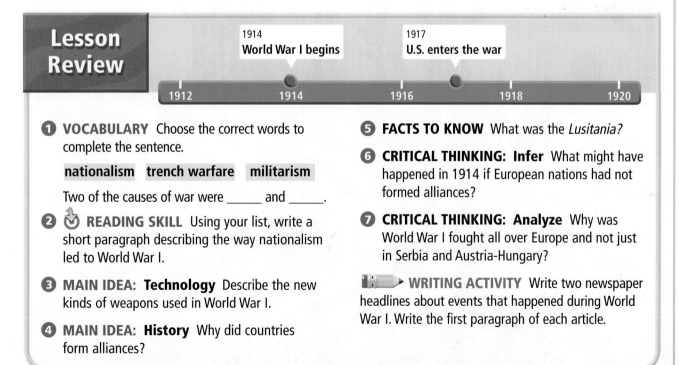

Lesson Review

1914 — World War I begins
1917 — U.S. enters the war

1912   1914   1916   1918   1920

1. **VOCABULARY** Choose the correct words to complete the sentence.

   nationalism   trench warfare   militarism

   Two of the causes of war were _____ and _____.

2. **READING SKILL** Using your list, write a short paragraph describing the way nationalism led to World War I.

3. **MAIN IDEA: Technology** Describe the new kinds of weapons used in World War I.

4. **MAIN IDEA: History** Why did countries form alliances?

5. **FACTS TO KNOW** What was the *Lusitania*?

6. **CRITICAL THINKING: Infer** What might have happened in 1914 if European nations had not formed alliances?

7. **CRITICAL THINKING: Analyze** Why was World War I fought all over Europe and not just in Serbia and Austria-Hungary?

WRITING ACTIVITY Write two newspaper headlines about events that happened during World War I. Write the first paragraph of each article.

Over There!

How did a popular song help win a war? In April, 1917, headlines blared the news: The United States had declared war on Germany and entered World War I. Europeans had been fighting for almost three years, and the Allies badly needed the help of American soldiers.

On a train to New York City, American songwriter George M. Cohan read those war headlines. Cohan was famous for patriotic songs such as "You're a Grand Old Flag" and "Yankee Doodle Dandy." Now a new patriotic song began to form in his mind. It was a song to inspire Americans to join the war effort. He built the chorus around a simple three-note bugle call. The title "Over There" came to him.

The song's message was a simple one: "We're coming! Help is on the way!" The message lit a fire of determination in people, inspiring many Americans to enlist in the army.

American soldiers on a ship heading to Europe.

Over There

George M. Cohan

1 O-ver there,____ o-ver there,____ Send the word, send the word o-ver there,____ That the

2 Yanks are com-ing, the Yanks are com-ing, The drums rum-tum-ming ev-'ry where.____ So pre-pare,____ say a prayer____ Send the word, send the word to be-ware,____ **3** We'll be o-ver, we're com-ing o-ver, And we won't come **4** back 'til it's o-ver o-ver there. O-ver there.

1 *Over there* means across the ocean in Europe, especially France, where most of the fighting was taking place.

2 A message of encouragement to the Allies that the "Yanks"—the Americans—were on their way.

3 A warning to the enemies to watch out.

4 A proud claim that Americans would not come home until the war was over.

▲ "Over There" became the most popular song of World War I and was even translated into French. By the end of the war, more than two million copies of the sheet music for the song had been sold.

Activities

1. **THINK ABOUT IT** Why do you think "Over There" was translated into French?

2. **REPORT IT** Interview someone who lived in the time of World War II or the Vietnam War. Ask about war songs. Then write the title of one song and explain its purpose.

 Technology Find more primary sources at Education Place. www.eduplace.com/kids/hmss05/

Skillbuilder

Understand Point of View

▶ **VOCABULARY**

point of view

A point of view is the way someone thinks about an issue, an event, or a person. Point of view is affected by experiences and beliefs. As someone grows and has new experiences, that person's point of view can change.

Understanding different points of view can help you understand others' actions. It can also help you form your own opinions. Part of being a good citizen is respecting others' points of view.

"I am bitterly opposed to my country entering the war, …War brings no prosperity to the great mass of common and patriotic citizens…We are taking a step today that is fraught with [full of] untold danger…We are going to run the risk of sacrificing millions of our countrymen's lives."

- Senator George W. Norris

"We know that in such a government [as Germany's]… we can never have a friend; and that in the presence of its organized power…there can be no assured security for the democratic governments of the world…The world must be made safe for democracy."

- President Woodrow Wilson

Learn the Skill

Step 1: Identify the writer or speaker's point of view.

Step 2: Find out who is writing or speaking. Do you know any experiences that may have influenced the writer or speaker?

Step 3: Summarize the writer or speaker's point of view in your own words. If you know about the person's experiences, explain how they might have influenced his or her point of view.

Practice the Skill

Read the passages on page 310 about the debate over whether the United States should enter World War I. Then answer the questions.

1 What is George Norris's point of view?

2 What words tell you what Norris believes?

3 What is Woodrow Wilson's point of view?

4 What events that you have read about might have affected Wilson's point of view?

Apply the Skill

Choose a topic below or one of your own. Write a paragraph expressing your point of view on the subject. Describe any personal experiences that affect your point of view.

- Students are excellent volunteer workers, and they should be required to do volunteer work as part of their education.

- A state tax on all movie tickets and movie rentals has been suggested. The money would go toward supporting school libraries across the state.

Americans and the War

VOCABULARY

rations
propaganda
armistice
isolationism

Vocabulary Strategy

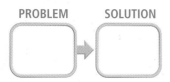
isolationism

Isolationism is related to a word that means island. An island is isolated, or far away, from other lands.

READING SKILL
Problem and Solution
Note the problems the United States faced in making enough supplies for soldiers and the solutions it found.

PROBLEM   SOLUTION

STANDARDS

SS5H4a U.S. fight against Germany

Build on What You Know When you have a hard job to do, other people can help you get it done. In the same way, Americans worked together to get things done during World War I. Ordinary people, as well as soldiers, helped the Allies fight the war.

The Home Front

Main Idea World War I changed life in the United States.

American soldiers needed many things to fight World War I. They needed ships and trucks. They needed small weapons, such as pistols, and large weapons, such as cannons. They needed uniforms, gas masks, and helmets. All of these things were provided by working Americans.

Businesses and workers made a huge effort to support the soldiers. During the war, the United States produced more war supplies than any other country ever had before.

African American Workers
Thousands of African Americans helped with the war effort. In this photo, champion riveter Charles Knight (left) puts together a ship.

The War Effort

To create more supplies for the soldiers, the government set limits on the amount of some goods civilians could have, such as meat. These limits are called **rations.** The things people did not use could be given to soldiers.

The government used propaganda to remind civilians to help with the war effort. **Propaganda** is information that is used to shape people's thinking. For example, the United States needed to send food to the soldiers, so the government printed posters urging civilians to eat less.

The United States needed millions of workers to make all the supplies for the soldiers. Many men, however, were serving in the military. Employers had to find new workers to fill the jobs at factories.

During the war, thousands of African Americans left the South to work in northern cities where the factories were. African Americans earned good wages in these factory jobs. They also earned respect because they were helping to win the war. But they still faced prejudice in the North, as they had in the South.

Women in the Workforce

The war brought new opportunities for women, too. Many women took jobs that had been open only to men. Women made weapons, repaired cars, delivered the mail, and directed traffic.

People changed their opinion of what women could do when they saw how well women worked in jobs that had been held by men. At this time, only men had suffrage, or the legal right to vote. The work women did convinced people that this was unfair. Demonstrations for women's suffrage also helped build support. In 1919, the Senate passed the Nineteenth Amendment to the Constitution. The states approved it in 1920. Women could finally vote throughout the United States. A woman of the time said,

66 **The greatest thing that came out of the war was the emancipation [freedom] of women, for which no man fought.** 99

REVIEW Which two groups of Americans took new jobs during World War I?

The War Ends

Main Idea World War I changed the boundaries of Europe.

The United States joined the war in 1917. By then, the Central Powers and the Allies were exhausted from three years of fighting. About one million American soldiers went to France. The strength of this force helped the Allies win important battles. Eventually, the Central Powers realized that they could not win the war and signed an armistice. An **armistice** is an agreement to stop fighting. The war ended on November 11, 1918.

In January 1919, leaders of the Allied countries met in France to write a treaty. President **Woodrow Wilson** was one of those leaders.

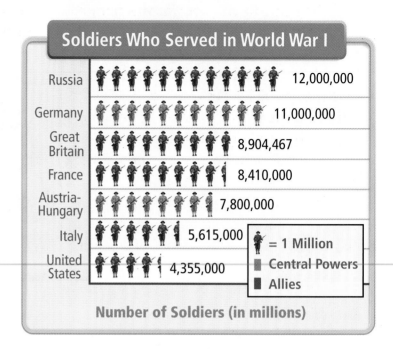

Soldiers Who Served in World War I

Russia	12,000,000
Germany	11,000,000
Great Britain	8,904,467
France	8,410,000
Austria-Hungary	7,800,000
Italy	5,615,000
United States	4,355,000

= 1 Million
Central Powers
Allies

Number of Soldiers (in millions)

SKILL **Reading Graphs** Which side had more soldiers during the war, the Allies or the Central Powers?

Effects of War The war changed the borders of Europe and created new countries.

Europe after World War I

LEGEND
Formerly Russia
Formerly Austria-Hungary

FINLAND
NORWAY
SWEDEN
North Sea
ESTONIA
IRELAND
DENMARK
EAST PRUSSIA (Ger.)
LATVIA
LITHUANIA
GREAT BRITAIN
NETH.
BELG.
GERMANY
POLAND
RUSSIA (SOVIET UNION)
LUX.
CZECHOSLOVAKIA
ATLANTIC OCEAN
FRANCE
SWITZ.
AUSTRIA
HUNGARY
ROMANIA
ITALY
Black Sea
PORTUGAL
YUGOSLAVIA
BULGARIA
SPAIN
ALBANIA
TURKEY
GREECE
Baltic Sea
Mediterranean Sea

km 0 200 400
mi 0 200 400

The Treaty of Versailles

The treaty to end the war was named the Treaty of Versailles (VEHR sy), after the French palace in which it was signed. Several European leaders blamed Germany for the fighting in Western Europe. These Allied leaders used the Treaty of Versailles to punish Germany. The Germans lost colonies, gave land to France, and paid money to Allied countries.

Wilson did not want to punish Germany, but he supported the treaty because it created the League of Nations. Through the League, nations would try to solve their problems peacefully. Members of the League also promised to protect one another if war did start.

Wilson asked the United States Senate to approve the Treaty of Versailles. The Senate refused. The senators thought the League of Nations might cause the United States to be pulled into future wars. Also, many Americans were horrified by the destruction of World War I.

Some began to believe in isolationism. People who believe in **isolationism** want to stay out of world events. After World War I, the United States would avoid alliances and conflicts whenever it could.

REVIEW What effect did the Treaty of Versailles have on Germany?

Lesson Summary

United States	Europe
Economy grew	Allies win with help from U.S. troops
New jobs for African Americans and women	Treaty of Versailles changed Europe

Why It Matters ...

After World War I, the United States took part in reshaping the borders and alliances of Europe.

Lesson Review

1918 — World War I ends
1919 — Treaty of Versailles
1920 — League of Nations

1917 | 1918 | 1919 | 1920 | 1921

1 **VOCABULARY** Why did **isolationism** in the United States grow after the **armistice** of World War I? Explain in a short paragraph.

2 **READING SKILL** How did ordinary people help the United States **solve** the **problem** of producing supplies for soldiers?

3 **MAIN IDEA: Economics** Why did African Americans and women have more job opportunities during World War I?

4 **MAIN IDEA: Citizenship** In what ways did United States civilians help win the war?

5 **EVENTS TO KNOW** Describe two results of the Treaty of Versailles.

6 **TIMELINE SKILL:** Was the League of Nations formed before or after World War I?

7 **CRITICAL THINKING: Decision Making** What were the consequences of the United States' decision to enter World War I?

HANDS ON

ART ACTIVITY Americans had to use less resources during the war to help the war effort. What resource do you think Americans should use less of today, and why? Make a poster supporting your idea.

315

POSTERS AND THE WAR

Uncle Sam wants you! That was the message of one of the most famous posters of World War I. The government used posters to attract volunteers to the military and get people involved in other ways. A special committee created the posters. During the war, they printed millions of copies and sent them throughout the country.

The posters were so successful that the government used similar posters to build public support for later programs. Even today, the United States military uses posters to bring in volunteers.

Tanks
Some posters used the danger and drama of war to attract volunteers.

Women and the War
Nearly 10,000 women served as nurses overseas during the war.

I WANT YOU
FOR U.S. ARMY
NEAREST RECRUITING STATION

Uncle Sam
The name "Uncle Sam" was a symbol of the United States before World War I. But posters made the symbol more powerful than ever. The artist who painted this image used himself as the model. Uncle Sam is shown with the same features in cartoons and posters today.

Activities

1. **DRAW YOUR OWN** The government still needs volunteers. Draw your own poster that calls on young people to serve their community or their nation.

2. **PRESENT IT** Find an example of a poster that you think is persuasive. Write a one-page paper describing the poster and explaining why it is persuasive. If possible, display the poster.

 Technology Visit Education Place for more primary sources for this unit. www.eduplace.com/kids/hmss05/

Visual Summary

1.–4.  Write a description of each item named below.

Adding New Land

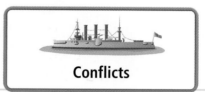

Conflicts

Alaska	Hawaii	Spanish-American War	World War I
_____	_____	_____	_____
_____	_____	_____	_____
_____	_____	_____	_____

Facts and Main Ideas

✔ **TEST PREP** Answer each question with information from the chapter.

5. **Geography** What resources were discovered in Alaska after it became a U.S. territory?

6. **Economics** Why did President Roosevelt want to build the Panama Canal?

7. **History** What is trench warfare?

8. **History** In what ways did World War I change the lives of African Americans and women?

9. **Government** Why didn't the United States join the League of Nations?

Vocabulary

✔ **TEST PREP** Choose the correct word from the list below to complete each sentence.

yellow journalism, p. 299
alliance, p. 304
rations, p. 313
militarism, p. 304

10. During World War I, Americans were allowed _____ of certain goods so that more supplies could be sent to soldiers.

11. The Allied Powers were an _____ during World War I.

12. Some newspapers in the United States used _____ to exaggerate news.

13. Some Europeans believed _____ was the best way to protect their empires.

1898
Spanish-American War

1901
Roosevelt elected

1914
World War I begins

1919
Treaty of Versailles

1895　　1900　　1905　　1910　　1915　　1920

Apply Skills

✓ **TEST PREP** **Citizenship Skill** Read the quote below from Mark Twain about the Spanish-American War. Then use what you have learned about point of view to answer each question.

> "...this is the worthiest [war] that was ever fought, so far as my knowledge goes. It is a worthy thing to fight for one's freedom; it is another sight finer [better] to fight for another man's. And I think this is the first time it has been done."

14. What was Twain's point of view?

　A. It was wrong for the United States to go to war.

　B. It was right for the United States to go to war.

　C. This was the longest war ever fought.

　D. This was the hardest war ever fought.

15. Which of the following reasons does Twain give for his point of view?

　A. The war would be bad for the honor of the United States.

　B. The war would be good for the U.S. economy.

　C. The United States would gain more freedom.

　D. It is good to fight for the freedom of others.

Critical Thinking

✓ **TEST PREP** Write a short paragraph to answer each question.

16. **Draw Conclusions** How did winning the Spanish-American War make the United States more powerful?

17. **Summarize** In what ways did life change for Americans during World War I?

Timeline

Use the Chapter Summary Timeline above to answer the question.

18. When was the Treaty of Versailles signed?

Activities

 Connect to Georgia Learn about men and women from Georgia who served overseas during World War I. Write a speech to honor one of these Georgians.

 Writing Activity Write a personal essay about why you think the contributions of civilians were so important to the American war effort.

 Technology
Writing Process Tips
Get help with your essay at
www.eduplace.com/kids/hmss/

319

The 1920s and 1930s

Vocabulary Preview

broadcast

In the 1920s, people began to listen to radio **broadcasts.** Listeners heard news, music, comedy, and mystery stories. **page 331**

aviator

Amelia Earhart was a famous **aviator** of the 1920s. She and other pilots made daring flights in early airplanes. **page 332**

Chapter Timeline

1917
Prohibition begins

1920
Women gain the vote

1927
Lindbergh's flight

1915

1920

1925

Reading Strategy

Predict and Infer Before you read each lesson, use this strategy.

Quick Tip Look at the lesson title and the pictures. What can you infer about the events?

depression

A **depression** began in the late 1920s. This slowdown in the economy affected the lives of many, even those who had once had luxuries.
page 337

hydroelectricity

Dams built in the 1930s used water power to create **hydroelectricity** for homes in rural areas. The prefix hydro- means water.
page 346

1929
Stock market crash

1932
Franklin D. Roosevelt elected

1930   1935

A Growing Economy

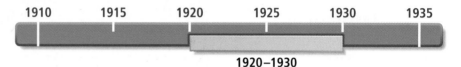

| 1910 | 1915 | 1920 | 1925 | 1930 | 1935 |

1920–1930

Build On What You Know How do you feel when you have a lot of energy? You probably feel like you can do anything. That's how many people felt after World War I. They put their energy into making life in the United States more prosperous.

Changes in Production

Main Idea The U.S. economy grew during the 1920s.

After World War I ended, people turned their attention away from world problems. They elected a popular new President, **Warren G. Harding**, in 1920. He believed that Americans were tired of war. His election message was "Back to Normalcy." For many, this meant they could stop thinking about the war and go back to their homes and jobs.

The economy of the United States went through a boom after World War I. A **boom** is a period of fast economic growth. One reason for the boom was an increase in international trade during and after the war. Most European nations had borrowed money from the United States during the war. When the war ended, their repayments of these debts helped the United States become the richest country in the world.

New Homes In the 1920s, many people had enough money to buy their own homes for the first time.

Car Sales, 1921–1929

Year		
1921	🚗🚗	
1925	🚗🚗🚗🚗	
1929	🚗🚗🚗🚗🚗	

🚗 = 1 million cars

SKILL **Reading Graphs**
About how many cars were sold in 1925?

Ford Cars Henry Ford and his son sit in one of Ford's early cars, built in 1905.

The Automobile Industry

The entrepreneur **Henry Ford** added to the boom by making cars in a new way. When he founded Ford Motor Company in 1910, his company's factories began using mass production. Mass production means using machines to make many products at once.

To produce large numbers of cars, Ford set up assembly lines. An **assembly line** is a long line of workers and equipment. Each group of workers on an assembly line does one job. For example, the first group might line up two pieces of the car. The next group connects the pieces with bolts.

This way of organizing work is called **division of labor.** When a company uses division of labor, each worker or group of workers has one small task in a big project. Using these methods, Ford's factories could produce cars more quickly and inexpensively than they had before mass production.

Because Ford spent less money to make his cars, he could charge lower prices for them. He could also pay his workers more and still earn a profit. Low prices and higher wages meant more people could buy Ford's cars.

Other industries copied Ford's methods of production. Companies mass-produced everything from sewing machines to refrigerators on assembly lines. As each industry grew, it hired more workers. These workers used the money they earned to buy consumer goods. Consumer goods are goods made to be sold to the public.

People bought consumer goods they had never owned before. For the first time, many Americans owned cars, vacuum cleaners, washing machines, and toasters.

REVIEW In what way did mass production change the economy?

Saving and Investing

In the 1920s, people looked for places to put their money. Many people kept money in savings accounts at banks. Banks hold people's savings and make loans to individuals and businesses. Banks in the 1920s, as today, loaned out the money in savings accounts. Businesses borrowed this money to improve their companies.

Other people invested money. To invest means to use savings in the hope of earning more money in the future.

Lots of Americans invested in stocks. A **stock** is a share of ownership in a company. Investors buy stocks at a certain price. When a company earns money, the value of its stock usually increases. Then the people who own stocks, also known as stockholders, can sell it at a higher price to earn money. When the value of the stock falls, however, the stockholder can lose money. The place where stocks are bought and sold is called a **stock market.**

Government in the 1920s

Main Idea The government encouraged economic growth during the 1920s.

The United States elected three Presidents in the 1920s: Warren G. Harding, **Calvin Coolidge**, and **Herbert Hoover**. These three leaders were similar. Each was a Republican and each encouraged strong economic growth in the United States. Calvin Coolidge expressed a belief held by all three of them when he said,

> 66 **The chief business of the American people is business.** 99

Coolidge wanted the government to act like a business. For example, he kept government spending low. He did this so that the government would take in more money than it was spending. President Coolidge also cut taxes. He believed that if taxes were lower, people would have more money to save and invest.

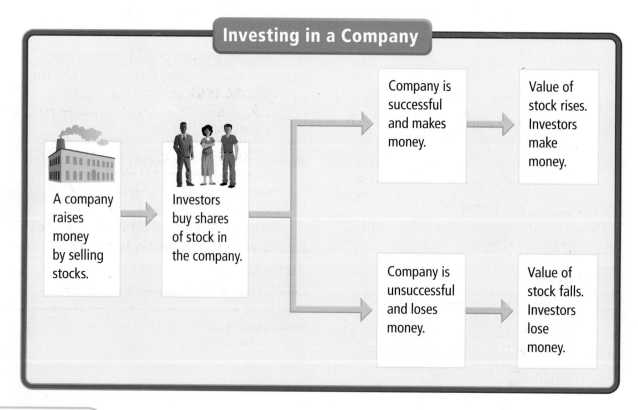

Investing in a Company

A company raises money by selling stocks. → Investors buy shares of stock in the company. →

Company is successful and makes money. → Value of stock rises. Investors make money.

Company is unsuccessful and loses money. → Value of stock falls. Investors lose money.

Herbert Hoover was elected President in 1928. Hoover believed that the government should not do too many things to change the economy. He believed that real economic growth came from the hard work of ordinary people.

Candidates
Campaign buttons and stamps told voters what presidential candidates stood for.

Hoover thought hard workers were the source of America's prosperity. In the 1920s, people thought this prosperity would last forever.

REVIEW How did Calvin Coolidge encourage economic growth?

Lesson Summary

- The American economy boomed during the 1920s.
- Mass production helped the economy grow.
- Some Americans invested in the stock market during the 1920s.

Why It Matters...

Mass production, assembly lines, and division of labor are used in United States businesses today.

Lesson Review

1910	1920	1928
Ford first uses mass production	Harding elected	Hoover elected

1900 — 1910 — 1920 — 1930 — 1940

1 **VOCABULARY** Use the terms **division of labor** and **assembly line** in a paragraph about how these methods were used in business.

2 **READING SKILL** Check your **prediction** against what you have read. How did the strong economy affect Americans?

3 **MAIN IDEA: Economics** Why did Americans buy more consumer goods in the 1920s than ever before?

4 **MAIN IDEA: Government** What views did Presidents Harding, Coolidge, and Hoover share?

5 **PEOPLE TO KNOW** How did **Henry Ford** change the way cars were made?

6 **TIMELINE SKILL** How many years after Harding was elected President did Hoover win the presidential election?

7 **CRITICAL THINKING: Decision Making** What might have been the opportunity cost for someone who decided to invest in the stock market in the 1920s? Remember that an opportunity cost is the thing you give up when you decide to do or have something else.

WRITING ACTIVITY Write a news article informing people of the economic boom in the 1920s. Answer the questions *Who?, What?, Where?, Why?,* and *When?*

Mass Production

Henry Ford's most successful automobile was the Model T. By today's standards it was boxy, and it came in only one color—black. But people bought it eagerly because it was well made and inexpensive. More than 15 million Model Ts were sold between 1909 and 1927.

Before the Model T, cars had been made one at a time by small groups of workers. The Model T was made in factories using mass production. Because the cost of making cars this way was lower, the cars could be sold at a lower price.

The assembly line was the secret to Ford's success. In assembly lines like the one shown here, each worker was trained to do a specific step, such as attaching the roof to the body of the car. These efficient methods lowered the price of the Model T from $850 to $290.

> " *I will build a car for the great multitude. It will be large enough for the family, but small enough for the individual to run and care for. It will be constructed of the best materials, by the best men to be hired, after the simplest designs that modern engineering can devise.* "
>
> —Henry Ford

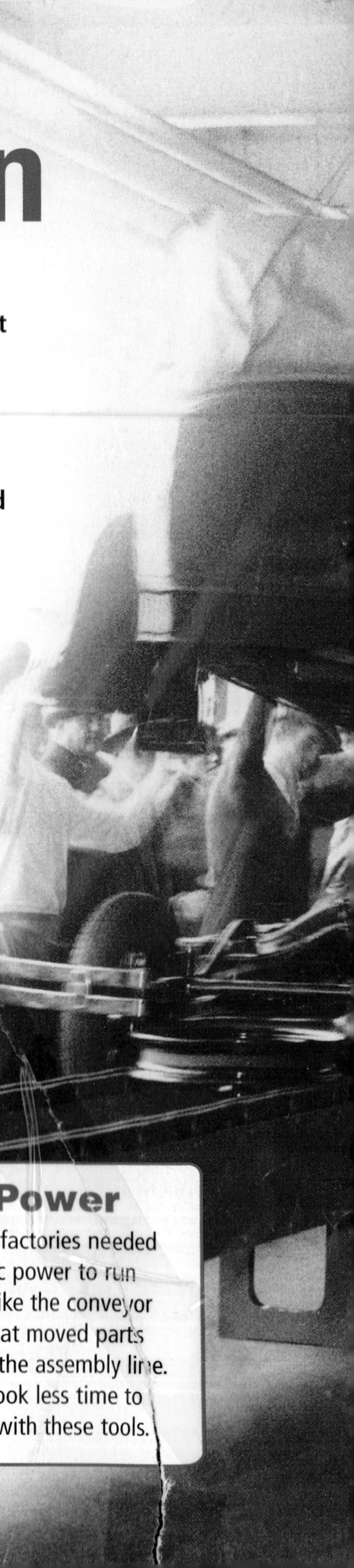

Power

Ford's factories needed electric power to run tools like the conveyor belt that moved parts along the assembly line. Cars took less time to make with these tools.

Parts

Each part of the Model T was cut to the exact size and shape as every other part like it. All the parts in a single car fit together like the pieces of a puzzle. Workers could put them in place quickly.

Price

Ford saved money in every way he could. If a part could be made smaller, it was. The savings on each part might be less than a penny. But the savings on millions of parts added up.

Activities

1. **STEP INTO IT** Why was electricity important to Ford's assembly line? Look at the photograph and find things that used electricity.

2. **ACT IT OUT** With other students, demonstrate how to make an object, such as a paper envelope, on an assembly line using supplies in your classroom. Describe what you've learned about creating an assembly line.

The Roaring Twenties

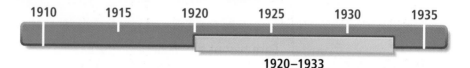

| 1910 | 1915 | 1920 | 1925 | 1930 | 1935 |

1920–1933

Build on What You Know How often do you ride in a car, listen to the radio, or see clothes being cleaned in a washing machine? These inventions first became popular in the 1920s.

Technology Changes Lives

Main Idea During the 1920s, the United States became more urban, and new technology changed the way people lived.

In the early 1900s, most people in the United States lived on farms or in small country towns. During World War I, rural people began moving to cities in large numbers. Instead of making a living by farming, they took jobs in factories and other businesses. By 1920, more Americans lived in urban areas than in rural areas.

Many people also bought cars for the first time in the 1920s, especially those built on **Henry Ford's** assembly lines. The number of cars on the road more than doubled between 1920 and 1929.

VOCABULARY

broadcast
aviator
prohibition

Vocabulary Strategy

aviator

The word **aviator** comes from a word meaning bird. Both birds and aviators can fly.

 READING SKILL
Main Idea and Details
As you read, note details that support the first main idea in this lesson.

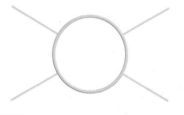

STANDARDS

SS5H3b Wright brothers
SS5H4b Cultural developments in the 1920s
SS5G1b Locate Kitty Hawk, NC

Changing Cities Electricity lights up the busy city streets of Richmond, Virginia, in 1921.

SKILL **Reading Visuals** What are some ways that electricity was used in Richmond in 1921?

Effects of New Technology

With cars, people traveled long distances more easily. Farmers in rural areas could drive to bigger towns for supplies. Families spent vacations touring the United States in their cars. Dirt roads were paved. Gas stations, billboards, and motels lined these highways.

Electricity also changed life at home. In 1920, about 35 percent of homes had electricity. Ten years later, 70 percent had electricity. Most homes with electricity were in urban areas.

Electric appliances made household chores easier. Vacuum cleaners and washing machines gave people, especially women, more free time. Before the invention of the washing machine, a woman could spend an entire day doing the laundry for her family.

Women in the Twenties Women smile as they hand in ballots to vote for President in 1920.

A Changing Society

Main Idea New kinds of music, art, and literature became popular in the 1920s.

The 1920s became known as the Roaring Twenties. People felt life was "roaring" forward like a speeding car. Women began to do things that they had not done in the past. Some played sports, went to college, and worked outside their homes in many types of jobs.

Like men, women drove cars for the first time. A few even flew airplanes. Young women called flappers cut their hair short and wore knee-length skirts instead of skirts that went down to their ankles. Most important, women enjoyed new rights. In 1920, the Nineteenth Amendment was ratified, giving women the right to vote in national elections.

REVIEW What were two ways women's lives changed during the 1920s?

Jazz and the Harlem Renaissance

Music was changing too. A new type of American music called jazz became popular. Jazz is a style of music that uses a lot of improvisation. That means musicians decide which notes to play as they perform. **Louis Armstrong**, a singer and trumpeter, helped to make jazz popular in the 1920s. Jazz fit that decade so well that it was sometimes called the Jazz Age.

Jazz has been influenced by many cultures, but it began among African Americans who lived in the South.

When enslaved Africans came to America, they brought many musical styles with them. Over time, some of these musical styles developed into jazz.

Harlem, a neighborhood in New York City, was famous for jazz. In the 1920s, Harlem became a center for African American musicians, artists, and writers, such as the poet **Langston Hughes.** They painted pictures of and wrote about African Americans. This period became known as the Harlem Renaissance (rehn ih SAHNS). A renaissance is a time when there is new interest in art, literature, music, and learning.

People of the ROARING TWENTIES

Duke Ellington
He was a bandleader who played the piano and composed songs that are still performed today.

Radio
The first radio signal to cross the Atlantic Ocean was sent by Guglielmo Marconi in 1901. By the 1920s, people listened to music, news, and dramas on radios like this one.

Joan Crawford
She was a movie star. Here she does a popular dance of the 1920s called the Charleston.

New Kinds of Entertainment

The first radio broadcast in the United States was in 1920. A **broadcast** is a program sent out over a radio or television station. In this first broadcast, station KDKA in Pittsburgh reported that **Warren Harding** had been elected President. Soon radio stations all over the country aired news reports and other programs. Families gathered around the radio each night to listen to music, comedy shows, and mystery stories. Radio commercials advertised everything from toothpaste to cameras. By 1925, more than two million homes owned radios.

Some of the most popular programs were sports broadcasts. Audiences cheered as **Babe Ruth** became the first baseball player to hit 60 home runs in a season, and as **Jack Dempsey** fought fearlessly in the boxing ring.

Helen Wills Moody was a famous tennis player in the 1920s. She won her first tournament when she was only 17 years old. Moody went on to win many more championships and Olympic gold medals as she showed the world that women could be great athletes.

Movies became a favorite form of entertainment during the Roaring Twenties. By 1924, movie studios in Hollywood, California, made more than 700 films a year. People crowded into theaters to watch the newest romance, adventure, and comedy films. At first, movies were silent. In 1927, the first movie with sound, called a "talkie," appeared, and movies became even more popular.

REVIEW What kinds of radio programs did people listen to during the 1920s?

Babe Ruth
Many people still think of Babe Ruth as the greatest baseball player of all time.

F. Scott Fitzgerald
His most famous novel, *The Great Gatsby,* was published at the height of the Jazz Age.

Zora Neale Hurston
She took part in the Harlem Renaissance by writing short stories and novels about African Americans.

The Wright Brothers Orville Wright made the first successful airplane flight at Kitty Hawk, North Carolina, on December 17, 1903. Wilbur Wright watched from the ground.

Early Aviators

The **Wright Brothers** made the first successful airplane flight in 1903 at Kitty Hawk, North Carolina. It lasted only a few minutes, but it showed Americans that flying was possible. In the 1920s, aviators began to fly long distances. An **aviator** is a person who flies an airplane.

In 1927, **Charles Lindbergh** became the first person to fly alone across the Atlantic Ocean. People listened to radio reports of his daring flight, and he became a hero. **Amelia Earhart** was another aviator who set many flying records. Earhart inspired other brave and independent women to follow their dreams.

In 1921, **Bessie Coleman** became the first African American woman to earn a pilot's license. Coleman learned to fly in France because flight schools in the United States would not teach an African American woman. When she returned, she thrilled crowds with her flying stunts.

Problems of the 1920s

Main Idea Discrimination and crime were problems in the 1920s.

Although the United States was changing, women, African Americans, Asian Americans, and Mexican Americans still faced prejudice. So did immigrants. Some Americans treated anyone different from themselves unjustly.

A group of mostly white men called the Ku Klux Klan spread hatred against immigrants, African Americans, Jewish people, and Catholics. The Klan had as many as five million members by the mid-1920s.

Klan members dressed in robes and hoods to hide their faces. They attacked and sometimes killed people they felt were "un-American." Brave people spoke out against the Ku Klux Klan, and by 1929 its membership had decreased.

Prohibition

Another source of problems in the 1920s was the Eighteenth Amendment to the Constitution. This amendment was ratified in 1917. It made selling and drinking alcoholic beverages against the law in the United States.

The time that this law was in effect is called the Prohibition Era. **Prohibition** means the act of forbidding something. During the Prohibition Era, criminals made and sold alcohol. These illegal activities led to violence in many cities. Prohibition was repealed, or ended, with the Twenty-first Amendment in 1933.

Farmers also struggled in the 1920s. They had grown and sold large amounts of crops during World War I and had borrowed money to buy more farmland. After the war, the Allies no longer needed these crops. As demand decreased, farm prices dropped.

Many farmers could not earn enough to pay back the money they had borrowed. Some were forced to sell their farms and look for other kinds of work.

REVIEW Why was Prohibition repealed?

Lesson Summary

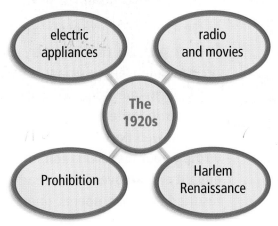

Why It Matters...

The prosperity of the 1920s brought with it new forms of entertainment, such as radio and movies, that are still enjoyed today.

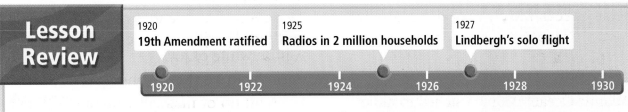

Lesson Review

1920	1925	1927
19th Amendment ratified	Radios in 2 million households	Lindbergh's solo flight

1920 — 1922 — 1924 — 1926 — 1928 — 1930

1. **VOCABULARY** Match each vocabulary word with its meaning:

   broadcast **aviator** **prohibition**

   (a) person who flies an airplane; (b) the act of forbidding something; (c) radio or television program

2. **READING SKILL** In what new ways did people use their cars in the 1920s? Use **details** to support your answer.

3. **MAIN IDEA: Technology** What effect did electricity have on people's home life?

4. **MAIN IDEA: Culture** What was the Harlem Renaissance?

5. **PEOPLE TO KNOW** Who was **Charles Lindbergh,** and what goal did he accomplish?

6. **TIMELINE SKILL** When was the Nineteenth Amendment ratified?

7. **CRITICAL THINKING: Analyze** New technology changed life in the 1920s. What new inventions are changing life in the United States today? Explain your answer.

HANDS ON

CHART ACTIVITY Use library resources to find out more information about the athletes, aviators, and artists from this lesson. Create a chart listing their accomplishments.

THE Harlem Renaissance

In the 1920s, the air of Harlem, in New York City, seemed full of poetry and the rhythms of jazz. A new generation of African American musicians and writers was getting people's attention.

African American poets, novelists, painters, and musicians came together in Harlem and other cities to share their ideas and their art. They showed how they felt about being black in a white world. They wrote about discrimination, their anger over slavery, and their need for equality. The movement spread to other cities. This outpouring of talent resulted in books, poems, operas, and plays—many of which are read and performed today.

The poets Georgia Johnson and Langston Hughes got their start during this period. Hughes loved listening to jazz and the blues. He wrote much of his poetry so it could be spoken to a jazz beat.

GEORGIA DOUGLAS JOHNSON (1886–1966)

Georgia Douglas Johnson began her career as a school teacher. She published her first book of poems in 1918. She said she wore a writing tablet and pencil on a string around her neck, "so when an idea, a word, a line for a poem comes, I jot it down." Johnson invited young writers to her Washington, D.C. home and encouraged them. Many famous writers came, including Langston Hughes.

Souvenir

A little hour of sunshine,
   A little while of joy,
We winnow in our harvesting
   From all the world's alloy.

None, none, are so benighted,
   Who journey up life's hill,
But have some treasured memory,
   Which lives all vibrant still.

— *Georgia Douglas Johnson*

Dream Variations

LANGSTON HUGHES (1902–1967)

Langston Hughes was born in Missouri. He began writing poetry in eighth grade and was selected class poet. Hughes first came to New York to study engineering, but soon gained recognition for his poetry. He once worked in a restaurant and left three poems on a table where a famous poet was dining. Impressed, the poet helped Hughes get his poems published. Hughes wrote books of poetry, plus stories, novels, plays, musicals, and operas— a total of around 60 books.

To fling my arms wide
In some place of the sun,
To whirl and to dance
Till the white day is done.
Then rest at cool evening
Beneath a tall tree
While night comes on gently
    Dark like me—
That is my dream!

To fling my arms wide
In the face of the sun,
Dance! Whirl! Whirl!
Till the quick day is done.
Rest at pale evening . . .
A tall, slim tree . . .
Night coming tenderly
    Black like me.

—Langston Hughes, 1926

King Oliver
Creole Jazz
Band, 1923

Activities

1. **TALK ABOUT IT** Listen to someone read aloud "Dream Variations." Explain how the poem is like music.

2. **WRITE ABOUT IT** Choose one of the poems on these pages. Write a paragraph explaining what the poem means to you.

The Great Depression

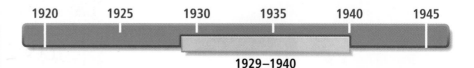

| 1920 | 1925 | 1930 | 1935 | 1940 | 1945 |

1929–1940

Build on What You Know Have you heard people use the terms "good times" and "hard times"? What do those terms mean to you? Life was difficult in the 1930s. For many Americans, these were hard times.

The Economic Depression

Main Idea Economic problems in the United States increased after the stock market crashed in 1929.

During the 1920s, many Americans believed the boom would last forever. They borrowed money to buy consumer goods and to invest in the stock market. They didn't know that the good times were about to end.

Then in October 1929, the stock market crashed. That means the total value of all the stocks in the stock market fell very quickly. Panicked stockholders sold their shares for whatever price they could get. Thousands of people and businesses lost money.

After the Crash
This man tries to sell his car just a few days after the stock market crash of 1929.

U.S. Unemployment

Number of People (in millions)

12
10
8
6
4
2
0

1929 1931 1933 1935 1937 1939

Year

SKILL **Reading Graphs** In which year were the most people unemployed? About how many people were out of work during that year?

Unemployed Americans People sold apples on street corners or did odd jobs to make small amounts of money during the Depression.

The Economy Slows Down

The stock market crash caused people to feel less confident in the economy. Store owners ordered fewer goods from factories because customers were buying fewer things. Fewer orders caused factories to fire workers. Unemployment increased. **Unemployment** is the number of people who are looking for a job but can't find one. Unemployed people had little money to spend, so more businesses closed. Within a few years, millions of people became unemployed, and many companies went out of business.

This period of unemployment and hardship is called the Great Depression. A **depression** is a time when people can't find work and many businesses close. The Great Depression lasted through the 1930s. Other countries were in a depression at this time, too. All over the world, people lost jobs. Factories and businesses closed.

Several things led to the worst depression in United States history. One cause of the Depression was that many people, especially farmers, were in debt. **Debt** is money that one person owes to another. People could no longer buy as many new homes or consumer goods as they had in the 1920s.

Bank failures were another cause of the Great Depression. In the early 1930s, thousands of banks went out of business. People who had money in these banks lost all their savings. Banks could no longer make loans to businesses. Problems on farms and the failures of banks added to an already slowing economy. The result was the Great Depression.

REVIEW Why did factory workers lose their jobs during the Great Depression?

Hard Times for Americans

Main Idea The Great Depression caused much hardship.

The Depression was a time of suffering for many people. The poet **Langston Hughes** said,

> 66 Everybody in America was looking for work. Everybody moving from one place to another in search of a job. 99

While not everyone was out of work, about 25 percent of the people who wanted to work were unemployed by 1932. Almost everyone knew someone who was looking for a job.

Thousands of people without jobs lost their homes because they could not pay their debts. Many built shanties, or shacks, out of cardboard boxes, broken-down cars, and scraps of wood. Clusters of these shacks were called shantytowns. Shantytowns sprang up all across the United States.

Charities and religious groups donated free meals to hungry people. A **charity** is an organization that helps people in need. People who did not have money for food lined up at soup kitchens and formed bread lines to wait for free bread and other food.

The Impact on Farmers

The Great Depression was especially hard on tenant farmers and sharecroppers in the South. Tenant farmers paid rent to live and farm on land owned by another person. Sharecroppers were tenant farmers who had so little money that they paid a share of the crops they grew to the landowner. Many tenant farmers and sharecroppers could not pay rent, so they had to leave.

A severe drought on the Great Plains in the early 1930s made things worse for farmers. So little rain fell that crops could not grow. Few plants held the dry soil in place, and winds blew loose dust and dirt across the Plains. Dust storms ruined crops and covered homes in soot.

Thousands of families living in this area, called the Dust Bowl, went to California to look for work on ranches and in orchards. Many Mexican families living in the United States were forced to move back to Mexico.

Tough Times This photograph taken by Dorothea Lange shows the suffering many farm families faced.

Culture in the 1930s

Many artists expressed the suffering during the Great Depression through photographs, music, and writing. **Dorothea Lange** was a photographer who took pictures of people who were hurt the most in the Depression. **Woody Guthrie** wrote songs about the hardships faced by people who left the Dust Bowl.

Other artists and athletes helped Americans to forget their struggles. People still listened to the music of **Duke Ellington** and other bands. **Margaret Mitchell**, a writer from Atlanta, wrote the novel, *Gone With the Wind*. In 1939, it was made into a popular movie.

Woody Guthrie

Jesse Owens, a track star, was also a hero of the 1930s. He won four gold medals in the 1936 Olympics. Owens, the grandson of an enslaved African, inspired many Americans to achieve their best.

REVIEW Why did people build shantytowns and stand in bread lines during the Depression?

Lesson Summary

- The economic boom of the 1920s was followed by a depression in the 1930s.
- After the stock market crash of 1929, people bought fewer goods and factories fired workers.
- Millions of Americans were without jobs, hungry, and homeless during the Depression.

Why It Matters ...

The Great Depression was a big event in recent history. Many people remember living through the Depression.

Lesson Review

1929
Stock market crash

1932
Unemployment at 25%

| 1929 | 1930 | 1931 | 1932 |

1. **VOCABULARY** Use the words **unemployment** and **depression** in a paragraph showing how these terms were related to each other in the 1930s.

2. **READING SKILL** Why were bank failures one **cause** of the Depression?

3. **MAIN IDEA: Economics** Why did many businesses close in the 1930s?

4. **MAIN IDEA: History** Why did many farmers from the Great Plains move to California during the Great Depression?

5. **EVENTS TO KNOW** What happened during the stock market crash of 1929?

6. **TIMELINE SKILL** How many years after the stock market crash did unemployment reach 25%?

7. **CRITICAL THINKING: Infer** In what ways do you think the Great Depression affected school children?

HANDS ON

MATH ACTIVITY Predict what the graph on page 337 would look like if it started in 1923. Then create a new graph with this information: 1 million unemployed people in 1923, 1.5 million unemployed people in 1925, and 1.5 million unemployed people in 1927. Compare the new graph with your prediction.

The Dust Bowl

They were called "black blizzards." Between 1933 and 1937, about 350 fierce dust storms swept through the Great Plains. People ran for shelter from swirling dust and dirt so thick it blocked the sun. The storms ruined crops and covered land and homes with dust.

The southern part of the Great Plains wasn't always known as the Dust Bowl. Before settlers moved there, the region was grassland. But farming harmed the land. Cattle ate too much grass, and plowing destroyed the grass that held the soil in place. When drought hit the region, the soil became very dry. Strong winds blew the dry soil into great clouds of dust.

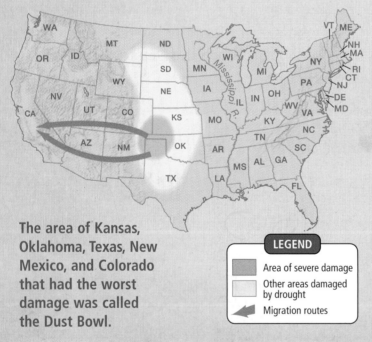

The area of Kansas, Oklahoma, Texas, New Mexico, and Colorado that had the worst damage was called the Dust Bowl.

LEGEND
- Area of severe damage
- Other areas damaged by drought
- Migration routes

1

Ruined Farms
Dust storms carried away the topsoil, the part of the soil that was best for growing crops. This ruined millions of acres of wheat and other crops.

2

On the Road

Unable to make a living, many families from the Dust Bowl region headed west. By 1940, 2.5 million people had left the Great Plains. They found work along the way when they could.

3

A New Life

The San Joaquin (wah KEEN) Valley is a rich farming area in California. Newly arrived families moved from farm to farm picking fruits, vegetables, and cotton.

Activities

1. **TALK ABOUT IT** What caused dust storms in the 1930s?

2. **DEBATE IT** Debate whether a Dust Bowl farmer should decide to move to California or keep farming on the Plains. Write a paragraph explaining your opinion.

Skillbuilder

Read Population Maps

Historians and geographers often want to know where people lived in the past and where they live now. Population maps can help. A **population map** shows where people live. By comparing population maps from two different time periods, you can see how settlement patterns have changed.

▶ **VOCABULARY**

population map

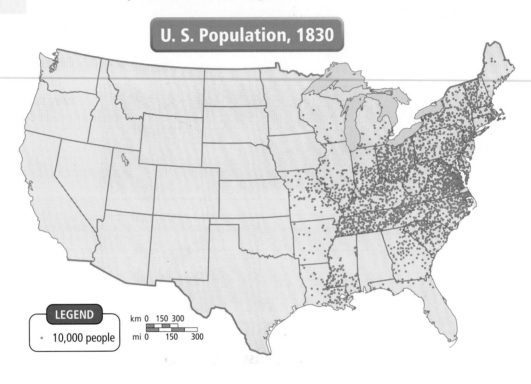

U. S. Population, 1830

LEGEND

· 10,000 people

km 0 150 300
mi 0 150 300

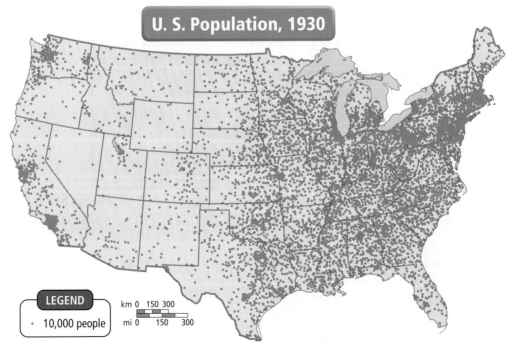

U. S. Population, 1930

LEGEND

· 10,000 people

km 0 150 300
mi 0 150 300

Learn the Skill

Step 1: Look at the two maps. Read each title. What is the subject and time period of each map?

U. S. Population, 1830

Step 2: Read the legend. It shows the number of people represented by each dot.

LEGEND
· 10,000 people

Step 3: Look at the dots on the maps. Areas with a lot of dots close together have many people living close together. Areas that have dots farther apart have fewer people.

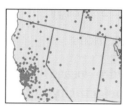

Step 4: Compare the two maps.

Practice the Skill

Use the two maps on page 342 to answer these questions.

1 Which regions of the country had the most people in 1830?

2 Which regions of the country had the fewest people in 1930?

3 Which regions of the country show the greatest population growth over time?

Apply the Skill

In a paragraph, describe the major changes in the United States settlement patterns between 1830 and 1930. Use information from the maps, as well as what you have learned about the history of this time period to explain some of these changes.

Roosevelt and the New Deal

| 1930 | 1932 | 1934 | 1936 | 1938 | 1940 |

1932–1939

Build on What You Know Have you ever helped someone in need? How did this make you feel? Many Americans needed help during the Great Depression. The federal government provided that help.

The Election of 1932

Main Idea Franklin D. Roosevelt was elected President because he gave Americans new hope during the Depression.

Herbert Hoover was President when the Great Depression began in the late 1920s. Hoover believed that the federal government should not play a big role in the economy. He thought the economy would improve on its own, as it had in the past.

The economy did not get better, though. Instead, it got worse. People continued to lose their homes and jobs. Many Americans started to think the government should do more to help. Hoover asked Congress to help struggling businesses and unemployed workers. Congress made new laws that loaned money to banks, railroads, and other companies. Unfortunately, these laws did not improve the whole economy.

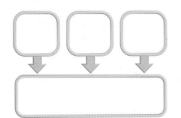
Herbert Hoover Some Americans blamed the poor economy on President Hoover. They urged him to take action.

Franklin D. Roosevelt This photograph shows President Roosevelt during his third term. He talks to a young friend while holding his dog, Fala.

Roosevelt Becomes President

Franklin Delano Roosevelt, a Democrat, ran for President against Hoover in the 1932 election. Roosevelt said, "I pledge you, I pledge myself, to a new deal for the American people."

Roosevelt thought the federal government should take action to end the Depression. He promised to create government programs to help people who were suffering. Americans believed these programs would help them. They elected Roosevelt as President.

When Roosevelt took office in 1933, he gave hope to many. He said,

> 66 **The only thing we have to fear is fear itself.** 99

Roosevelt wanted people to feel that the country's economy would soon improve.

The New Deal

Main Idea The federal government created programs that gave people food, shelter, and jobs during the Depression.

As soon as Roosevelt became President, he went to work to give the American people the "new deal" he had promised. He started a variety of government programs that became known as the New Deal. Some programs gave food and shelter to those in need. Others put people back to work. All were federal government programs that Roosevelt thought would help the economy. Congress quickly passed laws to put the New Deal into action.

Eleanor Roosevelt

Eleanor Roosevelt, the wife of the President, worked hard to get people, especially women, involved in New Deal programs. She traveled all over the country to learn about and see firsthand the problems caused by the Depression. Like her husband, she believed that the government should help people. She said,

> 66 **Government has a responsibility to defend the weak.** 99

The First Lady also spoke out for the rights of workers, African Americans, and children. She started programs like the National Youth Administration that created jobs for young people. She argued for laws that protected the rights of African Americans.

REVIEW How were Hoover's and Roosevelt's views about the federal government different?

New Deal Programs

One important New Deal program was the Civilian Conservation Corps, or CCC. Its goal was to create jobs and conserve, or protect, the natural environment. CCC workers planted trees, cleared hiking trails, and completed other conservation projects.

The Tennessee Valley Authority, or TVA, was another New Deal program. People working for the TVA built dams on the Tennessee River. The dams created hydroelectricity for rural areas in the Southeast. **Hydroelectricity** is electricity produced by moving water. The dams also prevented floods.

The Works Progress Administration, or WPA, hired people to build streets, parks, libraries, and schools. It paid artists to paint murals on public buildings and hired authors to write books about places in the United States.

Many New Deal programs continue today. The Social Security Act of 1935 is still in effect. **Social Security** provides money to people over the age of 65. Social Security also helps those who have disabilities and cannot work.

Some New Deal regulations still affect the economy. A **regulation** is a rule or law. Today, some regulations protect savings accounts in banks. Others protect workers by setting a minimum wage. A **minimum wage** is the lowest amount of money most workers can be paid.

President Roosevelt also used price incentives to improve the economy. He allowed the dollar to become worth less, which made it less expensive to pay debts. He also kept interest rates low. An interest rate is the amount people pay to borrow money. Low interest rates make it cheaper to borrow from banks. By making it easier to borrow and pay back money, Roosevelt helped Americans who were in debt.

Building Dams This mural shows workers building a dam as part of a New Deal project. It was painted by an artist hired by the WPA.

SKILL **Reading Visuals** What does this painting tell you about the amount of work involved in building dams?

The economy improved during Roosevelt's presidency, but by 1939, millions of people were still out of work. Even so, the New Deal gave Americans hope. Never before had the federal government created so many programs to provide jobs for people. Ever since Roosevelt's presidency, the federal government has played a larger role in the economy.

REVIEW What does the Social Security Act do?

New Deal Programs
The WPA provided jobs for about 2 million people.

Lesson Summary
President Hoover hoped the economy would improve without government action, but it did not. Franklin D. Roosevelt promised a "new deal" for the American people and was elected President in 1932. Roosevelt created government programs, called the New Deal, to help people through the Depression. Many of them still exist today.

Why It Matters ...
The New Deal was the beginning of a more active role for the federal government in the economy.

Lesson Review

1932
Roosevelt elected President

1935
Social Security begins

| 1932 | 1933 | 1934 | 1935 |

1 **VOCABULARY** Use the words **regulation** and **minimum wage** in a paragraph about the New Deal.

2 **READING SKILL** What **conclusion** did you come to about the effect of the New Deal? Support your conclusion with details.

3 **MAIN IDEA: History** What did Franklin D. Roosevelt believe about the role of the federal government in the nation's economy?

4 **MAIN IDEA: Government** Describe three of the jobs the New Deal created.

5 **TIMELINE SKILL** How many years after Roosevelt was elected President did Social Security begin?

6 **CRITICAL THINKING: Fact and Opinion** Was Eleanor Roosevelt's statement, "Government has a responsibility to defend the weak," a fact or an opinion? Explain your answer.

HANDS ON

SPEAKING ACTIVITY When Presidents run for reelection, they often give speeches telling people about their accomplishments as President. Write a short speech Roosevelt might have given when he ran for reelection in 1936. Prepare how you might act it out.

Eleanor Roosevelt

1884–1962

Champion of Equality

Eleanor Roosevelt believed in the equality of blacks and whites and all people.

Why was she admired for her knowledge, wisdom, and courage? Eleanor Roosevelt saw firsthand how citizens lived, and she listened to their concerns. During the worst times of the Depression, she traveled and met with southern blacks and migrant workers to find out about their struggles. She would talk over her experiences with her husband, President Franklin D. Roosevelt. Though she could not make laws, she could help shape New Deal programs.

She also shared her ideas with millions of readers. In her daily newspaper column, called "My Day," Roosevelt wrote about the rights of African Americans and women. She described the need for fair housing and fair working conditions.

In 1946, President Truman chose her to head the United Nations Human Rights Commission. In 1961, President John F. Kennedy made her head of the Commission on the Status of Women.

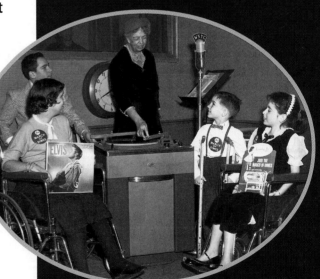

Concern for Others

Roosevelt often visited children with disabilities. Her own husband had overcome a disability.

" I could not, at any age, really be contented to take my place in a warm corner by the fireside and simply look on. **"**

—Eleanor Roosevelt

Activities

1. **TALK ABOUT IT** How did Eleanor Roosevelt work for **fairness** for other people?

2. **RESEARCH IT** Find out what happened in 1949 when Eleanor Roosevelt asked Marian Anderson to sing at the Lincoln Memorial. Use resources in your library.

 Technology Read more biographies at Education Place. www.eduplace.com/kids/hmss05/

Visual Summary

1–4. Write a description of each item named below.

Ecomonic Boom	Stock Market Crash	Great Depression	New Deal
	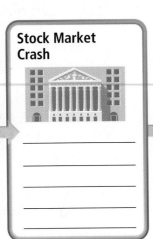	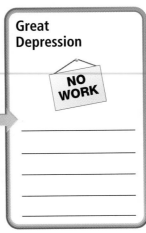	

Facts and Main Ideas

TEST PREP Answer each question with information from the chapter.

5. **Economics** What was the benefit of using assembly lines in Ford's car factory?

6. **Economics** How did mass production increase prosperity during the 1920s?

7. **History** What was the Harlem Renaissance?

8. **Geography** What and where was the Dust Bowl?

9. **History** What were two of the programs in President Franklin D. Roosevelt's New Deal?

Vocabulary

TEST PREP Choose the correct word to complete each sentence.

assembly line, p. 323
aviator, p. 332
debt, p. 337
charity, p. 338

10. Amelia Earhart was an _____ who inspired women to follow their dreams.

11. After the stock market crash, many farmers went into _____.

12. Henry Ford used an _____ to make his cars quickly.

13. People who could not buy food could sometimes go to a _____ for a free meal.

CHAPTER SUMMARY TIMELINE

1919 **Prohibition begins**	1920 **Women gain the vote**	1927 **Lindbergh's flight**	1929 **Stock market crash**	1932 **Roosevelt elected**

1915   1920   1925   1930   1935

Apply Skills

✔ **TEST PREP** **Map Skill** Use the 1890 U.S. population map below to answer each question.

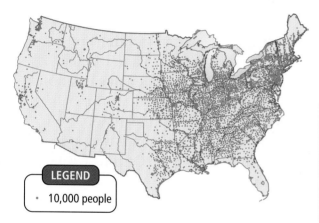

LEGEND

· 10,000 people

14. How many people does each dot represent?

   A. 1,000 people

   B. 5,000 people

   C. 10,000 people

   D. 100,000 people

15. What conclusion can you draw from the map?

   A. More people lived in the Southwest than in the Southeast.

   B. More people lived in the Northwest than in the Northeast.

   C. Most people lived in the western half of the country

   D. Most people lived in the eastern half of the country.

Critical Thinking

✔ **TEST PREP** Write a short paragraph to answer each question.

16. **Summarize** In what ways did women's lives change in the 1920s?

17. **Compare and Contrast** Compare President Roosevelt's and President Hoover's solutions to the Great Depression.

Timeline

Use the Chapter Summary Timeline above to answer the question.

18. Was Franklin D. Roosevelt elected President before or after the stock market crash?

Activities

 Connect to Georgia President Franklin Delano Roosevelt thought of Georgia as a second home. Do research and write a report on his connection to Georgia.

 Writing Activity Write a story about a family living in the Dust Bowl. Describe some of the difficulties they faced.

 Technology
Writing Process Tips
Get help with your story at
www.eduplace.com/kids/hmss/

Review and Test Prep

Vocabulary and Main Ideas

✓ **TEST PREP** Write a sentence to answer each question.

1. What actions did the United States take in the early 20th century that could be seen as following a policy of **imperialism?**

2. In what way did **alliances** help to start World War I?

3. What was **propaganda** used for by the United States government during World War I?

4. In what way was **unemployment** related to the Great Depression?

5. Why was the 1920s called the **Prohibition** Era?

6. How was **division of labor** used in Henry Ford's factories?

Critical Thinking

✓ **TEST PREP** Write a short paragraph to answer each question.

7. **Compare and Contrast** What are some ways in which the Spanish-American War and World War I were alike? What are some ways in which they were different?

8. **Synthesize** Explain how the New Deal helped people in the United States during the Great Depression. Use details from the unit to support your answer.

Apply Skills

✓ **TEST PREP** **Citizenship Skill** Read the quote below from President Roosevelt about the New Deal. Then use what you know about point of view to answer each question.

"Of course we will continue our efforts for young men and women so that they may obtain an education. Of course we will continue our help for the crippled, for the blind, … our insurance for the unemployed, our security for the aged. Of course we will continue to protect the consumer. "

9. What is Roosevelt's point of view?

   A. He thinks consumers do not need to be protected.

   B. He believes that government should continue to help people.

   C. No effort should be made to help young people.

   D. He does not think that unemployed people should have insurance.

10. What words tell you what Roosevelt believes?

   A. "we will continue our efforts"

   B. "they may obtain"

   C. "put it to use"

   D. "young men and women"

Connect to Georgia

Unit Activity
GEORGIA

Give a Presentation

- Research how New Deal programs helped Georgians during the Great Depression.

- Prepare an oral or multimedia presentation about the New Deal in Georgia.

- Include photographs, drawings, or primary sources as part of your presentation.

Personal Finance
GEORGIA

In this unit, you read that some people save money by putting it a savings account in a bank. People also invest money in the stock market. (p. 324)

Compare and contrast the benefits of saving money in a bank and investing it in the stock market. Why might people choose one option over the other? If you had extra money, which option would you choose? Why?

CURRENT EVENTS
WEEKLY (WR) READER

Connect to Today

Make a display of people in the news who do courageous things.

- Find information about at least two people who have shown courage.

- Find photographs of them or draw pictures. Write the name of each person below his or her picture.

- Discuss with a partner why you chose each person and display the pictures in your classroom.

Technology
Weekly Reader online offers social studies articles. Go to:
www.eduplace.com/kids/hmss/

Read About It

Look for these Social Studies Independent Books in your classroom.

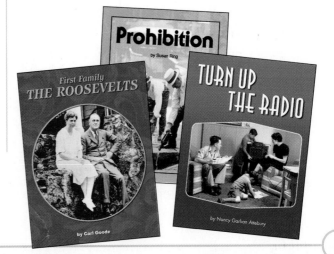

UNIT 6

Modern America

The Big Idea

How does a person inspire others?

"*Ask not what your country can do for you —ask what you can do for your country.*"

President John F. Kennedy,
Inaugural Address, 1961

Dwight D. Eisenhower
1890–1969

This general and future President led the largest invasion in history to defeat Germany during World War II. The success of the Allies depended on what he and his troops did on D-day.
page 377

I LIKE IKE

History Makers

Rosa Parks
1913–2005

When she refused to give up her seat on a bus, Parks challenged Alabama's laws. Her arrest and the boycott that followed it inspired people to protest unfair laws.

page 407

John F. Kennedy
1917–1963

The youngest President ever elected, Kennedy started programs to help people all over the world. He also urged his country to put a person on the moon.

page 392

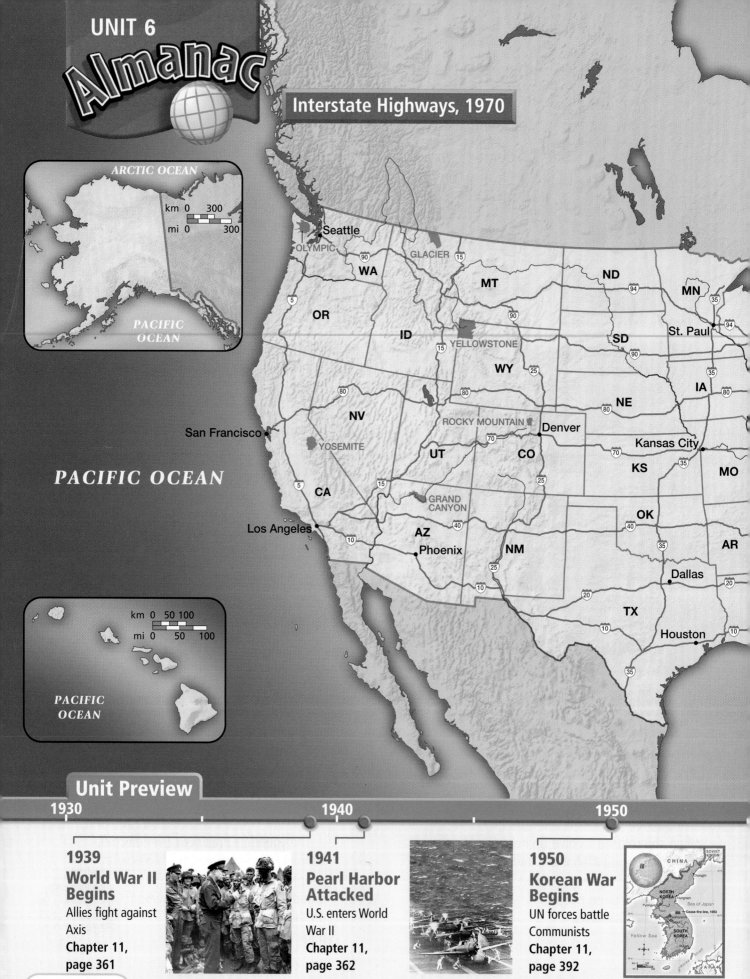

ARCTIC OCEAN

km 0   300
mi 0   300

PACIFIC
OCEAN

Seattle
OLYMPIC
GLACIER
90
WA
15

MT
ND
94
MN
35

OR
5
90

ID
15
YELLOWSTONE
SD
90
St. Paul
94

WY
25
35
IA
80

80
NE
80

NV
ROCKY MOUNTAIN
Denver
70
Kansas City

San Francisco
YOSEMITE
70
KS
35
MO

PACIFIC OCEAN

UT
CO
25

CA
15
GRAND
CANYON
25
OK
40
AR
35

Los Angeles
5
40
AZ
Phoenix
NM
25
Dallas
20

10
20
TX
10
Houston
10

10
35

km 0 50 100
mi 0 50 100

PACIFIC
OCEAN

Unit Preview

Map labels

ME
VT
NH
MA
95
NY
RI
CT
90
95
WI
MI
Detroit
94
75
Chicago
IN
OH
PA
NJ
Philadelphia
80
90
75
70
95
MD
DE
Washington, D.C.
55
65
IL
WV
70
64
64
KY
VA
64
95
75
55
NC
GREAT SMOKY MOUNTAINS
TN
SC
40
65
20
MS
AL
GA
20
75
95
55
65
10
Jacksonville
LA
75
New Orleans
FL
95

ATLANTIC OCEAN

N
NW NE
W E
SW SE
S

Gulf of Mexico

km 0   150   300
mi 0   150   300

LEGEND
- ▮ Major national park
- ―90― Interstate highway
- • Major city, 1970

Connect to Today

Highway Travel, 1960

Trip	Travel Time
Los Angeles–New York	51 hours
Dallas–Chicago	17 hours
Atlanta–Seattle	48 hours

Air Travel Today

Trip	Travel Time
Los Angeles–New York	5 hrs., 5 min.
Dallas–Chicago	2 hrs., 15 min.
Atlanta–Seattle	5 hrs., 30 min.

In what ways do you think faster travel affects individuals? In what ways does it affect business?

CONNECT to GEORGIA

Research a famous Georgian and his or her contributions to the state or the nation between 1940 and 1970. With another classmate, act out an interview of this person.

Timeline

1960

1970

1965
Vietnam War Begins
First U.S. troops sent to Vietnam
Chapter 12, page 422

1969
Moon Landing
Astronauts land on moon
Chapter 12, page 415

A Time of Conflict

Technology

e • **glossary**
e • **word games**
www.eduplace.com/kids/hmss05/

Vocabulary Preview

mobilize

After the attack on Pearl Harbor, people in the United States started to **mobilize** for war. They began to get ready to fight.
page 370

newsreel

People who went to a movie during World War II saw a **newsreel** at the beginning of the show. This short film supplied news about the war.
page 372

Chapter Timeline

1941 U.S. enters World War II		1944 D-day	1945 V-J Day

1940   1942   1944

Reading Strategy

Monitor and Clarify As you read, use this strategy to check your understanding.

Quick Tip Stop to check that you understand what you are reading. Reread, if necessary.

aircraft carrier

The United States used **aircraft carriers** during World War II. Planes can take off from and land on these large ships. **page 378**

capitalism

The United States economy is based on **capitalism.** People and businesses, not the government, decide what goods and services to make and sell. **page 384**

1950
Korean War begins

| 1946 | 1948 | 1950 |

World War II

1930   1935   1940   1945   1950   1955   1960   1965

1933–1941

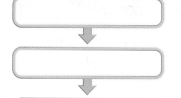
Build on What You Know Can you tell when a storm is coming? The wind is strong, the sky turns dark, and you hear thunder far away. In the 1930s, many people saw war coming like storm in the distance.

Start of the War

Main Idea The rise of powerful dictators led to World War II.

After World War I, people hoped for peaceful times. But nations around the world had serious problems in the 1930s. The Great Depression ruined their economies. Thousands of people had no work and struggled to make a living. As things grew worse, people turned to strong leaders to solve their problems.

A German leader named **Adolf Hitler** said that he could solve his country's problems. He led a political party called the National Socialists, or Nazis. The Nazis believed in fascism (FASH iz uhm). Under **fascism,** the government controls the economy, culture, and all parts of people's lives.

In 1933, the Nazis took power in Germany. Hitler ruled as a dictator. A **dictator** is a ruler who has total control of a country and its people. Hitler wanted to build a power-ful military and make Germany a strong nation.

Dictators Adolf Hitler of Germany (right) and Benito Mussolini of Italy (left) led political parties that believed in fascism.

A Growing Threat

Fascism and similar movements gained strength in other countries. In Italy, Benito Mussolini ruled as a dictator during the 1930s. In Japan, nationalist leaders took control. They wanted Japan to take over other Asian countries.

The leaders of Germany, Italy, and Japan believed in racism. **Racism** is the idea that one race, or group of people, is better than other races. Hitler blamed the Jewish people for Germany's problems and sent many German Jews to prison.

Germany, Italy, and Japan began to invade other countries. They also formed an alliance to defend each other. These three countries were called the Axis Powers, or the Axis.

In 1938, Hitler annexed, or added, Austria to Germany. Within a year, Germany had taken over Czechoslovakia as well. Next, Hitler made a secret agreement with **Joseph Stalin**, the leader of the Soviet Union. Under the agreement, Germany and the Soviet Union promised not to attack each other. This let Hitler plan attacks on other countries.

Germany Invades Poland

Great Britain and France formed an alliance known as the Allied Powers, or the Allies. The Allies tried to stop Germany by signing an agreement with Hitler.

Hitler promised not to invade any more countries. In return, the Allies agreed to let Germany keep the land it had already taken.

Hitler broke his promise. On September 1, 1939, Germany attacked Poland. The Allies then declared war on Germany. Italy and Japan soon declared war on the Allies.

The Allies could not stop the German army. By the end of 1941, Germany controlled most of Europe. Only Britain had not fallen. German airplanes bombed parts of London and other cities. British Prime Minister **Winston Churchill** inspired people to keep fighting:

> 66 **We shall go on to the end. We shall fight in France, we shall fight on the seas and oceans . . . we shall never surrender.** 99

REVIEW How did the Allies try to stop Germany before September 1, 1939?

Listening to Churchill The British heard Churchill's speeches on the radio. The Prime Minister (above) gave people hope during the dark days of war.

America Enters the War

Main Idea The Japanese attack on Pearl Harbor brought the United States into World War II.

At the beginning of the war, most Americans believed in isolationism. They remembered how terrible World War I had been. They hoped to avoid fighting in Europe again. However, President **Franklin D. Roosevelt** wanted to help the British. He sent military equipment and supplies to Britain.

President Roosevelt also worried about Japan's new nationalism. By 1941, Japanese troops had invaded China. Japanese leaders planned to conquer other Asian countries to get valuable resources such as tin, rubber, and oil.

Japanese Prime Minister **Hideki Tojo** (heh DAH kee TOH JOH) knew that only the United States Navy was strong enough to stop Japan. Japanese leaders planned to destroy the U.S. Navy in a surprise attack.

Japanese Attack on Pearl Harbor

Pearl City

Ford Island

U.S. Naval Air Station

Submarine Base

U.S. Naval Station

LEGEND
Japanese bombers
Sunk or damaged ship

km 0 — 1
mi 0 — .5

JAPAN Pearl Harbor UNITED STATES

PACIFIC OCEAN

Pearl Harbor This map of the American naval base of Pearl Harbor shows some of the ships attacked by Japan.

SKILL Reading Maps How many American ships were sunk or damaged in the attack?

Take Off Japanese planes take off from a ship in the Pacific Ocean and head for Pearl Harbor.

The Attack Japanese planes bomb the American ships docked at Pearl Harbor.

Wreckage Many ships and airplanes were destroyed in the attack.

Pearl Harbor

On the morning of December 7, 1941, Japanese airplanes bombed Pearl Harbor, a U.S. naval base in Hawaii. The U.S. Pacific fleet suffered terrible damage and thousands of soldiers and sailors died.

Americans were stunned by the attack on Pearl Harbor. Most believed that the country had no choice but to fight back. President Roosevelt called for war against Japan. He told Congress that the day of the attack was "a date which will live in infamy." Infamy means that something is known as shocking and evil.

Franklin Roosevelt
After the surprise attack on Pearl Harbor, President Roosevelt signed a declaration of war on Japan.

The day after Pearl Harbor, Congress declared war on Japan. Three days later, the leaders of Germany and Italy declared war on the United States. The United States had entered World War II.

REVIEW Why did Congress declare war on Japan?

Lesson Summary

- The Axis Powers—Germany, Italy, and Japan—invaded other countries.

- Britain and France formed the Allies.

- Japan attacked Pearl Harbor and Congress declared war on Japan.

Why It Matters ...

Dictators invaded other countries while trying to control the world. The United States was in danger after the attack on Pearl Harbor.

Lesson Review

| 1933 | 1939 | 1941 |
| Hitler takes power | Germany invades Poland | Pearl Harbor |

1930   1935   1940   1945

1. **VOCABULARY** Use the words **fascism** and **dictator** in writing two newspaper headlines about the events leading up to World War II.

2. **READING SKILL** Choose an event from your chart and explain why you think it had a part in starting World War II.

3. **MAIN IDEA: Government** What type of government did Germany and Italy have before World War II?

4. **MAIN IDEA: History** Why did the United States enter World War II?

5. **EVENTS TO KNOW** Why did Japan bomb Pearl Harbor?

6. **TIMELINE SKILL** How long after Hitler took power did Germany invade Poland?

7. **CRITICAL THINKING: Decision Making** What was the opportunity cost of the U.S. decision to remain neutral at the beginning of World War II?

WRITING ACTIVITY Use library resources to research any leader in World War II. Write a brief summary of this person's role during the war.

Remember Me

by Irene N. Watts

Jews living in Germany in the late 1930s were in danger. Many Jewish children were sent away for their safety, like the girl in this story.

The author, Irene N. Watts, writes about a family, the Kohns, who live in Berlin. Nazi secret police have just torn through the Kohns' house, and the family is worried. They've decided that Marianne, age 11, should go to England for her protection. The author had a similar experience when she was sent away from Berlin in 1938.

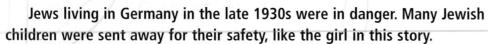

Nothing had prepared Marianne for this — not the taunts in the street, nor the smashed Jewish shops, not her mother's anxious warnings not to draw attention to herself, nor her father's disappearance — nothing. And yet, why was she surprised? Why hadn't she expected this? This was what it was like being a Jew in Germany. You couldn't even close your front door against the Gestapo . . . . Marianne watched as her mother packed her suitcase . . . .

"This transport is a rescue operation for children. A Kindertransport. The grown-ups must wait their turn. There are bound to be other opportunities for us to leave."

"You mean, I have to go by myself? No! Absolutely no. I'd have to be crazy to agree to something like that. I won't leave you all."

Mrs. Kohn said, "Marianne, I think you have to. You see, I can't keep you safe anymore. I don't know how. Not here in Berlin, not in Dusseldorf, or anyplace else the Nazis are . . . . One day it may be safe to live here again. For now, we must take this chance for you to escape to a free country."

Jewish children
in Liverpool Station ▶
in London, England

The guard pushed his way through the corridor. "Next stop — Liverpool Street Station. All change," he called.

The train slowed to a shuddering halt, expelling two hundred apprehensive, weary children. Steam from the engine misted behind them like a morning fog.

The children climbed down onto the platform. Not knowing what to do next, they formed an untidy line.

Eleven-year-old Marianne took Sophie's hand. "Come on, we have to wait with the others. Stay close beside me," she said.

Passersby stared at them curiously. Porters pushing trolleys shouted: "Mind your backs." A few photographers began taking pictures — "Smile," they said. A light flashed, or was it winter sunshine coming through the glass-domed roof of the station?

"Like animals at the zoo," Marianne said to the boy standing next to her.

"We'd better smile all the same, make a good impression," he said.

"Wipe your face, Sophie; it's got smuts on it from the train," Marianne told her.

"Are we going to our new families now?" Sophie asked, spitting on her grubby handkerchief and handing it to Marianne, who scrubbed at Sophie's cheeks.

"Soon."

Marianne wasn't ready to think that far ahead. It was only twenty-four hours ago that she'd said good-bye to her mother in Berlin. Today was December 2, 1938, and she was in London — the whole English Channel between her and her parents. The station overwhelmed her with its incomprehensible words and signs.

"A friend of my father's supposed to be meeting me. I don't even know what he looks like. Do you know who's taking you in?" the boy next to her said.

"I don't know anything. I can't even remember how I got here. Don't you feel like we've been traveling for a thousand years?" said Marianne.

"A thousand years, the thousand-year Reich, what's the difference? We're here, away from all that," the boy said. "They can't get us now."

An identification label spiraled down onto the tracks. A woman wearing a red hat climbed onto a luggage trolley facing them.

She tucked a strand of hair behind her ear, and spoke to the children in English, slowly, and in a loud voice, adding to the confusion of sounds around them. "I am Miss Baxter. I am here to help you. Welcome to London. Follow me, please."

She climbed down. Nobody moved. Miss Baxter walked slowly along the length of the line, smiling and shaking hands with some of the children. Then she headed up the platform to the front of the line, took a child's hand, and began to walk. She stopped every few moments, turned and beckoned, to make sure the others were following.

"Come on, Sophie, keep up," said Marianne. She could hear some women talking about them and shaking their heads, the way mothers do when you've been out in the rain without a coat.

"See them poor little refugees."

"Look at that little one. Sweet, isn't she?"

"More German refugees, I suppose. Surely they could go somewhere else?"

Marianne understood the tone, if not the words. Except for "refugee."

"We'll have to try to speak English all the time," Marianne told Sophie.

"But I don't know how. I want to go home," Sophie said.

Marianne was too tired to answer.

A girl dragging her suitcase along the platform said, "This is the worst part, isn't it? Do hurry up, Bernard, we'll be last. Vati said, 'Stay together.'" She called to the small boy trailing behind them, then turned to Marianne and said, "That's my little brother. Why do boys always dawdle?" They waited for the small boy to catch up.

"Look! A man gave a penny." Bernard held out a large round copper coin. "He said, 'Here you are, son.'"

"How do you know what he said? You don't speak English. You're not supposed to speak to strangers," his sister scolded.

"I suppose they're all strangers here and we are too," said Marianne. "I mean, we don't know anyone, do we?"

"No," said the girl and her lip trembled.

"Sorry," said Marianne. "I only meant . . . ." She didn't say any more, and they hurried to catch up to the other children.

Activities

1. **TALK ABOUT IT** What help does a child need when coming to another country? How could you help a newcomer like Marianne?

2. **ACT IT OUT** Using the dialogue from the story, act out the scene at the train station. If possible, use props such as a suitcase and a coin.

Skillbuilder

Analyze the News

▶ **VOCABULARY**

news article

editorial

You just read about events during World War II. To learn about current world events, you can use the radio, television, newspapers, or the Internet. As you listen to or read these different news sources, you need to evaluate the information carefully. The steps below will help you to analyze news sources.

Learn the Skill

Step 1: Identify the kind of article you are listening to or reading.

- A **news article** describes a recent event. It answers the questions *Who, What, Where, When,* and *Why*. Its purpose is to inform people.

- An **editorial** presents an opinion about an issue or an event. It can present facts, but an editorial's main purpose is to persuade its audience.

Step 2: Decide whether the article has a point of view. Although news articles are mostly factual, writers sometimes present a point of view. Editorials always have a point of view.

Step 3: If possible, double-check the article's facts in another source.

Practice the Skill

Read the following article about the attack on Pearl Harbor. Then answer the questions.

ATTACK ON PEARL HARBOR!

For days, U.S. officials met with Japanese leaders to try to keep peace. During that time, the Japanese military was secretly preparing an attack. On Sunday, December 7, starting at 7:40 A.M., almost 360 war planes swooped out of the sky and destroyed 8 warships in Pearl Harbor. In less than three terrible hours, almost 2,400 American lives were lost. It was a sad day in American history. It is now time for war. Now that we have declared war, Americans will show the world that we are not afraid.

1 What kind of article is it?

2 What facts are given? What opinions are given?

3 How would you describe the writer's point of view?

Apply the Skill

Choose a current event that interests you. Find an article about it. You might select something from a newspaper, magazine, television program, or website. Then answer the questions below.

1 What type of article did you find? How do you know what type it is?

2 What facts are given? How can you double-check them?

3 Are there any opinions? What are they? How do you know they are opinions?

The Home Front

1930   1935   1940   1945   1950   1955   1960   1965

1941–1945

Build on What You Know Have you ever had to work hard to get homework or chores done on time? During World War II, the whole country had to work hard to make the things it needed for the war.

Building an Army

Main Idea The United States military needed people and supplies to fight World War II.

The United States armed forces had grown weaker during the 1920s and 1930s. Armed forces are a nation's military. In 1941, the military was unprepared for a big war. When Japan attacked Pearl Harbor, the United States had to mobilize for war. Mobilize means to get ready to fight.

Americans joined the armed forces after Pearl Harbor. They were also drafted. More than 15 million Americans of all backgrounds served in the military during the war.

Women in the Military Over 100,000 women served in the armed forces. Some worked as nurses or clerks. Others drove trucks or flew supply airplanes.

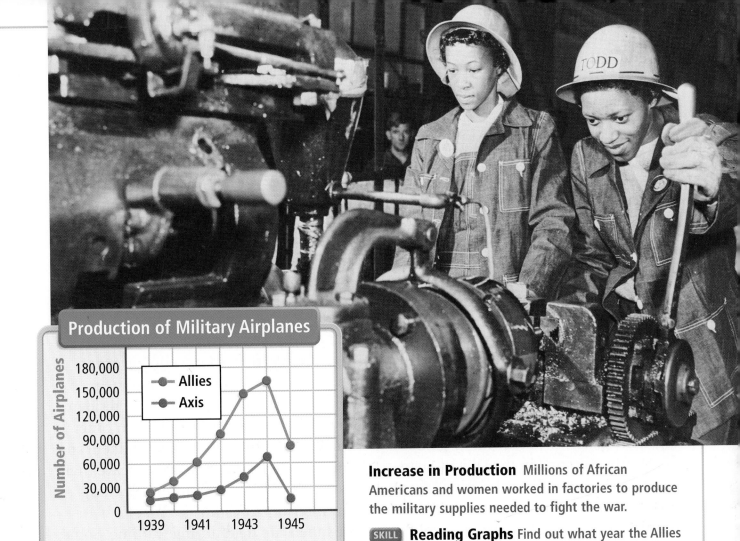

Production of Military Airplanes

Number of Airplanes (vertical axis): 0, 30,000, 60,000, 90,000, 120,000, 150,000, 180,000
Year (horizontal axis): 1939, 1941, 1943, 1945

- Allies
- Axis

Increase in Production Millions of African Americans and women worked in factories to produce the military supplies needed to fight the war.

SKILL **Reading Graphs** Find out what year the Allies produced the most airplanes.

War Supplies

These new soldiers needed uniforms, guns, airplanes, and tanks. The federal government hired businesses to make these supplies. Some factories changed from making consumer goods to making military goods. The Ford Motor Company built airplanes and airplane engines instead of cars. United States factories made more war supplies than the other countries that were involved in the war. The United States built over 320,000 airplanes during the war. That was more than Germany, Italy, and Japan all built.

Scientists created new technologies for fighting the war. They improved helicopter and airplane design.

Women and African Americans

The federal government spent hundreds of billions of dollars on war supplies. Factories had to hire more workers to make supplies as quickly as possible. Many of these new workers were women and African Americans. Nearly seven million women and two million African Americans worked in factories in the United States during the war. The nickname "Rosie the Riveter" was given to the many women who worked in jobs that only men had held before.

REVIEW Why did the United States have to produce so many military supplies?

At Home in Wartime

Main Idea People made many sacrifices to help fight the war.

Although Americans disagreed about the war before 1941, Pearl Harbor united them. They knew how important it was to fight the Axis armies. Many organizations packed up supplies to send to soldiers overseas. Children collected pieces of metal and old tires, which factories reused to make military products.

People made sacrifices during the war years. Goods such as meat, sugar, and gasoline were rationed, or limited. The military needed these supplies for soldiers. Because less food was available to buy, families often planted their own vegetable gardens, called victory gardens.

Nearly everyone in the United States had friends or family in the armed forces. People paid close attention to the events of the war. They read newspaper reports and watched war newsreels in movie theaters. A **newsreel** is a short film about current events.

World War II affected American culture. Writers and artists expressed the country's feelings about this huge event. Many of the paintings, books, movies, and plays created during these years were about the war.

The music of the time was often about the war, too. Popular songs reminded listeners of loved ones stationed overseas. To forget their worries, people danced to swing and jazz music played by big bands in clubs and dance halls.

Japanese Americans

After Pearl Harbor, people worried that Japanese Americans would help Japan attack the United States. President **Franklin D. Roosevelt** signed an order forcing over 100,000 Japanese American men, women, and children to leave their homes and move to internment camps. An **internment camp** is a place where prisoners are held during wartime. Some Italian Americans and German Americans were also placed in internment camps.

Watching Newsreels Military filmmakers in the South Pacific (left) and around the world filmed the events of the war that people watched in the theaters.

Most of the people sent to internment camps were American citizens. Even though they lost homes and jobs, thousands of Japanese Americans fought for the United States. All the soldiers in the 442nd Regimental Combat Team were Japanese American. They fought bravely in Italy and France and won more medals than most military units in U.S. history.

REVIEW What did Americans at home do to help the war effort?

Lesson Summary

- Millions of soldiers join the fighting.
- African Americans and women produce war supplies.
- The U.S. enters the war
- Americans make sacrifices at home.
- Japanese Americans placed in internment camps.

Why It Matters ...

Facing great danger, Americans at home sacrificed and worked hard to help the Allies fight the war.

The 442nd Regimental Combat Team
These Japanese American soldiers won 4,667 medals and other awards for their brave fighting.

Lesson Review

1 VOCABULARY Match each vocabulary word with its meaning:

mobilize   newsreel   internment camp

(a) a short film showing current events; (b) a place where prisoners are held during wartime; (c) to prepare for war

2 READING SKILL Write a paragraph telling how women helped **solve** the **problem** of preparing for World War II.

3 MAIN IDEA: Technology What did businesses do to help the military?

4 MAIN IDEA: History Why was gasoline rationed, or limited, during the war?

5 FACTS TO KNOW What did the nickname "Rosie the Riveter" refer to?

6 CRITICAL THINKING: Analyze Why was it important for the United States to make war supplies as quickly as possible?

7 CRITICAL THINKING: Decision Making Why do you think many Japanese Americans decided to serve in the war?

MUSIC ACTIVITY Use library or Internet resources to find a popular World War II song. Write a paragraph explaining what you think the song says about life during the war.

Children and the Home Front

After the Japanese attack on Pearl Harbor, many Americans felt for the first time that the nation was in real danger. Young Americans worried too, so they stepped forward to help. They raised money and grew food in Victory Gardens. They also collected tin, rubber, and other materials. These materials were used to build airplanes, jeeps, weapons, and other war supplies. Some children even learned to search the skies with binoculars, looking for enemy aircraft.

In September, 1942, 4000 students gathered in Washington to hear Secretary of the Treasury Henry Morgenthau, Jr. call for their help. He said, "Tell the world: 'We are ready—ready for war, ready for victory, ready for peace.'"

Victory Gardens Posters like this one persuaded young people to plant Victory Gardens. At one Florida school, a student garden supplied vegetables for the lunchroom.

Paper Children collect paper and bundle it at a playground in Minnesota. Paper was recycled for the war effort.

Activities

1. **MAKE YOUR OWN** Some students showed their **patriotism** by making posters. Make a poster to express your **patriotism.**

2. **PRESENT IT** Sometimes being a good citizen means taking an unpopular stand. Research the "conscientious objectors" who decided they could not fight the war during these years. Present a brief report on what you learn.

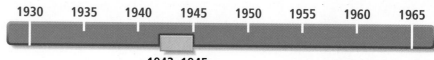

Winning the War

1930　　1935　　1940　　1945　　1950　　1955　　1960　　1965

1942–1945

Build on What You Know Think of some of the heroes you have read about in history. Many of them had to defend what they believed in. During World War II, millions of people around the world fought and died to defend freedom.

VOCABULARY

aircraft carrier
atomic bomb
concentration camp

Vocabulary Strategy

| **aircraft** carrier |

An **aircraft carrier** is a military ship on which **aircraft** take off and land. This ship carries aircraft out to sea.

 READING SKILL
Cause and Effect What events led to victory for the Allies?

 STANDARDS

SS5H6b Major events in Europe and Pacific
SS5H6c Atomic bomb
SS5H6d Hirohito
SS5H6e Tuskegee Airmen

Battles in North Africa and Europe

Main Idea The Allies invaded Africa and Europe to defeat Germany and Italy.

During the 1930s, Germany, Italy, and Japan had been preparing for war. These Axis nations trained millions of soldiers and built tanks, aircraft, and warships.

When World War II began, the powerful Axis armies caught the rest of the world by surprise. **Adolf Hitler** and Germany quickly conquered much of Europe. The Germans also attacked the Soviet Union. Meanwhile, Japan's army and navy took control of much of the Pacific region, including the Philippines. The United States and its allies were stunned by the quick Axis victories. They needed time to recover and strike back.

In late 1942, the Allies began to move against the Axis. American soldiers joined the Allies in North Africa who were fighting German and Italian forces. For several months, the Allies fought the Germans in tank battles on the hot sands of the Sahara. The Axis troops in North Africa surrendered in May 1943.

Military Badge
This military badge is from the U.S. Army Airforce 9th Engineer Command.

Fighting in Italy

A month later, the Allies struck again. They crossed the Mediterranean Sea and attacked Axis soldiers on the Italian island of Sicily. In October 1943, the Allies invaded Italy's mainland. They moved north as the Germans retreated. Thousands of soldiers on both sides were killed or wounded in the fighting. A group of African American pilots, known as the Tuskegee Airmen, flew many successful missions over Italy.

About the same time, the Germans suffered terrible losses fighting in the Soviet Union. Allied airplanes also began to control the skies over Europe. By early 1944, Germany was in trouble. Soviet forces turned back the German invaders at the battle of Stalingrad. Afterwards, the Soviets began to push the Germans west.

Dwight Eisenhower Eisenhower was the leader of the Allied forces on D-day. In "D-day," D stands for the day or date of a planned military operation.

D-day and Victory

The next big blow came on June 6, 1944, known as D-day. On that day, nearly 200,000 Allied soldiers invaded northern France. Before the battle, General **Dwight D. Eisenhower** inspired his soldiers. He said,

> 66 **The hopes and prayers of liberty-loving people everywhere march with you . . .** 99

Although many Allied troops died in the fighting, one million soldiers landed in France within 10 days. This landing allowed the Allies to begin to move toward Germany itself.

At the same time, Soviet soldiers were advancing on Germany from the east. In May 1945, Germany was forced to surrender. The Allies declared May 8 Victory in Europe Day, or V-E Day.

REVIEW Why was D-day important?

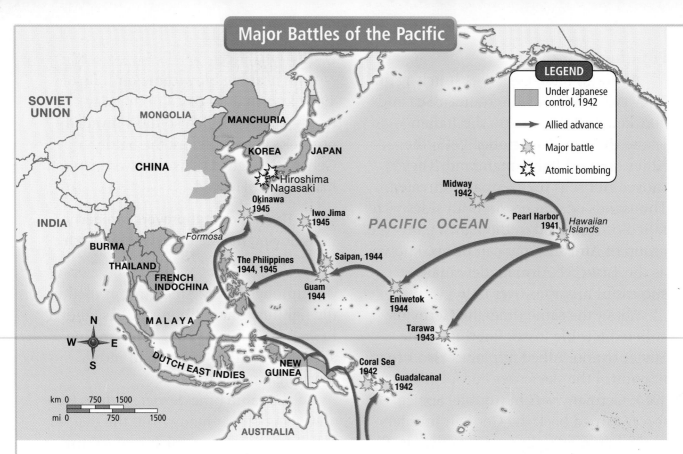

Major Battles of the Pacific

LEGEND

Under Japanese control, 1942

→ Allied advance

✴ Major battle

✴ Atomic bombing

SOVIET UNION

MONGOLIA

MANCHURIA

CHINA

KOREA   JAPAN

Hiroshima
Nagasaki

Okinawa
1945

INDIA

Formosa

BURMA

THAILAND

FRENCH INDOCHINA

The Philippines
1944, 1945

Iwo Jima
1945

PACIFIC OCEAN

Midway
1942

Pearl Harbor
1941   *Hawaiian
Islands*

Saipan, 1944

MALAYA

N
W   E
S

Guam
1944

Eniwetok
1944

Tarawa
1943

DUTCH EAST INDIES

NEW GUINEA

Coral Sea
1942

Guadalcanal
1942

km 0   750   1500
mi 0   750   1500

AUSTRALIA

Pacific Battles Allied forces fought their way across thousands of miles as they moved against Japan. It took three years to get as close as Okinawa.

SKILL **Reading Maps** Which battles took place in 1942?

Fighting in the Pacific

Main Idea The Allies fought to push Japan's army and navy back across the Pacific Ocean.

The end of fighting in Europe did not mean that World War II was over. The Allies also faced Japan in the Pacific region. After their attack on Pearl Harbor, the Japanese won many victories. By early 1942, they controlled a large part of the western Pacific and eastern Asia.

In June 1942, the Allies had a major victory over Japan. American forces led by Admiral **Chester Nimitz** won the Battle of Midway. In this important battle, the United States used aircraft carriers.

An **aircraft carrier** is a large ship that carries airplanes far from land. The ship is so large that the planes can take off from and land on the deck. At the battle of Midway, United States planes sank four Japanese aircraft carriers and shot down many Japanese airplanes.

The victory at Midway gave America more power in the Pacific. The Japanese, however, still held islands in the region.

To defeat Japan, the Allies used a plan they called island hopping. In island hopping, the Allies skipped over some islands guarded by the Japanese and captured others. Each island the Allies took over became a place from which to attack islands closer to Japan.

Island Battles

The island hopping began in August 1942 when the Americans invaded Guadalcanal. For most of the next three years, the battles continued. The United States and the Allies captured New Guinea, Iwo Jima (EH woh JEE muh), and many other islands.

The Japanese launched a large fleet to stop the American navy from freeing the Philippines. The two navies met and fought in Leyte (LAY tee) Gulf in those islands. The Japanese suffered heavy losses. So many of their ships were destroyed, and so many Japanese sailors died, that the Battle of Leyte Gulf ended Japan's ability to fight major naval battles.

Code Talkers at Work The code talkers used Navajo bird names for warplanes and called bombs "eggs."

Code Talkers

Navajo code talkers played an important role in the Pacific fighting. The code talkers were Navajo Indians who had joined the United States Marines. They used the Navajo language to create a secret code that the Japanese could not understand. The code talkers sent important messages and orders between Allied leaders and soldiers.

REVIEW Why was the battle of Midway important?

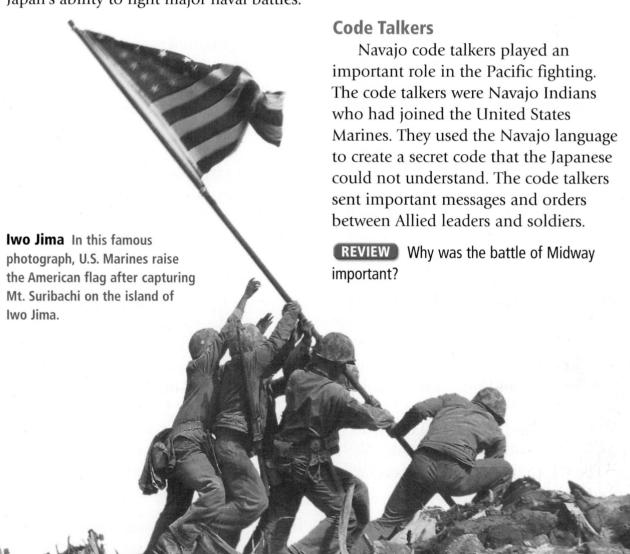

Iwo Jima In this famous photograph, U.S. Marines raise the American flag after capturing Mt. Suribachi on the island of Iwo Jima.

Watch This watch stopped at the exact time the atomic bomb was dropped on Hiroshima.

A Changed World

Main Idea Millions of people died during World War II, and many cities were destroyed.

Although people were happy that World War II was over, they had to face the destruction the war had caused. Many soldiers and civilians had been killed in the war. Cities across Europe and Asia lay in ruins. European civilians had no homes, no food, and no jobs.

The Holocaust

As the fighting ended, Allied soldiers discovered one of the worst horrors of the war. In Europe, the Nazis had killed millions of people in concentration camps. A **concentration camp** is a place where large numbers of people are held prisoner and forced to work. At the camps, men, women, and children were beaten, starved, and killed.

Victory Over Japan

By the summer of 1945, American forces were close enough to Japan to invade the island nation. However, President **Harry Truman** believed that many people would die in an invasion. He chose a different plan. The United States had developed a new weapon in secret, the atomic bomb. An **atomic bomb** is a powerful bomb that can destroy an entire city. President Truman hoped that the atomic bomb would end the war.

On August 6, 1945, an American airplane dropped an atomic bomb on the city of Hiroshima, Japan. The pilot said:

> 66 **We turned back to look at Hiroshima. The city was hidden by that awful cloud . . .** 99

The explosion killed nearly 100,000 people. Three days later, the United States dropped an atomic bomb on Nagasaki, another Japanese city. The emperor of Japan, **Hirohito** (HIHR oh HEE toh), soon surrendered. August 14, 1945, became known as Victory in Japan Day, or V-J Day.

Identity Card Cyrla Rosenzweig from Poland was sent to a concentration camp because she was Jewish. She was later rescued.

Prisoners These people were prisoners at a Nazi concentration camp. Allied soldiers freed them when the soldiers captured the camp.

Many of those killed were Jews, the people Hitler had blamed for Germany's problems. German soldiers arrested and killed Jews in the countries that Germany invaded. About twelve million people, six million of them Jews, died or were killed in concentration camps. This mass murder is known as the Holocaust. **Winston Churchill** said the Nazis were guilty of

66 **the greatest and most horrible crime ever committed in the whole history of the world.** 99

REVIEW What was the Holocaust?

Lesson Summary

● The Allies defeated German and Italian forces in North Africa and Europe.

● The Allies fought Japan in many battles on islands in the Pacific.

● The United States dropped two atomic bombs on Japanese cities to end the war.

● The Nazis murdered millions of people in concentration camps.

Why It Matters ...

The Allies fought for years because they were determined to win. With victory, they freed large parts of the world from fascism.

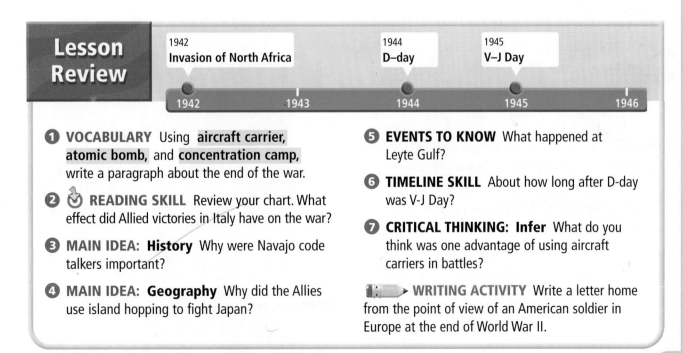

Lesson Review

1942 Invasion of North Africa	1944 D–day	1945 V–J Day

1942 — 1943 — 1944 — 1945 — 1946

❶ **VOCABULARY** Using **aircraft carrier, atomic bomb,** and **concentration camp,** write a paragraph about the end of the war.

❷ **READING SKILL** Review your chart. What effect did Allied victories in Italy have on the war?

❸ **MAIN IDEA: History** Why were Navajo code talkers important?

❹ **MAIN IDEA: Geography** Why did the Allies use island hopping to fight Japan?

❺ **EVENTS TO KNOW** What happened at Leyte Gulf?

❻ **TIMELINE SKILL** About how long after D-day was V-J Day?

❼ **CRITICAL THINKING: Infer** What do you think was one advantage of using aircraft carriers in battles?

▸ **WRITING ACTIVITY** Write a letter home from the point of view of an American soldier in Europe at the end of World War II.

D-DAY

The largest and most powerful sea invasion in history was about to begin. It was D-day. On June 6, 1944, over 150,000 Allied troops waited anxiously in southern England. Crossing the English Channel in boats loaded with troops would be tough. The Channel often had high wind and waves.

Early in the morning, under cover of darkness, close to 6,500 ships and landing craft headed into the rough waters for France. At the same time, hundreds of Allied war ships and bombers pounded German troops in France.

The Allied troops landing in Normandy met fierce German resistance, but they fought with great courage. They gained control of the beaches, and by the end of June, about 850,000 Allied troops had arrived in France.

Paratroopers
D-day began with thousands of paratroopers landing behind enemy lines to help the invasion.

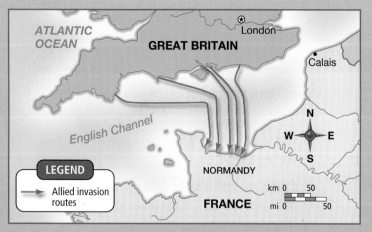

Troops from the United States, Canada, and Great Britain crossed the English Channel. They landed at five different beaches.

Landing Craft
Landing craft could motor right onto the beach to unload soldiers, tanks, and vehicles.

Greeting French Citizens
People were overjoyed when they saw the Allied soldiers, who had come to take back France from the Nazis.

Activities

1. **TALK ABOUT IT** Look at the pictures of the landing craft used to carry troops across the English Channel. Why do you think the Allies were worried about bad weather?

2. **PRESENT IT** Find information about U.S. General Dwight D. Eisenhower or British General Bernard Montgomery. Share your findings in an oral report.

The Cold War

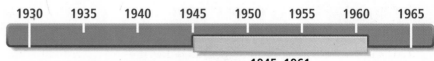

1930	1935	1940	1945	1950	1955	1960	1965

1945–1961

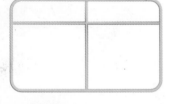
Build on What You Know You know that countries usually use armies to fight wars. After World War II, there was a new kind of war. Countries fought this war mostly with words and ideas.

Roots of the Cold War

Main Idea The Cold War began as World War II ended.

The Soviet Union and the United States worked together to win World War II. After the war, however, their differences pushed them apart. By 1947, they were fighting each other in a war of words and ideas. This war was called the Cold War.

Different Systems

The United States and the Soviet Union had different ideas about economics and government. People in the United States live under capitalism. In **capitalism,** ordinary people and businesses control the production of goods and services. The United States' economy is also called a market economy. In a **market economy,** individuals and businesses make most economic decisions.

Contrasting Economies Look to see who makes decisions in each system.

Economic Systems

Command	Market
Government planners decide what to produce.	Businesses decide what to produce, based on consumers' choices.
Consumers' choices are limited by government decisions.	Consumers' choices reflect their own economic wants and needs.

Communism

In the Soviet Union, however, people lived under communism. Under **communism,** the government controls production and owns the nation's natural and capital resources. The government often tells people where to live and work. This economy is called a command economy because the government makes most economic decisions and can command what will be produced.

The two countries also had different forms of government. The United States is a democratic country where people vote for their leaders. In the communist Soviet Union, the people had no control over the government.

Under Soviet communism, citizens had few rights and little freedom. During the early Cold War years, **Joseph Stalin** ruled the country. Stalin was a dictator. His government arrested people who spoke out against communism.

The Iron Curtain

When World War II was over, the Allies shared control of Germany. The Soviet Union controlled the eastern half of the country. The United States, Britain, and France governed the western half. Germany's capital of Berlin was in the Soviet part of Germany. It was also divided. The Soviet Union had power over East Berlin, and the Allies controlled West Berlin.

After the war, the Soviet Union set up communist governments in much of Eastern Europe. With help from the United States, Western Europe stayed democratic. **Winston Churchill** said that Europe was divided by an "iron curtain." This iron curtain was a symbol of the differences between communist and noncommunist countries.

REVIEW What area did the Soviet Union take control of after World War II?

Allied Leaders Although Winston Churchill, Harry Truman, and Joseph Stalin shared a three-way handshake in 1945, their alliance did not last.

The Iron Curtain

LEGEND
- Communist countries
- Noncommunist countries
- The Iron Curtain

km 0 200 400
mi 0 200 400

Berlin Wall
East Berlin
West Berlin

Europe Divided This map shows the Iron Curtain that divided Europe after World War II. **SKILL** **Reading Maps** Which country is split into eastern and western parts?

NATO

In 1947, President **Harry S. Truman** decided that the United States should help other countries protect themselves against communism. President Truman told Congress,

66 **I believe that we must assist free people to work out their own destinies [futures] in their own way.** 99

On April 4, 1949, leaders of the United States, Canada, Britain, and most of the noncommunist countries of Europe formed an alliance. The alliance was called the North Atlantic Treaty Organization, or NATO. NATO countries hoped that the alliance would keep the Soviet Union from forcing communism on other countries.

Conflicts in Europe Grow

Main Idea The Soviet Union and the United States struggled to control Berlin.

The city of Berlin was at the heart of the Cold War struggle. In June 1948, the Soviet Union tried to take control of the whole city. The Soviets blocked off all the roads and railroads that led into West Berlin. They hoped this blockade would make the other Allies leave the city.

Leaders of the United States and Britain refused to leave. To break the blockade, they decided to fly food and supplies into the city. Each day, airplanes brought thousands of tons of supplies to the trapped people of West Berlin. One German wrote, "The sound of the engines was like music to our ears." This action became known as the Berlin Airlift.

The Concrete Wall
The Berlin Wall divided neighborhoods and families. Few East Berliners managed to escape after it was built.

The Berlin Wall

During the 1950s, many people from East Berlin escaped into the West. They wanted freedom and better lives. Communist leaders tried to stop them from leaving. On August 13, 1961, the Soviets closed the entrances to East Berlin and began to build the Berlin Wall. This concrete wall divided the communist part of Berlin from the rest of the city.

REVIEW How did the United States and Britain help end the blockade of Berlin?

Lesson Summary

The Cold War was a war of ideas between the communist Soviet Union and the democratic United States. During the Cold War, the United States and other countries tried to stop the spread of communism. These countries struggled with the Soviet Union to control Berlin.

Why It Matters...

The Cold War was the beginning of a long tense period between the United States and the Soviet Union.

Lesson Review

1948 **West Berlin blocked**   1949 **NATO formed**   1961 **Berlin Wall built**

1945   1950   1955   1960   1965

1 VOCABULARY Write a short paragraph describing the economy of the United States, using **capitalism** and **market economy.**

2 READING SKILL Explain the differences in the way goods and services are controlled under capitalism and communism.

3 MAIN IDEA: Geography Why did the Soviet Union block West Berlin's roads and railroads in 1948?

4 MAIN IDEA: History Why did the United States help form NATO?

5 FACTS TO KNOW What was the Iron Curtain?

6 TIMELINE SKILL How many years after the blockade of West Berlin was the Berlin Wall built?

7 CRITICAL THINKING: Decision Making What were the consequences of the United States' decision to fly food and supplies to Berlin in 1948? Would it create friends and enemies?

HANDS ON
ART ACTIVITY Create a poster that West Berliners might have made to thank the Allies for the supplies they brought.

The Berlin Airlift

All roads are blocked. Nothing can come in, and nothing can go out. Food, fuel, and medicines are running out, and people wonder how long they and their neighbors can survive.

This happened in West Berlin in the summer of 1948. The Soviet Union had cut off all routes into the city by land and water. The people of West Berlin were hostages to the Soviet blockade.

There was still one way into West Berlin—by air. In just two days, the United States, Great Britain, and France began an emergency airlift. Planes flew over West Berlin day and night, dropping supplies by parachute. For the next year, pilots delivered more than 2,300,000 tons of supplies to people in West Berlin in over 278,000 flights. The planes brought something else to West Berlin during the airlift. They brought hope to the tired, hungry people of that city.

The Candy Hero

An American pilot named Gail S. Halvorsen became known as the "Candy Bomber" during the airlift, because he dropped candy to German children from his aircraft. He had another nickname, as well. As a signal to children on the ground, he would wiggle the wings of his plane. Soon Halvorsen began receiving letters addressed to "Uncle Wiggly Wings."

Special Delivery A young boy holds a box of candy, complete with parachute, dropped by Uncle Wiggly Wings.

Supplies Delivered in Berlin Airlift (in tons)

Food:	536,705
Coal:	1,586,029
Other:	202,775
Total:	2,325,509

Which supply did the Allies deliver the most? Why?

Activities

1. **THINK ABOUT IT** How did "Uncle Wiggly Wings" show that he was a **caring** person?

2. **WRITE ABOUT IT** Berlin lived through some of the most frightening events of the 20th century. Use your library to find out more about Berlin from 1950 to today. Write a story about one important event.

Communism Spreads

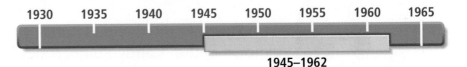

1930   1935   1940   1945   1950   1955   1960   1965

1945–1962

Build on What You Know Have you ever wondered about events that happen in other countries? During the Cold War, Americans tried to understand events taking place in the world outside the United States. They watched the changes taking place across the globe.

Communism Around the World

Main Idea Communism spread rapidly after World War II.

After World War II, Americans were worried about the Soviet Union and the spread of communism. The Soviet Union brought communism to large parts of Europe. United States leaders feared that the Soviets wanted to spread communism to the entire world.

Events in Asia made Americans even more concerned. The Soviets gave money and supplies to a communist army during a civil war in China. In 1949, **Mao Zedong** (mow DZUH DUNG) led the Chinese Communists to victory. The Soviet Union and China were two of the largest nations in the world. Now, both were communist.

Mao Zedong He ruled communist China for 27 years, becoming one of the most powerful political leaders of the 20th century.

VOCABULARY

arms race
nuclear war
anti-communism

Vocabulary Strategy

arms race

In an **arms race,** countries try to make **arms,** or weapons, faster than any other country.

READING SKILL

Draw Conclusions Note facts and details that will help you come to a conclusion about the effect of the Cold War on the United States.

STANDARDS

SS5H6f United Nations
SS5H7b Korean War
SS5H7c McCarthy, Khrushchev
SS5H8a Cuban Missile Crisis

School Drills During the Cold War, schoolchildren were taught to get under their desks in case of emergency.

Nuclear War

There was another reason many people were worried about the spread of communism. In 1949, the Soviet Union built its own atomic bomb. Like the American atomic bombs, the Soviet bombs could destroy entire cities.

United States leaders did not want the Soviet military to be stronger than the U.S. military. Scientists worked to develop bigger bombs and missiles, called nuclear weapons. The Soviets tried to equal them. This contest was called an arms race. An **arms race** is a race between nations to build more powerful weapons.

People around the world were afraid that the arms race might lead to a nuclear war. A **nuclear war** is a war in which powerful nuclear weapons are used. Such a war between the two countries could destroy all life on earth. Some people in the United States prepared for a possible attack by building bomb shelters and storing food.

Anti-communism in America

During the 1950s, fear of communism grew throughout the United States and led to anti-communism. **Anti-communism** was a movement to stop the spread of communism and communist ideas.

Senator **Joseph McCarthy** was an anti-communist. He said that secret communists worked in the United States government. He claimed that they were spying for the Soviet Union. McCarthy made up most of these claims, but some were true.

Anti-communists in Congress began to search for communists. Hundreds of government employees lost their jobs as a result. A few were found guilty of being spies, but most were innocent. Anti-communists also accused some actors, teachers, and writers of supporting communist ideas. Many lost their jobs or were prevented from working.

REVIEW Who was Joseph McCarthy?

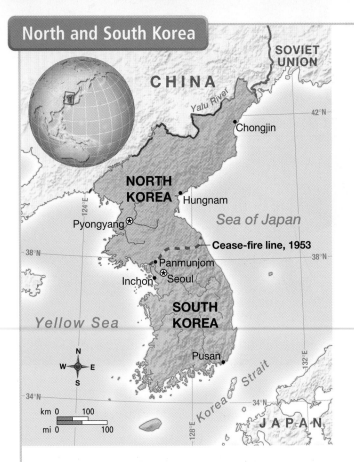

Korean War North and South Korea are on a peninsula bordering China and the Soviet Union.

SKILL **Reading Maps** In which country is Seoul the capital city?

Cold War Conflicts

Main Idea During the Korean War and the Cuban missile crisis, the Cold War was no longer just a war of ideas.

During World War II, the United States, along with its allies, took the lead in creating a plan for a new international organization to keep peace in the world. The organization was called the United Nations (UN), and its plan was ratified after the war, in October 1945. More than 50 nations joined the United Nations.

The UN faced one of its first challenges in Korea. After World War II, the Asian nation was divided in two.

The Korean War

South Korea was a republic supported by the United States. North Korea had a communist government supported by the Soviet Union. In June 1950, North Korean troops invaded South Korea. U.S. leaders thought the Soviet Union had helped plan the attack.

The United States convinced the United Nations to defend South Korea. Soldiers from 16 nations joined the fight, but the United States sent the most troops. American General **Douglas MacArthur** led the UN forces.

After fierce fighting, the UN troops pushed the North Koreans out of South Korea. Then communist China, North Korea's neighbor, sent soldiers to help the North Korean army. The Korean War dragged on, and thousands of American soldiers died. In 1953, the two sides finally agreed to stop fighting. North and South Korea remained divided.

The Cuban Missile Crisis

Communists also took power in Cuba. Cuba is an island nation 90 miles south of the United States. In 1959 **Fidel Castro** led a revolution in Cuba. The Soviet Union, led by Nikita Khrushchev, helped Castro set up a communist government in Cuba.

In October 1962, the United States discovered that the Soviet Union was secretly putting powerful missiles in Cuba. These missiles could easily reach the United States. Worse, they were large enough to carry a nuclear bomb. President **John F. Kennedy** feared a surprise attack and ordered a blockade of Cuba. American warships surrounded the island. The ships prevented Soviet ships from getting in.

John F. Kennedy President Kennedy (right) talks to his brother, Attorney General Robert Kennedy, in October 1962.

The Soviets refused to take their missiles out of Cuba. For days, nuclear war seemed possible. Finally, Khrushchev decided to remove the missiles. In return, President Kennedy promised not to attack Cuba. This conflict is known as the Cuban missile crisis. After the crisis, leaders on both sides agreed to work together to prevent nuclear war.

REVIEW What did President Kennedy do to end the Cuban missile crisis?

Lesson Summary
- China became a communist country after World War II.
- The United States led the fight against communist troops in the Korean War.
- The Cuban missile crisis was a dangerous struggle between the United States and the Soviet Union.

Why It Matters...
For many years, the Cold War brought the world close to nuclear war.

Lesson Review

1949	1953	1962
Communists control China	Fighting in Korean War ends	Cuban missile crisis

1945　　　1950　　　1955　　　1960　　　1965

1. **VOCABULARY** Choose the correct word to complete the sentence.

   arms race　anti-communism　nuclear war

   The _____ between the United States and the Soviet Union led people to fear _____.

2. **READING SKILL** What effect did fear of communism have on the United States?

3. **MAIN IDEA: Government** Where did communism spread after World War II?

4. **MAIN IDEA: Geography** Why did the Korean War begin?

5. **EVENTS TO KNOW** Why was the Cuban missile crisis dangerous to the United States?

6. **TIMELINE SKILL** How many years after the Korean War was the Cuban missile crisis?

7. **CRITICAL THINKING: Fact and Opinion** Why did many Americans believe that there were communists in the U.S. government?

▶ **WRITING ACTIVITY** Write an opinion paragraph about the arms race that someone might have written during the Cold War.

COMMUNISM SPREADS

The first communist country was founded less than a century ago. In 1917, communist leaders in Russia took control and renamed their nation the Soviet Union.

The Soviet Union was the only communist country for decades. After World War II, however, many nations came under communist rule. Soviet-style government spread to Eastern Europe, China, and other countries. Look at the chart below to see how many people lived under communist rule in 1962.

The spread of communism shaped much of 20th-century history. Many Americans believed that the United States should keep communism from spreading. The United States built military bases around the world. Never before had the United States kept so many armed forces in distant countries.

People Under Communist Rule

Year	Number of People (approximate)	Percentage of World's Population (approximate)
1932	200 million	10 percent
1962	1 billion	35 percent

C A N A D A

ALASKA (U.S.)

ARCTIC OCEAN

GREENLAND (DENMARK)

SOVIET UNION

ATLANTIC OCEAN

ICELAND

UNITED KINGDOM

NORWAY

WEST GERMANY

DENMARK

FRANCE

EAST GERMANY

PORTUGAL

POLAND

SPAIN

CZECHOSLOVAKIA

HUNGARY

ITALY

ROMANIA

MOROCCO

ALBANIA

GREECE

BULGARIA

TURKEY

LIBYA

IRAN

SAUDI ARABIA

PAKISTAN

EAST PAKISTAN

SOVIET UNION

MONGOLIA

JAPAN

NORTH KOREA

SOUTH KOREA

C H I N A

TAIWAN

NORTH VIETNAM

PHILIPPINES

THAILAND

SOUTH VIETNAM

INDIAN OCEAN

THE COLD WAR, 1962

United States and its allies

Communist countries

Non-aligned countries

Activities

1. TALK ABOUT IT Count the number of communist and non-communist countries on this map. Were there more communist or non-communist countries?

2. CONNECT TO TODAY China was one of the biggest countries to become communist. Use library and Internet resources to find out what China's government is like today.

Visual Summary

1.–4.  Write a description of each item named below.

Axis Powers

_____

_____

_____

_____

D-day, June 6, 1944

_____

_____

_____

_____

Berlin Wall

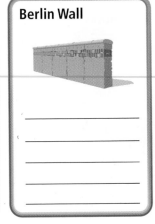

_____

_____

_____

_____

Korean War

_____

_____

_____

_____

Facts and Main Ideas

✔ **TEST PREP** Answer each question with information from the chapter.

5. **History** Which event caused the United States to enter World War II?

6. **Citizenship** What did people in the United States do to help the war effort?

7. **History** What was the Holocaust?

8. **Government** What was the difference between the forms of government in the United States and the Soviet Union?

9. **Geography** Why was the United States so worried about the Soviet Union's missiles in Cuba?

Vocabulary

✔ **TEST PREP** Choose the correct word from the list below to complete each sentence.

dictator, p. 360
racism, p. 361
mobilize, p. 370
arms race, p. 391

10. Adolf Hitler was the _____ in control of Germany.

11. The United States and the Soviet Union competed in an _____ to build weapons.

12. After Pearl Harbor, the United States decided to _____ for war.

13. Germany encouraged _____, the idea that one race or group of people is better than all others.

Apply Skills

☑ **TEST PREP** **Reading and Thinking Skill** Read the article below. Then answer each question.

Berlin Needs Our Help!

The Soviet Union has set up a blockade of Berlin, Germany. Their government does not want the United States, Britain, or France to have power in the city. Some Americans say we should let the Soviet Union have the city. I strongly disagree. We cannot let the Soviet Union take over Europe. It is our responsibility to save Berlin.

14. Which of the following statements describes the type of article above?

    A. It is an editorial because it tries to convince readers to agree with it.

    B. It is an editorial because it contains no facts.

    C. It is a news article because it contains only facts.

    D. It is a news article because it answers *Who, What, When, Where,* and *Why.*

15. Which of the following summarizes the writer's point of view?

    A. The United States should let the Soviet Union take over Berlin.

    B. The United States, Britain, and France should not have any power in Berlin.

    C. The United States has a responsibility to help Berlin.

    D. The writer does not state his or her point of view.

Critical Thinking

☑ **TEST PREP** Write a short paragraph to answer each question.

16. **Infer** Do you think that the United States would have joined the war if the Japanese had not bombed Pearl Harbor? Why or why not?

17. **Draw Conclusions** Do you think it was important for the United Nations to become involved in the Korean War? Explain your reasons.

Timeline

Use the Chapter Summary Timeline above to answer the question.

18. About how many years after V-J Day did the Korean War start?

Activities

 Connect to Georgia Find out about life in Georgia during World War II. Write lyrics to a patriotic song about the sacrifices and contributions Georgians made to support the war.

 Writing Activity Write a short story about someone living in Berlin during the airlift. Describe how the person felt and how it affected his or her views of the United States and the Soviet Union.

 Technology
Writing Process Tip
Get help with your story at
www.eduplace.com/kids/hmss/

397

Vocabulary Preview

veteran

When soldiers came home from the war, families welcomed them. Each soldier who left the army to return to civilian life became a **veteran.** page 402

nonviolent protest

African Americans used **nonviolent protest** to change unjust laws. Many college students protested by sitting at lunch counters that did not serve African Americans. page 407

Chapter Timeline

1960		1964	1965
John F. Kennedy elected		Civil Rights Act	U.S. enters Vietnam War

1960   **1962**   **1964**

Reading Strategy

Question Use this strategy as you read the lessons in this chapter.

quick Tip Stop and ask yourself questions. Do you need to go back and reread?

space race

The Soviet Union and the United States competed in the **space race.** Both tried to be the first to send people into space and land on the moon. **page 415**

demonstration

Citizens who want to express their opinions may hold a **demonstration.** Such marches were held during the Vietnam War. **page 424**

1968
Richard M. Nixon elected

1966   1968   1970

The Boom Years

| 1945 | 1950 | 1955 | 1960 |

1949–1959

Build on What You Know Imagine life without
modern appliances such as televisions and automatic
washing machines. In the 1950s, many people were buying
these kinds of appliances for the first time.

Government in the 1950s

Main Idea The 1950s were a time of great economic growth.

When World War II ended, millions of soldiers
returned home to the United States. They needed jobs and
places to live. President **Harry Truman** wanted to help.

In 1949, he brought his Fair Deal program to Congress.
It included laws to create jobs and build houses. Other laws
in the Fair Deal were written to help African Americans get
equal treatment when voting and applying for jobs.

President Truman worked hard to pass the Fair Deal
laws, but Congress did not vote for most of them. Many
Americans did not agree with Truman's view that people
needed the government's help. Most of the difficulties of
the Depression and war were over. People were looking
for a new kind of leadership.

President Harry Truman
He led the country through the
final months of World War II.

Eisenhower's Election

In 1952, **Dwight D. Eisenhower** was elected President. Eisenhower was a war hero who had led the Allied troops in Europe during World War II. As President, he helped end the Korean War in 1953. During his two terms as President, Eisenhower was very popular.

Eisenhower was well-liked not only because he was a war hero. People liked his warm personality. They called him "Ike" and wore buttons that said "I Like Ike."

One of Eisenhower's biggest contributions was to transportation. He saw that a system of four-lane highways would help the economy. Better roads would allow people and goods to move more freely through the states. Military supplies and soldiers would also be able to travel quickly across the country to defend it against attack. Eisenhower worked with Congress to pass the Federal-Aid Highway Act of 1956. The act provided over $32 billion to build 41,000 miles of modern highways.

Dwight Eisenhower His supporters wore buttons such as this one during the election campaign.

Under Eisenhower's leadership, the economy grew rapidly. In 1956, Eisenhower ran for re-election. His campaign slogan was "peace, progress, and prosperity." **Prosperity** means economic success, such as earning a good income. Eisenhower won a second term. The American people looked forward to the peace and prosperity Eisenhower promised.

REVIEW What made President Eisenhower so popular?

Building the Interstate System Workers level the land and lay the foundation for a new highway.

Americans at Home

Main Idea In the 1950s, the baby boom and new consumer goods changed Americans' way of life.

The biggest boost to the United States economy in the 1950s came from millions of World War II veterans. A **veteran** is a person who has served in the military. These veterans were eager to buy houses, settle down, and start families.

During the Great Depression and World War II, many couples had put off getting married and having children. America's new peace and prosperity changed that. So many new families were started after the war that the country had a baby boom. The **baby boom** was the increase in the number of babies born after World War II. During the 1950s, the population of the United States grew by over 28 million people. More babies were born in the five-year period between 1948 and 1953 than had been born in the previous 30 years!

Housing and Consumer Goods

The population grew so fast that builders could hardly keep up with the increased demand for homes. Builders met the demand by creating large housing developments. Houses in these developments often looked alike and were built very close together.

Factories and businesses could barely keep up with the demand for items such as washing machines, clothes dryers, and televisions. As prices dropped, families bought more of these consumer goods.

As businesses grew, workers earned more income. (Money earned is called income.) Families had more choices about what to buy, and many created a budget. A budget is a plan for saving and spending income. Income can be saved in places such as a bank savings account. Income can be used to pay expenses, such as buying a home or a car. Income can also be spent on entertainment, such as a movie or a baseball game.

Growing Suburbs During the baby boom, people needed inexpensive housing. They found it in suburbs such as this one in Levittown, Pennsylvania.

Television changed the way people learned about the world around them. Before television, people couldn't watch world events as they happened. They listened to the radio, read newspapers, or went to movie theaters to see filmed news reports. With television, entertainment and news from far away came right to people's living rooms. Television made the country and the world seem smaller.

Family and the Television Families gathered to watch shows such as this circus show. By 1960, almost nine out of ten homes had a television.

In the 1950s, there was progress in medicine, too. Polio is a disease that crippled many children. In 1956, Dr. **Jonas Salk** developed a vaccine to prevent polio. A **vaccine** is a medicine to protect people against a disease. Because of Salk's vaccine, polio is no longer a threat in most countries.

REVIEW What was the effect of the baby boom on home building?

Lesson Summary

- Truman's Fair Deal tried to help veterans and other Americans.
- President Eisenhower, a war hero, focused on helping the economy grow.
- Veterans married, had families, and helped create a baby boom.
- New consumer goods and technology made the economy grow rapidly.

Why It Matters ...

In the 1950s, consumer goods and suburbs became even more important in people's daily lives. They continue to be important today.

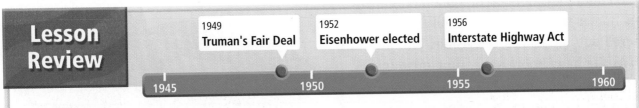

Lesson Review

| 1949 | 1952 | 1956 |
| **Truman's Fair Deal** | **Eisenhower elected** | **Interstate Highway Act** |

1945   1950   1955   1960

1 VOCABULARY Show that you know what **baby boom** and **prosperity** mean. Write a paragraph using these words.

2 READING SKILL Which **events** show reasons for Eisenhower's popularity?

3 MAIN IDEA: History What was Truman's Fair Deal?

4 MAIN IDEA: Geography What did President Eisenhower do to improve transportation in the United States?

5 PEOPLE TO KNOW Who was Dr. **Jonas Salk** and what did he do?

6 TIMELINE SKILL Who was elected first, President Eisenhower or President Truman?

7 CRITICAL THINKING: Analyze Did the baby boom affect the United States economy? Explain your answer.

WRITING ACTIVITY Many people bought televisions in the 1950s. Write a journal entry by someone watching television for the first time.

The Baby Boom

Babies! Millions and millions of new babies! How would all these new babies affect the American economy?

In the 1950s, the United States population grew by over 30 million in just 10 years.

This rapid increase in population had a powerful impact on the U.S. economy. It created a large demand for new houses. Between 1950 and 1960, over 15 million new homes were built.

All over the country, thousands of people found work in the home-building industry. Millions more worked to meet the demand for the materials needed to build and furnish new homes for baby boom families. Factories poured out appliances, televisions, and furniture.

As the baby boom generation grew up, the demand for new goods and services continued, helping to create one of the longest periods of economic growth in U.S. history.

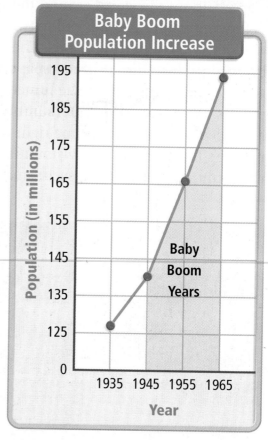

Baby Boom You can see on the chart that the population grew faster and faster after the end of World War II.

In the 1950s, more babies were born in America than at any other time in its history.

New Housing

New Homes (in thousands)

2,000
1,750
1,500
1,250
1,000
750
500
250
0

1945 1950 1955 1960 1965
Year

New Homes This view from the air shows new homes in the 1950s. Mass production was used to build inexpensive homes. That is why they all look similar.

Housing Boom The difference between 1945 and 1950 is huge. Compare this graph to the graph on page 404. How are they related?

Activities

1. **LIST IT** Make a list of the furniture and other things a family might need to set up a new house.

2. **DESIGN IT** What invention would help families today? Write a description of your invention and sketch it.

Civil Rights

Build on What You Know Sometimes, when a problem is hard to solve, you need to try something new. In the 1950s and 1960s, African Americans found new ways to get people to recognize their rights.

The Movement Begins

Main Idea In the 1950s, United States Supreme Court decisions helped guarantee the rights of African Americans.

The end of slavery was not the end of inequality for African Americans. Nearly 100 years after the Civil War, black Americans still struggled for freedom. State laws and discrimination greatly limited their civil rights. **Civil rights** are the rights that countries guarantee their citizens. Some civil rights are the right to vote, the right to equal treatment, and the right to speak out.

VOCABULARY

civil rights
desegregation
nonviolent protest

Vocabulary Strategy

desegregation

The prefix **de-** in the word **desegregation** means "the opposite of." Desegregation means doing away with segregation, or the separation of races.

 READING SKILL
Cause and Effect Make notes on what happened as a result of events in the civil rights movement.

CAUSES	EFFECTS

STANDARDS

SS5H8b Civil Rights movement
SS5H8c Assassination of King
SS5G1b Locate Montgomery, AL

Thurgood Marshall Civil rights lawyer Marshall is sitting in front of the Supreme Court. He argued a case against school segregation there. He would later serve as a Supreme Court justice.

School Segregation Ends

In the early 1950s, many places in the United States were segregated. Segregated means separated by racial or ethnic group. In some cities, African Americans could not use the same restaurants and schools as whites. Segregation was legal, but many people believed that it should not be. Segregation took away the important civil right of equal treatment. African Americans went to court to end this inequality.

In 1954, the parents of **Linda Brown** went to court against the Board of Education of Topeka, Kansas. They argued that because Linda went to a segregated school, she was not getting the same education as white students. Civil rights lawyer **Thurgood Marshall** brought the case to the United States Supreme Court. The Court decided that school segregation was illegal under the Constitution.

Desegregation was ordered in all public schools. **Desegregation** means ending the separation of people by racial or ethnic group.

The Montgomery Bus Boycott

In Montgomery, Alabama, buses were segregated. City law said that African Americans had to sit in their own section, usually at the back of the bus. In 1955, an African American woman named **Rosa Parks** refused to give up her seat on a crowded bus and go to the back. The police arrested Parks.

Members of Rosa Parks's church organized a protest. They asked all African Americans in Montgomery to boycott, or stop using, the buses. For over a year, the city's African Americans walked, rode bicycles, and shared cars.

Montgomery, Alabama

Rosa Parks Her courageous act in Montgomery, Alabama, helped the civil rights movement in the South.

A minister from Atlanta, Georgia, named Dr. **Martin Luther King Jr.** helped lead the boycott. He inspired many people with his courage and powerful speeches. King believed in nonviolent protest. **Nonviolent protest** is a way of bringing change without using violence. King said that even if people were hurt or arrested, they must not fight back. The protesters did not fight back or give up. In late 1956, the Supreme Court ruled that segregation on buses was illegal.

REVIEW What was the goal of the Montgomery Bus Boycott?

Civil Rights Victories

Main Idea African Americans won many civil rights victories in the 1960s.

In the 1950s, most restaurants and stores in the South had sections that were for "whites only." In 1960, four African American college students decided to challenge this inequality. They sat at a "whites only" lunch counter and refused to leave until they were served. People all over the country heard about this protest, called a sit-in. African Americans held sit-ins in 54 cities. The sit-ins forced the restaurants and stores to make a choice— close down or treat African Americans equally. For the first time, many businesses agreed to serve African Americans.

The Freedom Rides

In 1960, the Supreme Court made segregation in bus stations illegal. To test this rule, small groups of civil rights protesters traveled by bus through the South. They called themselves Freedom Riders. To show that segregation wasn't legal anymore, they used restrooms, bus waiting rooms, and restaurants that were once for "whites only."

In Alabama, mobs of people who were against desegregation attacked the Freedom Riders. Some people in state and local government supported the mobs. **Eugene "Bull" Connor,** the police chief of Montgomery, Alabama, once waited for 15 minutes before sending his officers in to stop an attack there.

Civil Rights, 1950–1963

Linda Brown In 1954, Linda Brown (front) and her parents brought a case against school segregation to the United States Supreme Court and won.

We Will Not Leave This photo shows a sit-in at a lunch counter in Charlotte, North Carolina, in 1960. The counter has just been closed, and everyone is waiting to see what happens next.

The governor of Alabama, **George Wallace,** defended what Connor had done. The violence did not stop the Freedom Rides. Instead, over 1,000 people joined the Freedom Riders.

In 1963, civil rights leaders called for more protests in Alabama. Martin Luther King Jr. was arrested while leading protests in the city of Birmingham and jailed. He defended the protests in his "Letter From Birmingham Jail," in which he said,

> 66 **Injustice anywhere is a threat to justice everywhere.** 99

King was finally released after almost two weeks. He then organized a children's protest known as the Birmingham Children's Crusade.

Bull Connor's police attacked the marchers and children with sticks, police dogs, and powerful blasts of water from fire hoses. Television coverage of the attacks shocked the nation.

In May 1963, the Sixteenth Street Baptist Church in Birmingham was bombed. The church was an important gathering place for civil rights marchers. Four African American girls were killed.

In June 1963, Governor Wallace tried to prevent two black students from signing up for classes at the University of Alabama. The federal government sent in police to make sure the students could attend the school.

REVIEW What was the purpose of the restaurant sit-ins?

Jailed in Birmingham Martin Luther King Jr. stares through the bars of his cell. He is waiting to be released from the Birmingham jail, where he wrote his letter.

Resisting Change Governor George Wallace (right) wanted to keep black students from attending the University of Alabama. He is speaking with a member of the National Guard.

March on Washington On August 28, 1963, people from all over the country joined together in protest and song during the march. Martin Luther King Jr. made his "I Have a Dream" speech that same day.

The March on Washington

In 1963, Congress was discussing a bill to end segregation in the United States. To show support for the bill, King and other civil rights leaders organized a protest march in Washington, D.C. Over 200,000 people took part. King gave his most famous speech at the march. He said,

> ❝ I have a dream that my four little children will one day live in a nation where they will not be judged by the color of their skin, but by the content of their character. ❞

More people joined the cause of civil rights after the Washington march.

Gains and Losses

Main Idea The civil rights movement won victories in Congress.

President **Lyndon Johnson** worked with Congress to pass the Civil Rights Act of 1964. The law banned segregation in schools, workplaces, and public places such as restaurants and theaters. Laws and customs that had kept people of different races apart were beginning to change.

The changes did not happen easily. African Americans in the South still faced many challenges. In Selma, Alabama, civil rights marchers protested laws that made it almost impossible for African Americans to vote. The police attacked the marchers.

The attacks made more people want the laws changed. President Johnson called the protests in Selma a major step in "man's unending search for freedom."

Congress passed the Voting Rights Act in 1965. The law made it illegal to prevent or hinder citizens from voting because of their racial or ethnic backgrounds.

In 1968, five years after the March on Washington, Martin Luther King Jr. was assassinated. Many people reacted to the news with anger and violence. With King's death, the civil rights movement lost one of its most important leaders. However, over time King became a symbol for peaceful change.

The civil rights movement inspired other groups to work for change. In the early 1960s, Mexican Americans **Cesar Chavez** and **Dolores Huerta** (hoo EHR tah) formed a farm workers union. They wanted to improve conditions for farm workers in California.

Women also formed a national organization to work for equal rights. American Indian groups in the 1960s took bold action. All of these groups continued working for equal rights.

REVIEW What did the Civil Rights Act do?

Lesson Summary

The United States Supreme Court declared school segregation laws unconstitutional. Martin Luther King Jr. led nonviolent protests that helped spread the message of the civil rights movement. The civil rights laws of the 1960s made it illegal to segregate schools and workplaces. They also made it illegal to discriminate against people because of their race when they tried to vote.

Why It Matters ...

The struggle for civil rights gave equal treatment to more Americans and made the country a better place in which to live.

Lesson Review

1955 — **Montgomery Bus Boycott**   1963 — **March on Washington**   1965 — **Voting Rights Act**

1950 — 1954 — 1958 — 1962 — 1966

❶ **VOCABULARY** Write two sentences about the fight for civil rights using the words **desegregation** and **nonviolent protest.**

❷ **READING SKILL: Cause and Effect** Using your chart, write one **effect** of the restaurant sit-ins.

❸ **MAIN IDEA: Citizenship** Give two examples of civil rights that are guaranteed by the Constitution.

❹ **MAIN IDEA: History** What court case in the 1950s won a victory over segregation?

❺ **PEOPLE TO KNOW** Who was **Rosa Parks** and what did she do to help end segregation?

❻ **TIMELINE SKILL** What law was passed after the March on Washington?

❼ **CRITICAL THINKING: Evaluate** Is nonviolent protest a powerful way to bring about change? Explain your answer.

HANDS ON

ART ACTIVITY Think about the people who fought for civil rights such as the right to equal treatment. Create a picture of a civil rights leader showing what he or she did.

Dr. Martin Luther King Jr.

(1929–1968)

It is August 28th, 1963. Thousands of people have marched from the Washington Monument to the Lincoln Memorial. Folk singers have performed, and civil rights leaders have spoken to the crowd. Now Dr. Martin Luther King Jr. steps forward to the podium.

Dr. King has written part of the speech only hours ago. He has given other parts before. He looks out at the crowd. So many people have joined together in one place in the cause of equality and justice.

Throughout his life, Dr. King worked for civil rights for all Americans. He was dedicated to bringing about change through nonviolent protest. In Montgomery and Birmingham, he led boycotts and protests to desegregate buses and lunch counters.

As Dr. King begins to speak, the people cheer. Of the many speeches given on this day, this is the one that most will remember. People join hands as they listen to his message of freedom.

Major Achievements

1957
Travels thousands of miles and gives over 200 speeches

1963
Leads March on Washington and gives "I Have a Dream" speech

1963
Meets with President Kennedy about civil rights

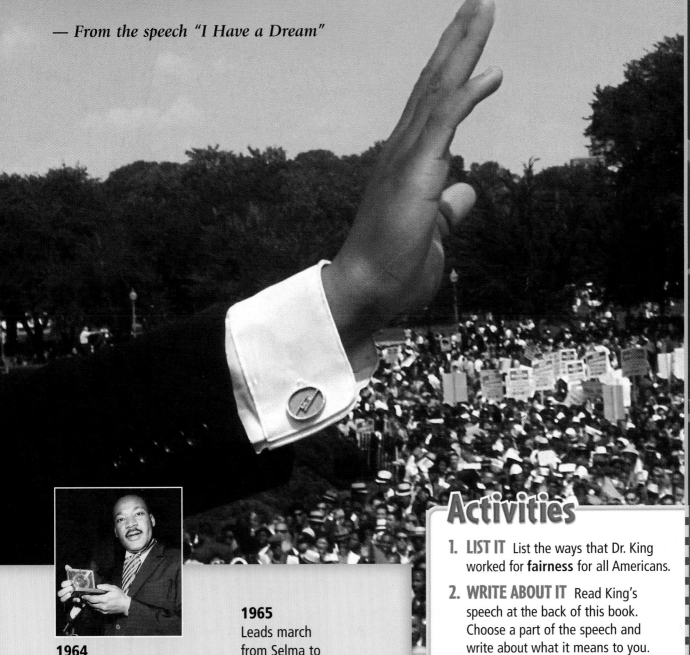

"When we allow freedom to ring, when we let it ring from every village and every hamlet, from every state and every city, we will be able to speed up that day when all God's children, black men and white men, Jews and Gentiles, Protestants and Catholics, will be able to join hands and sing in the words of the old Negro spiritual: "Free at last! Free at last! Thank God Almighty, we are free at last!"

— From the speech "I Have a Dream"

1964
Wins Nobel Peace Prize

1965
Leads march
from Selma to
Montgomery

Activities

1. **LIST IT** List the ways that Dr. King worked for **fairness** for all Americans.

2. **WRITE ABOUT IT** Read King's speech at the back of this book. Choose a part of the speech and write about what it means to you.

Technology Read about other biographies at Education Place. www.eduplace.com/kids/hmss05/

413

Life in the 1960s

1955   1960   1965   1970

1957–1969

VOCABULARY

space race
welfare
generation

Vocabulary Strategy

generation

Think about the baby boom generation. A **generation** is a group of people around the same age.

READING SKILL

Main Idea and Details
Write details that support the idea that the United States and the Soviet Union competed in outer space.

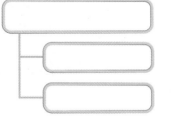

Build on What You Know On television, you have probably seen pictures taken from outer space. Imagine a time when human flight in space was still a dream. In the 1960s, this dream finally came true.

The Kennedy Years

Main Idea John F. Kennedy led the country through a time of change in the early 1960s.

In 1960, **John Fitzgerald Kennedy** became the youngest United States President ever elected. Kennedy encouraged Americans to do great things. He said,

" . . . ask not what your country can do for you—ask what you can do for your country. **"**

President Kennedy believed that citizens could change society for the better and wanted young people to help too. He introduced programs to improve life in the United States. He called these programs the New Frontier. Kennedy also wanted to help people in foreign countries. One of his programs, the Peace Corps, was very popular with college graduates. The Peace Corps sent volunteers to teach children, grow food, and help start businesses in countries around the world. The Peace Corps still exists.

John F. Kennedy This photo shows the President at his inauguration, where he encouraged Americans to serve their country.

The Space Race

While Kennedy was President, the United States entered the space race. The **space race** was competition between the United States and the Soviet Union to send people into outer space.

The Soviet Union won the first victory of the space race. In 1957, a Soviet rocket sent *Sputnik I* into outer space. *Sputnik I* was the first manufactured object ever to circle the earth in space. Its launch surprised the world. The Soviet Union also won the race to send the first person into space. In April 1961, Soviet cosmonaut **Yuri Gagarin** (yoo ree guh GAHR ihn) orbited, or went around, the earth in a space capsule.

The United States space program rushed to catch up. A month after Gagarin's flight, astronaut **Alan Shepard** blasted off in a Mercury space capsule. He did not circle the earth, but he was the first American to go into outer space. **John Glenn** made a flight similar to Gagarin's in February 1962. He orbited the earth for six hours in a space capsule called *Friendship 7*.

President Kennedy promised that the United States would beat the Soviet Union to the moon. The Apollo moon program fulfilled that promise. On July 20th, 1969, **Neil Armstrong** and **Buzz Aldrin** landed on the moon, telling people on Earth,

> 66 That's one small step for a man, one giant leap for mankind. 99

For the first time in history, a human being had set foot on another world.

REVIEW Who was the first person to orbit the earth?

Moon Rocket The Saturn 5 booster launched astronauts on many missions to space and the moon. It was filled with about a million gallons of fuel for each launch.

Lyndon B. Johnson Vice President Johnson was sworn in as President on an airplane the same day that John F. Kennedy was assassinated.

A Changing Nation

Main Idea American culture and politics changed in the 1960s.

President Kennedy did not live to see the moon landing. He was assassinated in 1963 in Dallas, Texas. People were shocked and saddened by the sudden death of their young leader. Some lost hope in Kennedy's plans to make society better. Others were determined to carry on his vision.

Vice President **Lyndon Baines Johnson** was sworn in as President. He asked Americans to work for a society that "...demands an end to poverty and racial injustice." Johnson started a government program called the Great Society and said that there should be a "war on poverty." Welfare was an important part of Johnson's plan. **Welfare** is a government program that helps people who are in need.

Great Society programs provided food, shelter, and medical care to people who couldn't pay for them. They also gave people an education and job training.

Another leader of the 1960s was **Robert F. Kennedy**, the brother of President Kennedy. In 1968, he ran for President. Kennedy supported civil rights and aid for the poor. However, he was assassinated during the campaign. His death, coming after those of his brother and Martin Luther King Jr., left the nation stunned. It was also a loss to those who supported his ideals.

Robert Kennedy had been popular with young people. The generation of children born during the baby boom became teenagers in the 1960s. A **generation** is a group of people born at about the same time. Many of these young people wanted to end injustice and poverty. A song by **Bob Dylan** described how they felt. "The Times, They Are A-Changin'," he sang, and many Americans agreed with him.

The Beatles Paul McCartney, George Harrison, Ringo Starr, and John Lennon (left to right) were members of the world's most famous band.

1960s Culture

Teenagers of the baby boom generation wanted to change American culture as well as politics. They loved rock 'n' roll. By the 1960s, rock 'n' roll was the most popular music of young people.

In the 1960s, artists were expressing themselves in new ways. A movement called "pop art" (popular art) used designs of everyday objects, comic strips, and advertisements. **Andy Warhol** and others wanted to show that advertising had too much influence over people.

Pop Art Andy Warhol's works often show large-sized images of everyday items such as this can of soup.

Warhol's paintings made fun of people's fascination with consumer goods, television, and magazines.

REVIEW What kind of music was most popular with teenagers during the 1960s?

Lesson Summary

Political Change	Cultural Change
President Kennedy started New Frontier.	The baby boom generation grew up.
Sputnik I launched the space race.	Rock 'n' roll became most popular music.
President Johnson started Great Society.	Artists tried new ideas, such as "pop art."

Why It Matters ...

The space race marked the beginning of human exploration of outer space. The baby boom generation changed the popular music and art of the country.

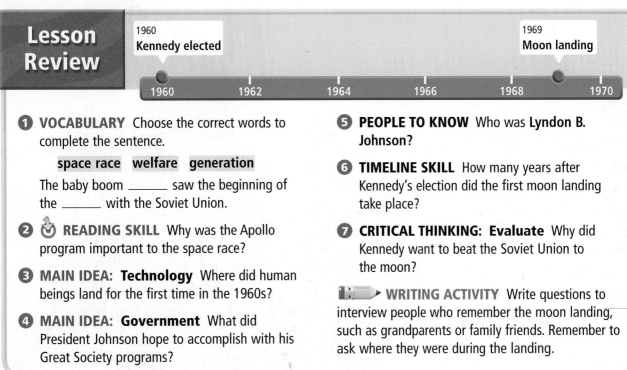

Lesson Review

1960
Kennedy elected

1969
Moon landing

| 1960 | 1962 | 1964 | 1966 | 1968 | 1970 |

1 **VOCABULARY** Choose the correct words to complete the sentence.

space race   welfare   generation

The baby boom _____ saw the beginning of the _____ with the Soviet Union.

2 **READING SKILL** Why was the Apollo program important to the space race?

3 **MAIN IDEA: Technology** Where did human beings land for the first time in the 1960s?

4 **MAIN IDEA: Government** What did President Johnson hope to accomplish with his Great Society programs?

5 **PEOPLE TO KNOW** Who was **Lyndon B. Johnson?**

6 **TIMELINE SKILL** How many years after Kennedy's election did the first moon landing take place?

7 **CRITICAL THINKING: Evaluate** Why did Kennedy want to beat the Soviet Union to the moon?

WRITING ACTIVITY Write questions to interview people who remember the moon landing, such as grandparents or family friends. Remember to ask where they were during the landing.

A Walk on the Moon

How did the first moon landing bring people together?
On the night of July 20, 1969, a family gathers around a TV set with
neighbors. It is six hours after the Apollo 11 moon landing, and the
astronauts still haven't stepped outside the lunar module.

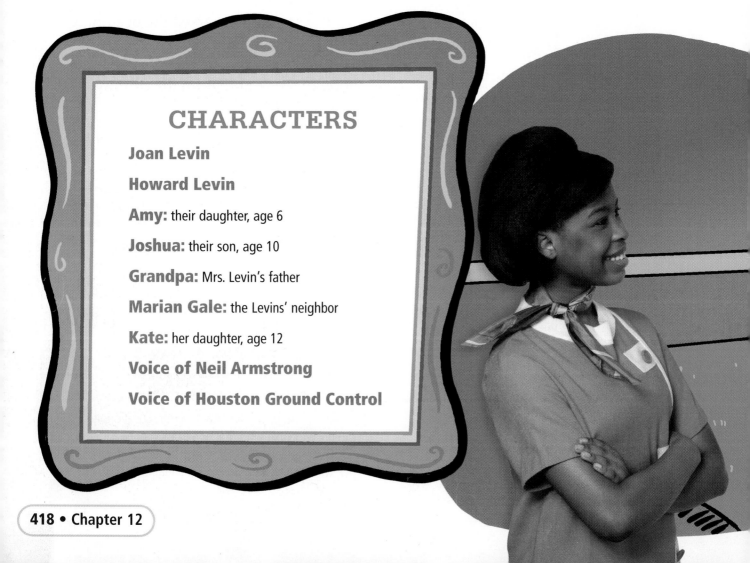

CHARACTERS

Joan Levin

Howard Levin

Amy: their daughter, age 6

Joshua: their son, age 10

Grandpa: Mrs. Levin's father

Marian Gale: the Levins' neighbor

Kate: her daughter, age 12

Voice of Neil Armstrong

Voice of Houston Ground Control

Amy Levin: When are they going to walk on the moon? My eyes keep closing.

Joan Levin: I know it's late, honey, but try to stay awake.

Grandpa: Then you'll be able to tell your grandkids, "I watched people walk on the moon."

Amy: Why is it taking so *long?*

Kate: The astronauts have been resting. Then they have to put on their space suits. They have to run tests to make sure the LEM will be able to lift off.

Amy: What's a LEM?

Josh: Lunar Excursion Module.

Kate: That's the smaller spaceship they landed in. It was attached to the main spaceship, which is orbiting the moon with another astronaut.

Josh: So the two astronauts on the moon will take off in the LEM and link up with the main spaceship again.

Grandpa: Then, if all goes well, they'll come back to earth.

Joan Levin: Of course all is going to go well, Dad!

Mrs. Gale: So, who's going to film the first person to come out?

Grandpa: Maybe the man in the moon.

Josh: Very funny, Grandpa.

Kate: They said they have a remote control TV camera attached to the outside of the LEM.

Howard Levin: These kids know everything!

Joan Levin: Look! They're showing the lunar module! The hatch is opening!

Joshua: He's coming out!

Voice of Neil Armstrong: "OK, Houston. I'm on the porch."

Voice of Ground Control: "Roger, Neil."

Marian Gale: I can't believe what I'm seeing!

Amy: *(yawning)* Why is he moving like that? He's so stiff.

Josh: Look at that space suit. You'd be stiff, too.

Howard Levin: He's almost at the bottom of the ladder.

Voice of Neil Armstrong: "OK, I'm going to step off the LEM now . . . That's one small step for a man. One giant leap for mankind."

Everyone claps and cheers.

Josh: Wow, I think the TV reporter is crying!

Joan Levin: It's a very moving thing, Josh.

Grandpa: You know, I was Josh's age when the Wright brothers flew the first airplane. And now this.

Kate: Hey, let's go outside and look at the moon!

Howard Levin: That's a great idea, Kate.

Josh: It's just a crescent. I doubt if we'll see the astronauts.

Kate: Very funny, Josh.

Marian Gale: *(looking up)* Wow. I can't believe there's someone walking around up there. I'll never look at the moon the same way again.

Joan Levin: Anybody ready for bed? Amy's sound asleep.

Joshua: Not me!

Kate: I want to watch the whole moon walk. Can we, Mom?

Marian Gale: Well . . .

Howard Levin: Why not? Let's all stay up. It's not every day a person takes a walk on the moon.

Activities

1. **TALK ABOUT IT** What are the most important news events that you've seen on television? Why were they important?

2. **REPORT IT** Interview someone you know who remembers watching the first moon landing on television. Write a report that includes details about what they remember.

421

War in Vietnam

| 1950 | 1955 | 1960 | 1965 | 1970 | 1975 |

1954–1973

VOCABULARY

overthrow
demonstration
cease-fire

Vocabulary Strategy

demonstration

The word **demonstration** comes from **demonstrate.** To demonstrate is to show clearly. A demonstration is a gathering of people showing how they feel.

READING SKILL
Compare and Contrast
Take notes on the different views that people had about the war in Vietnam.

FOR	AGAINST

Build on What You Know Sometimes reaching a goal looks easy when you start. Then it turns out to be very hard to accomplish. In the early 1960s, United States leaders thought winning a war in the Southeast Asian country of Vietnam would be easy. It turned out to be very hard.

The Conflict in Vietnam

Main Idea The United States fought a war against communism in Vietnam.

During the Cold War years of the 1950s and 1960s, the United States tried to stop the spread of communism. In the early 1950s, the United States had fought to keep communism from spreading from North to South Korea. Within a few years, United States leaders became worried that Vietnam might fall to communism. Look at the map on the next page to see where Vietnam is.

Vietnam had been a French colony since the 1880s. The Vietnamese wanted independence from the French and won it in 1954. The French and Vietnamese agreed to split the country into North and South Vietnam. The North was governed by communists, the South by non-communists.

In the early 1960s, a group of communists in South Vietnam began trying to overthrow the non-communist government there. To **overthrow** is to remove from power. The communist fighters in South Vietnam were called the Vietcong. North Vietnam supported them.

At first, the United States military only sent advisors and supplies to help South Vietnam's government. In 1965, the United States began sending soldiers to fight.

Fighting Increases

The North Vietnamese army joined the Vietcong in attacks against United States troops. As the fighting increased, President **Lyndon B. Johnson** sent more troops to help South Vietnam.

The U.S. troops used advanced technology. They had tanks and bombers. They had helicopters for quickly moving troops around. The Vietcong did not have such weapons. They fought in small groups and used the jungle as a place to hide in and attack from.

Better technology did not give United States troops a clear advantage against the small fast-moving bands of Vietcong soldiers. Even though the U.S. military had bigger and more powerful weapons, the Vietcong controlled most of South Vietnam.

REVIEW What did the Vietcong do to fight against the technology of the United States military?

Vietnam, 1959–1975

CHINA

Red River

⊕ Hanoi

20°N

LAOS

NORTH VIETNAM

Gulf of Tonkin

110°E

Vientiane

Mekong River

Demilitarized Zone

THAILAND

15°N

South China Sea

SOUTH VIETNAM

CAMBODIA

Phnom Penh ⊕

⊕ Saigon

N
W   E
S

Gulf of Thailand

10°N

Mekong Delta

10°N

km 0   100   200
mi 0   100   200

A Divided Country In 1954, Vietnam was divided into the North and the South. The dividing line between them was called the Demilitarized Zone.

Troops in Vietnam American troops used the speed of helicopters to move quickly between bases and battlefields.

No to War Thousands march down Pennsylvania Avenue in Washington, D.C., to protest against the Vietnam War.

Troops Increase By 1968, over 500,000 United States troops were in Vietnam. **SKILL** **Reading Graphs** About how many U.S. soldiers were in Vietnam during 1966?

The Antiwar Movement

Main Idea People in the United States disagreed about the Vietnam War.

As the fighting in Vietnam continued, the costs of the war grew. More and more soldiers were dying, and the United States government was spending billions of dollars. Television brought images of war right into people's living rooms. Nearly every night, viewers watched soldiers fighting dangerous battles. They saw the terrible effect of the United States air bombings on civilians. People's feelings about the war grew stronger, whether they were for the war or against it.

Americans strongly disagreed about whether the United States should be sending troops to South Vietnam.

Some believed that the United States should not interfere in a war between the people of North and South Vietnam. Others thought that the United States had to stop communism wherever it spread.

The draft was used to choose which young men would go to war. Many young men feared the draft. They did not want to be sent to Vietnam to fight in a war they thought was wrong.

Citizens from many parts of the country protested at antiwar marches and demonstrations. A **demonstration** is a gathering of people who want to express their opinions to the public and to the government. About 250,000 antiwar protesters held a demonstration at the United Nations in New York City in May 1967. By this time, even members of Congress were speaking out against the Vietnam War.

Getting Out of Vietnam

Richard Nixon became President in January 1969. He started to bring troops home from Vietnam. At the same time, U.S. planes increased the bombing of North Vietnam. The United States also began bombing Cambodia, a country west of South Vietnam. Many communist fighters had bases there.

In 1973, North Vietnam, South Vietnam, and the United States signed a cease-fire. A **cease-fire** is an agreement to stop all fighting. The U.S. soldiers in Vietnam went home. Once the U.S. soldiers were gone, the communists began attacking again. Two years later, North Vietnam defeated South Vietnam.

For a long time after the war ended, people felt its effects. Over 55,000 Americans had died. The nation had lost its battle to stop communism in Vietnam.

Strong opinions about the war still divided people. In 1982, the Vietnam Veterans Memorial in Washington, D.C., was built to recognize the contributions of veterans who had fought in Vietnam.

REVIEW Why did many people in the United States protest against the war in Vietnam?

Lesson Summary

- The United States sent troops to Vietnam to fight against the communist Vietcong and North Vietnam.

- In the late 1960s, many people in the United States protested against the war.

- In 1975, two years after U.S. troops left, North Vietnam defeated South Vietnam.

Why It Matters ...

The Vietnam War deeply divided people and cost many American and Vietnamese lives.

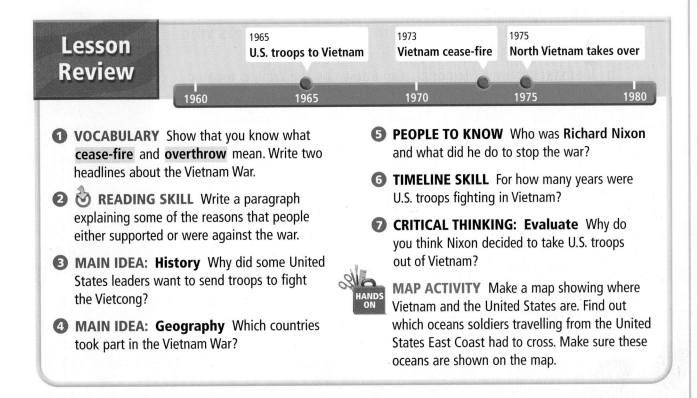

Lesson Review

| 1960 | 1965 | 1970 | 1975 | 1980 |

1965 **U.S. troops to Vietnam**

1973 **Vietnam cease-fire**

1975 **North Vietnam takes over**

❶ **VOCABULARY** Show that you know what cease-fire and overthrow mean. Write two headlines about the Vietnam War.

❷ **READING SKILL** Write a paragraph explaining some of the reasons that people either supported or were against the war.

❸ **MAIN IDEA: History** Why did some United States leaders want to send troops to fight the Vietcong?

❹ **MAIN IDEA: Geography** Which countries took part in the Vietnam War?

❺ **PEOPLE TO KNOW** Who was **Richard Nixon** and what did he do to stop the war?

❻ **TIMELINE SKILL** For how many years were U.S. troops fighting in Vietnam?

❼ **CRITICAL THINKING: Evaluate** Why do you think Nixon decided to take U.S. troops out of Vietnam?

HANDS ON **MAP ACTIVITY** Make a map showing where Vietnam and the United States are. Find out which oceans soldiers travelling from the United States East Coast had to cross. Make sure these oceans are shown on the map.

THE
VIETNAM
VETERANS
MEMORIAL

Nearly ten years after the last American troops had left Vietnam, there was still no memorial to honor soldiers who had died there. In 1982, a memorial was built.

The Vietnam Veterans Memorial, also known as the Wall, is located on the National Mall in Washington, D.C. The Wall is V-shaped, with one side pointing toward the Lincoln Memorial and the other pointing toward the Washington Monument.

The name of each American who died or was missing during the Vietnam War is on the Wall. The soldiers' names are grouped by their time of service in Vietnam to make it easier for veterans to find the names of people who served with them.

The polished black granite of the Wall reflects the grass and trees around the monument. The quiet atmosphere makes the Vietnam Veterans Memorial a place to remember and respect those who gave their lives in service to their country.

Maya Lin

The Vietnam Veterans Memorial was designed by Maya Lin from Ohio. She was 21 when she won a competition for the best memorial design. Lin designed the memorial to work peacefully with the landscape. She hoped it would help people to heal after the war.

Activities

1. **THINK ABOUT IT** How did Maya Lin show **respect** for veterans in her design of the Vietnam Veterans Memorial?

2. **WRITE IT** Poetry is a way to honor events and sacrifices. Write a short poem about the soldiers honored by the memorial.

427

Skillbuilder

Categorize

▶ **VOCABULARY**

category

Putting pieces of information into categories can help you organize the information. A **category** is a group of similar things. Categories allow you to make connections between ideas or facts. Placing information in categories also helps you study.

Learn the Skill

Step 1: Choose the best categories to use for the information you want to organize. Your categories might be based on time, place, people, events, ideas, or objects.

Things to Do After School
Finish math worksheet
Clear table after dinner
Play on computer
Clean room
Read social studies lesson
Play soccer

Step 2: Think about each piece of information and decide which category to put it in.

Things to Do after School		
Homework	Chores	Fun
Finish math worksheet	Clear table after dinner	Play on computer
Read social studies lesson	Clean room	Play soccer

Step 3: Use the information in your chart to draw conclusions. You might decide to do your homework first, then do the fun things, and complete your chores after dinner.

Practice the Skill

Copy the chart below. Then look at the list of events and categorize each one as a social change, economic change, or political change. The first three have been done for you. Some events may fit into more than one category. What conclusions can you draw from the categorized information?

Social Change	Economic Change	Political Change
Rock 'n' roll becomes popular	Americans buy new consumer products	Eisenhower elected President

- Eisenhower elected President
- Americans buy new consumer products
- School desegregation ordered by Supreme Court
- Montgomery bus boycott

- Rock 'n' roll becomes popular
- President Kennedy assassinated
- President Johnson announces War on Poverty
- Antiwar protests held
- Popularity of television increases

Apply the Skill

Research six events that occurred in your state during the 1950s or 1960s. Categorize the events as social, economic, or political changes. Then make a chart of the events and their categories. Events may fit into more than one category.

Visual Summary

1–4.  Write a description of each event named below.

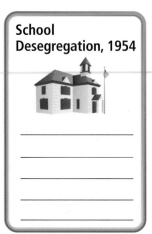

School Desegregation, 1954

_____

_____

_____

_____

_____

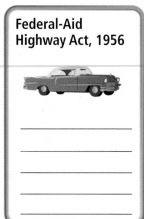

Federal-Aid Highway Act, 1956

_____

_____

_____

_____

_____

John Glenn's flight, 1962

_____

_____

_____

_____

_____

Cease-fire in Vietnam, 1973

_____

_____

_____

_____

_____

Facts and Main Ideas

✓ **TEST PREP** Answer each question with information from the chapter.

5. **Economics** What effect did veterans and the baby boom have on the economy in the 1950s?

6. **Citizenship** How did the passage of the Civil Rights Act of 1964 affect the lives of African Americans?

7. **Government** What was the Voting Rights Act of 1965?

8. **History** What was *Sputnik I*, and what did it cause the United States to do?

9. **Geography** What advantages did the Vietcong have over U.S. troops in Vietnam?

Vocabulary

✓ **TEST PREP** Choose the correct word from the list below to complete each sentence.

> **prosperity,** p. 401
> **space race,** p. 415
> **welfare,** p. 416
> **demonstration,** p. 424

10. When people gather to express their opinions it is called a _____.

11. People can earn a good income during a time of _____.

12. The moon landing was part of the _____.

13. The Great Society programs included _____, which helped people in need.

1960 Kennedy elected	1964 Civil Rights Act	1965 U.S. enters Vietnam War	1968 Nixon elected

1960   1962   1964   1966   1968   1970

Apply Skills

☑ **TEST PREP** **Study Skill** Read the lists below. Then use what you have learned about categorizing to answer each question.

1. John F. Kennedy	2.
New Frontier	Great Society
Peace Corps	Civil Rights Act

14. What would be the correct name for the second category?
   A. Harry Truman
   B. Lyndon Johnson
   C. Dwight Eisenhower
   D. Richard Nixon

15. Which of the following items would best fit under the category John F. Kennedy?
   A. Vietnam Veterans Memorial
   B. Fair Deal
   C. polio vaccine
   D. space race

Critical Thinking

☑ **TEST PREP** Write a short paragraph to answer each question.

16. **Draw Conclusions** What impact did the Vietnam War have on the United States?

17. **Summarize** What were Martin Luther King Jr.'s ideas about nonviolent protest?

Timeline

Use the Chapter Summary Timeline above to answer the question.

18. In what year were U.S. soldiers sent to fight in Vietnam?

Activities

Connect to Georgia Research civil rights in Georgia during the 1950s and 1960s. Write newspaper headlines for four events that took place in Georgia as part of the civil rights movement.

Writing Activity Use library resources to learn more about the 1963 March on Washington. Write a description of the event and the effect of Dr. King's speech.

Technology
Writing Process Tips
Get help with your description at
www.eduplace.com/kids/hmss/

Review and Test Prep

Vocabulary and Main Ideas

✓ **TEST PREP** Write a sentence to answer each question.

1. Why were many people in the world worried about **nuclear war** during the Cold War?

2. Why was **nonviolent protest** an important part of the **civil rights** movement?

3. What happens when countries **mobilize** for war?

4. What are some of the **civil rights** that people fought for in the twentieth century?

5. Why do people honor **veterans?**

6. Why might life be difficult in a country ruled by a **dictator?**

Critical Thinking

✓ **TEST PREP** Write a short paragraph to answer each question.

7. **Compare and Contrast** How are communism and capitalism similar? How are they different?

8. **Synthesize** How did events that occurred at the end of World War II lead to the Cold War? Use details from the unit to support your answer.

Apply Skills

✓ **TEST PREP Study Skill** Read the article about nuclear weapons. Then use what you know about analyzing the news to answer each question.

Countries should not be pointing nuclear missiles at each other. It's too dangerous. During the Cuban Missile Crisis, the entire world could have been destroyed. The Cold War is over now, and it is time for the world's most powerful nations to get rid of nuclear weapons. The world would be a safer place.

9. What kind of article is this?

   A. a news article

   B. a story

   C. an editorial

   D. a letter to the editor

10. What is the writer's point of view?

    A. The United States needs more nuclear weapons.

    B. Nuclear weapons are dangerous and we should get rid of them.

    C. Nuclear weapons bring world peace.

    D. The Cuban Missile Crisis showed how nuclear weapons make the world safer.

Connect to Georgia

Interview a Famous Georgian

- Research the contributions of a famous Georgian to the state or the nation in the 1940s, 1950s, or 1960s.

- With a partner, write interview questions and answers about the person's life and achievements.

- Act out the interview for the class.

In this unit, you read that some people use personal budgets to make decisions about spending and saving. (p. 402)

Suppose you earned $10 a week raking leaves. You want to buy a jacket that costs $25. Make a budget showing how you could save and spend your money for four weeks. When will you be able to afford the jacket?

Compare your budget to someone else's. How were your decisions about saving and spending similar? How were they different?

Connect to Today

Have a discussion about role models in the news.

- Find information about two people you think would be good role models.

- Make cards with the name of the person on one side, and the person's actions and ideas on the other.

- Trade cards with a partner, trying to identify each person before turning the card over to read the name.

Technology
Weekly Reader online offers social studies articles. Go to:
www.eduplace.com/kids/hmss/

Read About It

Look for these Social Studies Independent Books in your classroom.

UNIT 7

Linking to the Present

The Big Idea

What do all people in the United States share?

"America is woven of many strands. Our fate is to become one, and yet many."

-Ralph Ellison

Dolores Huerta

What did this teacher do to help her students? She left teaching to start the Farm Workers Association. By improving working conditions for farm workers, she helped their children, too.
page 443

History Makers

Ronald Reagan
1911–2004

The 40th President of the United States made many Americans feel confident and positive about their country. Reagan strengthened the U.S. military and helped to end the Cold War. **page 448**

Daniel Inouye

This son of immigrants showed his patriotism when he fought in World War II. As a senator for more than 40 years, he has worked to improved education and health care for all Americans. **page 486**

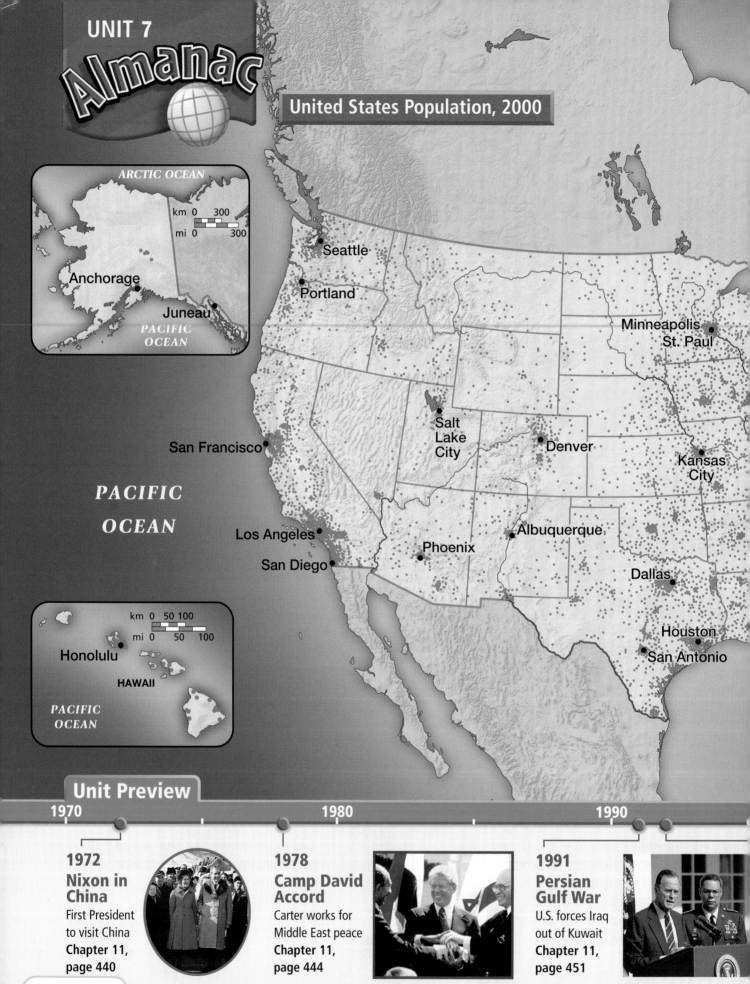

United States Population, 2000

ARCTIC OCEAN

km 0   300
mi 0   300

Anchorage

Juneau

PACIFIC
OCEAN

Seattle

Portland

Minneapolis
St. Paul

San Francisco

PACIFIC

OCEAN

Salt
Lake
City

Denver

Kansas
City

Los Angeles

San Diego

Albuquerque

Phoenix

Dallas

Houston

San Antonio

km 0   50 100
mi 0   50 100

Honolulu

HAWAII

PACIFIC
OCEAN

Unit Preview

1970   1980   1990

1972
Nixon in China
First President to visit China
Chapter 11, page 440

1978
Camp David Accord
Carter works for Middle East peace
Chapter 11, page 444

1991
Persian Gulf War
U.S. forces Iraq out of Kuwait
Chapter 11, page 451

Boston

Detroit

Chicago Cleveland Philadelphia New York

Cincinnati

St. Louis Washington, D.C.

Norfolk

Nashville Charlotte

Memphis

Atlanta

New Orleans

Miami

L. Superior

L. Michigan

L. Huron

L. Erie

L. Ontario

Gulf of
Mexico

N NE
NW E
W SE
SW S

LEGEND
• 10,000 people

km 0 150 300
mi 0   150   300

2000   **2010**

1992
NAFTA Signed
Canada, U.S., and
Mexico agree to
free trade
Chapter 12,
page 476

2001
September 11
Terrorists attack
the United States
Chapter 11,
page 466

Connect to Today

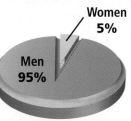

Women's Education, 1970

1970
Estimated number
of women receiving
law degrees: 805

Women
5%

Men
95%

Women's Education Today

2000
Estimated number
of women receiving
law degrees: 17,511

Women
46%

Men
54%

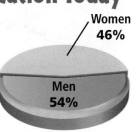

Today, there are almost as many women
getting law degrees as men.

How might other careers have changed
during the same time period?

CONNECT to **GEORGIA**

Write a Citizen's Letter about something
you would like to improve in your
community or in Georgia.

Vocabulary Preview

Technology

e • **glossary**
e • **word games**
www.eduplace.com/kids/hmss/

accord

President Carter convinced leaders of Israel and Egypt to sign a peace agreement. This important **accord** is called the Camp David Accord. **page 444**

coalition

The United States and its UN allies formed a group to fight in the Persian Gulf. This **coalition** of countries won the war. **page 451**

Chapter Timeline

1974
Richard Nixon resigns

1980
Ronald Reagan elected

1989
Fall of the Berlin Wall

1970   1975   1980   1985   1990

Reading Strategy

Monitor and Clarify As you read the lessons in this chapter, use this strategy to check your understanding.

Stop and ask yourself whether what you are reading makes sense. Reread, if you need to.

free-trade agreement

Nations make a **free-trade agreement** to increase trade with other countries. A treaty on trade removes tariffs, making it easier and less expensive to trade. **page 461**

popular vote

The vote of each citizen is counted in the **popular vote.** This number gives the total votes received by each candidate. **page 465**

1992
Bill Clinton elected

2001
September 11 attacks

1995   2000   2005

Challenges of the 1970s

| 1970 | 1975 | 1980 | 1985 | 1990 | 1995 | 2000 | 2005 |

1970–1979

VOCABULARY

resign
migrant worker
accord

Vocabulary Strategy

migrant worker

Migrate means to move. A **migrant worker** is someone who moves in search of work.

READING SKILL

Sequence List in order the events that happened during the 1970s.

1	
2	
3	
4	

Build on What You Know When you start school each year, you face a lot of changes: a new grade, a new teacher, and new classmates. Changes in the 1970s included two new Presidents and several new rights movements.

The Nixon Years

Main Idea The major events in Nixon's presidency included his trip to China, the oil crisis, and Watergate.

In 1968, **Richard Nixon** was elected President. Nixon focused on world events for much of his presidency. His biggest success was improving the United States' relations with the two largest communist countries: China and the Soviet Union. The United States had not traded with China since 1949, when China became communist. In 1972, Nixon became the first U.S. President to visit China, where he met with Chinese leader **Mao Zedong.** This meeting led to more contact and trade between the two countries.

That same year, Nixon traveled to the Soviet Union. He and Soviet leaders signed an agreement to limit the number of nuclear weapons each country made.

Nixon in China While in China, Nixon toured the Great Wall of China, an important cultural landmark.

STANDARDS

SS5H9a U.S. efforts at Middle East peace

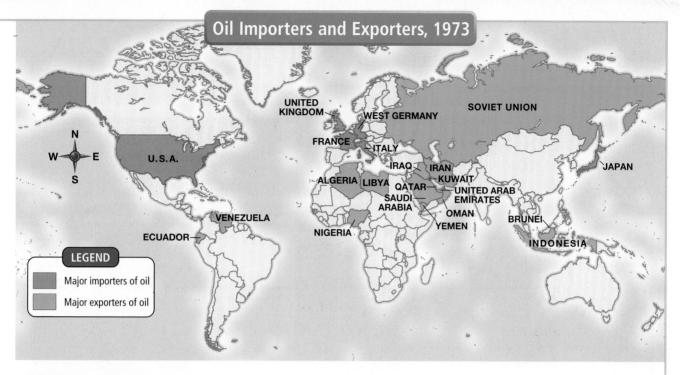

Oil Importers and Exporters, 1973

UNITED KINGDOM
WEST GERMANY
SOVIET UNION
FRANCE
ITALY
IRAQ
IRAN
JAPAN
U.S.A.
ALGERIA
LIBYA
QATAR
KUWAIT
UNITED ARAB EMIRATES
SAUDI ARABIA
OMAN
VENEZUELA
ECUADOR
NIGERIA
YEMEN
BRUNEI
INDONESIA

N
W E
S

LEGEND
- Major importers of oil
- Major exporters of oil

Oil Trade The United States is one of the biggest oil importers in the world.

SKILL **Reading Maps** What are three other big oil importers?

The Oil Crisis

Not all international relationships went well during Nixon's presidency. In 1973, a war started in the Middle East. The countries of Egypt and Syria attacked the country of Israel.

The United States was Israel's ally during the war. Many of the oil-producing countries in the Middle East supported Egypt and Syria. These countries decided to punish the United States for helping Israel. They knew the United States imported their oil, so they decided to produce much less oil. When the supply of oil went down, the price went up.

The rise in oil prices caused the price of gasoline and other fuels to go up. Because businesses had to pay more for fuel to make or transport their products, they charged their customers more. This caused an overall increase in prices, which is called inflation. The oil crisis ended after five months, but inflation remained a problem for many more years.

Nixon Resigns

The president faced another problem. In 1972, Nixon, a Republican, ran for reelection. Some people working for his reelection broke into the Democratic Party's offices in the Watergate building in Washington, D.C. They were caught stealing information from the Democrats.

Nixon said he did not know about the break-in. Investigators learned that he had lied and was trying to cover up the crime. The whole event became known as Watergate.

In 1974, Nixon resigned as President because of the Watergate scandal. To **resign** means to give up your job. He was the first U.S. President ever to resign. Vice President **Gerald Ford** took over as President. He urged Americans to put Watergate behind them, saying,

66 **Our long national nightmare is over.** 99

REVIEW Which events caused inflation during the 1970s?

RIGHTS MOVEMENTS OF THE 1970s

Women's Movement Women's rights groups held marches in cities around the country, including Washington, D.C.

American Indian Rights After protests by American Indians, the government formed a committee to solve problems facing Indian nations.

A Time of Change

Main Idea In the 1970s, women, farm workers, American Indians, and other groups worked for equal rights.

During the 1970s, different groups of people wanted the government to protect their rights. Women had won the right to vote in 1920. By the 1970s, however, women still did not have the same rights as men. For example, men usually were paid more than women for the same kind of work. Some businesses hired men instead of women, even though the women who wanted the jobs were just as qualified as the men.

Women of the 1970s spoke out. Leaders such as **Gloria Steinem** wrote books and essays with strong views about the importance of equality.

Women's Rights

Many women supported the National Organization of Women (NOW) in its fight for women's rights. NOW worked hard to pass an amendment to the Constitution, called the Equal Rights Amendment (ERA). This amendment would have guaranteed rights for women. However, the Equal Rights Amendment did not pass and become law.

The women's movement succeeded in many ways. The number of women serving in state legislatures doubled between 1975 and 1988. By the late 1980s, 40 out of 50 states required equal pay for men and women doing the same work. Many women began holding jobs in business and government that had been open only to men.

Farm Workers' Rights Cesar Chavez (holding sign) urged people not to buy fruits and vegetables grown on farms with bad working conditions.

Consumer Rights Ralph Nader led the movement to protect consumers from unsafe products.

Other Groups Seek Rights

American Indians, many of whom lived on reservations, faced problems, too. Most reservations did not provide good health care and education. Many had high unemployment. American Indian groups wanted more control over what happened on their reservations.

American Indians also wanted the U.S. government to honor earlier treaties it had signed with them. These treaties had promised to protect the rights of Indians and honor their sacred lands. In the 1970s, the government returned sacred land in New Mexico to the Taos Pueblo Indians, recognized Indian fishing rights in Washington State, and settled land claims in Alaska.

Migrant workers were another group working for their rights. A **migrant worker** is a person who moves from place to place to find work, mostly on farms. Big farm companies paid migrant workers very little and did not provide health care. **Cesar Chavez** (SAY sahr CHAH vehz) and **Dolores Huerta** (doh LOH rehs WEHR tah) led the migrant workers movement in California. Migrant workers' protests forced some farm companies to improve working conditions.

Another group, led by **Ralph Nader,** worked to protect consumers' rights. Those efforts helped create laws to improve the quality and safety of consumer products, such as cars.

REVIEW What were two goals of the Indian rights movement?

The Carter Years

Main Idea President Carter struggled with inflation at home while he encouraged peace in the Middle East.

By 1976, people in the United States were angry with the government because of Watergate and inflation. Voters wanted a change. In the presidential election that year, Democrat **Jimmy Carter** from Georgia ran against Ford. During the election, Carter promised to end scandals in government. Carter won the election and became the nation's 39th President.

Like Nixon, President Carter was more successful dealing with problems between nations than problems in the United States. In 1978, he invited the leaders of Israel and Egypt to a meeting at Camp David in Maryland. The two countries had been enemies for 30 years, but Carter helped get their leaders to sign a peace agreement. This achievement was known as the Camp David Accord. An **accord** is another word for agreement.

Economic Problems

Carter also struggled with the problem of inflation in the United States. To solve the problem, he tried to limit government spending and raise taxes, but his approach did not work. Oil-producing countries in the Middle East raised the price of oil again. By 1980, oil prices were more than double the price in 1977, when Carter became President.

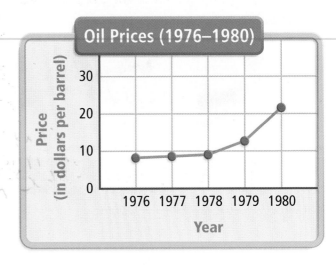

Oil Prices (1976–1980)

SKILL **Reading Graphs** About how much did the price of oil increase between 1978 and 1980?

The Camp David Accord
President Carter (center) helped Anwar Sadat, President of Egypt (left), and Menachem Begin, Prime Minister of Israel (right), sign a peace agreement.

By the end of Carter's term, people in the United States wanted a change in government again. Republican **Ronald Reagan** ran for President in 1980 and won the election.

After leaving office, Carter continued to work for peace and human rights around the world. This work and the Camp David Accord helped him win the Nobel Peace Prize in 2002.

REVIEW What were President Jimmy Carter's successes?

Nobel Peace Prize
This prize is awarded each year to people who have contributed to world peace.

Lesson Summary
- Watergate forced President Nixon to resign.
- Women, American Indians, migrant workers, and other groups worked for their rights.
- President Carter helped create the Camp David Accord that led to peace between Israel and Egypt.
- During the 1970s, inflation caused economic problems.

Why It Matters . . .
The changes in the United States during the 1970s still affect the way Americans think about their rights and their government.

Lesson Review

1972 Watergate break-in	1974 Nixon resigns	1976 Carter elected

1972 — 1973 — 1974 — 1975 — 1976 — 1977

1 **VOCABULARY** Choose a word to complete each sentence below.

resign   accord

Carter helped Israel and Egypt sign an ____.
Nixon had to ____ as President.

2 **READING SKILL** What did lower oil production in the Middle East lead to in the United States?

3 **MAIN IDEA: Citizenship** What changes did the women's movement bring in the 1970s?

4 **MAIN IDEA: History** What event started Watergate?

5 **PEOPLE TO KNOW** Who was **Gerald Ford** and what did he do in 1974?

6 **CRITICAL THINKING: Generalize** What could you say was true of all the groups who fought for their rights during the 1970s?

7 **CRITICAL THINKING: Draw Conclusions** What effect did Watergate have on people in the United States?

SPEAKING ACTIVITY Prepare notes for a short speech about equal rights. Include reasons why equality is important and how to work for it.

Women's Rights Movement

For much of our history, women's rights were unprotected. In the early 1800s, they were prevented from voting or holding political office. They had far fewer chances than men to get an education. If a woman owned property, it became her husband's when she married.

People's views of women's rights have changed a great deal in the past two hundred years. Today, women vote and hold political offices. They attend college as often as men and work as doctors, lawyers, and business leaders. The changes in women's rights did not come all at once. Look at this timeline to see some of the most important steps in the march toward women's equality in American life.

Women in the Workforce

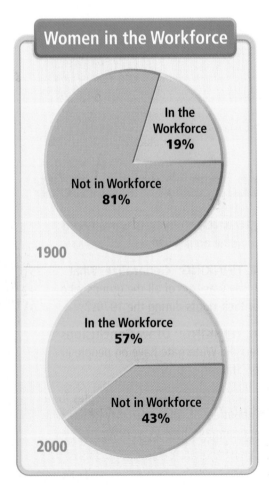

In the Workforce **19%**

Not in Workforce **81%**

1900

In the Workforce **57%**

Not in Workforce **43%**

2000

◀ How much did the percentage of women in the workforce grow in the 20th Century?

1878
Lawmakers defeat an amendment giving women the vote. The amendment is reintroduced in every session of Congress until 1919, when it passes.

1900
Every state has laws that allow married women some control over their property.

1840   1880

1848
Elizabeth Cady Stanton (below) helps organize the first women's rights convention held in Seneca Falls, New York.

League of Women Voters

1963
Betty Friedan (above) writes a book, *The Feminine Mystique*, which helps start the modern women's movement.

1963
Congress passes the Equal Pay Act, requiring equal pay for men and women doing the same jobs.

1981
Sandra Day O'Connor (above) becomes the first woman appointed to the U.S. Supreme Court.

1920
The 19th Amendment guarantees equal voting rights for women.

1920   1960   2000

1917
Jeanette Rankin (below) of Montana becomes the first woman elected to the U.S. Congress.

1976
U.S. military academies admit women.

Activities

1. **TALK ABOUT IT** If you were helping to pass the 19th Amendment, what would you say to leaders in Congress?

2. **ASK ABOUT IT** Interview a woman you know who remembers an event on this timeline. Ask why the event was important and what details she remembers. Write a one-page report of the interview.

The 1980s

1970　1975　1980　1985　1990　1995　2000　2005

1980–1992

VOCABULARY

deregulation
deficit
coalition

Vocabulary Strategy

deficit

Deficit is the antonym of surplus. A surplus is more than what is needed. A deficit is less than what is needed.

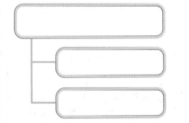

READING SKILL

Main Idea and Details
Note the details that support the first main idea.

Build on What You Know Have you ever been walking and not sure you were on the right path? Many people in the United States felt this way in 1980. They elected Ronald Reagan to change the direction of the country.

Reagan Becomes President

Main Idea President Reagan cut taxes and government spending on many programs, while building a stronger military.

For many people, the late 1970s were a time of disappointment. The United States faced many challenges, including a weak economy. When **Ronald Reagan** ran for President in 1980, he tried to change the country's mood. He spoke about

66 the great confident roar of American progress. **99**

Before Reagan, many Presidents tried to use government programs as a way to help people. For example, President Johnson's Great Society programs used government money to pay for health care, job training, and housing. Presidents in the 1960s and 1970s kept those programs and added new ones of their own.

President Reagan People in the United States knew Ronald Reagan as a popular actor before he became President.

 STANDARDS

SS5H9a Collapse of the Soviet Union, Persian Gulf War
SS5E2c Government function

Reagan's Economic Ideas

Reagan had a different view of the function of government. He wanted to spend less on some government programs because he believed that many of them did not work well. For example, some large government housing projects failed to give safe, comfortable homes to people who moved into them. Reagan also thought that people had become too dependent on the government. He said, "Government is not the solution to our problems; government is the problem."

Reagan also believed that a strong economy would help people more than government programs could. He wanted to use the government to help businesses grow. At the end of his term as President, 20 million more Americans had jobs than when he took office.

To help businesses be more productive, Reagan removed many government rules about what businesses could or could not do. Removing these rules is called **deregulation.** Because government rules often cost businesses money, deregulation helped slow inflation.

Military Spending

During Reagan's presidency, the government spent less money on some government programs and much more money on the military. Reagan believed that a strong military would keep the United States safe during the Cold War with the Soviet Union.

Building up the military, however, was expensive. The added spending left the United States with a large budget deficit. When the government spends more money than it collects in taxes in a particular year, it has a **deficit,** or shortage. In the 1980s, the deficit grew to the highest it had ever been.

REVIEW Why did President Reagan spend government money on the military?

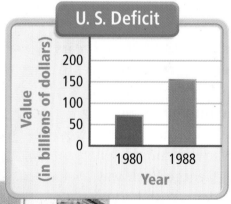

U. S. Deficit

National Debt
A billboard in New York City showed how much the national debt increased every second. The debt is the sum of all yearly deficits.

SKILL Reading Charts
About how much did the deficit change between 1980 and 1988?

449

International Events

Main Idea After the Cold War ended, the United States fought a war in the Middle East.

The Soviet Union was in trouble in the 1980s. Its command economy could not provide enough jobs, goods, and housing for most people. The cost of the arms race made the failing economy worse. Soviet leaders had spent a large amount of money building expensive weapons to compete with the United States.

Mikhail Gorbachev (mihkh uh EEL GAWR buh chawv) became the Soviet leader in 1985. Gorbachev decided to slow down the arms race by building a better relationship with the United States.

The Cold War Ends

Reagan and Gorbachev first met in 1985. They met several more times over the next two years to discuss ending the arms race. In 1987, they signed a treaty that lowered the number of nuclear weapons each country had. Slowly, the Cold War was ending.

In 1988, **George Bush** was elected President. Bush had been Reagan's Vice President for eight years. While Bush was President, the Soviet government and economy became weaker and weaker.

Soviet weakness gave the people in Eastern Europe and the Soviet Union the chance to break free from their communist rulers. Large groups of people joined protests in the streets of Eastern European cities. One by one, the communist governments in Eastern Europe fell from power. The most dramatic example was when the Berlin Wall came down and East and West Germany were reunited.

Finally, the Soviet Union itself fell apart. Many of its regions split away to form independent countries. The Russian people elected a new, non-communist government, and the Cold War was over.

Germany Reunited The Berlin Wall separated East Germany from West Germany for 28 years. In 1989, people on both sides of the wall helped bring it down and reunite the nation.

George Bush and Colin Powell As a top advisor under President Bush (left), General Powell (right) was in charge of the Persian Gulf War.

The Persian Gulf War

Although the Cold War was over, President Bush faced a new conflict in the Middle East. **Saddam Hussein** (SAHD uhm hoo SAYN) was the leader of Iraq. In 1990, his army invaded the neighboring country of Kuwait. Hussein planned to capture that country's oil fields.

Bush asked other countries in the United Nations to form a coalition to stop Iraq. A **coalition** is a group of allies that work together to achieve a goal.

In 1991, the United States led the coalition in a war against Iraq. The Persian Gulf War lasted about seven weeks. The coalition won the war quickly using advanced weapons and highly trained soldiers. Hussein remained in power, which worried leaders in the United States in the years to come.

REVIEW How did President Reagan help end the Cold War?

Lesson Summary

Reagan increased military spending and created a large deficit. During Bush's presidency, the Cold War ended.

Why It Matters ...

The Cold War ended when communists lost control of Eastern Europe and the Soviet Union.

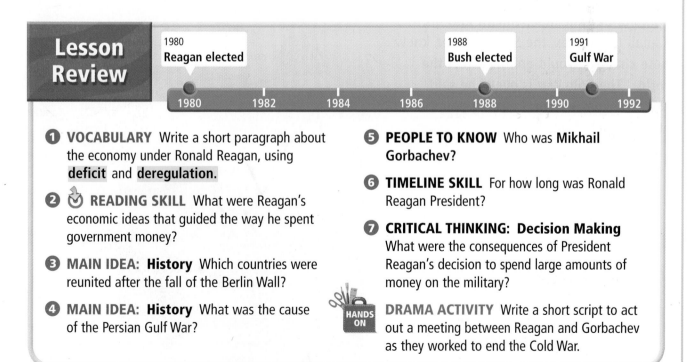

Lesson Review

1980 — **Reagan elected**
1988 — **Bush elected**
1991 — **Gulf War**

1980 1982 1984 1986 1988 1990 1992

1. **VOCABULARY** Write a short paragraph about the economy under Ronald Reagan, using **deficit** and **deregulation.**

2. **READING SKILL** What were Reagan's economic ideas that guided the way he spent government money?

3. **MAIN IDEA: History** Which countries were reunited after the fall of the Berlin Wall?

4. **MAIN IDEA: History** What was the cause of the Persian Gulf War?

5. **PEOPLE TO KNOW** Who was **Mikhail Gorbachev?**

6. **TIMELINE SKILL** For how long was Ronald Reagan President?

7. **CRITICAL THINKING: Decision Making** What were the consequences of President Reagan's decision to spend large amounts of money on the military?

HANDS ON **DRAMA ACTIVITY** Write a short script to act out a meeting between Reagan and Gorbachev as they worked to end the Cold War.

The Fall of Communism

Latvia

Latvia became a free nation after years of being part of the Soviet Union. In one town, citizens pulled down a statue of Vladimir Lenin, a founder of the Soviet Union.

In the mid-1980s, few people guessed that the Cold War would end in just a few years. The conflict between the United States and the Soviet Union had lasted for 40 years.

By the late 1980s, however, Soviet-style communism was in crisis. Its economy could no longer compete with the market economies of democratic nations. As its economy failed, Soviet political strength also collapsed.

In Eastern Europe, nations such as Poland broke free from Soviet control. Soon the Soviet Union itself broke apart and several republics became independent nations. Mikhail Gorbachev, the Soviet leader, knew these changes would greatly affect the world. "The Cold War is over," he said. "We are experiencing a turning point in international affairs."

Poland

During the 1980s, Lech Walesa led Solidarity, a union that opposed Poland's communist government. In 1990, he was elected President of Poland.

Russia

U.S. President Ronald Reagan and Soviet leader Mikhail Gorbachev met in 1988 to discuss common interests. Here they are standing in Red Square in Moscow, Russia's capital city.

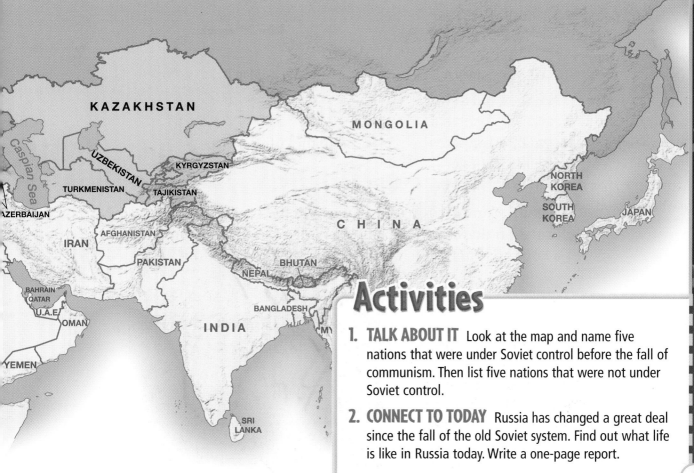

LEGEND	
■	Russia, 1991
□	Countries formerly under Soviet control

RUSSIA

KAZAKHSTAN

MONGOLIA

Caspian Sea

UZBEKISTAN

KYRGYZSTAN

TURKMENISTAN

TAJIKISTAN

AZERBAIJAN

NORTH KOREA

SOUTH KOREA

JAPAN

IRAN

AFGHANISTAN

CHINA

BAHRAIN

QATAR

U.A.E.

OMAN

PAKISTAN

NEPAL

BHUTAN

BANGLADESH

YEMEN

INDIA

SRI LANKA

Activities

1. **TALK ABOUT IT** Look at the map and name five nations that were under Soviet control before the fall of communism. Then list five nations that were not under Soviet control.

2. **CONNECT TO TODAY** Russia has changed a great deal since the fall of the old Soviet system. Find out what life is like in Russia today. Write a one-page report.

Skillbuilder

Compare Maps with Different Scales

▶ **VOCABULARY**

map scale

A map scale compares distance on a map to distance in the real world. People use maps with different scales for different reasons. Sometimes, you may need to see many details on a map or a small area of land. Other times, you need to see a large area or don't need many details. The two maps on the next page have different scales and show different information.

Learn the Skill

Step 1: Read the scales on the two maps. For each map, see how many miles equal one inch.

Map A   Map B

Step 2: Compare the scales. Note the differences.

Step 3: Compare the information on the two maps. What information does each map show? Which map gives a broad view of a large area, and which focuses on a smaller location?

Step 4: Think about what you want to learn. Identify which map presents the information you need.

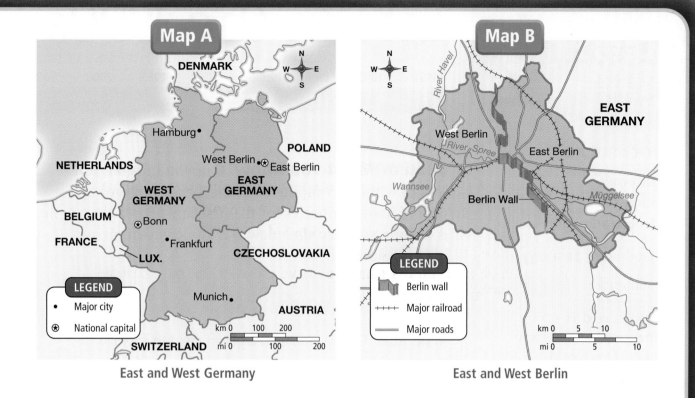

Map A

DENMARK

Hamburg

NETHERLANDS

West Berlin • ⊛ East Berlin

POLAND

WEST GERMANY

EAST GERMANY

BELGIUM

⊛ Bonn

FRANCE

• Frankfurt

LUX.

CZECHOSLOVAKIA

Munich •

AUSTRIA

LEGEND

• Major city

⊛ National capital

SWITZERLAND

km 0   100   200

mi 0   100   200

East and West Germany

Map B

River Havel

West Berlin

River Spree

EAST GERMANY

East Berlin

Wannsee

Berlin Wall

Müggelsee

LEGEND

Berlin wall

+++++ Major railroad

——— Major roads

km 0   5   10

mi 0   5   10

East and West Berlin

Practice the Skill

Use the two maps above to answer these questions.

1 What is the map scale for Map A?

2 What is the map scale for Map B?

3 Which map would you use to find the distance from Munich to East Berlin? Use a ruler to find that distance.

4 Which map would you use to find the approximate length of the Berlin Wall? Use a ruler and a piece of string to find that length.

Apply the Skill

Compare the two resource maps on pages 15 and 549. Write a paragraph explaining when and why you might use each of the maps. Be sure to describe the map scale, the amount of detail, and the purpose of each map.

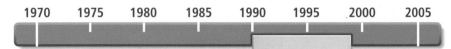

Life in the 1990s

1970   1975   1980   1985   1990   1995   2000   2005

1990–1999

VOCABULARY

Internet
high-tech
free-trade agreement

Vocabulary Strategy

inter**net**

When you read the word **Internet,** think of the way strings of a net are all connected. The Internet connects computers all over the world.

READING SKILL

Categorize As you read, categorize the changes that occurred in the U.S. economy.

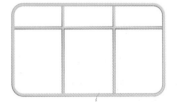

Build on What You Know Can you imagine your school without computers? In the 1990s, millions of people used computers for the first time. For these people, computers opened up a new way of doing things and learning about the world.

Clinton's Presidency

Main Idea Clinton wanted the government to improve the economy and settle conflicts around the world.

The victory in the Persian Gulf War made **George Bush** a popular President. By 1992, however, the United States' economy had stopped growing. Many people lost their jobs. As unemployment grew, Bush lost support.

In 1992, **Bill Clinton** defeated Bush in the presidential election. During his election campaign, Clinton told voters that the government should focus on the economy now that the Cold War was over.

Clinton and Albright President Clinton chose Madeleine Albright to be Secretary of State, the most important job a woman had ever held in government.

STANDARDS

SS5H9b Impact of computers and Internet
SS5E1d Voluntary exchange: G8
SS5E1e Trade: NAFTA
SS5E2a-c Private business, banks, government

Clinton's Economic Ideas

Clinton was a Democrat. In many ways he was like earlier Democratic Presidents. He believed that one function of government was to use social programs to help people. However, the budget deficit from the 1980s made it hard to spend money on new programs. Also, the Republicans who controlled Congress did not want more government programs. For these reasons, Clinton asked for only small increases in spending for education, health care, and other public services.

The economy grew again during Clinton's years as President. Inflation remained low. Businesses hired more workers. With more people working, the government collected more taxes. By 1998, the budget deficit had turned into a budget surplus. When the government collects more money than it spends, the money left over is a surplus.

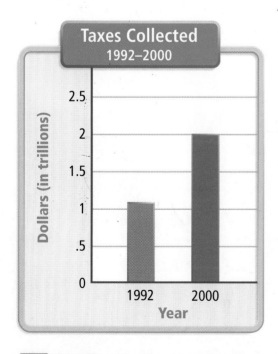

Taxes Collected
1992–2000

SKILL **Reading Graphs** About how much more money did the government collect in 2000 than in 1992?

World Events

Clinton acted as a peacemaker in several conflicts around the world. In Northern Ireland, Catholics and Protestants had been fighting for many decades. In 1998, Clinton helped with peace talks there. He also tried to end conflict in the Middle East.

The Balkan region in eastern Europe was another trouble spot during Clinton's presidency. Fighting there started when the former communist country of Yugoslavia split apart. Several ethnic groups battled each other as they tried to form new nations in the area. In the 1990s, the United States and other countries sent soldiers to try to stop the fighting.

Clinton Impeached

Clinton was reelected in 1996. His second term as President was hurt by a scandal. Some people in the United States believed that the President had lied in court about his private life. The House of Representatives voted to impeach him. To impeach means to charge a government official with a crime or other serious wrongdoing.

Clinton became the second President ever to be impeached. The first one was **Andrew Johnson** in 1868. The Senate held a trial to decide whether Clinton was guilty. They found him not guilty.

REVIEW In which places did President Clinton help settle conflicts?

A Changing Economy

Main Idea During the 1990s, the economy grew quickly.

During the 1990s, the United States had the longest period of economic growth in its history. The economic boom lasted for 10 years. Many people had more income to save, spend, or invest. In 2000, the stock market reached an all-time high.

Changes in computer technology boosted the economy in the 1990s. Inventors made computers better, faster, and less expensive. One inventor named **Bill Gates** developed computer programs to use in homes, classrooms, and businesses. Another inventor, **Marc Andreesen,** developed programs that allowed people to view websites on the Internet. The **Internet** links computers around the world with each other.

New Technology

Millions of people bought computers for their homes in the 1990s. These were known as personal computers. As the technologies improved, people found new uses for their computers. Through the Internet, they began to shop, send e-mail, and get information of all kinds.

The growing computer industry was part of a boom for high-tech (high-technology) businesses. **High-tech** businesses develop or use the most recent knowledge and equipment. They make products such as cellular phones and Internet software.

New technologies have made the U.S. economy more productive. Computers play a big role in most businesses. For example, computers now control much of the work on car assembly lines. Computer control makes production quicker, safer, and less expensive.

Computer Evolution

1946

ENIAC ENIAC was the first electronic digital computer. It weighed 30 tons and filled a large room. Even though it was a breakthrough at that time, it had less computing power than a digital watch does today.

Changes in Jobs

As the United States economy changed, jobs changed, too. During the 1990s, the number of people working in service jobs increased. People with service jobs provide information or perform tasks for others. For example, the functions of banks include providing people and businesses with savings accounts, checking accounts, and loans.

At the same time, the number of people who worked in manufacturing decreased. Computers and other machines helped businesses produce more goods with fewer workers. Some companies moved their factories overseas, where they could make their products at a lower cost. Farmers also used more machinery to grow food, so fewer workers were needed on farms.

Service Jobs

Number of Jobs (in millions)

1990   2000

Year

SKILL **Reading Graphs** About how many more people worked in service jobs in 2000 than in 1990?

The changing economy gave many people new opportunities. People with more education benefited the most. They had the skills and knowledge that they needed to become more productive. Many of these people saw their wealth grow quickly in the 1990s.

REVIEW What effect did computers have on the economy in the 1990s?

1977

Personal Computer The Apple II was one of the first personal computers manufactured in large numbers for use at home.

1981

Laptop Companies started creating computers that could be carried around and placed anywhere, including someone's lap.

1993

PDA These tiny computers were first sold in 1993. They run on batteries and hook up to personal computers. They can send and receive e-mail, search the Internet, and play movies and music.

A Connected World

Main Idea Technology, transportation, and trade have helped create a world where countries depend on one another.

During the 1990s, new technologies changed people's lives all over the world. Improved communication and better transportation brought individuals around the world closer than ever before.

New technologies, such as the Internet and cellular phones, made this change possible. Today, we take high-tech communication for granted, but communication has not always been so quick and easy. In the 1830s, it took four weeks for news to travel by ship between the United States and England.

Individuals now learn about events all over the world almost as soon as they happen. They can communicate with others no matter where they are. Some have even used telephones and computers on Mount Everest, the tallest mountain on Earth.

Transportation and Trade

Today, airplanes take people and products to any place in the world. Better communication and transportation have increased trade among nations. Many American businesses trade with companies in other nations. In the automobile industry, for example, parts are imported from many countries.

Trade between individuals or countries is called voluntary exchange. Every year, leaders from the United States, Canada, France, Italy, Germany, Britain, Japan, and Russia meet to discuss many issues, including trade. This group is known as the Group of 8, or G8. If G8 nations increase voluntary exchange, all of the nations can benefit. For example, if the United States buys oil from Russia, both nations gain. The United States gains oil, and Russia gains income.

Inside a Car Businesses around the world cooperate to make many of the products people use today.

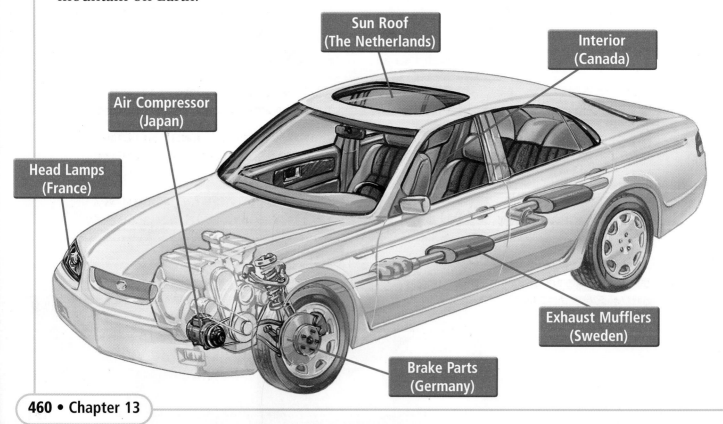

Sun Roof (The Netherlands)

Interior (Canada)

Air Compressor (Japan)

Head Lamps (France)

Exhaust Mufflers (Sweden)

Brake Parts (Germany)

Trade Agreements

Since the end of World War II, the United States has worked to increase voluntary exchange through free-trade agreements. A **free-trade agreement** is a treaty designed to increase trade by removing taxes or tariffs. When trade increases, the economy of each nation usually becomes stronger.

In 1994, the United States, Canada, and Mexico started the North American Free Trade Agreement, or NAFTA. NAFTA removed almost all of the taxes on goods traded among the countries. Without taxes, imported products began to cost less, and consumers bought more of them. Because of NAFTA, trade among the three countries increased greatly.

REVIEW In what ways did better communication change life for people during the 1990s?

Lesson Summary

- During the 1990s, the economy grew quickly.
- Clinton tried to settle conflicts around the world.
- Computers and high-tech businesses contributed to the economic boom of the 1990s.
- Better communication and transportation have increased trade among nations.

Why It Matters . . .

The technologies developed during the 1990s will have effects on people and businesses for years to come.

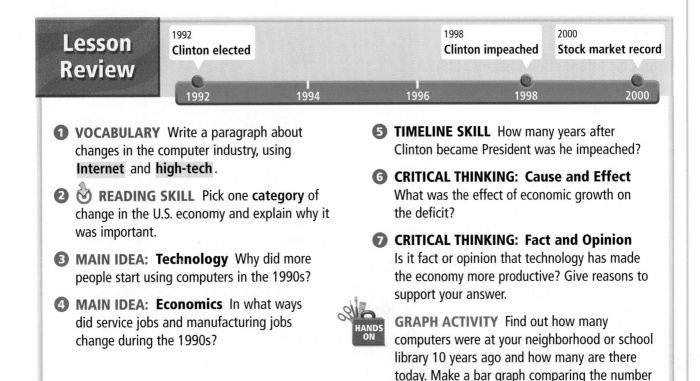

Lesson Review

| 1992 Clinton elected | | 1998 Clinton impeached | 2000 Stock market record |

| 1992 | 1994 | 1996 | 1998 | 2000 |

1. **VOCABULARY** Write a paragraph about changes in the computer industry, using **Internet** and **high-tech**.

2. **READING SKILL** Pick one **category** of change in the U.S. economy and explain why it was important.

3. **MAIN IDEA: Technology** Why did more people start using computers in the 1990s?

4. **MAIN IDEA: Economics** In what ways did service jobs and manufacturing jobs change during the 1990s?

5. **TIMELINE SKILL** How many years after Clinton became President was he impeached?

6. **CRITICAL THINKING: Cause and Effect** What was the effect of economic growth on the deficit?

7. **CRITICAL THINKING: Fact and Opinion** Is it fact or opinion that technology has made the economy more productive? Give reasons to support your answer.

HANDS ON

GRAPH ACTIVITY Find out how many computers were at your neighborhood or school library 10 years ago and how many are there today. Make a bar graph comparing the number of computers for both years.

High-Tech Geography

Where am I? The question seems simple, but the answer has not always been easy. Explorers and navigators need to know exactly where they are on Earth. Old technologies gave them only part of the answer. But in the 1990s, highly detailed maps and images of the world became possible.

A **high-tech** geography system called the Global Positioning System (GPS) uses satellites orbiting Earth to send information to computers on land. The information provides the latitude, longitude, and elevation for every square yard on Earth's surface. Geographic Information Systems (GIS) can combine several maps to create layers of information.

There are many uses for such detailed information. GIS can help track wildlife migrations and plan transportation in cities. Firefighters also use GIS to battle forest fires.

This smokejumper is headed into a fire zone in Montana.

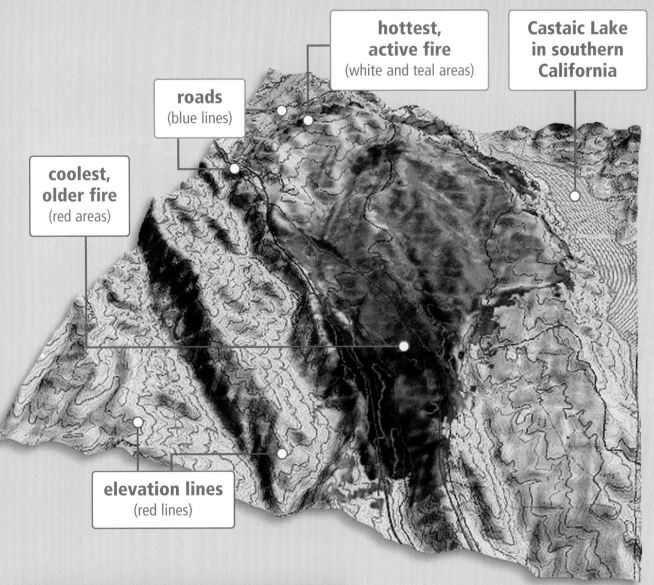

hottest, active fire (white and teal areas)

Castaic Lake in southern California

roads (blue lines)

coolest, older fire (red areas)

elevation lines (red lines)

▲ This infrared color image was made using GIS technology. Combined with a roadmap, it lets firefighters know the best routes for moving people away from the fire.

Smokejumpers use new technology to decide where to dig trenches to contain the fire.

Activities

1. **TALK ABOUT IT** Discuss other kinds of emergencies in which having a detailed map could save lives.

2. **PRESENT IT** Find out how new technologies can help track wildlife migrations or plan transportation in cities. Present the information in a report.

Twenty-First Century Begins

VOCABULARY

millennium
popular vote
Electoral College
terrorism

Vocabulary Strategy

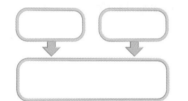
| popular vote |

Popular means "of the people." The **popular vote** is the vote of the people.

READING SKILL

Cause and Effect As you read, take notes on the reasons for the outcome of the 2000 presidential election.

| 1970 | 1975 | 1980 | 1985 | 1990 | 1995 | 2000 | 2005 |

2000–2005

Build on What You Know Many people celebrate each birthday, but some birthdays seem more important than others. Many people felt that the year 2000 was a special birthday for the whole world.

The 2000 Election

Main Idea The year 2000 brought one of the biggest parties ever and an unusual presidential election.

On December 31, 1999, people spent New Year's Eve listening to music, dancing, and watching fireworks. Parties around the world celebrated the beginning of a new century and a new millennium. A **millennium** is a period of 10 centuries, or 1,000 years. Although the new millennium actually began on January 1, 2001, people celebrated when the year 2000 began.

The 2000 election was one of the closest elections in United States history. The Democratic candidate was **Al Gore**, the Vice President under President Clinton. The Republican candidate was **George W. Bush**. He was the son of former President **George Bush**.

New Year's 2000 The New Year's celebrations of 2000 were some of the biggest ever.

Popular versus Electoral Votes

A presidential election has two steps. The first step is the popular vote. The **popular vote** is the vote of individuals. The next step is the Electoral College. The **Electoral College** is made up of represent-atives, called electors, from each state who vote for the President and Vice President.

The candidate who wins a state's pop-ular vote wins all of that state's Electoral College votes. To become President, a candidate must win the Electoral College vote. Under this system, it is possible for a candidate to win the popular vote but lose the electoral vote.

The election of 2000 was an example of a very close popular and electoral vote. In Florida, the popular vote was so close that the candidates disagreed on who had won. The disagreement went to the U.S. Supreme Court. The Court stopped the state from recounting the popular vote. **George W. Bush** was declared the winner of Florida's popular vote.

George W. Bush In 2000 he won one of the closest presidential elections in U.S. history. His re-election in 2004 was not that close.

By winning Florida's popular vote, Bush also won the state's electoral votes, allowing him to win the election. Four years later, in 2004, Bush again ran for President. This time, it was clear that Bush won both the popular and the electoral votes. He began his second term as President in January 2005.

REVIEW What is the difference between the popular vote and the electoral vote?

Electoral Votes, 2000

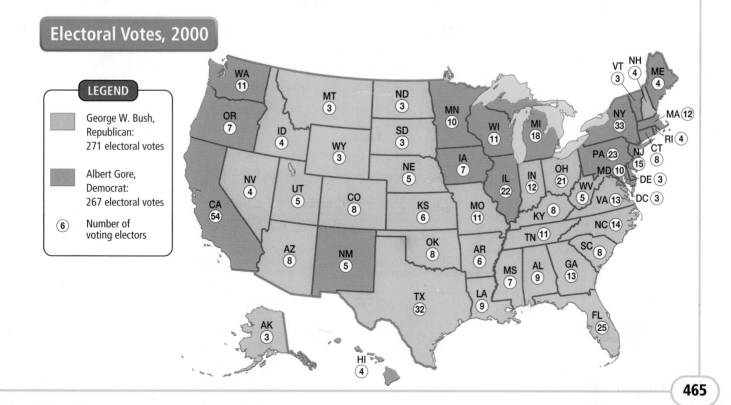

LEGEND

George W. Bush, Republican: 271 electoral votes

Albert Gore, Democrat: 267 electoral votes

(6) Number of voting electors

WA 11 · OR 7 · MT 3 · ND 3 · MN 10 · VT 3 · NH 4 · ME 4 · NY 33 · MA 12 · RI 4 · ID 4 · WY 3 · SD 3 · WI 11 · MI 18 · PA 23 · NJ 15 · CT 8 · NV 4 · UT 5 · CO 8 · NE 5 · IA 7 · IL 22 · IN 12 · OH 21 · MD 10 · DE 3 · CA 54 · KS 6 · MO 11 · WV 5 · VA 13 · DC 3 · KY 8 · NC 14 · AZ 8 · NM 5 · OK 8 · AR 6 · TN 11 · SC 8 · MS 7 · AL 9 · GA 13 · TX 32 · LA 9 · FL 25 · AK 3 · HI 4

Attack on the Nation

Main Idea The terrorist attacks of September 11, 2001, started a new era for the people and government of the United States.

On September 11, 2001, several acts of terrorism were carried out against the United States. **Terrorism** is the use of violence against ordinary people to achieve a political goal.

On that day, terrorists hijacked four airplanes. They crashed two planes into the World Trade Center in New York City. The two buildings caught fire and fell. Terrorists crashed a third plane into the Pentagon, the nation's military headquarters outside of Washington, D.C. The fourth plane crashed in Pennsylvania.

Nearly 3,000 innocent people were killed in these attacks. The United States found out that the terrorists belonged to a group from the Middle East called al-Qaeda (al KY duh). Their leader was **Osama bin Laden** (oh SAH mah bihn LAH dehn). Bin Laden and his followers strongly opposed the United States' involvement in the Middle East.

Bush told the military to prepare for war. He said,

> 66 While the price of freedom and security is high, it is never too high. Whatever it costs to defend our country, we will pay. 99

Afghanistan and Iraq Both countries are in the Middle East region.

SKILL **Reading Maps** Where is Afghanistan located in relation to Iraq?

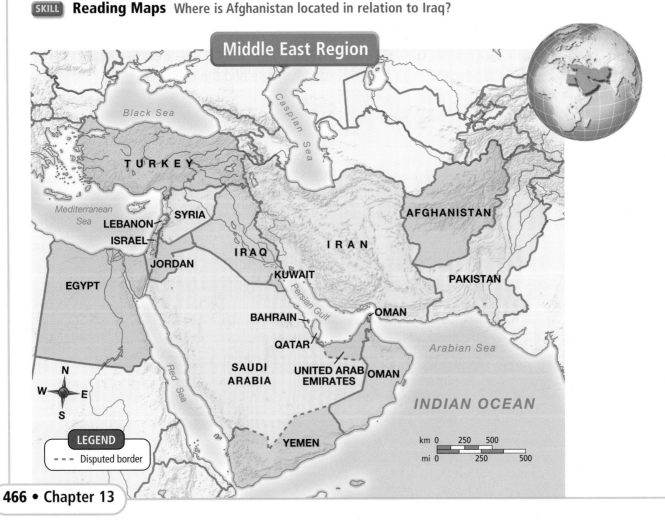

Middle East Region

War in Afghanistan and Iraq

Osama bin Laden's headquarters was in the country of Afghanistan in southwest Asia. Bush accused the government of Afghanistan of hiding bin Laden and his followers. In October, 2001, the United States led a coalition of nations into a war in Afghanistan.

The war lasted for three months. The United States defeated Afghanistan's government and military but did not capture bin Laden. New leaders in Afghanistan formed a government that was supported by the United States.

In 2003, Bush turned his attention to the nation of Iraq in the Middle East. **Saddam Hussein** was still in power there. During the 1990s, the United Nations tried to inspect places in Iraq to see whether Hussein had destroyed his most dangerous weapons. Bush did not believe that Hussein had disarmed. In March 2003, the United States invaded Iraq. American forces defeated Hussein's army and arrested the Iraqi leader.

The U.S. military stayed in Iraq to help form a new government. Some Iraqis helped build the new government, but others fought against it.

REVIEW How did the United States respond to the terrorist attacks of September 11, 2001?

Lesson Summary

2000	George W. Bush elected President
September 11, 2001	Terrorist attacks
2001	War in Afghanistan
2003	War in Iraq

Why It Matters . . .

The terrorist attacks of September 11, 2001, deeply affected people in the United States and the world.

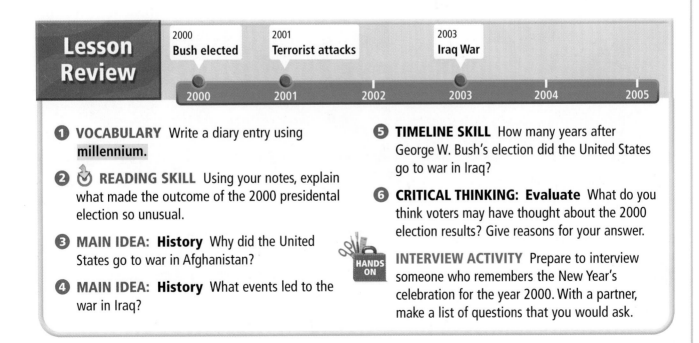

Lesson Review

2000 Bush elected   2001 Terrorist attacks   2003 Iraq War

2000   2001   2002   2003   2004   2005

❶ **VOCABULARY** Write a diary entry using **millennium.**

❷ **READING SKILL** Using your notes, explain what made the outcome of the 2000 presidental election so unusual.

❸ **MAIN IDEA: History** Why did the United States go to war in Afghanistan?

❹ **MAIN IDEA: History** What events led to the war in Iraq?

❺ **TIMELINE SKILL** How many years after George W. Bush's election did the United States go to war in Iraq?

❻ **CRITICAL THINKING: Evaluate** What do you think voters may have thought about the 2000 election results? Give reasons for your answer.

INTERVIEW ACTIVITY Prepare to interview someone who remembers the New Year's celebration for the year 2000. With a partner, make a list of questions that you would ask.

9/11 HEROES

News of the attacks on September 11, 2001, shocked the nation. As thousands of New Yorkers fled the city, hundreds of police and firefighters rushed to the burning World Trade Center to help survivors. Search and rescue teams went to New York City from all over the country, along with emergency medical crews. For these professionals, responding to this act of terrorism was the hardest job in their careers.

Ordinary citizens wanted to help, too. Truckers and work crews came to remove the tons of rubble from the collapsed buildings. Volunteers donated blankets, food, and other goods for people affected by the tragedy. Many people raised money for the effort. Together, people worked to comfort their fellow citizens and help them recover from the terrible blow.

Kids Step Forward

Students collected money to help the victims of the attacks. At a Saltillo, Mississippi, elementary school, students raised $971.00 in one day.

Run for Funds

This Michigan firefighter went to Washington, D.C., to take part in a fundraising race. The race was dedicated to the victims of the attacks.

On the Scene
Three firefighters raise the United States flag at the World Trade Center shortly after the 9/11 attacks.

©2001 The Record (Bergen County, NJ), www.groundzerospirit.org

Activities

1. DRAW IT Many people have ideas for a memorial for the victims of the September 11th attacks. Draw your idea for a memorial.

2. WRITE ABOUT IT The students from Saltillo, Mississippi, deserved a thank you note for their hard work. Write a letter the mayor of New York City might have written to them.

Visual Summary

1.–4. ✏️ Describe what you learned about each President named below.

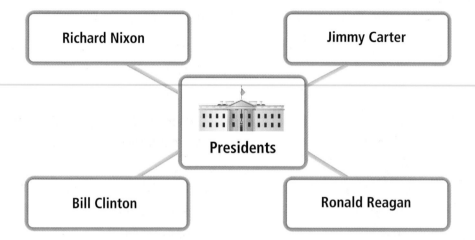

Richard Nixon

Jimmy Carter

Presidents

Bill Clinton

Ronald Reagan

Facts and Main Ideas

✅ **TEST PREP** Answer each question with information from the chapter.

5. **Citizenship** Name two groups of people who worked for equal rights in the 1970s.

6. **Government** Why did President Carter win the Nobel Peace Prize?

7. **History** Which two leaders signed agreements that led to the end of the arms race?

8. **Economics** Which three countries are part of NAFTA?

9. **Government** In what way was the 2000 presidential election unusual?

Vocabulary

✅ **TEST PREP** Choose the correct word from the list below to complete each sentence.

resign, p. 441
deficit, p. 449
high-tech, p. 458
terrorism, p. 466

10. Many _____ inventions led to improvements in medicine and business.

11. The use of violence against ordinary people to achieve a political goal is called _____.

12. Richard Nixon was the first U.S. President ever to _____.

13. The government spent more than it collected in taxes, which created a _____.

CHAPTER SUMMARY TIMELINE

1974	1980	1989	2001
Nixon resigns	Reagan elected	Fall of the Berlin Wall	September 11 attacks

1970   1975   1980   1985   1990   1995   2000   2005

Apply Skills

☑ TEST PREP **Map Skill** Compare the map of Afghanistan below to the map of the Middle East region on page 674. Then answer each question.

14. What can you learn from the map above that you can't learn from the map on page 674?

　A. the distance between Kabul and Kandahar

　B. the major rivers in the Middle East

　C. the locations of battles in the war in Afghanistan

　D. the distance between the capitals of Iran and Iraq

15. Which map would you use to learn the names of the countries that border Saudi Arabia?

Critical Thinking

☑ TEST PREP Write a short paragraph to answer each question.

16. **Cause and Effect** What were the effects of the rise in oil prices in the 1970s?

17. **Summarize** How has the world become more interdependent in recent years?

Timeline

Use the Chapter Summary Timeline above to answer the question.

18. Was Reagan elected before or after the fall of the Berlin Wall?

Activities

Connect to Georgia Find out about the life of President Jimmy Carter. Write a biography about his achievements for Georgia and for the country.

Writing Activity Write a persuasive essay to a student explaining why he or she will need a good education to succeed in an interdependent world.

Technology

Writing Process Tips
Get help with your essay at
www.eduplace.com/kids/hmss/

Chapter 14

America Today and Tomorrow

Technology
e • glossary
e • word games
www.eduplace.com/kids/hmss/

Vocabulary Preview

province

The United States is made up of 50 states, but Canada has political regions called **provinces.** Each province has a capital and a government.
page 474

heritage

The ideals of democracy and human rights are part of the history of the United States. The Liberty Bell is a symbol of this **heritage.**
page 487

Chapter Timeline

1821
Mexican independence

1867
Canadian independence

| 1800 | 1850 | 1900 |

Reading Strategy

Summarize As you read, use the summarize strategy to focus on important ideas.

quick Tip It helps to reread sections and put them in your own words.

responsibility

Americans have many rights. They also have a **responsibility** to follow the laws of the United States.
page 492

volunteer

People, no matter what their age, can help others by being a **volunteer.** Doing work to help others without being paid is an American tradition. **page 492**

1992
NAFTA signed

1950 — 2000

Neighbors in North America

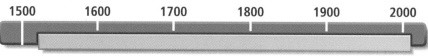

| 1500 | 1600 | 1700 | 1800 | 1900 | 2000 |

1521–present

Build on What You Know You and your neighbors share the same street. The United States and its neighbors, Canada and Mexico, share the same continent. The three countries also share similar histories.

Canada

Main Idea The United States and Canada have similar histories and are important trading partners.

Canada is the United States' neighbor to the north. Canada is large in area, but it has only 32 million people. In comparison, the United States is smaller in area, but it has 285 million people. Canada's capital is Ottawa. The country has three territories and ten provinces. A **province** is a political region that is similar to a state.

Canada and the United States share a 5,500-mile border that stretches from the Atlantic Ocean to the Pacific Ocean and along the eastern side of Alaska. Thousands of cars and trucks from both the United States and Canada cross the border every day.

Canadian Flag The maple leaf symbolizes the land and people of Canada. Red and white are Canada's official colors.

VOCABULARY

province
multicultural
maquiladora

Vocabulary Strategy

multi**cultural**

The prefix **multi-** in the word **multicultural** means many. A multicultural country has many cultural traditions within it.

READING SKILL
Compare and Contrast
As you read, take notes on the similarities and differences among the three countries in North America.

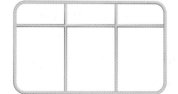

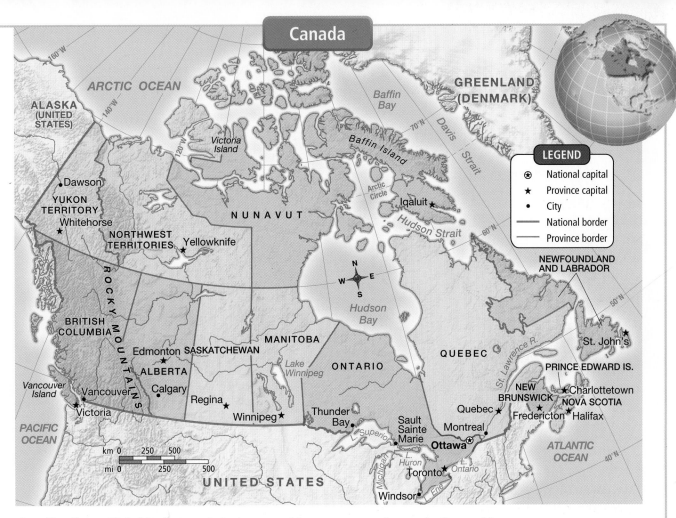

Canada

ARCTIC OCEAN

ALASKA (UNITED STATES)

GREENLAND (DENMARK)

Baffin Bay

Victoria Island

Baffin Island

Davis Strait

•Dawson

YUKON TERRITORY
★Whitehorse

NORTHWEST TERRITORIES

N U N A V U T

Arctic Circle

Iqaluit ★

Hudson Strait

LEGEND

⊛ National capital
★ Province capital
• City
— National border
— Province border

•Yellowknife

NEWFOUNDLAND AND LABRADOR

BRITISH COLUMBIA

Hudson Bay

St. John's ★

Vancouver Island

Edmonton SASKATCHEWAN
★
ALBERTA

MANITOBA

Lake Winnipeg

O N T A R I O

Q U E B E C

St. Lawrence R.

PRINCE EDWARD IS.

Vancouver•
•Calgary

Regina•

•Winnipeg ★

Thunder Bay•

NEW BRUNSWICK
Quebec ★

Charlottetown
NOVA SCOTIA

Victoria•

PACIFIC OCEAN

km 0   250   500
mi 0   250   500

Sault Sainte Marie
Montreal•
Ottawa ⊛

Fredericton★ •Halifax

ATLANTIC OCEAN

L. Superior

L. Michigan

L. Huron

Toronto•
L. Ontario

L. Erie

Windsor•

U N I T E D   S T A T E S

Our Northern Neighbor Canada is the second largest country in area in the world.

Canada's History and Culture

The history of Canada is similar to the history of the United States. The first people to live in Canada were native peoples, such as the Cree, Huron, and the Inuit, who are also known as Eskimos. Like the United States, Canada was colonized by Europeans. At first, the colonists were mainly French. In 1754, France and Britain began a war for control of North America. France lost, and the British gained control of Canada.

In 1867, Canada separated from Britain and became a self-governing country. It has a representative democracy, with powers divided between the provinces and a federal government. Canada also belongs to the Commonwealth of Nations, a group of countries that were once part of the British Empire.

The French influence is still strong in Canada, especially in the province of Quebec. In Quebec, most people speak French or both French and English. Throughout Canada, French and English are official languages.

Native peoples are an important part of Canadian society. The Inuit have their own territory called Nunavut.

Canada also has many immigrants from Europe, Asia, and South and Central America. In Canada, one out of six people is an immigrant. With so many immigrants, Canada is a multicultural society. **Multicultural** means having many cultural traditions.

REVIEW Why is French one of the two official languages in Canada?

Ottawa, Canada's Capital Canada's representatives meet in the Parliament building in Ottawa. Street signs in parts of Canada are in both French and English.

Canada and the United States

In 1992, Canada signed the North American Free Trade Agreement (NAFTA) with the United States and Mexico. NAFTA is an agreement among these three countries to increase trade. The agreement says that the countries will remove tariffs and taxes for the products they sell to each other. Today, the United States and Canada trade more with each other than with any other countries.

The United States buys oil, electricity, lumber, car parts, and paper from Canada. The United States sells cars, machines, chemicals, and other products to Canada. The two nations also work together to deal with environmental problems that affect both countries.

One example is reducing pollution that blows from the American Midwest into Canada. They also work together to improve the quality of the water in the Great Lakes. The Great Lakes form part of the border between the two countries.

Canada's Exports

Fish/shellfish	
Oil	
Natural gas	
Lumber/wood products	
Farm animals and products	

SKILL **Readings Charts** Which of Canada's exports are taken from the ground?

Mexico

Main Idea Mexico was colonized by the Spanish, but it has been an independent country since 1821.

Mexico is the United States' neighbor to the south. The 2,000-mile border between the United States and Mexico stretches from California to Texas. About 103 million people live in Mexico. Mexico City is the capital of Mexico and is one of the largest cities in the world.

The country has 31 states and one federal district. In northern Mexico, the land includes a central plateau with basins and ranges. This area is warm and dry. The south has mountains and tropical rain forests that cross Mexico's southern border with Belize and Guatemala.

Mexico's History

Mexico has a rich history. The Mayas and Aztecs were some of the first peoples in Mexico. They built large, beautiful cities and used technologies, such as irrigation, that were advanced for their time. Irrigation helped them have large farms.

Spanish explorers began coming to Mexico in the early 1500s. By the 1520s, the Spanish started to conquer and settle Mexico. Like the United States, Mexico fought a war for its independence. In 1821, Mexico defeated the Spanish and became an independent country. Since 1910, Mexico has had a representative government that gives a lot of power to the President.

REVIEW How and when did Mexico gain its independence?

Our Southern Neighbor Mexico is the most populated Spanish-speaking country in the world. **SKILL** **Reading Maps** Which Mexican states border the United States?

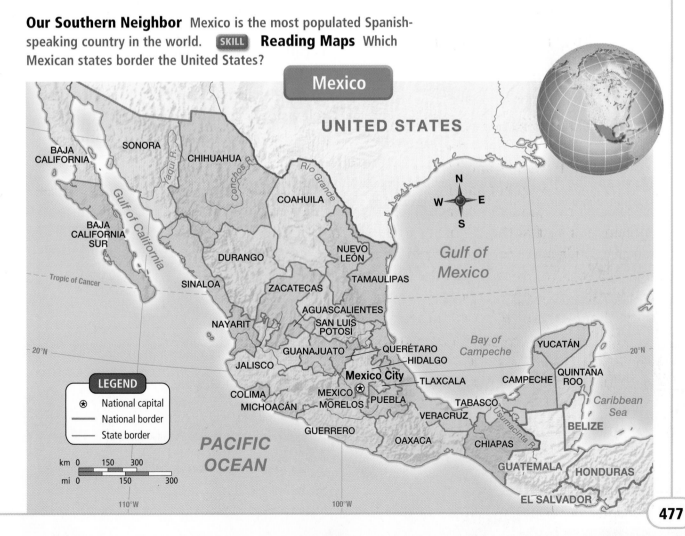

Mexico

477

Mexican Culture

Mexico's people have a Spanish and Indian heritage. Most Mexicans are mestizo (meh STEE zoh), which means people of both Spanish and Mexican Indian ancestry. Spanish is the official language, but many Indian languages are also spoken. Most Mexicans are Catholics, and the Catholic Church has shaped Mexico's culture in many ways.

Many Mexicans live in small villages in the countryside, where farming is an important part of life. Even more Mexicans live in busy modern cities. Most Mexican cities have a Spanish-style central square or plaza. Art inspired by the country's Indian heritage decorates many public places.

Mexico and the United States

Mexico and the United States have different cultures, but the two countries have had close contact for more than 150 years. Because much of the southwestern United States was once part of Mexico, Mexican arts, food, and building styles are common in California, Texas, Arizona, and New Mexico.

Many Mexicans immigrate to the United States. Immigration provides workers for the U.S. economy and gives jobs to Mexicans. Immigration can cause problems, however, especially when it is done illegally. The two countries work together to try to reduce illegal immigration across their shared border.

Mexico and the United States have important economic ties. Since the 1970s, businesses in the United States and other countries have built factories in Mexico near the U.S. border. This kind of factory is called a **maquiladora** (mah kee lah DOH rah). Thousands of Mexicans work in maquiladoras. They put together cars, televisions, computers, and other products that are sold all over the world.

Mexican Flag The three stripes symbolize from left to right independence, religion, and union. The flag flies over Mexico City's central plaza (below).

NAFTA

In 1992, Mexico signed NAFTA with the United States and Canada. Afterward, its trade with the two countries greatly increased. Today, Mexico's most important trading partner is the United States. Mexico is the United States' second most important trading partner after Canada.

Mexico's Exports

Farm crops	
Oil	
Farm animals and products	
Precious metals	
Iron	

SKILL **Reading Charts** Which of Mexico's exports are the same as Canada's exports?

The United States buys oil and minerals from Mexico. It sells machines, car parts, and farm equipment to Mexico. Partly because of NAFTA, the three countries will have close ties for a long time to come.

REVIEW What are some of Mexico's connections with the United States?

Lesson Summary

- British and French cultures are part of daily life in Canada.
- Spanish and Mexican Indian cultures are part of daily life in Mexico.
- Canada, Mexico, and the United States signed NAFTA to increase trade among the three countries.

Why It Matters ...

The United States, Canada, and Mexico are neighbors in North America. They all gain from trade and cultural sharing across the borders.

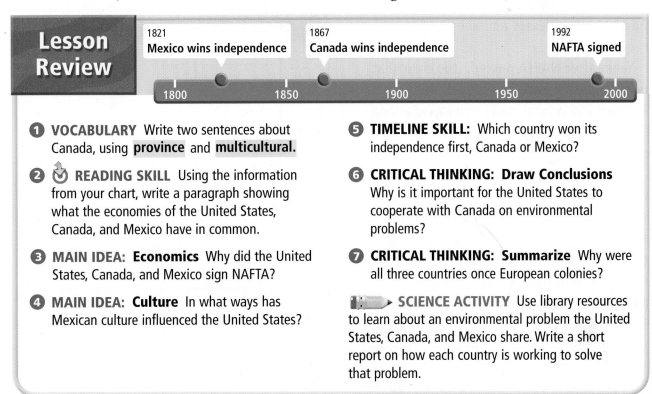

Lesson Review

1821	1867	1992
Mexico wins independence	Canada wins independence	NAFTA signed

1800　1850　1900　1950　2000

1. **VOCABULARY** Write two sentences about Canada, using **province** and **multicultural.**

2. **READING SKILL** Using the information from your chart, write a paragraph showing what the economies of the United States, Canada, and Mexico have in common.

3. **MAIN IDEA: Economics** Why did the United States, Canada, and Mexico sign NAFTA?

4. **MAIN IDEA: Culture** In what ways has Mexican culture influenced the United States?

5. **TIMELINE SKILL:** Which country won its independence first, Canada or Mexico?

6. **CRITICAL THINKING: Draw Conclusions** Why is it important for the United States to cooperate with Canada on environmental problems?

7. **CRITICAL THINKING: Summarize** Why were all three countries once European colonies?

SCIENCE ACTIVITY Use library resources to learn about an environmental problem the United States, Canada, and Mexico share. Write a short report on how each country is working to solve that problem.

THE EFFECTS OF NAFTA

Before NAFTA was signed into law, no one knew how free trade would affect the U.S. economy. Plenty of people had opinions, though. Some people warned that Americans would lose jobs if trade became freer. They predicted that more companies would move their factories to Mexico.

Most economists believed NAFTA would be good for each country. They believe free trade helps businesses and keeps prices low for consumers.

Years after NAFTA passed, it is clear that North American trade has grown. Between 1993 and 2001, total trade between Canada, Mexico, and the United States more than doubled.

Most leaders in Canada, Mexico, and the United States have been pleased by the increase in trade. However, some report that NAFTA has not helped to create enough jobs. Other nations will watch NAFTA's effects carefully. If free trade works in North America, they may want similar agreements with the United States.

LUMBER Canada's forests are the largest in North America. Wood and wood products from those forests are important exports.

Trade between the U.S. and Canada
1993–2001

Dollars (in Billions) / Year

- Exports to Canada
- Imports from Canada

Canada is our nation's biggest trading partner. About how many billions more in exports were traded from 1993 to 2001?

AUTOMOBILES Cars and car parts are important to North American trade. Car parts from the United States are put together in this Mexican factory.

OIL In recent years, Mexico has become a leading oil exporter. Most of its oil exports go to its NAFTA trading partners.

Trade between the U.S. and Mexico
1993–2001

- Exports to Mexico
- Imports from Mexico

Dollars (in Billions)

150
125
100
50
25
0

1993 1995 1997 1999 2001

Year

After NAFTA, Mexican imports to the United States more than tripled between 1993 and 2001.

Activities

1. **LIST IT** List three questions to ask other students about the information in the charts.

2. **GRAPH IT** Create a bar graph from the line graphs, comparing Canadian and Mexican trade with the United States.

481

Skillbuilder

Resolve Conflicts

In Lesson 1, you read about how the United States works with Canada and Mexico to resolve and avoid conflicts. A **conflict** is a disagreement. To resolve, or settle, a conflict, people sometimes need to compromise. Use the steps below to help resolve conflicts.

▶ **VOCABULARY**
conflict

Learn the Skill

Step 1: Describe the conflict.

Your class has decided to give the school a gift, but you cannot agree on what to give.

Step 2: Identify what each person or group wants and why they want it. Look for shared goals.

One group wants to donate musical instruments to the school band. A second group wants to buy art supplies and paint a mural. A third group wants to give books to the library.

Step 3: Brainstorm possible solutions. Look for more than one way to make the most people happy.

The class could split the money between buying a few musical instruments and painting a small mural. You could instead think of a fourth gift that would please everyone.

Step 4: Compromise and agree to one of the solutions. Some people may have to change what they want in order to resolve the conflict.

Practice the Skill

Read about a brief conflict between the United States and Canada. Then answer the questions about how it was resolved.

The governments of Canada and the United States wanted a way for large ships to travel more easily from the Atlantic Ocean to the Great Lakes. In the early 1950s, Canada began building dams and canals on the St. Lawrence River. However, it became too expensive for Canada to complete the work alone. The United States agreed to help but wanted to control the project. Canada did not want the United States to have complete control.

The two governments compromised. Each country agreed to build different parts of the waterway. Each government would then take part of the profits from the project. In June, 1959, Queen Elizabeth of Great Britain and President Eisenhower opened the St. Lawrence Seaway.

1 What was the conflict between Canada and the United States?

2 How were the goals of the two countries similar?

3 In what way was the solution a compromise?

Apply the Skill

Use your library or the Internet to research a conflict between two groups in the United States today. Identify the conflict and the goals of each side. Then suggest and evaluate possible resolutions of the conflict.

United States Today

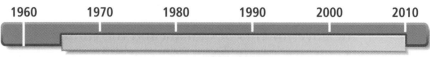

1960   1970   1980   1990   2000   2010

1965–2010

Build on What You Know You know that each of your classmates has special ideas, talents, likes, and dislikes. Each person contributes to your class. The same is true for the United States. There are almost 300 million people living in the United States, and each person contributes to the country in some way.

A Nation of Immigrants

Main Idea Immigrants come to the United States from all over the world.

Throughout its history, the United States has attracted many millions of immigrants. Some people come to the United States to escape poverty and to make a better life. Others come as refugees looking for political or religious freedom. A **refugee** is a person who escapes war or other danger and seeks safety in another country.

A Diverse Nation In the United States, about one out of ten people are immigrants. Many more are children or grandchildren of immigrants.

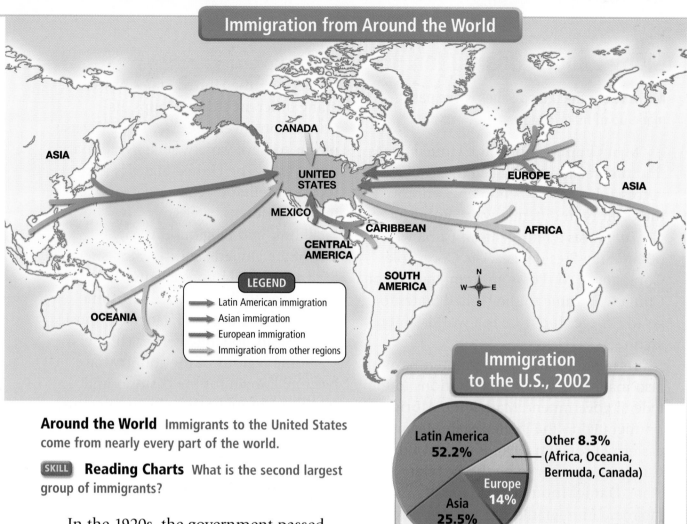

Immigration from Around the World

CANADA

ASIA

UNITED STATES

MEXICO

CARIBBEAN

CENTRAL AMERICA

SOUTH AMERICA

EUROPE

ASIA

AFRICA

OCEANIA

LEGEND
→ Latin American immigration
→ Asian immigration
→ European immigration
→ Immigration from other regions

N W E S

Immigration to the U.S., 2002

Latin America 52.2%

Other 8.3% (Africa, Oceania, Bermuda, Canada)

Europe 14%

Asia 25.5%

Around the World Immigrants to the United States come from nearly every part of the world.

SKILL **Reading Charts** What is the second largest group of immigrants?

In the 1920s, the government passed laws that limited immigration to the United States. From the 1920s to the 1960s, most immigrants came from only Europe or Mexico. In 1965, Congress passed a new law, allowing more immigrants from Latin America, Asia, the West Indies, and Africa to come to the United States.

Spanish-speaking immigrants come from Central and South America and from the Caribbean region. In the 1960s, when Cuba became a communist country, Cuban refugees came to the United States. During the 1980s, refugees fled wars in El Salvador and Nicaragua and settled in this country.

Today, almost one-third of immigrants to the United States are Asian. They come from countries such as India, China, and the Philippines.

Where Immigrants Settle

Immigrants often settle in communities where other people from their home countries live. Most of these communities are in cities. Los Angeles, New York, Chicago, and other cities attract large groups of immigrants.

Many immigrants from Latin America settle in California, Texas, and Florida. Like all immigrants, Latin Americans influence the government and culture in the places where they settle. For example, many Cuban immigrants have settled in Miami. Cuban Americans affect the politics, economy, and culture of Miami and Florida.

REVIEW Why did immigration to the United States change after 1965?

Many People, One Nation

Main Idea The United States is one nation made up of many peoples.

Many immigrants to the United States find the freedom they need to start successful careers. Their talents improve the country in different ways. **Roberto Goizueta** was a refugee from Cuba who became the President of The Coca-Cola Company. **I. M. Pei** is an immigrant from China who came to the United States to go to college. Today he is a world-famous architect.

Immigrants and their children have also made important contributions to the federal government. **Madeleine Albright** immigrated to the United States from eastern Europe. In 1996, President Bill Clinton chose her to be the Secretary of State. **Daniel Inouye** is the son of Japanese immigrants and a senator from Hawaii. He is the third longest-serving member of the Senate.

Ethnic Diversity

Because the United States has so many different ethnic groups, its population is very diverse. To be diverse means to have variety, such as cultural differences. The United States is also the most religiously diverse country in the world.

Ethnic and religious diversity is one of the United States' greatest strengths. Each individual brings talents, skills, and knowledge to the nation. Each ethnic group adds its art, food, language, music, and customs to United States culture.

Some regions of the country have become known for the customs and traditions brought there by immigrants. For example, bluegrass music in the Appalachian Mountain region was influenced by the music of Scots-Irish immigrants. Today, bluegrass is heard and enjoyed all over the United States and is now a part of our national culture.

Roberto Goizueta He led an international company with branches in more than 200 countries.

Madeleine Albright She was the first woman to hold the job of Secretary of State.

I. M. Pei He designed part of the National Gallery in Washington, D. C.

Our Common Heritage

Although the United States has a lot of diversity, all of its people share a democratic heritage. A **heritage** is something that is passed down from one generation to the next. The Constitution and Bill of Rights are part of that heritage. This shared heritage helps unite our large population.

One motto of the United States is:

❝E pluribus unum.❞

A **motto** is a short statement that explains an ideal or a goal. This phrase means "out of many, one."

"E pluribus unum" is written on coins and government buildings across the United States. The motto is a reminder that the original thirteen colonies formed one country. Today, fifty states form one democratic nation, with a culture that is as rich and diverse as the people who live in it.

REVIEW What do all U.S. citizens share?

Motto on Money
American coins are a daily reminder of the motto "E pluribus unum."

Lesson Summary

After immigration laws changed in 1965, more immigrants started coming to the United States from Latin America, Asia, and Africa. Many of them come to escape poverty or war and to make a better life. They add to the country's society, politics, and economy. In addition to diverse cultures, people in the United States share a common democratic heritage.

Why It Matters ...

Because of the country's diversity, people in the United States have the opportunity to learn about different cultures.

Lesson Review

1965
Immigration laws change

1960   1970   1980   1990   2000   2010

1 VOCABULARY Write a paragraph about immigration to the United States, using **refugee** and **heritage.**

2 READING SKILL In what way did the change in immigration laws in 1965 affect immigration from Asian countries?

3 MAIN IDEA: Geography Look at the chart on page 485. From which area do most immigrants to the United States come?

4 MAIN IDEA: Citizenship What does "E pluribus unum" mean and what meaning does it have for the United States today?

5 PEOPLE TO KNOW Who is **Daniel Inouye** and what has he done in public life?

6 CRITICAL THINKING: Synthesize What are some contributions immigrants make to United States society?

7 CRITICAL THINKING: Decision Making What were the effects of the government's decision in 1965 to change immigration laws?

HANDS ON

ART ACTIVITY Identify several ethnic groups in the United States. Make a construction paper quilt with one square for each group. Draw a picture on each square that shows something of that group's culture.

In America

★ ★ ★

What is the experience of immigrants or their children in the United States? These poems show the points of view of people from many cultures.

What is a Green Card? To begin with, it is not green. It is the size of a driver's license and gives a person permission from the government to live and work permanently in the United States.

Speak Up

by Janet S. Wong

You're Korean, aren't you?

Yes.

Why don't you speak Korean?

Just don't, I guess.

Say something Korean.

I don't speak it.
I can't.

C'mon. Say something.

Halmoni. Grandmother.
Haraboji. Grandfather.
Imo. Aunt.

Say some other stuff.
Sounds funny.
Sounds strange.

Hey, let's listen to you for a change.

Listen to me?

Say some foreign words.

But I'm American, can't you see?

Your family came from somewhere else.
Sometime.

But I was born here.

So was I.

Green Card Fever

by Bobbi Katz

NEW AMERICANS
Coast to Coast, 1995

We come from
    Haiti,
        Nevis,
            Pakistan,
      India,
            Afghanistan—
            Romania,
        El Salvador,
      China,
    Cuba,
Ecuador—
    Ghana,
      Mali,
          Katmandu—
        the Phillippines,
            St. Kitts,
               Peru—
                 Thailand,
              Israel,
                   Palestine,
              Turkey,
           Greece,
            the Levantine—
        Guatemala,
      Mexico …

We ALL know where we want to go!
Working, striving, trying hard—
where life depends on a
GREEN CARD!

Activities

1. **TALK ABOUT IT** Read aloud the words of each character in "Speak Up." Then discuss what it feels like to be that character.

2. **WRITE YOUR OWN** Write a poem that is a conversation between a recent immigrant and someone whose grandparents were immigrants.

Citizenship and Democracy

VOCABULARY

naturalization
register
responsibility
volunteer

Vocabulary Strategy

responsibility

Responsibility, meaning duty, is related to "respond." Citizens in a democracy must respond to their duties.

READING SKILL

Classify As you read, put information under these two category headings: Rights and Responsibilities.

Build on What You Know You know that a car needs an engine to run. Democracy is the engine that keeps the United States running. The actions and choices of people in the United States give the nation and the government the power to move forward.

Citizenship

Main Idea Living in a democracy brings rights and duties.

Being a citizen of a democracy like the United States is special. In most countries throughout history, ordinary people have had no role in their government. This is true for some countries even today. In a democracy, all people have a role. The choices they make help shape the government and culture.

One thing that is special about democracy is that its citizens have many rights. Rights are freedoms protected by law. The United States government is supposed to guarantee and protect these rights.

People who come to the United States from other countries can become citizens and vote. They go through a legal process called naturalization. **Naturalization** is the process of becoming a citizen by learning the laws of the country and the rights and duties of citizens.

A Guide to Naturalization

Studying Citizenship Immigrants going through naturalization study the laws and history of the United States using a book like this one.

 STANDARDS

SS5CG1a Responsibilities of citizens
SS5CG1b Freedoms granted by Bill of Rights
SS5CG3b Voting rights amendments

Voting and Other Rights

Voting is one of the most important rights American citizens have. By voting, citizens help choose leaders and give direction to the government. At age 18, citizens can register to vote. To **register** means to sign up. Citizens also have the right to run for political office.

The Bill of Rights is made up of the first ten amendments to the Constitution. These amendments include the right to speak freely, the right to practice any religion, and the right to a fair trial in court.

Voting Rights Amendments

Other amendments that protect the voting rights of citizens have been added to the Constitution. The Fifteenth Amendment gave voting rights to African American men. The Nineteenth Amendment guaranteed women the right to vote. The Twenty-third Amendment gave people who live in Washington, D.C., the vote in Presidential elections. The Twenty-fourth Amendment banned poll taxes, which people had to pay in order to vote. The Twenty-sixth Amendment said that everyone 18 years of age or older could vote.

REVIEW At what age can citizens register to vote?

Rights of Citizens

Vote
Join groups of your choice
Express opinions freely
Practice religion of choice
Have a fair trial
Own property and businesses
Not be discriminated against in jobs and housing

Naturalization Ceremony These immigrants are about to become United States citizens. When they do, they will enjoy all the rights listed in the chart to the left.

Personal	Civic
These actions improve your life and the lives of others.	These actions help make a democratic system work.
Educate yourself	Vote
Respect others	Obey laws
Help in your community	Pay taxes
Set a good example	Serve on juries

Two Kinds of Duties
It should be up to citizens to improve their own lives and the lives of others. They must also work to preserve the government.

SKILL Reading Charts
What kind of responsibility is paying taxes?

Citizens' Responsibilities

Main Idea Citizens in a democracy have important responsibilities.

In the United States, citizens have a lot of freedom. That does not mean people can do anything they want. Along with rights, citizens also have a responsibility to the country. A **responsibility** is a duty that someone is expected to fulfill.

In a democracy, it is up to the people to create an orderly and caring society. Representatives of the people write the nation's laws. Everyone must then obey the laws. When people obey laws, they help build a safe community. When they disobey laws, they often hurt others and make the community a dangerous place. Obeying the law is an important duty that puts the common good of the country first.

Paying taxes is another important responsibility. Taxes help our government pay for public goods and services. These goods and services include public parks, police, firefighters, roads, and many others. Citizens also have responsibilities to serve on juries in law courts and to vote. Men over the age of 18 have the responsibility of registering for the military.

Responsibilities of Young People

Young people have responsibilities as citizens, too. They are expected to go to school. The knowledge that students gain in school helps prepare them to make thoughtful decisions about public issues and to be good citizens.

Every day, government officials make decisions about issues such as safety, pollution, and schools. Citizens cannot expect their government to do everything, however. Ordinary people can also do their part by becoming volunteers. A **volunteer** helps other people without being paid. Volunteers help make their communities better places to live.

Young people can volunteer in hundreds of ways. For example, a third-grade class in Maryland collects gifts for children who need to stay at the local hospital. Leslie Lenkowsky, who is the leader of the Corporation for National and Community Service, said:

66 **Organizations of every type in every community depend on the time and talent of volunteers.** 99

Preserving Democracy

The future of the United States depends on the strength of its democracy. In a democracy, all citizens have a responsibility to be involved in the life of their communities and country. Some citizens do this by becoming active in politics. Other citizens vote, stay informed about issues, or run for political office.

Speaking Out Even before young people can vote, they can express their opinions to political leaders.

Being informed helps young people make good choices when, as adults, it comes time to vote. In big and small ways, each person can contribute to democracy and make the United States a better country.

REVIEW In what ways can learning about issues prepare young people to be good citizens?

Lesson Summary

- Being a citizen of a democracy means having rights and responsibilities.
- The Bill of Rights lists many of the rights United States citizens have.
- Citizens also have responsibilities to help create an orderly, caring society.
- Even though they cannot vote, young people have responsibilities to their communities and country.

Why It Matters ...

Good citizenship is necessary for a strong country and for safe communities.

Lesson Review

1 **VOCABULARY** Use **naturalization** and **register** in a paragraph. Explain why these terms are important for citizenship.

2 **READING SKILL** Use your notes to explain how citizens' responsibilities help preserve democracy.

3 **MAIN IDEA: Government** In what way are taxes used to help maintain a democracy?

4 **MAIN IDEA: Citizenship** Why is obeying the law important for the common good?

5 **FACTS TO REMEMBER** What part of the Constitution lists many of the rights of United States citizens?

6 **CRITICAL THINKING: Fact and opinion** Is it fact or opinion that government protects the rights of citizens? Give reasons for your answer.

7 **CRITICAL THINKING: Draw Conclusions** Why is it important for citizens to vote?

CITIZENSHIP ACTIVITY Write a personal essay explaining why it is necessary for citizens to be involved in their communities.

Citizen Sara

What rights and responsibilities go along with being a citizen? Sara has just turned 18; now she can register to vote. Her brother Will goes to Town Hall with her, and they see examples of democracy in action.

TV Reporter

Characters

Sara: age 18

Will: her brother, age 10

Supporter #1

Supporter #2

Supporter #3

TV Reporter

Senior Citizen

Frankie: Will's friend, age 11

Lisa: Will's friend, age 10

Mr. Addison: the principal of Will's school

Town Clerk

Petitioner

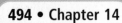

Senior
Citizen

Sara: I am so excited, Will.

Will: You already told me.

Sara: I know, but I have to say it again. I'm on my way to register to vote for the first time! I can't believe it!

Will: I can't believe I agreed to come along just to take your picture.

Sara: It's history! A photo for my scrapbook.

Will: Hey, what's happening over there?

Supporters: (*chanting*) More money for schools! More money for schools!

Sara: Oh, this must be about Question 3 that the town will be voting on.

Supporter #1: Say "yes" to raising more money for our schools!

Supporter #2: Say "yes" to keeping programs such as Art and Spanish!

Supporter #3: Say "yes" to a better education for our kids!

Will: Look, a TV reporter is interviewing someone. (*He takes a picture.*)

TV Reporter: What is your opinion about Question 3?

Senior Citizen: I don't like to lose those programs. But if the vote is yes, the town is going to raise our taxes again! Some of us can't afford to pay more taxes.

Will: We'd better go, Sara. The clerk's office closes in a half hour.

Sara: That's why being a citizen is great. Each of us gets to express our opinion. I guess I'd better find out more about Question 3. I want to make a good decision when I vote on it next month.

Will: Let's cut through Ames Park. It's faster.

Sara: Okay. Hey, look at all those people in the park. What's going on?

Frankie: Yo, Will! Did you forget?

Lisa: Today is "Keep Ames Park Beautiful Day!"

Mr. Addison: That's right. It's our big **volunteer** cleanup effort.

Sara: Wow! It looks like a lot of townspeople turned out today.

Mr. Addison: The more the merrier, Sara! Are you two going to join us?

Will: Uh…sure! Look, I even brought my camera!

Mr. Addison

Sara

Will

Sara: But first he has to take my picture. I'm on my way to register to vote.

Mr. Addison: Good for you, Sara! We'll see both of you later.

Will: There's no escaping now.

Sara: Oh, come on. It feels good when you give your time to make your community better.

Will: I know. I'm just kidding. Look, here we are at Town Hall.

Frankie

Sara: The town clerk's office is through this door.

Town Clerk: Hello, can I help you?

Sara: Yes, please! I'm here to register to vote.

Town Clerk: May I see your identification? Fill out this form and sign at the bottom.

Will: (*Taking their picture*) Say cheese!

Town Clerk: You're all set, Sara. Now remember—and I tell this to everyone— a vote is a citizen's most powerful tool. Use it well.

Sara: I will, starting next month!

Will: Congratulations, sis. I have to say, I'm a little envious. (*They walk outside.*)

Petitioner: Excuse me, would you mind signing our petition? We want to convince the town government to put a stoplight at Elm and South Streets.

Will: I'll sign that petition!

Sara: That's the spirit, Citizen Will.

Will: Thanks, Citizen Sara. Now let's go clean up the park.

Activities

1. **TALK ABOUT IT** How do Sara and Will show their sense of **responsibility**?

2. **WRITE ABOUT IT** As a citizen, what issues do you care about? Choose a national or local issue and write a letter to a government official about it.

Visual Summary

1.–3. ✏️ Write a description for the three topics named below.

Life in the United States	
NAFTA — **Trade with Canada and Mexico**	
Diverse Population	
Rights and Responsibilities	

Facts and Main Ideas

✓ **TEST PREP** Answer each question with information from the chapter.

4. **History** What effect did the 1965 immigration laws have on immigration to the United States?

5. **Citizenship** What are two rights and two responsibilities that citizens of the United States have?

6. **History** Which European nation controlled Mexico until 1821?

7. **Citizenship** Why is the diversity of the United States one of its strengths?

8. **Economics** Which nations signed NAFTA?

Vocabulary

✓ **TEST PREP** Choose the correct word from the list below to complete each sentence.

province, p. 474
refugee, p. 484
register, p. 491

9. A person who escapes war and seeks safety in another country is a _____.

10. When U.S. citizens turn 18, they can _____ to vote.

11. Quebec is a _____ of Canada where French influence is still strong.

CHAPTER SUMMARY TIMELINE

1821 Mexico's independence	1867 Canada's independence			1992 NAFTA
1800	1850	1900	1950	2000

Apply Skills

 TEST PREP Citizenship Skill Read the paragraph below and use what you have learned about resolving conflicts to answer each question.

> Rivers are part of the border between the United States and Mexico. Floods and pollution affect cities in both countries. The International Boundary and Water Commission works in both countries to prevent floods and to build sewage treatment plants. By cooperating, the countries make sure they both have clean water.

12. What issue might cause conflict between the United States and Mexico?

    A. Floods and pollution affect the United States.

    B. Floods and pollution affect both countries.

    C. Floods and pollution affect neither country.

    D. Sewage treatment plants are too expensive to run.

13. Why is an international organization a good way to resolve a conflict?

    A. It does what is best for the United States.

    B. It does what is best for Mexico.

    C. It does what is best for both countries.

    D. It does what is best for the world.

Critical Thinking

TEST PREP Write a short paragraph to answer each question.

14. **Compare and Contrast** How are the United States and Canada alike and different?

15. **Synthesize** What role does government play in guarding the rights of citizens?

Timeline

Use the Chapter Summary Timeline above to answer the question.

16. Which country gained independence first, Canada or Mexico?

Activities

 Connect to Georgia Research immigration to Georgia over the last fifty years. Write a poem to describe Georgia's rich cultural heritage.

Writing Activity Write a personal narrative about a time when you met your responsibilities as a citizen. You may wish to describe your work as a volunteer.

 Technology
Writing Process Tips
Get help with your essay at www.eduplace.com/kids/hmss/

499

Review and Test Prep

Vocabulary and Main Ideas

✔ **TEST PREP** Write a sentence to answer each question.

1. Why did **migrant workers** and other groups fight for their rights in the 1970s?

2. What effect did **free-trade agreements** have on the U.S. economy in the 1990s?

3. Why did the **popular vote** and the **Electoral College** vote create a conflict in the 2000 presidential election?

4. What is the **heritage** that all U.S. citizens share, and why is it important?

5. Why is it important for people to **register** to vote?

6. What rights and **responsibilities** do U.S. citizens have?

Critical Thinking

✔ **TEST PREP** Write a short paragraph to answer each question.

7. **Evaluate** Why was the end of the Cold War an important event in American history?

8. **Cause and Effect** What has been the effect of immigration on the culture of the United States? Use details from the unit to support your answer.

Apply Skills

✔ **TEST PREP** Map Skill Use the map of North and South America to answer each question about map scales.

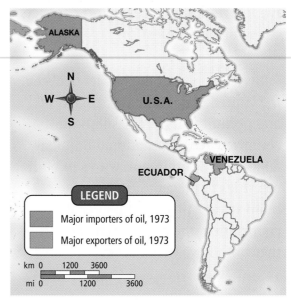

9. What can you learn from this map that you can't learn from the map of Canada on page 683?

   A. the distance from Quebec to Toronto
   B. the names of the provinces of Canada
   C. the distance from Venezuela to Alaska
   D. the oil producing provinces in Canada

10. What can you learn from the map on page 683 that you can't learn from this map?

   A. the name of the largest country in South America
   B. the names of the Great Lakes
   C. the distance from Ottawa to Mexico City
   D. the major oil producing countries in North America

Connect to Georgia

Unit Activity

GEORGIA

Write a Citizen's Letter

- Think about something that you would like to improve in your community or in Georgia.

- Write a letter to the editor of a newspaper, or to an elected leader.

- Describe your improvement and why you would like to see this change.

- Send your letter.

Mayor Kay Brown
Town Hall

Dear Mayor Brown,
  I would like to complain about the litter on Main Street. There is only one trash barrel on the corner of Main Street and Elm.

Personal Finance

GEORGIA

In this unit, you read that the federal government has a deficit when it spends more money than it takes in. (p. 449) The government borrows money and pays interest on the deficit.

Individuals who borrow money also have to pay interest. Suppose an adult borrowed $300 from a bank for ten years. If the bank charged $15 interest each year, what would be the total amount of interest? How much money would the person owe at the end of ten years?

CURRENT EVENTS
WEEKLY (WR) READER

Connect to Your Community

Design a volunteer project that your class can do together.

- Find information about volunteer projects that students are doing around the country.

- Find out about issues in your school or community. Who or what needs your help?

- Design a volunteer project to deal with the issue or help solve the problem. Present it to your class.

Technology

Weekly Reader online offers social studies articles. Go to: **www.eduplace.com/kids/hmss/**

Read About It

Look for these Social Studies Independent Books in your classroom.

Clean and Clear

CITIZENS OF THE WORLD

What Is the Media?

ESA DOMNAUER

by Julia Mercado

by Julia Jones

References

Citizenship Handbook

Resources

Pledge of Allegiance

*I pledge allegiance to the flag
of the United States of America
and to the Republic for which it stands,
one Nation under God, indivisible,
with liberty and justice for all.*

Spanish

Prometo lealtad a la bandera de los Estados Unidos de América, y a la república que representa, una nación bajo Diós, indivisible, con libertad y justicia para todos.

Russian

Я даю клятву верности флагу Соединённых Штатов Америки и стране, символом которой он является, народу, единому перед Богом, свободному и равноправному.

Tagalog

Ako ay nanunumpa ng katapatan sa bandila ng Estados Unidos ng Amerika, at sa Republikang kanyang kinakatawan, isang Bansang pumapailalim sa isang Maykapal hindi nahahati, may kalayaan at katarungan para sa lahat.

Arabic

ادين بالولاء لعلم الولايات المتحده الامريكيه والى الجمهوريه التي تمثلها دولة واحدة تؤمن باللة متحدة تمنح الحرية والعدالة للجميع

Chinese

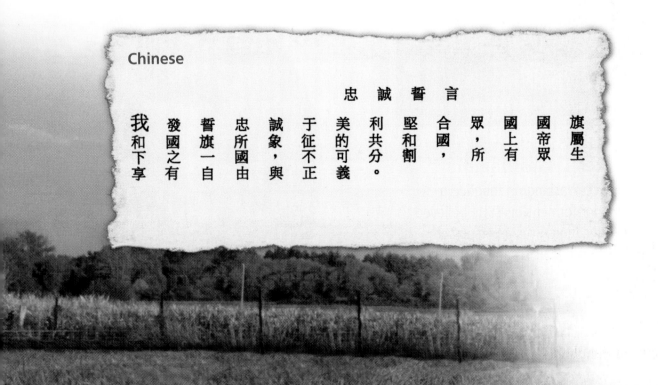

誓言 忠誠
我和下享
發國之有
誓旗一自
忠所國由
誠象，與
于征不正
美的可義
利共分。
堅和割
國上有
眾，所
國帝眾
旗屬生

Character Traits

Character includes feelings, thoughts, and behaviors. A character trait is something people show by the way they act. To act bravely shows courage, and courage is one of several character traits.

Positive character traits, such as honesty, caring, and courage, lead to positive actions. Character traits are also called "life skills." Life skills can help you do your best, and doing your best leads to reaching your goals.

Clara Barton
Courage Barton went into battle to help Union soldiers in the Civil War. She risked her own life to help those who had been wounded.

Booker T. Washington
Respect Washington founded a school for former slaves. He believed that education gives a person self-respect and gains respect from others.

Courage means acting bravely. Doing what you believe to be good and right, and telling the truth, requires courage.

Patriotism means working for the goals of your country. When you show national pride, you are being patriotic.

Responsibility is taking care of work that needs to be done. Responsible people are reliable and trustworthy, which means they can be counted on.

Respect means paying attention to what other people want and believe. The "golden rule," or treating others as you would like to be treated, shows thoughtfulness and respect.

Fairness means working to make things fair, or right, for everyone. Often one needs to try again and again to achieve fairness. This requires diligence, or not giving up.

Civic virtue is good citizenship. It means doing things, such as cooperating and solving problems, to help communities live and work well together.

Caring means noticing what others need and helping them get what they need. Feeling concern or compassion is another way to define caring.

Historical Documents

Pilgrims are shown writing the Mayflower Compact while still aboard the ship.

The Mayflower Compact (1620)

". . . We whose names are underwritten, . . . Having undertaken, for the Glory of God, and Advancement of the Christian Faith, and Honor of our King and Country, a Voyage to plant the first Colony in the northern Parts of Virginia; Do by these Presents, solemnly and mutually, in the Presence of God and one of another, covenant and combine ourselves together into a civil Body Politick, for our better Ordering and Preservation, and Furtherance of the Ends aforesaid: And by Virtue hereof do enact, constitute, and frame such just and equal Laws, Ordinances, Acts, Constitutions, and Officers, from time to time, as shall be thought most meet and convenient for the general Good of the Colony; unto which we promise all due Submission and Obedience. . . ."

Mr. John Carver	Mr. Samuel Fuller	Edward Tilly
Mr. William Bradford	Mr. Christopher Martin	John Tilly
Mr. Edward Winslow	Mr. William Mullins	Francis Cooke
Mr. William Brewster	Mr. William White	Thomas Rogers
Isaac Allerton	Mr. Richard Warren	Thomas Tinker
Myles Standish	John Howland	John Ridgdale
John Alden	Mr. Steven Hopkins	Edward Fuller
John Turner	Digery Priest	Richard Clark
Francis Eaton	Thomas Williams	Richard Gardiner
James Chilton	Gilbert Winslow	Mr. John Allerton
John Craxton	Edmund Margesson	Thomas English
John Billington	Peter Brown	Edward Doten
Joses Fletcher	Richard Britteridge	Edward Liester
John Goodman	George Soule	

Pitt's Speech to Parliament on the Stamp Act (1766)

"The Americans have not acted in all things with prudence and temper. They have been wronged. They have been driven to madness by injustice. Will you punish them for the madness you have occasioned? Rather let prudence and temper come first from this side. I will undertake for America, that she will follow the example. . . .

Upon the whole, I will beg leave to tell the House what is really my opinion. It is, that the Stamp-Act be repealed absolutely, totally, and immediately; that the reason for the repeal should be assigned, because it was founded on an erroneous principle."

William Pitt

Burke's Speech to Parliament on Conciliation with America (1775)

"The proposition is peace. Not peace through the medium of war; not peace to be hunted through the labyrinth of intricate and endless negotiations . . . It is simple peace, sought in its natural course and in its ordinary haunts. . . .

Let the colonies always keep the idea of their civil rights associated with your government — they will cling and grapple to you, and no force under heaven will be of power to tear them from their allegiance. But let it be once understood that your government may be one thing and their privileges another, that these two things may exist without any mutual relation — the cement is gone, the cohesion is loosened, and everything hastens to decay and dissolution. . . .

Magnanimity in politics is not seldom the truest wisdom; and a great empire and little minds go ill together."

Edmund Burke

In the Declaration of Independence, the colonists explained why they were breaking away from Britain. They believed they had the right to form their own country.

Members of the Continental Congress are shown signing the Declaration of Independence.

The opening part of the Declaration is very famous. It says that all people are created equal. Everyone has certain basic rights that are "unalienable." That means that these rights cannot be taken away. Governments are formed to protect these basic rights. If a government does not do this, then the people have a right to begin a new one.

Forming a new government meant ending the colonial ties to the king. The writers of the Declaration listed the wrongs of King George III to prove the need for their actions.

Colonists said the king had not let the colonies make their own laws. He had limited the people's representation in their assemblies.

The Declaration of Independence

In Congress, July 4, 1776

The unanimous declaration of the thirteen United States of America

Introduction*

When, in the course of human events, it becomes necessary for one people to dissolve the political bonds which have connected them with another, and to assume, among the powers of the earth, the separate and equal station to which the laws of nature and of nature's God entitle them, a decent respect to the opinions of mankind requires that they should declare the causes which impel them to the separation.

Basic Rights

WE hold these truths to be self-evident: That all men are created equal, that they are endowed by their Creator with certain unalienable rights; that among these are life, liberty, and the pursuit of happiness; that, to secure these rights, governments are instituted among men, deriving their just powers from the consent of the governed; that whenever any form of government becomes destructive of these ends, it is the right of the people to alter or to abolish it, and to institute new government, laying its foundation on such principles, and organizing its powers in such form, as to them shall seem most likely to effect their safety and happiness. Prudence, indeed, will dictate that governments long established should not be changed for light and transient causes; and accordingly all experience hath shown that mankind are more disposed to suffer, while evils are sufferable, than to right themselves by abolishing the forms to which they are accustomed. But when a long train of abuses and usurpations, pursuing invariably the same object, evinces a design to reduce them under absolute despotism, it is their right, it is their duty, to throw off such government, and to provide new guards for their future security. Such has been the patient sufferance of these colonies; and such is now the necessity which constrains them to alter their former systems of government. The history of the present King of Great Britain is a history of repeated injuries and usurpations, all having in direct object the establishment of an absolute tyranny over these states. To prove this, let facts be submitted to a candid world.

Charges Against the King

HE has refused his assent to laws, the most wholesome and necessary for the public good.

HE has forbidden his governors to pass laws of immediate and pressing importance, unless suspended in their operation till his assent should be obtained; and, when so suspended, he has utterly neglected to attend to them.

HE has refused to pass other laws for the accommodation of large districts of people, unless those people would relinquish the right of representation in the legislature, a right inestimable to them, and formidable to tyrants only.

HE has called together legislative bodies at places unusual, uncomfortable, and distant from the depository of their public records, for the sole purpose of fatiguing them into compliance with his measures.

HE has dissolved representative houses repeatedly, for opposing, with manly firmness his invasions on the rights of the people.

*Titles have been added to the Declaration to make it easier to read. These titles are not in the original document.

HE has refused for a long time, after such dissolutions, to cause others to be elected; whereby the legislative powers, incapable of annihilation, have returned to the people at large for their exercise; the state remaining in the mean time, exposed to all the dangers of invasions from without and convulsions within.

HE has endeavored to prevent the population of these states; for that purpose obstructing the laws for the naturalization of foreigners; refusing to pass others to encourage their migration hither, and raising the conditions of new appropriations of lands.

HE has obstructed the administration of justice, by refusing his assent to laws for establishing judiciary powers.

HE has made judges dependent on his will alone, for the tenure of their offices, and the amount of payment of their salaries.

HE has erected a multitude of new offices, and sent hither swarms of officers to harass our people and eat out their substance.

HE has kept among us, in times of peace, standing armies, without the consent of our legislatures.

HEhas affected to render the military independent of, and superior to, the civil power.

HE has combined with others to subject us to a Jurisdiction foreign to our constitution and unacknowledged by our laws, giving his assent to their acts of pretended legislation:

FOR quartering large bodies of armed troops among us;

FOR protecting them, by a mock trial, from punishment for any murders which they should commit on the inhabitants of these states;

FOR cutting off our trade with all parts of the world;

FOR imposing taxes on us without our consent;

FOR depriving us, in many cases, of the benefits of trial by jury;

FOR transporting us beyond seas, to be tried for pretended offenses;

FOR abolishing the free system of English laws in a neighboring province, establishing therein an arbitrary government, and enlarging its boundaries, so as to render it at once an example and fit instrument for introducing the same absolute rule into these colonies;

FOR taking away our charters, abolishing our most valuable laws, and altering fundamentally the forms of our governments;

FOR suspending our own legislatures, and declaring themselves invested with power to legislate for us in all cases whatsoever.

HE has abdicated Government here, by declaring us out of his protection and waging war against us.

HE has plundered our seas, ravaged our coasts, burned our towns, and destroyed the lives of our people.

HE is at this time transporting large armies of foreign mercenaries to complete the works of death, desolation, and tyranny, already begun with circumstances of cruelty and perfidy scarcely paralleled in the most barbarous ages, and totally unworthy the head of a civilized nation.

HE has constrained our fellow-citizens, taken captive on the high seas, to bear arms against their country, to become the executioners of their friends and brethren, or to fall themselves by their hands.

The king had made colonial assemblies meet at unusual times and places. This made going to assembly meetings hard for colonial representatives.

In some cases the king stopped the assembly from meeting at all.

The king tried to stop people from moving to the colonies and into new western lands.

The king prevented the colonies from choosing their own judges. Instead, he sent over judges who depended on him for their jobs and pay.

The king kept British soldiers in the colonies, even though the colonists had not asked for them.

King George III

The king and Parliament had taxed the colonists without their consent. This was one of the most important reasons the colonists were angry at Britain.

The colonists felt that the king had waged war on them.

The king had hired German soldiers and sent them to the colonies to keep order.

British soldiers became a symbol of British misrule to many colonists.

The colonists said that they had asked the king to change his policies, but he had not listened to them.

The writers declared that the colonies were free and independent states, equal to the world's other states. They had the powers to make war and peace and to trade with other countries.

The signers pledged their lives to the support of this Declaration. The Continental Congress ordered copies of the Declaration of Independence to be sent to all the states and to the army.

Congress ordered copies of the Declaration of Independence to be sent to all the states and to the army.

HE has excited domestic insurrections amongst us, and has endeavored to bring on the inhabitants of our frontiers, the merciless Indian savages, whose known rule of warfare is an undistinguished destruction of all ages, sexes, and conditions.

Response to the King

IN every stage of these oppressions we have petitioned for redress in the most humble terms; Our repeated petitions have been answered only by repeated injury. A prince, whose character is thus marked by every act which may define a tyrant, is unfit to be the ruler of a free people.

NOR have we been wanting in our attentions to our British brethren. We have warned them from time to time, of attempts by their legislature to extend an unwarrantable jurisdiction over us. We have reminded them of the circumstances of our emigration and settlement here. We have appealed to their native justice and magnanimity; and we have conjured them, by the ties of our common kindred, to disavow these usurpations, which, would inevitably interrupt our connections and correspondence. They, too, have been deaf to the voice of justice and of consanguinity. We must, therefore, acquiesce in the necessity which denounces our separation, and hold them, as we hold the rest of mankind, enemies in war, in peace, friends.

Independence

WE, therefore, the representatives of the United States of America, in General Congress Assembled, appealing to the Supreme Judge of the world for the rectitude of our intentions, do, in the name and by authority of the good people of these colonies, solemnly publish and declare, that these United Colonies are, and of right ought to be, FREE AND INDEPENDENT STATES; that they are absolved from all allegiance to the British crown, and that all political connection between them and the state of Great Britain is, and ought to be, totally dissolved; and that, as free and independent states, they have full power to levy war, conclude peace, contract alliances, establish commerce, and do all other acts and things which independent states may of right do. And for the support of this declaration, with a firm reliance on the protection of Divine Providence, we mutually pledge to each other our lives, our fortunes, and our sacred honor.

NEW HAMPSHIRE
Josiah Bartlett
William Whipple
Matthew Thornton

MASSACHUSETTS
John Hancock
John Adams
Samuel Adams
Robert Treat Paine
Elbridge Gerry

NEW YORK
William Floyd
Philip Livingston
Francis Lewis
Lewis Morris

RHODE ISLAND
Stephen Hopkins
William Ellery

NEW JERSEY
Richard Stockton
John Witherspoon
Francis Hopkinson
John Hart
Abraham Clark

PENNSYLVANIA
Robert Morris
Benjamin Rush
Benjamin Franklin
John Morton
George Clymer
James Smith
George Taylor
James Wilson
George Ross

DELAWARE
Caesar Rodney
George Read
Thomas McKean

MARYLAND
Samuel Chase
William Paca
Thomas Stone
Charles Carroll
 of Carrollton

NORTH CAROLINA
Willam Hooper
Joseph Hewes
John Penn

VIRGINIA
George Wythe
Richard Henry Lee
Thomas Jefferson
Benjamin Harrison
Thomas Nelson, Jr.
Francis Lightfoot Lee
Carter Braxton

SOUTH CAROLINA
Edward Rutledge
Thomas Heyward, Jr.
Thomas Lynch, Jr.
Arthur Middleton

CONNECTICUT
Roger Sherman
Samuel Huntington
William Williams
Oliver Wolcott

GEORGIA
Button Gwinnett
Lyman Hall
George Walton

The Constitution of the United States

Preamble*

We the people of the United States, in order to form a more perfect Union, establish justice, insure domestic tranquility, provide for the common defense, promote the general welfare, and secure the blessings of liberty to ourselves and our posterity, do ordain and establish this Constitution for the United States of America.

ARTICLE I
Legislative Branch

SECTION 1. CONGRESS

All legislative powers herein granted shall be vested in a Congress of the United States, which shall consist of a Senate and House of Representatives.

SECTION 2. HOUSE OF REPRESENTATIVES

1. **Election and Term of Members** The House of Representatives shall be composed of members chosen every second year by the people of the several States, and the electors in each State shall have the qualifications requisite for electors of the most numerous branch of the State Legislature.

2. **Qualifications** No person shall be a representative who shall not have attained to the age of twenty-five years, and been seven years a citizen of the United States, and who shall not, when elected, be an inhabitant of that State in which he shall be chosen.

3. **Number of Representatives per State** Representatives ~~and direct taxes~~** shall be apportioned among the several States which may be included within this Union, according to their respective numbers, ~~which shall be determined by adding to the whole number of free persons, including those bound to service for a term of years, and excluding Indians not taxed, three fifths of all other persons.~~ The actual enumeration shall be made within three years after the first meeting of the Congress of the United States, and within every subsequent term of ten years, in such manner as they shall by law direct. The number of representatives shall not exceed one for every thirty thousand, but each State shall have at least one representative; ~~and until such enumeration shall be made, the State of New Hampshire shall be entitled to choose three, Massachusetts eight, Rhode Island and Providence Plantations one, Connecticut five, New York six, New Jersey four, Pennsylvania eight, Delaware one, Maryland six, Virginia ten, North Carolina five, South Carolina five, and Georgia three.~~

4. **Vacancies** When vacancies happen in the representation from any State, the executive authority thereof shall issue writs of election to fill such vacancies.

5. **Special Powers** The House of Representatives shall choose their speaker and other officers; and shall have the sole power of impeachment.

*The titles of the Preamble, and of each article, section, clause, and amendment have been added to make the Constitution easier to read. These titles are not in the original document.

**Parts of the Constitution have been crossed out to show that they are not in force any more. They have been changed by amendments or they no longer apply.

Historical Documents

George Washington watches delegates sign the Constitution.

Americans often use voting machines on election day.

Number, Term, and Selection of Members In each state, citizens elect two members of the Senate. This gives all states, whether big or small, equal power in the Senate. Senators serve six-year terms. Originally, state legislatures chose the senators for their states. Today, however, people elect their senators directly. The Seventeenth Amendment made this change in 1913.

Qualifications Senators must be at least 30 years old and United States citizens for at least nine years. Like representatives, they must live in the state they represent.

President of the Senate The Vice President of the United States acts as the President, or chief officer, of the Senate. The Vice President votes only in cases of a tie.

Impeachment Trials If the House of Representatives impeaches, or charges, an official with a crime, the Senate holds a trial. If two-thirds of the senators find the official guilty, then the person is removed from office. The only Presidents ever impeached were Andrew Johnson in 1868 and Bill Clinton in 1998. Both were found not guilty.

Election of Congress Each state decides where and when to hold elections. Today congressional elections are held in even-numbered years, on the Tuesday after the first Monday in November.

Annual Sessions The Constitution requires Congress to meet at least once a year. In 1933, the 20th Amendment made January 3rd the day for beginning a regular session of Congress.

Organization A quorum is the smallest number of members that must be present for an organization to hold a meeting. For each house of Congress, this number is the majority, or more than one-half, of its members.

SECTION 3. SENATE

1. *Number, Term, and Selection of Members* The Senate of the United States shall be composed of two senators from each State, chosen by the Legislature thereof, for six years; and each Senator shall have one vote.

2. *Overlapping Terms and Filling Vacancies* Immediately after they shall be assembled in consequence of the first election, they shall be divided as equally as may be into three classes. ~~The seats of the senators of the first class shall be vacated at the expiration of the second year, of the second class at the expiration of the fourth year, and of the third class at the expiration of the sixth year,~~ so that one-third may be chosen every second year; ~~and if vacancies happen by resignation, or otherwise, during the recess of the legislature of any State, the executive thereof may make temporary appointments until the next meeting of the legislature, which shall then fill such vacancies.~~

3. *Qualifications* No person shall be a senator who shall not have attained to the age of thirty years, and been nine years a citizen of the United States, and who shall not, when elected, be an inhabitant of that State for which he shall be chosen.

4. *President of the Senate* The Vice President of the United States shall be President of the Senate, but shall have no vote, unless they be equally divided.

5. *Other Officers* The Senate shall choose their other officers, and also a President pro tempore, in the absence of the Vice President, or when he shall exercise the office of the President of the United States.

6. *Impeachment Trials* The Senate shall have the sole power to try all impeachments. When sitting for that purpose, they shall be on oath or affirmation. When the President of the United States is tried, the Chief Justice shall preside: and no person shall be convicted without the concurrence of two-thirds of the members present.

7. *Penalties* Judgment in cases of impeachment shall not extend further than to removal from office, and disqualification to hold and enjoy any office of honor, trust, or profit under the United States: but the party convicted shall nevertheless be liable and subject to indictment, trial, judgement and punishment, according to law.

SECTION 4. ELECTIONS AND MEETINGS

1. *Election of Congress* The times, places and manner of holding elections for senators and representatives, shall be prescribed in each State by the legislature thereof; but the Congress may at any time by law make or alter such regulations, except as to the places of choosing Senators.

2. *Annual Sessions* The Congress shall assemble at least once in every year, ~~and such meeting shall be on the first Monday in December,~~ unless they shall by law appoint a different day.

SECTION 5. RULES OF PROCEDURE

1. *Organization* Each house shall be the judge of the elections, returns and qualifications of its own members, and a majority of each shall constitute a quorum to do business; but a smaller number may adjourn from day to day, and may be authorized to compel the attendance of absent members, in such manner, and under such penalties as each house may provide.

2. **Rules** Each house may determine the rules of its proceedings, punish its members for disorderly behavior, and, with the concurrence of two-thirds, expel a member.

3. **Journal** Each house shall keep a journal of its proceedings, and from time to time publish the same, excepting such parts as may in their judgement require secrecy; and the yeas and nays of the members of either house on any question shall, at the desire of one-fifth of those present, be entered on the journal.

4. **Adjournment** Neither house, during the session of Congress, shall, without the consent of the other, adjourn for more than three days, nor to any other place than that in which the two houses shall be sitting.

SECTION 6. PRIVILEGES AND RESTRICTIONS

1. **Pay and Protection** The senators and representatives shall receive a compensation for their services, to be ascertained by law, and paid out of the treasury of the United States. They shall in all cases, except treason, felony and breach of the peace, be privileged from arrest during their attendance at the session of their respective houses, and in going to and returning from the same; and for any speech or debate in either house, they shall not be questioned in any other place.

2. **Restrictions** No senator or representative shall, during the time for which he was elected, be appointed to any civil office under the authority of the United States, which shall have been created, or the emoluments whereof shall have been increased during such time; and no person holding any office under the United States, shall be a member of either house during his continuance in office.

SECTION 7. MAKING LAWS

1. **Tax Bills** All bills for raising revenue shall originate in the House of Representatives; but the Senate may propose or concur with amendments as on other bills.

2. **Passing a Law** Every bill which shall have passed the House of Representatives and the Senate, shall, before it became a law, be presented to the President of the United States; if he approve, he shall sign it, but if not, he shall return it, with his objections, to that house in which it shall have originated, who shall enter the objections at large on their journal, and proceed to reconsider it. If after such reconsideration two-thirds of that house shall agree to pass the bill, it shall be sent, together with the objections, to the other house, by which it shall likewise be reconsidered, and if approved by two-thirds of that house, it shall become a law. But in all such cases the votes of both houses shall be determined by yeas and nays, and the names of the persons voting for and against the bill shall be entered on the journal of each house respectively. If any bill shall not be returned by the president within ten days (Sundays excepted) after it shall have been presented to him, the same shall be a law, in like manner as if he had signed it, unless the Congress by their adjournment prevent its return, in which case it shall not be a law.

3. **Orders and Resolutions** Every order, resolution, or vote to which the concurrence of the Senate and House of Representatives may be necessary (except on a question of adjournment) shall be presented to the President of the United States; and before the same shall take effect, shall be approved by him, or, being disapproved by him, shall be repassed by two-thirds of the Senate and House of Representatives, according to the rules and limitations prescribed in the case of a bill.

Rules Each house can make rules for its members and expel a member by a two-thirds vote.

Journal The Constitution requires each house to keep a record of its proceedings. *The Congressional Record* is published every day. It includes parts of speeches made in each house and allows any person to look up the votes of his or her representative.

Pay and Protection Congress sets the salaries of its members, and they are paid by the federal government. No member can be arrested for anything he or she says while in office. This protection allows members to speak freely in Congress.

Restrictions Members of Congress cannot hold other federal offices during their terms. This rule strengthens the separation of powers and protects the checks and balances system set up by the Constitution.

Tax Bills A bill is a proposed law. Only the House of Representatives can introduce bills that tax the people.

Passing a Law A bill must be passed by the majority of members in each house of Congress. Then it is sent to the President. If the President signs it, the bill becomes a law. If the President refuses to sign a bill, and Congress is in session, the bill becomes law ten days after the President receives it.

The President can also veto, or reject, a bill. However, if each house of Congress repasses the bill by a two-thirds vote, it becomes a law. Passing a law after the President vetoed it is called overriding a veto. This process is an important part of the checks and balances system set up by the Constitution.

Orders and Resolutions Congress can also pass resolutions that have the same power as laws. Such acts are also subject to the President's veto.

SECTION 8. POWERS DELEGATED TO CONGRESS

Taxation Only Congress has the power to collect taxes. Federal taxes must be the same in all parts of the country.

1. *Taxation* The Congress shall have the power to lay and collect taxes, duties, imposts, and excises, to pay the debts and provide for the common defense and general welfare of the United States; but all duties, imposts and excises shall be uniform throughout the United States;

2. *Borrowing* To borrow money on the credit of the United States;

Commerce Congress controls both trade with foreign countries and trade among states.

3. *Commerce* To regulate commerce with foreign nations, and among the several States, and with the Indian tribes;

Naturalization and Bankruptcy Naturalization is the process by which a person from another country becomes a United States citizen. Congress decides the requirements for this procedure.

4. *Naturalization and Bankruptcy* To establish an uniform rule of naturalization, and uniform laws on the subject of bankruptcies throughout the United States;

Coins and Measures Congress has the power to coin money and set its value.

5. *Coins and Measures* To coin money, regulate the value thereof, and of foreign coin, and fix the standard of weights and measures;

6. *Counterfeiting* To provide for the punishment of counterfeiting the securities and current coin of the United States;

Copyrights and Patents Copyrights protect authors. Patents allow inventors to profit from their work by keeping control over it for a certain number of years. Congress grants patents to encourage scientific research.

7. *Post Offices* To establish post offices and post roads;

8. *Copyrights and Patents* To promote the progress of science and useful arts by securing for limited times to authors and inventors the exclusive right to their respective writings and discoveries;

9. *Courts* To constitute tribunals inferior to the Supreme Court;

10. *Piracy* To define and punish piracies and felonies committed on the high seas, and offenses against the law of nations;

Declaring War Only Congress can declare war on another country.

11. *Declaring War* To declare war, ~~grant letters of marque and reprisal,~~ and make rules concerning captures on land and water;

12. *Army* To raise and support armies, but no appropriation of money to that use shall be for a longer term than two years;

13. *Navy* To provide and maintain a navy;

14. *Military Regulations* To make rules for the government and regulation of the land and naval forces;

Militia Today the Militia is called the National Guard. The National Guard often helps people after floods, tornadoes, and other disasters.

15. *Militia* To provide for calling forth the militia to execute the laws of the Union, suppress insurrections and repel invasions;

16. *Militia Regulations* To provide for organizing, arming and disciplining the militia, and for governing such part of them as may be employed in the service of the United States, reserving to the States respectively the appointment of the officers, and the authority of training the militia according to the discipline prescribed by Congress;

National Capital Congress makes the laws for the District of Columbia, the area where the nation's capital is located.

17. *National Capital* To exercise exclusive legislation in all cases whatsoever, over such district (not exceeding ten miles square) as may, by cession of particular states, and the acceptance of Congress, become the seat of the government of the United States, and to exercise like authority over all places purchased by the consent of the legislature of the State in which the same shall be, for the erection of forts, magazines, arsenals, dock-yards, and other needful buildings;—and

Necessary Laws This clause allows Congress to make laws on issues, such as television and radio, that are not mentioned in the Constitution.

18. *Necessary Laws* To make all laws which shall be necessary and proper for carrying into execution the foregoing powers, and all other powers vested by this Constitution in the government of the United States, or in any department or officer thereof.

SECTION 9. POWERS DENIED TO CONGRESS

1. *Slave Trade* ~~The migration or importation of such persons as any of the States now existing shall think proper to admit, shall not be prohibited by the Congress prior to the year 1808, but a tax or duty may be imposed on such importation, not exceeding ten dollars for each person.~~

2. *Habeas Corpus* The privilege of the writ of habeas corpus shall not be suspended, unless when in cases of rebellion or invasion the public safety may require it.

3. *Special Laws* No bill of attainder or ex post facto law shall be passed.

4. *Direct Taxes* ~~No capitation or other direct tax shall be laid, unless in proportion to the census or enumeration herein before directed to be taken.~~

5. *Export Taxes* No tax or duty shall be laid on articles exported from any State.

6. *Ports* No preference shall be given by any regulation of commerce or revenue to the ports of one State over those of another; nor shall vessels bound to, or from, one State, be obliged to enter, clear, or pay duties in another.

7. *Regulations on Spending* No money shall be drawn from the treasury, but in consequence of appropriations made by law; and a regular statement and account of the receipts and expenditures of all public money shall be published from time to time.

8. *Titles of Nobility and Gifts* No title of nobility shall be granted by the United States: and no person holding any office or profit or trust under them, shall, without the consent of the Congress, accept of any present, emolument, office, or title, of any kind whatever, from any king, prince, or foreign state.

SECTION 10. POWERS DENIED TO THE STATES

1. *Complete Restrictions* No State shall enter into any treaty, alliance, or confederation; grant letters of marque and reprisal; coin money; emit bills of credit; make anything but gold and silver coin a tender in payment of debts; pass any bill of attainder, ex post facto law, or law impairing the obligation of contracts, or grant any title of nobility.

2. *Partial Restrictions* No State shall, without the consent of the Congress, lay any imposts or duties on imports or exports, except what may be absolutely necessary for executing its inspection laws; and the net produce of all duties and imposts, laid by any State on imports or exports, shall be for the use of the treasury of the United States; and all such laws shall be subject to the revision and control of the Congress.

3. *Other Restrictions* No State shall, without the consent of Congress, lay any duty of tonnage, keep troops, or ships of war in time of peace, enter into any agreement or compact with another State, or with a foreign power, or engage in war, unless actually invaded, or in such imminent danger as will not admit of delay.

ARTICLE II
Executive Branch

SECTION 1. PRESIDENT AND VICE PRESIDENT

1. *Term of Office* The executive power shall be vested in a President of the United States of America. He shall hold his office during the term of four years, and together with the Vice President, chosen for the same term, be elected as follows:

2. *Electoral College* Each State shall appoint, in such manner as the legislature thereof may direct, a number of electors, equal to the whole number of senators and representatives to which the State may be entitled in the Congress; but no

Slave Trade This clause was another compromise between the North and the South. It prevented Congress from regulating the slave trade for 20 years. Congress outlawed the slave trade in 1808.

Habeas Corpus A writ of habeas corpus requires the government either to charge a person in jail with a particular crime or let the person go free. Except in emergencies, Congress cannot deny the right of a person to a writ.

Ports When regulating trade, Congress must treat all states equally. Also, states cannot tax goods traveling between states.

Regulations on Spending Congress controls the spending of public money. This clause checks the President's power.

Complete Restrictions The Constitution prevents the states from acting like individual countries. States cannot make treaties with foreign nations. They cannot issue their own money.

Partial Restrictions States cannot tax imports and exports without approval from Congress.

Other Restrictions States cannot declare war. They cannot keep their own armies.

Term of Office The President has the power to carry out the laws passed by Congress. The President and the Vice President serve four-year terms.

Electoral College A group of people called the Electoral College actually elects the President. The number of electors each state receives equals the total number of its representatives and senators.

senator or representative, or person holding an office of trust or profit under the United States, shall be appointed an elector.

Election Process Originally, electors voted for two people. The candidate who received the majority of votes became President. The runner-up became Vice President. Problems with this system led to the 12th Amendment, which changed the electoral college system.

Today electors almost always vote for the candidate who won the popular vote in their states. In other words, the candidate who wins the popular vote in a state also wins its electoral votes.

3. *Election Process* ~~The electors shall meet in their respective States, and vote by ballot for two persons, of whom one at least shall not be an inhabitant of the same State with themselves. And they shall make a list of all the persons voted for, and of the number of votes for each; which list they shall sign and certify, and transmit sealed to the seat of the government of the United States, directed to the President of the Senate. The President of the Senate shall, in the presence of the Senate and House of Representatives, open all the certificates, and the votes shall then be counted. The person having the greatest number of votes shall be the President, if such number be a majority of the whole number of electors appointed, and if there be more than one who have such majority, and have an equal number of votes, then the House of Representatives shall immediately choose by ballot one of them for President; and if no person have a majority, then from the five highest on the list the said house shall in like manner choose the President. But in choosing the President, the votes shall be taken by States, the representation from each State having one vote; a quorum for this purpose shall consist of a member or members from two-thirds of the States, and a majority of all the States shall be necessary to a choice. In every case, after the choice of the President, the person having the greatest number of votes of the electors shall be the Vice President. But if there should remain two or more who have equal votes, the Senate shall choose from them by ballot the Vice President.~~

4. *Time of Elections* The Congress may determine the time of choosing the electors, and the day on which they shall give their votes; which day shall be the same throughout the United States.

Time of Elections Today we elect our President on the Tuesday after the first Monday in November.

Qualifications A President must be at least 35 years old, a United States citizen by birth, and a resident of the United States for at least 14 years.

5. *Qualifications* No person except a natural-born citizen, ~~or a citizen of the United States at the time of the adoption of this Constitution,~~ shall be eligible to the office of President; neither shall any person be eligible to that office who shall not have attained to the age of thirty-five years, and been fourteen years a resident within the United States.

Vacancies If the President resigns, dies, or is impeached and found guilty, the Vice President becomes President. The 25th Amendment replaced this clause in 1967.

6. *Vacancies* ~~In case of the removal of the President from office, or of his death, resignation, or inability to discharge the powers and duties of the said office, the same shall devolve on the Vice President, and the Congress may by law provide for the case of removal, death, resignation, or inability, both of the President and Vice President, declaring what officer shall then act as President, and such officer shall act accordingly, until the disability be removed, or a President shall be elected.~~

Salary The President receives a yearly salary that cannot be increased or decreased during his or her term. The President cannot hold any other paid government positions while in office.

7. *Salary* The President shall, at stated times, receive for his services a compensation, which shall neither be increased nor diminished during the period for which he shall have been elected, and he shall not receive within that period any other emolument from the United States, or any of them.

Oath of Office Every President must promise to uphold the Constitution. The Chief Justice of the Supreme Court usually administers this oath.

8. *Oath of Office* Before he enter on the execution of his office, he shall take the following oath or affirmation:—"I do solemnly swear (or affirm) that I will faithfully execute the office of President of the United States, and will to the best of my ability, preserve, protect and defend the Constitution of the United States."

SECTION 2. POWERS OF THE PRESIDENT

Military Powers The President is the leader of the country's military forces.

1. *Military Powers* The President shall be commander in chief of the army and navy of the United States, and of the militia of the several States, when called into the actual service of the United States; he may require the opinion, in writing, of the principal officer in each of the executive departments, upon any subject relating to the duties of their respective offices, and he shall have power to

grant reprieves and pardons for offenses against the United States, except in cases of impeachment.

2. Treaties and Appointments He shall have power, by and with the advice and consent of the Senate, to make treaties, provided two-thirds of the Senators present concur; and he shall nominate, and by and with the advice and consent of the Senate, shall appoint ambassadors, other public ministers and consuls, judges of the Supreme Court, and all other officers of the United States, whose appointments are not herein otherwise provided for, and which shall be established by law: but the Congress may by law vest the appointment of such inferior officers, as they think proper, in the President alone, in the courts of law, or in the heads of departments.

3. Temporary Appointments The President shall have power to fill up all vacancies that may happen during the recess of the Senate, by granting commissions which shall expire at the end of their next session.

SECTION 3. DUTIES

He shall from time to time give to the Congress information of the State of the Union, and recommend to their consideration such measures as he shall judge necessary and expedient; he may on extraordinary occasions, convene both houses, or either of them, and in case of disagreement between them with respect to the time of adjournment, he may adjourn them to such time as he shall think proper; he shall receive ambassadors and other public ministers; he shall take care that the laws be faithfully executed, and shall commission all the officers of the United States.

SECTION 4. IMPEACHMENT

The President, Vice President, and all civil officers of the United States, shall be removed from office on impeachment for, and conviction of, treason, bribery, or other high crimes and misdemeanors.

ARTICLE III
Judicial Branch

SECTION 1. FEDERAL COURTS

The judicial power of the United States shall be vested in one Supreme Court, and in such inferior courts as the Congress may from time to time ordain and establish. The judges, both of the Supreme and inferior courts, shall hold their offices during good behaviour, and shall, at stated times, receive for their services, a compensation, which shall not be diminished during their continuance in office.

SECTION 2. AUTHORITY OF THE FEDERAL COURTS

1. General Jurisdiction The judicial power shall extend to all cases, in law and equity, arising under this Constitution, the laws of the United States, and treaties made, or which shall be made, under their authority; to all cases affecting ambassadors, other public ministers and consuls; to all cases of admiralty and maritime jurisdiction; to controversies to which the United States shall be a party; to controversies between two or more States; between a State and citizens of another State; between citizens of different States; between citizens of the same State claiming lands under grants of different States, and between a State, or the citizens thereof, and foreign states, citizens or subjects.

Treaties and Appointments The President can make treaties with other nations. However, treaties must be approved by a two-thirds vote of the Senate. The President also appoints Supreme Court Justices and ambassadors to foreign countries. The Senate must approve these appointments.

Duties The President must report to Congress at least once a year and make recommendations for laws. This report is known as the State of the Union address. The President delivers it each January.

Impeachment The President and other officials can be forced out of office only if found guilty of particular crimes. This clause protects government officials from being impeached for unimportant reasons.

Federal Courts The Supreme Court is the highest court in the nation. It makes the final decisions in all of the cases it hears. Congress decides the size of the Supreme Court. Today it contains nine judges. Congress also has the power to set up a system of lower federal courts. All federal judges may hold their offices for as long as they live.

General Jurisdiction Jurisdiction means the right of a court to hear a case. Federal courts have jurisdiction over such cases as those involving the Constitution, federal laws, treaties, and disagreements between states.

The President delivers the State of the Union address each year.

The Supreme Court One of the Supreme Court's most important jobs is to decide whether laws that pass are constitutional. This power is another example of the checks and balances system in the federal government.

Trial by Jury The Constitution guarantees everyone the right to a trial by jury. The only exception is in impeachment cases, which are tried in the Senate.

Definition People cannot be convicted of treason in the United States for what they think or say. To be guilty of treason, a person must rebel against the government by using violence or helping enemies of the country.

Official Records Each state must accept the laws, acts, and legal decisions made by other states.

Privileges States must give the same rights to citizens of other states that they give to ther own citizens.

Return of a Person Accused of a Crime If a person charged with a crime escapes to another state, he or she must be returned to the original state to go on trial. This act of returning someone from one state to another is called extradition.

Every American has a right to a trial by jury. Jurors' chairs are shown below.

2. The Supreme Court In all cases affecting ambassadors, other public ministers and consuls, and those in which a State shall be party, the Supreme Court shall have original jurisdiction. In all the other cases before mentioned, the Supreme Court shall have appellate jurisdiction, both as to law and fact, with such exceptions, and under such regulations as the Congress shall make.

3. Trial by Jury The trial of all crimes, except in cases of impeachment, shall be by jury; and such trial shall be held in the State where the said crimes shall have been committed; but when not committed within any state, the trial shall be at such place or places as the Congress may by law have directed.

SECTION 3. TREASON

1. Definition Treason against the United States shall consist only in levying war against them, or in adhering to their enemies, giving them aid and comfort. No person shall be convicted of treason unless on the testimony of two witnesses to the same overt act, or on confession in open court.

2. Punishment The Congress shall have power to declare the punishment of treason, but no attainder of treason shall work corruption of blood, or forfeiture except during the life of the person attainted.

ARTICLE IV
Relations Among the States

SECTION 1. OFFICIAL RECORDS

Full faith and credit shall be given in each state to the public acts, records and judicial proceedings of every other State. And the Congress may by general laws prescribe the manner in which such acts, records, and proceedings shall be proved, and the effect thereof.

SECTION 2. PRIVILEGES OF THE CITIZENS

1. Privileges The citizens of each State shall be entitled to all privileges and immunities of citizens in the several states.

2. Return of a Person Accused of a Crime A person charged in any State with treason, felony, or other crime, who shall flee from justice, and be found in another State, shall on demand of the executive authority of the State from which he fled, be delivered up, to be removed to the State having jurisdiction of the crime.

3. Return of Fugitive Slaves No person held to service or labor in one State, under the laws thereof, escaping into another, shall, in consequence of any law or regulation therein, be discharged from such service or labor, but shall be delivered up on claim of the party to whom such service or labor may be due.

SECTION 3. NEW STATES AND TERRITORIES

1. **New States** New states may be admitted by the Congress into this Union; but no new State shall be formed or erected within the jurisdiction of any other State, nor any State be formed by the junction of two or more States, or parts of States, without the consent of the legislatures of the States concerned, as well as of the Congress.

2. **Federal Lands** The Congress shall have power to dispose of and make all needful rules and regulations respecting the territory or other property belonging to the United States; and nothing in this Constitution shall be so construed as to prejudice any claims of the United States, or of any particular State.

SECTION 4. GUARANTEES TO THE STATES

The United States shall guarantee to every State in this Union a republican form of government, and shall protect each of them against invasion; and on application of the legislature, or of the executive (when the legislature cannot be convened) against domestic violence.

ARTICLE V
Amending the Constitution

The Congress, whenever two-thirds of both houses shall deem it necessary, shall propose amendments to this Constitution, or, on the application of the legislatures of two-thirds of the several States, shall call a convention for proposing amendments, which, in either case, shall be valid to all intents and purposes, as part of this Constitution, when ratified by the legislatures of three-fourths of the several States, or by conventions in three-fourths thereof, as the one or the other mode of ratification may be proposed by the Congress; provided, ~~that no amendment which may be made prior to the year 1808, shall in any manner affect the first and fourth clauses in the ninth section of the first article;~~ and that no State, without its consent, shall be deprived of its equal suffrage in the Senate.

ARTICLE VI
General Provisions

1. **Public Debt** All debts contracted and engagements entered into, before the adoption of this Constitution, shall be as valid against the United States under this Constitution, as under the Confederation.

2. **Federal Supremacy** This Constitution, and the laws of the United States which shall be made in pursuance thereof; and all treaties made, or which shall be made, under the authority of the United States, shall be the supreme law of the land; and the judges in every State shall be bound thereby, anything in the Constitution or laws of any State to the contrary notwithstanding.

3. **Oaths of Office** The senators and representatives before mentioned, and the members of the several State legislatures, and all executive and judicial officers, both of the United States, and of the several States, shall be bound by oath or affirmation to support this Constitution; but no religious test shall ever be required as a qualification to any office or public trust under the United States.

New States Congress has the power to create new states out of the nation's territories. All new states have the same rights as the old states. This clause made it clear that the United States would not make colonies out of its new lands.

Guarantees to the State The federal government must defend the states from rebellions and from attacks by other countries.

Amending the Constitution An amendment to the Constitution may be proposed either by a two-thirds vote of each house of Congress or by a national convention called by Congress at the request of two-thirds of the state legislatures. To be ratified, or approved, an amendment must be supported by three-fourths of the state legislatures or by three-fourths of special conventions held in each state.

Once an amendment is ratified, it becomes part of the Constitution. Only a new amendment can change it. Amendments have allowed people to change the Constitution to meet the changing needs of the nation.

Federal Supremacy The Constitution is the highest law in the nation. Whenever a state law and a federal law are different, the federal law must be obeyed.

Oaths of Office All state and federal officials must take an oath promising to obey the Constitution.

ARTICLE VII
Ratification

Ratification The Constitution went into effect as soon as nine of the 13 states approved it.

Each state held a special convention to debate the Constitution. The ninth state to approve the Constitution, New Hampshire, voted for ratification on June 21, 1788.

The ratification of the conventions of nine States shall be sufficient for the establishment of this Constitution between the States so ratifying the same.

Done in Convention by the unanimous consent of the States present the seventeenth day of September in the year of our Lord one thousand seven hundred and eighty-seven and of the independence of the United States of America the twelfth. In witness whereof we have hereunto subscribed our names.

George Washington, President and deputy from Virginia

DELAWARE
George Read
Gunning Bedford, Junior
John Dickinson
Richard Bassett
Jacob Broom

MARYLAND
James McHenry
Daniel of St. Thomas Jenifer
Daniel Carroll

VIRGINIA
John Blair
James Madison, Junior

NORTH CAROLINA
William Blount
Richard Dobbs Spaight
Hugh Williamson

SOUTH CAROLINA
John Rutledge
Charles Cotesworth
*   Pinckney*
Charles Pinckney
Pierce Butler

GEORGIA
William Few
Abraham Baldwin

NEW HAMPSHIRE
John Langdon
Nicholas Gilman

MASSACHUSETTS
Nathaniel Gorham
Rufus King

CONNECTICUT
William Samuel Johnson
Roger Sherman

NEW YORK
Alexander Hamilton

NEW JERSEY
William Livingston
David Brearley
William Paterson
Jonathan Dayton

PENNSYLVANIA
Benjamin Franklin
Thomas Mifflin
Robert Morris
George Clymer
Thomas FitzSimons
Jared Ingersoll
James Wilson
Gouverneur Morris

Delegates wait for their turn to sign the new Constitution.

AMENDMENTS TO THE CONSTITUTION

AMENDMENT I (1791)*
Basic Freedoms

Congress shall make no law respecting an establishment of religion, or prohibiting the free exercise thereof; or abridging the freedom of speech, or of the press; or the right of the people peaceably to assemble, and to petition the government for a redress of grievances.

AMENDMENT II (1791)
Weapons and the Militia

A well-regulated militia, being necessary to the security of a free State, the right of the people to keep and bear arms, shall not be infringed.

AMENDMENT III (1791)
Housing Soldiers

No soldier shall, in time of peace, be quartered in any house, without the consent of the owner, nor in time of war, but in a manner to be prescribed by law.

AMENDMENT IV (1791)
Search and Seizure

The right of the people to be secure in their persons, houses, papers, and effects, against unreasonable searches and seizures, shall not be violated, and no warrants shall issue, but upon probable cause, supported by oath or affirmation, and particularly describing the place to be searched, and the persons or things to be seized.

AMENDMENT V (1791)
Rights of the Accused

No person shall be held to answer for a capital, or otherwise infamous crime, unless on a presentment or indictment of a grand jury, except in cases arising in the land or naval forces, or in the militia, when in actual service in time of war or public danger; nor shall any person be subject for the same offense to be twice put in jeopardy of life or limb; nor shall be compelled in any criminal case to be a witness against himself, nor be deprived of life, liberty, or property, without due process of law; nor shall private property be taken for public use without just compensation.

AMENDMENT VI (1791)
Right to a Fair Trial

In all criminal prosecutions, the accused shall enjoy the right to a speedy and public trial, by an impartial jury of the State and district wherein the crime shall have been committed, which district shall have been previously ascertained by law, and to be informed of the nature and cause of the accusation; to be confronted with the witnesses against him; to have compulsory process for obtaining witnesses in his favor, and to have the assistance of counsel for his defense.

AMENDMENT VII (1791)
Jury Trial in Civil Cases

In suits at common law, where the value in controversy shall exceed twenty dollars, the right of trial by jury shall be preserved, and no fact tried by a jury shall be otherwise reexamined in any court of the United States, than according to the rules of the common law.

Amendments to the Constitution

Basic Freedoms The government cannot pass laws that favor one religion over another. Nor can it stop people from saying or writing whatever they want. The people have the right to gather openly and discuss problems they have with the government.

Weapons and the Militia This amendment was included to prevent the federal government from taking away guns used by members of state militias.

Housing Soldiers The army cannot use people's homes to house soldiers unless it is approved by law. Before the American Revolution, the British housed soldiers in private homes without permission of the owners.

Search and Seizure This amendment protects people's privacy in their homes. The government cannot search or seize anyone's property without a warrant, or a written order, from a court. A warrant must list the people and the property to be searched and give reasons for the search.

Rights of the Accused A person accused of a crime has the right to a fair trial. A person cannot be tried twice for the same crime. This amendment also protects a person from self-incrimination, or having to testify against himself or herself.

Right to a Fair Trial Anyone accused of a crime is entitled to a quick and fair trial by jury. This right protects people from being kept in jail without being convicted of a crime. Also, the government must provide a lawyer for anyone accused of a crime who cannot afford to hire a lawyer.

Jury Trial in Civil Cases Civil cases usually involve two or more people suing each other over money, property, or personal injury. A jury trial is guaranteed in large lawsuits.

*The date after each amendment indicates the year the amendment was ratified.

AMENDMENT VIII (1791)
Bail and Punishment

Bail and Punishment Courts cannot treat people accused of crimes in ways that are unusually harsh.

Excessive bail shall not be required, nor excessive fines imposed, nor cruel and unusual punishments inflicted.

AMENDMENT IX (1791)
Powers Reserved to the People

Powers Reserved to the People The people keep all rights not listed in the Constitution.

The enumeration in the Constitution, of certain rights, shall not be construed to deny or disparage others retained by the people.

AMENDMENT X (1791)
Powers Reserved to the States

Powers Reserved to the States Any rights not clearly given to the federal government by the Constitution belong to the states or the people.

The powers not delegated to the United States by the Constitution, nor prohibited by it to the States, are reserved to the States respectively, or to the people.

AMENDMENT XI (1795)
Suits Against States

Suits Against the States A citizen from one state cannot sue the government of another state in a federal court. Such cases are decided in state courts.

The judicial power of the United States shall not be construed to extend to any suit in law or equity, commenced or prosecuted against one of the United States by citizens of another State, or by citizens or subjects of any foreign State.

AMENDMENT XII (1804)
Election of the President and Vice President

Election of the President and Vice President Under the original Constitution, each member of the Electoral College voted for two candidates for President. The candidate with the most votes became President. The one with the second highest total became Vice President.

The 12th Amendment changed this system. Members of the electoral college distinguish between their votes for the President and Vice President. This change was an important step in the development of the two party system. It allows each party to nominate its own team of candidates.

The electors shall meet in their respective States and vote by ballot for President and Vice President, one of whom, at least, shall not be an inhabitant of the same State with themselves; they shall name in their ballots the person voted for as President, and in distinct ballots the person voted for as Vice President, and they shall make distinct lists of all persons voted for as President, and of all persons voted for as Vice President, and of the number of votes for each, which lists they shall sign and certify, and transmit sealed to the seat of the government of the United States, directed to the President of the Senate; the President of the Senate shall, in the presence of the Senate and House of Representatives, open all the certificates and the votes shall then be counted; the person having the greatest number of votes for President, shall be the President, if such number be a majority of the whole number of electors appointed; and if no person have such majority, then from the persons having the highest numbers not exceeding three on the list of those voted for as President, the House of Representatives shall choose immediately, by ballot, the President. But in choosing the President, the votes shall be taken by States, the representation from each State having one vote; a quorum for this purpose shall consist of a member or members from two-thirds of the States, and a majority of all the States shall be necessary to a choice. And if the House of Representatives shall not choose a President whenever the right of choice shall devolve upon them, before the fourth day of March next following, then the Vice President shall act as President, as in case of the death or other constitutional disability of the President. The person having the greatest number of votes as Vice President, shall be the Vice President, if such number be a majority of the whole number of electors appointed, and if no person have a majority, then from the two highest numbers on the list, the Senate shall choose the Vice President; a quorum for the purpose shall consist of two-thirds of the whole number of senators, and a majority of the whole number shall be necessary to a choice. But no person constitutionally ineligible to the office of President shall be eligible to that of Vice President of the United States.

The Twelfth Amendment allowed parties to nominate teams of candidates, as this campaign poster shows.

AMENDMENT XIII (1865)
End of Slavery

SECTION 1. ABOLITION

Neither slavery nor involuntary servitude, except as a punishment for crime whereof the party shall have been duly convicted, shall exist within the United States, or any place subject to their jurisdiction.

SECTION 2. ENFORCEMENT

Congress shall have power to enforce this article by appropriate legislation.

AMENDMENT XIV (1868)
Rights of Citizens

SECTION 1. CITIZENSHIP

All persons born or naturalized in the United States, and subject to the jurisdiction thereof, are citizens of the United States and of the State wherein they reside. No State shall make or enforce any law which shall abridge the privileges or immunities of citizens of the United States; nor shall any State deprive any person of life, liberty, or property, without due process of law; nor deny to any person within its jurisdiction the equal protection of the laws.

SECTION 2. NUMBER OF REPRESENTATIVES

Representatives shall be apportioned among the several States according to their respective numbers, counting the whole number of persons in each State, excluding Indians not taxed. But when the right to vote at any election for the choice of electors for President and Vice President of the United States, representatives in Congress, the executive and judicial officers of a State, or the members of the legislature thereof, is denied to any of the male inhabitants of such State, being twenty-one years of age, and citizens of the United States, or in any way abridged, except for participation in rebellion, or other crime, the basis of representation therein shall be reduced in the proportion which the number of such male citizens shall bear to the whole number of male citizens twenty-one years of age in such State.

SECTION 3. PENALTY FOR REBELLION

No person shall be a senator or representative in Congress, or elector of President and Vice President, or hold any office, civil or military, under the United States, or under any State, who, having previously taken an oath, as a member of Congress, or as an officer of the United States, or as a member of any State legislature, or as an executive or judicial officer of any State, to support the Constitution of the United States, shall have engaged in insurrection or rebellion against the same, or given aid or comfort to the enemies thereof. But Congress may by a vote of two-thirds of each house, remove such disability.

SECTION 4. GOVERNMENT DEBT

The validity of the public debt of the United States, authorized by law, including debts incurred for payment of pensions and bounties for services in suppressing insurrection or rebellion, shall not be questioned. But neither the United States nor any State shall assume or pay any debt or obligation incurred in aid of insurrection or rebellion against the United States, or any claim for the loss or emancipation of any slave; but all such debts, obligations and claims shall be held illegal and void.

This etching shows a group of former slaves celebrating their emancipation.

Abolition This amendment ended slavery in the United States. It was ratified after the Civil War.

Citizenship This amendment defined citizenship in the United States. "Due process of law" means that no state can deny its citizens the rights and privileges they enjoy as United States citizens. The goal of this amendment was to protect the rights of the recently freed African Americans.

Number of Representatives This clause replaced the Three-Fifths Clause in Article 1. Each state's representation is based on its total population. Any state denying its male citizens over the age of 21 the right to vote will have its representation in Congress decreased.

Penalty of Rebellion Officials who fought against the Union in the Civil War could not hold public office in the United States. This clause tried to keep Confederate leaders out of power. In 1872, Congress removed this limit.

Government Debt The United States paid all of the Union's debts from the Civil War. However, it did not pay any of the Confederacy's debts. This clause prevented the southern states from using public money to pay for the rebellion or from compensating citizens who lost their enslaved persons.

SECTION 5. ENFORCEMENT

The Congress shall have power to enforce, by appropriate legislation, the provisions of this article.

AMENDMENT XV (1870)
Voting Rights

SECTION 1. RIGHT TO VOTE

The right of citizens of the United States to vote shall not be denied or abridged by the United States or by any State on account of race, color, or previous condition of servitude.

Right to Vote No state can deny its citizens the right to vote because of their race. This amendment was designed to protect the voting rights of African Americans.

SECTION 2. ENFORCEMENT

The Congress shall have power to enforce this article by appropriate legislation.

AMENDMENT XVI (1913)
Income Tax

The Congress shall have power to lay and collect taxes on incomes, from whatever sources derived, without apportionment among the several States, and without regard to any census or enumeration.

Income Tax Congress has the power to tax personal incomes.

AMENDMENT XVII (1913)
Direct Election of Senators

SECTION 1. METHOD OF ELECTION

The Senate of the United States shall be composed of two senators from each State, elected by the people thereof, for six years; and each senator shall have one vote. The electors in each State shall have the qualifications requisite for electors of the most numerous branch of the State legislatures.

Direct Election of Senators In the original Constitution, the state legislatures elected senators. This amendment gave citizens the power to elect their senators directly. It made senators more responsible to the people they represented.

SECTION 2. VACANCIES

When vacancies happen in the representation of any State in the Senate, the executive authority of such State shall issue writs of election to fill such vacancies: Provided, that the legislature of any State may empower the executive thereof to make temporary appointments until the people fill the vacancies by election as the legislature may direct.

SECTION 3. EXCEPTION

This amendment shall not be so construed as to affect the election or term of any Senator chosen before it becomes valid as part of the Constitution.

The Prohibition movement used posters like this to reach the public.

AMENDMENT XVIII (1919)
Ban on Alcoholic Drinks

SECTION 1. PROHIBITION

After one year from the ratification of this article the manufacture, sale, or transportation of intoxicating liquors within, the importation thereof into, or the exportation thereof from the United States and all territory subject to the jurisdiction thereof for beverage purposes is hereby prohibited.

Prohibition This amendment made it against the law to make or sell alcoholic beverages in the United States. This law was called prohibition. Fourteen years later, the 21st Amendment ended Prohibition.

SECTION 2. ENFORCEMENT

The Congress and the several States shall have concurrent power to enforce this article by appropriate legislation.

SECTION 3. RATIFICATION

~~This article shall be inoperative unless it shall have been ratified as an amendment to the Constitution by the legislatures of the several States, as provided in the Constitution, within seven years from the date of the submission hereof to the States by Congress.~~

AMENDMENT XIX (1920)
Women's Suffrage

SECTION 1. RIGHT TO VOTE

The right of citizens of the United States to vote shall not be denied or abridged by the United States or by any State on account of sex.

SECTION 2. ENFORCEMENT

The Congress shall have power to enforce this article by appropriate legislation.

AMENDMENT XX (1933)
Terms of Office

SECTION 1. BEGINNING OF TERMS

The terms of the President and Vice-President shall end at noon on the 20th day of January, and the terms of senators and representatives at noon on the 3rd day of January, of the years in which such terms would have ended if this article had not been ratified; and the terms of their successors shall then begin.

SECTION 2. SESSIONS OF CONGRESS

The Congress shall assemble at least once in every year, and such meeting shall begin at noon on the 3rd day of January, unless they shall by law appoint a different day.

SECTION 3. PRESIDENTIAL SUCCESSION

If, at the time fixed for the beginning of the term of the President, the President-elect shall have died, the Vice President-elect shall become President. If a President shall not have been chosen before the time fixed for the beginning of his term, or if the President-elect shall have failed to qualify, then the Vice President-elect shall act as President until a President shall have qualified; and the Congress may by law provide for the case wherein neither a President-elect nor a Vice President-elect shall have qualified, declaring who shall then act as President, or the manner in which one who is to act shall be selected, and such person shall act accordingly until a President or Vice President shall have qualified.

SECTION 4. ELECTIONS DECIDED BY CONGRESS

The Congress may by law provide for the case of the death of any of the persons from whom the House of Representatives may choose a President whenever the right of choice shall have devolved upon them, and for the case of the death of any of the persons from whom the Senate may choose a Vice President whenever the right of choice shall have devolved upon them.

SECTION 5. EFFECTIVE DATE

~~Sections 1 and 2 shall take effect on the 15th day of October following the ratification of this article.~~

Ratification The amendment for Prohibition was the first one to include a time limit for ratification. To go into effect, the amendment had to be approved by three-fourths of the states within seven years.

Women's Suffrage This amendment gave the right to vote to all women 21 years of age and older.

This 1915 banner pushed the cause of women's suffrage.

Beginning of Terms The President and Vice President's terms begin on January 20th of the year after their election. The terms for senators and representatives begin on January 3rd. Before this amendment, an official defeated in November stayed in office until March.

Presidential Succession A President who has been elected but has not yet taken office is called the President-elect. If the President-elect dies, then the Vice President-elect becomes President. If neither the President-elect nor the Vice President-elect can take office, then Congress decides who will act as President.

President Kennedy delivers his inaugural address in 1961.

SECTION 6. RATIFICATION

This article shall be inoperative unless it shall have been ratified as an amendment to the Constitution by the legislatures of three-fourths of the several States within seven years from the date of its submission.

AMENDMENT XXI (1933)
End of Prohibition

End of Prohibition This amendment repealed, or ended, the 18th Amendment. It made alcoholic beverages legal once again in the United States. However, states can still control or stop the sale of alcohol within their borders.

SECTION 1. REPEAL OF EIGHTEENTH AMENDMENT

The eighteenth article of amendment to the Constitution of the United States is hereby repealed.

SECTION 2. STATE LAWS

The transportation or importation into any State, territory, or possession of the United States for delivery or use therein of intoxicating liquors, in violation of the laws thereof, is hereby prohibited.

SECTION 3. RATIFICATION

This article shall be inoperative unless it shall have been ratified as an amendment to the Constitution by conventions in the several States, as provided in the Constitution, within seven years from the date of the submission hereof to the States by the Congress.

AMENDMENT XXII (1951)
Limit on Presidential Terms

Two-Term Limit George Washington set a precedent that Presidents should not serve more than two terms in office. However, Franklin D. Roosevelt broke the precedent. He was elected President four times between 1932 and 1944. Some people feared that a President holding office for this long could become too powerful. This amendment limits Presidents to two terms in office.

SECTION 1. TWO-TERM LIMIT

No person shall be elected to the office of the President more than twice, and no person who has held the office of President, or acted as President, for more that two years of a term to which some other person was elected President shall be elected to the office of the President more than once. But this article shall not apply to any person holding the office of President when this article was proposed by the Congress, and shall not prevent any person who may be holding the office of President, or acting as President, during the term within which this article becomes operative from holding the office of President or acting as President during the remainder of such term.

SECTION 2. RATIFICATION

This article shall be inoperative unless it shall have been ratified as an amendment to the Constitution by the legislatures of three-fourths of the several States within seven years from the date of its submission to the States by the Congress.

AMENDMENT XXIII (1961)
Presidential Votes for Washington, D.C.

Presidential Votes for Washington, D.C. This amendment gives people who live in the nation's capital a vote for President. The electoral votes in Washington D.C., are based on its population. However, it cannot have more votes than the state with the smallest population. Today, Washington, D.C. has three electoral votes.

SECTION 1. NUMBER OF ELECTORS

The District constituting the seat of government of the United States shall appoint in such manner as the Congress may direct:

A number of electors of President and Vice President equal to the whole number of senators and representatives in Congress to which the District would be entitled if it were a State, but in no event more than the least populous State; they shall be in addition to those appointed by the States, but they shall be considered, for the purposes of the election of President and Vice President, to be elec-

tors appointed by a State; and they shall meet in the District and perform such duties as provided by the twelfth article of amendment.

SECTION 2. ENFORCEMENT

The Congress shall have power to enforce this article by appropriate legislation.

AMENDMENT XXIV (1964)
Ban on Poll Taxes

SECTION 1. POLL TAXES ILLEGAL

The right of citizens of the United States to vote in any primary or other election for President or Vice President, for electors for President or Vice President, or for senator or representative in Congress, shall not be denied or abridged by the United States or any State by reason of failure to pay any poll tax or other tax.

SECTION 2. ENFORCEMENT

The Congress shall have power to enforce this article by appropriate legislation.

AMENDMENT XXV (1967)
Presidential Succession

SECTION 1. VACANCY IN THE PRESIDENCY

In case of the removal of the President from office or of his death or resignation, the Vice President shall become President.

SECTION 2. VACANCY IN THE VICE PRESIDENCY

Whenever there is a vacancy in the office of the Vice President, the President shall nominate a Vice President who shall take office upon confirmation by a majority vote of both houses of Congress.

SECTION 3. DISABILITY OF THE PRESIDENT

Whenever the President transmits to the President pro tempore of the Senate and the Speaker of the House of Representatives his written declaration that he is unable to discharge the powers and duties of his office, and until he transmits to them a written declaration to the contrary, such powers and duties shall be discharged by the Vice President as Acting President.

SECTION 4. DETERMINING PRESIDENTIAL DISABILITY

Whenever the Vice President and a majority of either the principal officers of the executive departments or of such other body as Congress may by law provide, transmit to the President pro tempore of the Senate and the Speaker of the House of Representatives their written declaration that the President is unable to discharge the powers and duties of his office, the Vice President shall immediately assume the powers and duties of the office as Acting President.

Thereafter, when the President transmits to the President pro tempore of the Senate and the Speaker of the House of Representatives his written declaration that no inability exists, he shall resume the powers and duties of his office unless the Vice President and a majority of either the principal officers of the executive departments or of such other body as Congress may by law provide, transmit within four days to the President pro tempore of the Senate and the Speaker of the House of Representatives their written declaration that the President is unable to discharge the powers and duties of his office. Thereupon Congress shall decide

African Americans vote in Selma, Alabama, in 1966.

Ban on Poll Taxes A poll tax requires a person to pay a certain amount of money to register to vote. These taxes were used to stop poor African Americans from voting. This amendment made any such taxes illegal in federal elections.

Vacancy in the Vice Presidency If the Vice President becomes President, he or she may nominate a new Vice President. This nomination must be approved by both houses of Congress.

Disability of the President This section tells what happens if the President suddenly becomes ill or is seriously injured. The Vice President takes over as Acting President. When the President is ready to take office again, he or she must tell Congress.

the issue, assembling within 48 hours for that purpose if not in session. If the Congress, within 21 days after receipt of the latter written declaration, or, if Congress is not in session, within 21 days after Congress is required to assemble, determines by two-thirds vote of both houses that the President is unable to discharge the powers and duties of his office, the Vice President shall continue to discharge the same as Acting President; otherwise, the President shall resume the powers and duties of his office.

AMENDMENT XXVI (1971)
Voting Age

Right to Vote This amendment gave the vote to everyone 18 years of age and older.

SECTION 1. RIGHT TO VOTE

The right of citizens of the United States, who are 18 years of age or older, to vote shall not be denied or abridged by the United States or by any state on account of age.

SECTION 2. ENFORCEMENT

The Congress shall have power to enforce this article by appropriate legislation.

AMENDMENT XXVII (1992)
Congressional Pay

Limit on Pay Raises This amendment prohibits a Congressional pay raise from taking effect during the current term of the Congress that voted for the raise.

No law, varying the compensation for the services of the senators and representatives, shall take effect, until an election of representatives shall have intervened.

The voting age was lowered to 18 in 1971.

from *The Federalist* (No. 10) (1787)

The two great points of difference between a democracy and a republic are: first, the delegation of the government, in the latter, to a small number of citizens selected by the rest; secondly, the greater number of citizens and greater sphere of country, over which the latter may be extended.

The effect of the first difference is, on the one hand, to refine and enlarge the public views, by passing them through the medium of a chosen body of citizens, whose wisdom may best discern the true interest of their country and whose patriotism and love of justice will be least likely to sacrifice it to temporary or partial considerations. . . .

By enlarging too much the number of electors, you render the representative too little acquainted with all their local circumstances and lesser interests; as by reducing it too much, you render him unduly attached to these, and too little fit to comprehend and pursue great and national objects. . . .

Extend the sphere and you take in a greater variety of parties and interests; you make it less probable that a majority of the whole will have a common motive to invade the rights of other citizens.

The Star-Spangled Banner (1814)

O say, can you see, by the dawn's early light,
What so proudly we hailed at the twilight's last gleaming,
Whose broad stripes and bright stars, through the perilous fight,
O'er the ramparts we watched were so gallantly streaming?
And the rockets' red glare, the bombs bursting in air,
Gave proof through the night that our flag was still there.
O say, does that Star-Spangled Banner yet wave
O'er the land of the free and the home of the brave?

On the shore, dimly seen through the mists of the deep,
Where the foe's haughty host in dread silence reposes,
What is that which the breeze, o'er the towering steep,
As it fitfully blows, half conceals, half discloses?
Now it catches the gleam of the morning's first beam,
In full glory reflected now shines on the stream;
'Tis the Star-Spangled Banner, O long may it wave
O'er the land of the free and the home of the brave!

O thus be it ever when free men shall stand
Between their loved homes and the war's desolation!
Blest with vict'ry and peace, may the heav'n-rescued land
Praise the Power that hath made and preserved us a nation.
then conquer we must, for our cause it is just,
And this be our motto: 'In God is our trust.'
And the Star-Spangled Banner in triumph shall wave
O'er the land of the free and the home of the brave.

Francis Scott Key wrote "The Star-Spangled Banner" in 1814 while aboard ship during the battle of Fort McHenry. The gallantry and courage displayed by his fellow countrymen that night inspired Key to pen the lyrics to the song that officially became our national anthem in 1931.

John F. Kennedy was the 35th President of the United States.

President Kennedy gives a speech. Jackie Kennedy is at his left.

from President John F. Kennedy's Inaugural Address (1961)

"In your hands, my fellow citizens, more than mine, will rest the final success or failure of our course. Since this country was founded, each generation of Americans has been summoned to give testimony to its national loyalty. The graves of young Americans who answered the call to service surround the globe.

Now the trumpet summons us again—not as a call to bear arms, though arms we need—not as a call to battle, though embattled we are—but a call to bear the burden of a long twilight struggle, year in and year out, 'rejoicing in hope, patient in tribulation'—a struggle against the common enemies of man: tyranny, poverty, disease, and war itself.

Can we forge against these enemies a grand and global alliance, North and South, East and West, that can assure a more fruitful life for all mankind? Will you join in that historic effort? . . .

And so, my fellow Americans: ask not what your country can do for you—ask what you can do for your country.

My fellow citizens of the world: ask not what America will do for you, but what together we can do for the freedom of man."

from Martin Luther King Jr.'s "I Have a Dream" Speech (1963)

"*I say to you today, my friends, that in spite of the difficulties and frustrations of the moment I still have a dream. It is a dream deeply rooted in the American dream.*

I have a dream that one day this nation will rise up and live out the true meaning of its creed: 'We hold these truths to be self-evident; that all men are created equal.'

I have a dream that one day on the red hills of Georgia the sons of former slaves and the sons of former slaveowners will be able to sit down together at the table of brotherhood. . . .

I have a dream that my four little children will one day live in a nation where they will not be judged by the color of their skin but by the content of their character.

I have a dream today. . . .

. . . From every mountainside, let freedom ring.

When we let freedom ring, when we let it ring from every village and every hamlet, from every state and every city, we will be able to speed up that day when all of God's children, black men and white men, Jews and Gentiles, Protestants and Catholics, will be able to join hands and sing in the words of the old Negro spiritual, 'Free at last! Free at last! Thank God Almighty, we are free at last!'"

In August 1963, while Congress debated civil rights legislation, Martin Luther King Jr. led a quarter of a million demonstrators on a march on Washington. On the steps of the Lincoln Memorial he gave a stirring speech in which he told of his dream for America.

Historical Documents

Presidents of the United States

George Washington **1**

(1732–1799)
President from: 1789–1797
Party: Federalist
Home state: Virginia
First Lady: Martha Dandridge Custis
Washington

John Adams **2**

(1735–1826)
President from: 1797–1801
Party: Federalist
Home state: Massachusetts
First Lady: Abigail Smith Adams

Thomas Jefferson **3**

(1743–1826)
President from: 1801–1809
Party: Democratic-Republican
Home state: Virginia
First Lady: Martha Jefferson Randolph
(daughter)

James Madison **4**

(1751–1836)
President from: 1809–1817
Party: Democratic-Republican
Home state: Virginia
First Lady: Dolley Payne Todd Madison

James Monroe **5**

(1758–1831)
President from: 1817–1825
Party: Democratic-Republican
Home state: Virginia
First Lady: Elizabeth Kortright Monroe

John Quincy Adams **6**

(1767–1848)
President from: 1825–1829
Party: Democratic-Republican
Home state: Massachusetts
First Lady: Louisa Catherine Johnson
Adams

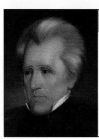

Andrew Jackson **7**

(1767–1845)
President from: 1829–1837
Party: Democratic
Home state: Tennessee
First Lady: Emily Donelson
(late wife's niece)

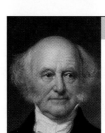

Martin Van Buren **8**

(1782–1862)
President from: 1837–1841
Party: Democratic
Home state: New York
First Lady: Angelica Singleton Van
Buren (daughter-in-law)

William Henry Harrison **9**

(1773–1841)
President: 1841
Party: Whig
Home state: Ohio
First Lady: Jane Irwin Harrison
(daughter-in-law)

John Tyler **10**

(1790–1862)
President from: 1841–1845
Party: Whig
Home state: Virginia
First Lady: Letitia Christian Tyler

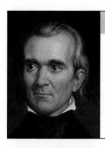

James K. Polk 11

(1795–1849)
President from: 1845–1849
Party: Democratic
Home state: Tennessee
First Lady: Sarah Childress Polk

Andrew Johnson 17

(1808–1875)
President from: 1865–1869
Party: Democratic
Home state: Tennessee
First Lady: Eliza McCardle Johnson

Zachary Taylor 12

(1784–1850)
President from: 1849–1850
Party: Whig
Home state: Louisiana
First Lady: Margaret Mackall Smith Taylor

Ulysses S. Grant 18

(1822–1885)
President from: 1869–1877
Party: Republican
Home state: Illinois
First Lady: Julia Dent Grant

Millard Fillmore 13

(1800–1874)
President from: 1850–1853
Party: Whig
Home state: New York
First Lady: Abigail Powers Fillmore

Rutherford B. Hayes 19

(1822–1893)
President from: 1877–1881
Party: Republican
Home state: Ohio
First Lady: Lucy Ware Webb Hayes

Franklin Pierce 14

(1804–1869)
President from: 1853–1857
Party: Democratic
Home state: New Hampshire
First Lady: Jane Means Appleton Pierce

James A. Garfield 20

(1831–1881)
President: 1881
Party: Republican
Home state: Ohio
First Lady: Lucretia Rudolph Garfield

James Buchanan 15

(1791–1868)
President from: 1857–1861
Party: Democratic
Home state: Pennsylvania
First Lady: Harriet Lane (niece)

Chester A. Arthur 21

(1830–1886)
President from: 1881–1885
Party: Republican
Home state: New York
First Lady: Mary Arthur McElroy (sister)

Abraham Lincoln 16

(1809–1865)
President from: 1861–1865
Party: Republican
Home state: Illinois
First Lady: Mary Todd Lincoln

Grover Cleveland 22 24

(1837–1908)
President from: 1885–1889 and 1893–1897
Party: Democratic
Home state: New York
First Lady: Frances Folsom Cleveland

Benjamin Harrison 23

(1833–1901)
President from: 1889–1893
Party: Republican
Home state: Indiana
First Lady: Caroline Lavina Scott
Harrison

William McKinley 25

(1843–1901)
President from: 1897–1901
Party: Republican
Home state: Ohio
First Lady: Ida Saxton McKinley

Theodore Roosevelt 26

(1858–1919)
President from: 1901–1909
Party: Republican
Home state: New York
First Lady: Edith Kermit Carow
Roosevelt

William Howard Taft 27

(1857–1930)
President from: 1909–1913
Party: Republican
Home state: Ohio
First Lady: Helen Herron Taft

Woodrow Wilson 28

(1856–1924)
President from: 1913–1921
Party: Democratic
Home state: New Jersey
First Lady: Edith Bolling Galt Wilson

Warren G. Harding 29

(1865–1923)
President from: 1921–1923
Party: Republican
Home state: Ohio
First Lady: Florence Kling Harding

Calvin Coolidge 30

(1872–1933)
President from: 1923–1929
Party: Republican
Home state: Massachusetts
First Lady: Grace Anna Goodhue
Coolidge

Herbert Hoover 31

(1874–1964)
President from: 1929–1933
Party: Republican
Home state: California
First Lady: Lou Henry Hoover

Franklin Delano Roosevelt 32

(1882–1945)
President from: 1933–1945
Party: Democratic
Home state: New York
First Lady: Anna Eleanor Roosevelt
Roosevelt

Harry S. Truman 33

(1884–1972)
President from: 1945–1953
Party: Democratic
Home state: Missouri
First Lady: Elizabeth Virginia Wallace
Truman

Dwight D. Eisenhower 34

(1890–1969)
President from: 1953–1961
Party: Republican
Home state: New York
First Lady: Mamie Geneva Doud
Eisenhower

John F. Kennedy 35

(1917–1963)
President from: 1961–1963
Party: Democratic
Home state: Massachusetts
First Lady: Jacqueline Lee Bouvier
Kennedy

Lyndon Baines Johnson 36

(1908–1973)
President from: 1963–1969
Party: Democratic
Home state: Texas
First Lady: Claudia Alta (Lady Bird)
Taylor Johnson

Richard M. Nixon 37

(1913–1994)
President from: 1969–1974
Party: Republican
Home state: California
First Lady: Thelma Catherine (Pat)
Ryan Nixon

Gerald R. Ford 38

(1913–)
President from: 1974–1977
Party: Republican
Home state: Michigan
First Lady: Elizabeth Bloomer Ford

Jimmy Carter 39

(1924–)
President from: 1977–1981
Party: Democratic
Home state: Georgia
First Lady: Rosalynn Smith Carter

Ronald Reagan 40

(1911–2004)
President from: 1981–1989
Party: Republican
Home state: California
First Lady: Nancy Davis Reagan

George Bush 41

(1924–)
President from: 1989–1993
Party: Republican
Home state: Texas
First Lady: Barbara Pierce Bush

William Clinton 42

(1946–)
President from: 1993–2001
Party: Democratic
Home state: Arkansas
First Lady: Hillary Rodham Clinton

George W. Bush 43

(1946–)
President from: 2001–
Party: Republican
Home state: Texas
First Lady: Laura Welch Bush

U.S. Presidents

Biographical Dictionary

The page number after each entry refers to the place where the person is first mentioned. For more complete references to people, see the Index.

A

Adams, Abigail 1744–1818, Patriot in the American Revolution (p. 77).

Adams, John 1735–1826, 2nd President of the United States, 1797–1801 (p. 77).

Addams, Jane 1860–1935, social worker who founded Hull House (p. 275).

Aldrin, Buzz 1930–, American astronaut; first person, with Neil Armstrong, to walk on the moon (p. 415).

Andreesen, Mark 1971–, inventor who developed programs allowing people to surf the Internet (p. 458).

Anthony, Susan B. 1820–1906, reformer who fought for women's rights.

Armistead, James 1748–1830, Patriot hero who spied on the British army.

Armstrong, Neil 1930–, American astronaut; first person to set foot on the moon (p. 415).

B

Bartholdi, Frédéric-Auguste 1834–1904, French sculptor who created the Statue of Liberty (p. 270).

Barton, Clara 1821–1912, nurse in Civil War; began American Red Cross (p. 185).

Begin, Menachem 1913–1992, prime minister of Israel who signed Camp David Accord (p. 444).

Clara Barton

Bell, Alexander Graham 1847–1922, invented the telephone (p. 259).

Berry, Chuck 1926–, rock 'n' roll musician (p. 416).

Bessemer, Henry 1813–1898, English scientist; invented process to convert iron to steel (p. 260).

Big Foot ?–1890, Ghost Dancer leader captured at Wounded Knee Creek (p. 249).

bin Laden, Osama 1957–, leader of a terrorist attack on the United States in 2001 (p. 466).

Black Kettle 1807?–1868, Cheyenne chief at Sand Creek Massacre (p. 247).

Bonaparte, Napoleon 1769–1821, French ruler who agreed to the Louisiana Purchase (p. 108).

Boone, Daniel 1734–1820, frontiersman who cut trail into Kentucky (p. 107).

Booth, John Wilkes 1838–1865, actor who assassinated Abraham Lincoln (p. 197).

Brady, Mathew 1823?–1896, American photographer during the Civil War (p. 186).

Breckinridge, John 1760–1806, supported spread of slavery; ran against Abraham Lincoln for President (p. 167).

Brown, John 1800–1859, abolitionist who led rebellion at Harpers Ferry (p. 159)

Brown, Linda 1943–, African American student who won Supreme Court decision forcing desegregation (p. 407).

Bruce, Blanche K. 1841–1898, African American planter and politician (p. 200).

Bush, George 1924–, 41st President of the United States, 1989–1993 (p. 450).

Bush, George W. 1946–, 43rd President of the United States, son of President George Bush (p. 464).

C

Calhoun, John C. 1782–1850, politician who supported slavery and states' rights (p. 143).

Calvert, Cecilius 1605–1675, Catholic leader of the Maryland colony; also called Lord Baltimore (p. 54).

Campbell, Ben Nighthorse 1933–, Northern Cheyenne chief and U.S. Senator.

Carnegie, Andrew 1835–1919, entrepreneur in the steel industry; philanthropist (p. 260).

Ben Nighthorse Campbell

Carter, Jimmy 1924–, 39th President of the United States, 1977–1981 (p. 444).

Cartier, Jacques 1491–1557, French explorer; sailed up St. Lawrence River (p. 38).

Carver, George Washington 1864–1943, teacher at Tuskegee Institute who used his discoveries to help poor farmers (p. 208).

Castro, Fidel 1926?–, communist leader of Cuba who took power in 1959 (p. 392).

Catt, Carrie Chapman 1859–1947, leader of women's suffrage movement (p. 280).

Champlain, Samuel de 1567–1635, French explorer; founded Quebec in 1608 (p. 46).

Chavez, Cesar 1927–1993, labor leader; founded the United Farm Workers (p. 411).

Chesnut, Mary 1823–1886, lived in South Carolina and kept a diary during Civil War (p. 189).

Churchill, Winston 1874–1965, British Prime Minister during World War II (p. 361).

Clark, George Rogers 1752–1818, captured three British forts during Revolutionary War (p. 79).

Clark, William 1770–1838, explored Louisiana Purchase with Lewis (p. 108).

Clay, Henry 1777–1852, proposed the Missouri Compromise and the Compromise of 1850 (p. 156).

Clinton, William J. 1946–, 42nd President of the United States, 1993–2001 (p. 456).

Cohan, George M. 1878–1942, American songwriter who wrote popular patriotic songs such as "Yankee Doodle Dandy" (p. 308).

Coleman, Bessie 1892–1926, aviator who became the first African American woman to earn a pilot's license (p. 332).

Columbus, Christopher 1451–1506, Italian navigator; reached the Americas (p. 37).

Connor, Eugene "Bull" 1897–1973, Alabama police chief who supported segregation (p. 408).

Coolidge, Calvin 1872–1933, 30th President of the United States, 1923–1929 (p. 324).

Cornwallis, Charles 1738–1805, English general in Revolutionary War; surrendered to Americans in 1781 (p. 78).

Cortés, Hernán 1485–1547, Spanish conquistador (p. 44).

Crawford, Joan 1904–1977, movie star of the 1920s (p. 330).

Crazy Horse 1849?–1877, Lakota chief who defeated Custer at Little Bighorn (p. 248).

Custer, George 1839–1876, army officer killed by Lakota at Little Bighorn in battle sometimes called Custer's Last Stand (p. 248).

Davis, Jefferson 1808–1889, president of Confederacy during Civil War (p. 168).

Dawes, William 1745–1799, Patriot who rode with Paul Revere (p. 72).

de Soto, Hernando 1500?–1542, Spanish explorer (p. 45).

Dempsey, Jack 1895–1983, famous boxer of the 1920s (p. 331).

Douglas, Stephen 1813–1861, supported popular sovereignty; ran against Abraham Lincoln for senate and President (p. 166).

Douglass, Frederick 1817–1895, abolitionist and writer; escaped from slavery (p. 149).

Du Bois, W.E.B. 1868–1963, educator who helped create the NAACP (p. 281).

Dylan, Bob 1941–, American folk singer and songwriter (p. 417).

Earhart, Amelia 1897–1937, aviator who became the first woman to fly across the Atlantic Ocean (p. 332).

Edison, Thomas A. 1847–1931, inventor of the light bulb, the moving-picture camera, and the phonograph (p. 259).

Eisenhower, Dwight D. 1890–1969, general in U.S. Army; 34th President of the United States, 1953–1961 (p. 377).

Ellington, Duke 1899–1974, jazz composer and musician of the Harlem Renaissance (p. 330).

Espey, Sarah Rousseau 1815–1898, lived in Alabama and kept a diary during Civil War (p. 170).

F

Ferdinand 1452–1516, king of Spain who paid for Columbus's voyage to find a westward route to Asia (p. 37).

Fitzgerald, F. Scott 1896–1940, American writer during the 1920s (p. 331).

Ford, Gerald 1913–, 38th President of the United States, 1974–1977 (p. 441).

Ford, Henry 1863–1947, automobile manufacturer; made cars on assembly line (p. 323).

Franklin, Benjamin 1706–1790, printer, writer, publisher, scientist, and inventor (p. 86).

Friedan, Betty 1921–, author of *The Feminine Mystique* and leader of women's rights movement (p. 447).

Benjamin Franklin

Fulton, Robert 1765–1815, civil engineer; built first profitable steamboat (p. 116).

 G

Gagarin, Yuri 1934–1968, Soviet cosmonaut; first person to travel in space (p. 415).

Gall 1840–1894, Lakota chief who fought at Little Bighorn (p. 248).

Garrison, William Lloyd 1805–1879, reformer and abolitionist (p. 149).

Gates, Bill 1955–, inventor who developed computer programs for use in homes, classrooms, and businesses (p. 458).

Glenn, John 1921–, first American astronaut to orbit the earth; U.S. Senator (p. 415).

Gompers, Samuel 1850–1924, founder of the AFL (American Federation of Labor) (p. 263).

Gorbachev, Mikhail 1931–, last president of the former Soviet Union (p. 450).

Gore, Al 1948–, Vice President under President Clinton; ran for President against George W. Bush (p. 464).

Grant, Ulysses S. 1822–1885, 18th President of the United States, 1869–1877; Union general in Civil War (p. 178).

Greene, Nathanael 1742–1786, American general in South during Revolutionary War (p. 78).

Grimke, Angelina 1805–1879, abolitionist and supporter of women's rights (p. 149).

Grimke, Sarah 1792–1873, abolitionist and supporter of women's rights (p. 149).

Guthrie, Woody 1912–1967, American singer and songwriter who wrote about the Dust Bowl (p. 339).

 H

Hamilton, Alexander 1755–1804, contributor to *The Federalist*; first Secretary of the Treasury (p. 86).

Harding, Warren G. 1865–1923, 29th President of the United States, 1921–1923 (p. 322).

Henry 1394–1460, Portuguese prince who started a school for navigation (p. 37).

Hirohito 1901–1989, emperor of Japan who surrendered during World War II (p. 380).

Hitler, Adolf 1889–1945, Nazi leader of Germany during World War II (p. 360).

Hoover, Herbert 1874–1964, 31st President of the United States, 1929–1933 (p. 324).

Houston, Samuel 1793–1863, first president of Republic of Texas (p. 122).

Hudson, Henry ?–1611, English navigator; gave name to Hudson River (p. 38).

Huerta, Dolores 1930–, labor leader; founded United Farm Workers with Cesar Chavez (p. 411).

Hughes, Langston 1902–1967, poet during the Harlem Renaissance (p. 338).

Hurston, Zora Neale 1891?–1960, African American writer during the Harlem Renaissance (p. 331).

Hussein, Saddam 1937–, former leader of Iraq (p. 451).

Zora Neale Hurston

Inouye, Daniel 1924–, senator from Hawaii (p. 486).

Isabella 1451–1504, queen of Spain, 1474–1504; supported and financed Columbus (p. 37).

Jackson, Andrew 1767–1845, 7th President of the United States, 1829–1837; encouraged Western expansion (p. 111).

Jefferson, Thomas 1743–1826, 3rd President of the United States, 1801–1809; wrote Declaration of Independence (p. 73).

Johnson, Andrew 1808–1875, 17th President of the United States, 1865–1869; impeached, then acquitted (p. 198).

Johnson, Georgia Douglas 1886–1966, poet during the Harlem Renaissance (p. 334).

Johnson, Lyndon 1908–1973, 36th President of the United States, 1963–1969; took office after Kennedy was assassinated (p. 410).

Joseph 1840?–1904, Nez Perce chief who tried to lead his people to Canada to escape white settlement (p. 248).

Kennedy, John F. 1917–1963, 35th President of the United States, 1961–1963; assassinated (p. 392).

King, Martin Luther, Jr. 1929–1968, civil rights leader; assassinated (p. 407).

Knight, Margaret 1838–1914, inventor of a machine that made paper bags (p. 259).

Lafayette, Marquis de 1757–1834, French; fought in American Revolution (p. 78).

Lange, Dorothea 1895–1965, documentary photographer (p. 339).

Latimer, Lewis 1848–1928, inventor who made improvements on the light bulb (p. 264).

Lazarus, Emma 1849–1887, wrote poem that appears on Statue of Liberty's base (p. 270).

Lee, Robert E. 1807–1870, commander of Confederacy (p. 176).

Lewis, Meriwether 1774–1809, explored Louisiana Purchase with Clark (p. 108).

Liliuokalani 1838–1917, last queen of Hawaii (p. 297).

Lin, Maya 1959–, Chinese American designer of the Vietnam Veterans Memorial (p. 427).

Lincoln, Abraham 1809–1865, 16th President of the United States; issued Emancipation Proclamation; assassinated (p. 164).

Lindbergh, Charles 1902–1974, first person to fly alone nonstop across Atlantic Ocean (p. 332).

Love, Nat 1854–1921, African American cowboy (p. 240).

Lowell, Francis Cabot 1775–1817, built first complete cotton spinning and weaving mill in the United States (p. 114).

MacArthur, Douglas 1880–1964, general who commanded the UN army in the Korean War (p. 392).

Madison, James 1751–1836, 4th President of the United States (p. 86).

Marion, Francis 1732?–1795, commander in American Revolution (p. 288).

Marshall, Thurgood 1908–1993, lawyer who successfully argued Linda Brown's case; first African American appointed to the U.S. Supreme Court (p. 406).

Mason, George 1725–1792, Virginia delegate at the Constitutional Convention (p. 86).

McCarthy, Joseph 1908–1957, U.S. Senator and leader of anti-communist movement (p. 391).

McCoy, Elijah 1843–1929, inventor of the oil cup, which kept machines running longer (p. 259).

Moctezuma 1480?–1520, Aztec emperor during Spanish conquest of Mexico (p. 34).

Monroe, James 1758–1831, 5th President of the United States, 1817–1825 (p. 110).

Moody, Helen Wills 1905–1998, famous tennis player of the 1920s (p. 331).

Morse, Samuel 1791–1872, invented telegraph code (called Morse Code) (p. 222).

Muir, John 1838–1914, nature lover who argued for conservation (p. 279).

Mussolini, Benito 1883–1945, Fascist leader of Italy during World War II (p. 360).

Nader, Ralph 1934–, leader of consumers' rights movement (p. 443).

Nimitz, Chester 1885–1956, leader of American navy in World War II victory at Battle of Midway (p. 378).

Nixon, Richard 1913–1994, 37th President of the United States, 1969–1974; resigned (p. 425).

Novello, Antonia 1944–, first woman elected U.S. surgeon general.

Antonia Novello

O'Connor, Sandra Day 1930–, first woman appointed to U.S. Supreme Court (p. 447).

Oglethorpe, James 1696–1785, founder of Georgia (p. 54).

Parks, Rosa 1913–2005, African American who refused to obey segregation laws in Alabama (p. 407).

Pei, I. M. 1917–, famous architect who emigrated from China (p. 452).

Penn, William 1644–1718, founder of Pennsylvania (p. 53).

Polk, James 1795–1849, 11th President of the United States, 1845–1849 (p. 123).

Polo, Marco 1254–1324, Italian merchant who worked in China and wrote a book about his travels (p. 36).

Ponce de Léon, Juan 1460?–1521, Spanish explorer of Florida (p. 40).

Powell, Colin 1937–, U.S. Secretary of State under President George W. Bush (p. 451).

Rankin, Jeanette 1880–1973, first woman elected to U.S. Congress (p. 447).

Reagan, Ronald 1911–2004, 40th President of the United States, 1981–1989 (p. 445).

Revels, Hiram R. 1822–1901, African American Senator during Reconstruction (p. 200).

Revere, Paul 1735–1818, rode from Boston to Lexington to warn Patriots that the British were coming (p. 72).

Rickenbacker, Eddie 1890–1973, American pilot; World War I hero (p. 307).

Rivera, Diego 1886–1957, Mexican artist whose murals decorate the National Palace in Mexico City (p. 34).

Rockefeller, John D. 1839–1937, entrepreneur and creator of Standard Oil Co. (p. 260).

Rolfe, John 1585–1622, English colonist; married Pocahontas (p. 51).

Roosevelt, Eleanor 1884–1962, fought for rights of women, children, and African Americans; wife of President Franklin D. Roosevelt (p. 345).

Roosevelt, Franklin D. 1882–1945, 32nd President of the United States, 1933–1945 (p. 345).

Roosevelt, Theodore 1858–1919, 26th President of the United States, 1901–1909 (p. 299).

Rosenberg, Anna 1902–1983, first female Assistant Secretary of Defense for the United States (p. 268).

Ross, John 1790–1866, Cherokee chief who led the fight against American Indian removal (p. 111).

Ruth, Babe 1895–1948, famous baseball player of the 1920s (p. 331).

S

Sacagawea 1787?–1812, Shoshone interpreter for Lewis and Clark (p. 108).

Sadat, Anwar 1918–1981, president of Egypt who signed Camp David Accord (p. 652).

Salk, Jonas 1914–1995, inventor of vaccine against polio (p. 403).

Santa Anna, Antonio López de 1795–1876, Mexican general and president during Texas revolution (p. 122).

Scott, Dred 1795?–1858, enslaved African American who sued for his freedom (p. 158).

Shays, Daniel 1747?–1825, led a rebellion of Massachusetts farmers (p. 85).

Shepard, Alan 1923–1998, first American astronaut to travel in space (p. 415).

Sherman, Roger 1721–1793, member of Constitutional Convention (p. 87).

Sherman, William Tecumseh 1820–1891, Union general in Civil War (p. 190).

Sinclair, Upton 1878–1968, muckraker who wrote *The Jungle*, a novel about meatpacking plants (p. 279).

Singleton, Benjamin 1809–1892, leader of the Exodusters who encouraged African Americans to move to Kansas (p. 232).

Singleton, Theresa archaeologist (p. 57).

Sitting Bull 1834?–1890, Lakota chief; fought at Battle of Little Bighorn (p. 248).

Slater, Samuel 1768–1835, set up cotton mill in Rhode Island (p. 114).

Squanto ?–1622?, Wampanoag who taught the Pilgrims to farm, hunt, and fish (p. 51).

Stalin, Joseph 1879–1953, leader of the Soviet Union during World War II (p. 361).

Stanton, Elizabeth Cady 1815–1902, organized first women's rights conference in Seneca Falls.

Starr, Ellen Gates 1859–1940, reformer who helped open Hull House (p. 275).

Steinem, Gloria 1934–, leader of women's rights movement (p. 442).

Stowe, Harriet Beecher 1811–1896, author of *Uncle Tom's Cabin* (p. 158).

 T

Tecumseh 1768?–1813, Shawnee chief; killed fighting for the British in War of 1812.

Tesla, Nikola 1856–1943, invented ways to create and send electricity (p. 268).

Tojo, Hideki 1884–1948, Japanese prime minister during World War II (p. 362).

Truman, Harry S. 1884–1972, 33rd President of the United States, 1945–1953 (p. 380).

Truth, Sojourner 1797?–1883, abolitionist and supporter of women's rights (p. 149).

Tubman, Harriet 1821?–1913, helped enslaved African Americans to freedom (p. 151).

Turner, Nat 1800–1831, led rebellion of enslaved people (p. 141).

 V

Van Lew, Elizabeth 1818–1890, spied for Union during Civil War (p. 189).

von Richthofen, Manfred 1892–1918, German pilot; World War I hero (p. 307).

 W

Walesa, Lech 1943–, leader of Solidarity; elected president of Poland after fall of communist government (p. 452).

Wallace, George 1919–1998, Alabama governor who supported segregation (p. 409).

Warhol, Andy 1928–1987, American artist (p. 417).

Washington, Booker T. 1856?–1915, first president of Tuskegee Institute (p. 208).

Washington, George 1732–1799, commanded Continental armies during Revolution; first President of the United States, 1789–1797 (p. 77).

Wheatley, Phillis 1753?–1784, African American poet (p. 77).

Whitney, Eli 1765–1825, inventor of the cotton gin (p. 115).

Williams, Roger 1603?–1683, founder of Rhode Island in 1636 (p. 52).

Wilson, Woodrow 1856–1924, 28th President of the United States, 1913–1921 (p. 306).

Woods, Granville 1856–1910, inventor who made improvements to the telephone, telegraph, and streetcars (p. 259).

Granville Woods

Wright, Orville 1871–1948, with the help of his brother, designed the first motorized plane to fly (p. 332).

Wright, Wilbur 1867–1912, with the help of his brother, designed the first motorized plane to fly (p. 332).

 Z

Zedong, Mao 1893–1976, leader of communist China (p. 390).

FACTS TO KNOW
The 50 United States

ALABAMA

22nd
Heart of Dixie
Population: 4,500,752
Area: 52,423 square miles
Admitted: December 14, 1819

ALASKA

49th
The Last Frontier
Population: 648,818
Area: 656,424 square miles
Admitted: January 3, 1959

ARIZONA

48th
Grand Canyon State
Population: 5,580,811
Area: 114,006 square miles
Admitted: February 14, 1912

ARKANSAS

25th
The Natural State
Population: 2,725,714
Area: 53,182 square miles
Admitted: June 15, 1836

CALIFORNIA

31st
Golden State
Population: 35,484,453
Area: 163,707 square miles
Admitted: September 9, 1850

COLORADO

8th
Centennial State
Population: 4,550,688
Area: 104,100 square miles
Admitted: August 1, 1876

CONNECTICUT

5th
Constitution State
Population: 3,483,372
Area: 5,544 square miles
Admitted: January 9, 1788

DELAWARE

1st
First State
Population: 817,491
Area: 2,489 square miles
Admitted: December 7, 1787

FLORIDA

27th
Sunshine State
Population: 17,019,068
Area: 65,758 square miles
Admitted: March 3, 1845

GEORGIA

4th
Peach State
Population: 8,684,715
Area: 59,441 square miles
Admitted: January 2, 1788

HAWAII

50th
The Aloha State
Population: 1,257,608
Area: 10,932 square miles
Admitted: August 21, 1959

IDAHO

43rd
Gem State
Population: 1,366,332
Area: 83,574 square miles
Admitted: July 3, 1890

ILLINOIS

21st
The Prairie State
Population: 12,653,544
Area: 57,918 square miles
Admitted: December 3, 1818

INDIANA

19th
Hoosier State
Population: 6,195,643
Area: 36,420 square miles
Admitted: December 11, 1816

IOWA

29th
Hawkeye State
Population: 2,944,062
Area: 56,276 square miles
Admitted: December 28, 1846

KANSAS

34th
Sunflower State
Population: 2,723,507
Area: 82,282 square miles
Admitted: January 29, 1861

KENTUCKY

15th
Bluegrass State
Population: 4,117,827
Area: 40,411 square miles
Admitted: June 1, 1792

LOUISIANA

18th
Pelican State
Population: 4,496,334
Area: 51,843 square miles
Admitted: April 30, 1812

MAINE

23rd
Pine Tree State
Population: 1,305,728
Area: 35,387 square miles
Admitted: March 15, 1820

MARYLAND

7th
Old Line State
Population: 5,508,909
Area: 12,407 square miles
Admitted: April 28, 1788

MASSACHUSETTS

6th
Bay State
Population: 6,433,422
Area: 10,555 square miles
Admitted: February 6, 1788

MICHIGAN

26th
Great Lakes State
Population: 10,079,985
Area: 96,810 square miles
Admitted: January 26, 1837

MINNESOTA

32nd
North Star State
Population: 5,059,375
Area: 86,943 square miles
Admitted: May 11, 1858

MISSISSIPPI

20th
Magnolia State
Population: 2,881,281
Area: 48,434 square miles
Admitted: December 10, 1817

MISSOURI

24th
Show Me State

Population: 5,704,484
Area: 69,709 square miles
Admitted: August 10, 1821

MONTANA

41st
Treasure State

Population: 917,621
Area: 147,046 square miles
Admitted: November 8, 1889

NEBRASKA

37th
Cornhusker State

Population: 1,739,291
Area: 77,358 square miles
Admitted: March 1, 1867

NEVADA

36th
Sagebrush State

Population: 2,241,154
Area: 110,567 square miles
Admitted: October 31, 1864

NEW HAMPSHIRE

9th
Granite State

Population: 1,287,687
Area: 9,351 square miles
Admitted: June 21, 1788

NEW JERSEY

3rd
Garden State

Population: 8,638,396
Area: 8,722 square miles
Admitted: December 18, 1787

NEW MEXICO

47th
Land of Enchantment

Population: 1,874,614
Area: 121,598 square miles
Admitted: January 6, 1912

NEW YORK

11th
Empire State

Population: 19,190,115
Area: 54,475 square miles
Admitted: July 26, 1788

NORTH CAROLINA

12th
Tarheel State

Population: 8,407,248
Area: 53,821 square miles
Admitted: November 21, 1789

NORTH DAKOTA

39th
Peace Garden State

Population: 633,837
Area: 70,704 square miles
Admitted: November 2, 1889

OHIO

17th
Buckeye State

Population: 11,435,798
Area: 44,828 square miles
Admitted: March 1, 1803

OKLAHOMA

46th
Sooner State

Population: 3,511,532
Area: 69,903 square miles
Admitted: November 16, 1907

OREGON

33rd
Beaver State

Population: 3,559,596
Area: 98,386 square miles
Admitted: February 14, 1859

PENNSYLVANIA

2nd
Keystone State

Population: 12,365,455
Area: 46,058 square miles
Admitted: December 12, 1787

RHODE ISLAND

13th
Ocean State

Population: 1,076,164
Area: 1,545 square miles
Admitted: May 29, 1790

SOUTH CAROLINA

8th
Palmetto State

Population: 4,147,152
Area: 32,007 square miles
Admitted: May 23, 1788

SOUTH DAKOTA

40th
Coyote State

Population: 764,309
Area: 77,121 square miles
Admitted: November 2, 1889

TENNESSEE

16th
Volunteer State

Population: 5,841,748
Area: 42,146 square miles
Admitted: June 1, 1796

TEXAS

28th
Lone Star State

Population: 22,118,509
Area: 261,914 square miles
Admitted: December 29, 1845

UTAH

45th
Beehive State

Population: 2,351,467
Area: 84,904 square miles
Admitted: January 4, 1896

VERMONT

14th
Green Mountain State

Population: 619,107
Area: 9,615 square miles
Admitted: March 4, 1791

VIRGINIA

10th
Old Dominion

Population: 7,386,330
Area: 42,769 square miles
Admitted: June 25, 1788

WASHINGTON

42nd
Evergreen State

Population: 6,131,445
Area: 71,303 square miles
Admitted: November 11, 1889

WEST VIRGINIA

35th
Mountain State

Population: 1,810,354
Area: 24,231 square miles
Admitted: June 20, 1863

WISCONSIN

30th
Badger State

Population: 5,472,299
Area: 65,503 square miles
Admitted: May 29, 1848

WYOMING

44th
Equality State

Population: 501,242
Area: 97,818 square miles
Admitted: July 10, 1890

DISTRICT OF COLUMBIA

No nickname

Population: 563,384
Area: 68 square miles
Incorporated: 1802

Geographic Terms

basin
a round area of land surrounded by higher land

bay
part of a lake or ocean extending into the land

coast
the land next to a sea or ocean

coastal plain
a flat, level area of land near an ocean

delta
a triangular area of land formed by deposits at the mouth of a river

desert
a dry area where few plants grow

▲ **glacier**
a large ice mass that moves slowly down a mountain or over land

gulf
a large body of sea water partly surrounded by land

harbor
a sheltered body of water where ships can safely dock

hill
a raised area of land, smaller than a mountain

island
a body of land surrounded by water

isthmus
a narrow strip of land connecting two larger bodies of land

lake
a body of water surrounded by land

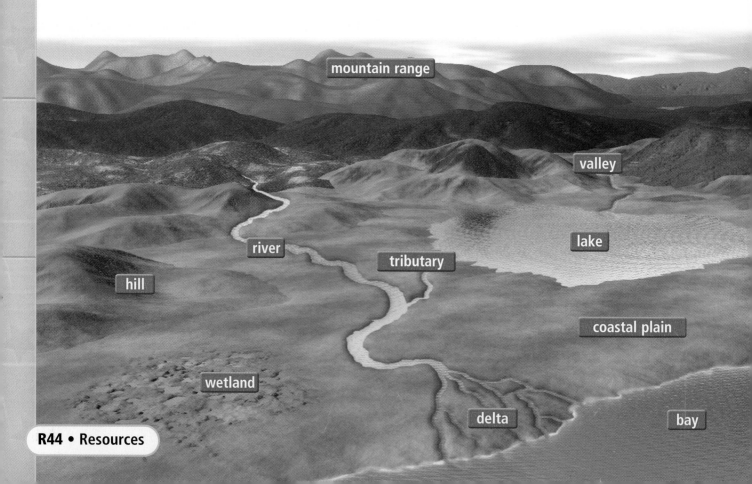

mountain range

valley

lake

river

tributary

hill

coastal plain

wetland

delta

bay

mesa
a wide flat-topped mountain with steep sides, found mostly in dry areas

mountain
a steeply raised mass of land, much higher than the surrounding country

mountain range
a row of mountains

ocean or sea
a salty body of water covering a large area of the earth

plain
a large area of flat or nearly flat land

plateau
a large area of flat land higher than the surrounding land

prairie
a large, level area of grassland with few or no trees

river
a large stream that runs into a lake, ocean, or another river

sea level
the level of the surface of the ocean

strait
a narrow channel of water connecting two larger bodies of water

tree line
the area on a mountain above which no trees grow

tributary
a river or stream that flows into a larger river

valley
low land between hills or mountains

volcano
an opening in the earth through which lava and gases from the earth's interior escape

wetland
a low area saturated with water

plateau

harbor

gulf

coast

strait

ocean

Atlas

ALB. —Albania
AZER. —Azerbaijan
BOS. & —Boznia &
HERZ. Herzegovina
CEN. AFR. —Central African
REP. Republic
DEM. REP. —Democratic Republic
OF CONGO of Congo
FR. —France
IT. —Italy
LIECH. —Liechtenstein
LUX. —Luxembourg
NETH. —Netherlands
N.Z. —New Zealand
REP. OF —Republic of
CONGO Congo
SERB. & —Serbia &
MONT. Montenegro
SLOV. —Slovenia
SWITZ. —Switzerland
U.A.E. —United Arab Emirates
U.K. —United Kingdom
U.S. —United States

Atlas

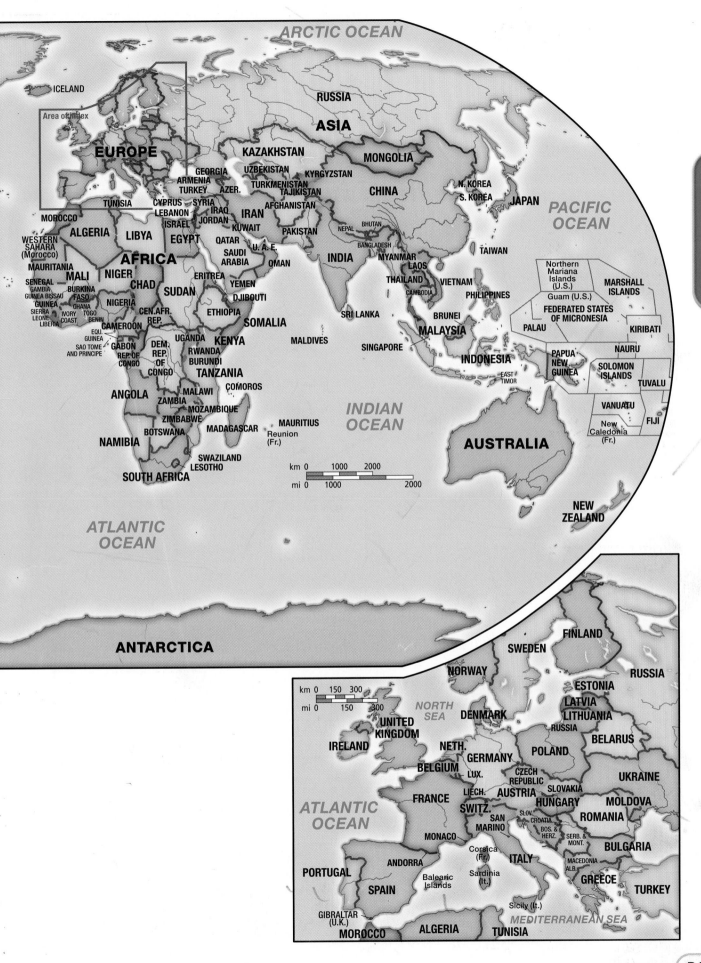

ARCTIC OCEAN

RUSSIA

ASIA

EUROPE

ICELAND

Area of index

KAZAKHSTAN

MONGOLIA

GEORGIA
ARMENIA
TURKEY
AZER.
UZBEKISTAN
KYRGYZSTAN
TURKMENISTAN
TAJIKISTAN
CHINA

N. KOREA
S. KOREA
JAPAN

PACIFIC
OCEAN

CYPRUS
LEBANON
ISRAEL
SYRIA
IRAQ
JORDAN
IRAN
AFGHANISTAN

TUNISIA

MOROCCO

KUWAIT

PAKISTAN

NEPAL
BHUTAN

TAIWAN

ALGERIA
LIBYA
EGYPT

QATAR
U. A. E.
SAUDI
ARABIA
OMAN

INDIA

BANGLADESH

MYANMAR
LAOS

WESTERN
SAHARA
(Morocco)

AFRICA

MAURITANIA

MALI
NIGER
CHAD

ERITREA

YEMEN

THAILAND

VIETNAM

CAMBODIA

Northern
Mariana
Islands
(U.S.)

MARSHALL
ISLANDS

Guam (U.S.)

FEDERATED STATES
OF MICRONESIA

SENEGAL
GAMBIA
GUINEA BISSAU
GUINEA
SIERRA
LEONE
LIBERIA

BURKINA
FASO
GHANA
IVORY
COAST
TOGO
BENIN
NIGERIA

SUDAN

CEN.AFR.
REP.

DJIBOUTI

ETHIOPIA

SOMALIA

SRI LANKA

MALDIVES

PHILIPPINES

BRUNEI

MALAYSIA

PALAU

KIRIBATI

NAURU

EQU.
GUINEA
SAO TOME
AND PRINCIPE
CAMEROON
GABON
REP. OF
CONGO
DEM.
REP.
OF
CONGO
UGANDA
RWANDA
BURUNDI

KENYA

SINGAPORE

INDONESIA

PAPUA
NEW
GUINEA

SOLOMON
ISLANDS

TUVALU

TANZANIA

ANGOLA

MALAWI
ZAMBIA
MOZAMBIQUE
ZIMBABWE

COMOROS

EAST
TIMOR

VANUATU

FIJI

MADAGASCAR

BOTSWANA

NAMIBIA

MAURITIUS
Reunion
(Fr.)

INDIAN
OCEAN

New
Caledonia
(Fr.)

AUSTRALIA

SWAZILAND
LESOTHO
SOUTH AFRICA

km 0   1000   2000
mi 0   1000   2000

ATLANTIC
OCEAN

NEW
ZEALAND

ANTARCTICA

Atlas

FINLAND

NORWAY

SWEDEN

RUSSIA

ESTONIA
LATVIA
LITHUANIA
RUSSIA

km 0   150 300
mi 0   150   300

NORTH
SEA

DENMARK

BELARUS

IRELAND

UNITED
KINGDOM

NETH.

GERMANY

POLAND

BELGIUM
LUX.

CZECH
REPUBLIC

SLOVAKIA

UKRAINE

ATLANTIC
OCEAN

FRANCE

LIECH.
SWITZ.
SAN
MARINO

AUSTRIA

HUNGARY

MOLDOVA

ROMANIA

MONACO

SLOV.
CROATIA
BOS. &
HERZ.
SERB. &
MONT.

BULGARIA

PORTUGAL

ANDORRA

Corsica
(Fr.)

ITALY

MACEDONIA
ALB.

GREECE

SPAIN

Balearic
Islands

Sardinia
(It.)

TURKEY

GIBRALTAR
(U.K.)

Sicily (It.)

MEDITERRANEAN SEA

MOROCCO

ALGERIA

TUNISIA

Atlas

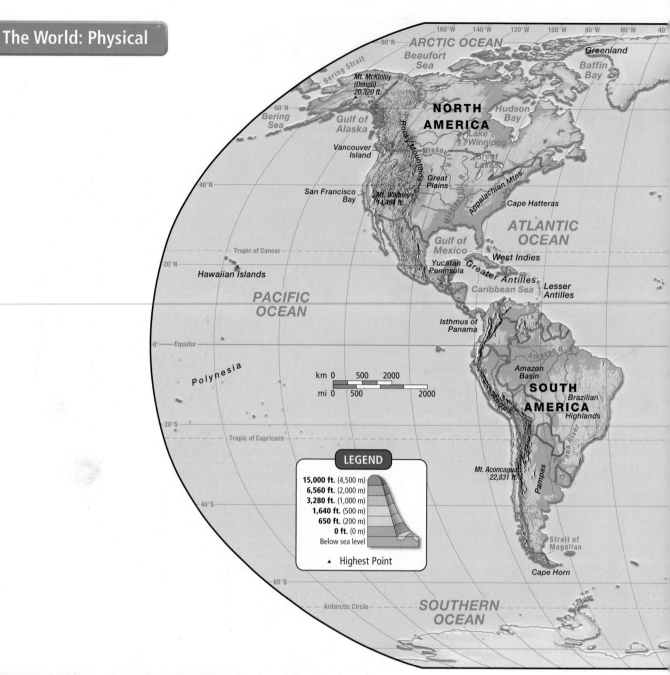

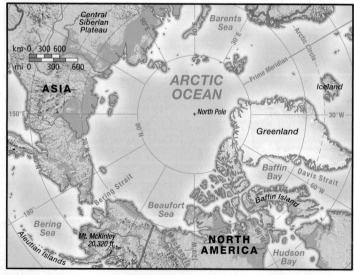

ARCTIC OCEAN

80°N

Barents
Sea

Central
Siberian
Plateau

Arctic Circle

Iceland

EUROPE

North
Sea

Northern European Plain

Ob River

Yenisey River

Ural Mountains

ASIA

60°N

Sea of
Okhotsk

Kamchatka
Peninsula

Volga River

Alps

Pyrenees

Mt. Elbrus
18,510 ft.

Aral
Sea

Amur River

Lake
Baikal

Gobi Desert

40°N

Sea
of
Japan

PACIFIC
OCEAN

Strait of
Gibraltar

Black Sea

Caucasus
Mountains

Atlas Mtns.

Mediterranean Sea

Plateau
of Tibet

Himalaya Mountains

Mt. Everest
29,035 ft.

East
China
Sea

Tropic of Cancer

Micronesia

20°N

SAHARA

Arabian
Sea

Bay of
Bengal

South
China
Sea

Philippine Islands

SAHEL

Niger River

Nile River

AFRICA

Congo River

Lake
Victoria

Great
Rift
Valley

Mt. Kilimanjaro
19,340 ft.

Sumatra

Borneo

Melanesia

Equator   0°

New Guinea

Strait of
Sunda

Java

**INDIAN
OCEAN**

Madagascar

Coral
Sea

Kalahari
Desert

Great
Sandy
Desert

Tropic of Capricorn

20°S

**ATLANTIC
OCEAN**

AUSTRALIA

Nullarbor
Plain

Darling River

Tasman
Sea

Cape of
Good Hope

Mt. Kosciusko
7,310 ft.

North Island

South Island

60°S

Antarctic Circle

ANTARCTICA

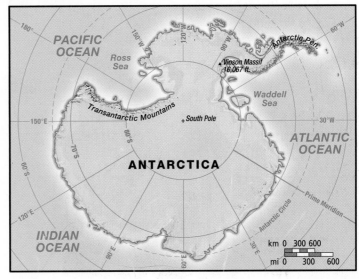

180°

**PACIFIC
OCEAN**

150°W

120°W

Antarctic Pen.

60°W

Ross
Sea

Vinson Massif
16,067 ft.

Transantarctic Mountains

South Pole

Waddell
Sea

150°E

80°S

**ATLANTIC
OCEAN**

30°W

60°S

70°S

ANTARCTICA

120°E

Prime Meridian

Antarctic Circle

30°E

**INDIAN
OCEAN**

90°E

60°E

km 0   300 600
mi 0   300   600

Western Hemisphere: Political

ARCTIC OCEAN

140°W

Beaufort Sea

Alaska (U.S.)

60°N

GREENLAND (DENMARK)

60°W

40°W

Hudson Bay

CANADA

Labrador Sea

60°N

Great Lakes

⊛ Ottawa

Great Salt Lake

40°N

UNITED STATES

⊛ Washington, D.C.

40°N

ATLANTIC OCEAN

Gulf of Mexico

Tropic of Cancer

Hawaii (U.S.)

BAHAMAS

Havana ⊛

CUBA

HAITI

DOMINICAN REPUBLIC

PUERTO RICO (U.S.)

20°N

MEXICO

Mexico City ⊛

Kingston

Santo

BELIZE

Belmopan

JAMAICA

Domingo

U.S. VIRGIN ISLANDS

ST. KITTS AND NEVIS

GUATEMALA

Guatemala City ⊛

Tegucigalpa

Port-Au-

Prince

ST. LUCIA

EL SALVADOR

San Salvador ⊛

Managua

BARBADOS

San José

GRENADA

HONDURAS

⊛ Caracas

PACIFIC OCEAN

NICARAGUA

Panama

City

VENEZUELA

Georgetown

Paramaribo

COSTA RICA

⊛

⊛ Cayenne

PANAMA

Bogotá

FRENCH GUIANA

(FRANCE)

COLOMBIA

SURINAME

0°

Equator

Galápagos Is.

(Ecuador)

ECUADOR

Quito ⊛

GUYANA

0°

French Polynesia

(France)

Lima ⊛

PERU

BRAZIL

La Paz ⊛

⊛ Brasília

BOLIVIA

20°S

Sucre ⊛

20°S

Tropic of Capricorn

PARAGUAY

CHILE

⊛ Asunción

N

W ✦ **E**

S

URUGUAY

Santiago ⊛

Buenos Aires ⊛

⊛ Montevideo

40°S

ARGENTINA

40°S

LEGEND

⊛ National capital

——— National border

km 0   500   1000

mi 0   500   1000

Falkland Islands

(U.K.)

South Georgia

(U.K.)

60°S

60°S

140°W

120°W

100°W

80°W

60°W

40°W

Western Hemisphere: Physical

GREENLAND

ARCTIC OCEAN

Beaufort Sea

Baffin Bay

Bering Strait

Davis Strait

Yukon R.

Mt. McKinley (Denali) ▲ 20,320 ft. (6,194 m)

Bering Sea

Gulf of Alaska

Hudson Bay

Labrador Sea

Coast Mountains

ROCKY MOUNTAINS

CANADIAN SHIELD

NORTH AMERICA

Great Lakes

Coast Ranges

Great Salt Lake

Range and Basin

Missouri R.

Mississippi R.

APPALACHIAN MOUNTAINS

ATLANTIC OCEAN

GREAT PLAINS

Death Valley -282 ft. (-86 m)

Mt. Whitney 14,495 ft. (4,418 m)

Coastal Plain

Rio Grande

Gulf of Mexico

Bahamas

Cuba

Hispaniola

Puerto Rico

Tropic of Cancer

Hawaiian Islands

Caribbean Sea

Lake Nicaragua

Lake Maracaibo

PACIFIC OCEAN

Line Islands

Galápagos Islands

Amazon R.

AMAZON BASIN

Equator

Marquesas

Society Islands

Cook Islands

SOUTH AMERICA

Tropic of Capricorn

Atacama Desert

Mt. Aconcagua 22,834 ft. (6,960 m)

Rio de la Plata

N
W   E
S

Valdés Peninsula -131 ft. (-40 m)

LEGEND

15,000 ft. (4,500 m)
6,560 ft. (2,000 m)
3,280 ft. (1,000 m)
1,640 ft. (500 m)
650 ft. (200 m)
0 ft. (0 m)
Below sea level

▲ Highest Point

Falkland Islands

South Georgia

Strait of Magellan

km 0   500   1000
mi 0   500   1000

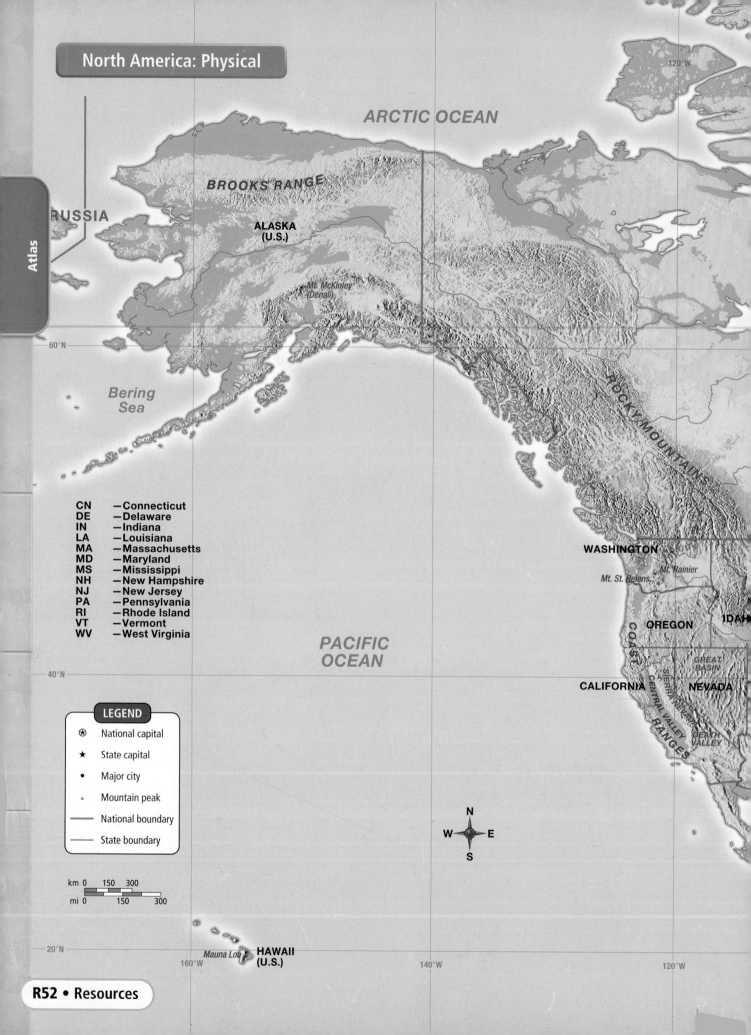

North America: Physical

ARCTIC OCEAN

120°W

BROOKS RANGE

RUSSIA

ALASKA
(U.S.)

Mt. McKinley
(Denali)

ROCKY MOUNTAINS

60°N

Bering
Sea

CN	—Connecticut
DE	—Delaware
IN	—Indiana
LA	—Louisiana
MA	—Massachusetts
MD	—Maryland
MS	—Mississippi
NH	—New Hampshire
NJ	—New Jersey
PA	—Pennsylvania
RI	—Rhode Island
VT	—Vermont
WV	—West Virginia

WASHINGTON

Mt. Rainier

Mt. St. Helens

OREGON   IDAH

COAST

PACIFIC
OCEAN

GREAT
BASIN

40°N

CALIFORNIA   NEVADA

SIERRA NEVADA

CENTRAL VALLEY

RANGES

DEATH
VALLEY

LEGEND

⊛ National capital

★ State capital

• Major city

▲ Mountain peak

—— National boundary

—— State boundary

N
W   E
S

km 0   150   300
mi 0   150   300

20°N

Mauna Loa   HAWAII
(U.S.)

160°W   140°W   120°W

Baffin
Bay

GREENLAND
(U.S.)

Labrador
Sea

60°W

60°N

Hudson
Bay

C A N A D A

Lake
Winnipeg

Great
Lakes

MONTANA   NORTH DAKOTA   MINNESOTA

St. Lawrence River

MICHIGAN

Ottawa ⊛   MAINE
NEW   VT   Mt. Washington
YORK   NH

SOUTH DAKOTA   WISCONSIN

MA
CT   RI

WYOMING

NEBRASKA   IOWA

ILLINOIS   IN   OHIO   PA   NJ

40°N

Missouri River

CENTRAL
PLAINS

WV   MD   DE
Washington, D.C.

UTAH   Pike's Peak

COLORADO   KANSAS   MISSOURI

KENTUCKY   VIRGINIA

Ohio River

APPALACHIAN MOUNTAINS

GRAND
CANYON   ARKANSAS   TENNESSEE   NORTH CAROLINA

ARIZONA   OKLAHOMA   SOUTH
CAROLINA

Arkansas River

ROCKY MOUNTAINS   GREAT PLAINS

NEW
MEXICO   MS   ALABAMA
LA   GEORGIA

TEXAS   GULF COASTAL PLAIN

ATLANTIC
OCEAN

Mississippi River

MEXICO

Rio Grande

FLORIDA

SIERRA MADRE OCCIDENTAL   SIERRA MADRE ORIENTAL

Gulf of
Mexico   B A H A M A S

C U B A

⊛ Mexico City

PUERTO RICO
(U.S.)

20°N

80°W   60°W

R53

United States: Political

ALASKA (inset)

ARCTIC OCEAN

RUSSIA

ALASKA

CANADA

Yukon R.

Fairbanks

Anchorage

Juneau

PACIFIC OCEAN

Aleutian Islands

km 0 250 500
mi 0 250 500

N
W E
S

Main map

Seattle
★ Olympia

WASHINGTON

Portland
★ Salem

Columbia R.

OREGON

IDAHO
★ Boise

Pocatello

Snake R.

Helena ★
MONTANA

Billings

WYOMING

Casper

Cheyenne ★

Reno
★ Carson City

Sacramento ★

San Francisco

NEVADA

Salt Lake City ★
Provo

UTAH

Colorado R.

COLORADO

Denver ★

Colorado Springs

Pueblo

PACIFIC OCEAN

CALIFORNIA

Las Vegas

Los Angeles

San Diego

ARIZONA

Phoenix ★

Tucson

Santa Fe ★
Albuquerque

NEW MEXICO

El Paso

Rio Grande

Gulf of California

MEXICO

LEGEND

⊗ National capital
★ State capital
• Major city
— National boundary
— State boundary

HAWAII (inset)

Kauai
Niihau
Oahu
Kailua
Honolulu
Molokai
Lanai
Maui
Kahoolawe

HAWAII

PACIFIC OCEAN

Hilo
Hawaii

km 0 50 100
mi 0 50 100

Atlas

CANADA

NORTH DAKOTA
★ Bismarck
• Fargo

MINNESOTA

SOUTH DAKOTA
• Pierre

St. Paul ★
Minneapolis •

L. Superior

WISCONSIN
Madison ★
Milwaukee •

MICHIGAN
Grand Rapids •
Lansing ★
Detroit •

L. Michigan
L. Huron
L. Erie

NEW HAMPSHIRE
VERMONT
Burlington • ★ Montpelier

MAINE
★ Augusta
• Portland
Concord ★
• Manchester
Boston ★

NEW YORK
Albany ★
• Rochester
Buffalo •

L. Ontario

MASSACHUSETTS
Hartford ★ • Providence
New Haven •

RHODE ISLAND
CONNECTICUT

St. Lawrence R.

IOWA
Cedar Rapids •
Des Moines ★

NEBRASKA
Omaha •
Lincoln •

ILLINOIS
Springfield ★

Chicago •

Indianapolis ★

INDIANA

OHIO
Columbus ★

Cincinnati •

Cleveland •

PENNSYLVANIA
Harrisburg ★
Pittsburgh •

Newark •
• New York
Trenton ★
Philadelphia •

NEW JERSEY
Dover •

DELAWARE

Baltimore •
Annapolis ⊛
Washington, D.C.

MARYLAND

KANSAS
Kansas City •
Topeka ★

Kansas City •
Jefferson City ★
St. Louis •

MISSOURI

Louisville •
Frankfort ★

KENTUCKY

WEST VIRGINIA
Charleston ★

Richmond ★
Norfolk •

VIRGINIA

Greensboro •
★ Raleigh

NORTH CAROLINA

OKLAHOMA
Tulsa •
Oklahoma City ★

Fort Smith •

ARKANSAS
Little Rock ★

Nashville ★
Memphis •

TENNESSEE

Birmingham •

Columbia •
★ Atlanta

SOUTH CAROLINA

Charleston •

Missouri R.
Mississippi R.
Ohio R.

TEXAS
Dallas •
Austin ★
Houston •
San Antonio •

LOUISIANA
Jackson ★

MISSISSIPPI

Montgomery ★

ALABAMA
⊛
Mobile •

GEORGIA
Savannah •

Tallahassee ★
Jacksonville •

Baton Rouge ★
• New Orleans

ATLANTIC OCEAN

FLORIDA
Tampa •

Gulf of Mexico

Miami •

BAHAMAS

km 0 100 200 300 400 500
mi 0   100   200   300   400   500

CUBA

United States: Physical

ARCTIC OCEAN

RUSSIA

Brooks Range

Bering Strait

Yukon R.

CANADA

Mt. McKinley
(Denali)
20,320 ft.

Alaska Range

Bering
Sea

Gulf of
Alaska

Kodiak Is.

Aleutian
Islands

km 0 250 500
mi 0 250 500

N
W   E
S

PACIFIC
OCEAN

San Francisco
Bay

Channel Islands

LEGEND

15,000 ft. (4,500 m)
6,560 ft. (2,000 m)
3,280 ft. (1,000 m)
1,640 ft. (500 m)
650 ft. (200 m)
0 ft. (0 m)
Below sea level

▲ Highest Point

Mt. Rainer
14,410 ft.

Mt. Hood
11,239 ft.

Columbia R.

COAST RANGE

CASCADE RANGE

COLUMBIA PLATEAU

BITTERROOT RANGE

Snake River

Missouri River

Yellowstone River

ROCKY MOUNTAINS

BIGHORN MTNS.

GREAT

Black
Hills

Badlands

Mt. Shasta
14,162 ft.

SIERRA NEVADA

CENTRAL
VALLEY

Sacramento R.

San Joaquin R.

COAST RANGES

BASIN
AND
RANGE

WASATCH RANGE

Green R.

PLAINS

Pikes Peak
14,110 ft.

Mt. Whitney
14,494 ft.

Death Valley
282 ft. below sea level

Mojave
Desert

Grand
Canyon

Painted
Desert

Colorado
Plateau

Colorado River

CONTINENTAL DIVIDE

SANGRE DE CRISTO MTNS.

Llano
Estacado

Sonoran
Desert

Gila River

Rio Grande

Pecos River

Edwards
Plateau

Gulf of California

MEXICO

PACIFIC OCEAN

Kauai

Niihau

Oahu

Molokai

Lanai

Maui

Kahoolawe

Hawaii

Mauna Kea ▲
13,796 ft.

Mauna Loa ▲
13,678 ft.

km 0 50 100
mi 0 50 100

CANADA

St. Lawrence River

Mesabi
Range

Lake Superior

Mt. Washington
6,288 ft.
White
Mtns.

Adirondack
Mountains

Lake Michigan

Lake Huron

Connecticut R.

Mississippi River

Des Moines River

Missouri River

L. Ontario

ALLEGHENY PLATEAU

Catskill
Mtns.

APPALACHIAN MOUNTAINS

Hudson R.

Nantucket
Martha's
Vineyard

Long Island

Sand Hills

Lake Erie

CENTRAL
PLAINS

Delaware River

Susquehanna River

Platte River

Delaware Bay

Ohio R.

Chesapeake
Bay

Wabash River

OZARK PLATEAU

Mt. Mitchell
6,684 ft.

Arkansas River

Cumberland Plateau

Tennessee R.

BLUE RIDGE MOUNTAINS

FALL LINE

ATLANTIC COASTAL PLAIN

Mississippi River

OUACHITA
MOUNTAINS

Red River

Savannah R.

Oconee R.

Sabine River

Tombigbee R.

Chattahoochee River

Altamaha R.

ATLANTIC
OCEAN

Brazos River

COASTAL

PLAIN

Alabama R.

Pearl River

Colorado River

GULF

Mobile
Bay

Pensacola
Bay

Galveston
Bay

Tampa
Bay

Gulf of Mexico

Everglades

BAHAMAS

Florida Keys

km 0   100   200   300   400   500

mi 0   100   200   300   400   500

CUBA

Gazetteer

Cumberland Gap Pass through the Appalachian Mountains (36°N, 83°W) p. 99

Dallas Large city in Texas (32°N, 96°W) p. 416

Delaware 1st state; capital: Dover (39°N, 76°W) p. R57

Delaware River Flows from New York to Delaware Bay (42°N, 75°W) p. R59

Denver Capital of Colorado (40°N, 105°W) p. R56

Egypt Country in North Africa; capital: Cairo (30°N, 31°E) p. 195

El Paso City in west Texas, on Rio Grande (32°N, 106°W) p. R56

England Country in western Europe; part of the United Kingdom (52°N, 2°W) p. R49

English Channel Arm of the Atlantic Ocean between western France and southern England (50°N, 1°W) p. 366

Erie Canal Artificial waterway extending from Albany to Buffalo, NY, completed 1825 (43°N, 76°W) p. 108

Europe 6th largest continent (50°N, 15°E) p. R49

Florida 27th state; capital: Tallahassee (31°N, 85°W) p. R57

France Country in western Europe (47°N, 1°E) p. R49

Georgia 4th state; capital: Atlanta (33°N, 84°W) p. 56

Germany Country in western Europe (51°N, 10°E) p. 305

Gettysburg Site in Pennsylvania of Civil War battle (40°N, 77°W) p. 180

Grand Canyon In Arizona, deep gorge formed by the Colorado River (36°N, 112°W) p. R58

Great Lakes Five freshwater lakes between the United States and Canada (45°N, 83°W) p. R59

Great Plains In central North America, high grassland region (45°N, 104°W) pp. R58–R59

Greensboro City in North Carolina (36°N, 80°W) p. R57

Guatemala Country in Central America (16°N, 92°W) p. R52

Gulf of Mexico Body of water along southern United States and Mexico (25°N, 94°W) p. R55

Havana Capital of Cuba (23°N, 82°W) p. 48

Hawaii 50th state; capital: Honolulu (20°N, 158°W) p. 297

Hiroshima City in Japan; destroyed by atomic bomb in 1945 (34°N, 132°E) p. 380

Hispaniola Island in the West Indies (18°N, 73°W) p. 38

Honolulu Capital of Hawaii (21°N, 158°W) p. R56

Houston City in Texas (30°N, 95°W) p. 7

Hudson River In New York; named for explorer Henry Hudson (43°N, 74°W) p. 49

Idaho 43rd state; capital: Boise (44°N, 115°W) p. R56

Illinois 21st state; capital: Springfield (40°N, 91°W) p. 158

Independence Town in Missouri at the start of the Oregon Trail (39°N, 94°W) p. 116

India Country in south Asia (23°N, 78°E) p. 38

Indiana 19th state; capital: Indianapolis (40°N, 87°W) p. R57

Iowa 29th state; capital: Des Moines (41°N, 93°W) p. R57

Italy Country in southern Europe (44°N, 11°E) p. 361

Iwo Jima Island in the Pacific Ocean; site of major battle in WWII (24°N, 141°E) p. 379

Jamestown, Virginia First permanent English settlement in Americas (37°N, 76°W) p. 52

Japan Island country off east coast of Asia (37°N, 134°E) p. R49

Kansas 34th state; capital: Topeka (39°N, 100°W) p. 157

Kentucky 15th state; capital: Frankfort (38°N, 88°W) p. 176

Lexington Site in Massachusetts of lst shots fired in Revolutionary War (42°N, 71°W) p. 72

London Capital of United Kingdom (52°N, 0°W) p. 382

Los Angeles City in California (34°N, 118°W) p. 15

Louisiana 18th state; capital: Baton Rouge (31°N, 93°W) p. 168

Maine 23rd state; capital: Augusta (45°N, 70°W) p. R57

Maryland 7th state; capital: Annapolis (39°N, 76°W) p. 56

Massachusetts 6th state; capital: Boston (42°N, 73°W) p. 54

Mediterranean Sea Inland sea surrounded by Europe, Africa, and the Middle East (35°N, 15°E) p. R51

Mexico Country bordering the United States to the south (24°N, 104°W) p. R52

Mexico City Capital of Mexico (19°N, 99°W) p. 34

Miami City in Florida (26°N, 80°W) p. R57

Michigan 26th state; capital: Lansing (46°N, 87°W) p. R57

Midway Group of islands in central Pacific Ocean; site of major battle in WWII (28°N, 177°W) p. 378

Milwaukee City in Wisconsin (43°N, 88°W) p. R57

Minnesota 32nd state; capital: St. Paul (45°N, 93°W) p. 16

Mississippi 20th state; capital: Jackson (33°N, 90°W) p. 168

Mississippi River Principal river of United States and North America (32°N, 92°W) p. R59

Missouri 24th state; capital: Jefferson City (38°N, 94°W) p. 157

Missouri River A major river in United States (41°N, 96°W) pp. R58–R59

Montana 41st state; capital: Helena (47°N, 112°W) p. 248

Montgomery City in Alabama (32°N, 86°W) p. R57

Montreal City in Quebec, Canada (46°N, 74°W) p. 48

Nagasaki City in Japan; severely damaged by atomic bomb in 1945 (33°N, 130°E) p. 380

Nauvoo, Illinois Starting point of Mormon Trail (40°N, 91°W) p. 116

Nebraska 37th state; capital: Lincoln (42°N, 102°W) p. 157

Netherlands Country in northwestern Europe; also called Holland (52°N, 6°E) p. R49

Nevada 36th state; capital: Carson City (40°N, 117°W) p. R56

New Hampshire 9th state; capital: Concord (44°N, 72°W) p. R57

New Jersey 3rd state; capital: Trenton (41°N, 75°W) p. R57

New Mexico 47th state; capital: Santa Fe (35°N, 107°W) p. R56

New Orleans City in Louisiana (30°N, 90°W) p. R57

New York 11th state; capital: Albany (43°N, 78°W) p. R57

New York City Large city in New York State (41°N, 74°W) p. 20

North America Northern continent of Western Hemisphere (45°N, 100°W) p. R48

North Carolina 12th state; capital: Raleigh (36°N, 82°W) p. 56

North Dakota 39th state; capital: Bismarck (46°N, 100°W) p. 18

North Korea Country in northeast Asia; capital: Pyongyang (39°N, 125°E) p. 392

Ohio 17th state; capital: Columbus (41°N, 83°W) p. R57

Ohio River Flows from Pennsylvania to the Mississippi River (37°N, 88°W) p. 98

Ohio River Valley Farming region west of the Appalachian Mountains (37°N, 88°W) p. 41

Gazetteer

Oklahoma 46th state; capital: Oklahoma City (36°N, 98°W) pp. R56–R57

Omaha Large city in Nebraska (41°N, 96°W) p. R57

Oregon 33rd state; capital: Salem (44°N, 122°W) p. R56

Oregon Territory Area from Rocky Mountains to Pacific Ocean (45°N, 120°W) p. 116

Pacific Ocean Largest ocean; west of the United States (0°, 170°W) p. R50

Panama Country in Central America (9°N, 80°W) p. 300

Panama Canal Canal across Isthmus of Panama, connecting the Caribbean Sea with the Pacific Ocean; completed 1914 (9°N, 80°W) p. 300

Pearl Harbor United States naval base; attacked by Japan (21°N, 158°W) p. 362

Pennsylvania 2nd state; capital: Harrisburg (41°N, 78°W) p. 55

Peru Country on the Pacific coast of South America (10°S, 75°W) p. R52

Philadelphia Large port city in Pennsylvania (40°N, 75°W) p. R57

Philippines Island country southeast of Asia (14°N, 125°E) p. 298

Pittsburgh Manufacturing city in Pennsylvania (40°N, 80°W) p. R57

Plymouth In Massachusetts; site of first Pilgrim settlement (42°N, 71°W) p. 53

Portugal Country in western Europe; capital: Lisbon (38°N, 8°W) p. 38

Promontory Point The place in Utah where the two halves of the Transcontinental Railroad met in 1869 (41°N, 112°W) p. 224

Puerto Rico A U.S. territory in the Caribbean; capital: San Juan (18°N, 67°W) p. 40

Quebec Province of Canada; capital: Quebec City (47°N, 71°W) p. 48

Rhode Island 13th state; capital: Providence (42°N, 72°W) p. R57

Richmond Capital city of Virginia; also was Confederate capital (38°N, 78°W) p. 75

Rio Grande River forming part of the Texas-Mexico border (26°N, 97°W) p. 115

Roanoke Island Island off the coast of North Carolina; site of first English colony in the Americas (37°N, 80°W) p. 48

Rocky Mountains Mountain range in the western United States (50°N, 114°W) p. R58

Russia Formerly part of the Soviet Union; capital: Moscow (61°N, 60°E) p. 304

Sacramento Capital of California (39°N, 122°W) p. 116

Sahara Large desert in northern Africa (20°N, 10°E) p. 376

St. Augustine, Florida Oldest European-founded city in U.S. (30°N, 81°W) p. 48

St. Lawrence River Links the Great Lakes to the Atlantic Ocean (49°N, 67°W) p. R59

St. Louis City in Missouri; on Mississippi River (39°N, 90°W) p. R57

Salem An early English settlement in Massachusetts (43°N, 71°W) p. 48

Salt Lake City Capital of Utah (40°N, 112°W) p. 116

San Francisco A major port city in California (38°N, 122°W) p. 20

San Salvador Caribbean island where Columbus landed (24°N, 74°W) p. 38

Santa Fe Capital of New Mexico (35°N, 106°W) p. 48

Saratoga New York site of an important American victory against the British in 1777 (43°N, 75°W) p. 80

Savannah Oldest city in Georgia (32°N, 81°W) p. 75

Seattle Large city in Washington State (48°N, 122°W) p. R56

Selma City of central Alabama; site of 1965 voter registration drive (32°N, 87°W) p. 410

Sierra Madre A system of mountain ranges in Mexico (27°N, 104°W) pp. R54–R55

Sierra Nevada Mountain range mainly in eastern California (39°N, 120°W) p. R58

South America Southern continent of Western Hemisphere (10°S, 60°W) p. R48

South Carolina 8th state; capital: Columbia (34°N, 81°W) p. 56

South Dakota 40th state; capital: Pierre (44°N, 100°W) p. 248

South Korea Country in eastern Asia on Korean peninsula; capital: Seoul (37°N, 127°E) p. 392

Soviet Union Large Communist country that split into separate republics in 1991; capital city: Moscow (61°N, 64°E) p. 314

Spain Country in Western Europe; capital: Madrid (40°N, 5°W) p. R49

Tennessee 16th state; capital: Nashville (36°N, 88°W) p. R57

Tenochtitlán Aztec city; present-day Mexico City (19°N, 99°W) p. 46

Texas 28th state; capital: Austin (31°N, 101°W) pp. R56–R57

Topeka Capital of Kansas (39°N, 95°W) p. 407

Trenton Capital of New Jersey (40°N, 75°W) p. R57

Tucson City in Arizona (32°N, 111°W) p. R56

United Kingdom England, Scotland, and Wales (57°N, 2°W) p. R49

United States Country in central and northwest North America (38°N, 110°W) pp. R56–R57

Utah 45th state; capital: Salt Lake City (40°N, 112°W) p. 54

Valley Forge George Washington's winter camp in 1777; near Philadelphia (40°N, 75°W) p. 118

Vandalia, Illinois Ending point of National Road (39°N, 89°W) p. 108

Vermont 14th state; capital: Montpelier (44°N, 72°W) p. 21

Vicksburg, Mississippi Site of Civil War battle (32°N, 91°W) p. 178

Vietnam Country in southeast Asia (18°N, 107°E) p. 423

Virginia 10th state; capital: Richmond (37°N, 81°W) p. R57

Washington 42nd state; capital: Olympia (48°N, 121°W) p. R56

Washington, D.C. Capital of the U.S. (39°N, 77°W) p. R57

West Indies Islands separating the Caribbean Sea and the Atlantic (19°N, 79°W) p. 40

West Virginia 35th state; capital: Charleston (38°N, 81°W) p. R57

Wisconsin 30th state; capital: Madison (40°N, 89°W) p. R57

Wyoming 44th state; capital: Cheyenne (43°N, 109°W) p. R56

Yorktown In Virginia; site of last major battle of Revolutionary War (37°N, 77°W) p. 81

Glossary

A

abolitionist (ab uh LIH shuhn ist) someone who joined the movement to abolish, or end, slavery. (p. 148)

accord (uh KAWRD) an agreement. (p. 444)

agriculture (AG rih kuhl chur) farming, or growing plants. (p. 31)

aircraft carrier (AYR kraft KAR ee ur) a large ship that carries airplanes far from land. The ship is so large that the planes can take off from and land on the deck. (p. 378)

alliance (uh LY uhns) an agreement nations make to support and defend each other. (p. 304)

annexation (an ihk SAY shuhn) the act of joining two countries or pieces of land together. (p. 122)

anti-communism (an tee CAHM uh nihz uhm) a movement to stop the spread of communist ideas. (p. 391)

Antifederalist (an tee FEHD ur uh lihst) someone who opposed the new Constitution. (p. 89)

armistice (AHR mih stihs) an agreement to stop fighting. (p. 314)

arms race (ahrms rays) a contest between nations to build more powerful weapons. (p. 391)

assassination (uh SAS uh nay shuhn) the murder of an important leader. (p. 197)

assembly line (uh SEHM blee lyn) a line of workers and equipment that puts a product together piece by piece. (p. 323)

assimilate (uh SIHM uh layt) to change a group's culture and traditions so that it blends with a larger group. (p. 250)

atomic bomb (uh TAHM ihk bahm) a powerful bomb that can destroy an entire city. (p. 380)

aviator (AY vee ay tur) a person who flies an airplane. (p. 332)

B

baby boom (BAY bee boom) the increase in the number of babies born after World War II. (p. 402)

bar graph (bahr graf) a graph that compares amounts of things. (p. 146)

barbed wire (bahrbd wyr) twisted wire with a sharp barb, or point, every few inches. (p. 241)

boom (boom) a period of fast economic growth. (p. 322)

boomtown (BOOM toun) a town whose population booms, or grows very quickly. (p. 125)

border state (BOHR dur stayt) a slave state that stayed in the Union. (p. 176)

boycott (BOI kaht) the refusal to buy, sell, or use certain goods. (p. 71)

broadcast (BRAHD kast) a program sent out over a radio or television station. (p. 331)

C

camp (kamp) a place where people live for a time in tents, cabins, or other rough shelters. (p. 184)

canal (kuh NAL) a waterway built for boat travel and shipping. (p. 116)

capital resource (KAP ih tuhl REE sawrs) a tool, machine, or building that people use to produce goods and services. (p. 8)

capitalism (KAP ih tuhl ihz uhm) an economic system in which ordinary people and businesses control the production of goods and services. (p. 384)

cash crop (kash krahp) a crop that people grow and sell to earn money. (p. 51)

casualties (KAHZ oo uhl teez) soldiers who are killed or wounded. (p. 178)

category (KAT ih gohr ee) a group of similar things. (p. 428)

cease-fire (SEES fyr) an agreement to stop all fighting. (p. 425)

charity (CHAR ih tee) an organization that helps people in need. (p. 338)

circle graph (SUR kuhl graf) a graph that illustrates how a part compares with the whole. (p. 146)

civil rights (SIHV uhl ryts) the rights that countries guarantee their citizens. (p. 406)

civil war (SIHV uhl wawr) a war between two groups or regions within a nation. (p. 169)

civilian (sih VIHL yuhn) a person who is not in the military. (p. 186)

coalition (koh uh LIHSH uhn) a group of allies that work together to achieve a goal. (p. 451)

Cold War (kohld wawr) a war of words and ideas. (p. 384)

colony (KAHL uh nee) a territory ruled by another country. (p. 45)

Columbian Exchange (kuh LUHM bee uhn ihks CHAYNJ) the movement of goods across the Atlantic Ocean after Columbus's first trip to the Americas. (p. 39)

communism (KAHM yuh nihz uhm) an economic system in which the government controls production and owns the nation's natural and capital resources. (p. 385)

compass rose (KUHM puhs rohz) a part of a map that shows the cardinal and intermediate directions. (p. 13)

competition (kahm puh TIHSH uhn) what occurs when more than one business tries to sell the same goods or service. (p. 261)

compromise (KAHM pruh myz) a settlement in which both sides give up something they want. (p. 87)

concentration camp (kahn suhn TRAY shuhn kamp) a place where large numbers of people are held prisoner and forced to work. (p. 380)

conclusion (kuhn KLOO zhuhn) a judgment or decision based on facts and ideas. (p. 120)

Confederacy (kuhn FEHD ur uh see) the name chosen by the states that left the Union at the time of the Civil War. (p. 168)

confederation (kuhn fehd ur AY shun) a type of government in which separate groups of people join together, but local leaders still make most decisions for their group. (p. 84)

conflict (KAHN flihkt) a disagreement. (p. 482)

congress (KAHNG grihs) a group of representatives who meet to discuss a subject. (p. 72)

consequence (KAHN sih kwehns) something that is a result of a decision or an action. (p. 82)

conservation (kahn sur VAY shuhn) the protection and wise use of natural resources. (p. 23)

convert (kuhn VURT) to convince someone to change his or her religion or beliefs. (p. 45)

corporation (kawr puh RAY shuhn) a business in which many people own shares, or parts, of the business. (p. 260)

corps (kawr) a team of people who work together. (p. 108)

cotton gin (KAHT n jihn) a machine that used wire teeth to clean seeds from cotton. (p. 115)

Cuban missile crisis (KYOO buhn MIHS uhl KRY sihs) a conflict during which the United States ordered the Soviet Union to remove missiles from Cuba. (p. 393)

culture (KUHL chur) the way of life that people create for themselves and pass on to their descendants. (p. 31)

debt (deht) money that one person owes another. (p. 337)

deficit (DEHF ih siht) a shortage. (p. 449)

delegate (DEHL ih giht) someone chosen to speak and act for others. (p. 86)

demand (dih MAND) the amount of something that people want to buy at certain prices. (p. 239)

demonstration (dehm uhn STRAY shuhn) a gathering of people who want to express their opinion to the public and the government. (p. 424)

depression (dih PREHSH uhn) a period when many people can't find work and many others have no money to keep businesses going. (p. 337)

deregulation (dee rehg yuh LAY shuhn) the removal of rules. (p. 449)

desegregation (dih SEGH rih GAY shuhn) ending the separation of people by racial or ethnic group. (p. 407)

desert (dih ZURT) to leave the army without permission. (p. 192)

dictator (DIHK tay tur) a ruler who has total power over a country and its people. (p. 360)

discrimination (dih skrihm uh NAY shuhn) the unfair treatment of particular groups. (p. 149)

division of labor (dih VIHZH uhn uhv LAY bur) when workers perform different parts of a large task. (p. 323)

doctrine (DAHK trihn) an official statement or position. (p. 110)

draft (draft) government selection of people to serve in the military. (p. 179)

drought (drout) a long period with little or no rain. (p. 233)

economic system (ehk uh NAHM ihk SIHS tuhm) a set of rules that influences the way a country uses its resources and produces goods. (p. 9)

ecosystem (EH koh sihs tuhm) a community of plants and animals, along with the surrounding soil, air, and water. (p. 23)

editorial (ehd ih TOHR ee uhl) a piece of writing that presents an opinion about an issue or event. (p. 368)

Electoral College (ih LEHK tur uhl KAH luhdj) representatives from each state who vote for the President. (p. 465)

emancipation (ih MAN suh pay shuhn) the freeing of enslaved people. (p. 180)

empire (EHM pyr) many nations or territories ruled by a single group or leader. (p. 44)

entrepreneur (ahn truh pruh NUR) a person who takes risks to start a business. (p. 114)

environment (ehn VY ruhn muhnt) the surroundings in which people, plants, and animals live. (p. 21)

ethnic group (EHTH nihk groop) a group of people who share a language or culture. (p. 268)

Exoduster (EHK suh duhs tur) an African American settler who called him or herself after Exodus, a book of the Bible. (p. 232)

expedition (ehk spih DIHSH uhn) a journey to achieve a goal. (p. 37)

extinct (ihk STIHNGT) when a certain type of plant or animal is no longer living. (p. 249)

fact (fakt) a piece of information that can be proved. (p. 284)

fascism (FASH ihz uhm) a system in which the government controls the economy, culture, and all other parts of people's lives. (p. 360)

federal (FEHD ur uhl) a system in which the states share power with the central government. (p. 86)

Federalist (FEHD ur uh lihst) a supporter of the Constitution. (p. 89)

forty-niner (FAHR tee NY nur) a miner who went to California in 1849. (p. 125)

free state (free stayt) a state that did not have slavery. (p. 156)

Freedmen's Bureau (FREED mehnz BYOOR oh) an organization that provided food, clothing, medical care, and legal advice to poor blacks and whites. (p. 198)

free-trade agreement (free TRAYD uh GREE muhnt) a treaty among countries that trade with each other. (p. 461)

frontier (FRUHN teer) the edge of a country or settled region. (p. 107)

fugitive (FYOO jih tihv) a person who is running away. (p. 158)

generation (jehn uh RAY shuhn) a group of people born and living at about the same time. (p. 416)

gold rush (gohld ruhsh) a movement of many people hurrying to the same area to look for gold. (p. 124)

habitat (HA buh tat) the area where an animal or a plant normally lives or grows. (p. 249)

heritage (HEHR ih tihj) something that is passed down from one generation to the next. (p. 487)

high-tech (hy TEHK) the most recent knowledge and equipment. (p. 458)

historical map (hih STOHR ih kuhl map) a map that shows information about places and events in the past. (p. 12)

home front (hohm fruhnt) all the people in a country who are not in the military during wartime. (p. 186)

homestead (HOHM stehd) a settler's home and land. (p. 231)

House of Burgesses (hous uhv BUR jihs iz) the first representative government in the English colonies. (p. 55)

human resources (HYOO muhn REE sohrs uhz) people and the skills and knowledge they bring to their work. (p. 8)

hydroelectricity (hy droh ih lehk TRIHS ih tee) electricity produced by moving water. (p. 346)

impeach (ihm PEECH) to charge a government official with a crime. (p. 199)

imperialism (ihm PIHR ee uh lihz uhm) the building of empires by adding colonies. (p. 298)

independence (ihn duh PEHN duhns) freedom from being ruled by someone else. (p. 73)

Indian Removal Act (IHN dee uhn ree MOO vuhl akt) a law ordering American Indians of all nations east of the Mississippi River to move west. (p. 111)

indigo (IHN duh goh) a plant that can be made into a dark blue dye. (p. 54)

Industrial Revolution (ihn DUHS tree uhl rehv uh LOO shuhn) a time marked by changes in manufacturing and transportation. (p. 114)

inset map (IHN seht map) a small map within a larger one that may show a close-up of an area or provide other information about it. (p. 12)

interchangeable parts (ihn tur CHAYN juh buhl pahrts) parts made by a machine to be exactly the same in size and shape. (p. 115)

interdependent (ihn tuhr dee PEHN duhnt) depending, or relying, on each other. (p. 17)

International Date Line (ihn tur NASH uh nuhl dayt lyn) an imaginary line that marks where the date changes. (p. 229)

Internet (IHN tuhr neht) a system that links computers around the world with each other. (p. 458)

internment camp (ihn TURN muhnt kamp) a place where prisoners are held during wartime. (p. 372)

interpreter (ihn TUR prih tur) someone who helps speakers of different languages understand each other. (p. 108)

Iron Curtain (EYE urn KUR tn) a symbol of the differences dividing communist and non-communist countries in Europe. (p. 385)

isolationism (eye suh LAY shuh nihz uhm) the belief that the United States should stay out of world events. (p. 315)

isthmus (IHS muhs) a narrow strip of land that links two larger pieces of land. It has water on both sides. (p. 300)

jazz (jaz) an American form of music that was started by African American musicians. (p. 330)

Jim Crow (jihm kroh) laws that segregated African Americans from other Americans. (p. 208)

labor union (LAY bur YOON yuhn) an organization of workers that tries to improve pay and working conditions for its members. (p. 262)

line graph (lyn graf) a graph that shows change over time. (p. 146)

Loyalist (LOI uh lihst) someone who was still loyal to the king. (p. 76)

map legend (map LEHJ uhnd) a part of a map that explains any symbols or colors on a map. (pp. 13, 454)

map scale (map skayl) a part of a map that compares distance on a map to distance in the real world. (p. 13)

maquiladora (mah kee lah DOH rah) a factory in Mexico near the U.S. border. (p. 478)

market economy (MAHR kiht ih KAHN uh mee) an economic system in which people and businesses make most economic decisions. (p. 384)

mass production (mas pruh DUHK shuhn) making many identical products at once. (p. 115)

Mayflower Compact (MAY flow ur KAHM pakt) the first written plan for self-government in North America. (p. 55)

merchant (MUR chunt) someone who buys and sells goods to earn money. (p. 36)

migrant worker (MY gruhnt WUR kuhr) a person who moves from place to place to find work, mostly on farms. (p. 443)

migration (my GRAY shuhn) a movement from one region to another. (p. 30)

militarism (MIHL ih tuh rihz uhm) the building of a strong military to frighten or defeat other countries. (p. 304)

millennium (muh LEHN ee uhm) a period of 10 centuries, or 1,000 years. (p. 464)

minimum wage (MIHN ih muhm waj) the least amount a worker in most types of jobs can legally be paid. (p. 346)

mission (MIHSH uhn) a religious community where priests taught Christianity. (p. 45)

mobilize (MOH buh lyz) to get ready to fight. (p. 370)

monopoly (muh NAHP uh lee) a company that has no competition. (p. 261)

Monroe Doctrine (MUHN roh DAHK trihn) a warning from President James Monroe to European nations not to start new colonies in the Americas. (p. 110)

motto (MAHT oh) a short statement that explains an ideal or a goal. (p. 487)

muckraker (MUHK rayk ur) someone who "rakes up," or points out, unpleasant truths. (p. 279)

multicultural (muhl tee KUHL chuhr uhl) having many cultural traditions. (p. 475)

nationalism (NASH uh nuh lihz uhm) devotion to one's country. (p. 304)

natural resource (NACH ur uhl REE sawrs) a material from nature, such as soil or water, that people use. (p. 7)

naturalization (nach ur uh lihz AY shuhn) the process of becoming a citizen by learning the laws of the country and the rights and duties of its citizens. (p. 490)

navigation (nav ih GAY shuhn) the science of planning and controlling the direction of a ship. (p. 37)

neutral (NOO truhl) not to take sides. (p. 76)

news article (nooz AHR tih kuhl) a piece of writing that describes a recent event. (p. 368)

newsreel (NOOZ reel) a short film about current events. (p. 372)

nonrenewable resource (nahn ree NOO uh buhl REE sowrs) a natural resource that cannot be replaced once it is used, such as oil. (p. 7)

nonviolent protest (nahn VY uh luhnt PROH test) a way of bringing change without using violence. (p. 407)

nuclear war (NOO klee ur wahr) a war in which powerful nuclear weapons are used. (p. 391)

opinion (uh PIHN yuhn) a personal belief. It expresses someone's thoughts or feelings and cannot be proved. (p. 284)

opportunity cost (ahp ur TOO nih tee kahst) the thing you give up when you decide to do or have something else. (p. 9)

overthrow (oh vur THROH) to remove from power. (p. 422)

Parliament (PAHR luh muhnt) the government that makes the laws in Britain. (p. 70)

Patriot (PAY tree uht) a colonist who opposed British rule. (p. 76)

persecution (pur sih KYOO shuhn) unfair treatment or punishment. (p. 266)

physical map (FIHZ ih cuhl map) a map that shows the location of physical features, such as landforms, bodies of water, or resources. (p. 12)

pioneer (py uh NEER) one of the first of a group of people to enter or settle a region. (p. 107)

plantation (plan TAY shuhn) a large farm on which crops are raised by workers who live on the farm. (p. 54)

point of view (poynt uhv vyoo) the way someone thinks about an issue, an event, or a person. (p. 310)

political map (puh LIHT ih kuhl map) a map that shows cities, states, and countries. (p. 12)

pollution (puh LOO shuhn) anything that makes the soil, air, or water dirty and unhealthy. (p. 22)

popular sovereignty (PAHP yuh luhr SAHV uhr ihn tee) an idea that the people who live in a place make decisions for themselves. (p. 157)

popular vote (PAHP yuh luhr voht) the vote of individual citizens. (p. 465)

prejudice (PREHJ uh dihs) an unfair, negative opinion that can lead to unjust treatment. (p. 224)

population map (pahp yuh LAY shuhn map) a map that shows where people live. (p. 342)

primary source (PRY mehr ee sawrs) firsthand information about an event, a place, or a time period. (p. 204)

productivity (proh duhk TIHV ih tee) the amount of goods and services produced by workers in a certain amount of time. (p. 115)

profit (PRAHF iht) the money a business has left over after all expenses have been paid. (p. 36)

progressives (pruh GREHS ihvs) reformers who think governments should make laws to protect workers, consumers, and citizens' rights. (p. 278)

prohibition (proh uh BIHSH uhn) the act of forbidding something. (p. 333)

propaganda (prahp uh GAN duh) information that is used to shape people's thinking. (p. 313)

proprietor (pruh PRY ih tur) a person who owned and controlled all the land of a colony. (p. 53)

prosperity (prah SPEHR ih tee) economic success and security. (p. 401)

province (PRAHV ihns) a political region of a country that is similar to a state. (p. 474)

Puritan (PYUR ih tn) someone who wanted to change, and purify, the Church of England. (p. 51)

racism (RAY sihz um) the idea that one race, or group of people, is better than other races. (p. 361)

railhead (RAYL hehd) a town where railroad tracks begin or end. (p. 239)

rapid transit (RAP ihd TRAN siht) a system of trains used to move people around cities. (p. 274)

ratify (RAT uh fy) to accept. (p. 88)

rations (RASH uhn) the limits on the amount of some goods civilians can have. (p. 313)

Reconstruction (ree kuhn STRUHK shuhn) the period when the South rejoined the Union. (p. 196)

refugee (REHF yoo jee) a person who escapes war or other danger and seeks safety in another country. (p. 484)

region (REE jehn) an area that has one or more features in common. (p. 14)

register (REHJ ih stur) to sign up. (p. 491)

regulation (rehg yuh LAY shuhn) a rule or law. (p. 346)

Renaissance (rehn ih SAHNS) a time when there is new interest in art, literature, music, and learning. (p. 330)

renewable resource (rih NOO uh buhl REE sawrs) a natural resource that can be replaced, such as wood. (p. 7)

repeal (rih PEEL) to cancel something, such as a law. (p. 333)

republic (rih PUHB lihk) a government in which the citizens elect leaders to represent them. (p. 122)

reservation (rehz ur VAY shuhn) land that the government set aside for American Indians. (p. 246)

resign (ree SYN) to quit one's job. (p. 441)

resource (REE sawrs) something people use to produce goods and services. (p. 7)

responsibility (rih sphahn suh BIHL ih tee) a duty that someone is expected to fulfill. (p. 492)

revolution (rehv uh LOO shuhn) an overthrow, or a forced change, of a government. (p. 72)

rights (ryts) freedoms that are protected by a government's laws. (p. 73)

scarcity (SKAIR sih tee) not having enough resources to provide all the things people want. (p. 9)

secession (sih SEHSH uhn) the withdrawal when a part of a country leaves or breaks off from the rest. (p. 164)

secondary source (SEHK uhn dehr ee sawrs) information from someone who did not witness an event. (p. 204)

sectionalism (SEHK shuh nuh lihz uhm) loyalty to one part of the country. (p. 143)

segregation (sehg rih GAY shuhn) the forced separation of the races. (p. 208)

self-government (sehlf GUHV urn muhnt) a government in which the people who live in a place make laws for themselves. (p. 55)

settlement house (SEHT uhl muhnt hous) a community center for people in cities. (p. 275)

sharecropping (SHAIR krahp ihng) a system in which landowners let poor farmers use small areas of their land, and in return, the farmers gave the landowners a share of the crop. (p. 207)

skyscraper (SKY skray pur) a very tall building. (p. 274)

slave state (slayv stayt) a state that permitted slavery. (p. 156)

slum (sluhm) a poor, crowded part of a city. (p. 274)

Social Security (SOO shehl sih KYOOR ih tee) a government program that provides money to people over the age of 65 and to those with disabilities. (p. 346)

sodbusters (SAHD buhs turz) name given to Great Plains farmers because they had to break through so much thick soil, called sod, in order to farm. (p. 234)

space race (spays rays) a competition between the United States and the Soviet Union to send people into outer space. (p. 415)

specialization (spehsh uh lih ZAY shuhn) when people make the goods they are best able to produce with the resources they have. (p. 16)

states' rights (stayts ryts) the idea that states, not the federal government, should make the final decisions about matters that affect them. (p. 143)

stock (stahk) a share of ownership in a company. (p. 324)

stock market (stahk MAHR kiht) the place where stocks are bought and sold. (p. 324)

stockyard (STAHK yahrd) a fenced area where large numbers of animals such as hogs and cattle are kept until they are used as food or moved to another place. (p. 273)

strike (stryk) the stopping of work by workers. (p. 262)

suffrage (SUHF rihj) the right to vote. (p. 110)

supply (suh PLY) the amount of something that people want to sell at certain prices. (p. 239)

tariff (TAR ihf) a tax on imported goods. (p. 142)

tax (taks) money that people pay to their government in return for services. (p. 70)

telegraph (TEHL ih graf) a machine that sends electric signals over wires. (p. 191)

tenement (TEHN uh muhnt) a rundown, poorly maintained apartment building. (p. 268)

terrorism (TEHR uh rihz uhm) the use of violence against ordinary people to achieve a political goal. (p. 466)

textile (TEHKS tyl) cloth or fabric. (p. 114)

timeline (tym lyn) a line that shows events in the order in which they happen. (p. 58)

time zone (tym zohn) a region that shares the same time. (p. 228)

tolerance (TAHL ur uhns) the respect for beliefs that are different from one's own. (p. 53)

total war (TOHT uhl wawr) the strategy of destroying an enemy's resources. (p. 191)

trade (trayd) the buying and selling of goods. (p. 16)

Trail of Tears (trayl uhv teers) the forced march of the Cherokee 1,000 miles west, during which many Cherokees died. (p. 111)

transcontinental (trans kahn tuh NEHN tuhl) crossing a continent. (p. 224)

treaty (TREE tee) an official agreement between nations or groups. (p. 79)

trench warfare (trehnch WAWR fair) a way of fighting in which soldiers fought from long narrow ditches, or trenches. (p. 305)

Underground Railroad (UHN dur ground RAYL rohd) a series of escape routes and hiding places to bring slaves out of the South. (p. 150)

unemployment (uhn ehm PLOI muhnt) the number of people without a job. (p. 337)

Union (YOON yuhn) another name for the United States. (p. 157)

United Nations (yoo NY tihd NAY shuhnz) an international organization of the United States and other countries. (p. 392)

vaccine (vak SEEN) a medicine to protect people against a disease. (p. 403)

veteran (VEHT ur uhn) someone who has served in the military. (p. 402)

volunteer (vahl uhn TEER) someone who helps other people without being paid. (p. 492)

wagon train (WAG uhn trayn) a line of covered wagons that moved together. (p. 124)

welfare (WEHL fayr) a government program that helps people in need. (p. 416)

wetland (WEHT land) a moist area such as a swamp or marsh that provides a home for wildlife. (p. 22)

yellow journalism (YEH loh JUR nuh lihz uhm) a kind of writing that exaggerates news to shock and attract readers. (p. 299)

Index

Page numbers with *m* after them refer to maps. Page numbers that are italicized refer to pictures.

Index

Acknowledgments

Permissioned Literature Selections

"Dream Variation," from The Collected Poems of Langston Hughes, by Langston Hughes. Copyright © 1994 by The Estate of Langston Hughes. Used by permission of Alfred A. Knopf, a division of Random House, Inc. and Harold Ober Associates Incorporated. Excerpt from First In Peace: George Washington, the Constitution, and the Presidency, by John Rosenburg. Copyright © 1998 by John Rosenburg. Reprinted by permission of The Millbrook Press, Inc. "Green Card Fever" from We The People, by Bobbi Katz. Text copyright © 2000 by Bobbi Katz. Used by permission of HarperCollins Publishers. Excerpt from the Speech, "I Have a Dream," by Dr. Martin Luther King Jr. Copyright © 1963 by Dr. Martin Luther King Jr., copyright renewed © 1991 by Coretta Scott King. Reprinted by arrangement with the Estate of Martin Luther King Jr., c/o Writers House as agent for the proprietor New York, NY. Excerpt from In the Days of the Vaqueros: America's First True Cowboys, by Russell Freedman. Text copyright © 2001 by Russell Freedman. Reprinted by permission of Houghton Mifflin Company. Excerpt from "Juan Ponce de Leon," from Around the World In A Hundred Years: From Henry The Navigator To Magellan, by Jean Fritz. Text copyright © 1994 by Jean Frtiz. Used by permission of G.P. Putnam's Sons, a division of Penguin Young Readers Group, a member of Penguin Group (USA) Inc., 345 Hudson Street, New York, New York, NY 10014. All rights reserved. Excerpt from Remember Me, by Irene N. Watts, published by Tundra Books of Northern New York. Copyright © 2000 by Irene N. Watts. Permission to reproduce work must be sought from originating publisher. Reprinted by permission. "Speak Up," from Good Luck Gold and Other Poems, by Janet S. Wong. Copyright © 1994 by Janet S. Wong. Reprinted with the permission of Margaret K. McElderry Books, an imprint of Simon & Schuster Children's Publishing Division. All rights reserved. Excerpt from Stealing Freedom, by Elisa Carbone. Text copyright © 1998 by Elisa Carbone. Reprinted by arrangement with Random House Children's Boosk, a division of Random House, Inc., New York, New York.

Photo Credits

COVER (Lincoln Memorial)© Dennis Brack. (capital)© Royalty Free/CORBIS. (map)© Granger Collection, New York. (compass) HMCo./Michael Indresano. (spine Lincoln memorial)© Peter Gridley/Getty Images. (backcover statue) © Connie Ricca/CORBIS. (backcover nickel) Courtesy of the United States Mint.

v (bkgd) Photodisc/Getty Images. vi (t) Alan Kearny/Getty Images. (b) The Art Archive/National Anthropological Museum Mexico/Dagli Orti. vii (t) (detail) Courtesy of the Trustees of the Boston Public Library: George Washington at Dorchester Heights, by Emmanuel Luetze. (b) The Granger Collection, New York. viii (t) Courtesy Don Troiani, Historical Miltary Image Bank. (b) Bettmann/CORBIS. ix (t) ©D. Robert & Lorri Franz/CORBIS. (b) Brown Brothers. x (t) © Bettmann/CORBIS. (b) ©Rick Souders/Index Stock Imagery. xi (t) © Courtesy Don Troiani, Historical Miltary Image Bank (b) Francis Miller/Time Life Pictures/Getty Images. xii (t) Mario Tama/Getty Images. xiii © Paul A. Souders/CORBIS. 0 (t) Musee National de la Renaissance, Ecouen, France/Bridgeman Art Library. (b) © Archivo Iconografico, S.A./CORBIS. 1 (tl) National Museum of Fine Arts, Madrid. (tr) The Granger Collection, New York. (bl) Granada Cathedral Photo: Oronoz (br) Photodisc/Getty Images. 2 (l) ©Giraudon/Art Resource, NY. (m) Time Life Pictures/Getty Images. (r) ©Archive Iconografica, S.A./CORBIS. 3 (l) North Wind Picture Archives.(r) Photodisc/Getty Images. 4 (l) ©Marc Muench. (r) ©Annie Griffiths Belt/CORBIS. 5 (r) ©David Muench. 6–7 ©Marc

Muench. 10–1 Courtesy Cannondale Bicycle Corporation. 11 (t) Culver Pictures. 14 Grant Heilman/Grant Heilman Photography, Inc. 16 (l) Courtesy Alabama Marble Company, Fayetville, Alabama. (r) Stephen St. John/Getty Images. 17 © Annie Griffiths Belt/CORBIS. 18–9 Graphics by Melvin L. Prueitt, Los Alamos, New Mexico. 20 Mark Segal/Panoramic Images, Chicago. 21 ©W.T. Sullivan III/Science Photo Library/Photo Researchers, Inc. 22 Tennessee Valley Authority. 28 (l) Wood Ronsaville Harlin, Inc. (r) Bibliotheque Nationale, Paris, France/Bridgeman Art Library. 29 (l) ©Archivo Iconografico, S.A./CORBIS. (r) The Granger Collection, New York. 33 Cincinatti Art Museum, Gift of General M. F. Force, Photo: T. Walsh. 36–7 Time Life Pictures/Getty Images. 36 ©Reunion des Musees Nationaux/Art Resource, NY. 41 ©North Wind Picture Archives. 44 ©Archivo Iconografico, S.A./CORBIS. 45 ©Jerry Jacka. 48 (l) ©Archive Iconografico, S.A./CORBIS. (r) ©North Wind Picture Archives. 48–49 ©DigitalVision/Picture Quest. 49 (t) ©North Wind Picture Archives. (b) ©North Wind Picture Archives. 50 © North Wind Picture Archives. 51 © Brownie Harris. 52–3 American Philosophical Society Library. 54 Metropolitan Museum of Art, Gift of Edgar William and Bernice Chrysler Garbisch, 1963 (63.201.3) Photograph © 1984 The Metropolitan Museum of Art. 56–57 Colonial Williamsburg Foundation. 56 (b) © Farrell Grehan/CORBIS. 64 (t) The Granger Collection, New York. (b) Smithsonian Institution, National Numismatic Collection, Douglas Mudd. 65 (tl)© Massachusetts Historical Society, Boston, MA, USA/Bridgeman Art Library. (tr)©Bettmann/CORBIS. (bl) Photodisc/Getty Images (digital composite). 66 (l) Independence National Historical Park. (m) ©Private Collection/Art Resource, NY. (r) Monticello/Thomas Jefferson Foundation, Inc. 67 (t) Andrea Pistolesi/Getty Images. (b) Dave Bartruff/Corbis/MAGMA. 68 (l) ©Bettmann/CORBIS. (r) The Granger Collection, New York. 69 (l) ©Bettmann/CORBIS. (r) ©North Wind Picture Archives. 71 Library of Congress. 73 Independence National Historical Park (detail). 74 (t) Independence National Historical Park. (bl) © Royalty-Free/CORBIS. (bm) © Ted Spiegel/CORBIS. (br) Monticello/Thomas Jefferson Foundation, Inc. 75 (t) Library of Congress. (b) National Museum of American History, Smithsonian Institution, Behring Center, Neg # 83-4689. 76 Fenimore Art Museum, Cooperstown, New York. Photo: Richard Walker. 77 (t) ©Bettmann/CORBIS. (b) (detail) The Metropolitan Museum of Art, Gift of John. Stewart Kennedy, 1897 (97.34) Photograph ©1992 The Metropolitan Museum of Art. 78 (t) The Granger Collection, New York. (b) New York Historical Society/Bridgeman Art Library. 79 The Granger Collection, New York. 84 (l) American Numismatic Society, 0000.999.29464. (r) The Granger Collection, New York. 85 The Granger Collection, New York. 86 Courtesy of National Constitution Center (Scott Frances, Ltd.) 87 AP/Wide World Photos. 91 ©The Corcoran Gallery of Art/CORBIS. 93 Painting by Hy Hintermeister, Photo: SuperStock. 96–7 Photodisc/Getty Images. 99 (t) Peter Gridley/Getty Images. (m) Andrea Pistolesi/Getty Images. (b) Photodisc/Getty Images. 100 (b) © Dennis Brack/Black Star Publishing/PictureQuest. 101 (b) © SW Productions/Brand X Pictures/PictureQuest. (br)Photodisc/Getty Images. 104 The Granger Collection, New York. 105 (l) Oldest known Lone Star Flag, Republic period. Collection of the Star of the Republic Museum. Gift of L. Cletus Brown, Jr. (r) Denver Public Library, Western History Collection. 106–7 Mark Segal/Panoramic Images/NGSImages.com. 107 (t) from the collection of Gilcrease Museum, Tulsa, Oklahoma. 108 (t) ©Giraudon/Art Resource, NY. (b) ©Burstein Collection/CORBIS. 109 (l) John Ford Clymer,'In the Bitteroots', Courtesy Mrs. John F. Clymer and The Clymer Museum. 110 ©Smithsonian American Art Museum,

Washington, DC/Art Resource, NY. 112 (l) © John Warden/SuperStock. (r) Jack Olson. 113 (l) © Shan Cunningham. (r) Jack Olson. 115 The Granger Collection, New York. 117 ©North Wind Picture Archives. 118–9 Eastern National. 120 Library of Congress, LC-USZC4-5940. 122 Oldest known Lone Star Flag, Republic period. Collection of the Star of the Republic Museum. Gift of L. Cletus Brown, Jr. 123 ©Steve Vidler/SuperStock. 125 Denver Public Library, Western History Collection. 134 (t) ©CORBIS. 135 (tl) Library of Congress, LCUSZ62-984. (tr) Library of Congress. (bl) National Museum of American History, Smithsonian Institution, Behring Center, Neg # 95-5528. (br) Photodisc/Getty Images. 136 © National Portrait Gallery, Smithsonian Institution/Art Resource, NY. (m) The Granger Collection, New York. (r) ©Scala/Art Resource, NY. 137 © Getty Images. 138 (l) © National Portrait Gallery, Smithsonian Institution/Art Resource, NY. (r) © Bettman/CORBIS. 139 (l) Picture Research Consultants, Inc. (r) The Granger Collection, New York. 140–1 Private Collection/Bridgeman Art Library. 142 The Granger Collection, New York. 143 ©National Portrait Gallery, Smithsonian Institution/Art Resource, NY. (frame) Image Farm. 145 ©Burke/Triolo/Brand X Pictures/PictureQuest. 148 South Carolina Confederate Relic Room and Museum. 149 (l) © National Portrait Gallery, Smithsonian Institution/Art Resource, NY. (m) ©National Portrait Gallery, Smithsonian Institution/Art Resource, NY. (r) ©Bettman/CORBIS. 151 ©Bettman/CORBIS. 156 The Granger Collection, New York. 158 (tl) Picture Research Consultants, Inc. (tr) Schlesinger Library, Radcliffe Institute, Harvard University. (b) The Granger Collection, New York. 159 The Granger Collection, New York. 164 ©Bettman/CORBIS. 165 (t) D. Muench/Robertstock.com. (b) Library of Congress. 166–7 State Historical Society of Illinois, Chicago, IL, USA/Bridgeman Art Library. 167 (t) Courtesy PictureHistory (digital composite). (b) Stanley King Collection .168 National Archives. 169 ©Scala/Art Resource, NY. 174 (l) Library of Congress, USZCN4- 49, G01231.(r) © Medford Historical Society Collection/CORBIS. 175 (l) Electricity Collection, NMAH, Smithsonian Institution, Neg # 74-2491. (r) Brown Brothers. 176 Cook Collection, Valentine Museum. 180 Library of Congress, USZCN4- 49, G01231. 181 Gettysburg National Military Park. 182 The Granger Collection, New York. 184 The Granger Collection, New York. 185 (l) Library of Congress. (r) Paragon Light, Inc. 186 The Granger Collection, New York. 187 Larry Kolvoord/The Image Works. 188 National Archives. 189 (t) The Granger Collection, New York. (b) © Private Collection /Art Resource, NY. 190 Library of Congress. 191 National Archives, 77-F-194-6-56. 192 (l) Tom Lovell/National Geographic. (r) National Museum of American History, Smithsonian Institution, Neg # 95-5515-7. 194 (l) Fort Loreto Museum, Puebla. (r) Electricity Collection, NMAH, Smithsonian Institution, Neg # 74-2491. 195 (tl) The Granger Collection, New York. (tr) Hulton Archive/Getty Images. (bl) The Granger Collection, New York. (br) ©Polak Matthew/CORBIS SYGMA. 196 The Meserve Collection/New-York Historical Society. 197 (l) Courtesy of the New York Historical Society, NYC. (r) New York Historical Society/Bridgeman Art Library. 201 ©CORBIS. (frame) Image Farm. 202 (t) © Medford Historical Society Collection/CORBIS. 202–3 Courtesy of the Charleston Museum, Charleston, South Carolina. 206-7 Brown Brothers. 208 (l) The Granger Collection, New York. (r) ©Dhimitri/Folio Inc. 209 Brown Brothers. 210 ©CORBIS. 210–11 ©CORBIS. 216 (t) ©National Portrait Gallery, Smithsonian Institution/Art Resource, NY. (b) Courtesy, National Museum of the American Indian, Smithsonian Institution, S01810. Photo by Carmelo Guadagno. 217 (tl) AP Wide World Photos. (tr) ©Bettman/CORBIS. (bl) Photodisc/Getty Images. (br) Houghton Mifflin wishes to thank the Crisis Publishing Co., Inc., the publisher of the magazine of the National Association for the Advancement of Colored People, for the use of this material first published in the December 1980 issue of Crisis. 218 (l) The Granger Collection, New York. (m) ©Stock Montage. 219 (l) Brown Brothers. (r) Hulton Archive/Getty Images. 220 (l) Courtesy of the Bancroft Library/University of California, Berkeley. (r) Nebraska State Historical Society. 221 (l) Library of Congress. (r) ©Tom Bean. 222 ©Stock Montage. 224 ©Stock Montage. 226 Courtesy of the Bancroft Library/University of California, Berkeley. 226–7 Courtesy of the Bancroft Library/University of California, Berkeley. 230 Library of Congress. 232 Nebraska State Historical Society. 233 Kansas State Historical Society, Topeka. 234 Nebraska State Historical Society Photograph Collections. 238 Collection of Dr. and Mrs. Edward H. Boseker. 240 ©The Newberry Library/Stock Montage. 242–3 Oakland Museum of California, Oakland Museum Kahn Collection. 245 Archives and Special Collections, New Mexico State University. 246 ©D. Robert & Lorri Franz/CORBIS. 247 Courtesy Colorado Historical Society CHS-X20087. 248 (t) Library of Congress. (b) Denver Public Library Western History Collection. 250 Cumberland County Historical Society, Carlisle, PA. 252–3 National Anthropological Archives, Smithsonian Institution. 252 (bl) National Postal Museum. (br) ©Bettmann/CORBIS. 253 (b) The Granger Collection, New York. 256 (l) Brown Brothers. (r) ©Laurie Platt Winfrey Inc. 257 (l) Brown Brothers. (r) Time Life Pictures/Getty Images. 258 The Granger Collection, New York. 259 (t) ©National Geographic Soceity. Courtesy of the Bell Family. (m) The Granger Collection, New York. (b) Brown Brothers. 260 (t) Laurie Platt Winfrey Inc. (b) ©Underwood & Underwood/CORBIS. 261 (l) Humble Oil & Refining Co., Houston/American Heritage Publishing Co. (r) ©Bettmann/CORBIS. 262 Brown Brothers. 263 Library of Congress, USZ62-19862. 264 (frames) Image Farm. (l) Science Museum, London, UK/Bridgeman Art Library. (ml) The Granger Collection, New York. (mr) National Museum of American History, Smithsonian Institution, acc.#1983.0458.90. (r) The Hall of Black Achievement at Bridgewater State College. Photo: Kindra Clineff. 265 © Schenectady Museum; Hall of Electrical History Foundation/CORBIS 267 (l) The Granger Collection, New York. (r) Laurie Platt Winfrey Inc. 268 ©Bettman/CORBIS. 270 (frame) Image Farm. (l) The Granger Collection, New York. 270–1 Laurie Platt Winfrey Inc. 272–3 Library of Congress, LC-USZ62-126464 DLC. 274 (l) Library of Congress, USZ62-16174. (r) The Granger Collection, New York. 275 Time Life Pictures/Getty Images. 276–7 Library of Congres, LC-D401-18671. 278 George Eastman House. 280 Brown Brothers. 281 Brown Brothers. 282–3 Library of Congress, LC-USF34-40820-D. 284 ©Underwood & Underwood/CORBIS. 290 (t) Culver Pictures. (b) ©Elfi Kluck/Index Stock Imagery. 291 (tl) Library of Congress LCUSZ-52-5515. (tr) Library of Congress. (br) ©Bettmann/CORBIS. 292 (l) New-York Historical Society, Neg #4305. (m) The Granger Collection, New York. (r) The Granger Collection, New York. 293 (t) Gehl Company/CORBIS/Magma. (m) Buddy Mays/CORBIS/Magma. (bl) Library of Congress. (br) Franklin D. Roosevelt Library, Hyde Park, NY. 294 (l) Puck, May 25, 1898. (r)Stockbyte. 295 (l) The Art Archive/Imperial War Museum. (r) Hulton Archive/Getty Images. 296 ©SuperStock. 297 ©Bettmann/CORBIS. 298 Library of Congress. 299 Franklin D. Roosevelt Library, Hyde Park, NY. 300 The Granger Collection, New York. 301 ©Will & Deni McIntyre/Photo Researchers, Inc. 302–3 © CORBIS 306 (r) The Granger Collection, New York. 307 The Granger Collection, New York. 308–9 ©CORBIS. 310 (t) Culver Pictures. (b) The Granger Collection, New York. 312 ©CORBIS. 313 Brown Brothers. 310 (t) Culver Pictures. (b) The Granger Collection, New York. 316 ©Swim Ink/CORBIS. 317 ©Swim Ink/CORBIS. 320 (l) ©Rick Souders/Index Stock Imagery. (r) ©Bettman/CORBIS. 321 (l) The Granger Collection, New York. (r) Tennesse Valley Authority. 322 ©CORBIS. 323 ©Bettmann/Corbis. 325 Stanley King Collection. 326–7 ©Bettmann/Corbis.328 Archives Charmet/Bridgeman Art Library. 329 ©Bettmann/Corbis. 330 (l) ©Rick

Souders/Index Stock Imagery. (m) Culver Pictures. (r) Culver Pictures 331 (l) Library of Congress/Bridgeman Art Library. (m) Culver Pictures. (r) The Granger Collection, New York. 332 The Granger Collection, New York. 334 New York Public Library/Art Resource, NY. 334–5 Hogan Jazz Archive, Howard-Tilton Memorial Library, Tulane University. 335 (r) National Portrait Gallery, Smithsonian Institution/Art Resource, NY. 336 The Granger Collection, New York. 337 ©Bettmann/Corbis. 338 Library of Congress, USF34-9058X. 339 Marjorie Guthrie, Committee to Combat Huntington's Disease. 340–1 Brown Brothers. 341 (l) Library of Congress, LSUSF33-11938-M3. (b) ©CORBIS. 344 © National Portrait Gallery, Smithsonian Institution / Art Resource, NY. 345 Franklin D. Roosevelt Library, Hyde Park, NY. 346 U. S. Department of Interiors-Mural. 347 The Granger Collection, New York. 348 © Bettmann/CORBIS. 349 Brown Brothers. 354 ©Bettmann/CORBIS. 355 (tl) William Philpott/Getty Images. (tr) AP Wide World Photos. (bl) ©Bettmann/CORBIS. 356 (l) ©CORBIS. (r) Naval Historical Center, US Navy (digital composite). 357 (t) Hulton Archive/Getty Images. (bl) ©Tim Page/CORBIS. (br) Project Apollo Archive, NASA, KSC-69PC-442. 358 (l) U. S. Air Force, courtesy National Air and Space Museum, Smithsonian Institution (SI 91-1471). (r) Newsfilm Archive, University of South Carolina. 359 (l) U.S. Navy Photo. (r) ©Bettmann/CORBIS. 360 Culver Pictures. 361 (l) Popperfoto/Robertstock.com. (r) Brown Brothers. 362 (t) Naval Historical Center, US Navy. (m) ©CORBIS. (b) ©Bettmann/Corbis. 363 Library of Congress. 365 ©Bettmann/Corbis. 370 U. S. Air Force, courtesy National Air and Space Museum, Smithsonian Institution (SI 91-1471). 371 Library of Congress, LC-USW33-025833-C. 372 (l) Culver Pictures. (r) Newsfilm Archive, University of South Carolina. 373 US Army Photography. 374 ©Minnesota Historical Society/CORBIS. 374–5 ©Minnesota Historical Society/CORBIS. 376 Courtesy Don Troiani, Historical Miltary Image Bank. 377 ©CORBIS. 379 AP Wide World Photos. 380 (t) © Brian Brake/Photo Researchers, Inc. (b) United States Holocaust Memorial Museum. 381 Margaret Bourke-White/Time Life Pictures/Getty Images. 382 U.S. Air Force Photo. 382–3 Brown Brothers. 383 (tl) Bettmann/CORBIS. (tr) Culver Pictures. 385 Imperial War Museum. 387 ©Bettmann/CORBIS. 388 © Bettman/CORBIS. 389 (l) AP Wide World Photos. (r) © CORBIS. 390 AP Wide World Photos. 391 ©Bettmann/CORBIS. 393 AP Wide World Photos. 398 (l) ©Bettmann/CORBIS. (r) ©Bruce Roberts/Photo Researchers, Inc. 399 (l) Project Apollo Archive, NASA, KSC-69PC-442 (r) Bernard Gotfryd/Woodfin Camp. 400 White House Historical Association (White House Collection) (23). 401 (t) Julian Wasser/Time Life Pictures/Getty Images. (b) ©Bettmann/CORBIS. 402 ©Bettmann/CORBIS. 403 Hulton Archive/Getty Images. 404 ©Bettmann/CORBIS. 405 AP Photo/Levittown Public Library 406 Hank Walker/Time Life Pictures/Getty Images. 407 ©Bettmann/CORBIS. 408 (l) Carl Iwasaki/Time Life Pictures/Getty Images. (r) ©Bruce Roberts/Photo Researchers, Inc 409 (l) ©Bettmann/CORBIS. (r) AP/Wide World Photos. 410 James P. Blair/National Geographic. 412–3 Francis Miller/Time Life Pictures/Getty Images. 412 (l) ©Bettmann/CORBIS. (r) Express Newspapers/Getty Images. 413 (b) AP/Wide World Photos. 414 U. S. Army Signal Corps. Photograph in the John Fitzgerald Kennedy Library, Boston. 415 Project Apollo Archive, NASA, KSC-69PC-442. 416 (t) ©Bettmann/CORBIS. (b) Bernard Gotfryd/Getty Images. 417 ©The Andy Warhol Foundation Inc./Art Resource, NY. 419 NASA. 423 ©Tim Page/CORBIS. 424 ©Wally McNamee/CORBIS. 426–7 ©James P. Blair/CORBIS. 427 Richard Howard/Time Life Pictures/Getty Images. 434 (t) Michael Smith/Newsmakers/Getty Images. (b) Hulton Archive/Getty Images. 435 (tl) The White House. (tr) AP Wide World Photos. (bl) ©Bettmann/CORBIS. (br) Photodisc/Getty Images. 436 (l, m) AP/Wide World Photos. (r) Diana Walker/Time Life Pictures/Getty Images. 437 (t) Artbase Inc. (b) Michael Rieger/FEMA/Getty Images. 438 (l) ©Wally McNamee/CORBIS. (r) AEF-Serge Attal/Getty Images. 439 (l) ©Bettmann/CORBIS. (r) Joe Raedle/Newsmakers/Getty Images. 440 AP/Wide World

Photos. 442 (l) ©Bettmann/CORBIS. (r) ©Wally McNamee/CORBIS. 443 (l) AP/Wide World Photos. (r) Time Life Pictures/Getty Images. 444 AP/Wide World Photos. 445 ©The Nobel Foundation. 446 ©Stock Montage. 447 (tl) Hulton/Archive/Getty Images. (tm) ©Bettmann/CORBIS. (tr) ©Wally McNamee/CORBIS. (b) ©CORBIS. 448 Dirck Halstead/Time Life Pictures/Getty Images. 449 Chris Hondros/Getty Images. 450 Reuters New Media Inc./CORBIS. 451 Diana Walker/Time Life Pictures/Getty Images. 452 (t) ©Reuters New Media Inc./CORBIS. (b) AP/Wide World Photos. 453 AP/Wide World Photos. 456 ©AFP/CORBIS. 458 ©Bettmann/CORBIS. 459 (t) Courtesy of Apple Computer, Inc. (bl) Walter Hodges/Getty Images. (br) Courtesy of palmOne, Inc. 462 ©Roger Archibald. 463 (t) Courtesy of V. Ambrosia (NASA-Ames Research Center). (b) ©Roger Archibald 464 ©CORBIS. 465 ©Reuters New Media Inc./CORBIS. 468 AP/Wide World Photos. 469 ©2001 The Record (Bergen County, NJ), www.groundzerospirit.org. 472 (r) (detail) Independence National Historical Park. 473 (l) Photodisc/Getty Images. (r) Jeff Greenberg/PhotoResearchers, Inc. 476 (t) ©Will & Deni McIntyre/Photo Researchers, Inc. (b) ©Carl & Ann Purcell/CORBIS. 478 (b) ©Jeremy Woodhouse/Masterfile. 480 Alec Pytlowany/Masterfile. 481 (l) ©Danny Lehman/CORBIS. (r) A. Ramey/PhotoEdit. 486 (l) Carl Mydans/Time Life Pictures/Getty Images. (m) ©AFP/CORBIS. (r) ©Maroon/FOLIO, Inc. 488 Kaz Chiba/Getty Images. 489 (t) Philip Lee Harvey/Getty Images. (b) Dick Luria/Getty Images. 491 George B. Jones III/Photo Researchers, Inc. 493 David Young-Wolff/PhotoEdit. R1 (bl) © Archivo Iconografico, S.A./CORBIS. (frame) Image Farm. (bkgd) Yann Arthus-Bertrand/CORBIS. (tr) Photo Library International/CORBIS. R2–R3 LWA-Dann Tardif/Crobis. R4 (l) © Bettmann/CORBIS. (l frame) Image Farm. (r) © CORBIS. (r frame) Image Farm. R6 The Pilgrim Society, Plymouth MA. R7 (t) Philip Mould, Historical Portraits Ltd., London, UK/The Bridgeman Art Library. (b) Royal Albert Memorial museum, Exeter, Devon, UK/The Bridgeman Art Library. R8 The Granger Collection, New York. R9 Royal Academy of Arts, London (detail). R10 Anne S. K. Brown Military Collection. R11 Independence National Historical Park (detail). R12 Benn Mitchell. R17 Dennis Brack. R18 Steve Dunwell. R20 Independence National Historical Park (detail). R22 The Granger Collection, New York. R23 Hulton Archive/Getty Images. R24 Picture Research Consultants, Inc. Archive. R25 (tr) Museum of American Political Life, University of Hartford. (br) U.S. Army Signal Core Photograph In The John Fitzgerald Kennedy Library, Boston. R27 Black Star. R28 Bob Daemmrich/ Stock Boston. R29 Maryland Historical Society. R30 (tl) Fabian Bachrach/Hulton Archive/Getty Images. (cl) Hulton Archive/Getty Images. R31 © Flip Schulke/CORBIS. R32–R35 White House Historical Association. R35 (George W. Bush) The White House. R36 (l) © CORBIS. (r) John Duricka/AP WIde WOrld Photo. R38 (t) © Bettmann/CORBIS. (b) © CORBIS. R40 AP Wide World Photo. R41 The Associated Publishers/New York Public Library. R44 Michael Melford/Getty Images. R45 © Craig Auress/CORBIS.

Assignment Photography

All Photography © HMCo./Angela Coppola. xxiv-xxv © HMCo./Ken Karp.

Art Credits

5 Luigi Galante. 24–25 Luigi Galante. 28 (l) Wood Ronsaville Harlin, Inc ©. 32 Nenad Jakesevic. 81 (t) Will Williams. 126–129 Nenad Jakesevic. 144–145 Inklink. 153–154 Beth Peck. 160–163 Will Williams. 198–199 Barbara Higgins Bond. 236–237 Pat Rossi. 271 Patrick Gnan. 309 William Brinkley 418–421 Dave Klug. 460 Matthew Pippin. 494–497 Dave Klug. Charts and Graphs by Pronk & Associates